Fantastic Shadows
Upon the Ground

FANTASTIC SHADOWS
UPON THE GROUND

★ ★ ★ ★ ★

THE THIRTY-FIFTH OHIO VOLUNTEER
INFANTRY IN THE CIVIL WAR

by

GREG FUGITT

LITTLE MIAMI PUBLISHING CO.
MILFORD, OHIO
2011

Little Miami Publishing Co.
P.O. Box 588
Milford, Ohio 45150-0588
www.littlemiamibooks.com

Printed in the United States of America on acid-free paper.

ISBN-13: 978-1-932250-88-6
ISBN-10: 1-932250-88-3

Library of Congress Control Number: 2011923182

To the Travelers

Garl Fugitt, Jeremy Heath, Paul Hesse, Kevin Dunaway, and Arnie Eaton

and

" . . . to him who is able to do immeasurably more than all that we ask or imagine, according to his power that is at work in us, to him be the glory . . . "

Contents

CHAPTER 1

To Render Some Service

July to September 1861

Bouncing Shadows

Night marches were always more subdued, but even so, the darkness was filled with the sound of motion. Thousands of feet shuffling through the course fields beside a north Georgia road, accouterments clanking against moving bodies, muffled voices, labored breathing, the hoofs of officers' horses, and the rattle of supply wagons mixed together in the unmistakable and unforgettable clamor of an army on the move. The column of men was like a huge snake that stretched and contracted as it moved along, so there was a constant stream of quiet but urgent orders. "Close up, there, close up," alternated with "Slow it down in the front." It was hard to see the surface of the road in the dark so a man's first step was too short and his second too long. Ruts and roots made the surface even more treacherous. Occasionally someone would lose his balance on the uneven ground and stumble into the man nearest him. Straps and belts, uncomfortable under the best conditions, cut even deeper into the shoulders and waist with each jarring step.

At times, the dense cedar thickets through which it passed gave the road the feel of a tunnel filled with thick, almost liquid dust kicked up by the wheels and animals of the corps supply train and artillery. Through the thick air, a continuous stream of sweaty, blue-clad soldiers from eleven different states trudged on hour after hour. The September night was cool, and every time the marching column stopped to rest, sweat turned to chill, so fence rails from some lonely field would be pulled down, fires started, and coffeepots came out. When the fire starters moved on, shadows bouncing along the trees, the next unit in line would feed the fires and the smoke added to the density of the air and irritated the eyes. In some places, fires burned on both sides of the road and tired soldiers stumbled blindly through the smoke. Buried deep among the column of dusty blue soldiers plodding along at a steady gait were the weary men of the Thirty-fifth Ohio Volunteer Infantry. They had marched all day to get to Crawfish Spring and then been ordered to march on into the night. With well over a thousand miles behind them, tiresome road marches were nothing new to these Buckeye soldiers, but this one was different. As they marched, the camp-fires of the rebel army were clearly visible to their right. Though they sensed it coming, they didn't yet know that in a few hours the regiment's two-year period as a bridesmaid was about to end a long way from home in a forested land on the banks of a creek called Chickamauga.

Pigs Under the Courthouse

In the spring of 1861, Hamilton, Ohio, was one of the older cities west of the Appalachian Mountains. Located about twenty miles north of Cincinnati astride the Great Miami River, until the middle of the eighteenth century the area was part of an immense wilderness covered with trees three- to four-feet thick. The forests of southwestern Ohio were claimed by the Shawnee tribe, but there were no Indian villages in the immediate vicinity. The game-filled forests were prolific hunting grounds and, when there was no hunting to occupy the tribes, the river was the roadway to war. French and British expeditions passed through the Miami Valley claiming the land for their respective kings, but neither party sought nor attempted any permanent settlement.[1]

During the early 1780s, white settlers began to appear along the banks of the Ohio in the vicinity of present day Cincinnati, but it was 1785 before anyone entered what was to become Butler County with an eye on settling it. In May of that year, Congress ordered the western lands to be surveyed and divided into townships and sections for sale to the public. Judge John Cleves Symmes of New Jersey purchased an immense tract that included Hamilton and Butler counties in 1788 and quickly sent men out to explore and mark his new venture. They explored the land between the two Miami rivers as far as Middletown, seven miles north of Hamilton. The native tribes who claimed the Miami Valley were not pleased with the influx of whites into their hunting grounds and began to resist. In 1791, hero of the Revolution Arthur St. Clair arrived at Fort Washington near present day Cincinnati with a dual commission as both territorial governor and general of an army intended to pacify the hostile tribes.[2]

Like so many locations related to America's westward expansion, Butler County originated in conflict. In preparation for his expedition into the far reaches of the Miami Valley, St. Clair sent a detachment north to build a fort

---

1. *History and Biographical Cyclopedia of Butler County, Ohio* (Cincinnati, Ohio: Western Biographical Publishing, 1882), 1.
2. Ibid., 2–4.

that was to be the link between his base at Fort Washington and the area he intended to campaign in. In September of 1791, Lt. Col. William Darke led a party of soldiers up the Great Miami and established a camp on the prairie on the western bank of the river about half a mile south of what is now downtown Hamilton. A few days later, General St. Clair came up river and laid out the site for a stockade he named Fort Hamilton in honor of his wartime colleague and secretary of the treasury, Alexander Hamilton. The new fort was directly on the bank of the river in a thickly wooded area. St. Clair, a successful general during the War of Independence, came in a distant second in his encounter with the western tribes. Plagued with inexperienced troops and a poor supply system, St. Clair lost more than half his men in November 1791 when his expedition was savaged by Indians, so for a few years, Fort Hamilton and its garrison were the edge of the frontier. St. Clair's successor, Gen. "Mad Anthony" Wayne, was imminently more successful in his efforts to subdue the native population. Wayne took nearly two years to make preparations before taking his force out to fight. His victory at Fallen Timbers in 1794 and the subsequent Treaty of Greenville in 1795 ended the Indian wars in Ohio, and within a year of Wayne's victory, the army decided it no longer needed to garrison the Miami Valley. All remaining military stores were sold to the public and the stockade and buildings that comprised Fort Hamilton were formally abandoned.[3]

The first settlers around Hamilton were mostly men from the armies of Generals St. Clair and Wayne, but the tide was coming in. Along all the routes from the east, people were moving. Some came by wagon over the few primitive roads, driving their livestock before them. Others came by raft or boat on the Ohio River from Pittsburgh. It was easier than walking but just as dangerous. Those who came by water sold their boats in Cincinnati and walked north to the lands of promise. Families on foot or in wagons required two to three days to reach the area around Fort Hamilton, and once there, they lived outdoors until they could get a shelter up. It was easier for those who chose to live by the banks of the river on the rich prairie lands. There was good soil away from the river as well, but the would-be farmers had to fight the forest for it first.[4]

The town of Middletown, already the site of the first church in the Miami Valley, a small hut erected by the Baptists, was laid out in 1802. On March 24, 1803, the General Assembly of the new state of Ohio established boundaries for several counties, one being Butler County named for Gen. Richard Butler. Butler was another hero of the Revolution who had been part of St. Clair's expedition. Not nearly as fortunate as his commander, Butler had been killed and scalped in St. Clair's defeat. The original county boundaries ran west from the

---

3.   Ibid., 4; Stephen D. Cone, *Biographical and Historical Sketches: A Narrative of Hamilton and its Residents from 1792 to 1896* (Hamilton, Ohio: Republican Publishing Co., 1896), 7.

4.   *Cyclopedia of Butler County*, 39.

bank of the Little Miami River to the state line and stretched north four townships from the Colerain bend in the Great Miami. By 1815, the county had shrunk to its current size with the founding of Preble County to the north, Warren County to the east, and as a matter of convenience, a northern shift of the southern boundary with Hamilton County. The county seat was originally planned for the west bank of the Miami across from the new east bank town of Hamilton, but the proprietor of the Hamilton town site, Israel Ludlow, offered free lots for county use if the commissioners would agree to move the seat across the river. They did, and the current courthouse stands where its original ancestor stood two hundred years ago.[5]

It was only natural that the first county government would make use of the abandoned fort, and even if they had wanted something better, nothing else was available. If they weren't exactly the best buildings for the job, Ohio was, after all, still wilderness, and the old fort was as good as it got. Until 1810, the county courts met in the former officer's mess. It was a sturdy building raised on large wooden blocks so that it sat three feet off the ground. Besides providing a suitable space for legal proceedings, it made a wonderful shelter for the community's pigs and sheep who escaped the hot sun by lying underneath it. The clerk of courts also occupied a log building in the fort until he decided he could function just as well and much more comfortably from his own home. A new courthouse was built and first used in the spring of 1817 and a few years after that, the clerk was able to move from his home into the newly built offices adjacent to it.[6]

The old powder magazine served as the first county jail until 1809. It proved to be imminently unsuited to the purpose. Nearly all the prisoners incarcerated there escaped its confines, so it was no surprise that the first building erected on the public square in Hamilton was a new stone jail. It was much roomier than the old powder magazine with cells for criminals downstairs and space for a courtroom and a small debtors prison on the upper floor. A local historian described the new jail as "neither a model of elegance or convenience," and even though the building successfully held the majority of criminals placed there, quite a few still managed to get out early and undetected. Not until 1846 did the county build a truly secure jail.[7]

Butler County was hardly a sophisticated place in the early eighteen hundreds and for good reason. Roads and bridges were few or nonexistent. Clearing land was backbreaking work and farming it wasn't any easier. Transportation of goods was prohibitively expensive. No luxury items like silverware and glass came in nor could farmers get produce and stock to market. The people ate what they grew and made their own homes, utensils, tools,

5. *Cyclopedia of Butler County*, 32; George C. Crout, *Middletown Diary* (Middletown, Ohio: George C. Crout, 1965), 367.

6. *Cyclopedia of Butler County*, 35–36.

7. Ibid., 35–36.

clothes, and shoes. If they were lucky to have one nearby, the preacher might help educate their children. If not, they did it themselves or accepted illiteracy as a fact of life. Living on the edge of civilization was a risky business and it took strong, hardy people to make it work; the kind of people who didn't worry about pigs and sheep under the courthouse.

In spite of the hardships, or most likely because of them, development of Butler County from howling wilderness to rural landscape was fairly rapid. In 1807 the town of Hamilton contained two stores, one tavern, one doctor, one lawyer, and two "houses of entertainment." Across the river in Rossville, there were only four buildings, one of which was a combination tavern and ferry house. New settlers began to move in and ten years into the nineteenth century, 242 people lived in Hamilton, 84 called Rossville home, and it was not unusual to see Indians in town to trade. The first school was opened in 1809, and in 1814 a weekly newspaper began to roll off the city's first printing press. In 1819, the Miami Bridge Company erected a sturdy span between Rossville and Hamilton. Only the second bridge in the state, it was an impressive, enclosed structure with two driving lanes and two walking lanes.[8]

Higher education came to the Miami Valley with the founding of Miami University. The original plan for the subdivision of the Northwest Territories had called for one section in each township to be set aside to benefit education. The first lots for the town of Oxford were sold in 1810, and the money from the purchase of designated lots was used as an endowment for Miami University in 1811. From the start, students from the north and southwest were attracted by the college's high academic standards.[9]

The county's social and economic life began to flourish in the 1820s. A Thespian Club was founded in 1822 to provide theater for the inhabitants but was essentially taxed out of existence by the end of the decade. Communication grew with the establishment of newspapers in Oxford and Middletown and with improved transportation. One of Ohio's greatest advantages was direct access to the Ohio River and the Great Lakes. The development of the state's canal system extended that advantage to inland Butler County. The Miami Canal was opened from Middletown to Cincinnati in 1827, and within two years, the waterway was open to Dayton, as well. For the first time, the county had access to substantial external markets for its goods through Cincinnati. On the other side of the coin, items previously not available in the county could now be brought in at a price people were willing to pay.[10]

---

8. *Cyclopedia of Butler County*, 35–36; Cone, *Biographical*, 8–12, 23; Jim Blount, *Rossville: Hamilton's West Bank* (Hamilton, Ohio: Past/Present/Press, 1994), 19–21; James Schwartz, *Hamilton, Ohio: Its Architecture and History* (Hamilton, Ohio: American Printing, 1986), 122; Stephen D. Cone, *A Concise History of Hamilton, Ohio* (Middletown, Ohio: G. Mitchell, 1901), 90–91.

9. Ralph J. McGinnis, *The History of Oxford, Ohio* (Oxford, Ohio: Stewart Press, 1930), 7, 10.

Butler County began to prosper in the 1830s. Oxford was incorporated in the first year of the decade. Middletown followed suit three years later, but the change was not to everyone's liking. Fears of higher taxes prevented the town council from forming for four more years. According to the 1830 census, 1,072 people made Hamilton their home. Rossville was also flourishing, having placed even more emphasis on mercantile interests than her sister across the river, and 629 more people lived in that town. In 1831, the two towns counted over 120 businesses between them including lawyers, doctors, numerous stores, taverns, saloons, restaurants, hotels, carpenters, cabinetmakers, wood-turners, wheelwrights, masons, tanners, saddlers, hatters, tailors, watchmakers, silversmiths, and blacksmiths. The next decade saw the addition of bakers, pork packers, drug stores, candlemakers, shoemakers, barbers, gunsmiths, and stovemakers, the city's first fire company, and its first counterfeiters. The first county fair was held in 1832 and, in 1838, a huge countywide celebration was held on Independence Day. Industry also began to make its appearance in the 1830s. Two Hamilton companies, Herring-Hall and MacNeale and Urban began manufacturing safes and James Graham built a paper mill on the river just south of Hamilton in 1832. In the same decade, grisly but vital work began in two slaughterhouses. By the end of the decade, Middletown had nearly 1,000 citizens, but like Oxford, it remained primarily an agricultural town.[11]

Industrialization expanded rapidly in the 1840s. A canal system was constructed in Hamilton in 1845 to bring hydraulic power to the city's mills and factories. The Beckett Paper Mill was established on the hydraulic in 1848 and quickly became a major regional supplier of newsprint. The impact of the Miami-Erie Canal was overwhelmingly evident by 1840. In that year the port at Hamilton saw 2,108,269 barrels of pork, over 20,000 barrels of flour, 13,000 barrels of butter, and 200,000 pounds of other goods go down stream to the markets of Cincinnati. The traffic wasn't one way. The county imported over 4 million pounds of various goods to feed its growing society. Agriculture was still the primary source of income for most Butler countians, but it too began to become intertwined with the industries that were popping up. Barley was a major crop and nearly all of it went to local breweries.[12]

It was also in the 1840s that sectionalism, and more specifically, the extension of slavery into federal territories became the dominant theme of Ohio politics. Large numbers of emigrants from Virginia, Kentucky, and North Carolina, as well as the commerce that went down river, had always ensured close ties between Ohio and the South, so slavery was a contentious issue. The

10. Cone, *Biographical*, 12–14; Schwartz, *Hamilton*, 66, 79; Crout, *Middletown*, 28, 139; Christine Dee, *Ohio's War: The Civil War in Documents* (Athens, Ohio University Press, 2006), 1.

11. Cone, *Biographical*, 25; Schwartz, *Hamilton*, 67–68; Cone, *Concise*, 99; McGinnis, *Oxford*, 13.

12. Schwartz, *Hamilton*, 74, 106; Crout, *Middletown*, 69.

Northwest Ordinance had outlawed slavery in Ohio even before statehood, but that had not translated into racial equality. The great majority of Ohioans, including those in Butler County, believed blacks were inferior to whites, and a series of Black Laws restricted the liberty of free blacks in the state until 1849. To be sure, there were vocal groups that advocated abolition and actively assisted runaway slaves, but they represented only a small fraction of the total population. Cincinnati had its own abolitionist movement, but few members could be found in the counties north of Cincinnati. But even the majority of Ohioans who opposed abolition perceived that the political power of slaveholding states was growing, and this vague fear served to muddle the situation even more. The once monolithic sympathy for the South and its institutions began to crack. The Whigs and Democrats were the two main political parties of the decade. As a general rule, predominantly rural areas of the state, where suspicion of banks, tariffs, and manufacturing interests ran higher, tended to favor the Democrats. Butler County, in spite of its growing industrial base, was mostly rural and agricultural, and therefore solidly Democratic. When war with Mexico flared in 1845, the county's response was uneven. An infantry company was raised with great fanfare in Hamilton and Middletown, but the war didn't even create a ripple in Oxford. Of the men who did go off to Mexico, several would be heard from again in 1861.[13]

Continued industrial expansion was the dominant feature of the decade before the Civil War. The Erwin brothers opened a paper mill in Middletown in 1852 that boasted the largest paper machine in the western states. In Hamilton, the Schuler and Benninghofen Mill began producing woolen goods in 1853. In addition to clothing, they supplied felts to the local paper mills. The great railroad expansion of the 1850s boosted the county's economy. By 1851, the Cincinnati, Hamilton, & Dayton Railroad was operating along the established commercial corridor, and Oxford gained access to the road with the opening of the Junction Railroad in 1858. By 1860, Ohio had more miles of track than any other state in the Union, and the railroads had already had a dramatic impact on commercial activity. Goods that used to go north and south by water now went east and west on the rails. Churches in Butler County were active and prevalent. Inhabitants could choose between Presbyterian, United Church of Christ, Lutheran, Catholic, Episcopal, Methodist, African Methodist Episcopal, Baptist, and Disciples of Christ congregations. Recognizing their mutual dependencies, Rossville and Hamilton merged in 1855 with the west bank town becoming the First Ward of the City of Hamilton. It was an exciting time to be a Butler countian.[14]

On the eve of war, Butler County and its people had much in common with most other people in the developing Midwest. Still rural in character, the growth of commerce and industry was beginning to leave distinctive marks on

13. Dee, *Ohio's War*, 7–8; Schwartz, *Hamilton*, 74, 106; Crout, *Middletown*, 69.
14. Blount, *Rossville*, 19–21.

the people and their attitudes. In its nearly sixty years of existence, Butler County had grown from a few hundred inhabitants to almost thirty-six thousand. Hamilton had grown to more than seventy-two hundred and Middletown had burgeoned to more than two thousand residents. The river that separated the two parts of Hamilton was spanned by two bridges, one toll and one free, and the Miami-Erie Canal still carried goods to other parts of the state even though more and more business was migrating to the railroad. Together, they transported a variety of goods to Cincinnati, the largest city in Ohio at the time, and from there to the rest of the nation.[15]

The Viper Warmed Into Vitality

That nation had been gnawing itself apart for years. The sectional differences that existed even before the American Revolution had been smoothed over during the first forty years of the nation's life, but the spirit of good will began to fade rapidly in the second decade of the nineteenth century. States rights politics were generally stronger in the South than in the North and became the first major area of conflict between the two regions, but always lurking beneath the surface was slavery, the one matter no one seemed willing to compromise on. Every new decade brought a new and deeper crisis. Missouri's application for statehood, the Nullification crisis with South Carolina, and the annexation of Texas followed each other in rapid succession. Wars usually bring at least temporary unity to nations, but the Mexican War only highlighted the sectional split. The South strongly supported the war, while the New England states strongly opposed it.

Ohio, with strong ties north and south, was at the center of the growing conflict. It was the Kansas-Nebraska Act that tipped the balance across the state. The doctrine of popular sovereignty increased the fear that slave states might gain control of the Senate and dominate national politics. The political fallout of this growing fear was a remarkable coalition of antislavery Democrats, former Whigs, Free-Soilers, and Know-Nothings that became Ohio's Republican Party in 1855. State Republicans startled the entire nation by managing to get their candidate, Salmon P. Chase, elected governor late that same year, and when Republican presidential candidate John C. Fremont carried the state in 1856, it was obvious that a political realignment had taken place. Out in Kansas, a complete unwillingness to compromise brought open warfare among proslavery and antislavery forces, and out of this cauldron of hate boiled one of the best haters of all, a man named John Brown. Ohioans had mixed feelings about Brown's raid, but there was no doubt farther south where the raid became the last straw for the slave states. The Election of 1860 sealed the South's belief

15. *Cyclopedia of Butler County,* 35–36.

in Northern aggression, and Abraham Lincoln's peace initiatives never had a chance.[16]

Historians have debated the true causes of the Civil War for more than a hundred years, but one county historian stated, "The remote cause was negro slavery; the immediate cause was States rights, so called, pushed to an unnatural and dangerous extent." The statement was written with the benefit of twenty years hindsight. The reality was that, right up to the last minute, many of Butler County's citizens still sympathized with the southern states. But, when those states began to secede, sympathy for the South faded quickly. The first cannonball that arched high into the sky over Charleston Harbor and burst over Fort Sumter required everyone to make a choice. With very few exceptions, the people in Butler County chose the Union.[17]

The news of Fort Sumter spread across the county like a flash fire. The bells of the Neptune Fire Company in the First Ward were used to call the people of Hamilton together. The agitated crowd that gathered that day was unanimous in its verdict. Traitors were trying to destroy the nation, and an impassioned call was made to sustain the Union. In addition, the meeting called on the state legislature to appropriate one million dollars, an immense sum of money for the time, to arm and equip military units. Before the meeting broke up, Judge Scott expounded on the righteousness of the Union cause. "Why is it worse to war against a domestic rather than a foreign foe?" he asked. "Foreign nations may have no cause for gratitude toward us, but these rebel States, who owe all their prosperity and greatness to the fostering hand of the general government—like the viper warmed into vitality in the bosom of its benefactor— have turned their deadly fangs upon their own country with the wicked design of destroying it. What punishment can be too severe for such ingratitude and outrage?" Stoking already inflamed emotions, the Hamilton *Intelligencer* declared that the bombardment of Fort Sumter by "traitors of the Southern Confederacy and their misguided dupes" had "fired the Northern heart to a pitch of indignant enthusiasm never before equaled since the days of the Revolution." On April 15, President Lincoln called for seventy-five thousand volunteers and recruiting stations opened at once.[18]

Only three days after the call for volunteers, the Jackson Guards, commanded by Capt. John P. Bruck, left Hamilton to become Company K of the First Ohio Infantry. On the same day, fifty more men left for Cincinnati. Led by W. C. Margedant, later to become the most famous mapmaker in the Union army, this contingent of Germans became part of the Ninth Ohio Infantry. A second company was ready to go by the twentieth. Captain Rossman's Hamilton Guards, soon to be Company F, Third Ohio Infantry, fared better than their predecessors as the citizens of the city had had time to prepare an appropriate

---

16. Dee, *Ohio's War*, 8–10.
17. *Cyclopedia of Butler County*, 207.
18. Cone, *Biographical*, 330, *Cyclopedia of Butler County*, 207.

sendoff. The ceremony opened with a prayer followed by the presentation of a national flag to Captain Rossman. Miss Kate Campbell, representing all the young ladies of the city, handed a silk banner to the captain and admonished the assembled company to "stand by it with your lives, if necessary." In accepting the banner, Rossman promised to "bring it back with no lost laurels, with no tarnished fame" even if its "symmetry be destroyed by the elements and by strife."[19]

Feelings of patriotism were at a fever pitch, and the rest of the county followed suit. William C. Dine and J. W. C. Smith opened an office for recruiting on April 20. Posters tacked up around the city read:

TO THE RESCUE!

Our patriotism is invoked. Our country calls. "The Stars and Stripes" must be protected—the banner which has floated in honor and glory in every land and on every sea. We have therefore opened

"Recruiting Quarters"

in this city for a company of volunteers. Come boys! Turn out! Let the enemies of our country hear from us in thunder tones!

J.W.C. Smith

Wm. C. Dine

Hamilton, O., April 20th, 1861

Dine and Smith failed in their first attempt to enter the army, but Dine was to try again later.[20]

Over the span of a few days, nearly every community made public resolutions of their patriotism. The people of Port Union pledged to never shrink from war and to form their own militia company. At Jones Station, the promise was to teach traitors that a free people would never yield their birthright. The largest meeting of all was held on April 24 in Hamilton and was carefully organized. On that day, nearly every house in the city had a flag flying and every community in the county had sent representatives to the gathering. While the crowd was harangued by various speakers, a handpicked committee went off to prepare resolutions. The committee was a high powered one that included former sheriff and prominent attorney Ferdinand Van Derveer along with local engineer John S. Earhart. They returned with no less than ten resolutions to be put before the people.[21]

Volunteers continued to enlist. A group of Miami University students formed the University Rifles. Two companies formed in Middletown—one infantry and one artillery. In Hamilton, Minor Millikin helped form a cavalry

19. *Cyclopedia of Butler County*, 208; Cone, *Biographical*, 331–32.

20. J. W. C. Smith and William C. Dine Broadside, 20 April 1861, VFM4101, Ohio Historical Society, Columbus.

21. *Cyclopedia of Butler County*, 209–10, 215.

company, and a company of home guards was formed in each of the city's three wards. The first units stayed in hotels and drilled in the streets until the fairgrounds were turned into Camp Hamilton where a rowdy bunch of recruits hanged Jefferson Davis in effigy. Recruiting continued throughout the spring and summer with the formation of the Butler Grays, the Union Rifles, the Reeder Cadets, and the Butler Pioneers. While new companies were being formed, the companies that had signed on for ninety days were finishing their enlistment. [22]

Resolved

While several Ohio regiments wrested the western part of Virginia away from the Confederacy, the Third Ohio sat at Camp Dennison for three months. When the call was made for three hundred thousand three-year men, several of the men from Hamilton intended to continue their service, but they weren't sure if their regiment, the Third Ohio, would be reenlisted. Besides, they had a better idea. They wanted to form an entire regiment made up of men from Butler and the surrounding counties that made up the Third Congressional District. They carried their proposal to Ferdinand Van Derveer in his law office. Van Derveer was the right man to approach. A lawyer, local politician, a veteran of the Mexican War, and a likely candidate to command a regiment, his presence would make it easier for all of those associated with him to get commissions, and in the end, all but one did. On July 11, 1861, a notice, accompanied by supporting editorials, was published in both the *Intelligencer* and the *Telegraph.*

"ATTENTION VOLUNTEERS!"

In accordance with notice previously given, a meeting was held in Hamilton, for the purpose of taking into consideration measures to organize a regiment in Butler county and adjoining counties.

On motion, George T. Earhart was called to the chair, and B. F. Miller was appointed secretary. The following resolution was offered and adopted:

Resolved, That a committee of five be appointed to draft a plan for organizing a regiment in Butler and adjoining counties, inviting the cooperation of all who are willing to assist in suppressing armed rebellion. J. C. Thoms, F. W. Keil, John S. Earhart of Butler; Joseph L. Budd of Warren, and George D. Hendricks, of Preble, were appointed said committee.

The committee in due time presented the following report, which was submitted: Since measures are on foot to organize an independent regiment in Butler and adjoining counties, which is simple, and attended with little expense, or loss of time:

22. *Cyclopedia of Butler County,* 212.

The regiment to consist of ten companies, of not less than eighty-three men, rank and file. The first ten companies fully organized will form a regiment. The position of honor will be assigned according to the date of tender of service after organized.

When companies have elected officers, they will march their companies before a magistrate, or other proper officer, where all shall take an oath to the effect that as soon as the regiment is fully organized, its service tendered and accepted by the war department, the companies will march to the place of rendezvous, and then be mustered into the service of the United States.

Captains of companies will report to the secretary at Hamilton, Ohio; and to avoid the expense of attending the regimental organization, it is suggested that the commissioned officers be empowered to cast the votes of their respective companies for field officers. It is not contemplated in the foregoing plan to parcel out the offices in the organization of the regiment, but to reward merit, and efficiency through open competition.

The committee, however, would recommend that the command of the regiment be tendered Capt. Ferdinand Van Derveer, who has seen service in the Mexican war; and whose military qualifications are fully recognized, and who, the committee is satisfied, would accept the command provided it be tendered him.

It will be seen from the foregoing plan that volunteers will not be taken from their employment, until the regiment is accepted by the government. It is hoped prompt action will be taken in the matter by the active and energetic young men of the county.

By Order of the committee.

George T. Earhart   B. F. Miller
President   Secretary" [23]

Other influential citizens contacted Governor Dennison and let it be known they supported Ferdinand Van Derveer for the position of colonel in the new regiment. The governor was amenable, formally commissioning Van Derveer on July 26, and recruiting kicked into high gear. The experiences of the regiment that was soon to become the Thirty-fifth Ohio Volunteer Infantry were being repeated all over the state. Competition for officer's appointments in new regiments was fierce. The power of patriotism was evident, but ambitious men hoped to translate wartime deeds into political or business success. The situation was also a bonanza for sitting politicians who could reward friends and supporters by recommending their appointment to the governor. In turn, the governor knew that his power to appoint officers was a wonderful way to support his own political career. Not only could he appoint his own friends and supporters, he could use his power to gain influence with other powerful men around the state. Modern Americans raised on the idea of a nonpolitical

---

23. Frederick W. Keil, *Thirty-fifth Ohio: A Narrative of Service from August, 1861 to 1864* (South Bend, Ind.: Archer, Housh and Co., 1894), 210–11.

military would be appalled at the overtly political character of the Civil War recruiting process. It was a questionable process for creating an army, and it sent many incompetent officers into the ranks, but given the number of men required and the speed with which they were needed, no better system was available. In spite of all the potential flaws, the process worked surprisingly well. In a matter of weeks, dozens of regiments were recruited and put into the field.

The day after the notice was printed in the *Intelligencer,* Nathaniel Reeder of Hamilton, a former militia officer, wrote to Governor Dennison beseeching him for a position in any regiment. He had recruited enough men to form an artillery company but had been informed by the adjutant general of Ohio that the state would receive no artillery companies from Butler County. Apparently convincing enough of his erstwhile cannoneers to take a crack at the infantry, he then informed the adjutant general that he had formed a new company but was told once again there were no available quotas for his county. Desperate to get into the war, Reeder tried once again and finally got his appointment as a captain of Company D. One of his officers was William Dine, who had also failed in his first attempt to recruit a company in April. Farther north in Montgomery County, Michael S. Gunckel had requested a permit to raise a company for the war. On August 1, the adjutant general sent his permit and asked how quickly he could produce the required men. Gunckel replied, "I could do so as soon as any man in this country—at least I so flatter myself. I might perhaps raise a company—say—in 10 days or by the middle of this month." Gunckel raised his company in the Germantown area, but there was more competition than he expected. Working the same area as Gunckel were eleven other officers actively recruiting for six other regiments. Gunckel's two weeks stretched into six, but he eventually became the captain of Company H.[24]

Those with local influence had the fast track. John S. Earhart, had developed war resolutions with Van Derveer back in April, immediately got permission to recruit his own company in Hamilton and became captain of Company C. Benjamin F. Miller, secretary of the committee that had recommended Van Derveer for command of a regiment, teamed with Frederick W. Keil to try and raise another company in that city. Eventually they combined their efforts with Earhart and became lieutenants in Company C. About the same time, Hamilton physician Henry Mallory rode the train to the state capital at Columbus in the hopes of obtaining a medical appointment but none were available. Wishing to be a part of the war in some way, he returned to Hamilton and got Van Derveer's permission to begin raising an infantry company in Butler County.[25]

It also helped to be acquainted with Governor Dennison. Henry Van Ness

24. Correspondence to the Governor and the Adjutant General of Ohio, 1861–1866, Series 147–1:117 and 147–3:97, Adjutant General of Ohio State Archives, Ohio Historical Society, Columbus; W. H. Beers, *The History of Montgomery County, Ohio* (Chicago: W. H. Beers and Co., 1882), 410.

Boynton was from a prominent family of Cincinnati abolitionists. Small in size and still young at twenty-six, Boynton was said to have looked like a sixteen-year-old boy trying to pass for eighteen. He had no prior military experience, but his education from the Kentucky Military Institute (KMI) was enough to induce Governor Dennison to appoint him a major. Ordered to report to Colonel Van Derveer, who apparently accepted him without complaint, Boynton quickly proved himself capable and earned the respect of the regiment. Boynton was reunited with fellow KMI graduate Samuel L'Hommedieu, until recently the adjutant at Camp Hamilton, now captain of Company G composed of men from Butler and Preble counties.[26]

Nepotism also played its part in the process. Colonel Van Derveer led the way by requesting Governor Dennison to appoint his brother John as quarter-master of the new regiment. D. M. Gans from the town of Eaton in Preble County had already served three months in the Twentieth Ohio and had come home to recruit a company of his own. Gans's father, wrote the governor on behalf of his son requesting that he be appointed captain of the company he was organizing. Gans's men eventually became Company E. Recruiting was helped immeasurably by the Union defeat at Bull Run two weeks after notice of recruiting was made. Electrified by the defeat, the people of Ohio began to realize "that serious work lay before [them]."[27]

The appearance of the new regiment was not welcomed by everyone, since it upset the plans of men already recruiting their own companies. William H. Eacott, also of Hamilton, had recruited a company for three-month service and offered it to the state, but the acceptance had been delayed. In the meantime, recruiting for the Thirty-fifth began, and sixty-five of his men enlisted for three years with the new regiment. No sooner had he been informed of their action, then Eacott received conditional acceptance of his ninety-day company from the adjutant general. Annoyed at being left out, Eacott reported, "This I regret because I prefer the regular organization through the state authorities." What was probably most annoying to Eacott was that his men went into the company of fellow Hamiltonian John Earhart, who had not been required to wait on the adjutant general's approval. Annoyed as he may have been, Eacott eventually became second lieutenant of Company B. H. P. Clough of Middletown found himself in a similar situation but responded differently. He had received permission from the adjutant general on August 31 to begin recruiting, but while Clough waited for a permit, Joel Deardorf had gotten a sizeable lead in collecting men around Middletown in Butler County. Seeing that Deardorf had a decided advantage over him. Clough chose not to complain or stew over the sit-

---

25. B. S. Bartlow, *Centennial History of Butler County, Ohio* (Indianapolis: B. F. Bowen Company, 1905), 356.

26. Keil, *Thirty-fifth Ohio*, 247.

27. Correspondence to the Governor and the Adjutant General of Ohio, 1861–1866, Series 147–3:97 and 147–3:111, Adjutant General of Ohio State Archives.

uation. He assisted Deardorf in recruiting a company to clear the way for his own efforts. Deardorf's men became Company K.[28]

There were also quite a few men returning from ninety-day service who were interested in reenlisting for three years. Some of them had no trouble. For others, it wasn't so simple. The indifferent efforts to muster out the three-month regiments combined with the quick detachment of many ninety-day officers to serve in or recruit for three-year regiments left some soldiers in a bureaucratic limbo. Sgt. C. H. Murray of Hamilton wrote directly to Adj. Gen. C. P. Buckingham, saying that he and fifty fellow soldiers had been sent home on furlough a few weeks before. The conditions of their leave stated that they "shall remain at home until regularly mustered out of service, or until further orders." The rest of their regiment had been sent to West Virginia where they had reenlisted for three years. The enlistment of the men on furlough had also expired, but since they no longer existed as far as their former regiment was concerned, they had neither received their discharges nor been paid. Most of them just wanted their money, but some of them wanted to reenlist. Sgt. George Earhart, another of the committee that had first approached Van Derveer, also wrote asking what was to be done with men from Company F of the Third Ohio. Their enlistment was also up, and they had not been discharged. Earhart bragged that he had been the orderly sergeant of his company and had already raised "the big end of a company," and if he could get the Third Ohio men released to reenlist, he could fill his company up. Sergeant Earhart never filled up his own company. He became second lieutenant of Company G.[29]

Of course, there was no way to keep the organization of the regiment from becoming political. Some of it was essentially harmless, but a more serious issue arose in Captain Gans's Company E. When Gans's father had extolled the virtues of his son to the governor, he had also recommended another Eaton man named William H. Kline for a commission. Klines had agreed to help Gans recruit with the understanding that he would be his first lieutenant. Along the way, they "associated" themselves with another young man, Edward Cottingham, formerly a private in the Twentieth Ohio, with the understanding that he would become second lieutenant. The problem apparently started when it became known that Gans's company was intended for the Thirty-fifth Ohio. Colonel Morton of the Twentieth Ohio, another Eaton area resident, had hoped to get Gans's men into his new regiment. The Twentieth had completed its three-month term and was reorganizing for three years. Gans's three-month service had been in the Twentieth and Morton expected he would rejoin it. Klines claimed that friends of Colonel Morton "in the spirit of reveng[e] commenced their operations to defeat our elections," presumably to influence the men into joining the Twentieth Ohio.

28. Correspondence to the Governor and the Adjutant General of Ohio, 1861–1866, Series 147–2:1, 147–5:20, and 147–8:144, Adjutant General of Ohio State Archives.

29. Ibid., Series 147–5:28 and Series 147–5:183.

In new regiments, company officers were elected to their position by the men of the company of which they were a member. In virtually every instance, it was understood by the men who were enlisted that the men doing the recruiting would be their officers. Once this was formalized by a rubber stamp election, the tally sheets were forwarded to the governor who generally abided by the results and issued commissions to the chosen men. That was what Kline had agreed to with Gans and what he had every expectation of happening, but it didn't work that way. Supposedly influenced by the cabal from the Twentieth, Cottingham broke the previous agreement and ran for first lieutenant rather than second. Cottingham won the canvas, and according to his own self-serving account, Kline "submitted to the result and worked hard as ever in raising the company content to take the 2nd place." When Kline also lost the election for second lieutenant, he got mad and requested that the governor do him justice and restore him to his rightful rank. Governor Dennison refused to intervene and the elections stood as they were. Appealing to the governor was a wasted effort. During the summer, the process for selecting officers had been changed. Realizing the inefficiency of officer elections, the state adjutant general had convinced Dennison to stop elections and appoint officers under his own authority. To his credit, Kline accepted the outcome and remained with the company and served out his full enlistment as a private.[30]

A second politically charged incident with potential for discord involved precedence. It was the accepted practice that companies were lettered in the order that they filled their quotas and were accepted into service, and the same stipulation had been part of the original resolution made just a few weeks before. In other words, the first company to be enrolled was designated "A" and the last was "K." Enrollment was the key. A company might be the first into camp, but if they had not yet met their enlistment quota, they could not be formally enrolled. Designation as Company A was also a matter of honor. Aside from being able to claim they were first to serve, Company A held the first position in regimental formations. There was competition among recruiters to be first and gain the honor of commanding Company A.

Capt. Thomas Stone, a partner in a local lumber company, believing his company had been enrolled first, was stunned to receive his commission as commander of Company "B." The designation of Company A had been awarded to Capt. Joseph Budd. Not only had Budd come into camp days after Stone, his company was from Warren County. In anger, Stone wrote one of those letters that should be left overnight and then rewritten. His letter to Governor Dennison was abrupt to the point of rudeness and even accusatory. Stone started by quoting regulations to Dennison, "the Commander in Chief of the Militia of Ohio," and laying out his version of the sequence of events. He accused Lieutenant Colonel Long, also of Warren County, of using trickery to

---

30. Ibid., 7:83; Whitelaw Reid, *Ohio in the War: Her Statesmen, Her Generals and Soldiers* (Cincinnati: Robert Clarke Co., 1895), 1:55.

get the state adjutant general to give his fellow citizen preference and could not even bring himself to use Budd's rank, referring to him over and over again as "Mr. Budd." Rising to a crescendo, Stone demanded of the governor, "—now—Sir do you consider this Good—Treatment is it Honorable—is it the treatment that you desire your men to get when they Sacrifice their little all Leave Home & friends—to do Battle for their Country—do you as Chief Magistrate of Ohio—Sanction & approve of this kind of underhanded mean Contemptible Trickery" [31]

Stone was careful not to burn all of his bridges. He was sure Colonel Van Derveer was "too much of a gentleman to engage in as mean a matter as I consider This to be," but it never seems to have never occurred to Stone that while defending his own honor, he had impugned that of the governor of Ohio. Stone closed his letter by saying, "Will you please—have the goodness to answer & Excuse anything amiss under my Present State of Excitement I may have wrote things that I should not." [32]

Capt. Thomas B. Stone, the disappointed commander of Company B.
AUTHORS COLLECTION

The letter had no affect, and there probably was something a little shady about the whole affair. The official rosters indicate that the men of Stone's company were enrolled a week before Budd's company was. Colonel Long and Captain Budd did make a trip to Columbus where Long certainly had influence and where Budd was able to receive his commission on the spot. Long was a bit of a conniver willing to cross boundaries to get his way. He also tried to get Adjutant George B. Wright removed so that Long's relative Charles W. Ellis, could take the adjutant's position. Long would certainly have been willing to pull strings to put his friend Budd in a position to claim precedence and Company A. Budd had also been one of the men who had first approached Van Derveer in July about commanding a regiment, and the colonel was no doubt inclined to support him, as well. The switch may indeed have been a technical violation of the rules, but Stone's acerbic response had offended the final judge in the matter and destroyed whatever chance he had for redress. Stone remained

---

31. Correspondence to the Governor and the Adjutant General of Ohio, 1861–1866, Series 147–8:131, Adjutant General of Ohio State Archives; *Williams Hamilton Directory for 1860* (Cincinnati: Williams Directory Co., n.d.).

32. Correspondence to the Governor and the Adjutant General of Ohio, 1861–1866, Series 147–8:131 and 147–11:155, Adjutant General of Ohio State Archives.

captain of Company B, and his discontent was to have negative affects on his company. [33]

Joseph Budd had come to Hamilton, Ohio, from New Jersey as a boy. At age seventeen, he had moved to Lebanon, Ohio, to enter the "mercantile profession." Budd had joined the local militia company, the Warren Guards, in 1857 and found he had a bit of a taste for the "military profession," as well. That taste had led him to raise his own company for the Thirty-fifth Ohio, and in the end, the choice of Budd over Stone proved to be correct. Budd served with distinction throughout the regiment's service. [34]

In spite of the ups and downs of the organizational process, things were beginning to shape up by the end of August. Having seen the pitfalls of accepting unfit men firsthand from previous service, most of the recruiters were not willing to take just anyone who showed up. By and large, they picked the men who appeared best able to stand up to the rigor of war. Recruits reportedly "were of a high order physically, and were of a class that endured the wear and tear of actual service remarkably well." They were the best the counties had to offer, men who were considered respectable citizens and were "not willing to compromise that standing while soldiers." In an age where politics was the quickest way to fame and fortune, Frederick Keil, writing years later, said recruits for the new regiment enlisted to be soldiers only and not as a stepping stone for personal ambition. Perhaps realizing the dubious quality of his statement in light of then established facts, he qualified if by saying that if any of them had political ambitions, they "had the good sense not to mention it." [35]

On August 7, 1861, the regimental officers received formal appointments from the governor. Charles L. H. Long, a thirty-three-year-old native of Warren County, became lieutenant colonel. Long had been born in Franklin, Ohio, but spent most of his life in Cincinnati. A printer by trade, Long has served in the Mexican War in the same regiment as Van Derveer and, also like Van Derveer, was an unsuccessful veteran of the California gold fields. He had previously organized a ninety-day company and been appointed major of the Fifth Ohio. In September, he had resigned that commission to accept the lieutenant colonel's position in the Thirty-fifth Ohio. [36]

Camps for volunteer soldiers were being established with great rapidity all over the country, but the speed with which they were being established made certain that the accommodations would be spartan at best. The Thirty-fifth Ohio reported to Camp Hamilton at the Butler County Fairgrounds, familiar to a great many of the men enlisting, and Companies A, B, and C were mustered in at Camp Hamilton on August 20 by Capt. T. I. Cram, a topographical engineer in the regular army. Company A had been recruited in Warren County, B

---

33. Ibid., 8:173.
34. Keil, *Thirty-fifth Ohio*, 240; Cone, *Biographical*, 346–47.
35. Keil, *Thirty-fifth Ohio*, 213.
36. Ibid., 235–36; Cone, *Biographical*, 345–46.

in Butler County, and C was made up of men from the city of Hamilton and Preble County. Officer's commissions from the governor began to arrive and each was instantly answered. Most of the responses were one line acceptances of the honor bestowed upon them, but Lieutenant Miller of Company C was more reflective in his acceptance notice. "In accepting the honor," he replied, "I do so not being insensible of the responsibility that rests upon me; and yet I hope I shall be able to render some service in aiding to put down the rebellion."[37]

By the time the Thirty-fifth moved in, the stables at the fairgrounds had been made into acceptable sleeping quarters by the addition of tons of straw and a little housekeeping. Food service was provided by Straub, Rerutti, and Co., on a sea of tables that could seat four hundred men at a time. For their efforts, Straub and Rerutti got thirty-five cents per man per day. The fairgrounds made acceptable barracks, but the stables and other buildings lacked one important feature. There was no open area for drilling. Because of that, Camp Hamilton was moved to the common north of the city in early September. The site had been selected specifically for its large, flat area imminently suitable for maneuvering soldiers. As part of the move, tents were issued for the first time and the men began to feel like they were in the army. On September 9, Companies D, E, F, and H were mustered in at the new camp by Capt. P. H. Breslin of the Eighteenth U.S. Infantry.[38]

The regimental adjutant, George Wright, requested blank morning report forms and things began to get businesslike. The rest of Van Derveer's staff was beginning to shape up as well. Doctors Perkins A. Gordon and Francis D. Morris agreed to serve as regimental surgeons, and men to serve in the various non-commissioned positions of the regimental staff were being identified. Even the regimental band was coming up to strength. On September 23, one more key position was filled. The field officers and company commanders in camp met to discuss the selection of a chaplain for the regiment. After their business was conducted, eleven of them requested in writing that the governor appoint Reverend John Woods to the position. It would prove to be an unhappy choice.

It was not until September 24 that the minimum number of companies to form a regiment was reached. On that day, Company G was mustered in by Captain Breslin. That ceremony was followed immediately by an identical one for the field officers and staff, and the Thirty-fifth Ohio Volunteer Infantry came into official existence.[39]

---

37. Correspondence to the Governor and the Adjutant General of Ohio, 1861–1866, Series 147–8:28, 147–8:33, and 147–8:148, Adjutant General of Ohio State Archives; Ohio Roster Commission, *Official Roster of the Soldiers of the State of Ohio in the War of the Rebellion, 1861–1866*, vol. 3 (Akron: Werner Co., 1886), 601–34 .

38. Dallas R. Bogan, *Warren County's Involvement in the Civil War* (Lebanon: Warren County Quickprint, 1991), 72.

39. Ohio Roster Commission, *Official Roster*, 601.

Farmers, Politicians, and Shopkeepers

The enlisted men who made of the vast majority of the regiment and who would bear the brunt of any fighting were not as well known as their officers. Coming from the Ohio counties of Butler, Montgomery, Preble, and Warren, they were for the most part ordinary citizens who had volunteered to do an extraordinary task. Farmers, politicians, shopkeepers, clerks, lawyers, carpenters, coopers, meat packers, schoolteachers, laborers, and all of the other occupations that made up the western states, they had all decided to take part in the defining moment of their nation. As they tried to come to grips with a situation so much larger than themselves, the continued unity or ultimate division of the United States of America rested on their shoulders at the mustering formation.[40]

The men came to enlist for a variety of reasons. For the most part, they signed up out of a general feeling of patriotism. They believed in the Union and that it was something worth fighting for, but they probably could not have explained it very well. The spirit of adventure and the possibility for personal glory had been the primary factor that brought most of them to recruiting offices. The fact that the war was being fought for a patriotic and just cause simply made it easier. Most also saw their participation in the war as a way of fulfilling their masculine obligation to protect their families and their homes. During the period of their enlistment, that sense of family they brought with them would permeate their company and regiment.[41]

Volunteer regiments were mustered in by regular army officers who traveled from place to place to bring new regiments into Federal service. For them, the muster was just another administrative duty that they had not sought out. For the men in the ranks, it was much more. Their new adventure was about to become official and they were feeling proud and excited. Little did they know that the ritual they were about to participate in was a shadow of things that had not yet come into sight. Each company was inspected by the mustering officer to ensure the men were fit for duty. Each name on the roster was called and answered to and then each man signed the roll and took the oath prescribed in the tenth Article of War. After the roll was called and signed, both the mustering officer and the company commander certified that the rosters and information were accurate and complete.

The last part of the ritual was by far the worst. Once they had formally enlisted, the companies were forced to stand in formation while the entire Articles of War were read to them tedious line by tedious line. Consisting in large part of the infractions a soldier might commit and the punishment for each, the reading had to have dampened the feeling of excitement if not altogether extin-

---

40. Bruce Catton, *America Goes to War* (New York: MJF Books, 1958), 66.
41. Ibid., 55; Reid Mitchell, *Civil War Soldiers* (New York: Viking Press, 1988), 17.

guishing it. Men who had been looking forward to the glories of war were given pause to reconsider what they had just done. Some of these newly sold men must have been appalled by what they had heard for the regimental rosters indicate several men present at the muster-in never received any pay and had no further mention of service. Those who stayed would hear it all again. Army regulations required the Articles of War to be read to the companies twice a year.

War has always been a game for young men, and the rosters of the Thirty-fifth Ohio reflected that. Of the 912 men who enlisted in the regiment in 1861, 80 percent were under the age of thirty, half were twenty-five or under, and one in three was under the age of twenty. An "uncommonly plentiful" number of eighteen year olds presented themselves to the recruiters, the uncommon plentifulness being explained by the fact that some of the teenagers professing to be eighteen were as young as sixteen. The youngest member of the regiment who was not a musician was Benjamin Miller. Only fifteen at the time he enlisted, he was later promoted to sergeant and served his full three years. After going over one particular company roster and noting with suspicion that over half of the men were listed as being eighteen, one of the mustering officers at Camp Hamilton remarked that 1843 "must have been a h——l of a year for boys!" After the war, the regimental historian wrote, "The nation in the hour of danger can depend on the boys, while it may not be so safe to say that concerning the men."[42]

While the large number of younger men in the ranks may seem to support his position, it is an unfair statement at best. It was not only the young men who enlisted. Many mature men also chose to volunteer and a strong argument can be made that they deserve the greater credit. With nothing to leave behind or lose, it is easy for a young man to sign away three years of his life and accept the risks of war. It is another thing entirely to leave behind a wife and children knowing that they may have to fend for themselves for the rest of their lives. Balancing responsibility to a family and responsibility to a nation has never been easy and a man who has never had to do it cannot fully understand the conflict. But having more to lose also gave these older men a better grasp of the issues involved, so it is not surprising that a large number of them, nearly two hundred, did choose to leave their homes and enlist in the new regiment. Over fifty of them admitted to being over the age of forty and another eight were fifty or older. The honor of being the oldest man in the regiment went to Wilkinson Beatty who was sixty-four years old when he enlisted. Beatty was apparently known to Van Derveer before the war, and the colonel considered him an excellent judge of horses.[43]

Regardless of whom they were, what they did for a living, or where they came from, very few of them had any real sense of what they had just signed up for. Alfred Amlin of Company H wrote a letter to his sister while at Camp

---

42. Keil, *Thirty-fifth Ohio*, 213; Ohio Roster Commission, *Official Roster*, 601–34.
43. Ohio Roster Commission, *Official Roster*, 628.

Hamilton that surely reflected the naiveté of most of his peers at that time. In addition to giving instructions for the corn harvest, Amlin said he was well and contented in camp. They had just finished an inspection that apparently went well enough. He expected that they would move from Camp Hamilton in a few days, but he wasn't really sure about that. In spite of expecting to move, he also thought he would be able to get home in "too or three weeks," but he wasn't sure about that either. They were starting to receive weapons, and Amlin was convinced that the Springfield musket he was to receive was the best rifle he had ever seen. Like all of his compatriots in the Thirty-fifth Ohio, Amlin was shortly to learn a lot about his ability to come and go and about the rifle he would have to use. For him, it was to be a school from which he would never graduate.[44]

There was a mountain of things that had to be done before the Thirty-fifth was ready for war. The companies had been mustered in individually and now had to be hammered into a single cohesive organization managed by a functioning staff. Van Derveer had staff officers, but they were not ready to perform the complete set of duties required. The main issue was training, and even though there was a smattering of Mexican War veterans among them, the man who had any formal military training was the exception. Staff officers had to learn how to deal with administration and logistics. Company officers had to learn how to lead the required company maneuvers but, at this point, not only did they not know the maneuvers, they didn't know how to lead anything. In spite of what they and their fellow citizens might have thought, an upstanding position in the community did not make a man a leader. Instinctive ability certainly was part of the equation, but the practical part of leadership had to be learned on the job. These same inexperienced, clueless officers were supposed to teach other military novices to be sergeants so they could teach the rest of the regiment to be soldiers. The soldiers were typical mid-nineteenth century Americans who saw no reason that being in the army made them any less free than they had been before enlisting. For the moment, the Thirty-fifth was little more than a partially organized mob of men who had a common purpose but no common method. All of the required skills and attitudes would come with time and countless hours of training. All of this training would be very time consuming, and while at Camp Hamilton, the Thirty-fifth Ohio would only be able to start the most rudimentary instruction. The war was also starting to consume things on its own, and one of those things was new regiments.

---

44.   Alfred Amlin correspondence, Smith Library of Regional History, Oxford, Ohio.

CHAPTER 2

Proceed With Your Regiment

September to December 1861

Close to Home

Bishop Polk's rash move on Columbus, Kentucky, on September 4, 1861, was the lever that set the wheel of war in motion in that state. Though certainly not his intent, Polk's lunge into the southwest corner of the state placed most of Kentucky firmly into Union hands. With the support of Kentucky's unionist legislature, the federal government immediately implemented a political and military occupation of the commonwealth. Bushwhacking and raiding would go on until the last days of the war, but within a matter of hours Kentucky's permanent place in the Union was secured.

War is a combination of routine and excitement with both at work simultaneously. The day-to-day administration of an army continues even in the midst of battle. So while there was great agitation in Kentucky, only a few miles away the Thirty-fifth Ohio was busy with the routine, frustrating task of coming into existence. Telegraphic messages flew through bare copper wires from Kentucky into Ohio, from Ohio to Washington, and back from Washington to both states. Anxious letters were borne from place to place in the pouches of couriers whose horses flew headlong along the roads and byways of Kentucky. Back in Hamilton, it was more likely expletives that flew around the camp as restless men finally began to realize they were in the army. While the War Department tried desperately to get an army into Kentucky, the Thirty-fifth Ohio, where only a handful of people really knew what was supposed to happen, was probably trying hard just to get through another day. What both parties needed but neither was going to get was time; time for one to meet the threat of a Confederate army and the other to learn what soldiering was all about.

It would be hard to argue that any volunteer officer in the nation was better prepared to turn raw volunteers into useful soldiers than Ferdinand Van Derveer. Born in Middletown on February 27, 1823, Van Derveer came from a family that had already been in America for over two hundred years. The Van Derveers had arrived in New York from Holland in 1645. During the American Revolution, Van Derveers had served the patriot cause, and Ferdinand's grandfather, Henry Van Derveer, had been a volunteer colonel in the government forces that suppressed the Pennsylvania Whiskey Rebellion of 1794. Peter Van Derveer, Ferdinand's father, had been trained as a physician in New York before deciding to seek his fortune in the west. He arrived in Middletown in 1819 and practiced on both sides of the Great Miami River. Peter spent a great deal of time in the saddle traveling to visit his patients and had more than one close call swimming his horse across the river. Well respected by his neighbors, Peter also served the community as an elder in the Presbyterian Church.[45]

Ferdinand was the oldest son of Peter and his second wife, Mary Ann Hubble, and received his formal education from Farmers College in College Hill north of Cincinnati. Very much a man of his time, he chose the law as his career. Not only a respected occupation, it was the stepping stone to influence and political power. As did most men of his day, Van Derveer believed that personal mobility was one requirement of success. After studying law in Ohio, he went to Memphis, Tennessee, where he was admitted to the bar in 1845. He stayed in that city only a brief time before returning to Hamilton to continue reading the law with a local attorney.[46]

The war with Mexico created a great deal of excitement in Butler County. The people of the county were predominantly Democrats and strongly supported what was generally accepted as a Democratic war. Democrats or not, most volunteers weren't really interested in the issues behind the conflict. There was a war on and they just wanted to be part of it. John B. Weller, the Hamilton lawyer who had taken Ferdinand Van Derveer on as an understudy, immediately announced that he was forming a rifle company for service in Mexico. Within forty-eight hours, the men of the county had filled the rosters, and when officers were elected, Weller was named captain. County Recorder James George, later to be closely associated with Van Derveer again, was elected first lieutenant and Oliver Whitherby won the post of second lieutenant. Weller's company was designated Company I, First Ohio Volunteers, and twenty-four-year-old Ferdinand Van Derveer was appointed orderly sergeant. Company I drained the city of its legal talent as no less than thirteen Hamilton attorneys enlisted. Whether or not this was a hardship was debatable, and one local wag was reported to have noted that "during their absence, Hamilton was more peaceable than it had ever been before." During the final organization of the regiment, Captain Weller was appointed lieutenant colonel and Lieutenant Whitherby became the regimental quartermaster. Lieutenant George stepped up

45. Keil, *Thirty-fifth Ohio*, 231; Ezra J. Warner, *Generals in Blue* (Baton Rouge: Louisiana State University Press, 1997), 522–23.

46. Keil, *Thirty-fifth Ohio*, 231; Warner, *Generals in Blue*, 522–23.

to take command of Company I.[47]

The regiment passed through New Orleans on July 2, 1846, before moving on to the mouth of the Rio Grande and a month of drilling at Brazos Santiago. The First Ohio having been called on to join Gen. Zachary Taylor's advance to Monterrey, it was at the Mexican village of Camargo that Van Derveer earned his first fame as a soldier. In his rounds of the regiment, he learned that the quartermaster, Lieutenant Whitherby, was keeping a barrel of whiskey in his tent where it could be closely watched and came to the conclusion that Company I could make much better use of the liquor than the quartermaster. With the able assistance of Pvt. Clem Murphy of Rossville, Van Derveer managed to steal the entire contents of the barrel at night and carry it off in buckets and camp kettles. The next morning, every member of the company was invited into the orderly sergeant's tent and given a tin cup of whiskey. Lieutenant Whitherby was furious when the theft was discovered, and when he learned who the thieves were, the fact that most of its members were drunk having made Company I the leading suspect, the former company officer got so mad he shortly resigned his commission and went home. The members of Company I, seeing the situation in an entirely different light, gratefully elected Van Derveer first lieutenant in Whitherby's place. It was Van Derveer's first promotion.[48]

His second elevation in rank came as the result of combat at the battle of Monterrey. As Company I assaulted the Mexican positions, Captain George and several other men in the company were wounded. Because George's wounds were serious enough that he was forced to resign, Van Derveer was elected captain and given command of the company. Monterrey was also the place where Van Derveer's deep concern for the men under his command first became apparent. Company I had lost three men killed during the battle and had buried them on the spot. Months later, when the company was leaving to be mustered out, Van Derveer had the three bodies exhumed and returned to Ohio where they were reinterred in Middletown.[49]

As an orderly sergeant and company commander, Ferdinand Van Derveer learned the myriad details of administering a military unit. It was the young lawyer's responsibility to ensure his soldiers were trained, fed, medicated, housed, and equipped. It was up to him to make sure rations were issued, weapons were inspected, and drill was conducted. Lost and damaged equipment had to be replaced, and company payrolls had to be accurately prepared and certified. Van Derveer had to make sure the company area was policed and that proper camp sanitation was maintained. It was up to him to ensure that company officers and sergeants were doing their jobs like they were supposed to. In the process of doing all of these things, Ferdinand Van Derveer discovered that

47. *Cyclopaedia of Butler County*, 199.
48. Ibid., 199–200.
49. Ibid., 200.

he had a knack for soldiering. It was also in Mexico that Van Derveer first observed career military officers. It is probable that one of the regulars that Van Derveer became acquainted with at Monterrey was a junior officer named George H. Thomas.[50]

In February 1847, Van Derveer volunteered to lead the rescue of three companies of the Second Ohio that were surrounded by fourteen hundred Mexican soldiers at the village of Marin. Arriving at the village after a long march, Van Derveer drove the Mexicans off with a few rounds of canister from his howitzers. They suffered no injury at the hands of the Mexicans, but their fellow Buckeyes besieged in the village mistook them for the enemy and wounded several before the necessary introductions could be made. Van Derveer's men, fatigued by a hard day's work, had just enough strength left to loot the village before falling asleep. The Second Ohio had been relieved, but the danger was far from over. The Americans started back for Monterrey the next morning, their every move shadowed by Mexican lancers. Learning that several hundred Mexican soldiers were collecting to his front and several hundred others were moving in behind him, Van Derveer continued the march on into the night. The column finally halted about two o'clock in the morning when everyone decided they would rather fight than keep walking. The night passed quietly and Company I was almost to Monterrey when they learned why. The Mexicans who had been trailing them had turned back for easier pickings. The men of the Second Ohio had marched much slower than Van Derveer and were again surrounded by the enemy.

Van Derveer immediately reversed his march and went at once to the aid of his fellow Buckeyes. Riding on ahead with two or three others, the young captain suddenly found himself face to face with over a hundred Mexican lancers. The handful of Americans "judged discretion the better part of valor" and stood staring at their enemies. The Mexicans were content to stare back until riding off when the rest of Van Derveer's force arrived. Van Derveer made contact with the ecstatic men of the Second Ohio and then attacked the Mexicans. In a letter to his father, the proud young officer wrote that it was "a beautiful little fight for twenty minutes; but the rascals would not stand." Casualties were light because "nearly every one of their bullets went over our heads. They always fire too high." When the Mexican force finally retreated, Van Derveer led the now unified command back to Monterrey. Company I was proud of its performance, but no one was there to congratulate them. Arriving in Monterrey, they found that the American garrison had moved to a new camp, and to make matters worse, the tents belonging to Van Derveer's men had been lost or stolen during the move.[51]

The rescue expedition was the last combat Van Derveer participated in but

---

50. Francis F. McKinney, *Education in Violence* (Chicago: Americana House, Inc., 1991), 491.

51. *Cyclopaedia of Butler County*, 200–201.

he was intimately involved in another interesting incident while the First Ohio was still at Monterrey. Two officers, James Fyffe and Carr White, got into a heated dispute over a company election and one challenged the other to a duel. Fyffe chose James Harrison to be his second, and White got Van Derveer involved by naming him as his own second. Since everyone knew General Taylor was strongly opposed to dueling, it was agreed that the actual confrontation would be delayed until after the regiment's enlistment expired in a few days. June 1 was set as the date and the place would be New Orleans. None of the participants had ever dueled before, so it was necessary for White to go out and buy pistols. On the day the two officers faced off, Van Derveer was selected to call off the count. As he gave the command, both officers fired and missed. Observers and the seconds quickly stepped in and convinced the two officers that honor had been served and there was no need to continue. To everyone's relief and satisfaction, the contest ended without bloodshed. Fourteen years later, all four duelists and seconds would become regimental commanders in the Union army. [52] [Note: Duelist Carr White commanded the Twelfth Ohio Volunteer Infantry in the Civil War. His opponent, James Fyffe, commanded the Fifty-ninth Ohio Volunteer Infantry. Secondly, James Harrison was appointed commander of the Eleventh Ohio Volunteer Infantry.]

War had been an exciting and educational experience for Ferdinand Van Derveer. He had observed how a regiment was recruited and put into the field and been exposed to both the practical and political aspects of organization. As an orderly sergeant and company commander, he had learned the administration and logistics of a military unit and how important it was to be sure soldiers were properly cared for. Experience as a line officer had shown him what it was like to be under fire, what it was like to command men in the field and in battle, and how to deal with volunteer soldiers. Above all, he had learned the value of discipline in a military unit. They were all lessons he would have opportunity to use later.

A bonafide war hero, Van Derveer cast a long shadow when he returned from Mexico. A huge celebration was held in Middletown on July 4, 1847, where Captain Van Derveer was presented with an engraved sword and spoke to the crowd in "a happy and appropriate strain." All of this increased his local reputation and benefited his law practice. Riding a wave of popularity, he was elected county sheriff in 1848, and in that same year, married Emily Gaylord of Cincinnati. Presiding over the opening of the new county jail was the high point of his two-year tenure in office, but it was not enough to get him reelected. A man named Yeargus had been arrested and jailed for threatening to murder his wife and burn his neighbor's house down. After several weeks of confinement, Van Derveer had given Yeargus the liberty of the jail yard and had left his cell unlocked at night. The ungrateful Yeargus had left the jail, walked to the tiny hamlet of Busenbark, and killed his wife just as he had threatened to do. The

52. *Cyclopaedia of Butler County*, 201–2.

negative publicity ruined Van Derveer's chances for reelection.[53]

The disappointment of being voted out of office led Van Derveer to try a new career. He purchased part ownership and became editor of the Butler County *Telegraph* in November 1849. He was known as "an able and forcible writer, and woe be it to the individual who incurred his displeasure," but Van Derveer sold his interest in the paper less than a year later in October of 1850. As a newspaperman, Van Derveer would have seen the almost daily reports of the fabulous discoveries being made in the gold fields of California and the allure of gold caused him to seek his fortune away from Butler County one more time. Late in 1850, he left Hamilton and his wife behind and headed west for the gold fields. It was a decision he later regretted for California was not the bonanza he had hoped for. The expectant Van Derveer had arrived in California much too late to take part in the big mining boom. All that he got from his sojourn in the west was emotional distress caused by separation from his wife, personal disappointment in a failed venture, and a greater appreciation of home. Returning from California in 1852, Van Derveer settled into a comfortable position as a local attorney and respected citizen. Until the summer of 1861, his ambitions all remained close to home. It took another war to change his mind. The patriotic spirit that was part of his heritage was aroused once again, and the thirty-nine-year-old attorney decided once more to offer his services to the nation.[54]

Whistling in the Dark

Amid the flurry of communications that accompanied the Union buildup in the commonwealth of Kentucky was one that started the regiment down the road to war. While the paperwork was being completed to muster the Thirty-fifth Ohio Volunteers into Federal service for three years, Colonel Van Derveer received a terse telegram from Governor Dennison. "You will consider yourself as under Gen. O. M. Mitchhell's orders." If Van Derveer wondered what the telegram portended, he did not have to wait long. The telegraph wires from Cincinnati began to heat up, and the Thirty-fifth Ohio's entry into the war was precipitate. Within a few hours, General Mitchel contacted Van Derveer directly. His first message of the day, as succinct as the governor's earlier message, warned Van Derveer to be ready to move at a moment's notice. Word went out and the men began to pack what gear they had. Shortly, another message arrived.

"Are you ready to proceed to Cincinnati with your regiment with the necessary arms and equipments to enter Kentucky, and hold the Covington and

53. Keil, *Thirty-fifth Ohio*, 217; Cone, *Biographical*, 344–45.

54. Cone, *Biographical*, 345; *Memorial Record of Butler County, Ohio* (Chicago: Record Publishing Co., 1894), 409–10.

Lexington railway? Answer."

Mitchel's second message, both demanding and imperative, let the regiment know what its first mission was to be. The nation's expanding railway network was fast becoming a vital circulatory system. Any advance into and beyond Kentucky would require the use of the railroads, and with the situation in Kentucky very much up in the air, seizing the roads before the Confederates captured or damaged them was absolutely vital. Mitchel's third message of the day escalated the urgency of the moment.

"Transportation will be furnished you at 12 o'clock tomorrow. Sit up all night, if necessary, to be ready. You will leave here at 2:30 p.m.—A secret—."[55]

The regiment was in no way ready for war. It had received a few days worth of individual and company drill, new uniforms, and personal accouterments, but some other significant items were missing—things like rifles. Whether or not the regiment sat up all night as General Mitchel suggested, the unit historian proudly recorded that, even though an early morning telegram moved the departure time up two hours, the regiment began its war on time. While the excited infantrymen waited to board the cars for the trip south someone decided they ought to at least have weapons before they were sent out. Many Civil War regiments went into the field carrying more than one kind of weapon, but the problem was much more prevalent in the west, where weapons stocks were fewer and farther between. Eight companies were issued Model 1842 .69 caliber Springfield smoothbore muskets and the two remaining companies got .58 caliber Enfields. Once armed, the companies climbed on board Cincinnati, Hamilton, & Dayton Railroad railcars and rolled south toward the Queen City of the West and the Ohio River. The excited novices received their first lessons on loading their muskets as the train pulled out of the station.[56]

Once in Cincinnati, the regiment had to unload and march down to the river. Cincinnati was a nervous place at the moment. In peace time, the Queen City of the West had been the gateway to the South but more recently people had worried it might become a city a few yards from a hostile border. Every regiment that passed through the city provided a little more assurance that they were safe. Regimental drill was still a future hope as the Thirty-fifth moved awkwardly through the streets. It was all quite disorganized, but the people cheered anyway, not for their soldierly appearance but rather for the potential they represented. As the regiment boggled its way through the city streets, more specific orders arrived.

"Col. Van Derveer:

SIR: You will proceed with your regiment and take possession of the Kentucky Cen-

---

55. Keil, *Thirty-fifth Ohio*, 217

56. Ibid., 1; Quartermaster General Report for 1862, Adjutant General of Ohio State Archives, Ohio Historical Society, Columbus; Brent Nosworthy, *The Bloody Crucible of Courage* (New York: Carroll and Graf Publishers, 2002), 183.

tral Railway, from Cynthiana to Lexington. You will probably find it unnecessary to send your guards beyond the town of Paris; of this you will be the judge. I desire you to report to these headquarters, each day, the condition of your command and any matter of interest. Telegraph me the result of your expedition tonight. In case you require aid telegraph. You are directed to inform citizens of Kentucky that you hold the railroad by the order of Gen. Robt. Anderson.

O. M. Mitchell

Brig. Gen. Commanding"[57]

On the other side of the Ohio River, things were different. The fact that Kentucky was a Union state meant nothing. Since their basis for deciding who supported the Union had as much to do with regional identity as it did with a profession of loyalty, nearly all of them saw Kentucky as a Southern state. Once across the broad waterway everyone felt like they were indeed on the fabled "dark and bloody ground" in the presence of the enemy. Most of the soldiers in the Thirty-fifth Ohio had come of age in the emotionally charged years between 1855 and 1860 and viewed the South with strong prejudice. The greeting the regiment received in Covington served to reinforce their opinions. A slave state, Kentucky held a large number of Confederate sympathizers who did not see the blue clad soldiers as saviors. Rather than cheers, the Buckeyes received curses. When they were told, "Go to _____ , you Yankee _____ !" it only fed the feeling of being in enemy territory. Boarding Kentucky Central cars at the Covington station, the men were introduced to another timeless aspect of military life; hurry up and wait. All the rushed movement had brought them to their jump-off point hours early. They had no choice but to wait for the appointed time of departure. There was some concern that word of the movement might reach Southern sympathizers along the route, so the telegraph office was seized and held to prevent any sabotage to the road.[58]

The lack of training and discipline among the regiment's new soldiers showed itself immediately in an expected way. Human nature has changed little over the centuries, and having just received new toys, the men of the Thirty-fifth wanted to play with them. As the train began chugging south, the men quickly came up with many plausible reasons for firing their newly acquired rifles. Some said it was to check to see if the vents were open. Others, having torn open a cartridge to inspect it contents, said it was to see if the coarse black powder would really fire. For whatever reason, rifle barrels began to appear out the doors and windows of the cars as they rolled through the countryside. Men excited at going to war began to fire at whatever targets presented themselves. As one officer put it, "It was simply impossible to prevent the snapping of caps."[59]

---

57. Keil, *Thirty-fifth Ohio*, 217–18.
58. Ibid., 1; Bell I. Wiley, *The Life of Billy Yank* (Baton Rouge: Louisiana State University Press, 1994), 96; Mitchell, *Civil War Soldiers*, 16.
59. Keil, *Thirty-fifth Ohio*, 1.

While it may have seemed impossible to a greenhorn lieutenant unsure of his ability and authority to control men he had known most of his life and who had only recently elected him to his position, Colonel Van Derveer suffered under no such delusions. His hard-earned sense of military discipline was offended at the unsoldierly popping of caps. To appease his anger and to further the professional development of his junior officers, the bristling colonel sent Major Boynton to deliver a stinging rebuke to company officers who allowed their men to experiment. This was only the first in a long string of corrections the regimental officers would receive from their colonel whose admonitions came with such frequency and detail that the lieutenants and captains of the regiment assumed they came straight from *Hardee's Tactics*.[60]

As the train neared Cynthiana around 10:00 p.m., Major Boynton toured the cars again commanding silence as the train entered the town. The men may have been responding to the earlier correction, or perhaps they were excited at the prospect of sneaking up on somebody, but not a voice was heard from the train as it entered the depot. When the train came to a stop, the soldiers bounded out of the cars and enthusiastically formed ranks. All a twitter at the new game they were playing, the men were actually looking forward to making a night march into the countryside, but most of the companies went no further that night. While most of the regiment settled in at the Cynthiana depot, Company C and Company H, with Colonel Long accompanying them, were put onto another train to be taken out to guard bridges and trestles farther down the track. Lieutenant Keil of Company C got off the train with twenty men at the first stop, a place known as Lair Station. Their mission was to guard a series of trestles spanning deep ravines near the south fork of the Licking River. Keil was ordered to "have your sentinels conceal themselves, and not make targets for prowling confederates; allow no colored person to come into your camp, be circumspect." [61]

These new soldiers had so much to learn. Three guards were posted after being given the orders for careful concealment. They wanted to be good soldiers, so they obeyed the letter of the order. When their relief arrived two hours later, the guards on duty were nowhere to be found. An unintended game of hide and seek was played until the relief finally gave up and whistled. Even after this "ally-ally-in-free," the guards did not speak or show themselves. They rustled bushes until the relief found them. No doubt there was some concern about being a target, but it is easy to imagine these young men lying in the nighttime shadows and grinning while their friends searched up and down for them. War was just an exciting game to be played at until it was time to go home.[62]

Keil's detail had brought no camp equipment with them, so the agent

---

60. Keil, *Thirty-fifth Ohio*, 2.
61. Ibid.
62. Ibid., 2

opened the station for their use. There was no bedding but the off-duty men could at least lie across sacks of grain, a much better cushion than the floor. All was quiet until 3:00 a.m. when a "fearful racket" caused everyone to scramble up, weapons in hand to repel whatever enemy force had fallen upon them. Anyone truly eager for a fight was to be disappointed. Among those sleeping on grain sacks was Pvt. Johnny Doyle, who in his sleep, had rolled off his perch into an assortment of buckets, brooms, and shovels.[63]

Several other details were placed along the railroad that night. After Keil's group was dropped off, the train continued on a few more miles and deposited Captain Gunckel and a detail from Company H at the next set of trestles at Stoner Creek. The rest of Company C was placed in two further locations. Lieutenant Miller with twenty men guarded a bridge near Aquia Run. Captain Earhart and the largest detail of sixty men were taken all the way to Paris to watch the bridges in the immediate vicinity of that city. Two days later, on September 28, General Mitchel reported to the Adjutant General of Ohio that Colonel Van Derveer's mission "has been successfully accomplished, the bridges are guarded, and our communications with Camp Dick Robinson are now secure." For the next eight weeks, the mission of the Thirty-fifth Ohio was to guard this thirteen-mile section of the Central Kentucky Railroad. At any one time, about 150 to 200 men were on guard detail. The rest of the regiment went into camp near Cynthiana and began training.[64]

Pushed Forward

On a bluff northeast of Cynthiana, a "substantial union man" named Frazer owned a plantation that became the regiment's first camp outside Ohio. In honor of Mr. Frazer's generosity, the camp bore his name. Camp Frazer was laid out facing north. The official entrance was at the northeast corner of camp adjacent the Old Falmouth pike. The first view visitors entering the camp had was of the guardhouse tent on their immediate right and the rest of the camp extending toward the southwest where the railroad formed the opposite edge of the encampment. Staff officers lived in the first northern most row of tents separated from the company commanders and officers by a grass strip, or street. Just behind the company officers, across another street, was the regimental band, those men who lived in a sort of suspended state, of the regiment but not really in it. In the same row was the commissary tent, conveniently located to issue rations. Behind the band and the commissary, the individual companies

63. Keil, *Thirty-fifth Ohio,* 3

64. Ibid., 7; U.S. War Department, *The War of the Rebellion: A Compilation of the Official Records of the Union and Confederate Armies,* Ser. no. 3, p. 552; Ser. no. 4, pp. 280–81.

set up their tents. Each company had two rows of tents facing each other and running perpendicular to the rows of officers in front of them. This same pattern of encampment was used throughout the war.

The companies not on guard duty began the tedious task of learning to be soldiers, and the first step in that process has been the same for centuries. They learned to march. No matter how quickly the men and their officers wanted things to go, learning the maneuvers required of the individual soldier, the company, and the regiment was a slow process. As one officer put it, "Time is an important factor in the work of disciplining troops; and only so much can be done within a given time, no matter how strongly the work is pushed forward." The Thirty-fifth Ohio had gone to war with only eight of its ten authorized companies. Company I apparently accompanied the regiment to Cynthiana even though they had not yet been formerly mustered. Company K was still recruiting in Butler County.[65]

In those early days of the war, the Thirty-fifth Ohio was truly on its own. There was no organized command structure between Colonel Van Derveer and the department commander. Whatever administrative and logistical support was needed had to be orchestrated by him, and the regiment needed almost everything. The blankets the men had received were in deplorable condition "not even good for mosquito bars, being entirely torn open." Colonel Van Derveer had them all condemned, but it did no good. There were no new blankets in store to replace them, so the old ones remained. The same situation existed with the regiment's dilapidated tents. Captain Stone of Company B wrote a letter to the Hamilton *Telegraph* requesting that citizens send blankets, quilts, and comforters, as well as providing instructions on how to make a bedroll from ticking. The men were using piled up straw that was uncomfortable and dirty.[66]

Officers fared much better than the men who served under them. The wives of Captain Gunckel and Lieutenant Smith came down for a visit. Mrs. Long and Mrs. Earhart were hardy enough to spend several days and nights in camp sleeping in their husband's tents. Colonel Van Derveer considered bringing his wife Emily to Cynthiana, perhaps because the rushed exit from Camp Hamilton had created some personal problems for him. "You think I intentionally deceived you when I left home," he wrote in a letter shortly after arriving in Camp Frazer. "You do me injustice dear wife, for I knew nothing further than I told you until I got to Cincinnati—the movement as you must know was a secret." In the end, Van Derveer decided it was best for Emily to remain home, because he believed the second parting would do both more harm than good. Even so, the colonel assured his wife that he was doing well. Camp life was pleasant and he had several friends around him to keep company. He had received many gifts of food and flowers from local women, but Van Derveer

65. Keil, *Thirty-fifth Ohio*, 7.

66. Gerald J. Prokopowicz, *All for the Regiment* (Chapel Hill: University of North Carolina Press, 2001), 36; Hamilton *Telegraph*, October 17, 1861.

playfully assured Emily that "these are all gifts of married ladies, so do not be uneasy." There was also a constant stream of dinner invitations, many of which had to be refused due to his ever increasing work load. There were more than enough administrative and training requirements to keep him busy all of the time.[67]

The focus of training in the early days was squad drill, also known as the "school of the soldier." During this part of the program, individual soldiers learned the most basic things like standing at attention, simple facing movements, how to march, and how to load and fire a musket. There were nine steps involved in firing a musket the way the army wanted a man to do it, and in the school of the soldier, each man repeated those steps until loading and firing a rifle became second nature.

Ferdinand Van Derveer wrote his wife that, "Cynthiana is a pleasant little town about the size of Middletown—We astonished them not a little when we took up our quarters in their midst—but now have got somewhat used to us— we treat all with politeness." Politeness not withstanding, the Yankee soldiers were not well received by the local citizens who generally supported the new Confederacy. Confederate recruiters were active in the area, and quite a few local men, strongly encouraged by their women, were stealing away to the south. At night, one detail always stood guard over the supplies at the train depot. Once darkness fell, the detail was essentially on its own, because the passwords for entry into camp were not given to its members. In early October, the depot guards heard a rumor that a local minister was preparing to slip away that same night to become a chaplain in the Confederate army. There was no way to get the information into camp without the sign and countersign, but the guards felt it was vital that Colonel Van Derveer know of the minister's flight.[68]

One "rather ingenious" but unnamed corporal, known for his ability in "working through difficult places," was assigned the risky task of slipping into camp to warn the Colonel. After nearly being caught several times, the young man got through the lines and made his way to the regimental commander's tent. Van Derveer was lying on his cot reading a newspaper by candlelight. The intrepid corporal started his report, fully expecting it to excite his commander and initiate a flurry of activity. Without looking up from his paper, the colonel interrupted the corporal's report to say, "D——n him, let him go. I don't know of a concern more in need of prayer than the confederate army!" As the colonel returned to reading his paper, having never looked up to see who was making the report, the deeply disappointed corporal backed quietly out of the tent to run the gauntlet back out of camp. Everyone later agreed the minister's prayers went unanswered, and never again did anyone bother Van Derveer with rumors

---

67. Van Derveer to wife, 30 September 1861, Van Derveer Family Collection, MS79-1010, Smith Library of Regional History, Oxford, Ohio.
68. Ibid.

of recruits going south.[69]

If the white population of Cynthiana generally avoided the Thirty-fifth, the local slaves were fascinated by the blue-clad soldiers and approached the camp in an unending stream. The Federal government was desperate to keep Kentucky loyal, and officers with free black servants had been forced to send them back to Ohio. Furthermore, orders were that the soldiers were not to fraternize with the slaves or allow them into camp. Local white citizens who openly espoused the southern cause could walk freely among the tents, but slaves friendly to the army were kept out. Day after day, they would approach the guards claiming to have useful information, and day after day, they were "courteously" turned away with the hope of being able to enter at some future date. Even so, for the first time, the officers and men of Thirty-fifth Ohio were faced with "the practical phaze of the negro question." Rather than fictional caricatures, they stood face to face with real black men and women.[70]

Like the great majority of men in the Union armies, the men of the Thirty-fifth Ohio displayed a general antipathy toward African Americans. Typical of mid-nineteenth-century Americans, their record of relations with the African Americans they came into contact with was a mixed one. They came from the old Northwest Territory which had always been free, and so opposed slavery, but that made them neither abolitionists nor supporters of racial equality. They did not believe in the equality of races, and almost unanimously, believed that whites were superior to blacks. That attitude was prevalent in their dealings with the runaway slaves and contrabands, which they generally referred to as "darkies," that they came into contact with as the war progressed. The soldiers sympathized with the contrabands and saw them as natural allies, but they never treated them as equals or fellow citizens.[71]

In Kentucky, the first contacts with local slaves were driven mostly by curiosity. It was not uncommon for the men to gather around while a black man told stories of living in bondage. One such incident occurred in Cynthiana when an older, broken down slave slipped quietly into camp. Several men gathered around while he told a pitiful story. The slave, named Jim, had been born in Virginia and his parents had been sold to a plantation in Georgia while Jim was still an infant. He had run away twice and carried horrible scars from being beaten and mauled by dogs. His leg had been broken to cripple him and keep him from running again. After a long tale of abuse and sorrow, Jim closed with the hopes that the Yankees would "whip de secesh, an' not go home til poo' ole Jim am free." Jim's story had a stronger impact on his listeners than any antislavery sermon they had ever heard. "The mere wreck that was left" was ample proof of the evils of slavery, and "the simple eloquence in which he narrated the

---

69. Keil, *Thirty-fifth Ohio*, 8–9

70. Ibid., 3–4

71. Wiley, *Billy Yank*, 109; Michael R. Bradley, *Tullahoma: The 1863 Campaign for the Control of Middle Tennessee* (Shippensburg, Pa.: Burd Street Press, 2000), 2.

sad tale of his wrongs softened the sternness with which we had ordered away from camp all his race." The men of the Thirty-fifth never saw him again, but they hoped that "old Jim lived long enough to hear the glad news of his freedom."[72]

If the men had a lot to learn, their officers were equally inexperienced, and their behavior often reinforced the idea that the war was a big game. Colonel Van Derveer determined to conduct a night alert to test the response of the regiment. The callow company commanders were informed of the drill, and "certain captains made too much fuss in attempting to impress upon the minds of their men, that there was imminent danger." Knowing full well there were no enemy forces within fifty miles of Cynthiana, "the guise was so thin, that the men saw though it, and laughed at the seeming concern of the officers." When the long roll was sounded, the fully alerted companies leapt into line with dizzying speed. The only excitement occurred when one soldier got gouged in the eye by a bayonet.[73]

Among the prevalent sympathy for the Confederacy, there were Unionists living in and around Cynthiana. While the men were generally unwilling to actively defend the Union, the loyal ladies were willing to do what they could. Having left Hamilton in such a rush, there had been no time for a formal flag presentation, and the regiment had only a smaller storm flag. The lack of a good national flag was noticed at a dress parade, and a discrete inquiry was made by a group of local women. They were concerned that there might be some reluctance to accept a flag made by Kentucky ladies. Colonel Van Derveer promptly replied that the men of the Thirty-fifth Ohio "respected the American flag, wherever found, no matter by whom made, and particularly so, when the gift and handiwork of patriotic Kentucky ladies." The complete list of women who worked on the flag was lost, but among them were Mrs. Delling, Mrs. George Morrison, Mrs. Frank Gray, Miss Pauline Ballingall, Mrs. Sallie Thompson, Miss Sallie Kimbrough, Mrs. J. S. Frizell, Mrs. Dickey, Mrs. Dr. W. O. Smith, Miss Mary January, and Miss Emma Tabor. The flag was presented in a ceremony at Camp Frazer and was placed in the custody of Color Sgt. Mark B. Price. The men of the Thirty-fifth Ohio were devoted to their flag. It was the symbol of their purpose and their unity. More than any words could, it symbolized what they had agreed to fight for. The Cynthiana flag was considered by the soldiers of the Thirty-fifth to be one of the finest flags in the western armies and was carried by the regiment throughout its service. When it became too tattered to fly, it was still carried proudly furled around its staff. Decades later, the men still remembered and praised the generous ladies of Cynthiana.[74]

---

72. Keil, *Thirty-fifth Ohio*, 4, 7; Wiley, *Billy Yank*, 115.

73. Keil, *Thirty-fifth Ohio*, 9.

74. Ibid., 10; U.S. War Department, *War of the Rebellion*, Ser. no. 4, p. 314; Mitchell, *Civil War Soldiers*, 20.

The Thirty-fifth Ohio had only been away from home for a few weeks, but already some men were getting homesick. In the case of Pvt. William McKean, a farm boy from Preble County, it was the smell of the autumn breeze that drove him to distraction. Turning his face into the wind, he said, "That smells like papaw time in Ohio, and I'd give three months of my three years enlistment for a good mess." When McKean applied for a pass the next day to go collect papaws, Captain L'Hommedieu told him there were none in Kentucky. McKean was not to be denied and replied, "Give me a pass and I'll bet you $10 I'll find some before I come back." L'Hommedieu, who granted the pass, was about to learn one of the unwritten laws of the army: If you want to get an officer in trouble, just do exactly what he told you to do. McKean missed roll call for the next three days, and on the fourth day, L'Hommedieu received a letter in the mail. It read:

Holden Cross Roads, Ohio

October 15, 1861

Dear Captain—I took your word for it that there were no papaws in Kentucky, so I did not look for them there, but I knew where there were plenty in Ohio and I was bound to have them if I had to come to Ohio to get them. Well, captain, I got them and I am satisfied, and if you will hold my job for me, I will be back in a few days and fill my contract.

Yours truly,

Wm. M. Mc---"

McKean did return, and just as he promised, he finished his enlistment with no further trouble.[75]

Yet another way that inexperience showed itself was in the handling of rumors. According to John White of Company F, the camp was "full of rumors about marching and a hundred other things, all of which are nothing but the idle wishes of some of the boys who give vent to them, and ere an hour they perambulate to the remotest corners of the camp as coming from headquarters." Later on, the men would be able to gauge the plausibility of rumors with aplomb, but in the naiveté of Kentucky, every rumor was assumed to be true. This fact was proven to everyone's detriment on at least one occasion. A soldier in the Thirty-fifth was rumored to have enlisted for the sole purpose of poisoning the water supplies of the regiment. The story seems extremely doubtful and the unit historian admitted that no incident of poisoning ever occurred, but the accused was actually tortured by his mates to get him to confess. When this effort failed, the men were forced to admit that he might be innocent, but they preferred to believe he was an "expert rascal."[76]

---

75. Benjamin Arnold, *Sunshine and Shadows in the Life of a Private Soldier* (Dayton, Ohio: Curt Dalton, 1995), 33–34.

Seasoning

Upon entering Kentucky at the end of September, the Thirty-fifth Ohio had been the vanguard of the army. But in just a few days, other regiments had leap-frogged past them and moved deeper into the state. Gen. George H. Thomas, former Mexican War acquaintance of Colonel Van Derveer and now the regional commander, placed his forces in a line stretching from Lexington to the Cumberland Gap. The two main roads into central Kentucky via London and Crab Orchard were guarded by Union regiments, and Thomas also had a reserve force with him at Camp Dick Robinson. All of his logistical support came by rail from Cincinnati to Nicholasville where supplies were loaded on wagons for distribution to units in the field. The overall commander of the state, General William T. Sherman, was concerned about the Union's ability to defend Kentucky. He could get but few troops from within the state, and had to depend upon "the raw levies of Ohio and Indiana, who arrive in detachments perfectly fresh from the county and loaded down with baggage." The Thirty-fifth Ohio was one of the raw levies Sherman was worried about. Thomas's communications had to remain open and to do that, the railroads had to be protected by the Thirty-fifth and others.[77]

In support of the general move forward, the regiment broke camp at Cynthiana on October 22 and moved by rail to Paris. Upon arrival, the regiment paraded through Paris, and the men were well aware of the contrast of that movement presented with their movement through Cincinnati the month before. The drill was paying off, and they were beginning to look and feel like soldiers. Their camp at Paris was also an improvement over Camp Frazer. The regiment set up its tents on the Bourbon County fairgrounds where there were buildings to store equipment and stables for the horses. The bluegrass pastures south of the camp provided excellent fields for drilling. The site became known as Camp Bourbon.[78]

The camp was an attractive location "high and rolling and thickly sodded with blue grass." When the men of the regiment commented on its beauty, the local citizens lost no time in explaining that the fairgrounds had been used to show the finest cattle, jacks, and mules in the country. Stock breeding was serious business in Bourbon County, with animals being brought in from as far away as Europe. The "intelligent stock raisers" of the county realized substantial profit from their breeding operations.[79]

It was at Camp Bourbon that the regiment reached full strength with the arrival of Company K and began to settle into the military routine. The regi-

76. Keil, *Thirty-fifth Ohio*, 11–12; Thirty-fifth OVI Collection, Butler County Historical Society, Hamilton, Ohio.

77. U.S. War Department, *War of the Rebellion*, Ser. no. 4, p. 333.

78. Keil, *Thirty-fifth Ohio*, 13.

79. Bogan, *Warren County's Involvement*, 50–52.

ment's day began with musicians sounding reveille between five and six o'clock, depending on the season, immediately followed by a roll call. As with nearly all regiments in the Union army, the majority of men were "reasonably prompt" about reporting for roll call, since failure to report led to time in the guardhouse. After the roll was called, the men had a few free minutes while the first sergeants prepared the morning report. Some used it to prepare for the day. Others tried to grab a few extra minutes of sleep before the breakfast call was sounded. The end of breakfast was the signal for two competing calls; sick call for the ill and fatigue call for the able. Ailing soldiers were marched to the surgeon for examination while those on fatigue duty performed activities such as policing the regimental area, digging latrines and drainage ditches, or chopping wood. The balance of the morning was spent in drill. After the noon meal, there was more drill, but in late afternoon, the men were released to prepare for the evening retreat.[80]

Training began to take on a more earnest tone. The heart and soul of this process, the force that controlled and guided all its actions, was Col. Ferdinand Van Derveer. It was his responsibility to ensure that all the officers, sergeants, and soldiers in the regiment were taught and mastered the necessary skills that would allow the Thirty-fifth Ohio to fight well. Van Derveer's Mexican War experience was of immense help in this task. Perhaps most important of all, Mexico had taught him how to manage and lead American volunteer soldiers. He understood that even though they had entered into a legally binding agreement to be soldiers for three years, they would always be civilians in blue uniforms that could behave in ways that completely baffled regular army officers. They could be stubborn, willful, disrespectful, profane, and abusive, but they could also be naive and childlike. Van Derveer, once an enlisted volunteer himself, understood all of this and accepted the men as they were, never trying to force them to become professional warriors. He had seen how West Point graduates who demanded military exactness in all things failed miserably when it came to leading volunteers and was able to persuade the men under him to accept his authority. He treated them respectfully, strictly, and humanely, but more than all of those, he demonstrated to them that he knew what he was doing. Sensing that their colonel trusted them, and convinced of his competence, Van Derveer's officers and men trusted him in return.

Van Derveer's efforts at discipline were fully supported by his two ranking officers, Lieutenant Colonel Long and Major Boynton. Long had learned from experience in Mexico and in the ninety-day Fifth Ohio to deal directly with the men under him and take nothing for granted. He was quite firm in manner, and the new soldiers responded to his methods. If Long was adept at controlling the volunteers, Major Boynton proved to be quite masterful. Boynton seemed to have everything stacked against him. He was a young man who appeared to be even younger than he was and an outsider thrust upon them by the governor.

80. Wiley, *Billy Yank*, 45–46.

Major Henry V. Boynton
ROGER D. HUNT COLLECTION AT USAMHI

Raised by a father who was both an ardent minister and abolitionist, Boynton graduated from Woodward College in Cincinnati before entering the Kentucky Military Institute. He had gone to KMI to get a degree in civil engineering, and his detail-oriented mind, religious upbringing, and military school background made him a strict disciplinarian.

For all of those reasons, the men should have naturally resisted Boynton's presence, yet they immediately took to him. Boynton had a personal manner that allowed him to exercise great authority without seeming to. His instructions seemed to be coming from a reasonable fellow named Henry rather than a major named Boynton, so the raw recruits of the Thirty-fifth took no offense at his many orders. Rather they willingly obeyed them, because they seemed to make such good sense. Boynton was also convinced of the efficacy of "equal and exact" justice. The regiment quickly learned that Major Boynton treated everybody fairly and consistently.[81]

The preparation of an infantry regiment for war was a very specialized task calling for a great deal of technical knowledge. The only place to get that knowledge was from experience and military manuals. The army had no organized officer training schools, and for the most part, each commander was left to his own devices in deciding how to train his men. Fortunately, there was some base of experience in the Thirty-fifth Ohio. Besides Van Derveer, both Lieutenant Colonel Long and Major Boynton could provide some expertise. Captain L'Hommedieu was another graduate of the Kentucky Military Institute and thoroughly familiar with drilling. But for the most part, officers and sergeants had to learn their jobs from books. In 1861, the primary training manual was *Hardee's Tactics*. A three volume, pocket-size set of books, Hardee's manual, officially titled *Rifle and Light Infantry Tactics*, was readily available and became an absolutely vital possession for every officer in the regiment.

As commander and head instructor, it was Van Derveer's responsibility to ensure that all officers were properly trained so that they could in turn train the sergeants. To this end, Van Derveer pushed his officers hard to learn their jobs, requiring them to study tactics regularly. They had to demonstrate their knowledge during daily drills, but Van Derveer expected more of his officers. After the training day ended for the soldiers, officers attended sessions where Van Derveer lectured them on things like outpost duty and the sword exercise, tested their knowledge of drill commands, and threatened them regularly, constantly reinforcing the need to become competent. He was assisted to a great degree by human nature. No officer wants to stand in front of the men he must command and look like an idiot. The desire to appear competent drove the junior officers to learn their jobs as quickly as possible, and it was not unusual to see them with their head buried deep in some tactics manual. One of the more popular references was *Scientific American* magazine, which did its bit for God and country by publishing articles about learning to shoot a rifle and

81. Keil, *Thirty-fifth Ohio*, 238.

other practical applications of warfare.[82]

But in the end, it all came down to drill. In the early days of the regiment's existence, drill had focused on simple facing and marching movements. The men of the Thirty-fifth had learned the various positions for carrying a rifle, how to load a rifle in "nine times," and how to march forward, to the rear, to the flank, and obliquely. As individuals learned the skills required of them, training shifted to company level maneuvers, and soon, it became time for the companies to learn to maneuver as a regiment. At this level, soldiers learned to move from marching formations into fighting formations and back. The maneuvers were very complicated and required constant practice until the companies learned how to move around each other. Since no one was entirely proficient, each day consisted of squad, company, and regimental level drill. As the lone garrison in the area, no training was conducted at a level higher than the regiment. Individual soldiers in the Thirty-fifth Ohio became adept, and the companies learned to maneuver as a unit, but their full development as a fighting unit was slightly retarded by their isolation. They did not have the chance to develop a sense of being part of a larger organization than their own regiment, which would be important in battle.[83]

When formed for battle, the companies lined up side by side in two ranks. Based on the letter of the companies, the order from left to right as they faced the enemy was A-F-D-I-C-H-E-G-K-B. The company commander stood at the right end of the front rank and the first sergeant stood behind him at the end of the second. Behind the ranks were the lieutenants and sergeants of each company acting as file closers. Their job was to direct and encourage the men in line and to make sure they remained in the ranks. The field grade officers were mounted and positioned themselves behind the lines. As was to be expected, the colonel placed himself in the center of the regiment about 150 feet behind the firing line. Nearby, the field musicians, not to be confused with the regimental band, stood ready to relay commands by drum and bugle. The major and lieutenant colonel were closer to the line and posted to the colonel's right and left. The adjutant and sergeant major, closer still to the firing line, were posted on each flank.

As long as the regiment stood in place, the commander had fairly good control of it, but as time would prove, this tight formation rarely lasted more than a few minutes in maneuvers against a real enemy. Depending upon the situation, the major or some designated company officer, who could only be controlled by messenger, would be in charge of skirmishers. The colonel was likely to move closer to the line to see what was going on, while the other staff officers would move to and fro behind the regiment to carry orders and give encouragement. Men on the firing line tended to spread out in movement, particularly when firing commenced.

---

82. Wiley, *Billy Yank*, 50, 53; Nosworthy, *Bloody Crucible*, 141, 151.
83. Prokopowicz, *All for the Regiment*, 47; Wiley, *Billy Yank*, 49.

Like soldiers everywhere, the men of the Thirty-fifth got tired of the incessant drilling and began to complain. The movements were definitely complicated, and the field manual did nothing to make things any clearer. "Before the military authorities authorize a certain military drill for the army, the author should be made to go through the drill prescribed; and become perfect in it personally; in that event much of the nonsense found in the work would be studiously eliminated. Hardee's two volumes would crawl into one, and not very large at that." The fact that the drill manual in use was authored by a general in the Confederate army no doubt added to the irritation, but there was no help for it. During the mid-nineteenth century, there was no other way for an army to get into a formation from which it could fight. The best hope for controlling a unit and massing its firepower in combat was the close order formation taught to the soldiers, so the drilling had to be endured. Because it was so complex, the system would only work if everyone performed his part correctly and could trust others to do the same.[84]

As the regiment prepared to fight, other things besides drill needed to be attended to. The logistical train was also being improved. Wilkinson Beatty went to Cincinnati to select horses for the regiment's wagon teams. Beatty, the oldest man in the regiment, was known as an excellent judge of horseflesh, so Van Derveer had been willing to argue with the mustering officer to get him enlisted. An independent operator, Beatty was also known for his ability to talk endlessly. "A habitual storyteller," Beatty could "manage several stories at the same time. It was no hardship for him, when in a chatty mood, to carry on six stories at once, and complete them all." His listeners found it more difficult to keep up with his tales. They were constantly trying to piece the parts of several stories together while keeping up with the raconteur.[85]

Arriving at the government corral in Cincinnati, Beatty was informed that he was expected to take whatever horses were brought out to him. He refused to accept that logic or those horses and argued long and loud with the quartermaster about which animals were fit and which were not. For the most part Beatty got what he wanted. He had to accept a few scrubs, but the rest were good, healthy animals. Later on, the train Beatty managed would seem amazingly extravagant, but in the fall of 1861, the regiment was assigned one six-horse team per company, and because they were operating independently of the rest of the army, they were assigned eight extra teams for transportation.[86]

The office of regimental quartermaster was a vital one requiring knowledge and the ability to manipulate an extremely bureaucratic system. Lt. John Van Derveer had been commissioned by his big brother as the Thirty-fifth Ohio's quartermaster, he had no previous experience and had to learn his job

84. Keil, *Thirty-fifth Ohio*, 13; Prokopowicz, *All for the Regiment*, 51; Donald A. Ritchie, *Press Gallery* (Cambridge: Harvard University Press, 1991), 114.

85. Keil, *Thirty-fifth Ohio*, 55–56.

86. Ibid., 14.

like everyone else. As a result, rations sometimes ran short and weren't always of the best quality. At Cynthiana, he had bought a batch of "sour" flour and baked it into bread, and the regiment subsequently nicknamed him "Sour Bread" Van Derveer. On another occasion while still in Kentucky, Company F was so upset by the condition of the meat ration that it refused to accept it. Conditions would improve with experience, but in Kentucky, among the rest of the regiment, suffering while Lieutenant Van Derveer learned his job, it was generally believed that if the quartermaster failed to quickly mend his ways, he should be "forcibly ejected from his office."[87]

Some of the deficiency in the food could be made up by visits to the sutler, Mr. Connor. Sutler could be a lucrative position, and the competition was fierce. Ten different men had applied for the sole right to serve as the regiment's convenience store, so a committee consisting of Lieutenant Colonel Long, Major Boynton, and Captain Budd was assembled to make the choice. Each apparently had his favorite, and nine separate votes were required before Connor was declared the victor. During the course of the war, the Thirty-fifth would have three different sutlers [88]

Another vital aspect of the regiment's preparation was what was known at the time as "seasoning." Not only did the men have to learn to fight, they had to get used to being in the army. That involved several things. They had to adjust to essentially living out of doors all the time. While this wasn't much of an adjustment for some, it was a big change for others. They had to get used to eating army rations, which were monotonous at best. They had to learn how to cook rations so that they were at least edible and to mend clothes. More than all of those, they had to get used to communal living, part of which involved sharing communicable diseases as quickly as possible. Illness was a fact of life for soldiers in the field, and during his three-year enlistment, the typical solider could expect to succumb to some illness about eight times. Once the inevitable wave of measles and chicken pox was over, the regiment would be much hardier and less prone to minor epidemics that could sap its strength. Existing records indicate that November 1861 was the sickest month of the war for the Union army, and at Paris, the Thirty-fifth Ohio's sick list increased rapidly to about two hundred men. Captain Parshall of Company F became sick as soon as the regiment left Hamilton, and was quite ill for over a month before returning to full duty. Four men died of disease while the regiment was guarding the Central Kentucky Railroad. The first, Pvt. Isaac Mann of Company B, died on October 10, less than a month from the time the Thirty-fifth entered active service. On November 21, the Hamilton *Telegraph* carried the death notice of Albert Mayhew, a nineteen-year-old private from Company D. Mayhew, "a young man very much respected in his company," had fallen ill on November 10. By the fifteenth, he was dead. His body was escorted home by 1st Sgt.

---

87. Bogan, *Warren County's Involvement*, 50–52.
88. Keil, *Thirty-fifth Ohio*, 219.

Alfred Morgan and turned over to family friends who carried it to Mayhew's mother. It was only the beginning. From that time on, the strength of the regiment began to dwindle and would never again reach anything resembling full strength.[89]

In a letter home, John White of Company F complained bitterly about surgeons Perkins A. Gordon and Francis D. Morris. According to White, they were "anything but satisfactory." He accused them of forcing people out of the hospital before they were well which only worsened the illness. White was also annoyed that the two men prescribed quinine and calomel for every ailment. As annoying as that may have been, it was in line with the medical practices of the day. Standard practice or not, White insisted that they would have been thrown out of town if they had treated their civilian patients the way they treated the soldiers of the Thirty-fifth. "Unless a different system of better nursing is pursued," he went on to say, "more of our brave boys will die from 'doctoring' than by the weapons of the enemy." White's was a prophetic statement, but Gordon and Morris were probably no better or no worse than other doctors in southwestern Ohio. As events would later prove, Gordon's professional qualifications, a medical degree from Western Reserve Medical College and eleven years in private practice, were quite good. In all likelihood, White was in large part exercising the soldier's right, and even obligation, to complain about his lot in life.[90]

Raw Material

After a few weeks, the men of the Thirty-fifth Ohio began to get impatient for action. They wanted to "see the enemy and smell powder." Like Cynthiana, Paris also contained a large number of Confederate sympathizers (Abraham Lincoln only got two votes in Paris in 1860), and groups of men would slip away at night to join the rebel army at Bowling Green. Home guardsmen would hear about a group preparing to leave and bring news to the camp. Having ignored individual defections at Cynthiana, Van Derveer was apparently unwilling to allow large groups to leave unmolested, and a company would be sent out to try and intercept them. Every move the Yankees made was shadowed and reported by southern sympathizers, so the rebel recruits always had plenty of warning. No would-be rebels were ever caught by the Thirty-fifth, and often as not they would find out from slaves that whatever group they were after had already gone. The desire for action and the frustration of being unable to catch rebel recruits led one corporal to pummel a local man for cheering Jeff Davis.[91]

---

89. Hamilton *Telegraph*, November 21, 1861; Wiley, *Billy Yank*, 124, 134.
90. Bogan, *Warren County's Involvement*, 50–52; Wiley, *Billy Yank*, 137–38.

Unfortunately for him, a shadowy figure named Steve Smith, chose this time to appear in Kentucky. Smith was known to the men, having arrived in Hamilton in the spring of 1861 with a story of how he had been driven out of the South for Union sympathies. After gaining the sympathy of the local residents, Smith had supposedly become heavily involved in a local group supporting secession. It was said he had passed out bills supporting Clement Vallandigham and had even attempted to establish the Knights of the Golden Circle in town. The regimental rumor mill said that Smith was a spy. Having become too well known at home to be of use there, the "secession squad" had given him "an endorsement to go elsewhere to do mischief." Smith entered Camp Bourbon wearing a stolen major's uniform and alternately masquerading as a member of General Sherman's staff or a newspaper correspondent and was mobbed as he walked among the tents. The boys "took the buttons and stripes from his coat, and shortened the legs of his pants somewhat" and were rather proud of themselves for showing restraint and not immediately hanging him. After being humiliated, Smith was hustled to the guardhouse where he was provided time "to arrange the facts for his next communication for his paper." Colonel Van Derveer claimed that Smith was kept locked up to protect him from further violence, but even if he pitied the man, he felt little sympathy for him. "This morning I sent Stephen Smith off to Cincinnati—I was sending Mr. Beatty with the sick and good for nothing horses and concluded to get Smith in the same load."[92]

As at Cynthiana, there were also loyal unionists in Paris who treated the Thirty-fifth well. The women of the city worked tirelessly in the hospitals, so that the regiment's sick later remembered their stay pleasantly. John White, in addition to complaining about the surgeons and quartermaster, also passed along some tidbits about the women of Paris and their ability to charm the officers of the Thirty-fifth. In his own company, Captain Parshall and 2nd Lt. Thomas Harlan, having been "continually exposed to cross-fires of bouquets," had been completely captured by the ladies of Old Bourbon. Neither providing specific instances nor directly accusing the officers of anything improper, White felt it necessary to say that Captain Parshall "leaves a happy family at home to mourn his loss." Harlan's case was not so offensive to White, the lieutenant being unmarried, and it was hoped that he would "survive the shock." White apparently thought more of 1st Lt. Joseph Thoms and declared him "crinoline proof." While providing an interesting glimpse into camp life in central Kentucky, White's stories tend more toward gossip than fact. No doubt they were in large part the product of envy, because a few lines lower in the same

91. Keil, *Thirty-fifth Ohio*, 15–16; Peter Cozzens, *This Terrible Sound* (Urbana: University of Illinois Press, 1992), 125; Thirty-fifth OVI Collection, Butler County Historical Society.

92. Keil, *Thirty-fifth Ohio*, 11–12; Hamilton *Telegraph*, October 29, 1861; Van Derveer, 28 October 1861, Van Derveer Family Collection.

letter, White stated that Parshall "was a stranger to fear, yet prudent, and the boys all like him." Thoms and Harlan were "good, well respected officers" and "owned as the best in any regiment."[93]

Every evening, a roll call, inspection, and dress parade were conducted. The dress parade was a dignified, colorful event intended to make the men proud of being soldiers. It began with the band marching down and back in front of the regiment, playing slowly one way and quickly the other. Each company first sergeant reported to Lieutenant Wright, the adjutant, who in turn reported to Colonel Van Derveer. The regiment then would conduct a brief but brisk "exercise in arms," before Van Derveer made remarks or passed on orders to his officers. On some occasions, official communications, orders, or even the findings of a court-martial were read to the assembled men prior to dismissing the regiment for the evening.[94]

The retreat was also an inspiration for local Unionists who would often come to camp to watch and visit. Paris was the home of Senator Garret Davis who formed a friendly acquaintance with Ferdinand Van Derveer. Van Derveer enjoyed spending evenings with Davis, and so it was that they arranged for the senator to speak to the assembled regiment. The men were marched to the senator's house for their obligatory oration, but in spite of Van Derveer's friendly feelings toward the senator, it was not an event remembered kindly by his officers or men. The regimental historian noted that everyone already knew of Davis's "fondness to talk upon all kinds and shades of topics," and then stating it more plainly, added that Davis "talked us tired; and we were only too glad when he got through telling how Kentucky soldiers marched to the defense of the great northwest during the Indian wars, and the war of 1812. [I]t was a good speech, but we wanted no more of that kind."[95]

The men of regiment had not been forgotten at home as one member of Company C learned when he got an unexpected package. Pvt. Benjamin Arnold of Company C had grown up in Montgomery County, Ohio, near Dayton. At the time of his enlistment, he had been living in a small village of fewer than five hundred people doing carpentry and hanging out with a group of local boys. Even though Arnold only knew him by reputation, there was an older man named Billy Blair who had been the butt of several jokes by the boys and so treated them all, stranger Arnold included, with disregard. Based on the tales of his friends, Arnold considered Blair to be a "cross-grained, crabbed old skin flint." One day in November, packages arrived in camp for the boys from Arnold's village. The townspeople had gathered up several useful items and sent them to their hometown boys for the oncoming winter.

Being a stranger to most people in town and only a temporary resident,

93. Bogan, *Warren County's Involvement*, 50–52.
94. Wiley, *Billy Yank*, 46–47.
95. Keil, *Thirty-fifth Ohio*, 17; Van Derveer to wife, 28 October 1861, Van Derveer Family Collection.

Arnold had not expected to receive anything and was surprised when his name was attached to a particularly large and heavy bundle. Upon opening the package, he was surprised to see that he had received a "Benjamin's mess." For everything the others had gotten, he had gotten two and they were of better quality. Down in the pile was a brief note:

"My Dear Boy —I am perhaps a stranger to you, but you are not unknown to me. I noticed when you left for camp that while all others had friends to bid them good-bye, you were neglected and alone, so I wish you to remember that you have a friend by the name of William Blair."

Stunned by the note and the package, Arnold was forced to reconsider previous testimony about Old Billy Blair. In his heart, he decided to "grant him a new trial, and on the strength of newly discovered testimony reverse the former decision."[96]

While soldiers found endless hours of drill physically demanding, it was not the labor of drill they disliked most. More than anything, they resented the unthinking submission it required of them. In Mexico, Ferdinand Van Derveer came to place great value on military discipline and so insisted upon a closer control of his soldiers than they were used to. Considering themselves to be citizen soldiers on a great adventure, the enlisted men felt some resentment of this situation, especially where it pertained to their ability to go into Paris after hours. Either failing to, or perhaps refusing to, understand that the only way Colonel Van Derveer could ensure proper training took place and that the regiment would be ready in the event of an emergency was to keep them close at hand, the men in ranks chafed and complained about being so tightly restricted. They were trapped in a paradox of their own making. Believing in the justice of their cause and that their own personal freedom was being threatened, they had joined an organization that required them to limit the personal autonomy they had enlisted to fight for. One man who had served under Van Derveer in Mexico felt the colonel had unfairly changed the rules. In Mexico, he related, the men could come and go as they pleased when not drilling. Now, in Paris, they were not permitted to leave camp to get a drink without a pass. Maintaining the traditional ideas of American soldiers since the Revolution, the men stuck in camp insisted that Van Derveer's rules contributed to loosening discipline rather than improving it. The way they saw it, men who never knew when their next opportunity would come, rather than just taking one "hotn" as they would normally, had no choice but to drink as much as they could which always caused trouble.[97]

Heavy drinking among the members of his regiment was a problem for Van Derveer. As John White put it, "'Old Bourbon Whiskey' is a welcome to all lovers of the ardent, and being in the immediate neighborhood where the vegetable grows, the boys occasionally indulge in it to their satisfaction." Those

---

96. Arnold, *Sunshine and Shadows*, 25–26.
97. Prokopowicz, *All for the Regiment*, 48; Mitchell, *Civil War Soldiers*, 57.

who returned to camp intoxicated were sent to the guardhouse and prohibited from ever again leaving camp, forcing them to sneak out when they wanted another drink. The problem was not limited to the enlisted men. Officers also drank heavily. To the amusement and disgust of the men, even Chaplain John Woods frequented the saloons, and by his low behavior, abrogated his responsibility as a spiritual leader. Woods tenure was as short as it was unsuccessful. He resigned on November 19, less than two months after joining the regiment.[98]

Van Derveer was also strict when it came to training and required endless sessions of drill. But he also understood that his men could only stand so much and was willing to try other more innovative techniques. When Major Boynton came up with a novel idea for training, Van Derveer readily agreed. In addition to the training benefits, Boynton's plan created a welcome break in the camp routine and supplemented the dull army diet. A rabbit hunt was organized in which the regiment would maneuver as if on a battlefield. Everyone was armed with clubs, skirmishers were deployed, and field musicians sounded appropriate calls. As the rabbits were driven out of their hiding places, the flank companies were turned inward to form a circular trap. Just as the ring was about to be completed, the organization broke down. A few excited men broke ranks to grab nearby rabbits and soon everyone was running every which way to get his own animal. Quite a large number of rabbits were captured, but the largest number had gotten away.

A second attempt was made, but was again unsuccessful. According to Lieutenant Keil, the men were "demoralized; and a promiscuous warfare was carried on for the remainder of the day." Once they had escaped the closing ring, the rabbits had scattered far and wide, and for the rest of the afternoon small clumps of men could be seen gathered around crevices and corn shocks or were seen running across the fields waving clubs as they chased elusive hares. Eventually, the hunt became a kind of public sport in which the local citizens came out and participated in or watched from the sidelines. For the moment, political differences were set aside and even Confederate sympathizers mounted on blooded horses joined in excitedly.[99]

Perhaps the regiment should have made better use of "that dog Jack." Jack wandered aimlessly into Camp Bourbon and quickly became an honorary member of Company B. A brown and white mutt of undetermined origin and ancestry, Jack was the only Kentuckian to serve in the Thirty-fifth. Lieutenant Keil said Jack howled annoyingly at night, was "not a pretty dog by any means, nor was he in any sense unusually smart, but he had good sense, for he stood by the Union." Jack was probably more intelligent than Keil gave him credit for. He was smart enough to stick with a good thing when he found it. Quickly becoming known throughout the regiment, Jack was received as a friend in every tent.[100]

98. Bogan, *Warren County's Involvement*, 50–52.
99. Keil, *Thirty-fifth Ohio*, 17–18.
100. Ibid., 222–23.

The hunter-gatherer instinct that had been plumbed from the depths of each man's heart was put to use in other ways. An apple orchard was raided and nuts were collected from trees in the area. As the afternoon shadows grew longer, men straggled back into camp in small groups, and as each group came in, Major Boynton recorded the tally. Some of the regiment's hunters "forgot to return, having found their way, by some means, to the far famed city of Paris." They were not, however, to enjoy its delights for long. They were brought in later in the evening by the provost patrol and "registered as guests" at the regimental guardhouse.[101]

Even though the well-organized plan for the hunt had degenerated in a community free-for-all, an important lesson had been communicated to the men in ranks. While the regimental formation had been maintained, the rabbits had been easily driven and corralled. But as soon as the men cast off discipline and broke ranks, most of the rabbits had escaped and a great deal of effort was required to track down and capture them. The value of maintaining the cohesion of a formation during maneuver was readily apparent to all.

Also somewhat less than satisfying was Company C's first attempt at target practice. Because loaded weapons and inexperienced soldiers were considered a risky combination, target practice was rare in 1861. Captain Earhart marched the company onto a nearby hill and had a six-by-one-foot board placed against the trunk of an old spreading walnut tree on the bluff across the ravine from his men. A white paper was placed on the board as the target to shoot at. One by one, each man in Company C, some ninety men, was called forward with his .69 caliber musket and directed to fire several shots at the target. Many of Company C's soldiers were hunters and could shoot squirrels out of a tree at some distance, so everyone expected to see the target shredded. At the end of the exercise, the branches of the walnut had been badly shot up and the bank around it was filled with lead slugs, but the target, the board, and even the trunk of the tree upon which the board rested, were untouched. Not a single shot had come even reasonably close to the target. The old muskets had proven to have quite different characteristics than a squirrel rifle, and the company returned to camp chastened by its experience. Captain Earhart was devastated and avoided talking to other officers lest he have to describe the results of the practice.[102]

Despite the errant aim of its soldiers, their general antipathy toward military discipline, and their untutored officers, after two months of service, the Thirty-fifth Ohio was well on its way to becoming a good outfit. All the right raw materials were there. The individual soldiers were willing enough, even if they did complain all the time. There were cowards and thieves among them, but a very solid core was already forming. Junior officers applied themselves earnestly at learning their new trade, an attitude that would pay handsome divi-

---

101. Ibid., 19.
102. Prokopowicz, *All for the Regiment*, 50; Keil, *Thirty-fifth Ohio*, 19–20.

dends many months in the future. Colonel Van Derveer was a proven commander and administrator, actively whipping his regiment into fighting trim. His two field officers had the right skills and experience to contribute meaningfully to the process. There would be bumps in the road and some very embarrassing moments, but the signs were all there. The Thirty-fifth Ohio was going to be a good fighting regiment.

CHAPTER 3

Up the Creek, Down the River

December 1861 to April 1862

Climb Into the Hills

Upon taking command, Maj. Gen. Don Carlos Buell reorganized the Army of the Ohio. Buell resented the way midwestern governors interjected themselves into the management of his army, so he attempted to dilute their influence by ensuring that each of the army's brigades contained regiments from two or more states. On November 30, 1861, the Thirty-fifth Ohio was placed in the army's Third Brigade along with the Second Minnesota, the Ninth Ohio, and the Eighteenth United States Infantry to be commanded by Col. Robert L. McCook of the Ninth Ohio. The Third Brigade was part of Brig. Gen. George Thomas's First Division. Thomas, a tall heavyset man in his mid-forties, was just setting out on his personal path to fame. Serious in manner, and radiating a kindly sternness, Thomas's was an impressive appearance. He had been side-ling forces toward the Tennessee border as they became available on the assumption that he would be invading East Tennessee soon. General Buell, whose desire was to invade central Tennessee rather than the eastern part of the state, became concerned that Thomas was getting too far forward, and he ordered the First Division to concentrate at Lebanon. As a result of Buell's orders, the Thirty-fifth Ohio left Paris on December 1, 1861, to join its brigade at Camp Dick Robinson near Danville, Kentucky. The regiment was to ride the train to Nicholasville and then march to the camp.[103]

They had just drawn new uniforms, so as the regiment marched out of Camp Bourbon, there was "but one thing to mar their joy at the prospect of getting themselves under a Southern sun and facing the enemies of their country." They hadn't been paid since they left Hamilton; therefore, there had been no

---

103. U.S. War Department, *War of the Rebellion*, Ser. no. 7, p. 460; Bruce Catton, *This Hallowed Ground* (New York: Doubleday & Co., 1956), 75.

money to send home. Every man was anxious to get on with the war, but it was hard for a family man to move farther away from home not knowing if his wife and children were adequately provided for. Some of them had already received letters describing severe difficulties at home from lack of support. These men who had sacrificed so much to defend the folks back home were deeply offended that their neighbors would allow their families to suffer deprivation. An effort was made by Butler County to set up a relief fund, but one commissioner voted against it, and the tax increase required a unanimous vote. After a blistering editorial in the newspaper, a deal was worked out, and before long formal relief programs were in place. In the meantime, many soldiers in the Thirty-fifth suffered the heartache of worry.[104]

The railroad grade from Lexington to Nicholasville was steep enough that the train had to be split in half. While one-half of the regiment rode on toward the town, the other waited until the locomotive returned. Because it was cold and snowing, the chilled men climbed down off the train to look for something to build fires with. As soon as it was known they were there, curious slaves came down to see the Yankee soldiers. There was a rail fence beside the track, and the slaves were asked whose fence it was. When one replied it was "Massa Breckinridge's," it was immediately dismantled and a fire kindled. No one bothered to ask which Massa Breckinridge it was. Assuming it to be the Confederate general, the men went to work to get every well-anchored post out of the ground. By the time the locomotive returned about midnight, the men had learned that the owner was not John C. Breckinridge but Dr. Breckinridge of the Danville Theological Seminary, but at that point, it no longer made any difference that Dr. Breckinridge was one of the strongest Union men in Kentucky. Every post and rail on the fence had already been fed to the flames. The men felt neither guilt nor any particular need to justify their actions, but they did agree that next time they would make a "closer examination before proceeding to that kind of work."[105]

At Nicholasville, the train was unloaded and the regiment prepared to march to Camp Dick Robinson at Danville. In later times, the veterans would laugh at how much baggage they had brought with them on the train. They would joke that the entire Fourteenth Corps didn't carry as much baggage to Atlanta as the Thirty-fifth Ohio did to Nicholasville. At the time, every piece of it seemed necessary and useful to its owner, but Colonel Van Derveer adamantly disagreed. As he looked at the boxes, bags, and stacks of material piled up at the depot, Van Derveer "warmed up." The regimental historian reported that Van Derveer "was usually very quiet, and choice in his use of good English; but here was an occasion where it cannot be said to be altogether wrong to

---

104. Prokopowicz, *All for the Regiment*, 39; Hamilton *Telegraph*, December 5, 1861; Mitchell, *Civil War Soldiers*, 67; Kenneth A. Hafendorfer, *Mill Springs* (Louisville: KH Press, 2001), 98.

105. Keil, *Thirty-fifth Ohio*, 23–24.

depart from the instructions laid down in the decalogue. It was rumored that on this occasion he did so depart, somewhat to the amusement of the men." The twenty-five wagons then available to the regiment were loaded with things the commander thought were necessary, regardless of what the owner believed. [106]

Once the wagons were loaded, everyone was permitted to get a few hours of sleep. Early the next morning, the Thirty-fifth Ohio again experienced one of the great mysteries of army life. The camp was awakened at the "unchristian" hour of 4:00 a.m. It had been a cold night, and everyone got up, stood around campfires, and waited for the order to move. For hours, they waited, and it was not until nine o'clock that the march to Danville began. No one knew why the march started so late. No one knew why the regiment had been awakened so early when everyone could have slept three hours more and still had plenty of time to get ready. All they knew was that indeed they had been awakened and had stood waiting for five hours. [107]

The trip from Nicholasville to Danville was the first real road march the Thirty-fifth Ohio had undertaken, and the men had as much to learn about packing as they did about fighting. All of them were carrying the standard equipment; haversack, cartridge box, cap box, rifle, bayonet, blanker, canteen, and haversack. Together, it all weighed about fifty pounds. The men had stuffed their haversacks full of things they honestly believed were essential and had added even more when Colonel Van Derveer commenced throwing stuff out of the wagons. During the first segment of the march, the overloaded "knapsacks reminded us of their presence, by their weighty importance." At the first halt, men began to take stock of what was in their packs, but they removed next to nothing. It all still seemed vital to their happiness, but another half hour of marching convinced them that something had to be done. At the next halt, things began to appear on the roadside; a portfolio with gilt-edged paper, a pocket inkstand, packets of old letters, etc. Still, the pack was unbearably heavy, and a second mental inventory was taken as the march continued. The load had to be made lighter, and the next halt found still more items, things like campfire song books, littering the road. Extra clothes and shoes were either discarded or given to curious slaves who had come to see the blue soldiers. By the end of the first day, few men were carrying anything more than one pair of pants, one shirt, one set of drawers, and a pair of socks. A long line of debris traced the regiment's route from Nicholasville to Danville, but one item was said to be conspicuous by its absence. There were no photographs. Every man had kept the picture of the sweetheart he had left behind. [108]

All of the above were just "personal items." The soldier also had to carry other required equipment. Canteens started out heavy but got lighter as the contents were consumed. Cartridge boxes contained forty rounds of .69 caliber

---

106. Keil, *Thirty-fifth Ohio*, 24.
107. Ibid., 25.
108. Ibid., 30–32.

ammunition. Looking at the size of these huge slugs, the men wondered if "the authorities thought that the Confederate soldiers were covered with the hide of a rhinoceros, to have given men such awful slugs of lead." At the end of the march, it was discovered that quite a few men had "lost" at least one package of ten bullets to some inexplicable cause. A soldier's rifle was a different story. There was nothing to be done to decrease its eleven-pound weight. Men who rode wagons or horses were the envy of every man on foot, and if a call had been made for cavalry recruits on that day, "there would have been no need for a motion to make it unanimous." The Thirty-fifth was beginning to learn what it really meant to be a soldier. As Bell Irvin Wiley put it, "the process of becoming a veteran was in large measure one of shedding." Extended road marches would soon be quite common, and as the men toughened up, they would become easier and easier to bear.[109]

If they disliked road marches, the men of the regiment were learning that camp life could be pleasant and even a little romantic. At the end of the day's march, camp was set up according to a never varying pattern. Rifles were stacked and tents erected. Once everyone had shelter, it was time for supper. Flickering fires, as many as a hundred at a time, cast dancing shadows across the tents and marked the positions of every company. Any available wood was used as fuel, but the most preferred was "solid sesech fence rails; a most excellent article to build quickly a hot fire." Pots and pans began to appear, and as the flames gave way to coals, beans boiled and frying bacon spread its alluring fragrance. In groups of six to twelve, soldiers sat "on the ground, tailor fashion, or on piles of rails, on stumps, [or] stones." It was a tranquil scene where the "jolly laugh; the bable of tongues; the disappearance of bacon, of coffee, and of hard tack, was a sight well worthy to be seen." In his book, *All for the Regiment*, Gerald Prokopowicz described the Army of the Ohio as a collection of "local, almost tribal, groups of volunteer soldiers." It was the evening gathering around the fires that best supports that visual image.[110]

The menu sometimes varied, but the one thing that never changed was coffee. Even when there was no food, the coffee would be prepared before every meal and at most halts. It was black and hot, and "strong enough to bear an egg, sweetened to suit with rich, yellow army sugar." Army coffee was, and still is, famous for its strength, but that was exactly the way the men liked it. "The black, strong coffee had no demoralizing effect on a man's digestive apparatus; that slander on coffee is only practiced in refined home society; where it is epidemic to say mean things of the soldier's cherished and respected beverage." The dark liquid became the constant staple of their diet. They would often bear the shortage of food with little complaint, but when there was no coffee, things got tense.[111]

---

109. Keil, *Thirty-fifth Ohio*, 31–32; Wiley, *Billy Yank*, 64.
110. Prokopowicz, *All for the Regiment*, 47; Keil, *Thirty-fifth Ohio*, 33.
111. Keil, *Thirty-fifth Ohio*, 33.

After the cooking was completed, half-burned fence rails were moved onto the coals, and more wood was piled on. Men gathered around the blazing fires and smoked cigars or pipes. The day's work was ended, and the pain of blisters and sore spots began to ease. "Good cheer, rich, mirth-provoking stories came one by one," and no one worried about the next day. As far as the tired soldiers were concerned, "sufficient unto the day is the evil thereof," and there was no cause to go "seeking for it, let it come all the way on its own accord; it will receive attention when it comes; until then enjoy the present hour." Some men would tell stories while others listened and commented or just watched the smoke waft up into the sky. It was a pleasant little world all to itself, and it could not be recreated in any other setting. Decades later, those who had experienced it would still long for those passing moments.[112]

The regiment reached Camp Dick Robinson that same day. The camp was located in a forest of very old trees, and everyone was a little awed by the possibility that Daniel Boone might have hunted deer in the same woods. It seemed a pleasant place, but no one had time to enjoy it. Encouraged by what appeared to be a Union withdrawal to Lebanon, the Confederates sent a force under Gen. Felix Zollicoffer through Cumberland Gap into Kentucky. While the Thirty-fifth Ohio slept through their first night in camp, General Thomas directed the regiment to move immediately to Somerset, Kentucky, to reinforce the brigade commanded by Gen. Albin Shoepf now threatened by a rebel army. Ordered to Dick Robinson to join their new brigade, the Thirty-fifth would not make the connection until the rest of the brigade arrived at Somerset in January. Before leaving camp, the wagons were scoured once again to make room for the men's heavy backpacks. This time it was the officers who lost out. Their mess chests, cots, campstools, and dress uniforms were sent to army warehouses. While they would miss the camp amenities they were used to, the loss of uniforms turned out to be a blessing in disguise. Forced to wear the ordinary blouse while their uniform coats were in storage, most of them came to find it more comfortable and continued to wear them for the remainder of their service.[113]

Leaving Camp Dick Robinson at noon on December 3, the regiment marched to Lancaster before halting for the night. In spite of being lightened by not having to carry their backpacks, the men had still suffered from the march. The hard-surfaced roads were tough on the feet and most men were afflicted with big watery blisters. The companies were quartered separately in several churches and other public buildings. The war was still a lark to these painfully inexperienced young men, and those spending the night in the courthouse conducted a mock trial. Charged with refusing a ride in an ambulance after having been politely invited to climb aboard, the perpetrator was sentenced to ride in the same ambulance for two days. In the churches, the padded deacon's pew

112. Keil, *Thirty-fifth Ohio*, 34.
113. U.S. War Department, *War of the Rebellion*, Ser. no. 7, p. 471; Keil, *Thirty-fifth Ohio*, 32; Catton, *Hallowed Ground*, 91.

was much sought after, but no one would lie on the mourner's bench. The brief stay in Lancaster also demonstrated how confusing the war in Kentucky could be. Some officers of the Thirty-fifth were invited to spend the night with various families and came away thinking the town was staunchly Unionist. The men and officers who stayed out in the town developed an entirely different opinion. They believed the inhabitants to be "sesech," and had they been permitted, "would have left Lancaster a cleaned out town."[114]

At noon the next day, the regiment passed through Stanford and began the climb into the hills of eastern Kentucky. They camped in the open just short of Hall's Gap, and the next morning, December 5, began to ascend into the hills. At the top of the ridge, the Thirty-fifth encountered a spectacular view. The entire bluegrass region spread out before them, and Stanford, Lancaster, and Danville were clearly visible in the distance. Continuing through the wild hill country, they met ambulances loaded with sick soldiers and a line of sutler's wagons headed for Danville. The word was that an attack was expected at Somerset, and the sick were being sent to the rear. The sutlers, seeking to protect their investment, went with them. Later in the day, a rumor came that the Confederates had already attacked and General Shoepf's forces were in trouble. Excited by the prospect of battle, the men forgot their fatigue and sore feet and stepped up the pace of the march. The acceleration was only temporary. When the initial enthusiasm wore off, feet started to hurt again and the pace returned to normal.[115]

On the night of December 5, camp was established at the village of Cuba. Cuba had seen its better days many years before and was not much more than a country store offering "jeans, kaliker, whiskey, and tobakker." A courier from General Shoepf met the regiment at Cuba with instructions to move on as quickly as possible. Shoepf also warned that enemy cavalry were roaming the area in search of the Thirty-fifth with the intent of preventing its arrival in Somerset. Pickets were posted and Van Derveer placed Captain Earhart in charge of them. In giving instructions to Earhart, the colonel said, "The occasion demands unusual caution. Rebels may move to attack us, and likewise, Gen. Shoepf may decide to fall back on us during the night; you will be particularly on your guard, and be sure what troops are approaching before firing on them." Pumped up at having been specifically selected for the task at hand, Earhart's bubble burst when Van Derveer added that the choice was made because "you possess caution in a greater degree than any officer in the line." Stung by the last comment, Earhart went out determined to "kick up a muss" if at all possible, but in spite of maintaining a personal watch all night, no opportunity presented itself. Even so, the game was becoming more and more exciting.[116]

---

114. Keil, *Thirty-fifth Ohio*, 26.
115. Ibid., 26–27.
116. Ibid., 27–28.

Late on December 6, the Thirty-fifth Ohio arrived at General Shoepf's camp. Shoepf, a Hungarian immigrant and veteran of the Prussian Army was used to the military pomp of European armies. His entire command was drawn up to greet the Thirty-fifth as it arrived, and there was a formal exchange of salutes. Minutes after the military courtesies were completed, Van Derveer put his men back on the road. After passing through Somerset, the regiment encamped on Hudson's Ferry Road about two and a half miles from Fishing Creek. The next day, Shoepf brought his entire command through town and set up a larger camp between the city and the camp of the Thirty-fifth.[117]

Fishing Creek was the physical barrier that separated the Union position at Somerset and the Confederate camp at Mill Springs. It ran generally south entering the Cumberland River several miles below Somerset, and for most of its course, the stream ran through a ravine whose steep sides left the stream in shadows most of the day. As much as three hundred feet deep in some places, there were only two places where it was practical to descend into the ravine and cross Fishing Creek. Confederate general Zollicoffer was just as interested in those crossings as General Shoepf. So it was that the Thirty-fifth was directed to picket the Upper Ford of the creek on the night of December 7.[118]

Trade Mark

The thirty men chosen for picket duty that night were placed under the charge of 1st Lt. William C. Dine of Company D. The men were posted in a line across the road to Fishing Creek about two miles west of the regimental camp. Company E of the First Kentucky (U.S.) Cavalry was posted across the creek. Duty in the presence of the enemy was still a new sensation, and with no previous experience in this sort of thing, the need for a constant vigil wasn't readily apparent. To the men at the relief posts, picket duty didn't seem to be any different than guard duty at Paris. They got bored waiting for their next turn on an outpost, and Lieutenant Dine didn't feel any compelling reason to keep the relief together. The waiting soldiers were getting hungry, the persimmons were ripening, and the old fields in the area contained quite a number of trees. Dine, never considering the possibility of an attack, allowed the men not on duty to roam the area in search of the tangy fruit.[119]

At about two o'clock on the afternoon of December 8, a mixed unit of Confederate cavalry approached the Upper Ford, and the Union cavalrymen fired at

117. Keil, *Thirty-fifth Ohio*, 28; Larry J. Daniel, *Days of Glory: The Army of the Cumberland, 1861–1865* (Baton Rouge: LSU Press, 2004), 51.

118. U.S. War Department, *War of the Rebellion*, Ser. no. 7, p. 11; Hafendorfer, *Mill Springs*, 95.

119. Keil, *Thirty-fifth Ohio*, 28.

them. Dine heard the shots and frantically began trying to pull his men back together. The first warning Dine and his pickets had that things were truly amiss was when several cavalrymen from the First Kentucky rushed past them followed a moment later by the rest of their company. The Union cavalrymen were determined to get as far away from the approaching rebel horsemen as they could. They had no intention of fighting and refused to stop even long enough to tell the bewildered Dine what he faced. The only help they gave him was to shout, "Run for it," as they streamed by. The behavior exhibited at Fishing Creek was apparently standard for Federal cavalry in southeastern Kentucky at the time, and in his report to General Thomas, General Shoepf complained, "The cavalry under my command, as usual, behaved badly. They are a nuisance, and the sooner they are disbanded, the better."[120]

Unchecked by the bolting Union cavalry picket, the rebel cavalry charged up the road and burst upon the scattered guards of the Thirty-fifth Ohio. Dine lined up the men at hand behind a fence, and they managed to fire three ragged volleys at the rebels as they retreated toward the woods. When the rebels got close in among them swinging sabers and firing pistols, the pickets broke and ran for the forest. The rebel horsemen rode around gathering up the Ohio troops they could get their hands on and shooting into the shadows at the Yankees they couldn't reach. Some of those captured were nabbed where they had been picking persimmons.[121]

The sound of gunfire from the direction of the creek alerted the camp that something was happening on the picket line. The long roll was sounded and the regiment quickly formed up to move in support of Dine and his men. Two companies were immediately sent down the road, but by the time they reached the picket line there was nothing to support. What was left of the detail had either scattered into the woods or lay on the ground bleeding. The rebel cavalry itself had become scattered in running down the pickets and left when the rest of the Thirty-fifth began to approach. Twenty-one-year-old Pvt. Isaac J. Gilbert of Company B was found dead, the first man of the regiment to die in battle, while Pvt. Bill Creager of Company G lay bleeding from wounds, and suddenly the war wasn't a game anymore. The images of noble combat generated by poets and novelists vanished immediately amid the reality of bloody comrades.[122]

Van Derveer's report on the incident was brief and to the point without any spin or sugarcoating. It described the action, specified when it took place, noted the size of both units involved, and the equipment used by the enemy force. In addition to one man killed and another wounded, fifteen soldiers of

120. U.S. War Department, *War of the Rebellion*, Ser. no. 7, p. 9; Hafendorfer, *Mill Springs*, 96.

121. Keil, *Thirty-fifth Ohio*, 28; U.S. War Department, *War of the Rebellion*, Ser. no. 7, pp. 9, 13; Hafendorfer, *Mill Springs*, 96.

122. Keil, *Thirty-fifth Ohio*, 29; U.S. War Department, *War of the Rebellion*, Ser. no. 7, p. 9.

the Thirty-fifth Ohio were captured by the rebels. The known enemy losses were one officer killed, one horse killed, and another horse captured. Van Derveer made it clear that his pickets had been driven in and dispersed by the rebels, but there was no hint of panic in his report, not even any real concern. As far as the colonel was concerned, the situation had been handled and all was well. Van Derveer's calm, matter-of-fact approach to his duties was becoming known to his superiors. In a letter home, Van Derveer also indicated the skirmish was a minor affair, but he added a few details he had not included in his report. The attacking force was said to be "several hundred strong," and the pickets had performed very well and "killed the officer in command and a number of their men and horses." As the commander of the regiment, Van Derveer understood the public relations aspect of his position. The folks back home were looking to him for reliable information about what was happening to their husbands, fathers, sons, and brothers. Having provided only verifiable facts to his headquarters, Van Derveer was willing to embellish the story just a little for the home audience.[123]

The men who had fled into the woods eventually made their way back to camp one by one. Lieutenant Dine, minus his sword, coat, and hat and looking "somewhat skeered," was among them. The lesson of readiness was learned. The men dug rifle pits that night, and from then until the end of the Atlanta campaign, digging became part of the camp routine. As the men learned, so did their colonel. Van Derveer realized that he had taken too much for granted. He assumed that the instructions that Lieutenant Dine had received were enough to keep him alert. The debacle reminded him that his officers were still very green and needed closer attention. From that moment on, Van Derveer paid personal attention to the proper posting of pickets and preparation of fortifications.[124]

Van Derveer had not mentioned the gathering of persimmons in his report, but word soon spread among the regiments at Somerset. Before long, the others were calling the Thirty-fifth Ohio the "Persimmon Regiment." At first, "the same was not very palatable," but after they had had time to think about it, it didn't seem so bad. As Lieutenant Keil of Company C wrote, "Trade marks posses a business value" that is respected in society, and the registration fee had been paid in blood. In no time, the title "Persimmon Regiment" became a matter of pride, and after the war, the veterans of the regiment fought to retain the right to be known as the "Original Persimmon Regiment."[125]

Poor Lieutenant Dine didn't handle the situation as well as the rest of the regiment. He had tried so hard to get into the war, and now he was in as far as any man could be. The rest of the men put the incident behind them, counting it as a lesson learned, and accepted the ribbing with good nature. Lieutenant Dine

---

123. U.S. War Department, *War of the Rebellion*, Ser. no. 7, pp. 9–10; Van Derveer to wife, 10 December 1861, Van Derveer Family Collection.

124. Keil, *Thirty-fifth Ohio*, 29.

125. Ibid.

either didn't learn from his mistakes or was too badly spooked by his experience. Civil War soldiers followed their officers because they respected them as men, not because they wore shoulder straps. In order to be an effective officer, Lieutenant Dine would have had to demonstrate physical courage, a demonstration he was apparently unable to make. When he resigned his commission the next year, the endorsements of his commanders were damning. Lieutenant Colonel Long stated that Dine's resignation would be a "great benefit to the service." Ferdinand Van Derveer was more critical. "I have no hesitancy in certifying that the discharge of Lieut. Dine will be of an advantage to his company and for the good of the service," Van Derveer wrote. "He is totally unfitted by education and manners for a command." General Steedman simply said, "He is morally unfit for any command."[126]

Pure and Unadulterated Rebels

General Shoepf kept his seven infantry regiments and cavalry busy patrolling the western bank of Fishing Creek. "Feesh" Creek, as pronounced by the locals, was not an easy stream to get across. Both sides of the small valley were skirted by steep, forested hills. Where the stream wound around one particular spur as it traversed the valley there was an easily usable ford. Each patrol required the regiment to descend the steep eastern slope of the valley, wade the cold water of the creek, and then climb back out of the valley. The first combat mission by the Persimmons was an attempt to ambush Confederate cavalry camped west of the creek. The idea was for a company of the First Kentucky Cavalry to draw the attention of the rebels and then lead them to the place where Thirty-fifth and Thirty-first Ohio waited in ambuscade concealed in the woods just below Logan's Cross Roads. Nothing came of the effort. The two regiments went to ground while the cavalry went out to entice the rebels. Much later the horse soldiers came back and reported there were no enemy troops in the area. The men of the Thirty-fifth believed the cavalry had ridden far enough to be out of sight and then hidden until it was time to return. There was no way to prove it, but it fit with their previous observation of the cavalry's performance.[127]

There were salt works known to be supplying the Confederates near the western bank of the creek, and on another cold December day, the Thirty-fifth Ohio marched up the east bank of the creek until it was adjacent to the salt works on the other side. Four companies descended to the valley floor where

126. Ohio Roster Commission,*Official Roster*, 612; Compiled service record, William C. Dine, 1st Lt., Co. D, 35th Ohio Inf.; Carded Records, Volunteer Organizations, Civil War; Records of the Adjutant General's office, 1780s–1917, Record Group 94; National Archives, Washington, D.C.; Catton, *America*, 53.

127. Keil, *Thirty-fifth Ohio*, 35; Hafendorfer, *Mill Springs*, 114.

Company A drew the dubious honor of wading the creek to destroy the manufacturing facility. Attempts to burn the place failed because the wood was thoroughly impregnated with salt, so kettles were smashed and the furnaces and buildings torn down. When they retraced their steps across the creek, Company A carried back with them "loads of the purest salt in any market."[128]

As had been the case in central Kentucky, there were many Confederate sympathizers in the Somerset area. These malcontents would declare they "were good union men in the presence of our troops," but turned into "pure and unadulterated rebels when not under the eye of our forces." Every Union troop movement was quickly conveyed to the Confederates. Even worse was the smuggling of useful supplies across the lines. There were many local Home Guard units in and around Somerset, so it was easy for a person to buy military supplies. All the buyer had to do was declare that the supplies were for the Home Guard and then smuggle them to the Confederates.

General Shoepf had been receiving information about arms being purchased in the northern part of the state and then being smuggled to Zollicoffer's rebels. Returning from a patrol across Fishing Creek one day, the Thirty-fifth ran into two blue-clad soldiers in a wagon as they were climbing up "the rough and precipitous hills" out of the valley. Suspicious of what the two soldiers might be doing, the wagon, carrying two coffins, was stopped and the men closely questioned. One of the soldiers produced identification papers that said he was a medical director and a set of orders signed by General Buell. The two coffins were said to be carrying the bodies of Union men who had died at Camp Dick Robinson and were being taken home. No one present had ever seen Buell's signature before, so there was no way to authenticate the order. The soldier's story seemed plausible, and both soldiers had the demeanor of men on a solemn mission. They were permitted to pass without an examination of the coffins.[129]

The Other Side

In January, General Thomas began his effort to drive the Confederates back through Cumberland Gap. Thomas began by moving the rest of his division to the western side of Fishing Creek between Somerset and the rebel camp at Beech Grove. The weather was cold and wet, and the unimproved dirt roads were in atrocious condition. After a week of slogging through thick mud, Thomas's troops arrived at Logan's Cross Roads with few supplies, and the division trains were mud-bound far to the rear. Thomas requested supplies be sent from the depots at Somerset, and Wilkinson Beatty and his wagon teams

---

128. Keil, *Thirty-fifth Ohio*, 36.
129. Ibid., 44.

were sent to deliver the needed victuals. Beatty had been ordered by Van Derveer to return to camp that same night, so when he arrived in Thomas's camp in
a driving rain, he was anxious to unload and move on. When the commissary
informed him that he could not unload his supplies because no place had been
prepared to store them out of the weather, Beatty took matters into his own
hands.

Unwilling to take no for an answer, Beatty wasted no more time with the
commissary. Knowing little of military protocol and caring even less, Beatty
walked directly past the unwary sentries posted at General Thomas's tent entering "without ceremony, and in his rattling, garrulous way demanded a place to
unload the stores" so he could return to camp as his colonel had ordered him to
do. General Thomas, from a well-to-do Virginia family, was known to be a
stern, taciturn man, but he took a shine to the Thirty-fifth Ohio's rustic wagon
master. Beatty's "entire innocence as to what was due person's of rank" amused
the taciturn general who must also have respected the older man's desire to
obey orders and the two men formed a friendly acquaintance. In the months
ahead, they were seen to chat informally on several occasions. It may be that
Thomas later spoke with Colonel Van Derveer about Beatty, because he authorized the wagon master to pick the teams for his headquarters wagons. The old
man repaid the general's confidence by obtaining "finer teams [than] were
found in any army, east or west."[130]

When Thomas arrived at Logan's Cross Roads near Mill Springs on January 17, 1862, only nine miles from the rebel force, his intention was to have
General Shoepf's forces join him. On January 18, the Thirty-fifth was ordered
to cross Fishing Creek and join Thomas, but no sooner than they had waded the
stream, they were ordered to return to their camp. Watching all this federal
movement, the new Confederate commander, Gen. G. B. Crittenden, decided
the wisest thing to do was to attack before the Union force was able to concentrate. On Sunday morning, January 19, the rebels made their assault.[131]

The sound of battle could be heard on the eastern side of Fishing Creek,
and the Thirty-fifth immediately began to prepare for battle, so as to be ready
to move as soon as the order came. When it did come, the Thirty-fifth Ohio left
camp first and "started pell-mell for the field." The weather had been very wet,
and the roads were almost impassable. Company A had been detailed to repair
the road north of Somerset, but when Lt. James Bone heard the sound of battle,
he decided he had to get there. Mounted, he was able to catch up with the rest
of the regiment before it had gotten too far along the road. As the Persimmons
hurried toward the fighting, they passed groups of army stragglers and civilians
moving away from the battle. Each group was interrogated as to how the fighting was progressing and each had a different story. Several people announced

---

130. Keil, *Thirty-fifth Ohio*, 55.
131. Ibid., 38; Abia M. Zeller to brother, 22 January 1862, Abia M. Zeller Papers,
VFM 1297, Ohio Historical Society, Columbus.

that General Zollicoffer had been killed, but only when one straggling soldier produced a lock of hair and claimed it came from the general's head did the Thirty-fifth take the news seriously.[132]

After battling the treacherous mud of the road, the Thirty-fifth Ohio still had to get across Fishing Creek. Arriving on its banks at noon, they found that the rains had swollen the creek so that it was no longer safe to cross. It didn't matter. There was a battle going on, and the Persimmons wanted in on it. So desperate were they to take part, that ropes were stretched across the dangerously rapid creek and attached to trees on either bank. Each man placed his cartridge and cap boxes at the end of his bayonet. Holding the rifle up with one hand and grasping the rope with the other, one by one, the men plunged into the swift, icy water. Wading through the swift current was a treacherous undertaking, and with only a few men able to cross at a time, an excruciatingly slow one. Once across, there were still several miles to cover, and the rest of the march was made without stopping.[133]

Union infantry crossing flood-swollen Fishing Creek near Somerset, Kentucky.
ALFRED E. MATHEWS LITHOGRAPH COLLECTION, OHIO HISTORICAL SOCIETY.

The Thirty-fifth Ohio made a similar crossing in an attempt to reach the Mill Springs battlefield.

While the Thirty-fifth trudged toward the battlefield, things were going well for the Union forces. Fighting had spread through the fields and woodlands beside Fishing Creek, and the initial advantage had been with the rebels.

---

132. Keil, *Thirty-fifth Ohio*, 37; Hafendorfer, *Mill Springs*, 434.
133. Keil, *Thirty-fifth Ohio*, 37–38; Zeller to brother, 22 January 1862, Zeller Papers.

The Union forces were hard-pressed, but at just the right moment, General Thomas's reserves, among them the Second Minnesota and Ninth Ohio, began to arrive. The Minnesota regiment had replaced the Fourth Kentucky in the line and at one point had been so close that only a rail fence separated them from their enemies. The Minnesotans captured the battle flag of the Fifteenth Mississippi Infantry, but more importantly, they had stopped the Confederate advance, providing the opportunity for the tables to be turned. Seeing an opening, Colonel McCook had ordered the Ninth Ohio to counterattack. McCook was seriously wounded, but the rebels were driven from the field and forced to flee through the timbered countryside. Thomas never forgot the contribution of the two regiments, and held a fondness for them, particularly the Second Minnesota, for the rest of the war.[134]

When the Thirty-fifth arrived on the field, the rebel army had already fled. After resting for about an hour, the regiment set off in pursuit of the defeated Confederates. Thomas's army reached the Confederate camp at Beech Grove the same night, but did not move on it until the next morning. Beech Grove, located in a bend of the Cumberland River near the entry of White Oak Creek, was fortified on the north, the only side by which it could be accessed. The Persimmons were in reserve behind the center along with the Twelfth Kentucky, Seventeenth Ohio, and Thirty-first Ohio. While the Union forces formed a line of battle, General Thomas climbed up on the Russell house to survey the fortifications through his "field-glass," and the artillery bombarded the enemy camp. At 7:40 a.m., after about fifty rounds were fired, the infantry advanced through the forest and found the camp empty. The rebels had crossed the river the night before burning the boats on which they crossed.[135]

Once inside the camp, the men of the Thirty-fifth had time to look around and see how their counterparts lived. They carefully examined the "miniature log cabins, chinked and plastered, with clapboard roofs, and wooden chimney's, log cabin style," and found them to be the best they had ever seen. These snug quarters looked very inviting after two days in the rain and mud. Sitting among the cabins was the same wagon that the regiment had stopped on the road only days before. It was empty now, and the Persimmons approached some nearby prisoners who were more than happy to tell them what had happened to the coffins. Rather than two bodies, the coffins had actually contained revolvers purchased in Cincinnati. After being repackaged in Lexington, the guns were smuggled to the Confederate camp. It was a lesson learned the hard way, and the rebels would require "smarter tricks to win later on during the war." Thomas's army immediately began to plunder the enemy camp, carting off whatever was useful. The Thirty-fifth Ohio missed the party. They were

134. Keil, *Thirty-fifth Ohio*, 39; Constantine Grebner, *We Were the Ninth* (Kent, Ohio: Kent State University Press, 1997), 85–86; Judson W. Bishop, *The Story of a Regiment* (St. Cloud: North Star Press, 2000), 78.

135. Keil, *Thirty-fifth Ohio*, 40; Hafendorfer, *Mill Springs*, 473, 476.

detailed to guard the public stores captured from the rebels and got almost none of the captured booty.[136]

With no way to get across the rain-swollen Cumberland, Thomas called the pursuit off and sent several regiments, including the Thirty-fifth Ohio, back to their camps at Somerset with orders not to halt until they got there. Later, they would find out that Thomas felt there was not enough food and forage at Beech Grove and that he feared rebel cavalry would try to raid the depots at Somerset while the troops were at Beech Grove, but that afternoon, all the Persimmons knew was that they were very tired. Weary from marching in the rain and mud for two days, they now had to repeat the process, covering eighteen miles and crossing Fishing Creek again in one afternoon and evening. The sloppy roads made it impossible to maintain unit formations. The regiment broke up into companies, and the companies disintegrated into squads of men fighting their way through the muck. As Lieutenant Keil put it, "There are times when men reach the limit of physical endurance." The men of the Thirty-fifth had reached that point, and only members fortunate enough to be mounted reached camp that night. The rest straggled in as best they could the next morning.[137]

The Persimmons transited the previous day's battlefield and got a good look at the wreckage left behind. By most standards it had been a small battle fought by amateur soldiers, but the men were "greatly impressed" by some of the things they saw. One cannon ball had gone completely through a green tree but left it standing. Every stump had several bodies lying nearby, men who had tried to use them for cover. Piles of discarded weapons, equipment, and food lay scattered along the roads. But there were other sights as well, and it was because of them that most of the men did not enjoy the visit. Many of the dead from both sides were still lying about and starting to swell, and a group of Michigan pioneers was in the process of collecting and burying the corpses. Rebel corpses were tightly packed in a mass grave where they lay with "faces turned upward, hands placed over the breast." Every building and shelter adjacent to the battlefield had been filled with wounded men, and surgeons were busy amputating limbs of the seriously wounded.[138]

At Mill Springs, the men of the Thirty-fifth learned one of the truths of war as they marched through the flotsam of battle. During a battle, soldiers would look indifferently upon the bodies of the wounded and slain, but once the fighting had ended, "there were few who could muster courage to look at sights like those to be seen at a surgeon's tent near a field hospital." All in all, It was "a ghastly looking sight" that was "more than most nerves could endure. Like the Pharisee we passed on the other side."[139]

---

136. Keil, *Thirty-fifth Ohio*, 44–45; Hafendorfer, *Mill Springs*, 482.

137. Keil, *Thirty-fifth Ohio*, 41; Hafendorfer, *Mill Springs*, 490.

138. Keil, *Thirty-fifth Ohio*, 42; Zeller to brother, 22 January 1862, Zeller Papers; Hafendorfer, *Mill Springs*, 500.

139. Keil, *Thirty-fifth Ohio*, 42; Arnold, *Sunshine and Shadows*, 1.

The remainder of Thomas's division eventually followed the Thirty-fifth back to Somerset, and for a while, Confederate prisoners were kept in the Thirty-fifth's camp. The main work of the day was collecting and sorting through the spoils of the battle. The 150 wagons, 12 guns, 1,000 horses and mules, and a herd of cattle made an impressive display, but with the exception of the cattle, the materiel was of inferior quality and not very useful. The wagons were of such varied style and construction that P. T. Barnum "would have promptly purchased the lot for his museum." Many of the more than one thousand horses and mules were deemed not fit for service and sent to the depot at Louisville for rehabilitation. The eleven captured artillery pieces were quite old and rejected for further service. The captured item that interested the Union soldiers the most was the body of Gen. Felix Zollicoffer. His body had been nearly stripped of its clothes and his hair nearly shorn off by soldiers seeking mementos of the battle. In his letter home describing the battle, Abia M. Zeller of Company H began with the greeting: "It is with great pleasure that I write to you to tell you that old Zollicoffer is dead and is no more." He also promised to send one of the dead general's vest buttons home.[140]

Individual ability was not evenly distributed in the Van Derveer family. While the men had an undying respect for Ferdinand Van Derveer, they did not feel the same way about his younger brother Henry, a sergeant in Company B. In early January, Lt. Ransford Smith had been appointed to the brigade commissary. Henry Van Derveer apparently got the idea that he should be appointed to replace Smith and began campaigning among his friends at home. Smith's permanent assignment to Company B was not affected by the detail, so there was in fact no open slot to fill, but the men of Company B were taking no chances. Having seen Henry Van Derveer in action, they wanted no part of him as an officer. Sixty-two of them got together and signed a letter to Governor David Tod. They informed the governor that Henry was inattentive to this duty and that none of them had any confidence in his ability to be an officer. In short, Henry was incompetent and the men of Company B wanted someone better.[141]

When You Please

Ferdinand Van Derveer struggled with illness throughout his Civil War service, and his first serious bout was in Somerset. He was sick enough that he moved out of camp and into town to recuperate. The illness provides an interesting insight into mid-nineteenth century medical practices. Van Derveer's primary

---

140. Zeller to brother, 22 January 1862, Zeller Papers; Hafendorfer, *Mill Springs*, 513; Daniel, *Days of Glory*, 54.

141. Correspondence to the Governor and the Adjutant General of Ohio, 1861–1866, Series 147–27:130.

medication appears to have been brandy. Other than helping him sleep, it may not have been very effective, since in a letter to his wife, the colonel said he had run out but was recovering just as well. On February 5, the regimental commander was convinced there would be no movement for at least a month. "Soldiers cannot live without provisions," he lectured his wife, "and the roads are so bad that it is impossible to carry sufficient to subsist an army beyond this point." He was wrong about the movement, but his estimate of road conditions proved quite accurate.[142]

The Thirty-fifth Ohio had expected that Thomas would continue his advance and enter East Tennessee, but back in Louisville, General Buell had other thoughts. On February 8, 1862, the regiment received orders to leave its camp at Somerset and march to Lebanon. The stubborn streak that ran up Ferdinand Van Derveer's back showed itself starkly at Somerset. The wagon train of the Thirty-fifth was still abnormally large, so it had been sent to Lebanon to pick up supplies for the entire brigade. The train returned to Somerset just as the order to leave the town was received. Col. Horatio P. Van Cleve of the Second Minnesota, the acting brigade commander while Colonel McCook recovered, ordered Van Derveer to bring the stores with him to Lebanon. The Thirty-fifth had its own equipment and baggage to carry, and if the brigade stores remained on the wagons, the regiment's gear would have to be left behind.

Van Derveer protested the order, declaring his unwillingness to leave until he had unloaded his wagons enough to carry his own regiment's equipment. Van Cleve promptly repeated the order, and once again Van Derveer "declined to move." Van Cleve was in no mood to deal with a subordinate's intransigence. He ordered Van Derveer placed under arrest and further ordered Lieutenant Colonel Long to immediately move the regiment to Lebanon. Colonel Long had no intention of going against the wishes of his own commander and also refused Van Cleve's order. Van Cleve's anger was growing, and he did not hesitate to place Long under arrest and order Major Boynton to assume command and make the movement. Boynton refused the order, as well, and was himself placed under arrest. With no field grade officer left to take command, the Thirty-fifth Ohio remained behind in its camp at Somerset while the rest of the brigade marched to Lebanon.

Lieutenant Keil, who recorded the incident in his history of the regiment, did not provide any other reason for Van Derveer's stubborn refusal to move than the lack of space for regimental stores. Perhaps Van Derveer's recent illness had made him peevish, but the distant observer can't help but believe there was more to it than that. There had to have been a way for the two commanders to settle the argument. Even if the other regiments were incapable of carrying the fresh stores, the stores could have been off-loaded and picked up later after the regiment had moved to Lebanon. Even making two round trips, the stores could have been gotten to Lebanon in a week. It would seem that the incident

142. Van Derveer to wife, 5 February 1862, Van Derveer Family Collection.

was a personal snit between two proud men who apparently didn't like each other; a contest of wills that would continue for several more days.

Van Cleve, known as a "competent, though non professional" officer, and by now completely exasperated, could not leave the Thirty-fifth at Somerset indefinitely. Accordingly, two days after the rest of the brigade had departed for Lebanon, he sent another order to Van Derveer. The order released Van Derveer and his subordinates from arrest and ordered the Thirty-fifth to join the brigade at Lebanon. In part, it read, "Do with the stores what you please; move when you please; take what route you please, and report to Lebanon when you please." Perhaps the most remarkable direction any colonel ever received, Van Derveer's astonishment and amusement can easily be read in his reaction to the new order. Using atypically "unscriptural language," Van Derveer muttered, "Damme, I'll obey that order."[143]

Van Cleve's liberal order had been written in sarcasm, and knowing that, Van Derveer was in no mood to be conciliatory. He was determined that even though they had started two days behind the rest of the brigade, the Thirty-fifth Ohio would be the first unit to arrive in Lebanon. Only the winter weather made such a vain goal possible. Seasonal rains had churned the roads into viscous soup that deepened and thickened with each unit that passed by. Wagon teams became stuck in the mud and would not move. Angry teamsters whipped the beasts and cussed incessantly, proving once again the old army adage that "no man could drive an army team and get to heaven." Every regiment in Thomas's division was stuck in the mud.

All except one, the Thirty-fifth Ohio. Colonel Van Derveer had something no other regiment had—Wilkinson Beatty. The old wagon master had made many trips between Somerset and Lebanon hauling supplies and knew every possible route between the two towns. The normal route to Lebanon, the one on which the rest of the division had foundered, skirted the headwaters of Fishing Creek and the hills around them. Cutting across the hills would greatly shorten the distance. It would also be an exhausting, arduous trek, but Van Derveer was determined to upstage Van Cleave. After consulting with Beatty, Van Derveer moved the Persimmons off the main road and set off into the hills.

As the story spread through the ranks, the regiment took on the determination of its commander. Details were sent ahead to repair the roads and wagon teams were doubled. When the teams faltered, they were dragged up the hills by brute force. Once a wagon reached the top, the team was disconnected and sent back down to help with other loads. Wagons that got stuck were levered out, or when necessary, pulled out by the men. On the afternoon of the third day, men toiling to move teams up the hill heard the men at the head of the line begin to shout, and as each group reached the top, they took up the cheer. Before them opened a "pleasant little valley, through which a small stream flowed," but what really caused the cheers to well up inside the men was what

143. Keil, *Thirty-fifth Ohio*, 49; Daniel, *Days of Glory*, 191.

they saw beyond the stream. Along the opposite bank of the stream ran a macadamized road, and once on the pike, the pace of the march picked up considerably. Even though there was a three-mile break in the macadamized surface, the hardest part of the march was over, and late on the next morning, the Thirty-fifth Ohio set up camp on the commons near Lebanon.

The Persimmons were lazing around their tents when the rest of the brigade trudged into town. It was a perturbed Van Cleave who rode up to Van Derveer's tent, but he was too proud to show it. The two men stared stonily at each other, neither willing to be the first to speak, until Van Cleave finally stated the obvious. "You are here?" Van Derveer, intent on maintaining his own independence, replied simply, "Yes." After another moment of cold silence, Van Cleave asked the question that could not be avoided. "How did you get through?" From behind his own stubborn mask, Van Derveer said, "Marched through." With that, Van Cleve turned his horse and rode away. Characteristically, Van Derveer only obliquely mentioned the event in writing his wife. "We arrived here yesterday at noon, all safe and sound," he wrote. "Our boys stood the trip very well, and beat all the other regiments up." From that point on, the two regimental commanders avoided each other. Any long-term conflict was prevented when Colonel McCook rejoined the brigade and Van Cleave received a promotion to brigadier general.[144]

The Thirty-fifth Ohio dressed well in Lebanon, because among the items in the regiment's wagons were new uniforms, but just as their commander had, the men were suffering from health problems. Van Derveer wrote that the men were "not quite as healthy as before they were paid—they are buying and eating too much trash." Sutler stores were not always the most sanitary food sources, and since sweets were rare in army rations, the men may have been making up for lost opportunities. It was also at Lebanon, Captain Mallory of Company I resigned his infantry commission to accept one as a senior surgeon in the Fourth Kentucky Cavalry. First Lieutenant Lewis was promoted to command the company, and 1st Sgt. Phillip Rothenbush was promoted to replace Lewis. Born and raised in Hamilton, Ohio, Rothenbush had attended local schools and worked as a drug store clerk prior to the war. In April of 1861, he had enlisted in the Third Ohio for ninety days but that regiment never left its original rendezvous. Rothenbush had been among the group from the Third Ohio who wanted to raise an entire regiment from Butler County. Enlisting in Company I, Rothenbush had been appointed first sergeant based on his previous experience and had performed well. He was commissioned at the first available opportunity and quickly proved a capable officer.[145]

The Persimmons were only in Lebanon for a day or two. Gen. Ulysses S.

144. Keil, *Thirty-fifth Ohio*, 50–51; Van Derveer to wife, 19 February 1862, Van Derveer Family Collection.

145. Cone, *Biographical*, 348; Van Derveer to wife, 8 February 1862, Van Derveer Family Collection.

Grant's unexpected capture of Forts Henry and Donelson extended the shadow of Union power deep into Tennessee, adding weight to General Buell's argument for an attack into the central part of the state. Buell ordered a concentration of forces at Bowling Green in preparation for an advance on Nashville. By the time the march started on February 19, the Confederate army was already hotfooting it into Tennessee. Instead of marching to Bowling Green, the regiment was turned northwest for Louisville. They were to board river steamers and travel to the Tennessee capital or some interim point from which an advance on the city could be made. The rain that had plagued them for weeks did not let up, and each night found the Thirty-fifth Ohio "a sorry looking set of boys . . . standing around huge log fires" trying to dry out. The long ascent of Muldraugh Hill was excruciatingly slow and at one point the regiment was forced to halt and move off the road because mired wagon trains had it completely blocked. On February 25, the regiment arrived in Louisville and began to board the riverboats. Being on the move was better than sitting in camp, but Ferdinand Van Derveer wasn't expecting much from it. "The news of the success of our arms on all fronts is encouraging—and although we are doing a great deal of marching, I think our prospect of getting into a fight is quite slim."[146]

How Are You, Old Fellow?

Among the steamers waiting to take on the brigade's soldiers was the *Jacob Strader*, purportedly the largest boat on the river, and capable of shipping the entire Ninth Ohio and Second Minnesota. The Eighteenth U.S. infantry was also able to board a single boat, but the Thirty-fifth Ohio was split between two smaller boats. Companies B, E, H, and K went aboard the *Belle Creole* while the *Franklin No. 3* took on Companies A, C, D, F, G, and I. The regiment was fully loaded on February 26, and on the twenty-seventh, the convoy of ships carrying Thomas's division set off for Nashville.[147]

Still uncertain as to whether Confederate commander Albert Sidney Johnston would fight for Nashville, the convoy halted briefly at the mouth of the Cumberland River before steaming further up the river. The only available drinking water came from the flooded river and caused several men to be sickened. The two steamers transporting the Persimmons were lashed together. More convenient for the regiment, it was a great annoyance to the riverboat captains. The captain of the *Belle* complained, that he was being held back by the *Franklin*. The captain of the *Franklin* "warmed up," and without consulting

146. Keil, *Thirty-fifth Ohio*, 52, 219; Van Derveer to wife, 19 February 1862, Van Derveer Family Collection.

147. Keil, *Thirty-fifth Ohio*, 52.

Van Derveer, cut loose and surged ahead leaving the *Belle* far downstream. "The spirit of racing had taken hold of the boatmen," and the captain of the *Belle* began to look for shortcuts through the flooded bayous. One such "shortcut" cost the *Belle* considerable time when it had to back track, but once back in the main channel, the *Belle* was able to catch and pass the *Franklin*, and continuing on, was able to outdistance every boat in the convoy except the huge *Jacob Strader*.[148]

The convoy reformed at Fort Donelson, since it was considered unsafe for individual boats to proceed beyond that place. The men were allowed to disembark while waiting at Fort Donelson and had the opportunity to explore the works and battlefield there. They found the terrain surrounding the fort very difficult to negotiate and in covering the route taken by Brig. Gen. Charles F. Smith's division used in its assault, were impressed that the "boys in blue forced their way under a heavy fire." They "examined every point about the rebel works" and came away feeling that in spite of the damage done by the gunboats, the fort should have been held much longer than it was. The lack of determination to do so the men blamed on the guilty conscience of Confederate general John Floyd, a former secretary of war who feared he would be mistreated if captured. The rest of the trip was uneventful, and Ferdinand Van Derveer recorded, "We had a pleasant trip here though somewhat crowded."[149]

Upon arrival at Nashville on March 2, they found the city was also crowded with an estimated seventy-five thousand Union soldiers. The Persimmon's first sight of the city was the still-smoldering Louisville and Nashville Railroad bridge, destroyed by the Confederates only a few weeks after it had been completed. There was evidence of the rebel's hurried attempts to destroy all property of military value throughout the city, but much was left behind. On and near the wharves, the men could see piles of cannon balls, stacks of railroad iron, and great bales of cotton. After the steamers were tied to the wharf, the first order of business was to unload the cargo and assemble the troops, and while this effort was under way, Lieutenant Keil of Company C and Lt. Joseph C. Thoms of Company F managed to slip away and see some of the city.[150]

They had met rebel sympathizers in Kentucky, but in Nashville, they came face to face with the real thing. The attitude of the locals was openly hostile, the women more so than the men. Ladies passing the two officers on the sidewalk took care to give them a wide berth going so far as to gather their skirts about them to ensure there was absolutely no contact with the northern invaders. Their efforts greatly amused Keil and Thoms who decided to see just how far the women of Nashville would go to avoid Yankees. Finding a place where

148. Ibid., 52–53; Zeller to Sir, 16 March 1862, Zeller Papers.

149. Keil, *Thirty-fifth Ohio*, 54; Van Derveer to wife, 7 March 1861, Van Derveer Family Collection.

150. Keil, *Thirty-fifth Ohio*, 54; Daniel, *Days of Glory*, 71; Van Derveer to wife, 7 March 1861, Van Derveer Family Collection.

packing cases restricted passage on the sidewalk to a narrow aisle, Thoms sat on the boxes on one side of the walk, and Keil perched himself on the other side. Shortly, a group of the "the little vixens came up and took in the situation." Much to the delight of the two lieutenants, the ladies halted and stepped off the sidewalk into the street flowing with mud and water. Determined to avoid the trap set for them, the women ambulated through the muck and mire until "they could conveniently regain the pavement." The Thirty-fifth was to find a similar reception throughout the city.[151]

In most instances, the hostility was impersonal, but it could also be very personal upon occasion. Wilkinson Beatty had also slipped away while the regiment was offloading from the riverboats. Apparently, his simple ways also included a fair amount of generosity. An old acquaintance happened to live in Nashville, and Beatty carried a letter for the man from his brother in Hamilton. Beatty went to the female boarding school the man operated in the city, knocked on the door and was ushered into the waiting room. When the director of the school entered, Beatty approached him in his usual friendly, direct way, declaring, "Why, how are you old fellow? It's been many, many years since I saw you" and stuck out his hand. To Beatty's chagrin, his former Buckeye friend turned out to be a complete convert to the southern cause and refused to shake the old teamster's hand. "I don't shake hands with men who come down here to despoil us," the schoolmaster declared disdainfully. "I regard you as an enemy, and the sooner you leave my premises the better it will suit me." The insult "made the blood boil in the veins of the hot headed Wilk" who withdrew but had no intention of letting the affront pass.

The Thirty-fifth Ohio went into camp with the rest of Thomas's division on March 5 about four miles west of Nashville on the Granny White pike. On March 7, McCook, promoted to brigadier general in January and once again back in command of the brigade, sounded the alarm, and the men were told to arm themselves with clubs. McCook was making use of Van Derveer's training technique from Paris, and the Ninth Ohio and Thirty-fifth Ohio were going on a rabbit hunt. The plan was to drive the rabbits out of the thickets into a field from three sides. The open fourth side of the field was the bank of the river, where it was hoped to trap the hares against the Cumberland and capture a great number of them. As with the first hunt, things did not go as intended.[152]

The cedar thickets were rather dense, and the troop formations were quickly broken with men scattering in squad-size elements. With great gaps in the ranks, there was no way to surround their prey. A large number of desperate rabbits rushed into the river to escape the hunters and most of them drowned. The Thirty-fifth apparently caught quite a few more than the forty-nine hares nabbed by the Ninth Ohio, but the total catch was not enough for anyone to have a good feast. There was some good-natured ribbing between the officers

151. Keil, *Thirty-fifth Ohio*, 55.
152. Grebner, *We Were the Ninth*, 91–92.

of the two regiments. When Major Boynton noted that the number of rabbits taken by the Thirty-fifth exceeded that of the Ninth, McCook joked, "That's quite natural. Your men are a set of darned hounds. Of course you can catch rabbits." For their part the Persimmons found the entire affair disappointing. Once cooked, the rabbits "had a butternut flavor" and the men did not enjoy the meal.[153]

The camp west of Nashville was a pleasant one with good water sources, so the men who had been sick on the boats perked up quickly when they got into a healthier environment. Some of the men believed the rebels were scared and would not fight again. Colonel Van Derveer told his wife, "It does seem that the war is about over—but we may be mistaken." Within the next two weeks, it became obvious he was indeed incorrect about the duration of hostilities, when the Confederate concentration around Corinth, Mississippi, became apparent. Buell's Army of the Ohio was ordered to join Gen. Ulysses S. Grant's Army of the Tennessee already camped around Pittsburgh Landing just above the Mississippi state line. On March 20, 1862, the Army of the Ohio, moving for the first time as a single unit, broke camp and headed toward Franklin. The early spring weather was very pleasant and the gentle breeze swayed the now blooming peach trees and young clover. The Persimmons later recalled that, "a more inviting landscape could scarcely be pointed out." It was as if "Spring and divine serenity seemed to have come together in the countryside."[154]

In order to move south to Franklin, the army had to pass through Nashville, and once the wagons were loaded, Wilkinson Beatty went ahead into the city alone. Going to the schoolmaster's residence with a "cowhide," he proceeded to whip the man who insulted him on his own veranda. When his anger was spent, Beatty exclaimed, "There, you infernal old traitor, take that, and see whether you can't be at least half decent, if you must be a traitor." After informing the beaten man he could not insult Union men at will, and that if he ever returned to Ohio, he would flog him again, Beatty left to rejoin the regiment. Still full of self-righteous indignation, he informed his commander what he had done. [Note: W. W. Bennett gives a different version in *A Narrative of the Great Revival Which Prevailed in the Southern Armies During the Late Civil War Between the States of the Federal Union.* Bennett says schoolmaster Reverend C. D. Elliot, was beaten by a "stout fellow of the 36th Ohio regiment" and was encouraged in the beating by a major on horseback who accompanied him.]

Van Derveer was not pleased. Calling him an old rascal, the colonel ordered Beatty to give his horse to another soldier and then take the man's place in the ranks. Sure that the provost guard would be looking for Beatty by the time the regiment got into Nashville, Van Derveer tried to hide him, but

---

153. Ibid., 92; Keil, *Thirty-fifth Ohio*, 19–20.
154. Keil, *Thirty-fifth Ohio*, 60; Zeller to Sir, 16 March 1862, Zeller Papers; Grebner, *We Were the Ninth*, 99; Van Derveer to wife, 14 May 1862, Van Derveer Family Collection.

"the garrulous old fellow wouldn't keep still." Not only did he keep repeating the story over and over, as wagon master, Beatty had never learned to march. He made such a poor showing at it that everyone was sure he would be easily spotted. The provost guards were on the lookout, but somehow the out of step Beatty went undetected. Once out of the city, he resumed control of the wagons.[155]

The Sad Results of War

One division of the Army of the Ohio, under the command of Gen. Ormsby Mitchel moved south toward Huntsville, Alabama, but the bulk of the army was to join General Grant at Pittsburgh Landing before advancing on to Corinth. General Thomas's division was the army's rear guard, and it was not until the third day of a march dusted by snow that the Thirty-fifth arrived at Spring Hill. The Confederates had destroyed the bridge across the Duck River, and the Persimmons waited five more days for a bridge to be built. On March 29 they moved forward several miles, but it was April 2 before they were able to cross the Duck and go into camp three miles from its banks. Ferdinand Van Derveer still thought the war would wrap up soon. "No enemy has yet been found and we begin to think none will be—The recent victories have so discouraged the rebels that they are ready to give up the contest." Others in the in the Duck River camp agreed. While there, one unnamed soldier from Company H who was known for having dreams that came true told Abia Zeller of his latest vision. He had dreamed that he would die on Saturday, there would be a battle on Sunday, and that peace would be declared in June.[156]

As the Thirty-fifth Ohio began to climb into the hills of southern Tennessee, the roads grew worse. The other regiments in the brigade were forced to remove their backpacks from their wagons and carry them to relieve the wagon teams, but the Thirty-fifth, blessed with much better animals, was able to march unburdened. There were some changes among the regimental staff officers on the march. Dr. Francis Morris, the assistant surgeon was having some health problems of his own. He had developed cancer of the tongue and went to Cincinnati to have surgery. He resigned for medical disability a few months later, but reenlisted in the Thirty-fifth the next year after recuperating. Signs of continuing turbulence in the chaplain's position also appeared. Joshua Hoblet, a minister from Mason, Ohio, had joined the regiment in January, and he had been chosen partly on the recommendation of Mrs. Van Derveer. In spite of his wife's involvement, there was a hint of disrespect in Ferdinand Van Derveer's

155. Keil, *Thirty-fifth Ohio*, 57–58; Daniel, *Days of Glory*, 77.
156. Keil, *Thirty-fifth Ohio*, 61; Zeller to Sir, 25 April 1862, Zeller Papers; Van Derveer to wife, 24 March 1862, Van Derveer Family Collection.

letters when he mentioned the new chaplain. "Mr. Hoblet has just given us a sermon and I with the rest feel comfortable—for soldiers who fight for their country and in a good cause we are told have a pretty sure time of it hereafter—Mr. Hoblet is going to Nashville this afternoon to visit our sick."[157]

As rear guard, Thomas followed the army's extensive wagon train so progress was painfully slow. When Confederate general Albert Sidney Johnston, knowing full well that he would be attacked as soon as Grant and Buell joined, decided to launch a preemptive strike against the Union forces camped near Pittsburgh Landing, the Thirty-fifth was still forty miles from the landing on the wrong side of the Tennessee River. When news of the fighting reached the First Division, still forty miles to the rear, Thomas's men put on a burst of speed. "No troops ever marched faster over almost impassable roads, or labored harder to cross swollen streams, without bridges or boats, than the division under Thomas." The men of the Thirty-fifth Ohio impatiently moved out into the fields and dense thickets to get around the wagon train that was slowing them up, but by noon, the men were rapidly tiring and the race seemed about to peter out. That changed when dull booms were heard from the direction of battlefield. "This spurred the men forward and added strength and endurance to wearied limbs," but try as they might, they could not go fast enough.[158]

On the night of Sunday, April 6, while the soldiers of Grant's army slept on the battle line in the rain, and the forward elements of Buell's army were arriving at Pittsburgh Landing, the Persimmons were spending the night standing in the rain around fence rail fires near Indian Creek. They went into bivouac without rations or tents, and when food did arrive, they had no way to prepare it in the pouring rain. The rain swelled the creek so that it could not be forded, and axes were used to drop trees across the water for men to cross. A few brave souls swam the flooded creek on horses so trees could be felled from both sides at the same time. The crossing, done by stretching ropes for support, was painfully slow, and the regiment did not arrive at Savannah until after dark on April 7. The next morning, they were packed tightly into transports and ferried across the river. Their clothes were still wet from the rain, and the cold wind blowing down the river chilled everyone.[159]

The fighting was over by then, but the landing was a scene of great turmoil. The first news the Thirty-fifth received about the battle were the rumors that floated everywhere. It was claimed that the army had been taken completely by surprise, which wasn't far from the truth, and that bad generalship had nearly lost the battle, which wasn't true at all. Most of the rumors were accepted at face value. As volunteers with barely six months service, they were still inclined to believe all regular army generals spent more time drinking than

157. Van Derveer to wife, 30 March 1862, Van Derveer Family Collection.

158. Keil, *Thirty-fifth Ohio*, 61–62; Daniel, *Days of Glory*, 78.

159. Keil, *Thirty-fifth Ohio*, 63; William Bircher, *A Drummer Boy's Diary* (St. Cloud: North Star Press, 2000), 19.

working. By the end of their enlistment, they would understand that even generals had to learn how to fight, and at Shiloh, both soldiers and generals had been inexperienced.[160]

As at Mill Springs, the Persimmons had the opportunity to view the Shiloh battlefield. Pvt. Benjamin Arnold and his friend Pvt. Bill Barnhiser, both of Company C, explored the battlefield on Tuesday, April 9. As soon as they crested the hill behind the landing, the "sad results of war" appeared on all sides. Immediately, they passed two men bearing a stretcher piled high with arms and legs. Many of the legs still had shoes on them. The stretcher bearers informed the two explorers that they were removing amputated limbs that had been "racked up like cord-wood" outside a nearby hospital. Burial parties made up mostly of volunteers from regiments who had fought in the battle were searching for dead and wounded comrades. While many of them conducted the grim work with "the tenderness of brothers," others made coarse jokes and cursed as they worked. To Arnold, it was proof of "how soon men's hearts become hardened when surrounded by misery and deprived of woman's presence."[161]

In passing over the area of the Confederate attack on Sunday morning, the dead of both sides lay side by side. Arnold and Barnhiser found a wrecked artillery battery with "men, horses, guns, and caissons, all entangled in one heap of destruction." While the wounded artillerymen had been attended to, three wounded horses still remained in harness where they had fallen. Arnold was saddened when he "heard the soft whinny of a horse (I had thought them all dead) calling for sympathy, for when I looked into his clear, brown eyes I could understand that he knew that I could give him nothing else." As they walked away from the battery, they were surprised to hear a voice say, "Hello, pardner."

The roving pair found two wounded Union soldiers lying between two fallen trees. The wounded men, one from the Eighth Missouri and one from the Sixth Ohio, had been placed there by comrades for protection as the fighting raged, but their protected position had concealed them from search parties. In spite of having been exposed to the weather without treatment for three days, they were "not suffering greatly except from thirst." Arnold and Barnhiser tried to make them more comfortable and then led a search party to their location. Leaving the wounded men to the care of their comrades, the two Persimmons moved on when Barnhiser noticed a man guarding a row of knapsacks. Arnold suggested they go "see what he has to say." The man was sitting on the ground resting with his back against a tree, rifle grasped tightly in his hands, but they found he had little to say. As they drew near, the pair could see the man with "wide-open eyes staring wildly down the line" was dead. Years later, Arnold told the story to a member of an Iowa regiment who claimed to know the dead

160. Keil, *Thirty-fifth Ohio*, 63.
161. Arnold, *Sunshine and Shadows*, 2.

man, who believing he had been only slightly wounded, had volunteered to return and guard his unit's baggage.[162]

While the Union dead were gathered up by friends and buried individually, slain Confederates were "gathered like sheaves of grain in a harvest field, into long windrows which extended almost as far as the eye could see." The tour had been a sobering event for Arnold and Barnhiser, and Arnold closed his description of it with this observation. "More than two years later, when General Sherman said, 'War was hell,' the whole world marveled and took it as something original. What a vast difference it makes in the perpetuity, either of words or of deeds, who speaks it or who does it. On the battlefield of Shiloh that day I heard more than a score of men say, while looking with horror upon the scene, 'This is hell.'"[163]

Ferdinand Van Derveer had also been affected by the horror of what he had seen. In writing to his wife several days after the battle to let her know he was still alive and well, he complained that the regiment had "yet to find its first fight," but what he wrote next surely did not comfort Emily. "There are a great many wounded fellows here, from four to five thousand—they are being placed on boats and removed to St. Louis, Louisville & Cincinnati—When I first came here there was dead men scattered through the woods for miles around—but now they are mostly buried." Van Derveer was never a fan of Ulysses S. Grant, and his dislike was first expressed after Shiloh. "Great shame is attached to Gen. Grant for his neglect and want of generalship—He is responsible for the lives of hundreds of his men—And should be very severely dealt with."[164]

The regiment had gone into a makeshift camp next to Pittsburgh Landing, where the constant noise and movement made for difficult sleeping. There was continuing disappointment that the Persimmons had missed their second battle. "We have had no fight yet," Colonel Van Derveer stated, "and do not expect any as the enemy, we hear will likely abandon Corinth—Our regiment will have to return home I fear without any laurels." Pvt. Abia Zeller and his comrades were thinking about the visionary whose dreams always came true. In a letter to his brother dated April 25, he said the man who had dreamed he would die on Saturday had done just that. He had dreamed there would be a big battle on Sunday, the day after he died, and there had been. [Note: There is no record of any member of Company H dying on April 5, 1862.] Now they were all hoping that the third part of the dream, that peace would be declared in June, would also come true. It didn't.[165]

---

162. Arnold, *Sunshine and Shadows*, 2–3.

163. Ibid., 4.

164. Van Derveer to wife, 12 April 1862, Van Derveer Family Collection.

165. Zeller to Sir, 25 April 1862, Zeller Papers; Van Derveer to wife, 28 April 1862, Van Derveer Family Collection.

CHAPTER 4

We Were Not in the Deal

May 1862

The Step Was A Little High

It was some time before the baggage came up. Having no tents, the Persimmons camped in the woods around the battlefield using the rapidly growing vegetation to provide the only shelter they had. For once, officers and men fared alike. "I am about as dirty as ever I was in my life," Colonel Van Derveer reported, "it is ten days since I had a clean shirt and I don't know how long it may yet be before I enjoy that luxury." Considering the minimal facilities, it was a pleasant campsite. The tulip poplars were in bloom, wildflowers were cropping up, and everything wore the green of spring. It rained about half the time, but the spring showers were mild and the warm sun filled the sky in between. As far as the soldiers could see, "all nature wore a smiling countenance."[166]

On April 24, the Thirty-fifth Ohio and the Eighteenth U.S. Infantry performed a reconnaissance southwest toward Monterey to try and find out exactly where the rebel forces were. Rebel pickets were posted at several places along the road, but each group retreated before the blue ranks after exchanging shots with the Thirty-fifth. After advancing six miles, the two regiments came upon an equal number of Confederate regiments in their encampment. The Persimmons formed a line of battle, and the men were ready for their first big fight, but as it turned out, the artillery did all the work. About fifty shells were fired into the enemy camp with no return fire by Confederate artillery. As the Federal cannons fired and the men in line of battle watched, the rebels burned their camp and "shoved off." The Thirty-fifth plundered and destroyed whatever had been left behind and then continued on the road toward Monterey. This small

---

166. Keil, *Thirty-fifth Ohio*, 68; Van Derveer to wife, 12 April 1862, Van Derveer Family Collection.

affair had been but a brief interlude, and the men had thought little enough of it. The entire incident would have been relegated to the ranks of all old war stories if it were not for *Harper's Weekly*.[167]

Several weeks after the skirmish, a full-page illustration appeared in *Harper's* purporting to show the Eighth Missouri Infantry charging over the Eighteenth U.S. Infantry to get into the rebel camp. The caption stated that the Eighteenth U.S. Infantry had refused to advance on the enemy so the Eighth Missouri had forged on alone. The story created outrage among the Persimmons who knew the Eighteenth U.S. was being libeled. During the assault on the camp, the Thirty-fifth had been in the second rank behind the regulars, so they knew the Eighteenth had been first into the camp and that no other regiment had charged through them. The Eighth Missouri had indeed been part of the reconnaissance, but they had been at least half a mile away and had not arrived until after the camp was captured. According to the regimental historian, the story was the fabrication of "some would be artist, [who] wanted to give the Eighth Missouri a send off, and make heroes of them, [and so] got up this illustration."[168]

Lieutenant Keil of Company C also wrote that the Eighth Missouri was well known for its foraging skills. According to Keil, the local inhabitants had much more to fear from the Missourians than the rebel army did. Apparently nothing was safe while the Eighth was in the vicinity and their efforts took on legendary proportions. "A story is told of one of Sherman's bummers who strayed off from the line of march seeking something to eat. He entered the house of an old sesech planter and said:

"Can I get something to eat?"

"No," said the planter, "I hav'nt a thing to give you, your men have stripped me of everything. Why they took off just now a blind mule, the last living thing on the plantation. I hav'nt a thing left on the entire plantation."

Then, with a deep sigh continued: "Thank God, there is one thing I possess that your soldiers can not deprive me of."

"What is that?" asked the soldier.

"Why, sir, they can't take from me my hope of eternal salvation."

The soldier contemplated the old planter for a moment, then said: "Just wait until the Eighth Missouri comes along."

No doubt the *Harper's Weekly* incident left a sour taste in the mouths of the Thirty-fifth when it came to the Eighth Missouri, but there was also a hint of jealousy, perhaps even respect, for the Eighth Missouri's ability to freely supply itself.[169]

Changes had been made in the western armies after Shiloh. Gen. Henry Halleck had combined the Armies of the Ohio, Mississippi, and Tennessee into

---

167. Keil, *Thirty-fifth Ohio*, 69; Zeller to Sir, 25 April 1862, Zeller Papers.
168. Keil, *Thirty-fifth Ohio*, 69.
169. Ibid., 69–70.

one huge mass, and for the one and only time in the war, he took command in the field. As part of that reorganization, General Thomas had been assigned to command the right wing of the army and his old division, having been transferred with him, was redesignated the Seventh Division. With a combined strength of 120,000, the Union army had at least twice as many men as the Confederates could assemble in front of them. Halleck's intention was to move south and capture the Confederate base at Corinth, Mississippi. After Shiloh, General Grant had come under political attack for having been surprised. To avoid having the same thing happen to him, Halleck moved very deliberately. "One of the most singular campaigns of the war" began when the army moved south on April 30. Operating on his theory that the North could win the war with little fighting by capturing southern territory, Halleck took over five weeks to advance nineteen miles, a distance that could have been covered with one forced march. It took nineteen days to cover the twelve-mile distance between Pittsburgh Landing and Monterey, and from the time the Persimmons left their camp near Shiloh, they camped at thirty-one different locations before entering Corinth.[170]

The regimental sutlers had stocked up while the army was in camp, and the sutler of the nearby Ninth Ohio, knowing well the proclivities of his clientele, had ordered a large stock of sauerkraut and lager beer from Cincinnati. The boys from Cincinnati planned a great celebration and beer kegs were hoisted on to homemade beer stands. Being a naturally generous bunch of fellows, the Ninth called for their friends in the Thirty-fifth Ohio to share their newfound abundance, and the Persimmons eagerly turned out, but the end result was disappointing. As Pvt. Benjamin Arnold of Company C stated, "The Thirty-fifth always stood in with the Ninth, so far as doing duty, fighting, and eating were concerned. But when it came to beer, we were not in the deal. So they gave us a generous share of the kraut, but when it came to the lager, they said, 'Nein.'"[171]

The Germans were shocked and greatly chagrined when the brigade received orders to move on the day the celebration was scheduled to commence. There was no way the great stock of barrels could be transported by wagon. The only way the beer could be moved was "to take it inwardly," and the Ninth Ohio went at it with just that intention. The United States was already involved in putting down one rebellion, and another was brewing if the Ninth didn't get its lager. Colonel McCook was a well-respected commander, and he earned the undying love of the Ninth Ohio that day by declaring that it would take less time to allow the party to go on than it would to put down the riot cancellation would definitely cause. He was able to convince new division commander Gen. Thomas W. Sherman of the matter by promising that the Ninth Ohio would be on the move before the sun went down or sooner if required. As it turned out, the Ninth marched out of camp before noon. As the now loaded

170. Keil, *Thirty-fifth Ohio*, 68; Arnold, *Sunshine and Shadows*, 5.
171. Keil, *Thirty-fifth Ohio*, 76; Arnold, *Sunshine and Shadows*, 5.

regiment marched out of camp, the Thirty-fifth Ohio, Second Minnesota, and Eighteenth U.S. Infantry lined up to give them "three cheers and a tiger" and joked that there was at least one full regiment in the brigade. The men of the Ninth apparently came through their binge none the worse for the wear. Private Arnold noted that as they set out down the road, "the only discernible difference in the men was that all the belts were buckled in the last notch, the step was a little high, and the time a little fast." The regimental band was apparently improved by the experience since all present affirmed that they had never played better.[172]

The long slow campaign for Corinth was a study in tedium interrupted at very irregular intervals by moments of excitement. Some days the regiment would only advance a quarter of a mile before going into camp, and on others, they actually marched backwards. The myriad camps were sparse. Spare clothes and writing materials were in storage somewhere behind them. All the soldiers carried with them were small items that would fit in their knapsacks and blankets. They were also carrying a lot of ammunition. Between what was carried in cartridge boxes and what was in knapsacks, each man was toting 160 rounds of heavy .69 caliber ammunition.[173]

Not In Suitable Attire

Much of the land between Pittsburgh Landing and Corinth was wet and swampy. Living and working in hot, humid malarial swamps where trees prevented the air from moving was not the healthiest place to be, and as Pvt. Abia M. Zeller wrote, there was plenty of water, but it was "nearer like dishwater. The boys nearly all of them have the diarea, it is very poor water but we have to shift." Wells were dug at each camp, but just about the time the well was cleared out, the regiment would move. Contaminated water sent thousands of soldiers to the hospital, and the Persimmons' sick list was as large as it would ever be. Companies were dwindling to skeleton crews, and the surgeons were becoming more and more concerned. Convinced that the men were not taking their daily dose of quinine as directed, the doctors went back to the "primitive remedy" they knew few men would refuse. Quinine was replaced with a daily ration of "Old John Barley Corn." Virtually everyone swallowed the drink on the spot, but a few didn't. Benjamin Arnold of Company C put his four ounces in his canteen every morning and then sold it for a quarter.[174]

Part of mess number 2 in Company C, Arnold and his messmates normally

---

172. Arnold, *Sunshine and Shadows*, 6.
173. Zeller to brother, 19 May 1862, Zeller Papers.
174. Arnold, *Sunshine and Shadows*, 17; Wiley, *Billy Yank*, 126; Zeller to Sir, 25 April 1862, Zeller Papers.

spent the evening around the fire talking and singing in a jovial mood, but one night, he approached the campfire to find his friends silent and depressed. They had just learned that one of their mess, Pvt. Joseph Robinson, left in the rear with a raging fever had died several weeks previous in the hospital at Indian Creek, Tennessee. While they grieved, the men in the mess next to them were having a jolly time. Led by Pvt. George Hime, "the wittiest boy in the company, everybody's friend," that mess spent the evening singing and joking.

The next morning, a crowd gathered around the tent where the neighboring mess lived. A fever had come over George Hime in the night, and a few hours later he was dead. The surgeons declared it to be black measles, and orders came to bury him immediately in the blanket he had died in. The tent and everything in it was to be burned. Hime's friends dug a grave and laid him to rest as tenderly as they could. "Shedding tears of genuine sorrow," they placed a piece of cracker box on the grave. Marked in pencil, it read simply:

George Hime
C, 35th Ohio
Aged 19 Years

Some time later, the bodies of those who died on the way to Corinth were disinterred and moved to the cemetery at Shiloh. All his friends could do was hope that the simple grave marker could still be read when the body was moved. It was, and Hime now rests in the National Cemetery at Shiloh.[175]

When the Thirty-fifth Ohio was being enlisted, the men had accepted the possibility of death in combat. Death from some unknown fever or strange disease had not been part of the deal. You could see an enemy standing on the other side of the field with his weapon pointed at you, but you couldn't see sickness as it crept up. But sickness was in fact part of the life of a soldier, and the men took an increasingly matter-of-fact view of it. Medicine as it was practiced in the 1860s was flawed, inadequate, and in some ways, barbaric. Soldiers were keen enough observers to recognize that, and hospitals became places to avoid. One of the things that bothered soldiers most about hospitals was not the treatment of the living, but the dubious treatment of those unfortunate enough to die in one. They believed wholeheartedly that the dead deserved a decent burial, but the assembly line operation of most hospitals didn't provide one.[176]

Shortly after Hime's death, Arnold was sent to the division hospital as part of a burial detail. For him "it was the saddest scene of my whole army life." Nine graves were required that day. Once they had been dug, the detail was sent to a small tent used as a morgue. The tent was full of swarming blue bottle flies, and the detail was "compelled to cut branches off the trees and brush them out while the dead were wrapped in blankets." The sergeant in charge of the detail counted and found that there were only six bodies. When he complained to the

175. Arnold, *Sunshine and Shadows*, 9–10.
176. Mitchell, *Civil War Soldiers*, 61–62.

hospital steward about digging three extra graves, he was told that there were "three in that little wall tent, but they are not dead yet."

While the sergeant raged at the steward over the inhumanity of digging graves before the sick men had even died, Arnold and some of the others went over to the wall tent and looked in. As with the other, bottle flies filled the tent, and beneath the insect swarm, three men, their faces shadowed by death, lay on blankets spread on the ground. Aghast at what they saw, Arnold and his companions cut branches to drive off the flies while berating the hospital stewards for their "neglect and hardness of heart." The only defense the stewards offered was, "If you fellows were in our places and saw this every day, as we do, you would become callused as we are." As bad as the situation was, things got even worse when someone called out, "Why this is Bill Calvin of Company K!" Calvin, who had been known as an athlete, up until four days prior had been the picture of health. Once the flies had been driven out, the three sick men became quite peaceful and died within minutes. Even knowing that the main hospital and all the surgeons had been moved the day before leaving the stewards to fend for themselves, Arnold was still appalled at what he had seen. Forty years later, he still hesitated to tell the story fearing that even then it might cause sorrow for those who had lost loved ones during the war.[177]

There were lots of ways to die in a war, and most of them did not involve combat. A certain amount of randomness has always been a part of life, but war tended to increase the likelihood of that random event. Disease could strike at anytime, but being in close proximity to hundreds of other men, all in various states of hygiene, increased the chance. It was the same with accidents. While at Pittsburgh Landing, Pvt. Martin Kelly of Company D fell in the Tennessee River and drowned. The same thing might have happened to him at home, but it didn't. It happened several hundred miles away in Tennessee, a place Kelly would not have been had it not been for the war.[178]

Benjamin Arnold's mess had a runaway slave named Jim Polk for a cook. An enterprising man, Polk wanted to borrow a dollar so he could buy lemons and sugar and "make a heap ob money selling lemonade." He had been sent to Arnold who was known to be a careful man with money and served as the unofficial banker for his mess. Arnold gave Polk money for lemons and provided sugar from the mess stores. Two hours later, Polk was back, having learned first hand that the Union soldier's dislike of slavery did not translate directly into fair treatment of runaway slaves. Excited when he returned, Polk told Arnold he would not need to borrow any more money. "Ise done awful well," he declared merrily, "Ise got jist all kinds ob money eben de long green." Upon closer inspection, the money Jim had collected turned out to be one dime, a ten-cent sutler check, four pieces of yellow pasteboard, and one green colored advertisement that Polk had taken to be a greenback. Arnold's only comment

177. Arnold, *Sunshine and Shadows*, 10–11.
178. Ohio Roster Commission, *Official Roster*, 614.

was that the two men who had paid with the dime and the sutler's check obviously hadn't been in the army very long.

Jim Polk turned out to be a better gambler than businessman. In general, the servants taken in by the men were not well looked after. They were poorly clothed, rarely paid, and verbally abused. So, when Polk came to camp one day with an army blouse, two shirts, a pair of shoes, a hat, and a bright red bandana, the men in Arnold's mess took note. When asked where all of this plunder had come from, Jim secretively said he had "dun skinned" another runaway. If Arnold's mess had any doubts about Jim's story, they were removed shortly afterwards. Captain L'Hommedieu walked up with his own cook who "was not in suitable attire for an evening reception," wearing only a pair of blue army pants. It was L'Hommedieu's cook that had been skinned, and in the irate officer's presence, Jim had no choice but to return everything he had won.[179]

Like A Hungry Hound

Army life agreed with that dog Jack, and he was learning to be a good soldier. No loafer, Jack was always in camp, night or day, and always ready for duty. Being a well-behaved animal, he avoided the "chuck-luck gang," and his name was never found on the guardhouse log. It was also noted that he never played "old soldier," never reported on sick call to avoid a march, and always reported on time to receive his rations. When the rations were skimpy, Jack would go out and find something he liked. Sometimes it came from a "comrade's haversack. But, in this he did no more than others who were not dogs!"[180]

When the regiment moved out of the swamps, the daily medicinal ration was ended, and whiskey was difficult to come by. Whiskey was considered contraband for enlisted men. Officers and enlisted men with orders from their company commander could purchase it from the sutler, but the prices were exorbitant. Even so, the soldiers were very creative in finding ways to get what they wanted. One method was simple deception. The sutlers couldn't sell whiskey to soldiers, but they could sell patent medicine that had about the same contents and effect. Another way to get alcohol was to steal it from the sutlers. Because of the high prices they charged, soldiers had little sympathy for the roving salesmen. In their minds, looting the sutler was equivalent to looting Southern property. On one occasion, a member of Company C stole a case of canned oysters from the sutler. Amidst the hurried preparations to cook and eat the oysters before the sutler discovered his loss, Pvt. Alfred Mehan, an Irishmen, opened the first can and announced, "Be dad, yees needn't fear the sutler reporting his loss to the colonel." Rather than oysters, each can contained con-

---

179. Arnold, *Sunshine and Shadows*, 14–15; Wiley, *Billy Yank*, 115.
180. Keil, *Thirty-fifth Ohio*, 223.

traband whiskey.[181]

Another soldier from Company C, known as Gully, developed his own way of getting the whiskey he craved. Claiming he suffered from an old ailment that could be treated only with whiskey, Gully convinced Captain Earhart to give him an order so he could purchase a bottle from the sutler. After giving himself a hefty dose of the medicine, he lay down and went to sleep with the bottle under his head for safekeeping. He awoke some time later to find the bottle gone. With a look of sorrow on his face, he informed Earhart that someone had stolen his medicine and requested that the company be searched. The captain was doubtful that the contents would last more than a few minutes when passed among the rest of the company, but Gully was certain whoever stole the bottle would keep it all. "Well, then," said the captain, "just wait a while and the guilty party will expose himself." An hour or so later, an orderly reported to Colonel Van Derveer and handed him a note that read:

"Colonel, one of your men who declares himself able to lick all creation is threatening the peace of the army, and, as orders are strict against bringing on an engagement, you had best send a guard to take charge of him.

M. B. Walker
Colonel Commanding Thirty-first Ohio"[182]

Once they had moved out of the swamps, the regiment camped in the cotton fields of an abandoned plantation. As the latest tent city sprung up in the cleared fields, visitors from home, thousands of them, came to visit. They were blue house martins, familiar to every farm boy from Ohio, and they reminded the regiment of springtime at home. The martins inspected the men and their tents closely, chattering the while. Men were making birdhouses out of cracker boxes and mounting them around camp, and the makeshift houses were soon teeming with birds. A symbiotic relationship developed between man and beast, and when the regiment moved to a new campsite, the birds moved with them.[183]

A new sutler, William C. Ellis of Dayton, arrived in camp just in time for payday. Each private had received two months pay, and while the money lasted, the sutler and the gamblers would be very busy. Ellis and his clerks were taking in money so fast they couldn't keep an accurate count. One clerk's account would be short $700 while the other would have $1,500 more than he should have. Regardless of the count, the sutlers were making huge profits. A can of peaches that normally went for well under a dollar sold for as much as $1.50. The soldiers remembered the preserves and other sweet things they had at home and hankered for them, so they had no choice but to pay the high prices. When the sutler set those wonderful things out for display, the longing became

---

181. Arnold, *Sunshine and Shadows*, 18.
182. Ibid., 19–20.
183. Ibid., 21.

a craving that had to be satisfied at any cost.[184]

Benjamin Arnold had not had any of his favorite food, mackerel, for over a year. While walking through the camp of the Tenth Kentucky, he caught a whiff of his favorite dish and began to "follow the scent like a hungry hound." Learning that the Tenth Kentucky's sutler had mackerel for sale, Arnold purchased two at the outrageous price of twenty-five cents each. Crazed by his homesick appetite, he couldn't take his eyes off the two fish as he walked back to his own camp. But no sooner than he had gotten back to his own tent, Private Arnold was selected for an emergency detail and barely had time to grab his rifle and other gear. There was no time to cook the fish and he certainly couldn't take it with him. It was just as certain that if he left the fish in his tent, they would be long ·gone by the time he got back.

Desperate over what to do with his mackerel, he thought of Pvt. Moses Holsaple, a Dunkard who surely could be trusted with the fish while Arnold was gone. Arnold was placed on a picket for the night at two hours on and four hours off. When he was on duty, he thought about his mackerel and the miracle of the two fishes he had learned in Sunday School. On his last turn off duty, he dreamt of cooking the mackerel while he slept. In his dreams "they had greatly increased in size" and "the odor that arose filled the air with a delicious fragrance." He dreamed that hundreds of hungry soldiers were drawn by the aroma and stood with hands out to receive their share. The fish in the pan kept growing larger and larger "until they threatened to fill the whole universe."

Arnold was awakened by an explosion and expected to find bits of mackerel scattered everywhere. Instead, he found that the explosion had been caused when he had been hit over the head with a rubber blanket. The grinning soldier who had smote him had come to relieve him of duty. Rushing back to his tent to recover his fish, Arnold was puzzled when people began to congratulate him on his return. He wondered for a moment if he had been promoted, but his thoughts quickly returned to his fish. When he couldn't find them, he went in search of their protector, Moses Holsaple. When queried, Holsaple, "as meekly and coolly as it would have been possible for Moses of old," responded that another private, Alf Mehan, had come in from picket and told Holsaple that Arnold was dead. Assuming Arnold would no longer need the mackerel, Holsaple and Mehan had eaten them.[185]

Both disappointed and furious at the plot against him and his fish, Arnold would have "licked the whole gang" if he had been able to. Arnold never again entrusted anything of value to his Dunkard messmate, but he still found Holsaple to be a useful companion, if not quite as honest as had been hoped. Shortly after he perpetrated the fish scam, Holsaple went to get the sugar ration for his mess. One of the kettles he carried was filled to the top, but the other was only about half full. The commissary clerk, John M. Bradstreet, also trusted Holsa-

---

184. Arnold, *Sunshine and Shadows*, 22–23.
185. Ibid., 29–30.

ple, and didn't pay any attention when Holsaple stopped next to the whiskey barrel. The lid was off, and Holsaple dipped the half-filled kettle of sugar into the barrel and collected about two gallons of whiskey. No one complained about Holsaple's petty thievery on that occasion, nor did they complain about the loss of the sugar. The whiskey Holsaple brought back was worth at least twenty-five dollars.[186]

Foraging, legal or not, did provide some variety in the diet of the Thirty-fifth Ohio. In the swamps, there had been whortleberries to gather. They were large and delicious, but the Confederates had picked most of them before they retreated. In the drier lands, there being many thickets in the region, wild plums were abundant. Even though they were "quite puckery to the taste," they were a welcome addition for men anxious for any kind of change. The stewed plums were relished by both armies and the supply seemed unlimited.[187]

Poor Benjamin Arnold continued to have bad luck when it came to food. The shadow of despondency had recently descended on 1st Sgt. Leonard Allen of Company C. Suffering from a severe case of separation anxiety, he had refused food and taken to sitting up all night to brood on his inability to get home to his wife. After several days of this behavior, he approached Pvt. Benjamin Arnold and asked for a favor. Arnold had been in the army long enough to know that the first sergeant wasn't really asking, and perhaps he just wanted to help the despondent man, so he agreed to do whatever he could for the first sergeant. Allen gave Arnold a half dollar and sent him to get a beef liver from the regimental butcher, Pvt. Jeff Debolt, also a member of Company C.

Allen was highly pleased when Arnold returned with the liver. "I suppose," the first sergeant said, "you can eat liver nicely fried, can't you?" Arnold replied that he was fond of liver, so Allen told him to "get a pan and fry it nice and brown. But first let's do things right while we are at it." Now Arnold was directed to go the hospital kitchen and get a cup of flour while Allen held the liver. Arnold was beginning to get suspicious and "went with some misgivings, wondering the while whether or not this was not another mackerel game," but when he returned, Allen was still there with the liver. Feeling guilty for having misjudged the first sergeant, Arnold started a fire while Allen sliced and breaded the liver.

His own mouth now watering over the thought of fried liver, Arnold used two pans to make the job go quicker. "I fried liver and the sergeant ate," Arnold recorded. "As soon as a piece was browned it was on his fork and I imagined I could hear the hot stuff sizzle as he gulped it down." When the last pan was on the fire and each piece that came out of the pan was still going down Allen's throat "like pebbles in a cray-fish's hole," Arnold's misgivings returned. He badly wanted to ask the first sergeant which part was his, but "modesty prevented it." The delay was fatal. Allen dumped the last of the meat on his plate

186. Arnold, *Sunshine and Shadows*, 31.
187. Ibid., 38.

and began to gobble it down. Desperate, Arnold said, "Where in thunder does mine come in?" The first sergeant's only response was to express amazement that Arnold had not saved some for himself. Arnold's anger overcame his better judgment for the moment, and "what I said to the sergeant on that occasion I could not repeat at this time with a clean conscience, neither would it be appropriate." Allen took it all in stride and spoke only of how good the liver had made him feel. He told Arnold that he was "awful sorry that you got left, but I'll tell you what to do: there's some flour left, make yourself some gravy."

The next morning at roll call, First Sergeant Allen was missing. Sitting up brooding night after night, "battling between right and wrong, between honor and dishonor," the first sergeant had finally come to a decision. Having made that decision, his appetite had returned, and he had eaten his meal of liver. During the night, Allen took "French leave," and was never again seen by the members of Company C.[188]

The liver was gone forever, but Arnold got some recompense for the loss of his fish on another date. He and Moses Holsaple were on picket duty one predawn morning. They had been assisted in staying awake all night by lice that kept them scratching, but all else was forgotten when they heard a rooster crow. The call of that rooster represented change; change from a diet of bacon and hard tack to one of chicken stew. Holsaple quietly moved over to where Arnold was posted and whispered that he was going to have that rooster or bust but didn't want to be shot "for a Johnnie" when he came back through the lines. Much wiser after his recent experiences, Arnold spoke plainly, "Hold on, Mose. I'm not to be trusted tonight unless it means pards." Holsaple crawled out into no man's land in search of the bird. As an old farm hand, he was able to skillfully imitate the call of the rooster and the flopping of wings. The rooster was enticed to draw near, and Arnold was able to hear the rooster's demise. Arnold made no further comment on the incident, so it is safe to assume Holsaple stuck to their deal.[189]

Theft of food was a common practice, though it was most often practiced against other regiments. John G. Baxter, another of Arnold's messmates was known for his ravenous appetite. When rations were pooled, there was always plenty to go around. But when rations were issued separately, Baxter ate all of his on the first day and starved for the next two. To satisfy his hunger, Baxter slipped into the camp of the Tenth Kentucky, only a hundred yards from the Persimmons. The commander of the Kentucky regiment was John M. Harlan, who was to become a Supreme Court justice after the war, and was known to keep a well-supplied larder. Baxter entered into a conspiracy with mess cook Jim Polk. While Polk distracted Harlan's cook, Baxter raided the mess chest and returned with several hams and other fat things.[190]

---

188. Arnold, *Sunshine and Shadows*, 35–36.
189. Ibid., 37–38.
190. Ibid., 31.

Colonel Van Derveer was well liked by his troops. He cared about what happened to them, and because of that, he worked them hard and held them under tighter control than in most regiments. His soldiers chafed under the restriction but were beginning to understand it was because their commander wanted to keep them healthy and make sure they were always prepared to fight. They had also learned that they could expect fair treatment from him in every situation. Pvt. Frank Brown of Company C was caught "foraging," a minor offense, but one that Van Derveer punished since it was still generally unacceptable in the spring of 1862. When the next camp was set up, Brown and several other minor offenders were sent to erect the colonel's tent. The first attempt was slipshod, and Van Derveer lost no time in expressing his displeasure over its slackness. Witnesses said that "music filled the air and words were spoken that did not sound like 'Well done,' etc." The miscreants went back to work, and by the time they were done, a small crowd had gathered in hopes of seeing the colonel let loose on them again. The colonel inspected the structure closely, and found that the tent was as taught as a drumhead.

The bespectacled commander had the men brought before him as the crowd looked on in anticipation of his next philippic. "Boys," Van Derveer began sternly, "I promised you fellows a dose of extra duty that you would remember as long as you live, and I'm going to make that promise good this morning." When he called to the contraband that cooked for him, a runaway Van Derveer called Horace Greely, to get his pistol out of the mess chest, the offenders and the crowd must have become apprehensive. The smiling cook returned and placed a black bottle in Van Derveer's hand. While the crowd looked on, the colonel handed the bottle to the men who had erected his tent and told them to drink heartily. Brown took his swallow when the bottle came his way, and upon returning to his own tent, sought out his messmate and best friend. "Johnnie," he declared solemnly, "there's just three people in the big world that I love better than you." When the curious Johnnie inquired as to who those three people might be, Brown responded, "Mamy Brown, Granny Brown, and Colonel Ferd Van Derveer."[191]

The colonel was not as understanding with Chaplain Hoblet, who still had not reported back to the regiment after visiting the hospitals in Nashville. In a letter partly intended to scold his wife for recommending the chaplain, Van Derveer wrote, "I have no news from Mr. Hoblet—I think he has treated us very shabily—He is pretending he has been ordered to stay at Nashville—that may be all true—but he would not have been so ordered unless he had desired it —And he could have the order revoked if he wanted to. But now the men have lost all confidence in him—he left just when we were beginning to have hard times—and expecting a fight—And I doubt if he could do any good if here—I have been disappointed in him." The annoying issue of the chaplain's official status would drag on for months.[192]

---

191. Arnold, *Sunshine and Shadows*, 26–27.
192. Van Derveer to wife, 25 May 1862, Van Derveer Family Collection.

The Most Disagreeable Task

For the men of the Thirty-fifth Ohio who had to endure it, the Corinth campaign was a harsh, distressing experience. Comfort was almost unknown since
there was always something disagreeable to ruin or take away any amenities
that might have been available. The soldiers were perpetually half mad from
the heat or nearly dead from being overworked. They lived in hot canvas tents,
the food was of questionable quality, and when they weren't involved in mind-
less digging or on some other fatigue detail, the inescapable inactivity was stifling. Even so, the Persimmons were becoming more and more familiar with
military life and steadily learning the finer arts of active campaigning.

As the Thirty-fifth arrived in the vicinity of Monterey, Mississippi, eight
miles from Corinth, the Confederate pickets were "rather bold, in fact saucy,"
continually sniping at the advancing Federal troops. General Halleck began his
siege of Corinth at Monterey while he was still miles from the city. From then
on, the Thirty-fifth had plenty of work to do, but none of it was the glorious
activity they had all imagined when they enlisted. The line of advance followed
by the Thirty-fifth Ohio ran through another swamp. A corduroy road had to be
built through the muck, and to complicate matters, Halleck insisted that preparations be made for retreat as well as advance, which required several roads to
be built.[193]

Road building in the swamps of Mississippi was about the most disagreeable task that anyone could be assigned. The canopy of trees created a stifling,
shadowy world inhabited by many disagreeable things. Working in black, slimy
water up to the waist was both distasteful and dangerous. Aside from the danger of the construction work, there were snakes slithering about, mosquitoes
that carried malaria, and man-killing bacteria that permeated the soupy sub-
stance. A few roads did run through the swamps, but they were simple dirt
roads that sunk into the mire when even the lightest traffic moved over them.
Logs ten feet wide were cut and dragged through the muck to be laid side by
side on the existing roadbed. In some places, the mud was so deep that several
layers of logs were required to make them passable. There were not always
suitable trees nearby, and timber would have to be cut and brought in. In those
instances, several men would be required to carry each log through the oozing,
scum covered water. The work was slow, backbreaking, and seemingly endless.
Wherever the road left solid ground, it had to be corduroyed, and when things
went well, a dozen logs extended the road a dozen feet.[194]

Some days, getting out of the swamp was no better. The roads that covered
dry ground were just as dusty as the swamp roads were wet. The heat in Mississippi was worse than anything the Persimmons had experienced back home in

193. Keil, *Thirty-fifth Ohio*, 70; Arnold, *Sunshine and Shadows*, 6–7.
194. Prokopowicz, *All for the Regiment*, 117.

Ohio. The sandy soil turned into dry powder in the heat, and the dust was quite often ankle deep. The dry roads were usually narrow and lined by tall pine trees that blocked the sun but also prevented any air from moving beneath them. At times it was like moving through a dust-filled tunnel, and it was not uncommon for men to swallow so much dust that it made them nauseous.[195]

It was in the swamps of Mississippi that Benjamin Arnold lost the last few items that remained from those sent to him by his generous benefactor, Billy Blair. The regiment had piled knapsacks in the morning when deployed as skirmishers. When they returned in the evening, the packs were nowhere to be found. The man left to guard them said they had been used to fill potholes in the road so an artillery battery could pass. The men were too tired and too busy to complain about the loss for long. Including the Thirty-fifth, there were four regiments in McCook's brigade, and every night two regiments were placed on picket duty and two remained in camp. The two regiments in camp were not loitering. Each camp the brigade established was required to be fortified, so the privates of the Thirty-fifth spent a lot of time digging.[196]

The rank and file were frustrated by the slow movement, but most frustrating of all was this daily requirement for entrenchment. "We are busy," wrote Abia Zeller. "Every day we have no rest neither day nor night. We have to be on the wach all the time. You can't trust to go away from camp 15 minutes for fear you will be detailed to do something." General Halleck expected the rebels to attack daily and was ready to put his army on the defensive at a moment's notice. No one else believed the rebels would fight another battle in the open. The soldiers were convinced that the rebels had learned their lesson at Mill Springs and Shiloh and would wait and fight from the fortifications surrounding their base at Corinth. But no one at army headquarters was much interested in what the enlisted men thought. As one member of the Thirty-fifth put it, "A soldier in the ranks is supposed by many to be an automaton; oblivious to conditions and surroundings." The soldiers knew that was a foolish notion and that every regiment in the army had men who given the chance could have taken the place of any colonel or general. Within the Thirty-fifth Ohio "each officer from Colonel to Captain knew just where the brains were to be found."[197]

One of the qualities that have always distinguished American soldiers from others is their desire to know why a particular order is given. The men of the Civil War armies were just as insistent on being led in a sensible fashion. They learned very quickly when it was necessary to entrench and when it wasn't. Nothing was more annoying than to dig useless trenches, but when danger was afoot "a soldier with nothing more than his bayonet and a tin cup would beat a Rocky Mountain badger to safety." Digging night after night, with rifles stacked nearby reminded one soldier of "the building of the walls of Jerusalem." [198]

---

195. Catton, *Hallowed Ground*, 126.
196. Arnold, *Sunshine and Shadows*, 26.
197. Ibid., 7; Zeller to brother, 19 May 1862, Zeller Papers.

During the glacial advance of the Union army toward Corinth, Company C was detailed to division headquarters as provost guard. Under most circumstances, it would have been a comfortable detail, but under Gen. Thomas W. Sherman, known to the men as "Granny" Sherman, it was an onerous assignment. Sherman was a fussy, cranky, crabby regular officer very much aware of his prerogatives as division commander. Sherman made sure he had the maximum number of staff officers permitted and issued an interminable stream of orders. The problem for Company C was that the orders were often contradictory.

The first morning of duty was enough to exasperate the officers and men assigned to the provost. Sherman ordered that three guards be placed over his own horses and the horses of his staff. No sooner than the guards had been positioned, when the general demanded that two guards be removed right away. One guard for horses was plenty. Immediately after the two guards were removed, Sherman sent word that two sentries should be placed before his tent so it wouldn't be unguarded when he left it. Two men were placed at the general's tent in time to receive word that the general had decided he didn't want any guard for the horses, since there was no purpose to put a guard over horses that were securely fastened. A guard would only be needed at night. Just as the company officers were admitting that the general's last order made sense, another one arrived. The general demanded that the sentries placed near his tent be removed. He didn't want them listening and watching him all the time. Thus it went, day after day. The only letup came when the army was on the march.[199]

The one redeeming quality that the Company C detail noticed about Granny Sherman was his equitable distribution of justice. The monotonous pace of the advance led bored soldiers to seek some form of stimulation. Enlisted men fanned out far and wide to forage and to shoot whatever stray farm animals they came across. Likewise, officers would go out in groups and take target practice with their revolvers. All of this shooting had gotten to the point that General Sherman felt compelled to ban the discharge of all firearms when the division halted near Blackland. The provost guard was directed to enforce the order, and patrols from Company C scoured the division's area looking for violators.

Not long after the order was publicized, firing was heard near the headquarters and General Sherman sent the provost detail out to arrest whoever it was. The provost officer politely informed the general that he knew exactly who was doing the shooting. It was members of the general's own staff. "That makes no difference," shouted the general. "Arrest them and bring them to me.' Upon being informed that they were under arrest, one of the staff officers moaned, "There will be h——l to pay," but they all dutifully reported as ordered. Sherman was impatiently waiting and upon their arrival immediately

198. Arnold, *Sunshine and Shadows*, 7.
199. Keil, *Thirty-fifth Ohio*, 73–74.

launched into an extended, stinging rebuke. According to Lieutenant Keil, "it would be impossible to describe [Sherman's] indignation. He exhausted his vocabulary of epithets at the members of his staff; then fell back to replenish like a battery of artillery when its ammunition is exhausted." During the tirade, Sherman's large staff waited "good humouredly," and when the general "could replenish his caisson no longer," they all immediately went to their quarters as ordered. After the staff had retreated, Sherman turned back to the provost and said, "Be vigilant, and arrest all officers, no matter what rank they hold. I will see whether my orders are not obeyed."[200]

An Infernal Racket

During the period of General Sherman's imposed quiet, there were days when it seemed impossible that two large armies faced each other. "The bright sunlight comes streaming through the rich foliage of the trees. Birds are flitting from branch to branch, while calling affectionately to their mates. A few squirrels are ambling overhead cautiously while they look down upon the vast throng of men who have so suddenly come into possession of their late domain." One day, a shot shattered the tranquil setting and the birds and squirrels disappeared. A large fox squirrel, wounded and dying, stumbled into the clearing and expired. Immediately, a soldier unknown to the Thirty-fifth rushed out, grabbed the squirrel, and stuffed it under his shirt. The hunter, a private from the Twelfth Kentucky was almost immediately arrested and taken before his regimental commander. The Thirty-fifth found out later that the soldier did not deny his guilt but offered a compelling defense for his actions. "Colonel, I could in nowise help shootin' that thar squirrel, for the very sight of him made me long to be down in Turkey Creek bottoms in Old Kaintuck, and if I hadn't shot that bushy-tailed beauty I'd have desarted for sure. I can stand all other temptation, Colonel, except squirrel." The Kentuckian got off with a severe lecture and then went back to camp to cook his squirrel.[201]

As the two armies bedded down each night, their pickets were within a stone's throw of each other, often no more than "the width of a field apart." Opposing pickets traded shots, but casualties from gunshots were rare. On the night of May 20, the rebels made an attempt to break the line of Union pickets and see what was behind it. The regiment was awakened from its sleep and put into line of battle to support the pickets if needed. The Union pickets fought back stoutly, and Confederate raiders were repulsed without the help of the rest of the regiment. As Abia Zeller put it, "No siree, not a time could they do it," and when things quieted down, the regiment went back to bed. [202]

200. Keil, *Thirty-fifth Ohio*, 74.
201. Arnold, *Sunshine and Shadows*, 13.

The next night, the two sides traded artillery fire. The Union gunners opened the exchange, but the Confederates quickly joined in. The results of the Federal barrage were not observed, but the rebel shelling was ineffective. Only one enemy shell reached the camp of the Thirty-fifth Ohio. It hit the ground and skipped through a tent without exploding. The tent was unoccupied at that moment, and no one was injured. It was one of many similar instances. "We have had almost daily skirmishes with the rebels," one officer reported. "And scarce a day passes without the firing of muskets and cannon."[203]

As the Union army drew closer to Corinth, the rebel pickets began to back off a little, starting rumors that they were sending troops and supplies away from the city. The men, sensing that a battle was near, expected fighting to commence as soon as the entire army was in position around Corinth. Individual soldiers became jittery as they began to consider their mortality. In a letter to his brother, Abia Zeller wrote, "I am well more so than heretofore. I hope that I can fight and come out of this battle safe and sound again."[204]

On May 29, the Thirty-fifth Ohio threw up breastworks one thousand yards away from the fortifications that surrounded the Confederate base. Part of Company C drew picket duty for the division that night and took up watch posts that were within "point-blank musket range" of the enemy line. Only the thick vegetation prevented them from eyeballing their foes. Just after dark, the pickets heard the rebels moving around and prepared for an attack. The Persimmons could see nothing in the dark shadows to their front, but after the initial commotion, it got quiet again. In fact, as time wore on, the area to their immediate front got more and more quiet. In contrast to the quiet close in, the sound of locomotives could be heard from the city.[205]

The pickets, coached by the railroaders among them, noticed that they could tell not only which direction the trains were moving but how heavily loaded they were. Trains coming into the station seemed to be lightly loaded, but when they left, they were obviously straining. The movement of trains continued throughout the night, and the Persimmons on picket decided the rebels were evacuating. Their opinion was confirmed at about 4:00 a.m. when "a most infernal racket was heard in the direction of Corinth." The still morning air was rent with the sounds of explosions as the Confederates destroyed the stores they couldn't carry off. Someone yelled, "Good golly, I'll bet the Confederacy has bust her boiler," and cheers rang out all around. Gen. Pierre G. T. Beauregard, knowing all along that he could never hope to defeat the huge force inching up to his lines, had evacuated Corinth when an attack became inevitable.[206]

The explosions brought soldiers all along the line to their feet. Pickets and

202. Zeller to brother, 19 May 1862, Zeller Papers.
203. Ibid.; Van Derveer to wife, 25 May 1862, Van Derveer Family Collection.
204. Zeller to brother, 19 May 1862, Zeller Papers.
205. Keil, *Thirty-fifth Ohio*, 71.
206. Ibid., 1; Arnold, *Sunshine and Shadows*, 39.

those men still in camp expected momentarily to receive word to move forward. The noise of the explosions died away, the sun rose in the east, and the front grew deathly calm, but no word came. The Thirty-fifth and the other regiments of McCook's brigade formed ranks, ready to move on an instant's notice, but the waiting continued. Restless Colonel McCook finally got tired of the inaction and ordered the brigade forward toward the enemy lines. Excited at finally moving, the men rushed forward with a yell. As impatient as McCook had been, other commanders had been even more so, and several units beat the Thirty-fifth into the city.[207]

The men of Company C still on picket duty were caught in a ridiculous situation. They could not leave their posts until formally relieved. So, while the rest of the regiment passed through and approached the outskirts of the city, the pickets hung out in the woods. The supposed forward line of the division was now well to the rear and falling farther behind by the minute. Rather than being the first to know what the enemy was up to, they would now be the last. [208]

Presently, General Sherman came looking for McCook's brigade but didn't find it. He and his staff continued to seek the missing brigade without success and eventually ended up at the picket line. When informed that McCook had moved his brigade into the city, Sherman was livid. Because he had received no orders to advance, McCook was going to catch it for taking action on his own. Sherman's anger was overruled in the end by common sense. All along the line, individual commanders had realized what was happening and moved into the city without waiting for orders. Eventually, even General Halleck was stirred, and a general forward movement and pursuit was ordered.[209]

Climbing over the abandoned breastworks that had been the cause of their slow advance into Corinth gave the Persimmons a strange feeling. The first thing they discovered was several rows of cast off clothing. Rather than leave new clothing stores behind, the Confederates had issued them, and the men had changed clothes while standing in ranks. The discarded rags had been dropped where they stood, leading to jokes that the rebels had stripped naked to run faster. A little farther on, the Thirty-fifth waded through the muck created when the Confederates dumped thousands of drums of molasses on the ground rather than leave them for the Yankees.[210]

The not overly ambitious pursuit ordered by Halleck proved unsuccessful. Sweating profusely in the stifling heat, the men realized that the rebels had enough of a head start that the pursuit was likely to come to naught except for scaring the rebels further into Dixie. In struggling through the molasses spill, the regiment had gotten the sugary stuff on their shoes and pants. Some men had tried to take some of the syrup with them and had smeared it on their

207. Keil, *Thirty-fifth Ohio*, 71; Arnold, Sunshine and Shadows, 39.
208. Keil, *Thirty-fifth Ohio*, 71.
209. Ibid., 71–72.
210. Arnold, *Sunshine and Shadows*, 39–40.

clothes in the process. Plodding along in the sweltering heat, they were assailed by swarms of flies. Bombastic Gen. John Pope sent word that he had captured twenty thousand prisoners. Upon reaching Rienzi, Mississippi, the Thirty-fifth had been assigned the task of collecting and forwarding those twenty thousand as they were brought in. After a week of waiting in the woods of Mississippi, they had collected about fifty prisoners. Not only was the number disappointing, the prisoners themselves proved to be rather uncommunicative. No good rumors were to be had from any of them.[211]

The effect of the long, tiresome advance to Corinth was apparent in Ferdinand Van Derveer. On June 1, he couldn't remember what day of the week it was but he thought it might be Sunday. There was also a growing feeling of disappointment among the Persimmons. To the men of the Thirty-fifth Ohio, it seemed as if they might never get into combat. At Mill Springs, they were on the wrong side of the creek, and at Shiloh, the wrong side of the river. In both cases, they had missed the battle by a few hours. Now at Corinth, they had missed a battle again because of the dilatory advance of General Halleck. Disappointed at missing another chance to fight, their colonel wrote that "the expected battle of Corinth has turned out to be no battle at all; and the enemy after keeping up a resistance and skirmishing fight for ten days, night before last left Corinth and its camps in a great hurry. We had been gradually approaching the place on three sides, and on Thursday our Brigade went within a thousand yards and threw up entrenchments—In a day or two at most the fight would have commenced in earnest, but the rebels became nervous and could not wait." A few days later, he added, "Anyhow, things indicate that there will be no fighting here—And the fact is that , there never is any fighting where our regiment goes—here we have been spoiling for a fight for many months—lways close up—never behind orders a moment, but still no one to knock the chip off one's shoulder—it has become so apparent that I frequently hear our boys say, that were we go, the enemy is soon to get away." The regret was twofold. The regiment had enlisted to fight and did not want to go home before they had been in at least one battle. Likewise, there was a growing maturity within the ranks. They had been soldiers long enough to lose their initial enchantment with war and to know they would much rather be at home. They now realized that the only way to get home was to end the war by defeating the Confederate army. Every delay in getting into battle extended the war and their absence from home.[212]

211. Keil, *Thirty-fifth Ohio*, 72; Arnold, *Sunshine and Shadows*, 40.
212. Van Derveer to wife, 1, 9 June 1862, Van Derveer Family Collection.

Fading Sunshine

Still believing the war could be won without too much fighting, Halleck settled down to occupy Confederate territory. In a matter of days, he had scattered his huge army across northern Mississippi. General Buell was ordered to take the Army of Ohio and capture Chattanooga, but included in the orders was the requirement to repair the Memphis and Charleston Railroad as he went. On June 13, the army was again reorganized. Gen. Henry W. Halleck had been named commander in chief of all Union armies and gone to Washington. His successor, Gen. Ulysses S. Grant did away with the wings of the army as Halleck had constituted them. General Thomas returned to the command of his division, which was once more designated the First Division of the Army of the Ohio. Unfortunately for Thomas, Grant would harbor hard feelings in the years to come, but as far as Ferdinand Van Derveer was concerned, the change came none too soon. He considered Gen. Thomas Sherman "a most consummate humbug," and had at one point considered resigning to get away from him.[213]

After the brief pursuit of the rebel army, the Thirty-fifth went into camp about a mile east of Corinth along the Memphis and Charleston Railroad. It was an unhealthy and unpleasant site, and everyone rejoiced when the regiment moved a little further east where the ground was much nicer and where there was a good spring for water. There wasn't a whole lot to be done immediately after the capture of Corinth. The regiment was required to supply details for preparing and stocking warehouses in the city, and while the men assigned to the detail may not have enjoyed them, the officers liked the details very much. Once they had reported to their assigned area and gotten the work started, they were free to do as they pleased. What pleased them was to explore the town and its immediate surroundings.[214]

Lieutenant Keil of Company C found the meals at the Tishomingo House to be the most enjoyable aspect of the stay in Corinth. Corinth had suffered somewhat from the affects of being a Confederate garrison town, but the owner, realizing that the Yankee army was a source of ready cash, had immediately opened the hotel up to them. The food prepared at the hotel located at the intersection of the Memphis and Charleston and Mobile and Ohio railroads was not at all remarkable, consisting mainly of cornbread and bacon. What Keil enjoyed most was "the variety the table afforded. This variety was not in edibles, but in table cloths and dishes." Multiple cloths were required to cover one table, and on any table, no two cloths were the same color. The tableware was in a similar state. Each setting came from a variety of sets, most of which were chipped and cracked. The only thing that was consistent at the Tishomingo House was the price of a meal. Breakfast, lunch, and supper all cost the same.[215]

---

213. Van Derveer to wife, 13 June 1862, Van Derveer Family Collection.
214. Keil, *Thirty-fifth Ohio*, 72.

As commissary sergeant, Joseph Claypool expected to spend a lot of time in warehouses, but as things turned out, he got to join the officers at the Tishomingo House. On June 2nd, he was promoted to second lieutenant in Company B. While promotions were more and more based on merit, Claypool's rise in rank showed that politics was still part of the equation. Clearly a capable man, he had been promoted once already to his current position, Claypool's campaign for promotion to officer ranks began in the winter of 1862. In early March, Lt. Col. Fred C. Jones of the Twenty-fourth Ohio had written Governor Tod on Claypool's behalf. Having known Claypool since he was a boy, Jones was "happy to have the opportunity of bearing testimony to his bearing and conduct as an officer and a gentleman" and could "conscientiously recommend him as in every way qualified to make a good and efficient officer." Colonel Van Derveer agreed, describing Claypool as being "young, intelligent, and qualified to fill the place with credit to the State and usefulness to the service." Claypool also got support from the home front when John A. Gano, editor of the Cincinnati *Daily and Weekly Commercial*, also wrote to Tod to say that the young sergeant had enlisted "from purely patriotic motives." He had seen the letter sent by Van Derveer and one by Major Boynton and hastened to add that these recommendations "could not have been had inconsiderately." Claypool's opportunity for promotion finally came when Capt. Thomas Stone resigned.[216]

Stone had been nursing a grudge for a long time. He had never forgotten that he had been relegated to Company B when Joseph Budd had been given precedence and command of Company A, and the feud between the two of them had been simmering for ten months. The fact that Budd was obviously well thought of and set to advance at the first opportunity certainly fed Stone's resentment. The final straw occurred in May 1862 when Budd wrote a letter to C. P. Buckingham, the state adjutant general. Budd had become aware that Stone's date of rank was one week before his own. Technically, that made Stone superior to Budd, even though Budd had always been considered and treated as the regiment's senior captain. Budd could not see how Stone's commission could properly be dated prior to his, and requested that the error be corrected. To prove his claim, Budd was prepared to provide the testimony of all three field officers, the adjutant and several company officers. It was too much for Stone. Seeing that Budd's overwhelming support precluded his own advancement, Stone submitted his resignation and it was accepted. [217]

The official reason for Stone's resignation was ill health. In his certificate, Surgeon Perkins A. Gordon said he had prepared the document because Stone had "applied for a certificate of disability on which to ground his resignation." Stone was looking for a way out, and Gordon was willing to give him one. In

---

215. Keil, *Thirty-fifth Ohio*, 73.

216. Correspondence to the Governor and the Adjutant General of Ohio, 1861–1866, Series 147–34:12.

217. Ibid., Series 147–33:10.

describing Stone's ailments, Gordon listed the standard complaint of chronic diarrhea. He also included chronic rheumatism, dyspepsia, and most interesting of all, "hypochondriasis." Gordon further stated that Stone would "not be fit for duty during the remainder of the time for which he was enlisted." It seems that Stone had made himself so unpopular, that the good doctor, soon to have his own popularity issues, was going to make sure the certificate was so strongly stated that there was no chance of it being turned down.[218]

It is unfortunate that Stone's resentment seems to have had a negative impact to the other officer's in Company B. William Eacott was working his own grudge over not getting a company for himself in the initial organization of the regiment. No doubt he and Stone spent many hours complaining to each other about how they had been treated. When Ransford Smith was promoted to captain, Eacott's resentment increased until he finally resigned in January 1863, but not before poisoning the newly promoted Claypool. It may have been that Claypool planned to resign all along once he got his commission, a common thing during the war, but the fact that he resigned the same day Eacott did seems too coincidental. Ransford Smith had been promoted to captain but was still on detail with the brigade staff, but then he too resigned from the army in February of 1863. First Sgt. Joseph Henninger watched as the officers shuffled in and out of his company. When Eacott and Claypool resigned, Henninger was promoted to first lieutenant.[219]

Made of more steadfast stuff than the others, Henninger finally provided consistent leadership to Company B. A farm boy who got most of his education through personal reading, Henninger became a stonemason, a cooper, and then a carpenter. By the time the war started, the thirty-two year old had been running his own contracting business for seven years. Henninger remained with the company most of the way through the Atlanta campaign.[220]

The Corinth campaign, while involving little or no fighting for most of the participants, had been hard on the men. The heat and unhealthy climate had worn down many men used to a milder climate. Benjamin Arnold had been suffering periods of sickness ever since wading Fishing Creek in January. He had been left behind when the regiment left Somerset and spent most of February and March in the hospital. The experience was enough to convince him that hospitals were very bad places, and Arnold was terrified at the thought of entering another one. Arnold had struggled along with his company, and his friends had done what they could to doctor him themselves. Believing that their friend was better off with them than with the doctors, they had even pulled duty for him so the surgeons would not be able to see his condition, but on June 11th,

---

218. Compiled service record, Thomas Stone, Capt., Co. B, 35th Ohio Infantry; Carded Records, Volunteer Organizations, Civil War; Records of the Adjutant General's office, 1780s–1917, Record Group 94; National Archives, Washington, D.C.

219. Ohio Roster Commission, *Official Roster*, 605.

220. *Cyclopedia of Butler County, Ohio*, 385.

Arnold was unable even to get out of bed. When the brigade was ordered to move several days later, Arnold's condition could no longer be hidden, and he was sent to a hospital in Corinth where he remained for the rest of the month.[221]

Fortunate to be placed under the care of a conscientious hospital steward, Arnold survived several days of delirium, during which he imagined he was at home in scenes of bright sunshine. At the very end of his period of unconsciousness, shadows descended. Arnold dreamed that he had died and been buried. His messmates had then dug him up and brought him back into the hospital. The dream ended as his friends were cursing the doctor for allowing him to be buried alive. With that, Arnold returned to consciousness and found that the "sunshine had faded and the shadows were falling." When he had recovered enough to walk, he went down to the Tishomingo House where there was good clear water, but the well was guarded and reserved for the use of commissioned officers only. Other nearby wells were murky with minerals, so Arnold began to ask officers to fill his canteen for him. All refused until an old friend from home, Lt. W. W. Shoemaker of the Fourth Ohio Cavalry came by. Years later, Shoemaker told Arnold that after viewing Arnold's condition that day, he had not expected to see him alive again.[222]

---

221. Arnold, *Sunshine and Shadows*, 41; Wiley, *Billy Yank*, 139.
222. Arnold, *Sunshine and Shadows*, 46–47.

CHAPTER 5

Brothers No More

June to August 1862

A Highly Annoying Thought

The Thirty-fifth Ohio and the rest of McCook's brigade had gone into camp expecting to remain there for some time. Their expectations proved to be unfounded when General Buell was ordered to capture Chattanooga. Done quickly, it would have been a bold stroke, but Buell was just as cautious as Halleck. The advance turned out to be another leisurely movement, but it had been more than two months since the Persimmons had done any hard marching. The unhurried walk to Corinth had often covered less than a mile per day, followed by weeks in camp, but the first march beside the railroad to Iuka was done at a fast pace. The hot June weather caused dozens of men to fall out along the way.[223]

Iuka, about twenty miles east of Corinth on the Memphis and Charleston Railroad, was a resort town known for its mineral springs. The war had cut into the tourist business, and with the arrival of the Yankees, "the fashionable southron did not materialize." Only one of the town's hotels remained open, and the landlord's distaste for soldiers in blue was apparent to all. Once it was known that he did not enjoy receiving Yankees, the men of the Thirty-fifth swarmed his dining room, demanding to be fed. The food the men made for themselves in camp was just as good, or better, than the poor fare at the hotel, but the men went back time after time just to annoy the owner. Iuka was remembered for another reason as well. The paymaster arrived and everyone received two months pay in brand new postal currency. As other units pushed forward to Iuka, the Thirty-fifth continued its march to the east. The summer heat was brutal, and the march was conducted in short, relatively easy stages. The movement generally commenced about 4:00 a.m. and ended at about 11:00

---

223. Keil, *Thirty-fifth Ohio*, 76.

a.m. The hottest part of the day was spent lounging in the shade. It was a relatively pleasant journey, because there was an abundance of clear, cool springs along the route, so every camp was well watered.[224]

At Dixon Spring, the Persimmons camped on a plantation whose owner was away in the Confederate army, and his family fully expected the Yankees to treat them severely. To try and protect their property as much as possible, the plantation slaves were sent out to gather the pigs, cattle, and chickens in close to the house where they could be watched and kept out of the way of marauding soldiers. The slaves talked freely as they went about their business, and by the time they were done, the Thirty-fifth knew the complete history of the family, the names of their grown daughters, and even the names of each daughter's boyfriend in Beauregard's army. Standing orders prevented the Thirty-fifth from taking what they wanted while at the plantation, and as much as they wanted to "forage," they obeyed their orders. Ever after, the Persimmons, sure that some other troops would clean the plantation out just the way they wanted to, believed they had lost a golden opportunity. After leaving Company F at Buzzard's Roost to guard a railroad trestle, the regiment moved on to Tuscumbia, Alabama. General Thomas had made the city his headquarters, and all troops not working on the railroad were garrisoned nearby.[225]

Northern troops believed that they came from a culture superior to that of the South, so it isn't surprising that the Persimmons stationed at Tuscumbia considered it a small, old-fashioned, and even somewhat dilapidated town. Though some of the houses were shaded or vine covered and surrounded by large shrub-filled gardens, the town was considered unremarkable at best. What they found most interesting was the local method for paving public streets. They were covered in dog fennel, and when in full bloom, were quite aromatic. Long known as one of the premier cotton growing areas of the south, the war had brought radical changes to Tuscumbia. Cotton had not turned out to be nearly as valuable to the Confederacy as had been hoped. Efforts to create a worldwide shortage and stir up support in Europe had failed, and by the time the Confederate government removed the ban on its sale overseas, the blockade made exporting it very difficult. Also, cotton could not be eaten, and just then, the Confederacy needed food crops to feed its people and its armies. Corn had been planted in most of the cotton fields.[226]

The men of the Thirty-fifth, a large percentage of them farmers, were impressed with neither the soil around Tuscumbia nor the corn crop it produced, it being "rather puny in appearance with only one stalk in a hill." They were also unimpressed by the grand plantation houses they saw. While beautiful in their own right, the houses were surrounded by squalid huts inhabited by the owner's slaves. The poverty and wretchedness that surround the manor

---

224. Keil, *Thirty-fifth Ohio*, 76–77.
225. Ibid., 76–77; Bircher, *Story of a Regiment*, 23; Daniel, *Days of Glory*, 92.
226. Keil, *Thirty-fifth Ohio*, 79–80.

house left an overall impression of unattractiveness. They noticed the same effect at work with the women who remained on the plantations. They might be dressed in stunning finery, but the slave women who followed them around were dressed in filthy rags. It further reinforced the Persimmons feelings of superiority over the Southerners, because they could see the ugliness of slavery that was apparently invisible to Southern whites.[227]

As the Buckeyes watched the slaves toiling among the scrawny plants, another realization struck them. All of the field hands were women. By using female slaves, the Confederacy was able to use nearly all of its able-bodied black men to support its army with menial tasks, thus freeing up nearly every white man for active service in the army. The direct connection between slavery and the war was a new and highly annoying thought and was one of the reasons that white soldiers were generally unsympathetic to blacks. Just because the men hated slaveholders, and even slavery, didn't mean they had any particular love for the slaves themselves. Ferdinand Van Derveer, for one, was opposed to abolition and believed that abolitionists were "enemies of the constitution." The official policy of the Army of the Ohio was not to interfere with the rights of slaveholders, particularly those considered loyal to the Union. Buell, a former slaveholder, wanted as little to do with slaves as possible, but regardless of their personal opinion of African Americans, from that point on the Persimmons saw things in a more practical light. They were convinced that removing the Confederacy's slave labor force was one way of destroying the rebellion. This attitude eventually prevailed across the Army of the Ohio, and later the Army of the Cumberland, and when the Emancipation Proclamation was announced, the men generally accepted it without complaint, because they no longer viewed freeing the slaves as a social or moral issue. It was just another way of ruining the Confederacy.[228]

The camp at Tuscumbia was pleasant enough. In spite of the hot summer days and the fact that there was no shade other than tents, the heat was never really oppressive. With the exception of a few hours in the morning and evening, a good steady breeze blew all day and kept the heat in check. The men of the regiment found that it was actually better to camp in the open than in the pine forests that provided uninterrupted shade. The trees knocked the breeze down and left the air in the forests still and muggy. The breezes in the open fields kept the camp cooler than the shade did.[229]

Benjamin Arnold rejoined the Thirty-fifth Ohio while it was at Tuscumbia and was cheered wildly upon arrival, because the hospital had reported him dead. His stay was short. On July 19, Arnold was discharged with a surgeon's

227. Keil, *Thirty-fifth Ohio*, 77–78; Mitchell, *Civil War Soldiers*, 100–101.

228. Keil, *Thirty-fifth Ohio*, 77–78; Prokopowicz, *All for the Regiment*, 124; Wiley, *Billy Yank*, 112; Mitchell, *Civil War Soldiers*, 14–15; Bradley, *Tullahoma*, 3; Van Derveer to wife, 1 August 1862, Van Derveer Family Collection.

229. Keil, *Thirty-fifth Ohio*, 79; Mitchell, *Civil War Soldiers*, 15.

certificate of disability stating he had suffered from chronic diarrhea for four months and that he would likely never fully recover from its effects. Arnold had grown very close to the men of his company, but the parting of ways was not a sad one. The sadness came later when the Thirty-fifth came home for the last time and Arnold realized how many of his friends and acquaintances had been lost.[230]

Many Conflicting Opinions

The rest of the Army of the Ohio had begun to cross the Tennessee River and move toward Chattanooga at the end of June. The Thirty-fifth Ohio, along with the rest of Thomas's division remained behind in Tuscumbia. Their mission was to protect the Memphis and Charleston Railroad between Iuka, Mississippi, and Decatur, Alabama, a stretch of tracks that was very vulnerable to Confederate raids. General Halleck's vision of supplying the advance on Chattanooga using the railroad had proven to be a pipe dream. Rebel raids destroyed bridges and trestles as fast as Thomas's men could repair them, and when the tracks were open, the great dearth of rolling stock kept the flow of supplies to a trickle. Even dedicating two hundred wagons to the supply train didn't help. Within the Union ranks, the shortage of competent staff officers also took its toll on logistical operations. In July and August, rations became scarce.[231]

It was at Tuscumbia that the Thirty-fifth celebrated its first Independence Day in service. While typical of the times, it was further proof that the volunteer armies of the Civil War were still very civilian in character. Originally General Thomas had intended to limit the celebration to firing a salute at noon, but the colonels of the nearby regiments, all volunteers and civic leaders accustomed to giving and receiving public orations on that day, requested they be allowed to gather the troops for that purpose. Thomas agreed and the troops were assembled that evening. Col. Speed Fry of the Fourth Kentucky read the Declaration of Independence to the assembly and made comments to the affect that their Southern brothers should be treated mildly. Col. James Steedman of the Fourteenth Ohio, Colonel Harlan of the Tenth Kentucky, and Colonel Connelly of the Seventeenth Ohio all harangued the troops with similar themes. It was all too much for Colonel McCook, an ardent abolitionist. When his turn to speak came, he jumped to his feet and cried out, "The Union must be preserved, the rebellion crushed. The secessionists are our brothers no more, they

---

230. Arnold, *Sunshine and Shadows*, 46; Compiled service record, Benjamin Arnold, Pvt., Co. C, 35th Ohio Inf.; Carded Records, Volunteer Organizations, Civil War; Records of the Adjutant General's office, 1780s–1917, Record Group 94; National Archives, Washington, D.C.

231. Prokopowicz, *All for the Regiment*, 117–18, 124; Daniel, *Days of Glory*, 93–94.

are enemies: ours and the nation's. If they will not submit peaceably, they must be exterminated. My men and I are ready to do just that, even if it means the south is to be laid waste." McCook's remarks set off "some pretty lively sparring" among the various speakers on the podium. General Thomas, the professional soldier who always kept his emotions in check, had been sitting near the speaker's stand all evening. No doubt wishing he had never agreed to allow the assembly, Thomas remained calm until the embarrassment became too great. Rather than interject himself in the arguments, Thomas used his power of position to suggest that it was time to return the troops to camp. The senior officers on the dais got the hint, and the celebration ended early. As the regiments began to march off, Thomas remarked to one of his staff officers, "If the boys can't keep within bounds, they must omit celebrating the 4th of July hereafter."[232]

It may have been that General Thomas felt like Colonel McCook needed more constructive employment, because a few days later, McCook was ordered to take the Thirty-fifth Ohio and Ninth Ohio on a reconnaissance to the Muscle Shoals in the Tennessee River. More specifically, McCook was to inspect Hog Island, known to be the location of a guerilla camp. The march was made at night, but it was a quick one, and the Persimmons suffered greatly in muggy weather. According to the regimental historian, "If the troops had waded the Tennessee River their clothing could not have been wetter."

The regiment was halted in a grove of trees about a mile from Hog Island. Before making a movement, McCook consulted several slaves working in the immediate vicinity, and they informed him that there was "nobody thar." Taking the slaves at their word, McCook and Colonel Van Derveer rode out to the islands with only their orderlies to verify the camp was indeed empty. They reported that the island was still there, but that the hogs had departed. After resting in the shade for the rest of the day, the Thirty-fifth marched back the way it had come. Similar missions were conducted around Tuscumbia, and while they provided little military benefit, the men looked forward to them as a way of seeing the country and enjoyed the break in the routine.[233]

The Persimmons did not enjoy the people around Tuscumbia nearly as much. The region was fervently secessionist, and while the shooting war had moved on, the personal war continued unabated. It was the attitude of the townspeople that was the problem. Secessionist to the core, the locals took every opportunity to snub the Northern soldiers among them. They would gather at certain locations where the Yankee invaders were openly "cussed and discussed." For their part, the men of the Thirty-fifth took advantage of every possible opportunity to annoy their unwilling hosts. Wherever the local citizens would gather to socialize and complain, the Persimmons would sit in benches or lounge under trees nearby. As the Yankees moved in, the locals would quickly decide they had business elsewhere and the gathering would break up.

---

232. Keil, *Thirty-fifth Ohio*, 78; Grebner, *We Were the Ninth*, 104.
233. Keil, *Thirty-fifth Ohio*, 78–79.

The men of the Thirty-fifth loftily declared their actions were intended to break up a "nest of treason plotters," but admitted that the real reason was because they knew how greatly it irritated their enemies.[234]

At times, the irritation worked the other way. A rumor came to the attention of General McCook that some rebel soldiers were visiting a home in Tuscumbia. McCook ordered Colonel Van Derveer to arrest every man in the house and bring them to brigade headquarters. The regimental officer of the day, Lieutenant Andrew of Company I, took a detail and encompassed the house. A very thorough search of the place was conducted, but the only male on the premises was an elderly crippled man. Interpreting his orders strictly, Andrews had the protesting man carried back to McCook, who was anything but happy and demanded, "What the deuce do you bring a crippled man to me for?" When reminded that his order was to bring all men at the house to headquarters, McCook scowled and ordered the man returned. The irritation now belonged to Andrews and his men. The young lieutenant remarked, "It was fun for the boys to carry him to the colonel's tent; but it was h——l to get him back. That was so much like work."[235]

Soldiers in war want nothing more than to get it over with, and they generally don't care how it's accomplished, just so it is. Particularly, soldiers don't want politics to interfere, knowing that it can have only one effect, delay. General Buell refused to allow his soldiers to live off the land, believing that the war must be directed at the Confederacy's army, not its people. He felt the best way to regain the loyalty of the citizens of Alabama was to scrupulously respect their rights. It was a policy soon to be proven fallacious, and one that badly damaged the commanding general's credibility with his troops. But in the meantime, it was the practice of the army at Tuscumbia to ensure that widows and families without support, in other words, those with husbands and fathers in the Confederate army, were adequately fed. This charity was practiced by issuing commissary rations to those in need, a practice that outraged the soldiers of the Thirty-fifth, themselves already on very short rations.[236]

The soldiers, more concerned about the fathers and husbands than the wives and children, saw it differently. "We fed the families of rebel soldiers, so that they could fight us with more assurance, knowing that their families were being taken care of, while they were trying to shoot us. It was done for humanity's sake. How much humanity was there in the shot aimed at union soldiers, by the very families we fed?" If the Union army refused to feed the families of rebel soldiers, those soldiers would eventually desert to come home and care for them, themselves. The Confederate army would be weakened and the war would be over that much sooner. The truth of the matter was that the Persim-

---

234. Keil, *Thirty-fifth Ohio*, 80.

235. Ibid., 89.

236. Prokopowicz, *All for the Regiment*, 121; Keil, *Thirty-fifth Ohio*, 80; Daniel, *Days of Glory*, 100.

mons had become hardened to the point that nothing less than total victory was acceptable. The next step from that position was that any action contributing to the victory was acceptable. As the Union army made war, innocent children were going to starve, unprotected women were going to suffer, and quite a few families were going to lose everything they had, but in the pursuit of victory, they were valid targets. Never reconciling themselves to the idea of providing material support to the families of active rebels, the Persimmons and their compatriots in the Ninth Ohio sometimes took matters into their own hands.[237]

During the Persimmon's stay in Tuscumbia, fires sometimes broke out in the homes of the town's most vocal secessionists. No one ever seemed to know how they started, but as soon as one did, the Ohio soldiers would rush to assist with "rescue and salvage." Laboring mightily, the men "carried beds out-of-doors" and "threw glasses and porcelain out of windows" to prevent them from burning. At one fire, the volunteer firemen "were passionately solicitous to save from incineration the beehives" in one widow's yard. In the confusion attendant to heroic firefighting, the honey disappeared and the perpetrator was never caught. Seeing the incident as simple justice, the men of Thirty-fifth and the Ninth kept the identity of the honey thief a secret for decades. It was not until thirty years later that it was suggested that Pvt. Crittendon Cox of Company E *might* be able to shed some light on the details.[238]

While the Thirty-fifth Ohio perambulated around Alabama, two Company F soldiers captured at Fishing Creek six months before had finally been paroled in May. Pvts. Thomas Halloway and William Keys were both in poor health after their imprisonment. Keys wasn't really sure what he was supposed to do. The "many conflicting opinions as to what is required" caused him to finally give up and request instructions directly from the governor in early July. He was still weak but willing to leave Waynesville and report to Columbus for whatever service he was able to perform. There was just one small catch. If Keys was required to report in person, the governor would have to "send me a pass as it is now more than ten months since I entered the service and I have never yet received a cent from anybody or person for my services."[239]

Keys was apparently in much better shape than his compatriot. Later in the same month, Private Halloway's doctor prepared a certificate describing his greatly deteriorated health and had it notarized. Dr. Joshua Stevens of Lebanon reported that Halloway was "indisposed & under treatment by me" for some indecipherable disease and diarrhea. Halloway's condition was such that "he has not yet so far recovered as to admit to his ability to be mustered into active service," but there was hope. The young soldier was "improving & I hope will

237. Keil, *Thirty-fifth Ohio*, 81; Mitchell, *Civil War Soldiers*, 91, 108; Catton, *America*, 21.

238. Keil, *Thirty-fifth Ohio*, 81; Grebner, *We Were the Ninth*, 106.

239. Correspondence to the Governor and the Adjutant General of Ohio, 1861–1866, Series 147–41:31.

soon be restored to health & efficiency."[240]

Both Keys and Halloway returned to the regiment in late summer or fall of 1862. In July, Keys was the stronger of the two and seemingly the most likely to fully recover, but it didn't work out that way. Halloway continued to gain strength and survived Chickamauga, Missionary Ridge, and the Atlanta campaign. When Company F mustered out, Halloway was standing in the ranks. Keys was not. Never fully regaining his health, Keys again became seriously ill in the fall of 1863 and died in a Chattanooga hospital in January 1864.[241]

No Evil Intent

General Thomas's headquarters issued Special Orders No. 10 on July 19. "That portion of the Third Brigade, Brig. R. L. McCook commanding, posted at Tuscumbia, will move it's train across the Tennessee River at Florence on Wednesday, the 23d instant, the troops crossing the following day. They will make preparations to march from Florence to Huntsville, Ala., via Athens, with five days' rations for each regiment, two days' cooked and carried in the haversacks." Not all of the Thirty-fifth Ohio was in Tuscumbia. "The two companies of the Thirty-fifth Ohio Volunteers posted at Cherokee, on being relieved, will march at once to Florence, crossing the river, and rejoin their regiment."[242]

The Thirty-fifth made note of the fact that they crossed the Tennessee River the same place Andrew Jackson had on his journey to fame at New Orleans. In Florence on Sunday night, July 27, some of the Persimmons, feeling like they ought to go to church while they had the chance, joined a fairly sizable number of Union soldiers who were like-minded. The Federal soldiers entered the church quietly, sat wherever seats were available, and "deported themselves in a gentlemanly manner." They had come to worship, but the local minister, Reverend Mitchell, was apparently unable, or more likely, unwilling to separate politics from spiritual matters. He led off his prayer by asking a blessing on Jefferson Davis. This annoyed the Union soldiers, but they were in church and let the insult pass. What came after, however, was more than they could tolerate. In a very "bitter and insulting way," the minister proceeded to ask God to bring His wrath upon the invading Yankees and drive them from the South.

When the minister completed his prayer, a group of officers, led by Colonel Harlan of the Tenth Kentucky, quietly got up and left. The rest of the Union soldiers, equally offended, followed them out. The minister imagined his

---

240. Correspondence to the Governor and the Adjutant General of Ohio, Series 147–41:85.

241. Ohio Roster Commission, *Official Roster*, 620.

242. U.S. War Department, *War of the Rebellion*, Ser. no. 23, p. 187.

prayer had been heard and answered, and his church happily cleared of the Northern pest, but Colonel Harlan wasn't so easily dispensed with. He went immediately to General Thomas and got permission to arrest the minister. He and many of the men who had been at worship returned to the church while the service was still in progress. The minister paused in his sermon as the body of blue clad soldiers moved up the aisle toward him. As the congregation began to murmur uncertainly, Colonel Harlan spoke directly to the man in the pulpit.

Mr. Mitchell, we, soldiers of the army of the United States, entered your place of worship this morning; we came in quietly and took seats in order to listen to the discourse you intended to deliver here this day; we were gentlemanly; we made no disturbance; we insulted no one; we had no evil intent; yet, we had scarcely taken our seats, when you proceeded to grossly insult us because we were soldiers in the army of the United States. I am directed by the general in command to arrest and bring you to his headquarters. You will, therefore, come down from the sacred desk which you have dishonored, and go with us as ordered.

The congregation murmured but acquiesced quietly, and Mr. Mitchell was provided the opportunity to engage in prison ministry at the Nashville penitentiary. Ferdinand Van Derveer thought he got off easy. "My vote would be to hang him."[243]

The first stirrings of understanding of the intense desire of Southern slaves to be free appeared in camp outside Florence. The Emancipation Proclamation had yet to be issued, but the slave population was already convinced that blue was the color of freedom, and they "besieged" the Union camps in search of a way out of their bondage. Their masters knew their intentions and kept a very close watch. It was difficult for most to steal away, but they desperately sought out any opportunity, and for some, it worked. A slave of local planter Mr. Harris named Henry "made arrangement" with Sgt. Samuel Hippard of Company C. In exchange for help in escaping, Henry agreed to cook for the sergeant's mess. The plan was for Henry to hide out in his master's cornfield, which was adjacent to the Thirty-fifth's camp, and wait for the regiment to move.

Even such a simple plan almost came to naught. The corn crop was ripening, and the men of the Thirty-fifth enjoyed any addition to army rations. They helped themselves freely to Mr. Harris's roasting ears, and Harris made an official complaint. After an army commission was appointed to assess the damage to the Harris fields, the members dutifully accompanied the owner on an inspection of the crop. Henry was kept busy trying to avoid his master and the commission while they passed to and fro in the cornfield. Eventually, the regiment left camp, and Hippard stowed Henry on the company baggage wagon under a pile of knapsacks. After a full day of baking beneath the sun-heated baggage, Henry emerged and accompanied Sergeant Hippard and his messmates throughout the reminder of the regiment's enlistment.[244]

---

243. Keil, *Thirty-fifth Ohio*, 81–82.
244. Ibid., 82–83.

In Strict Accordance With the Usage of War

Col. Robert McCook had fallen seriously ill while in Tuscumbia, but when orders came to move to Decherd, Tennessee, he gamely left his sickbed to accompany the Third Brigade in a carriage. The August weather was very hot, so marches were limited to the cool hours of the day. The regiment would step off at 4:00 a.m. and go into camp after six hours of marching. On August 5, the brigade was approaching Winchester, Tennessee. The Thirty-fifth Ohio was in the lead with the brigade topographical engineer acting as guide. The engineer "was not as well informed as to the route to be taken as he might have been," and in the midst of the march, the regiment went the wrong way at a fork in the road. McCook was following the Thirty-fifth in an ambulance in which a cot had been arranged. Seeing that the Thirty-fifth had gone the wrong way, he sent an orderly to correct them and then continued down the correct branch of the road placing his party in front of the main body of troops. Some of those present on the day felt that McCook was "very careless in his mode pf traveling."[245]

An hour later, the Thirty-fifth, now trailing McCook's party, was toiling up a hill when Major Boynton pounded up on his horse and alerted Colonel Van Derveer that the brigade commander's party was under attack. Van Derveer immediately rushed ahead with Company C. The relief force encountered a few of the rebel raiders, but they fled when Company C fired a few shots in their direction. Van Derveer found the wagons accompanying McCook on fire and his ambulance lying overturned on the side of the road. McCook was nowhere to be seen but was soon found in a nearby cabin, having been shot and left to the care of the family there. His wounds were very serious, so it was decided he could not be moved.[246]

McCook's advance party had been scattered when the rebels attacked. McCook had pulled up at a farmhouse trying to get information on water sources. A sergeant and three men were riding half a mile ahead scouting for possible camp sites and were the first to be attacked. Seeing the guerillas in pursuit of his scouts, McCook had ordered his wagons turned around and had attempted to reach the Thirty-fifth Ohio. After the rebel bushwhackers, over a hundred strong, had quickly overtaken the advance party, one of them rode up and shot McCook where he lay in his ambulance. Capt. Hunter Brooke and a black servant carried the mortally wounded colonel to the house by the road to care for him. The guerillas followed and captured Brooke, but the servant dived out a window and escaped. Major Boynton was riding some distance behind the brigade commander, also in search of water and a place to camp. Boynton saw

---

245. Van Derveer to wife, 7 August 1862, Van Derveer Family Collections.
246. Keil, *Thirty-fifth Ohio*, 83–84; U.S. War Department, *War of the Rebellion*, Ser. no. 22, p. 840.

the guerillas, now between him and the brigade commander's party, attack McCook and rode for help. Unencumbered by wagons and mounted on a fleet horse, Boynton kept ahead of his pursuers and arrived safely at the regiment to give warning.[247]

Every man in the brigade was enraged at the news, and in his report, Van Derveer explained why. "In reply to the oft-repeated cry of 'Stop!' 'Stop!' [McCook] rose in his bed and exclaimed, 'Don't shoot; the horses are running; we will stop as soon as possible.' Not withstanding this surrender those riding within a few feet by the side of the carriage fired, one ball passing through his hat and one inflicting a mortal wound." As he continued, Van Derveer removed all doubt that McCook had been murdered. "The condition of General McCook could not but have been known to the attacking party, as he was on his bed, divested of all outer clothing, except a hat used as a shade, and the curtains of the carriage raised on all sides. Infuriated by this cowardly assassination, many of the soldiers of the brigade spread themselves over the country before any measures could be taken to check them." It was the Ninth Ohio, McCook's own regiment that sought immediate revenge. They set out to punish whomever they could find, and their officers were unable to restrain them. A rumor spread that the guerillas had been cheered as they passed a particular house near the road and the inhabitants, a woman and her grown daughter, were given thirty minutes to vacate the house with whatever they could carry. An hour later, the house was a smoking ruin. Slaves pointed out houses that supposedly belonged to members of the guerilla band, and the Ninth set fire to them as well, hanging some of the owners in the process. As the senior regimental commander, it fell to Ferdinand Van Derveer to get the Germans back under control. He finally succeeded, but pillars of smoke from burning houses stretched for some distance.[248]

General Thomas had watched Ferdinand Van Derveer closely for several months, and his growing respect for the Ohioan was evident in the report he made to General Buell. "[McCook's] regiment was very much enraged, and before they could be stopped burned and destroyed some four or five farmhouses; but Colonel Van Derveer, by great exertions, succeeded in subjugating them to discipline before night, and they are now quiet." Thomas echoed the sentiments of the Thirty-fifth Ohio toward McCook when he praised their brigade commander for his performance at Mill Spring and went on to say, ""He was affable in his manners and a courteous gentleman. A brave officer and a congenial friend is lost to this division." Thomas directed that a badge of mourning be worn for thirty days in McCook's honor.[249]

---

247. Keil, *Thirty-fifth Ohio*, 85–86; U.S. War Department, *War of the Rebellion*, Ser. no. 22, pp. 839–840.

248. Keil, *Thirty-fifth Ohio*, 84; U.S. War Department, *War of the Rebellion*, Ser. no. 22, pp. 840–41.

249. U.S. War Department, *War of the Rebellion*, Ser. no. 22, p. 839.

Senior army commanders were upset by the behavior of the Ninth Ohio, but the Thirty-fifth Ohio was entirely sympathetic. As far as they were concerned, "the revenge taken by the [Ninth Ohio] on the country around, may have been severe; but in strict accordance with the usage of war. The citizens were in accord with the acts of the guerilla band and boldly avowed the same." Even Colonel Van Derveer, the man credited with restoring order on the scene said, "The rebels have been made to pay dearly for this, we burned every house within three miles of this place." As far as they were concerned, the local citizens who supported the rebellion had gotten what they deserved. When McCook died two days later, the entire brigade escorted his body to the railroad station for shipment back to Cincinnati.[250]

The shadow of fear passed over the entire region around Winchester with the news of the approach of the avenging angels in the Ninth Ohio. The fears of the population were groundless. The Ninth was a good regiment and, once having spent its anger and been brought back under control, was in no danger of breaking away again. The people of Salem and Winchester didn't know that, and when they learned the brigade was about to arrive in their city, they begged the army for additional protection. As the Thirty-fifth entered Winchester, they noticed that there seemed to be an unusual number of sentries posted around the town, and many citizens approached them cautiously to ask which regiment was the Ninth. The Ninth Ohio was marching at the rear of the brigade that day, and the longer it took for them to arrive, the greater the tension grew. The city was completely astir when the Ninth's band marched into town playing Prussian military music. It might have been that the Ninth was trying to show that they were not outlaws, or perhaps they wanted to make a further impression on the populace. Whatever the reason, the Germans from Cincinnati marched into the city in perfect order, looking as fine as any regiment in the army. They passed though without breaking step, and the entire city breathed a sigh of relief when they marched out of sight.[251]

By August 31, the Thirty-fifth Ohio had reached Decherd, Tennessee, astride the Nashville and Chattanooga Railroad after a leisurely march from Winchester via Pelham Gap. One of the young men who dropped his pack and surveyed yet another Southern town was an unusual new recruit from Wayne Township in Warren County. Joseph W. O'Neall was all but illiterate and was beginning his second enlistment. Neither of those things was really remarkable. There was a fair number of Persimmons who had served in ninety-day regiments before joining the Thirty-fifth and many more who could barely read or write. Two things made O'Neall stand out from the rest, only one of which was known at the time. Unlike any other Persimmon, O'Neall had recent combat experience, a fact that was known. What they didn't know was that both of his

---

250. Keil, *Thirty-fifth Ohio*, 84; Van Derveer to wife, 7 August 1862, Van Derveer Family Collection.

251. Keil, *Thirty-fifth Ohio*, 85.

enlistments were fraudulent. O'Neall had first gone for a soldier with the Fifty-fourth Ohio in the fall of 1861. Even though he fought with the regiment at the battle of Shiloh, they cut him loose shortly afterwards when it was learned he was only fifteen years of age, a fact he conveniently failed to report at the time he joined up. He had gone home, cooled his heels for several weeks, got tired of that, and reenlisted in Company A of the Thirty-fifth Ohio. O'Neall again reported that he was eighteen when he signed the roster, a number that included two birthdays he had not yet had.[252]

Preparing for what appeared to be a long stay, runaway slaves, other contrabands, and even some local citizens were put to work on fortifications. While all of this activity was underway, Confederate general Braxton Bragg and the Army of Tennessee were beginning a march of their own. Their goal was nothing less than the complete reconquest of Tennessee and Kentucky.[253]

252. Bogan, *Warren County's Involvement*, 12.
253. Grebner, *We Were the Ninth*, 109; Bishop, *Story of a Regiment*, 95; Keil, *Thirty-fifth Ohio*, 90.

CHAPTER 6

It Was That or Nothing

September 1862 to February 1863

Too Long Coming Up

The Thirty-fifth Ohio had been at Decherd, Tennessee, for fifteen days when word was received that Gen. Braxton Bragg and the Confederate Army of Tennessee had left Chattanooga headed for Nashville. Most of Thomas's division was sent to block Pelham Gap and force Bragg to take a more inconvenient route. Poor staff work within the Army of the Ohio combined with destructive raids by Confederate cavalry had left the army short on supplies. The fortunate Persimmons found themselves in a beautiful valley filled with fine cornfields, "and excellent use was made of the advantages thus afforded. Never did roasting ears disappear more rapidly." First Lt. Lewis Lambright of Company K became known for two things at Pelham Gap; his capacity for eating corn and his theory on ending the war, the latter being supported by the former. Known to eat at least nine ears of corn per setting, Lambright announced his belief that there were two practical ways to end the war. The first was to "whip the rebels in the field." The second way was to "damage them in store," or in other words, eat all of their food. Lambright expounded that the quickest way to end the war was to combine the two efforts.[254]

The attitude toward foraging was changing, partly from need and partly from the ever hardening attitude of the soldiers. They had always believed they should be able to take what they needed from rebel farms, and higher levels of command were beginning to agree. On August 20, Gen. James B. Steedman, appointed to replace the murdered McCook, suddenly called an unscheduled halt beside a huge orchard filled with ripe peaches and then appeared not to notice while the regiments in his new command picked it clean. Bragg's advance cut the railroad to Nashville, and the Thirty-fifth Ohio went on half

---

254. Prokopowicz, *All for the Regiment*, 114; Keil, *Thirty-fifth Ohio*, 90.

rations on August 22. Shortly afterwards, Capt. Samuel L'Hommedieu of Company G led a detail whose official mission was to scout the country beyond the gap. The unofficial part of his mission was to "spy out the condition of the smokehouses in that part of the confederacy." L'Hommedieu was considered one of the best at the second task, "being a good judge of nice ham and bacon," and his scouting party worked diligently at their assigned task. Their success nearly unhinged them when they ran into the colonel of a Kentucky regiment and his own detail out on the same mission.

When it was discovered that the efforts of L'Hommedieu and his men had been blessed much more abundantly than that of the Kentuckians, L'Hommedieu was placed under arrest for having already done what the colonel wanted to do. But even arrest did not prevent the Buckeye captain from completing his mission. An old-fashioned family carriage "with bent wooden springs over which strong leather straps were fastened to support the carriage body" was located and loaded with smokehouse bounty. Lacking stock to pull the carriage, the men became beasts of burden by attaching a rope to the coach's pole. When they came into camp everyone agreed "the gang reminded a person of an old styled fire engine company on a run for a fire." They also agreed the fresh ham and bacon went well with the roasting ears.[255]

After a week in their bountiful valley, the corn and smokehouses were left behind as Buell and Bragg began their race for Louisville. Having been very smoothly bypassed by Confederate dexterity, Buell's first objective was to keep Bragg from capturing the depots at Murfreesboro and Nashville, and from opposite sides of the mountains, the two armies dashed northward. Buell intended to move all of the stores in the more exposed depots into the relative security of Nashville and sent his forces rushing ahead into the gaps through the mountains to prevent Bragg from reaching them first. Confident that the forces at Nashville could withstand a siege, the bulk of the army would shadow the rebel army as it moved north into Kentucky.

The Thirty-fifth passed through Manchester, a town that had suffered occupation by both armies, on September 1 and reached Hoover's Gap the next day. There, the Army of the Ohio waited for Gen. Alexander McD. McCook, the brother of former commander Robert McCook, and his division to arrive from McMinnville. The Persimmons remembered their camp at the Gap for the stately beech trees that surrounded it. Once McCook's division had arrived and the stores were loaded onto Nashville bound trains, the rest of the army followed. After a two-day halt at Murfreesboro to allow the depots there to be emptied, the regiment continued north on the morning of the September 7 arriving at its designated campsite below Nashville by two o'clock in the afternoon. It had been a hard march over paved roads on an "exceedingly hot" day, and when Colonel Van Derveer called the halt, only one officer and thirty enlisted men remained with him. The rest, footsore and exhausted, were scat-

---

255. Keil, *Thirty-fifth Ohio*, 90–91; Grebner, *We Were the Ninth*, 111.

tered on the road behind him. It was not a day the Persimmons remembered with pride. Except for the emergency return from Mill Springs to Somerset, it was their worst showing on the march of the entire war.[256]

As he sat in his tent at Nashville, Van Derveer was generally displeased. The entire summer campaign had been discouraging for him. He did not know what to expect next, since "under Buell's administration every thing is uncertain—we may stay a few months or leave in two hours. His plan of campaigning, does not suit the army, whatever the people at home may think of it." Furthermore, the Buckeye colonel believed that all the effort to hold unnecessary railroad lines, and doing what amounted to protecting rebel property, was entirely wasted, "but our brigade does little of that—We came for the purpose [of] fighting—and don't propose to do anything else of we can help it." Van Derveer was even unhappier with his chaplain. Hoblet had gone to Nashville to visit the sick four months before and was now determined to stay there. No one in the regiment had seen him again. The colonel and the minister met in the city to discuss the situation. After their meeting, Van Derveer reported that he had been polite and had not insisted that Hoblet return to the regiment. He did not know what Hoblet intended to do and no longer cared. It had become obvious that Hoblet "evidently is not suited for the Chaplaincy of our regiment—and having deserted us for so long a time—he will not receive a very flattering welcome."[257]

Bragg's opportunity to recapture the Tennessee capital was lost as soon as Buell occupied the city. Shunning any fight at Nashville, the Army of Tennessee continued on toward Kentucky, leaving Buell no choice but to follow. At the request of Union governor Andrew Johnson, General Thomas's First Division was left behind to guard the city against a return of Bragg's army. The Thirty-fifth, camped along the Lebanon pike, spent a week working feverishly on fortifications in the vicinity of Fort Negley. While the rest of their comrades dug into the red clay, the regimental band was heading home. The War Department had decided that the expense involved in maintaining so many bands was unjustified and ordered all regimental bands to be mustered out. Only the field musicians, drummers assigned to each company, were kept in service. When it became obvious that Bragg's entire army was in Kentucky, Buell called for Thomas to rejoin the rest of the Army of the Ohio at Louisville. The orders met with great satisfaction among the Persimmons who were growing concerned that they would miss yet another battle.[258]

Just before leaving Nashville, Van Derveer, apparently under pressure from his wife, had his photograph taken. In the letter in which he transmitted the photograph, he told his wife how homesick he had been and that it had affected his appearance. "I have had a photograph of myself taken when I was laboring

256. Keil, *Thirty-fifth Ohio*, 92.

257. Van Derveer to wife, 8 September 1862, Van Derveer Family Collection.

258. Keil, *Thirty-fifth Ohio*, 92; Ohio Roster Commission, *Official Roster,* 602.

under a severe attack [of homesickness]—the face as cadaverous as a colored ghost and as long as a three hour sermon—I only send it to you to show you how miserable I look at such times—I intend to get some good looking fellow to sit for me someday so that I may have a pretty picture."[259]

Col. Ferdinand Van Derveer, taken in
September 1862 at Nashville, Tennessee.
AUTHOR'S COLLECTION

After a year of service, the regiment had learned how to travel light. Tents were left standing in front of Fort Negley, and all surplus baggage was stuffed inside when the Thirty-fifth left Nashville at 4:00 p.m. on September 15. Halting at Edgefield for the night, the men looked and felt ragged. Rapid campaigning always created shortages as the army moved away from its established depots, and Buell's march through Kentucky was perhaps the worst of all. The limestone roads wore away shoe leather, and blankets were in very short supply. After an early start, they made Holiday Springs by the night of the sixteenth, and once on the improved surface of the Louisville pike, were able to enter Bowling Green, Kentucky, on the September 18. Weary and worn, the Persimmons remained at Bowling Green for a day to rest and make new march arrangements. To keep the main road clear for the fighting units, Wilkinson

259. Van Derveer to wife, 13 September 1862, Van Derveer Family Collection.

Beatty's wagon team joined the rest of the division trains on a different route along the Green River. The night of the nineteenth found the Persimmons at a place called Bell's Tavern near Cave City. A persistent drought had drained the land of moisture, and water was getting harder and harder to find. Near Bell's Tavern, there was a cool spring at the bottom of a deep natural rock pit, and for the whole time they were there, the line to make the one-hundred-foot descent to the pool in the shadowy depths of the pit never ended. After resting a day, Thomas's division finally caught up with the rest of the Army of the Ohio at Woodland on the twenty-first.[260]

The Thirty-fifth almost had its first battle that night. As the brigade came into Woodland, General Steedman was fooled by its size. Believing it was only another village on the road to his true destination, Steedman continued on through town in a direction that would have brought him into the rebel lines and "stirred up the chaps." Fortunately, someone on Buell's staff saw the brigade march through and a messenger was sent to bring Third Brigade back into town where it belonged.[261]

The Confederate invasion had greatly disrupted Union logistics, and distribution of food became erratic. In preparation for resumption of the march, the men were ordered to load three days cooked rations in their haversacks. At Nashville, they had been issued a good supply of flour and some coffee and sugar, but no salt. Raiding fruit orchards along the way had helped greatly, but at Woodland, all that was left was flour to bake into bread. There was one other small problem. There were no ovens, Dutch ovens, or any similar devices for baking, and the Persimmons were forced to make use of what was available. After mixing flour and water, some of the men put the dough on heated boards to bake. Others used hot stones or heated metal plates. In all cases, the unskilled combination of flour, water, and heat produced unappetizing results. "This was the occasion when we lived on unleavened bread. It cannot be said that it was palatable, but it was that or nothing."[262]

The Thirty-fifth was back on the road on September 21. The Persimmons experienced worse single days on the march, but for endurance, nothing ever compared to the weeklong, hot, dry march through Kentucky. Movements were irregular, sometimes made during the day, sometimes during the night. There was little water along the route, as the summer drought had dried up even the most dependable ponds and creeks. Over-heated men oozed sweat from every pore as the army trod along. The salty liquid ran into their eyes and dripped off the nose and chin, leaving men constantly thirsty and desperate even enough to drink water contaminated by animal carcasses. Making matters worse, the dust

---

260. Keil, *Thirty-fifth Ohio*, 92–93; Bircher, *Drummer Boy's Diary*, 25; Wiley, *Billy Yank*, 61–62.

261. Keil, *Thirty-fifth Ohio*, 93.

262. Ibid.; Bircher, *Drummer Boy's Diary*, 25; Bishop, *Story of a Regiment*, 97; Grebner, *We Were the Ninth*, 113.

of the army's passing was horrendous. The limestone dust kicked up from the roads was suffocating. As much as six inches deep at times, it was so thick that it was often hard to see even a few feet to the front.[263]

Bragg gained the lead, and Buell was desperately trying to catch up and keep him from capturing Louisville. Passing through Munfordville, the men of the Thirty-fifth met troops from the Eighty-ninth and Ninety-third Indiana regiments whose unfortunate soldiers had been surrounded at Munfordville, captured, and then paroled. Rather than denigrate them for having surrendered, the men of the Persimmons felt respect for the unhappy men. These Hoosiers, who had only recently enlisted and were only partly trained, had been surrounded by greatly superior forces that they had no hope of defeating, yet they had fought anyway, delaying Bragg's advance for two days before being forced to give in. At a time when the entire army was frustrated with Buell's refusal to turn and give battle, these raw recruits had "showed fight, and did their duty well for new troops," and the men in ranks were convinced that the blame for their predicament lay higher up. "Buell was too long coming up to render assistance."[264]

Having delayed long enough for Buell to get around in front of him, General Bragg seemed to see Union forces everywhere he looked, and at Elizabethtown, the Confederate commander began to move toward the east to link up with the smaller Confederate army under Kirby Smith. Camping a few miles from the Confederates on the night of September 23, the men of the Thirty-fifth Ohio were not at all happy. The army's wagon train could not keep up with the marching columns. They had run out of food during the day and would have been glad for more of the unappetizing bread they had made at Woodland, but the nearest source of resupply was still twenty-one miles away on the Ohio River. Soldiers spent the night "nursing the gripes of hungry stomachs, and bathing blistered feet."

With no reason to stay in camp, the Thirty-fifth Ohio made an early start. Hungry and desirous of ending their long march, they set off with a will. It was common for dogs to join the army on the march, and leaving Nashville, a loose pack of them had joined the column. They, too, had suffered, and very few of them were left, many having died from the heat or fallen out along the way. So anxious were the men to get to the river, the regiment left the road and struck out on a direct line for the Ohio. Many of the men, having worn theirs out on the road, were without shoes, and it was a sore-footed bunch that found themselves standing on the banks of the Ohio River at 2:00 p.m. on September 25. They had been promised that boats and rations would meet them at the mouth of Salt River, but there were no boats at the landing. Looking around for anything edible, the men discovered several potato patches, and saved the owners "the expense of digging, but they did not realize financially as they had prom-

---

263. Prokopowicz, *All for the Regiment*, 147–48.
264. Keil, *Thirty-fifth Ohio*, 94; Prokopowicz, *All for the Regiment*, 149.

ised themselves in their dreams." A steamboat arrived at the landing about sunset but made no attempt to land. The captain was afraid to approach the famished soldiers that crowded the landings. The boat crews tossed some bread, ham, and bacon from the boat into the crowd. Lieutenant Keil described the scene as "more than interesting" and said any farmer who had cut up corn in his fields and thrown it to half-starved hogs would fully understand what ensued. Eventually, the crowd was brought under control, and an orderly distribution of rations was made.[265]

All of Louisville was in an uproar at the approach of Bragg's army, and there was a rush to quickly get as many troops into the city as possible. For once, the exigencies of war worked in favor of the Thirty-fifth. After boarding steamers with the Ninth Ohio, they cruised into the city where they were greeted by cheering crowds. Hastened off the riverboats and placed in the lines around the city, they remained in place for several days, replacing worn clothing and eating everything they could get their hands on to make up for all the meals they had missed on the march. They desperately wanted to visit the numerous hotels, restaurants, and groceries in Louisville, but having no cash, could only stand in the buildings' shadows while others entered. Their feasting was limited to what could be gotten from the commissary.[266]

The long, forced marches endured during the race to Louisville had a weeding-out effect. The chronically ill and those unable to endure the physical strain had long since been left behind. Those who remained were lean and tough, but they were far fewer than the number that had left Ohio a year before. Like the rest of the Army of the Ohio, they were dirty, their clothes were ragged, and their rifles were rusted. It was easy to tell them apart from the Louisville garrison troops who were clean and shiny. One day, while the regiment idled in the lines around Louisville, a brigade of men looking all new and fresh marched up and began to settle into the brickyard on the right of the Thirty-fifth Ohio's position. As it turned out, the Persimmons, now used to depleted numbers, were mistaken about the size of the new unit. Rather than a brigade, their new neighbors were Hoosiers of the Eighty-seventh Indiana Infantry, just arrived by rail from Indianapolis. An able administrator, General Buell refused to make new brigades with the new regiments arriving daily. Like all the others, the Eighty-seventh Indiana had been assigned to an experienced brigade, in this case the Third Brigade, and they were to remain comrades in arms for the next two years. [267]

Other reorganizations took place while the army was at Louisville. The expanded Army of the Ohio was organized into three separate corps. General

---

265. Keil, *Thirty-fifth Ohio*, 94; Bircher, *Drummer Boy's Diary,* 26; Bishop, *Story of a Regiment*, 97; Grebner, *We Were the Ninth*, 113.

266. Keil, *Thirty-fifth Ohio*, 95.

267. Ibid., 95–96; Prokopowicz, *All for the Regiment*, 151, 152; Van Derveer to wife, 24 July 1862, Van Derveer Family Collection.

Thomas became Buell's second in command, and the Third Corps, to which the Third Brigade was assigned, was taken over by Charles C. Gilbert. Gilbert was chosen to replace Gen. William Nelson who had been murdered by fellow Union general Jefferson C. Davis. It was a confusing situation. At the time he was chosen for command of Third Corps, Gilbert was officially a regular army captain. Buell believed Gilbert was a major general, but the War Department said he was only a brigadier general. As it turned out, he was still just a captain, because the Senate refused to confirm his promotion to any kind of general. Gilbert was a strict, by-the-book, professional disciplinarian who had never served in a line unit, had no understanding of volunteer soldiers, and desired none. He quarreled with other officers over meaningless trivia and was known to snoop into individual soldier's personal baggage. Shortly after the army left Louisville, Gilbert tried to take the colors from an exhausted Indiana regiment that didn't present the proper courtesy to him while they slept. Almost as soon as he took command, he became an object of scorn for every soldier in his corps.[268]

The Army of the Ohio, under its new corps commanders, moved out of the lines around Louisville on October 1, 1862. The Third Brigade was now in the Third Division under the command of General Shoepf, well known to the Thirty-fifth from their time in Somerset. Shoepf's division, forming the extreme right of the army, moved south toward Bardstown on the Preston Street Plank road. The effort to regain Kentucky from the Confederates had begun.[269]

The movement initiated a crisis of morale in the Thirty-fifth Ohio. The men had expected to be paid while in Louisville, since at least one of the other regiments in the brigade had been. The realization that they were starting a new campaign before the paymaster arrived made them angry. Other grudges took the opportunity to resurface. The Persimmons knew that new recruits were being paid substantial bonuses for enlisting. The general belief was that all the available funds had been used to pay enlistment bounties and that none was left over to pay the old soldiers. Just as aggravating was the fact that several officers had been allowed to go on leave, apparently some had also gone without approval, and there was a shortage of officers as the regiment marched toward the enemy. Up and down the column, men began to shout, "Paymaster," and grumble loudly among themselves. While this conduct was "somewhat unsoldier-like," it was nothing more than a louder than usual grumbling and the men still carried on willingly enough. The officers of the regiment handled the situation by ignoring it. As one put it, "all that could be done was to let them indulge until satisfied."[270]

Buell was moving cautiously to ensure his units advanced in concert. The regiment stopped at McCauley's Creek the first day and went on to Shepards-

---

268. Daniel, *Days of Glory*, 138.
269. Keil, *Thirty-fifth Ohio*, 96.
270. Ibid., 97; Bircher, *Drummer Boy's Diary*, 26.

ville the next. The rebels evacuated Bardstown as the Union army approached, and from then on the advance elements of the army were in close contact with Bragg's rear guard. After stopping overnight at the village Fredericksburg, the Thirty-fifth arrived in Springfield on October 6. At Springfield, when it appeared that the rebels were going to finally contest the advance, General Steedman put the brigade in line of battle and swept up the hill on the other side of town. Confederate artillery fired a few rounds near the Thirty-fifth, but other than to create a little excitement, the shells had no effect. That night, the regiment camped on Buck Creek. Once in camp, Company B Pvt. Andrew Bane of Port Union, Ohio, decided to do a little exploring in the surrounding countryside. His curiosity cost him his life. A band of rebel cavalry came across him as he walked, killed him, and left him lying on the ground. [271]

Moving along the Springfield road to Chapel Creek the next day, the weather was working against the Persimmons. Temperatures were unseasonably hot and the dust in the road was deeper than the water in the creeks. The lack of water was a driving concern for the marching men whose only sources were pools and puddles of warm, putrid liquid that even horses refused to drink from. Some men were using spoons to get muddy water from nearly dry pools and straining it through handkerchiefs. More and more, movements were dictated by the availability of water.[272]

Seldom Witnessed by Man

Both armies concentrated near Perryville, but neither commander had a clear idea of what was supposed to happen next. The Thirty-fifth Ohio was in the valley formed by Doctor's Creek about three miles west of the village. Skirmishing had been going on regularly since the sixth, and on the morning of October 8, the two armies began to fight over the pools of water still remaining in the creeks. The Confederates made a vigorous attack on Gen. Alexander McCook's corps. As Ferdinand Van Derveer recorded it, "Quite a severe fight occurred between the forces under General Alex McCook and the rebel army at this place on Wednesday—the battle lasted the greater part of the day—in which the losses were very severe on both sides." McCook's men "fought nobly but were at length compelled to fall back before superior numbers." Neither army commander had planned to fight that day, but the battle that developed proved to be as brutal and as costly as any fought during the war. McCook's First Corps and Gilbert's Third Corps met near the Springfield pike where the

271. Keil, *Thirty-fifth Ohio*, 97, 257; Bircher, *Drummer Boy's Diary*, 26–27; Ohio Roster Commission, *Official Roster*, 606; Daniel, *Days of Glory*, 144; Van Derveer to wife, 11 October 1862, Van Derveer Family Collection.

272. Daniel, *Days of Glory*, 144.

road crossed Chapel Creek. As the battle opened, the Thirty-fifth and the rest of Shoepf's division were a mile behind the firing line. Waiting on the hill, they could see down into the valley where the fighting was going on. Everyone began checking weapons and cartridge boxes in preparation for joining the battle, but once again, no orders came. General Shoepf got tired of waiting and requested permission to go support McCook's men.[273]

At 4:00 p.m., Steedman was directed to bring his brigade down into the valley and be prepared to support McCook. Steedman rode ahead to view the situation, but there was no order to proceed to the battle line. It was obvious to the Persimmons that their presence was needed, but they were forced to wait helplessly as the sun dipped ever lower in the sky. The fighting had begun early in the morning, but the shadows had grown long before orders finally arrived directing the Third Brigade to support McCook's firing line. Hustling down the road behind Battery I, Fourth U.S. Artillery and in front of the Second Minnesota, the Thirty-fifth passed other brigades still waiting for orders. All around them was the confusion that exists behind the front line in any battle. "The valley presented a scene of bustle and commotion: ammunition trains were pushing to the front; ambulances passing to the rear with wounded men; aides and orderlies were urging onward their jaded steeds, while stragglers seemed intent on but one idea—getting to the rear." The movement of feet on the dry roads created great clouds of dust that settled on the marching men. As they approached the front, powder smoke began to drift down on them and the sound of musketry became sharper and clearer. The regiment passed Generals McCook and Steedman as the former instructed the latter.[274]

The Persimmons had missed Mill Springs and Shiloh, and they were anxious to get into the battle at Perryville. They believed they were as capable and as brave as their compatriots in the Ninth Ohio and Second Minnesota, and they wanted the chance to prove it. They wanted to beat the Confederate Army of Tennessee and send it reeling back southward. Behind it all was the desire to end the war as quickly as possible, and the only way to do that was crush the rebellion by fighting, and they were willing to accept the danger necessary to make it happen.[275]

The Confederate assault had driven the Third Corps' lines back and separated the divisions of Sheridan and Rousseau. General Steedman could see that the Federal line in front of the Russell House and fallen back leaving an artillery battery unsupported, and he determined to move his brigade up to prevent the loss of the guns. The Third Brigade would close the gap to stop the onrushing rebels if no one else would. Cresting the low hill just behind the battle lines, the Persimmons heard cannon balls screech by overhead and could look

273. Keil, *Thirty-fifth Ohio*, 98; Bishop, *Story of a Regiment*, 100; Catton, *Hallowed Ground*, 175; Van Derveer to wife, 11 October 1862, Van Derveer Family Collection.

274. Keil, *Thirty-fifth Ohio*, 98–99; Daniel, *Days of Glory*, 156.

275. Mitchell, *Civil War Soldiers*, 76–77.

out and see the rebel batteries across the way. After passing through a cornfield, the Thirty-fifth went into line of battle on a bench at the edge of the woods behind the Eighteenth U.S. and Ninth Ohio. The position was within easy range of the Confederate regiments reforming to continue their attack, and three rebel batteries quickly opened fire and were joined by the rifles of the enemy infantry. Steedman ordered the men to lie down to avoid the worst of the fire but not to return fire until the rebels actually attacked. Borrowing a phrase from an earlier time, he ordered his men not to fire until they could see the whites of the rebel's eyes. A standoff developed. Not being able to clearly see the Union battle line, the Confederates suspected an ambush was being laid for them. Rather than advance, they began firing heavily to try and force the Union force to return fire and show their positions. Shot, shell, and canister whistled through the air, and minié balls fell among the prone men like "the falling of nuts on a frosty fall morning, under a heavy wind storm."[276]

The Persimmons endured this rain of lead for at least an hour and a half. According to Ferdinand Van Derveer, the Thirty-fifth was "for several hours exposed to as severe a fire as ever I experienced—the enemy played upon us with two or three batteries filling the air with exploding shells and plowing up the ground with solid shot—add to this the flanking fire of musketry and you have some idea of our position." About sundown, Union batteries began to return fire, and as night fell, Lieutenant Keil of Company C waxed poetic. "The moon soon thereafter rose directly over the rebel batteries, and added grandure to the scene. The skies were cloudless, and the little stars peered down upon the scene, with a friendly sparkle. The flash of cannons, the exploding of shells in their angry course, the incessant rattle and roar of musketry under the mellow moonbeams, gave to this scene an interest seldom witnessed by man." The firing gradually died down and finally petered out about 8:00 p.m.[277]

The regiment spent the night lying on its arms in line of battle. Other than an occasional picket firing at imagined rebels, the night was still. When dawn came, the reason for the quiet became apparent. The rebel army was gone. Bragg had had enough and abandoned his offensive a few miles short of the Ohio River. The Persimmons came through their brush with battle virtually unscathed. For all its ferocity, the enemy fire of the evening before had been entirely ineffective. Although the regiment "lay exposed to it for hours, not one of our men was injured—Some were shot through their caps and clothes—some struck by spent balls and pieces of shell, but all escaped safe." The only casualties that Colonel Van Derveer felt compelled to report were four men, Lt. Joseph S. Claypool and three privates, who were captured when they walked into the rebel lines by mistake. They were paroled and released little more than a week later.[278]

---

276. Keil, *Thirty-fifth Ohio*, 100.

277. Ibid., 100; Van Derveer to wife, 11 October 1862, Van Derveer Family Collection.

Perryville had not exactly been a repeat of Mill Springs, Shiloh, and Corinth, but it had not been much of a battle for the Thirty-fifth Ohio. The entire campaign had been disappointing. In the matter of a month, they had watched the Union army give back most of the territory it had required a year to capture. They had walked hundreds of miles for no good purpose, as far as they could see, and not been paid when they expected to. There was a general sense of mismanagement felt in the ranks. Their commander was just as unhappy. He wrote home that, "While Buell remained in a house several miles to the rear and many of our divisions stood idly by, longing for employment— McCook's men fought nobly." The Thirty-fifth Ohio had been forced to once again wait while a battle raged nearby, but for the first time, they had actually made it to the field in time to participate. And even if they had never fired a shot at the enemy, they had been under enemy fire for an extended period. "My men behaved splendidly," their commander said, "and never flinched for a moment." That experience would stand them in good stead in the future. [279]

A Sensible Word on Any Subject

The Federal pursuit of Bragg's retreating Confederates began on October 9, the day after Perryville, but there seemed to be no haste in it. Buell, believing Bragg was preparing to fight again, held his units close. The Thirty-fifth moved along the Harrodsburg pike only as far as Nevada Station and did not move again for two days. After a frustrating month of retreating and a leaderless battle, the easy pace of the pursuit "was conducted in a way to correspond with the management in the field." It was a week before the Thirty-fifth arrived at Crab Orchard several miles southeast of Lancaster, Kentucky. While passing through Lancaster on the fourteenth, the brigade conducted another communal foraging binge, this time at a distillery. The owners having been declared Confederate sympathizers, their property was fair game, and the men considered the quantity of whiskey consumed as recompense for what they had recently been through. Knowing that the rebel army was already approaching the Tennessee state line, the men were not surprised when the pursuit was officially ended. By October 20, the Persimmons had begun to retrace their route of the month before, passing through Lebanon, Campbellsville, Green River, and Cave City. [280]

The pace of the march had gradually picked up as the pursuit continued.

278. Keil, *Thirty-fifth Ohio*, 101; U.S. War Department, *War of the Rebellion*, Ser. no. 22, p. 1076; Van Derveer to wife, 11 October 1862, Van Derveer Family Collection.

279. Van Derveer to wife, 11 October 1862, Van Derveer Family Collection.

280. Keil, *Thirty-fifth Ohio*, 102; Grebner, *We Were the Ninth*, 116; Daniel, *Days of Glory*, 167.

For the old hands that had made the march from Alabama to Kentucky just a few weeks before, chasing Bragg was no big deal. For the Eighty-seventh Indiana, on its first campaign, the marching was a lot tougher. When a halt was called, the foot-sore Hoosiers would spread out under the trees that lined the roads of Kentucky. The veterans of the Thirty-fifth noticed that the boys from Indiana always seemed to seek out walnut trees, and immediately after plopping down, would pass the time by hulling and cracking walnuts. The Eighty-seventh Indiana was quickly dubbed the "Walnut-crackers," and at first they were not pleased with their new moniker. But then they learned the story of Fishing Creek and how the Thirty-fifth came to be the "Persimmon Regiment" and "made good use of it." From that point on, there was a lot of good-natured ribbing on both sides. "It was the 'Walnut-crackers' vs. 'The Persimmon Regiment,' and it would be hard to say which had the better." [281]

The baggage left behind in Nashville six weeks before caught up to the regiment at Lebanon, but a lot of it was missing. Much of what did arrive was in bad shape, and after being unseasonably warm the weather was now turning colder. Winter clothing would soon be necessary, so at New Market, with snow on the ground, General Steedman refused to move until his men were properly supplied. The refusal was part of an ongoing conflict between General Buell and Steedman, who had actively conspired with other officers to have the commanding general replaced. On November 2, the regiment once again marched into Bowling Green and made camp. Things began to look up on November 3. The paymaster finally arrived, and the Persimmons learned that General Buell had been relieved on October 30. Maj. Gen. William S. Rosecrans now commanded the army and had decided to shift the army's base of operations back to Nashville. The Thirty-fifth Ohio and the Third Brigade, now posted to the Third Division, Center, Fourteenth Army Corps, were assigned to assist in that effort by supporting the repair of the Louisville and Nashville Railroad. [282]

On November 6, General Steedman led his Third Brigade across a broken landscape of steep hills toward Mitchellville, Tennessee. Several members of Company I did not make the trip. A clique of unhappy soldiers had formed in that company, and six of them decided they had had enough of the army and its hard times. Thomas Price and William Llewellyn slipped out of camp on the night of November 3. After seeing their friends abscond successfully, George Jenkins, Solomon Mantelbaum, Wakefield Martindale, and Charles Sherde decided to follow them on the night of November 5. For Price, it turned out to be the mistake of a lifetime. Captured and brought before a court-martial, he was sentenced to be shot. Fortunately for him, Abraham Lincoln had qualms about shooting citizens who had volunteered for his armies. Price's sentence was commuted to hard labor, and he was sent to the Dry Tortugas for the duration of the war. [283]

---

281. Keil, *Thirty-fifth Ohio*, 246.
282. Ibid., 102; Grebner, *We Were the Ninth*, 117; Daniel, *Days of Glory*, 130.

Wagons had to be double-teamed as the column climbed onto the highland rim, and the skill of the teamsters was tested daily. The war was becoming harsher with foraging having gone from being a crime to being a official military function. Wagons could only carry small loads and the region supported few farms, so the quartermasters and those assisting them were kept busy. Useful items were confiscated, but the owners were given a quartermaster's certificate for the value of the items taken. The owner could be reimbursed when their loyalty to the Union was proven. The area was soon awash in these certificates, and even though the region was filled with confirmed secessionists, the men never doubted that all had been paid. As one Company C officer put it, "When a matter of dollars and cents is involved, it is easy to prove loyalty."[284]

Pvt. Henry Moser of Company G had managed to get a furlough and arrived in Hamilton on November 13. The twenty-five-year-old Moser, a native of Neuhausen, Switzerland, had come to the United States as a child, and was fluent in German. As soon as Moser got home, he went to visit his girlfriend near Flenner's Corner in Butler County. Sarah Elizabeth Rogers, known as Sallie, was nineteen in 1862, strong willed, but level headed. She remained coy with Moser and flirted with several other men, but it was apparently Henry who held sway in her heart.[285]

The young couple had their photographs taken, separately since to be photographed together would have been very forward, and exchanged gifts. Sallie bought Henry a Bible and wrote her name in it. She also added a biblical quote, "The Lord watch between me and thee when we are absent one from the other." (Genesis 31:49) They took a coach ride to church on a cold Sunday morning, "such as required good wrapping and a narrow buggy," and the "conversation was very pleasant, I'll never forget what Henry asked me." Moser left Hamilton on November 24, and Sallie consoled herself with the memories of their buggy ride.[286]

Back in Tennessee, the Third Brigade had been assigned to assist in clearing South Tunnel on the Louisville and Nashville Railroad (L&N) near Gallatin, Tennessee. As part of Bragg's invasion, fabled Confederate raider John Hunt Morgan was assigned to raid the L&N at Gallatin to cut off Buell's source of supply from Louisville. After seizing the twin tunnels at Gallatin, Morgan set about preventing their use by Federal forces. In South Tunnel, a captured freight locomotive was run at high speed into cross ties that had been piled across the tracks in the center of the tunnel. The wrecked train caught on fire and spread to supporting timbers. The slate rock into which the tunnel had been cut contained a fair amount of coal, so the fire smoldered for days. By the time

283. *Cyclopedia of Brown County, Ohio*, 230.

284. Keil, *Thirty-fifth Ohio*, 102–3.

285. Sarah Elizabeth Rogers Papers, "Country Life During the Civil War," Butler County Historical Society, Hamilton, Ohio, 4.

286. Ibid., 4–5.

it had burned out, the heat had caused huge chunks of slate to break off the roof and walls of the tunnel, blocking it completely.

On the north side of the tunnel, where trains could still approach, an L&N work train and crew worked to clear debris from the opening. Trains could not reach the south end of the tunnel, and it was here that detachments of soldiers began to clear the mass of rock from the shaft. Starting on November 13, the men worked in shifts using handcars to remove the debris, and after only a few days, much of the tunnel had been cleared of large debris. Men not working on the tunnel were assigned the task of unloading cargo from trains at Mitchellville and reloading then into wagons bound for Gallatin and Nashville. On November 23, new orders arrived. The Eighty-seventh Indiana and Ninth Ohio were to remain at the tunnel until the work was done. The Thirty-fifth Ohio, Second Minnesota, and the Eighteenth Infantry were to go to the Cumberland River ford located south of Gallatin and support the Thirty-first Ohio which was already in position to guard the crossing.[287]

The movement was made at night, and arriving at the ford at 1:00 a.m., they found the Thirty-first Ohio behind improvised fortifications but learned that the danger of Confederate raiders had passed. Resting for three hours, the march was continued up to Cairo and then to Cunningham's Ford still farther upstream. An island at Cunningham's Ford made it one of the best places to cross the Cumberland River. As such, it was favored by John Hunt Morgan for the starting point of his raids behind Union lines. A camp was established in a wood filled with old poplar, oak, and hickory trees. Assuming its rebel owner valued it greatly, "the men took a fiendish delight in cutting down those stately oak and poplar trees."[288]

Morgan's successful raid on Gallatin had made the commander there fearful of his return, so a steady stream of alerts came to Colonel Van Derveer who commanded the post at the ford. On one particular night, a courier, "his horse all afoam," brought news that Morgan was definitely going to attack the camp at Cunningham's Ford the next morning at sunrise. There were several units guarding nearby fords, so Van Derveer called them all together to discuss plans for a defense of the camps. According to the regimental historian, the council was "an amusing affair" due to the commander at Gallatin continually "crying wolf," and the fact that the forces reported to be at Morgan's disposal greatly outnumbered what was possible. Rather than creating concern, repeated, unfulfilled warnings caused this latest one to be taken very lightly.

The meeting started off on a lighthearted note and degenerated into slapstick comedy when the major commanding the Eighteenth Infantry battalion sent a message that he was too busy fortifying his camp to attend. He further stated that he "could hold his position one hour and a half, without support." The assembled officers apparently found this precise claim quite humorous.

---

287. Keil, *Thirty-fifth Ohio*, 103; Bishop, *Story of a Regiment*, 103.
288. Keil, *Thirty-fifth Ohio*, 103–104.

The jokesters among them "had the floor, and it was next to impossible to get in a sensible word on any subject before these wags would head off the speaker with some ludicrous remark, and set the grave 'council of war' in a roar of laughter." The fact that serious-minded Colonel Van Derveer allowed this to go on is a good indication that he was not overly concerned about the threat he faced.

The most exposed position belonged to the Second Minnesota, now commanded by Col. James George. George and Van Derveer were old friends. Back in Hamilton, Van Derveer had served under him in the Mexican War. After the war, George had moved to Minnesota and been commissioned in that state's forces when the Southern rebellion began. The Second Minnesota was on the far side of the river on top of a small hill making it an excellent artillery target. In spite of that tactical difficulty, the position had to be held if the ford was to be defended and denied to the enemy. After discussing the situation, Colonel George provided his proposed solution to the problem. Speaking to his old friend Van Derveer, George announced, "Colonel, I think, if the rebels open up on me, I'll right oblique down the ravine and let Morgan shell and be d——d." It was common sense approach to the problem, but in this crowd of all volunteer officers, it set the jokesters to work once again. They mockingly reproved the colonel from Minnesota for his use of such precise military language and for using profanity on "an occasion that demanded the most serious conduct."[289]

It was not until 1:00 a.m. that the council finally broke up. Having made all the jokes they could think of and still finding little to be truly concerned about, the officers returned to their own camps to await developments. The only definitive action taken was to order Lieutenant Keil, the officer of the day, to remain extra vigilant. The night passed without incident, and "Phoebus drove his chariot up the heavens in quietness—no sound of strife broke in on the stillness of that tranquil fine December morning." Morgan had chosen to attack the Federal garrison at Hartsville on December 6. The unit stationed there was a new regiment and the Thirty-fifth Ohio naturally assumed Morgan had avoided a confrontation with veteran troops in favor of the inexperienced men at the town.[290]

An important part of Van Derveer's mission at Cunningham's Ford was to actively watch for Confederate activity. On December 10, the colonel sent eight men to scout out any enemy activity in the vicinity. The scouts, four from the Eighteenth Infantry, two from the Second Minnesota, and two from the Thirty-fifth Ohio, all armed only with pistols, were led by Sgt. Ephraim Day of Company G. The second soldier from the Thirty-fifth was Pvt. Thomas P. Williams of Company F. After crossing the Cumberland River, the men walked southwest along the road until they were about two miles from Lebanon. They

---

289. Keil, *Thirty-fifth Ohio*, 104–105.
290. Ibid., 106.

stopped at "a house occupied by an intelligent woman" who was awakened and asked where the southern army was. Day and Private Primrose of the Eighteenth Infantry claimed to be deserters seeking rebel troops to surrender to and be paroled. The woman complimented the two men for their decision and told them to proceed to Lebanon where there were "no Union men, but plenty of friends to them." From Lebanon, the woman said, the nearest Confederate troops were at Black Shop, eighteen miles from Lebanon. The lady claimed the force there was twenty-two thousand strong and commanded by Morgan and Gen. Kirby Smith. The party went down the road a little further before deciding it was time to return to camp.[291]

They stopped one more time at a nearby house to ask for information. It was then 4:00 a.m. on December 11, and three of Day's men refused to go on until they had eaten breakfast. The party had been resting for about fifteen minutes when it was suddenly surrounded by twenty enemy soldiers and forced to surrender. Day once again claimed to be a deserter, and the Confederate officer in charge of the enemy patrol said he would have to take them back to his camp to be paroled. The rebel officer confirmed that it was at Black Shop and that Morgan was in command there. The rebels apparently accepted the story of desertion. They took away the men's pistols but otherwise treated them kindly. Along the way, Day also learned that Morgan was in the habit of sending scouting parties along the southern bank of the Cumberland every few days. After "making an excuse to step aside," the intrepid pair of Day and Primrose ran into the bushes and escaped, the only members of the scouting party to get away. Williams was never heard from again. Day and Primrose reported back to Van Derveer and their information was dutifully passed on to General Thomas.[292]

A new attitude arrived at Gallatin in the form of Abraham Landis. Landis, a forty-one-year-old doctor from Millville, Ohio, joined the regiment as an assistant surgeon in November. A man of strong beliefs, Landis enlisted out of patriotism and ardent abolitionist sentiments. With the possible exception of Henry Boynton, public support for abolition in the Thirty-fifth Ohio was somewhat less than enthusiastic. The same sensitivity that supported his racial beliefs gave Landis an interest in the people around him. While working in the hospital at Gallatin he picked up on the growing weariness and pessimism among the citizens of Tennessee. He began to believe the citizens of the Volunteer state might just volunteer to rejoin the Union if given the chance. Landis's experience ran the gamut of all new soldiers. He innocently wrote of the natural beauty of the area around Gallatin and, feeling homesick, asked his wife to write him a nice, long letter. Only a few weeks after joining the army, the good doctor was afflicted with severe erysipelas that required a twenty-day furlough to overcome.[293]

Dr. Landis got several opportunities to observe the new approach toward

---

291. U.S. War Department, *War of the Rebellion*, Ser. no. 30, p. 157.
292. Ibid.; Ohio Roster Commission, *Official Roster*, 621.

subsistence that had created changes in the logistical operations of the Thirty-fifth Ohio. The primary means of supplying the regiment was now foraging. The Persimmons were expected to supplement their rations with items seized in the local vicinity. Parties were sent out daily to collect produce and livestock, and Private Debolt who had been designated as the regimental butcher, slaughtered them. After a few weeks in the vicinity, "the articles sought" were becoming scarce on the south side of the river, and it was necessary to begin looking on the far side of the Cumberland for foodstuffs to seize. The decision was supported by the sight of sheep grazing daily on the far bank. Having gained fame for his foraging skills while at Decherd, Captain L'Hommedieu was again chosen to "test the richness of the land on that side" of the river.

The detail quickly rounded up three heifers, but the real targets of the hunt were the sheep so often seen on the hills across the river. L'Hommedieu set up a skirmish line to gradually herd the sheep into a confined area where they could be easily captured. Everything seemed to be going well, but the owner of the sheep, an older woman living nearby, had been keeping an eye on the Yankees as they moved onto her land. Just as the circle around the sheep was about to be closed, the woman "rushed into the field and reached for the bottom of her dress, raising it up with both hands, flopping the same vigorously like the buzzard his wings, crying: "Shoo, s-h-o-o, s—h—o—o." Both sheep and men were startled by the woman's arrival. The sheep took off running and the men began to laugh. By the time the men remembered what they were there for, the sheep had once again scattered thought the gaps in the line, and only the three heifers reached Debolt that day.[294]

Change of Affairs

The issue of manpower had become very critical after the Perryville campaign. The constant wastage would go on until the very last days of the regiment's enlistment, and even though the problem would never be solved, some efforts were made. Absenteeism had been rampant under Buell. Of the roughly seventy-four thousand men assigned to the Army of the Ohio when Rosecrans arrived, over thirty-two thousand were absent, nearly sixty-five hundred without permission. The new general immediately cracked down, canceling furloughs and clearing the hospitals of men avoiding duty. Regiments throughout the army sent teams back to their hometowns to both recruit and look for deserters. The group assigned to this task from the Thirty-fifth included Capt. Andrew J. Lewis of Company I, 1st Lt. Lewis F. Daugherty of Company A, 2d

---

293. Lincoln Landis, *From Pilgrimage to Promise* (Westminster, Md.: Heritage Books, 2007), 12, 15.

294. Keil, *Thirty-fifth Ohio*, 106.

Lt. David W. Schaeffer of Company H, 1st Sgt. Richard Foord of Company K, Sgts. Robert J. Livingston and James R. Frost, both of Company B and Sergeant Van Horn of Company I. While at home in Middletown, Ohio, First Sergeant Foord began a diary that he kept up until July 1864.[295]

Born in Sittingbourne, England, in 1841, Foord had migrated to the United States in 1852. After serving an apprenticeship in Elmwood, Illinois, Foord moved to Middletown where he was working as a carpenter when the war broke out in April 1861. He enlisted for ninety days in the Twelfth Ohio, and when that enlistment expired, the twenty-one-year-old Foord reenlisted in Company K of the Thirty-fifth Ohio. Based on his previous experience, he was made first sergeant. In Middletown on leave, Foord spent time with friends and visited his fiancée, Miss Laura J. Webster. After more than a year in the army, he thoroughly enjoyed socializing with the people of his hometown and attending church and considered the opportunity a "blessed privilege." Like the rest of the Persimmons, Foord was tired of the war. As he contemplated the end of his leave, Foord wrote, "God grant the time may not be far distant when I may be enabled to stay home and this awful war brought to a favorable close." The key was the favorable close. As much as he and the others wanted to come home, they would fulfill the commitment they had made.[296]

The recruiting mission was based out of Camp Dennison, northeast of Cincinnati. While his duties kept him in camp most of the time, Foord was able to make brief visits to Middletown thanks to the regular schedule of passenger trains between Cincinnati and Middletown. Foord was responsible for taking care of the recruits that were forwarded to Camp Dennison for mustering. He drew bedding and rations for the new men, but the three veteran sergeants generally ate their meals elsewhere. Foord, Frost, and Livingston spent as much time away from camp as they could. They visited nearby Milford and Cincinnati to see the sights and find edible food. They preferred to eat meals in the homes of friends and acquaintances, but a person could only take advantage so often. Captain Lewis was staying in a boarding house in Cincinnati, where Foord sometimes joined him for meals. Also in Cincinnati, he ate at the Gall House, the Burnett House, and the Gibson House, the latter being by far the favorite based on the number of mentions it received. Foord even went to the train depot for some meals, afterwards watching the trains as they came and went. The day that he would be forced to go back on army rations was coming soon, but Foord was in no hurry.[297]

The recruiting effort was winding up as January started, but there were as yet no definite arrangements to return to the regiment. First Sergeant Foord liked to read, and on days and evenings when he had little to do, he often lay on

---

295. Daniel, *Days of Glory*, 185; Richard H. Foord Papers, MSS. 1238, (1–21 January 1863), Center for Archival Collections, Bowling Green State University, Bowling Green, Ohio.

296. Foord Papers, 4 January 1863.

297. Ibid., 1–20 January 1863.

his bunk with a book. While at Camp Dennison, he read a dime novel called *General McClellan's Female Spy*. As often as he was able, Foord rode the train to Middletown to visit his friends, get his boots repaired, and to pay off a debt. As was to be expected, he visited Laura on every trip, and the two of them spent their time attending church, Sunday school, prayer meetings, and church sponsored concerts, a well-established pattern in their relationship. On Monday, January 19, Foord told all of his friends good-bye and left for Camp Dennison. His next trip home would be under vastly different circumstances.[298]

As final preparations were made to return to the regiment, movements became more restricted, Foord and the others were only able to get into Cincinnati for a few hours at a time. On January 21, the new recruits, five of them, were mustered in and issued clothing. Once clothed in blue, the recruits were deposited at the Columbia Street barracks and the veterans went out to eat. While waiting for transportation, the recruiting party continued their jaunts into the Queen City of the West. The loose lines of authority and casual relationships inherent in an army of volunteers were in full effect, and it was common for the officers and sergeants to visit restaurants and make sightseeing trips together. On the twenty-third, Foord was able to make one last dash to Middletown and spend two hours with his family and make a very brief visit to Laura.[299]

On January 24, Foord wandered through the Fifth Street Market (now known as Findlay Market) and that afternoon, the veterans and new recruits of the Thirty-fifth Ohio boarded the steamer *Ohio No. 3* and stowed their baggage. Everyone was in good spirits when the riverboat got underway at 8:00 p.m. The excitement of returning to the regiment combined with thoughts of home kept First Sergeant Foord from sleeping. "I stayed on deck until 10 o'clock," he wrote, "then came into the cabin and turned in with Sgnt. Frost—could not get to sleep for a good long while. Quite a change of affairs since last Sabbath Morning. I woke up at 3 A.M. and found the boat at anchor." A dense fog delayed arrival at Louisville until 9:00 a.m. Foord's heart was still back in Middletown, and as soon as the boat stopped, he wrote a letter to Laura, then went ashore with Lieutenant Schaeffer to mail it. The boat laid over long enough for Foord to tour the town, eat some oysters, visit some sick Persimmons in the Louisville hospital, and go to church. It was also long enough for one of the new recruits, Fred Reis, to desert. A perfunctory search was made, but Reis was not seen again.[300]

The *Ohio No. 3* lay at Louisville several days. Word had come that the Confederates had forces on the Cumberland River, so a convoy was being gathered to make the passage safer. The weather had turned cold, and it was no longer pleasant to walk on deck, but there wasn't much to do indoors. Foord took

298. Foord Papers, 1–20 January 1863.
299. Ibid., 21– 23 January 1863.
300. Ibid., 23–26 January 1863.

the opportunity to write another letter to Laura, view the canal around the Falls of the Ohio, watch soldiers from regiments heading south load onto their transports, and read a novel called *Mountain Patrol*. There were some official duties to perform. Lieutenant Daugherty, Sergeant Vanhorn, and Foord were sent into Louisville to draw rations and took the opportunity to ride the streetcars. Somewhere along the way, they also did a little trading, exchanging rice and beans for soft bread and salt pork for ham.[301]

Foord had a bit of the entrepreneurial spirit and knew from experience what it was that soldiers wanted. He also knew that three of the newly arrived regiments had just been paid. On the last day of January, he made yet another trip into Louisville and bought a large supply of stationary and began to peddle it to the soldiers around him. Before the market finally dried up two days later, he had cleared thirty dollars. While he was selling paper, a Michigan regiment had boarded the *Ohio No. 3* and taken over the berths below decks. Foord and his mates found themselves sleeping in the boat's barbershop. The weather had warmed a little, and Foord strolled around the deck for a while. His thoughts were still of home. "Evening was very beautiful," he wrote before retiring. "A splendid moonlight night—I sincerely wished I was home so I could go to church but no it cannot be so now I must take things as they come."[302]

The boat finally left Louisville on February 2, but not before Foord got off one more letter to Laura. The next day was very cold, and all the stored water on board was frozen. After ten days, life on a riverboat was beginning to wear thin. For reasons he did not provide, First Sergeant Foord got into a fight with a captain from the Nineteenth Kentucky Infantry. The two were separated before either got hurt, and being volunteers, no one thought to press charges. The boat made several stops for coal and provisions during the trip, but nothing struck Foord as interesting until they reached Fort Donelson in Tennessee. There had been a skirmish with the rebels the day before, and everyone wanted to go ashore and see the results. The boats remained tied up overnight to avoid any Confederates still lurking near the river.[303]

Foord went ashore the see the fort for himself the next morning. The freedom soldiers had to wander around is sometimes startling. The first sergeant walked over the field where the fighting had occurred and noticed "some pretty hard looking sights." Having seen all he wanted to in the fields, he moved on to a house where thirty captured rebels were confined. The guards there apparently didn't mind showing their prizes, and Foord was able to talk with one prisoner at length. Hoping to cash in once again, he bought another stock of stationary from a sutler. As interesting as it had been, First Sergeant Foord's little trip almost got him into trouble. While he was away, the *Ohio No. 3* had gone downstream to take on coal. It cost Foord fifty cents to be rowed down in a

---

301. Foord Papers, January 27–30, 1863.

302. Ibid., January 31–February 1, 1863.

303. Ibid., February 3–4, 1863.

skiff, but he more than made up the expense in paper sales.[304]

The fleet of riverboats, now numbering about fifty, steamed away from Fort Donelson at 10:00 a.m. on February 6. It was a beautiful day. Nothing else was happening, so the men were able to enjoy the slow journey up the Cumberland River, and that evening, the officers of the Nineteenth Michigan gave a concert. At about 5:00 p.m. on February 7, the flotilla finally arrived at the Nashville wharves. Captain Lewis went ashore and learned that the regiment was camped about twelve miles from the city. It would be the day after next before transportation could be arranged, so Foord and Sergeant Frost spent the day meandering about the city. They had a very tasty breakfast, visited friends on the familiar riverboat *Jacob Strader*, and had supper in a local saloon. It had all been very expensive, but in describing the day in his diary, Foord related the philosophy of the veteran soldier, "Who cares for expenses while the money lasts?"[305]

After one last night on the riverboat, the old campaigners and new recruits climbed onto wagons sent to carry them to camp. Before leaving Nashville, Foord mailed a valentine to Laura. Arriving in camp about 6:00 p.m. on February 9, the returning party was warmly greeted and was pleased to find most everyone well. Foord, after having had supper with Captain Deardorf, got a few minutes to enjoy himself. One of the things that men on leave always did was bring back packages from home. Because of the length of his stay, and because it was an officially sanctioned mission, Foord had been able to bring back quite a pile of baggage. That first night back in camp, he had the pleasure of distributing twenty boxes of food, clothes, gifts, photographs, and letters from home.[306]

Strolling Parties

While the recruiters were still in Ohio, the Third Brigade had been ordered to reassemble at Pilot Knob southwest of Gallatin on the Louisville and Nashville Railroad, and the Thirty-fifth had marched away from Cunningham's Ford on December 22, 1862. Their stay in the vicinity of Pilot Knob was a bit of a mystery to the Persimmons. As far as they could tell, their job was to patrol the area and collect "strolling parties that were on enterprises not considered strictly legitimate, and deliver the chaps to the kind hospitalities of the provo-marshal." The one benefit of the assignment was its closeness to the well-stocked Franklin plantation. Mr. Franklin, an avowed Confederate, lived on the plantation with his daughter, who was very vocal in support of the Confederacy. For-

304. Foord Papers, 5 February 1863.
305. Ibid., 6–8 February 1863.
306. Ibid., 9 February 1863.

aging parties enjoyed their visits to the Franklin place. They got to annoy an enemy civilian, look at his pretty daughter, and find just about anything they needed. Finding what they needed was becoming easier, now that foraging had become an officially sanctioned sport. Ferdinand Van Derveer cheerfully told his wife, "It would make you wonder to see how hard hearted I have become— I go with or send out parties to the farms and villages around, take their horses or grain, without saying so much as by your leave." [307]

Christmas 1862 was a busy time. General Rosecrans and the Army of the Cumberland began a winter advance toward the Confederate position at Murfreesboro, southeast of Nashville. At the same time, rebel John Hunt Morgan began his Christmas raid. Morgan crossed the Cumberland at now unguarded Cunningham's Ford, and the garrison at Gallatin moved out on a belated mission to watch the crossing. The Thirty-fifth Ohio was sent to Gallatin to replace the departed garrison. The movement was in the opposite direction the rest of the army was taking, and when the battle of Stones River was fought, the regiment was still ensconced at Gallatin. Tennessee was not the only place that the killing was going on. Henry Moser received a letter from home informing him that Enos Scudder, a friend of both he and Sallie, had been mortally wounded at Arkansas Post. The war was still going on, but it seemed to the Persimmons that they weren't doing much to help it along. [308]

The Nashville and Chattanooga Railroad (N&C) had suffered greatly during the war and was in no condition to supply the army now camped at Murfreesboro. Until the N&C was ready to carry the load, other means had to be found to subsist Rosecran's soldiers. Morgan's latest raid having run its course, the Thirty-fifth was sent from Gallatin to operate a gristmill on Bledsoe Creek. The Confederates had stockpiled grain at the mill but had been forced to abandon it during their retreat after the battle at Perryville. In addition to his skills as a forager, Captain L'Hommedieu had operated a flour mill for G. W. Tapscott prior to the war, so his Company G was assigned the task of grinding the captured grain. When the immediately available stock was used up, parties were sent out to gather all that could be found. Colonel Van Derveer led an expedition toward Hartsville that included a large number of wagons for transporting confiscated grain and was so fortunate as to come across several farmers bringing grain to the mill. They had no idea it was under new management and were summarily relieved of 90 percent of their loads. While the area was being "well cleaned out of grain" and the mill was converting all that "sesech wheat into good union flour," a local Unionist came to Van Derveer with information. This "private source" reported that part of the rebel army was "moving rapidly toward Kentucky" and was seizing all the horses and mules to mount its soldiers. [309]

---

307. Keil, *Thirty-fifth Ohio*, 107; Van Derveer to wife, 11 January 1863, Van Derver Family Collection.

308. Rogers Papers, "Country Life," 9.

The organization of the Third Brigade changed while the Persimmons were at Pilot Knob. The Eighteenth U.S. Infantry was reassigned to a newly formed brigade of regular army regiments. Throughout the war, volunteer troops tended to look down on regular troops because of the way they willingly put up with severe military discipline that no free man should tolerate. The volunteers in the Thirty-fifth Ohio and the three other volunteer regiments were no different, and no doubt, the Eighteenth U.S. felt more comfortable surrounded by its own kind. Still, the regulars had been part of the brigade since its organization a year before, and there was some sense of loss as the others watched them break camp and march away on December 23.[310]

On January 16, the Third Brigade marched to Nashville and set up camp on a hill about a mile from the state capital as the winter weather turned sour. "We came here yesterday through a cold driving rain—since then we have bitter snow hail or rain continually—certainly it is about as unpleasant soldiering just now as I have experienced during the war." It was a nice camp site, but living in the cold was hard work. The Thirty-fifth's commander wrote, "The weather is quite cold—it keeps one of us busy all the time to make fires." A few pickets went out daily, but there was little else to do. The Persimmons apparently enjoyed the idleness and were in generally good health, but within ten days, they were back on the road.[311]

A new camp near Antioch Church was set up nine miles south of Nashville, but within days, the campsite was moved closer to nearby Concord Church. By the time the regiment settled in there, things had changed. When the Army of the Ohio became the Army of the Cumberland in January, General Steedman was promoted to command the division, and on January 30, Ferdinand Van Derveer was promoted to brigade command. The four infantry regiments commanded by Van Derveer's were joined by Battery F, Fourteenth U.S. Artillery. The batteries assigned to the brigade would change with time, but the Second Minnesota, Ninth Ohio, Thirty-fifth Ohio, and Eighty-seventh Indiana would remain the heart of the brigade for another year and a half. The Persimmons also lost a good officer to promotion.[312]

An engineer by training, General Rosecrans created an engineering corps for the Army of the Cumberland. He accomplished its creation by force, ordering each regiment in the army to detail men from its own dwindling supply. Capt. John S. Earhart had also been a highly skilled and respected civil engineer in civilian life. He had worked on local road building projects and the construction of the hydraulic system for the city of Hamilton. He surveyed the route of the Cincinnati, Hamilton, & Dayton Railroad and was appointed the

309. Keil, *Thirty-fifth Ohio*, 108; Grebner, *We Were the Ninth*, 120; U.S. War Department, *War of the Rebellion*, Ser. no. 30, p. 307.

310. Keil, *Thirty-fifth Ohio*, 107.

311. Van Derveer to wife, 16, 24, January 1863, Van Derveer Family Collection.

312. Ibid., 16, 30 January 1863.

chief engineer for the Ohio division of the Junction Railroad. The greatest monument to his engineering talents was a huge seventeen arch stone viaduct across the Great Miami River in Hamilton. [Note: The viaduct still stands and is one of the more remarkable features of Hamilton, Ohio.] At the time the war started, Earhart was the chief engineer for the Miami and Erie Canal. Earhart was offered the position of topographical engineer on General Steedman's brigade staff, and as it fit well with his skills and interests, he accepted. Several weeks after assuming his new position, Earhart was reassigned to the same position at the division level where he worked on General Brannan's staff. The engineering position was a detail, and Earhart officially remained part of the regiment, but Company C never saw him again.[313]

Having all of his subordinate units in camp together made training and administration easier, but two sores that had nagged the Thirty-fifth Ohio for many months continued to fester; pay and chaplains. "We expect the paymaster in a short time—though only to pay for two months—there is now due the regiment five months pay, and they should have it at once—The Government has been very negligent about this matter—the men might get along well enough, but their wives and children at home need the money." Van Derveer had his own financial concerns, so he understood why it was such an important issue. The second issue, Chaplain Hoblet's status, was just as annoying to the colonel. "I have seen Mr. Hoblet several times, he is still in Nashville—this morning before he left, he promised to resign—he does not appear to feel as if he had done his duty to the regiment." In fact, Hoblet clearly had not. He had enlisted to provide spiritual guidance to the men of the Thirty-fifth Ohio, and he had not been with them for a year. The issue of pay dragged on to the end of the regiment's enlistment, but the chaplain's situation ended on February 2 when Hoblet finally did the right thing. "Mr. Hoblet came out to see us yesterday and tendered his resignation which we have very definitely forwarded to Gen. Rosecrans for his approval." Van Derveer's disappointment over the situation was so great, that he wrote to his wife, "Pray dearest, do not let it be known that he has resigned—we would be troubled by applicants for his place—for we do not wish for many more Chaplains."[314]

There weren't many good roads in Middle Tennessee, and the few there were radiated out of Nashville. Nolensville, astride one of those roads, was an unremarkable place. As far as the Persimmons were concerned, the only notable thing about the village was "the difference of opinion held by its liquor men, in spelling." One proprietor's sign said *tipling shop* while another's read *tippling shop*. No one ever found out if there was a difference in the products offered, since both owners had left before the Union army arrived, taking all their stock with them. The Thirty-fifth essentially took over the town. Concord

---

313. Daniel, *Days of Glory,* 189; Bartlow, *Centennial,* 874.

314. Daniel, *Days of Glory,* 189; Bartlow, *Centennial,* 874; Keil, *Thirty-fifth Ohio,* 107; Van Derveer to wife, 30 January 1863, Van Derveer Family Collection.

Church was used as a military court, and the regiment camped astride the turn-pike at the toll gate. Every night, pickets were posted about half a mile from camp, with the reserve remaining near the tollgate. The war had moved south of Nashville, and as far as anybody could tell, it would stay there for some time. Even so, rebel raiders and patrols were active in the region, and there was a steady stream of local citizens who wanted to go into the capital. Most of them were turned back at the tollgate. Escaped slaves and contrabands were another matter. Colonel Van Derveer had them pressed as teamsters.[315]

Part of Van Derveer's brigade camped on the front lawn of the plantation owned by Col. Joel A. Battle, commander of the Twentieth Tennessee Infantry in Bragg's army. Before the war, Battle had sent his son, Joel, Jr., to Miami University in Oxford, and many of the Persimmons were acquainted with him. Colonel Battle had been captured at Shiloh and sent to the prison camp at John-son's Island on Lake Erie. Paroled in the fall of 1862, he had been permitted to visit his home in Davidson County. From Battle's wife, Adeline, friends of Joel, Jr., learned that the Miami alumnus had served as his father's adjutant, had been wounded at Mill Springs, and then killed at Shiloh. The Second Min-nesota was encamped on her front lawn, but Mrs. Battle remained in the home. Even after her parlor was turned into a military courtroom and the center table was cleared of its mementos to be used as the judge's bench, she remained to protect what was left until forced to leave by military order.[316]

The morale problems among the officers of Company B continued. It had started in August 1861 when Captain Stone and Lieutenant Eacott both felt cheated. Stone believed his rightful position had been stolen by Captain Budd's appointment as commander of Company A. Eacott had hoped to have his own company, but when Earhart and Keil of Company C proved better recruiters, he had to settle for a lieutenant's rank. The two of them had supported each other's anger until both resigned on the same day in June 1862. Smith had played poli-tics to get his promotion to lieutenant in Company B, and he had been around Stone and Eacott just long enough to be poisoned by their attitude. Now a cap-tain and in command of the company, Smith used his connections to get out of the army the same way he got his promotion. When he resigned on February 24, Van Derveer wrote, "It is an unusual thing to have a resignation accepted except for physical disability, or for some grave offence—but the Captain it appears has his friends in Washington who have helped him."[317]

There was good news and bad news from home as February ended. The good news was that Ohio soldiers on active service with the army would now be permitted to vote in state elections. Previously denied this fundamental right of all male citizens, they would now be able to vote and exert some influence on matters that directly affected them. The first piece of bad news was that

315. Foord Papers, 10–20 February 1863.
316. Keil, *Thirty-fifth Ohio*, 108–109.
317. Van Derveer to wife, 24 February 1863, Van Derveer Family Collection.

Congress had passed a conscription bill obligating military service to all men from age twenty to forty-five. While this seemed like a good thing, with regimental strength constantly dwindling, it was also an indication that the war would not be over soon.

The second bit of bad news came from the Copperheads. Butler County had been a stronghold for peace Democrats since the war started, so Copperheadism was a personal issue for many of the men in the Thirty-fifth. Democrat Clement Vallandigham, the acknowledged leader of the Copperhead movement was the elected U.S. representative for Butler, Montgomery, Preble, and Warren counties, the four counties from which the regiment had been recruited. Vallandigham had a strong following in all four counties, but it was in traditionally Democratic Butler County that he had overwhelming support. Many of the men in the Thirty-fifth had voted for Vallandigham, and they had friends and family that strongly supported the peace Democrat. Henry Moser certainly did. Sallie Rogers was a pacifist and vehement supporter of Vallandigham. In her diary, she described reading the congressman's "great Peace Speech of Jan. 15th, 1863," and became concerned that the abolitionists would take over the House and Senate. Not afraid to declare her beliefs, Sallie wore a "Butternut pin" proudly and "had to talk quite saucy to keep up with my opposers," but she never considered taking the pin off. There were many others like Miss Rogers, and it was reasonable to expect that many of the Persimmons would at least have been sympathetic to Vallandigham and his supporters.[318]

But the war had changed their perspective. Having been in service for well over a year, the citizen volunteers of the Thirty-fifth Ohio had become soldiers. Their military experiences were beginning to blur their connection with civilian life, and the hardships they had faced had hardened attitudes as well as bodies. One of the things that permitted the soldiers to accept the difficulties of life at war was the belief that they had the support and respect of their fellow citizens at home. When the homefolks seemed to show disrespect for the soldiers and their efforts, they resented it strongly and took it as a particularly personal grievance. The soldiers in the field were fully committed to the mission of restoring the Union, and they expected the folks at home to behave the same way. Ferdinand Van Derveer spoke for them all when he said, "but of all the parties in our country I regard as the meanest and most pitiful those men in the north now advocating the cause of the rebels, and are too cowardly to go and help them." The colonel actually knew men who had gone south to fight for his convictions and regarded them "with a thousand times more' respect—than those others who only talk treason and keep their worthless carcasses out of harms way." In the minds of the Persimmons, the Copperheads were not the legitimate opposition. They were traitors trying to destroy the army and the nation. The regiment was assembled, and a resolution prepared by several Ohio colonels was read aloud by Colonel Long. The address somewhat belligerently

---

318. Rogers Papers, "Country Life," 10–12; Grebner, *We Were the Ninth*, 122–23.

*Sallie Rogers, outspoken supporter of Clement Vallandigham
and fiancée of Pvt. Henry Moser.*
BUTLER COUNTY HISTORICAL SOCIETY

demanded that private citizens remain true to the cause of freedom just as the army was doing. If the Copperheads would not desist in their treasonous activities, and the people of Ohio were unwilling to stop them, the army would. After the reading, a vote was taken and the Persimmons gave their unanimous support.[319]

Other than a visit by the division inspector general, not much out of the ordinary happened at Nolensville, but two exciting things did occurred. After several previous requests, the Persimmons were finally allowed to turn in their old 1842 model smoothbore muskets and replace them with new Springfield rifles, most likely the 1861 model. The best feature of the rifle depended on whose opinion was asked. The officers, who carried only side arms, believed the Springfield rifle was a fine, accurate weapon. The enlisted men, whose primary weapon was a rifle, thought the best thing was its smaller caliber and reduced weight. The .58 caliber minié ball fired from the Springfield weighed about half as much as the .69 caliber bullets they had been carrying, and a thousand miles of marching had taught them that a couple of pounds here or there could make all the difference.[320]

The second event was probably not as important in the long run, but it was definitely more exciting at the time. On March 3, General Steedman, newly promoted to division command, was ordered to perform a reconnaissance along the Chapel Hill road where the Confederate cavalry brigade under Gen. Philip Roddey of Alabama was camped near Lewisburg. He was to cross the Harpeth River and make a juncture with additional troops from Murfreesboro. When the Thirty-fifth Ohio arrived at the crossroads designated as the meeting place, only Steedman's troops were there. His orders called for a return to Nolensville if the meeting was missed, but after waiting through the night, Steedman decided to continue on with the men on hand. As the move commenced on the fourth, skirmishers from the Thirty-fifth and the other regiments in the brigade traded shots with their rebel counterparts. When the brigade came within site of the rebel camp on the opposite side of the Harpeth River, the Thirty-fifth went into line of battle and advanced steadily toward the riverbank. At the river's edge, the lines hesitated. It was January and the water was very cold, but when Steedman rode up and down the lines shouting, "Forward," the men jumped into the shallow water and waded across.[321]

Roddey's men had not expected the Yankees to cross the cold river and conducted a "hasty skedaddle." The Persimmons found the enemy camp well stocked, and everything that could be loaded was placed onto wagons. Every-

319. Grebner, *We Were the Ninth*, 122–23; Foord Papers, 23 February 1863; Mitchell, *Civil War Soldiers*, 56, 64, 66, 74, 82, 85; Daniel, *Days of Glory*, 252; Van Derveer to wife, 1 May 1862, Van Derveer Family Collection.

320. Keil, *Thirty-fifth Ohio*, 109; Wiley, *Billy Yank*, 63.

321. Keil, *Thirty-fifth Ohio*, 109; U.S. War Department, *War of the Rebellion*, Ser. no. 34, p. 127.

thing that wouldn't go on a wagon, including the shanties the rebel soldiers had been living in, was "fed to the flames." Once the fires were well along, the brigade marched back to the Harpeth and went into camp for the night. The rebels did not take even this small reverse lightly and sought to trap the Federal raiders. When word of their movements had come to General Thomas at Murfreesboro, he sent a courier to warn Steedman. Thomas's orders required the brigade to immediately place the Harpeth River between themselves and the approaching rebels. Rousted out at midnight, the Thirty-fifth made their way slowly across the river on trees felled across the water as a makeshift replacement for the destroyed bridge. As the last men crossed over at first light, rebel skirmishers began to appear on the opposite bank.[322]

The brigade did not return to Nashville. General Rosecrans had won his battle and felt his army needed a recovery period in established camps. He also knew that Tennessee roads were notorious for being impassable when wet from winter and spring rains. Halting at Triune on March 6, the Thirty-fifth Ohio set up camp in what became semipermanent quarters.[323]

322. Keil, *Thirty-fifth Ohio*, 110.
323. Bradley, *Tullahoma*, 7.

CHAPTER 7

Things Were All in Good Condition

March to June 1863

Settling in

As the Thirty-fifth Ohio prepared its new camp, the Civil War in Tennessee was settling into a seasonal lull. The Army of the Cumberland assumed positions around Nashville and Murfreesboro. Its counterpart, the Confederate Army of Tennessee, had established a line south of the Duck River anchored at Tullahoma. A range of steep hills north of the Duck River created a barrier between the armies that was pierced by roads at Liberty Gap and Hoover's Gap, both of which were protected by Confederate forces at Columbia, Shelbyville, Manchester, and McMinnville. Cavalry from both armies regularly raided behind the lines of the other, but there was a break in large scale maneuvering after February 1863. The Third Brigade's camp two miles north of the hamlet of Triune, halfway between Franklin and Murfreesboro, was "in a grove on a high and commanding hill" near good supplies of wood and water. All of the units of the Third Division were nearby and every effort was made to fortify the camp against enemy attack. The Thirty-fifth and the other regiments in the brigade supplied one-hundred-man details daily to work under the engineers laying out the works.[324]

First Sergeant Richard Foord of Company K had some difficulty getting back into the swing of things after his return from leave and recruiting duty. His first few days back in camp were spent talking to others about "the happy place I love," writing to his fiancée Laura, and fighting off a cold. He was lonesome and felt out of place, writing that "Camp Life doesn't suit me anymore—oh, I wish I was home again but that is played out now. I must forget all about it." Foord's homesickness was quite natural and no more than thousands of others

---

324. Bishop, *Story of a Regiment*, 109; Van Derveer to wife, 8 March 1863, Van Derveer Family Collection.

were feeling, and gradually, his duties and the familiar faces of the regiment helped drive it away.[325]

Foord relieved Sgt. Thomas C. Pearson who had filled in while he was gone, and began doing the myriad things any first sergeant must do. He drew rations from the commissary sergeant, distributing them to the individual messes of his company. He also drew and distributed clothing. One night was spent as commander of the picket relief force. Since his rifle had sat unattended for several weeks, it desperately needed cleaning. "It was very dirty and it was a big job to get it bright," so Foord was a bit surprised when it passed inspection the next day. Most of one morning was spent drawing lines across the blank pages of his morning report book. As the familiar routine fell back into place, Foord's uneasiness grew less and less.[326]

Another uneasy situation was settled in early March. First Sergeant Leonard Allen had taken "French leave" ten months before during the Corinth campaign. Allen immediately regretted his action and came to the conclusion that he could not live with himself until he had made things right. As soon as it was discovered he had left without authorization, Allen was reduced to the ranks in Company C. Unwilling to return to the Thirty-fifth and face the men he had abandoned, he began working through influential friends at home to develop another solution. The agreement that was finally reached was much more than Allen had any right to expect. He was formally discharged from the Thirty-fifth Ohio and was given a commission as first lieutenant in the Mississippi Marine Brigade. The former first sergeant–former deserter served honorably until the end of the war and few people in Company C ever knew the full story.[327]

Living Like Kings

The camp at Triune was the most comfortable the Persimmons ever had. In describing his own quarters, Colonel Van Derveer said, "As for me I am fixed comfortably enough—two tents 1 one room with a real board floor and a stove to keep us warm." That spring in Tennessee, waiting for the big push back into the Deep South, was about as good as it got. The nice grassy grove they occupied was churned into a "howling wilderness of mud" in less than a week, but a comfortable routine quickly appeared. They took turns at picket duty. There were company, regimental, and brigade drills to be done, fortifications to be built, and details to perform, but the men had a fair amount of leisure time and found a variety of ways to fill it, some positive and some not.

After spending a rainy night sleeping under India rubber blankets, the real

---

325. Foord Papers, 10–13 February 1863.
326. Ibid., 11–15 February 1863.
327. Arnold, *Sunshine and Shadows*, 36.

work of encampment began on March 8. Company streets were laid out according to regulations, and the process of pitching tents was begun. Just about the time the canvas was stretched out, orders came to form up for movement. The Triune camp would become the base for regular patrols and probes into Confederate controlled areas, and this was to be the first. The regiment marched to the Harpeth River, shelled some rebel cavalrymen, and returned to camp. The men found it all "rather provoking but had to go." Returning to camp, the men of Company K had supper and expected to sleep well after the day's activities but they were to be disappointed. The company was assigned picket duty and "had a benefit wading through the mud on the Franklin road but its all for the Union."[328]

Picket duty was one of the facts of life for the Thirty-fifth while in camp. Things were a lot different than they had been at Fishing Creek. Colonel Van Derveer paid much more attention to the security of the camp, and the officers and men now knew what was expected of them. They had also learned that picket duty wasn't always a bad thing and that some of the posts could be quite pleasant. Perhaps the most popular picket station while the Thirty-fifth was at Triune was the Jordan plantation. Mr. Jordan was a Union man who invited the officers and noncommissioned officers in for dinner and let them use the house as the reserve post when it rained. On one turn at Jordan's, First Sergeant Foord of Company K set up his shelter tent and spent the better part of the day reading. On another night, he was able to purchase an apple pie and custard and enjoy "quite a feast."[329]

Other nights on picket weren't quite as pleasant. Some nights it rained the entire time, causing the men on outpost to be miserable. When the rebels were known to be nearby, everyone would be up all night trying to stay alert. In between watching for any enemy scouts that might be lurking about, the men would tell stories and talk about home. The morning after an all night vigil could be just as long. Tired from a sleepless night, the men would have to clean weapons and equipment after returning to camp. On picket duty, everyone looked forward to the nights when the weather was clear and nothing much happened.[330]

The construction and maintenance of fortifications was a continuing effort that involved everyone in camp at one point or another. It was a labor shared by all the regiments in the brigade and by every company in each regiment. The initial work was done by the Second Minnesota the day after tents were first pitched. In the first two weeks of March, the work was intensive as Colonel Van Derveer pushed hard to secure his camp. Every day, details worked under the watchful eye of the engineers assigned to ensure the works were properly laid

---

328. Foord Papers, 8 March 1863; Bradley, *Tullahoma*, 45; Van Derveer to wife, 10 March 1863, Van Derveer Family Collection.

329. Foord Papers, 18 March, 5 April, 10 June 1863.

330. Ibid., 14–16 April 1863.

out and prepared. The men didn't particularly enjoy the work, but accepted its necessity, realizing that "if our fine Rebs call on us—we will give them a warm reception." The works consisted primarily of earth and log breastworks constructed above ground, but there was more to fortification than making walls. Company K was assigned to build a magazine for ammunition storage, the construction of which required a great deal of wood cutting, even after a nearby corncrib was dismantled for making the sills. The work of fortification was also unending. After the breastworks were complete, they had to be maintained, and there was always some little improvement to be made. Amidst all the digging, Pvt. Henry Moser of Company G had his twenty-fifth birthday on March 14. Sallie had not had time to write him a letter on that occasion. Both of them were greatly disappointed.[331]

Foraging was one duty the men usually looked forward to. It was a chance to get out of camp, see the countryside, and steal things without getting in trouble. On March 26, a huge foraging expedition involving all four regiments of the brigade and two hundred wagons set out for the Harpeth River. When they returned to camp on the Franklin pike, all two hundred wagons were full. Confederate cavalry made a show of attacking but never quite got around to doing it. A few days later, the entire brigade once again went foraging on the Starnes Plantation, owned by Col. James W. Starnes of the Fourth Tennessee Cavalry, but this time they took only sixty wagons which they filled with corn. The trip to the Starnes plantation demonstrated that foraging could also be hard work. The sixteen-mile trip and collection of the corn was done in about nine hours, and the men were tired out upon their return. There were many smaller expeditions and quite a few unsanctioned ones by individuals and small groups. Besides providing a little entertainment, foraging added variety to the army rations the regiment subsisted on.[332]

There were ways to dodge picket duty and stay off fortification details, but nobody could get out of drill. Whether it was squad, company, regimental, or brigade drill, everybody got drawn into it. Squad drill was used in small doses to touch up individual skills, but the focus was on fighting maneuvers. Company drill was usually led by an officer, and in most cases was preparation for a regimental drill to be held later in the day. With Colonel Van Derveer commanding the brigade, Lieutenant Colonel Long was the acting regimental commander. Regimental drill was conducted by him or by Major Boynton. On occasion, the drill was more specialized. Just before breaking camp in June, Major Boynton led the regiment in a skirmish drill. Ignored in the early days of their training, experience had shown the importance of skirmishing, and it had become part of the regular training regimen. As the shadows of winter turned into the bright light of spring, brigade and division level drills became more and more frequent. Since everyone, from private to general, had now learned

331. Foord Papers, 9–17 March, 14 May 1863; Rogers Papers, "Country Life," 11.
332. Foord Papers, 27–31 March 1863.

the business of soldiering, there was not nearly as much confusion and fewer mistakes in the maneuvering of units. For the men, the constant drill was a nuisance. As veteran campaigners, they were not excited about "playing soldier," but they tolerated it because it was a sure sign that a major campaign was coming.[333]

Another aspect of drilling was regularly scheduled inspections and parades. Inspections were the tool officers used to ensure that the equipment their men were supposed to have was present and in working order. An inspection was held every Sunday morning, and most often, they were rather informal and conducted by company or regimental staff officers. It was another situation entirely when the division staff came to inspect. When General Steedman inspected the Thirty-fifth Ohio on March 30, the entire regiment stood in ranks as the general made his rounds. After taking a brief look at the regiment as a whole, Steedman inspected individual soldiers. He looked closely at weapons, uniforms, equipment, of each man, and using the tip of his sword, poked around in their knapsacks. First Sergeant Foord reported that the Persimmons "made quite a grand display—things were all in good condition." Sometimes inspections took on a special air. On April 22, a liberty pole was placed in center of the camp, and Colonels Van Derveer and Long raised the flag while a band played.[334]

Part of the camp routine was the continuing administrative activities that go hand in hand with operating any large organization. Some activities, like policing the regimental area are familiar to modern veterans. Usually done one company at a time, the men got in line several feet apart and walked through the designated area picking up any trash and debris they came across. Rations had to be received and issued to each mess. Unlike modern armies, there was no mess hall. Each mess was responsible for storing and preparing its own food. Days were set aside, generally right before a major inspection or parade, to allow each man to do laundry. Manpower was still a problem. When the Thirty-fifth Ohio went into camp on March 7, there were about five hundred officers and men supposedly available, down from nine hundred in October, 1861. On April 11, Major Boynton held a special muster to find out the exact strength of the regiment and determine how many conscripts would be needed to fill the ranks. Some of the Persimmons may have had qualms against conscription, but all of them were glad to see it happen. Even if it did smack a bit of tyranny, it would bring more soldiers into the army, greatly increasing the chances of victory. There was an emotional aspect to their acceptance, as well. They had been in the field for a year and a half, and weren't too concerned if men who had stayed at home during that time now had to join them. Besides, had they all turned out earlier, the war might have ended already. [335]

---

333. Prokopowicz, *All for the Regiment,* 50; Foord Papers, 15 March–21 June 1863; Wiley, *Billy Yank,* 54.

334. Foord Papers, 15 March–21 June 1863; Wiley, *Billy Yank,* 47.

Receiving pay was of vital interest to the Persimmons, and a great deal of effort went into getting it done. Each company held a pay muster every other month. Upon hearing his name, each soldier called out "here," crisply brought his rifle to the carry position, and then returned to the order arms position. Pay-rolls were prepared, and once the mustering officer had accounted for every name on the roll, it was forwarded to the adjutant general in Washington, D.C., Generally, several weeks passed from the time of the muster to the time the men were actually paid, but it wasn't unusual for the paymaster to be months late. Payday always set off a flurry of activity. Some men seemed intent on spending their money as quickly as possible, so the sutler and gamblers would be very busy. Others, particularly those with families back home, were more careful. These men would keep a few dollars and send the rest home. Some, like First Sergeant Foord, continued to make regular payments on debts.[336]

But life in camp was not all work and military routine. The men had a fair amount of free time and used it in many ways. Quite a bit of time was spent in making things a little more livable. The regiment lived in square sided tents, and since there was plenty of wood in the region, they were likely shored up with log walls. Fireplaces or "California furnaces," dug into the ground provided heat. In early April, there was a "general renovation" of the Thirty-fifth Ohio's campsite. Tents were aired out and moved a short distance to a better piece of ground. Wood floors were put in to keep out most of the mud, and all in all, it wasn't a bad arrangement. As far as First Sergeant Foord was concerned, they were "living like kings." The only thing he regretted was that they had to do their own cooking. But that, too, was also a situation that could be remedied, and after a few days of looking, they found a contraband willing to take on the job.[337]

The Persimmons took a certain amount of pride in their humble dwellings. The longer they stayed in camp, the more elaborate their home improvements became. Late in their stay, the decision was made to erect an arbor through the regimental quarters. The arbor would make the camp more attractive and serve as a sort of porch on which the men could lounge when the weather permitted. One morning was spent collecting materials, and the arbor was erected the same afternoon. Construction of the arbor turned into a competition in which each company tried to outdo the others. It all looked nice when it was done, but unfortunately, the timing of the effort was atrocious. The day after it was done, the Thirty-fifth left the Triune camp for good.[338]

Food was ever on the minds of the soldiers. They spent a great deal of time looking for it, cooking it, talking about it, and even writing about it. Every once in a while, something good would be issued along with the usual rations, like

335. Foord Papers, 11 April 1863; Mitchell, *Civil War Soldiers*, 83–84.
336. Foord Papers, 10–11 April 1863; Wiley, *Billy Yank*, 48–49.
337. Foord Papers, 4–8 April 1863; Wiley, *Billy Yank*, 56–57.
338. Foord Papers, 22 June 1863; Wiley, *Billy Yank*, 58.

molasses, and a special meal would follow. The farms of central Tennessee provided great riches for invaders, and when the food obtained from foraging was combined with the issued rations, the men really did eat like kings. Meat was plentiful, and fried ham was a staple. It could be mixed with issued dried peas to make a nice pea soup. Other foods obtained by foraging were flapjacks, fruit pies, and buttermilk. In Triune, the Persimmons ate well, and they ate often.[339]

Armies have never been spiritually uplifting organizations, and some soldiers were dismayed by the level of immorality they experienced. Those with loftier views of humanity were appalled by the noisy behavior of their compatriots and the general absence of religious activity in camp. Upon enlisting, these men had viewed themselves and their fellow volunteers as virtuous patriots and were taken aback by the reality of being part of an organization of mortal men. The most often voiced complaints revolved around profanity, card playing, and drinking. Alcohol apparently created no problems of any significance, although Foord noted that after one issue things got a little out of hand with "all the boys drunk—and awful time in camp—frightening—whiskey is a bad thing." The issue of whiskey that created the awful time was made on March 9, two days after the Triune camp was set up. Foord made frequent entries in his diary directly related to ration issues, but no other mention of a whiskey issue is made.[340]

When it came to entertainment, the Persimmons mostly did the same kinds of things they would have done at home. First Sergeant Foord liked to play checkers and had regular partners in Corporals Henry B. Stetler and William I. Tillson. Music was also very popular, and even though the regimental band had been discharged, there were enough musicians in the regiment to keep an unofficial band going. The Thirty-fifth's band was given a tent in which to practice and gave many evening concerts. When they weren't playing, one of the other regimental bands might be. The Second Minnesota was known for its bugle band, and the Germans of the Ninth Ohio loved music so much, that they enlisted musicians as privates and agreed to make up the difference in pay among themselves. Materials were somewhat limited, but most of the men read whatever newspapers, magazines, and novels that were available. Other diversions were more strenuous. Company G apparently took the lead in organizing boxing matches and dances. The occasional horse race also drew large crowds.[341]

The soldiers of the Thirty-fifth Ohio also wrote letters to family and friends back home describing life in the army, things they had seen in the South, their hopes for an early end to the war, and giving instructions to wives and children left behind. They wrote on any kind of paper they could find. There was a lot of

---

339. Foord Papers, 14 March–16 April 1863.

340. Ibid., 9 March 1863, Mitchell, *Civil War Soldiers*, 73–74.

341. Foord Papers, 13 March–14 June 1863; Bishop, *Story of a Regiment*, 110; Grebner, *We Were the Ninth*, 128.

preprinted stationary available from sutlers and internal entrepreneurs like Richard Foord, but the folks at home received missives written on the backs of military forms, wallpaper, brown wrapping paper, and even the unused space on letters they had sent to their men in the army. Most of the preprinted stationary had patriotic symbols like flags, cannons, eagles, sentries on duty, and the goddess Liberty. It was a way of reminding homefolks of why they were away and how they felt about what they were doing.[342]

Their colonel had a lot to say about what he felt for the Copperheads at home. When his wife told him what they were saying, the editorial writer in him came to the forefront. "I am both surprised and mortified by the position taken by so many of the democrats at home," he wrote. "They may call this an abolition war if they please—but they cannot ignore the fact that it is a life and death struggle for the perpetuity of the best government the world ever knew – under which we have lived, prospered and been happy; enjoying civil and religious liberty without restraint. It is not a matter a great consequences now how the trouble originated—When a house is burning we first put out the fire, and then ask how it happened—We know now that war is upon us—that it was commenced by the rebels in Charleston when they dishonored our flag on Fort Sumter—and that unless the rebel lion is supressed we will have anarchy in the place of a government—and contiued fueds and civil wars in the place of law and order. I have no patience with the peace democrats of the north—A rebel who will boldly fight for his side I respect, in comparison with the sneaking backbiting traitor of the north who is too cowardly for any thing but cry for peace." No one ever had to guess where Ferdinand Van Derveer stood. [343]

By far, the most popular off-duty activity among the Persimmons was visiting with friends and neighbors. Sometimes a group of friends would walk and smoke together. Some of the walks were quite long, going as far as Triune and back. There were even instances when friends from home made it all the way to Tennessee. Sometimes the men would go to visit friends in other regiments in the brigade or other Ohio regiments in the division. The sutler's tent was also a popular gathering place, provided someone had money to spend. Usually, the visiting consisted of men gathering at a tent or around a fire to talk about home and "tell yarns." The campfire was a soldier's home away from home. It didn't matter if tents were set up or not, every halt produced fires that the men flocked to like moths. It was a place to cook food and, on cold nights, the men would approach it with outstretched hands, seeking its warmth. Even on warm nights, fires were started and men would gather. As Benjamin Arnold put it, "[The fire's] congenial glow invited companionship, because of a fire that once burned on a hearth at home."[344]

As with everyone else in camp, 1st Sgt. Richard Foord of Company K

---

342. Mitchell, *Civil War Soldiers*, 90.
343. Van Derveer to wife, 10 March 1863, Van Derveer Family Collection.
344. Foord Papers, 8–19 April 1863; Arnold, *Sunshine and Shadows*, 9.

found that some days were better than others. The regiment had been in camp at Triune less than a week when Company K, under Foord's direction was assigned to police the regimental camp. When Colonel Long inspected the work afterwards, he was highly displeased and ordered the company out to do it again. While the men picked up trash, Foord reported that Long "gave me fits for not doing it well the first time—didn't like it pretty well but had to submit." Foord might have forgotten that April 8, 1863, was his twenty-second birthday if Pvts. George W. Gilmore and Matthew McMahon had not burst into his tent and started "pulling my ears for me good."[345]

Foord continued his long distance romance with Laura Webster. Everyday, he waited for the mail to come in and worried when he got nothing from her ("No letter today. What can be the matter?"), and rejoiced when he did ("mail came and I received a good long letter from Laura—good news."). Laura seems to have written more often than Foord, but he wrote to her on a regular basis. Other than to say that one of Laura's letters was very patriotic, Foord did not record what they wrote to each other, but some diary entries comment that he got a "good" letter indicating that Laura said things he wanted to hear.

Foord was a conscientious man who took his responsibilities, both in the army and at home, seriously. Each payday, Foord always sent money to Middletown to pay his obligations there. He was worried about forming bad habits, once recording in his diary that he had "smoked and got very sick—did not sleep all night—that's good—I wish I would get sick every time I smoked." Foord also liked to go to church on Sunday after inspection whenever he could. The Thirty-fifth Ohio had not had much luck with chaplains. John Woods, unable to live up to his calling, had resigned after only two months. Joshua C. Hoblet had taken his place, but he too resigned just before the Persimmons arrived at Triune. With no one in the regiment to lead services, Foord would go to one of the other regiments when he heard someone was speaking there. He noted in his diary that April 30 had been designated as a day of prayer and fasting. As the weather turned warmer, Foord also reported that he had been struck down by a common illness of the season. "In camp all day—rather lazy—have the spring fever."[346]

Social Equals

The early months of 1863 were not a happy time for regimental Surgeon Perkins Gordon. After some complaints about his treatments in the early days of Kentucky, it became apparent that Gordon did have a pretty good idea what he was doing, but his methods eventually got him in trouble. Assigned to one of

---

345. Foord Papers, 8–30 April 1863.
346. Ibid.

the many hospitals in Nashville, Gordon and assistant surgeon Charles Wright had five other Persimmons stationed with them. Mordecai Cleaver, a private in Company F had been promoted to hospital steward. Pvts. Joshua Davis and Samuel Dennis of Company G, Charles Fisher of Company H, and John Leach of Company A were detailed to help the doctors care for sick soldiers of the Thirty-fifth and other regiments in the area. Coming from the same regiment and the same communities in Ohio, it was natural for the small group to form a pseudo-family and spend time together. This family routinely shared rations and ate meals together, and that's how Dr. Perkins found himself standing in front of a court-martial. He was accused of conduct prejudicial to good order and military discipline, misappropriation of hospital stores, and misuse of hospital property.

The origin of the charges is uncertain. Perhaps Dr. Gordon was guilty as charged, but the court-martial records aren't convincing. While guarding the Kentucky Central Railroad in the fall of 1861, only a few weeks into the regiment's enlistment, the soldiers in the regiment displayed some antipathy toward the doctor and the way he treated them, and descriptions of social activities among the officers of Thirty-fifth Ohio never include the doctor by name. So, it may have been that Perkins Gordon was a little difficult to get along with, and his lack of popularity may have contributed to his legal problems in the spring of 1863.

At the court-martial, government statements portrayed a man who made sure his own comforts were taken care at the expense of his subordinates and patients. It was said the surgeon took food from the hospital steward's rations while the regiment marched through Kentucky and Tennessee, that he took potatoes from his patient's rations in Nashville, and that after the battle of Perryville, he had used ambulances intended for transporting sick soldiers to carry his personal baggage. The defense witnesses painted a very different story. Assistant Surgeon Wright and the hospital stewards admitted that Dr. Gordon ate their rations, but it was done with their consent. It was common practice for the doctors and stewards to pool their rations and share meals. The soldiers and doctors thought nothing of it, and for those who questioned whether the officers should have mingled so closely with the stewards, the egalitarian Dr. Gordon made it clear that he considered any enlisted man to be the social equal of any officer, particularly in volunteer regiments. The stewards also made sure that the court understood that Gordon supplied medicine for patients with his own money and that many of the cooking utensils supposedly misappropriated for preparing Gordon's meals were also purchased with his personal funds. Steward Cleaver also informed the court that on at least one occasion, the fresh vegetables taken from hospital rations were used to treat the doctor's own case of scurvy.

There is another tantalizing clue to the possible reason behind the charges against Surgeon Gordon in the court-martial records. During his testimony on Gordon's behalf, Dr. Wright stated that some of the white sugar allegedly stolen from the hospital rations ended up in rum punch consumed at a social gathering led by Colonel Van Derveer and Lieutenant Colonel Long. The regimental officers had probably already heard stories of Gordon supposedly using hospital rations, and when he resisted their using hospital rations to entertain themselves, they probably considered him to be a hypocrite. Whatever the true reasons, Gordon was found guilty of conduct prejudicial to good order and military discipline and was sentenced to forfeiture of pay for one month.

As might be expected, Perkins Gordon lost interest in the Thirty-fifth Ohio after his conviction. During the summer of 1863, he applied for a position as Surgeon of U.S. Volunteers. Acceptance required Gordon to pass a very exhaustive qualification test covering subjects like chemistry, treatment techniques, and battlefield surgery. Perkins passed the test, but events prevented him from accepting his new commission. Sometime during the Tullahoma campaign, Gordon was felled by a severe sunstroke that left him an invalid. Unable to return to field duty, Gordon eventually resigned his commission in November. For the next critical year, medical services in the Thirty-fifth Ohio would be left the capable hands of Assistant Surgeons Charles Wright and Abraham Landis.[347]

Boys Would Rather Fight

Military operations slowed down considerably during the winter and early spring, but they did not stop completely. Small operations were carried on throughout the cold season by both sides. In particular, Confederate cavalry was very active throughout middle Tennessee, and on March 20, the Thirty-fifth Ohio, the Ninth Ohio, and two guns from Battery F, Fourteenth U.S. Artillery were sent to the Harpeth River in response to a report of rebel horsemen but found nothing. Other than a little physical conditioning, the twelve-mile march accomplished nothing. A few hours later, the entire brigade was called out again and put into line of battle. A rebel attack was expected, but as before, nothing materialized. The rebels were around, and they could be pesky when they wanted to. On March 23, there were signs of a rebel attack, and the brigade once again formed a line of battle. Just when everyone had decided the Confederates had moved away and were prepared to continue the normal routine, rebel sharpshooters would trade shots with Union pickets and keep everyone in line. At the end of the day, no one in camp had seen a rebel and frustration at not getting into a fight was high.[348]

Many a morning, the Persimmons would be placed in line at 3:00 a.m. to

347. Thomas P. Lowry and Jack D. Welsh, *Tarnished Scalpels* (Mechanicsburg: Stackpole Books, 2000), 90–94.

348. Foord Papers, 20–23 March 1863.

wait for attacks that never came. After three weeks of early rising to no purpose and spending all day working on fortifications, everyone wished "the Rebs would come if they intend to—our duty is rather hard now—boys would rather fight than do so much hard duty." The rebels were always nearby, but never close enough to engage. Twice in March Colonel Van Derveer took the entire brigade out to forage. The first time, Confederate cavalry appeared and lined up as if to attack, but when the brigade prepared to respond, they backed off. On April 1, friendly scouts reported an enemy force crossing the Harpeth. The alarm was sounded at midmorning and the Persimmons, joined by the Ninth Ohio and Second Minnesota, marched out beyond Triune to set an ambush, but as First Sergeant Foord reported, "they would not bite," and one more expedition ended without anything of interest happening.[349]

The Triune camp was the first time that the entire Third Brigade had camped at the same location for any appreciable time and could drill as a brigade. Colonel Van Derveer took advantage of the opportunity to conduct rigorous training. He was determined that the Third Brigade would be as powerful and have the best fighting qualities possible if it ever did go into battle. When General Buell had created his mixed-state brigades in late 1861, it had not necessarily created more cohesive units. Men who were citizens of the same state had a common bond that served to bring them closer, but the mixing of states often created rivalries among regiments in a brigade. While the Persimmons were on good terms with the Ninth Ohio, and had been for some time, their relations with the other regiments in the brigade had been more of a tolerant nature than a positive one. Brigade drill provided an opportunity to cement relations with the Second Minnesota and Eighty-seventh Indiana. During many hours of drill together, the regiments formed the bonds of common experience and learned that the other regiments shared the pride each felt in itself. They also learned to trust in their commander. Perhaps the most important factor in creating unity in mixed brigades was leadership, and Colonel Van Derveer's competence had long been established. If he drilled them long and hard, he did it with a sure hand, and the men in all four regiments came to believe in his ability and his concern for their welfare. After a month of hard work, Van Derveer proudly stated, "Mine is acknowledged to be one, if not *the* best brigade in the [A]rmy of the Cumberland—But it won't do to brag."[350]

There were instances that tested the warrior bonds. Foraging was now a standard practice, and everyone was eating well. Even so, soldiers are always hungry, more for variety than quantity, so petty theft of foodstuffs was common. Generally it wasn't practiced within the thief's own regiment, but that still didn't mean it was considered acceptable. On March 28, a member of the Thirty-fifth Ohio was caught stealing food in the camp of the Second Minnesota, perhaps because they were from a more distant state. In the ultimate dis-

---

349. Foord Papers, 2 April 1863.
350. Prokopowicz, *All for the Regiment*, 40.

play of contempt for a nineteenth-century military establishment, the men from Minnesota formally drummed him out of their camp. It may have been a setback in the development of closer relationships, but the Minnesotans apparently viewed it as the act of one individual and not as being characteristic of the entire Thirty-fifth.[351]

Aside from a few exchanges between rebel cavalry and Third Brigade pickets, the months of April and May were spent mostly in drill. One officer repined that "there has been a great and tiresome monotony in our life here for some time past," but there were some engaging activities from time to time. Scouting parties had noted that the plantation owned by John E. Tulles had a large barn full of hay and oats. After two years of war, Middle Tennessee had been stripped of most of its abundance. The vulnerable Louisville and Nashville Railroad was rarely able to carry supplies at full capacity, and it was becoming more and more difficult to feed men and beasts. On April 14, Major Boynton and a train of twenty-five wagons were sent to collect the barn's contents to be used as forage for the division's stock. Upon arriving at Mr. Tulles's barn, Boynton found it burned to the ground and the forage ruined and so reported to General Steedman. Maj. Gen. David Stanley had ordered his cavalry troopers to burn the houses of "all Citizens who have sons or near relatives in the Confederate service," thus the burning of the Tulles barn. Steedman wrote an angry letter to Fourteenth Corps Headquarters complaining of Stanley's action. Steedman was not mad because the barn had been burned; rather he was angry that the forage had not been removed before it was burned. The war was becoming less and less civil every day. [352]

There was a command shuffle In April. Gen. John M. Schofield became the Third Division commander replacing Steedman who had assumed command of a division in the Army of the Cumberland's Reserve Corps. The soldiers took to Schofield right away. Steedman had been in the habit of conducting numerous reconnaissance missions into the countryside. The men felt they were unproductive, and when foraging was not included in the mission, they were downright useless. Rather than conducting continual reconnaissance, Schofield began conducting brigade and division drills. The near constant movement of the army during the last year prevented these drills from being conducted regularly, and a fair amount of confusion attended the early ones. According to General Rosecrans's preference, the officers and men were instructed to hold fire until they were sure of hitting their target, aim low, and then go into the enemy with the bayonets. Over the span of weeks, they became more and more proficient, and the time was swift approaching when that proficiency would be vital. Bombarded daily by messages from Washington demanding that he attack the Confederate army under General Bragg, Rosecrans was strong-willed enough

---

351. Bircher, *Drummer Boy's Diary*, 37.

352. U.S. War Department, *War of the Rebellion*, Ser. no. 34, p. 241; Van Derveer to wife, 16 April 1863, Van Derveer Family Collection.

to resist the pressure for an immediate advance, but he had his own plans for an offensive when the spring rains ended.[353]

On the first of May, the Thirty-fifth Ohio was issued two-man shelter tents to replace the larger tents they had been using. The tents, made of light canvas, were issued in two halves about four feet square. Two men buttoned their halves together to make a shelter just large enough for both of them. If much smaller, the new tents were much easier to transport. No wagons were required. Each man merely folded up his half and put it in his pack. The tents were quickly dubbed "dog tents" because of their size and shape, and over time became known as "pup tents." Simple, lightweight, and adequate for temporary shelter, pup tents are a military success story. The same basic design is still in use by the U.S Army more than 140 years later.[354]

On May 10, after only a few weeks in command, General Schofield was promoted to command the Department of Missouri. When Schofield left for his new assignment, Gen. John M. Brannan assumed command of the division. A deeply religious man, Brannan had come to the Army of the Cumberland from duty on the South Carolina coast. The Cumberlanders looked down on the "paper collar" soldiers of the Eastern army, or anything resembling it, and Brannan was also an artillery officer with little infantry experience. The new commander was initially thought to be too stylish and too formal. That attitude would reverse itself with experience, but when the change first occurred, the men in ranks were not pleased.[355]

As June began, the Army of the Cumberland, thanks to the efforts of the Third Brigade and others, dominated the area around Triune, and signs of change began to appear. There was a general tightening up all around. Inspections by division staff officers became more frequent. Directions came to be prepared to move at any time with rations for ten days. There was a desperate need for cavalry and artillery horses, and the beautiful teams so carefully collected and groomed by Wilkinson Beatty had to be traded in for "scrubby" army mules. On the heels of this directive came another one to identify all nonessential baggage and send it to Nashville for storage. For a long time, the Persimmons had been able to carry a much larger amount of baggage than the other regiments around them. That luxury was gone forever. From that day on, the regiment was allotted three wagons for carrying necessary items and personal baggage was greatly restricted. Officers could carry up to eighty pounds on one mule. Enlisted men were not to be burdened with such luxury. They were restricted to one blanket, two pairs of drawers, two pairs of socks, one jacket, one pair of pants, one pair of shoes, and one hat. After putting on the clothes he would wear, each soldier had exactly one set of drawers and one pair

353. Grebner, *We Were the Ninth*, 125; Nosworthy, *Bloody Crucible*, 155; Bradley, *Tullahoma*, 11.

354. Grebner, *We Were the Ninth*, 125.

355. Ibid., 129; Daniel, *Days of Glory*, 239–40.

of socks to put in his knapsack.[356]

Gen. Gordon Granger, placed in command of the army's Reserve Corps, inspected the brigade and its camp on June 4. After the inspection, brigade and division drill was conducted for his benefit. While the review was going on, the sound of cannon fire was heard from the direction of Franklin. A rebel force had crossed the Harpeth River and moved on the Union garrison there.[357]

As the review came to a close at six o'clock, Granger directed that an investigation be made of the cannonading, and at 9:00 p.m. Colonel Van Derveer started the brigade for Franklin. It had been a hot and sultry day, and as it cooled off, clouds settled in for an extended rain. It was remembered ever after as the darkest night anyone had ever experienced. The surface of the road was uneven, wet, slippery, and invisible in the dark. Men were constantly losing their balance and falling. It took ten hours to make the march, and when the Persimmons reached the outskirts of town the next morning at dawn, they were tired, sleepy, and exasperated. Rather than attack the enemy works, Van Derveer ordered Battery F to bombard the Confederates, who apparently believed that Union commanders had decided to abandon Franklin and had invested the few defenders remaining there. Not prepared to fight for the town, the rebel raiders returned to the west side of the Harpeth. First Sergeant Foord reported that they had arrived "just in time to save the place—All was prepared to surrender." The rest of the day was used to reconnoiter the vicinity and drive off the few remaining Confederate scouts. On the morning of June 6, the brigade returned to Triune, finding "a splendid supper waiting for us which we devoured."[358]

On June 11, the rebels made a raid on the camp at Triune. Managing to capture about one hundred horses and mules, they were unwilling to press the attack. Both sides suffered minor casualties, and Colonel Van Derveer was apparently unwilling to go out and stir up a larger fight. For the next ten days, the finishing touches were placed on preparations for the upcoming campaign. Drilling was intensified, equipment was inspected, and clothing was replaced and made ready. After months in camp, the Persimmons were ready to move. The news from Virginia was bad, and the men of the Army of the Cumberland, having lost faith in the Army of the Potomac, had come to believe victory was up to them. When the word finally came down, the Thirty-fifth struck camp with alacrity.[359]

In the last week of June, the Thirty-fifth left Triune to begin its last journey

356. Bradley, *Tullahoma*, 46, 53; Keil, *Thirty-fifth Ohio*, 113; Grebner, *We Were the Ninth*, 129; Bishop, *Story of a Regiment*, 111.

357. Bishop, *Story of a Regiment*, 111.

358. Grebner, *We Were the Ninth*, 129; Foord Papers, 4–6 June 1863; U.S. War Department, *War of the Rebellion*, Ser. no. 34, p. 360.

359. Grebner, *We Were the Ninth*, 129; Foord Papers, 7–22 June; Catton, *Hallowed Ground*, 272; Daniel, *Days of Glory*, 242.

into the South on the Murfreesboro pike, arriving in that town the same day. After three months in camp, the march tired them out, but they were rewarded with a good campsite. They halted in a wheat field that had been cut and shocked providing comfortable beds of straw. Minus all the wagons they were used to, the Thirty-fifth had traveled lighter than ever before. The reductions were just the beginning. By campaign's end, they would be carrying little more than the clothes they were wearing.[360]

360. Foord Papers, 23 June 1863.

CHAPTER 8

No Dread in Their Minds

June to September 1863

The Rebs Had Departed

The drive south began Tuesday June 23, 1863. The land between Murfreesboro and the Confederate logistical base at Tullahoma provided less than ideal terrain for military operations. A line of hills several hundred feet high ran south of Murfreesboro, and the Army of the Cumberland had to cross them at one of four gaps, Hoover's, Liberty, Bellbuckle, or Guy's, since the roads and the railroad went through those same spots. Forty miles past the gaps, the deep and narrow Duck River offered few useful crossing points, and once across the Duck, things got even worse. Tennessee below the Duck River was a series of rocky hills and dense oak thickets rising up toward the Cumberland Plateau also known as the barrens. The ground was clay covered with a veneer of topsoil that had very little capacity for holding water. Fifteen miles below the Duck River, the Elk River ran down out of the barrens, providing the last barrier before Tullahoma.

The general movement of the Army of the Cumberland proceeded along four lines. General McCook's Twentieth Corps departed Murfreesboro for Liberty Gap as Thomas's Fourteenth Corps left the same town for Hoover's Gap. On the far left, General Crittenden's Twenty-first Corps moved on McMinnville. General Granger's Reserve Corps left Triune and headed for Shelbyville via Eagleville. Upon leaving their camps at Triune on June 24, a day after the cavalry advanced, General Brannan's division, including the Third Brigade, marched on the left flank of Granger's corps following a generally southern course on country roads. After participating in a feint toward Shelbyville, Brannan's division was to rejoin Thomas's corps at Hoover's Gap.[361]

The Third Brigade that marched behind Col. Ferdinand Van Derveer was a

---

361. Keil, *Thirty-fifty Ohio*, 114.

formidable force. The Second Minnesota, commanded by Van Derveer's old friend James George, and Gustav Kammerling's Ninth Ohio were proven combat veterans. No better regiments existed anywhere in the United States. The Thirty-fifth Ohio, under the ailing Lt. Col. Charles Long, had not yet been in a full-scale battle, but its men were experienced campaigners and skirmishers who had been under enemy fire more than once. Even the men of the Eighty-seventh Indiana, the newest regiment in the brigade, had been under fire at Perryville and could not be considered anything but veterans. In addition to his four infantry regiments, Van Derveer commanded three artillery batteries. They included the Fourth Michigan Battery under Capt. Josiah Church; Battery I, Fourth U.S. Artillery commanded by 1st Lt. Frank Smith; and Battery C of the First Ohio Light Artillery under Capt. Daniel Southwick.[362]

Steady rain began to fall on the morning the regiment set out, and it would be seventeen days before anyone again saw his shadow. It affected every man, mammal, milestone, movement, meal, and moment until the middle of July. If it wasn't raining, it was getting ready to. It soaked clothing and food and seeped into rifle barrels and trigger mechanisms. It permeated tents, destroyed roads, and made forbidding barriers of even small streams. The Persimmons walked in it, ate in it, slept in it, and fought in it. Days were spent watching water run off a hat rim and nights were spent in a vain effort to dry out.

The thin, sandy topsoil of the region sat loosely on top of a clay layer, and roads built on this substrate became a sticky morass in the presence of water. The continuing downpour quickly turned the roads into rivers of mud, and the regiment's baggage wagons became mired in the muck. When the regiment bivouacked for the night, the wagons were nowhere in sight, so the men built large campfires and stood around trying to dry out. It was midnight before the wagons arrived and shelter tents were erected. In spite of the rain, mud, and skirmishes with swarming rebel cavalry, spirits remained high. After weeks of drilling in camp, to be campaigning again was exhilarating. Every step taken was one step closer to ending the war. After making a brief mention of the rain, First Sergeant Foord of Company K noted that he had "a splendid supper and retired to dream of home and the gal I left behind."[363]

At midday on Thursday the twenty-fifth, Brannan's troops caught up with McCook's behind Liberty Gap near the village of Bell Buckle. The Twentieth Corps was then "contending for possession of the gap," but a large number of McCook's men had not yet arrived. To make up the shortfall, Brannan was ordered to remain at Liberty Gap in support of McCook's advance until the rest of his corps arrived. The Thirty-fifth Ohio went into line of battle and stacked arms. After a brief respite in the morning, the rain resumed in the afternoon, persisting until Brannan was relieved early in the evening. Some light was left,

---

362. U.S. War Department, *War of the Rebellion*, Ser. no. 34, p. 412.

363. Foord Papers, 24 June 1863; Grebner, *We Were the Ninth*, 130; Bradley, *Tullahoma*, 36.

so the march continued for several more miles before camp was established. First Sergeant Foord and Pvt. Anthony Korpal didn't particularly care to sleep on the wet ground, so they went in search of bedding. After a two mile hike, they found a farm and got straw to sleep on as well as cheese and a baloney sausage. On the way back, Foord fell into a rain-swollen creek and nearly drowned. No doubt the food was good, but the straw turned out to be wasted effort. By morning, the campground had become a shallow lake and everyone lay in the water. [364]

Wet roads always slowed a march, but in order to make the junction with Thomas's corps, Brannan's division was going to have to make some rapid movements. Baggage had already been greatly reduced at Triune, but the order went out to reduce even further. The Persimmons once again sorted through their packs and "many a nice and valuable thing was left behind." The requirement to once again leave behind valuable things set Lieutenant Keil of Company C to ruminating over the wasteful nature of armies. "An army is an engine for destruction—not of life only, but of property, no matter how valuable. The man whose 'bump' of destruction is not fully developed will never make a successful general."[365]

Company K experienced the full impact of the weather when they were detailed to guard a wagon train going to Murfreesboro for rations. With fifty-two wagons in train, the company left camp on Garrison Creek at 3:00 a.m. on Friday, June 26. After seven long, sopping, but uneventful hours on the road, the train arrived in Murfreesboro and began to load. While the teamsters and garrison troops loaded the wagons, the men of Company K took the opportunity to forage in the abundant surroundings of the depot. They scrounged some nice apple pies for dinner, but after only an hour at the depot, the wagon train turned back south. The rain was still falling in sheets and the roads were getting worse by the minute. The men had to slog along as best they could along the sides of the road, and at least one complained of losing his haversack full of food along the way. Company K stumbled through the mud all night and did not halt until 3:00 a.m. After breakfast and a couple hours of rest, they were back on the road at six o'clock and spent another drenched day marching in the mud beside the wagons. By the time they rejoined the regiment that afternoon, they all "looked pretty hard and tired of marching." But the day was still not over for the saturated men of Company K. The Thirty-fifth Ohio marched six more miles before halting at Manchester about 10:00 p.m.[366]

Rations were issued before the regiment moved out the next morning. By the time they reached Beech Grove at the northern entrance to Hoover's Gap, other units in Thomas's corps were moving into the gap and engaging the Con-

---

364. Keil, *Thirty-fifty Ohio*, 114; Foord Papers, 25 June 1863.

365. Keil, *Thirty-fifty Ohio*, 114.

366. Foord Papers, 26–27 June 1863; U.S. War Department, *War of the Rebellion*, Ser. no. 34, p. 450; Daniel, *Days of Glory*, 271.

federates attempting to block it. The Thirty-fifth ran into rebel pickets, drove them across a creek, and then went into camp behind its own line of pickets. Picket firing continued all night, and at one point a cannonball flew over the camp. No one was injured, but no one got any sleep either. At 3:00 a.m., the Persimmons were standing in line of battle and there they remained until after daylight, when a brief reconnaissance was made toward the creek after breakfast. After discovering nothing but tracks where Confederate cavalrymen had come to water their horses, the regiment stood waiting until nine o'clock when orders were at last received to move up into the gap.[367]

Thomas's regiments were working their way up both sides of the gap as fast as they could, but there were a lot of them still waiting. When the Thirty-fifth moved to the left to support some field artillery batteries ascending the ridge, they found themselves in a line of regiments six deep waiting to go up. As the climb into the hills began, things appeared to be quieting down. In particular, a Confederate battery that had been firing steadily had ceased and word spread that the rebels were abandoning the gap. No sooner than the news went out, a boom sounded from the woods only a short distance to the right of the regiment. The battery that everyone thought had retreated had only changed firing positions and was now in position to rake the Thirty-fifth's line. Before that could happen, Col. Moses Walker's First Brigade of Brannan's division, appeared in the trees and "came suddenly upon the saucy rebel battery, which considered it prudent to withdraw more hastily than it advanced."[368]

The most exciting event of the day involved Dr. Charles Wright, the regiment's assistant surgeon. Wright's horse, with him astride, got "in the way of a rebel cannonball" that passed clear through the beast. The animal was thrown violently by the force of the impact, and "the effect was to toss the doctor into the air some distance coming to the ground somewhat like a flying squirrel." As spectacular as it all had been, Dr. Wright picked himself up off the ground and was entirely unhurt. Soldiers are a tough crowd, and as Wright put his saddle on his shoulder and went to the rear, "the boys unmercifully guyed him." Part of the Fourth Ohio Cavalry came to support the advance, and skirmishing continued throughout the rest of the day during which several men were slightly wounded. Colonel Van Derveer was pleased with his men's performance. "Yesterday, our brigade took the advance and had a heavy skirmish most of the day—they done finely—we drove the enemy before us for several miles, without the loss of a man—Capt. L'Hommedieu got a buckshot through his leg—it will only disable him for a few days." Despite the excitement, the Persimmons spent most of the day lying on the sodden ground and, once again, most of the night trying to get their clothes dry.[369]

After the previous day's fighting, June 30 was a very quiet day. The men

---

367. Keil, *Thirty-fifty Ohio*, 114; Foord Papers, 28–29 June 1863.
368. Keil, *Thirty-fifty Ohio*, 114–15; Foord Papers, 29 June 1863; U.S. War Department, *War of the Rebellion*, Ser. no. 34, p. 450.

spent their time sleeping, writing letters, and even though they had been wet all week, some of them went swimming. When the Persimmons formed up on the morning of July 1, the weather was oppressive. The only breaks in the steady downpour were several violent thunderstorms that passed overhead at various times during the day. Creeks that would have been ankle high in normal times were running dangerously deep and swift. One sodden Buckeye trudging though the mud, high water, and wet brush noted that the entire "situation was abominable. *Reach Tullahoma, hit the enemy's fortifications, drive the enemy out of there, thrash him yet another time*—these hopes sustained us. We were sure of victory, would we but be released against him." The town of Tullahoma, so desired by the Union army, was a rough-hewn place. Built as a construction camp for the Nashville and Chattanooga Railroad less than fifteen years before, it consisted of a few dozen buildings on dirt streets. It had been the winter camp of Bragg's Army of Tennessee, but as the Persimmons took up positions along Crumpton's Creek, opposition was light and scattered.[370]

The greatly desired victory was not to be had. Civilians reported that the Army of Tennessee was evacuating the town, and at first light, it quickly became obvious that the rebels had slipped away in the night. The rear guard left behind by General Bragg was quickly overpowered and driven back. Van Derveer's Third Brigade led the advance during the day and was in constant contact with the enemy as they moved through the jack oak forests. Walking across wet ground as water dripped off the trees overhead ensured that everyone in the Thirty-fifth Ohio remained soaking wet. The small-scale fighting went on all day but casualties were few. As the Thirty-fifth entered Tullahoma late in the afternoon, "the entrenchments bravely stood their grounds, but the rebs had departed." The hapless Confederate rear guard was finally pushed across the Elk River, abandoning most of their equipment and rifles as they leapt in. The Persimmons watched as several of them drowned trying to swim the flooded stream. Another hundred, not desperate enough to enter the flood, were taken prisoner.[371]

Confederate general Bragg had taken his army across the Elk and burned the railroad bridge behind them. Brannan's division was one of two sent to immediately cross the Elk at Jones's Ford. The rain had raised the level of the river and the crossing was anything but easy. The men made bundles of their clothes and accouterments and stuck them on the end of their bayonets. Rifles, with bundles attached, were held at "support arms" with one arm while grip-

369. Keil, *Thirty-fifty Ohio*, 115; Bishop, *Story of a Regiment*, 113; U.S. War Department, *War of the Rebellion*, Ser. no. 34, p. 421; Van Derveer to wife, 30 June 1863, Van Derveer Family Collection.

370. Keil, *Thirty-fifty Ohio*, 115–16; Bradley, *Tullahoma*, 81; Daniel, *Days of Glory*, 274.

371. Keil, *Thirty-fifty Ohio*, 115–16, Foord Papers, 2 July 1863; Grebner, *We Were the Ninth*, 130; Bradley, *Tullahoma*, 86.

ping ropes strung across the river with the other. The trick was to balance the awkward bundle while leaning into the four-foot-deep current to stay upright. "The calm and the agile got themselves and their possessions to the other side. The shaky and the timid lost one thing or another, and some lost everything." During the three hours it took to get across, the scene at the crossing site was "mottley, and highly humorous to behold."[372]

Nothing of Importance Occurred

Brannan's division, along with that of Gen. Lovell Rousseau, crossed the river in good order on July 3 and quickly pushed the enemy picket line away from its banks. This action effectively ended the pursuit of Bragg's army. The river continued to rise, and no further units were able to cross that day. Rain had continued to fall since the day the Thirty-fifth left Triune, and the men no longer paid any attention to the water falling from the sky. They and everything they owned were soaked to the bone, so they simply stood in the rain making no attempt to get under any cover. Every stream in the region was running "bank full, while the roads were in a condition such that cannot be described." The Thirty-fifth Ohio and the other regiments on the south side of the Elk River were in a bit of a precarious position. They quickly ate up the rations they had with them, and supply trains could not get across the swollen river.[373]

On July 4, the regimental band rudely awakened the Persimmons by playing "Hail Columbia" in honor of Independence Day. All day long, the men played games, sang patriotic songs and fired several cannon salutes. The rations had been eaten up, so there wasn't much in the way of food to celebrate with. A foraging party went out but was only able to locate some potatoes. The regiment marched about two miles on the Winchester road and went into camp again. A couple of hogs were liberated that evening, but they were hardly enough, and everyone was hungry. Even so, the men weren't really concerned. They had experienced lean times during the Perryville campaign and had learned how to get by. They were convinced they would "not starve while there is anything in the land." On the fifth, foragers were able to find enough potatoes and a cow or two to keep them for another day. Pvt. Sylvester Clark was desperate enough to swim the river in search of food. In exchange for risking his life, he obtained a few potatoes and a young chicken. Any glumness over the shortage of food was overcome by news of the Union victory at Gettysburg.[374]

---

372. Keil, *Thirty-fifty Ohio*, 116; Grebner, *We Were the Ninth*, 131; Bishop, *Story of a Regiment*, 113.

373. Keil, *Thirty-fifty Ohio*, 116–17; Foord Papers, 3 July 1863; Catton, *Hallowed Ground*, 273.

Spirits fell a little on July 6. The rain had not let up in the least, so it had been a wet and sleepless night. Foragers found nothing but a few blackberries. The berries were added to a little left over beef that was roasted over fires. Even this small meal lifted everyone's spirits a little, leading First Sergeant Foord to say he still felt stout and could march if "it was particularly necessary." Still, the lack of food was having its effect. Foord was a spiritually minded man, but he admitted that he didn't feel much like praying just then. He went to bed early instead. [375]

On July 7, Major Boynton felt the time for sitting idly by was past. When the retreating rebels burned the railroad bridge, the structure had not collapsed. The beams on which the floor had rested were still intact. Boynton quickly organized a supply line where rations were transported across the river by men who "'cooned it across' pushing packages of supplies ahead of themselves" on the beams. It wasn't easy, but by "dint of perseverance and hard work," enough supplies were obtained to end the hunger. When the supply train arrived in camp at midnight, the famished men immediately emerged from their tents to get their share. There was no delay. Food preparation began immediately, and "cooking and eating commenced and continued until daylight."[376]

The fare was primarily hardtack and meat, but First Sergeant Foord declared it to be "a splendid breakfast. Best I ever had. Bully for crackers the Staff of life." Foord felt so good he went swimming that afternoon and cheered when a thirty-six-gun salute was fired for General Meade. Celebrations continued on July 8 with the announcement that Vicksburg had also fallen and the arrival of a wagon train laden with rations. Along with the food came a rumor, probably from news of John Hunt Morgan's great raid that the railroad had been torn up between Louisville and Nashville.[377]

The campaign to capture Chattanooga was as much one of logistics as maneuver. The Army of the Cumberland was short of transportation, and efforts to correct the situation had only been mildly successful. The reduction of regimental wagon teams had been one result, but the lack of transportation now resulted in a delay while the corn crop ripened. Unable to adequately supply itself with forage over the single rail line and country roads available, General Rosecrans was determined to wait for the corn crop to come in, so the army could subsist off the land. The weeks of waiting were a time of relative ease for the Thirty-fifth Ohio.

Drilling and inspections continued, but there doesn't appear to have been any extensive effort to prepare fortifications. Most of the time was spent making life a little easier. Rations were arriving regularly, but foraging details went out everyday. It was blackberry season, and large quantities of the fruit were

---

374. Foord Papers, 4–5 July 1863; Grebner, *We Were the Ninth*, 131.
375. Foord Papers, 6 July 1863.
376. Keil, *Thirty-fifty Ohio*, 117.
377. Ibid.; Foord Papers, 7–8 July 1863.

eaten fresh or stewed by the soldiers. Other meals, like fried crackers and potatoes, if less appetizing were much more simple to prepare. Poles and forked
sticks were cut by the thousands in order to make beds, and the men built
arbors and bowers over their tents to make them cooler. Informal gatherings
around the sutler's tent were common, while the band gave concerts in the evening. The war news was generally good, and everyone was in fine spirits.

Richard Foord's activities were typical of the few weeks between the capture of Tullahoma and the advance on Chattanooga. Life was easy, and his
diary contains frequent entries like "nothing to do" and "nothing of importance
occurred." On days when no drill was scheduled, Foord would read, visit, or
even go back to sleep after roll call. Free afternoons were spent at the sutler's
or swimming. Foord helped collect blackberries and built an arbor over his own
tent. When it was finished, he immediately tried it out by napping in its shadows for three hours. Foord was a man who enjoyed reading. On July 13, he
"took the Cincinnati paper into the woods and read all afternoon," and the next
day he "got a Nashville Union paper and perused it all morning." He wrote letters home, particularly to his fiancée Laura, and was quite pleased to receive a
photograph from her.[378]

The camp at Tullahoma provided opportunities for visiting friends and
family in the Sixty-ninth Ohio which had also been recruited in Butler County.
Dr. Landis got to spend some time with his brother, Frederick, discussing the
state of things. Over in Company K, First Sergeant Foord also enjoyed visiting
with friends from home. His friend, Lt. Jake Schaffer of the Sixty-ninth, came
by on more than one occasion. On one particular July day, Foord found Schaffer in a very expansive mood. "He looks well after his march and said he liked
soldiering—bully but *I can't see it*." Closer to home, Lt. David Stiles of Company K was on detail to brigade headquarters as the Commissary for Musters,
and Foord spent one morning with him.[379]

While the Persimmons were relaxing in camp, the folks back home were
having a little excitement. John Hunt Morgan's Confederate raiders were raising a ruckus in Indiana and Ohio, and Butler County was up in arms. Seven
hundred and three men from the city of Hamilton were formed into volunteer
militia companies on July 13. This group, larger than most regiments currently
in the field, needed a commander, and Capt. Ransford Smith, back in town
since March with his political connections, was selected for the job. Additional
volunteer militia from Butler, Preble, and Montgomery counties in Ohio
arrived in town followed by even more from Indiana, until more than five thousand men were wandering around in a city with a normal population of seventy-two hundred. The excitement ended as quickly as it started, when
Morgan's men moved on into eastern Ohio, and Smith and the others went back

---

378. Foord Papers, 8–21 July 1863.
379. Lincoln Landis, *From Pilgrimage to Promise* (Westminster, Md.: Heritage
Books, 2007), 16; Foord Papers, 15–19 July 1863.

to their normal routines.[380]

On July 15, Lt. Col. Charles Long, suffering from severe rheumatism, conducted the regimental drill. It was his last official function with the Persimmons. His resignation for medical disability was accepted on the seventeenth, and he left the same day. The regimental historian later noted that it could "be truthfully said that no one took a deeper interest, or was prouder of the organization than he." Those were probably polite words intended for later generations. Whether because of his extended illness or his conniving, Long had behaved in a way that most of the Persimmons didn't care for. The men were happy to see him go, and Colonel Van Derveer didn't seem to mind much either. "Col. L," he wrote to his wife, "had become very unpopular." [381]

Major Boynton was immediately promoted to take his place and Captain Budd of Company A was promoted to major. On July 18, the Thirty-fifth Ohio moved to Decherd, and there the paymaster finally caught up with them again. Each man received four months pay. The soldiers of Van Derveer's regiments were intimately familiar with the works they were occupying. They had built them when they passed through the town the year before under General McCook. On the July 25, the regiment made one more move to Winchester, again camping in the same field they had the year before. There they remained until the campaign to capture Chattanooga began. Reverend Charles Boynton of Cincinnati, the father of Major Boynton, visited the camp at Winchester and spoke to all of the regiments in the brigade. For the Persimmons, who had been without a chaplain for well over a year and had not heard a sermon in all that time, Boynton's presence was a bit of a novelty. Mr. Boynton, generally regarded as "a very good, kind, and pious man," drew sizable crowds when he spoke and some of the men wished he could stay on.[382] [Note: Charles Boynton, an active abolitionist in Cincinnati, went on to become chaplain of the U.S. House of Representatives in 1865.]

Of more worldly interest was a visit that Captain L'Hommedieu made to Colonel Van Derveer seeking assistance in a personal matter. L'Hommedieu knew Van Derveer was expecting a visitor from home soon, and he wanted the visitor to do him a favor. He had left a demijohn of whiskey in Louisville some time back, and he was hoping it could be brought to him in Tennessee. While it seems innocuous on the surface, the request was a fleeting glimpse into L'Hommedieu's future.[383]

---

380. Jim Blount, "Hamilton on alert as Confederate raiders bypass city," *Journal-News*, 9 July 2003.

381. Foord Papers, 17 July 17 1863; Keil, *Thirty-fifty Ohio*, 236; Van Derveer to wife, 20 July 1863, Van Derveer Family Collection.

382. Foord Papers, 17 July 1863; Grebner, *We Were the Ninth*, 132; Bircher, *Drummer Boy's Diary*, 42.

383. Van Derveer to wife, 8 August 1863, Van Derveer Family Collection.

I'll Find a Regiment That Will

In addition to the shortage of transportation, the geography of Tennessee presented still more natural obstacles to the Army of the Cumberland. The generally difficult nature of the terrain and the vastness of the area of operations made military operations in Tennessee problematic. The advance on Chattanooga was made over the Cumberland Plateau that stretched all the way to the banks of the Tennessee River. A barren range, it was described by those who passed through it as "a splendid primeval forest void of human habitation" that provided "a marvelous view of eastern Tennessee's handsome valleys." Beautiful as it was, it provided little in the way of forage. The forests seemed endless and the roads were mostly backwoods lanes. Once through the mountains, there was still the mighty Tennessee River to cross, and the mountainous terrain on the south side of the river would be the most difficult of all. Four main ridges below the city ran in a northeasterly direction separated from each other by narrow valleys. Creeks passed through each valley carrying runoff from the dry ridges into the river. Also south of the river was the Confederate Army of Tennessee, seemingly prepared to contest the Union advance. [384]

In the middle of August, Company C got bad news. Their company commander had died. Captain Earhart, a skilled engineer, had been detailed to the brigade staff as topographical engineer. His skill was so obvious that he had quickly been advanced to the division staff. While serving in what should have been a safer posting, Earhart had taken ill and died of a fever in Winchester, Tennessee, on August 10, 1863. The cause of his death was listed as an inflammation of the bowels, and Colonel Van Derveer reported that Earhart had suffered considerably before he died. General Brannan issued a special order to the division that described Earhart as a man of "zeal and undoubted ability" who had won the respect and admiration of everyone he had come in contact with. Brannan reported that the division had lost a capable officer and society had lost a "worthy and respected member."[385]

While the Persimmons waited and prepared for their next campaign, Capt. Nathaniel Reeder of Company D found himself in deep trouble through a series of confusing circumstances. He had not been with the regiment for more than a year. Left behind in the hospital at Somerset, Kentucky, in February 1862, Reeder had been on sick leave in either Hamilton or Louisville for the next four months. In August, Reeder had been ordered to return to his regiment, but the order was countermanded by General Boyle, and he was reassigned to the barracks in Louisville until April of the following year. Apparently no one in Louisville bothered to inform the Thirty-fifth Ohio of the situation, and the

---

384. Nosworthy, *Bloody Crucible*, 313, 315; Grebner, *We Were the Ninth*, 139.

385. Cone, *Biographical*, 347–48; Van Derveer to wife, 11 August 1863, Van Derveer Family Collection.

regiment had considered Reeder absent without leave the entire time. It is not clear where Reeder was in May of 1863, but in June, he was brought back to the Thirty-fifth Ohio under arrest. [Note: Butler county histories indicate that Reeder's wife died during the summer of 1863.] On August 12, 1863, Reeder was convicted by a general court-martial and dismissed from the army. Later, after the case was more carefully reviewed, Reeder got his commission reinstated, but he was lost to the Thirty-fifth forever.[386]

On August 16, the Thirty-fifth Ohio, along with the rest of Brannan's division, left the fortifications around Decherd. The move turned out to be a bit of a false start. After marching two miles in a terrible thunderstorm and finding the road completely jammed with units having precedence, the brigade moved off the road and set up camp in a nondescript location that Ferdinand Van Derveer described as "Sweetness Cove—Somewhere." The deluge rains of past weeks had finally ended and roads were passable. It was easy marching for the most part with plenty of blackberries, peaches, and cold spring water to nourish the masses. As the march continued, the regiment passed through University Point and camped on the grounds of the Southern Episcopal University. There was nothing in place yet except the foundation, but its great size was proof of its founders' lofty dreams. After passing through Jasper, Brannan's division halted along Battle Creek not far from Bridgeport, Alabama, on August 21. Brannan kept his men well back from the river as part of the effort to convince the Confederates that the army's main crossing would be at Chattanooga. It apparently had some effect, because Colonel Van Derveer, whose brigade was placed at the mouth of the creek, reported the next morning that five regiments of Confederate infantry posted on the opposite side of the river had left the night before in the direction of Chattanooga. Only one cavalry company remained on picket on the enemy's side of the river.[387]

Those rebel cavalrymen, not at all intimidated by being on their own, greeted the newcomers by peppering them with rifle fire. The distance prevented accuracy, but it was still annoying. The Third Brigade posted its own pickets and returned fire. After a couple of days of this useless activity, the opposing pickets came to an agreement and the exchanges of rifle fire were replaced with verbal ones. Persimmons on picket were greeted every morning with shouts of "Good morning, you d——d Yankees." After the pickets became more familiar with each other, the opposing sides bathed in the river without being harassed. Good swimmers on both sides would meet in the middle of the river to "swap lies, newspapers, and such while the pickets kept watch to see

386. *Cyclopedia*, 225; Compiled service record, Nathaniel Reeder, Capt., Co. D, 35th Ohio Inf.; Carded Records, Volunteer Organizations, Civil War; Records of the Adjutant General's office, 1780s–1917, Record Group 94; National Archives, Washington, D.C.

387. U.S. War Department, *War of the Rebellion*, Ser. no. 52, p. 113; Catton, *Hallowed Ground*, 275; Boynton, *Letters*, 11; Van Derveer to wife, 19 August 1863, Van Derveer Family Collection.

there should be no foul play or breech of confidence." Familiarity also brought a steady trickle of deserters from the south side of the river. One of them, a local man named Pendergrass, told Van Derveer that most of the troops on the south bank of the river had marched off toward Chattanooga after hearing erroneously that the Yankee army had already crossed at Bridgeport. Van Derveer also reported smoke from campfires on the opposite bank a short distance from where his brigade was camped.[388]

Work immediately began on a bridge across the creek and on rafts and dugouts for crossing the river. Erection of the bridge was the shared responsibility of Lt. Samuel House of Company A and Lt. Benjamin Miller of Company C. The plan was to build a crib in the middle of the stream and then place beams across the crib. Construction was accomplished by floating the frame at an anchor, and as each layer of logs was added, the crib sank into the creek. Once on the bottom, the entire structure would be anchored with stones. The mouth of the creek was filled rather deeply with backwater from the Tennessee River, and bridge building was no easy task while floating in midstream. During Lieutenant Miller's shift, the half-finished structure fell over into the creek, and logs drifted loosely across the water in all directions. Unfortunately for Miller, it happened just as Colonel Van Derveer walked by, and as one observer noted with great sarcasm, "the floating logs furnished a subject for complimentary remarks."[389]

The Persimmons did more than build bridges. In preparation for crossing the Tennessee River, the entire division was busy building just about anything that would float. They made huge dugout canoes from poplar trees and hid them out of sight in Battle Creek. Some of the canoes were big enough to carry fifty men and one raft was strong enough to carry artillery. Added to makeshift devices was a pontoon boat liberated from the locals some time before. Quite a flotilla had been prepared to get the Thirty-fifth Ohio and the rest of their division onto the rebel side of the river.[390]

On August 29, Colonel Van Derveer received orders to send troops across the Tennessee and reconnoiter crossings while driving off any rebel picket they encountered. It was quite a compliment as the Third Brigade troops would be the first Union soldiers to cross. Van Derveer offered the honor of being first to Colonel Bishop of the Second Minnesota, but Bishop felt that there was not sufficient means for getting safely over the river. Van Derveer, apparently perturbed, informed Bishop that "it's your privilege to accept the honor to cross first, but if not satisfied with the means at hand for crossing, I'll find a regiment that will." That regiment was the Thirty-fifth Ohio, and Captain L'Hommedieu's Company G was accorded the honor of being the first to cross the Ten-

---

388. Grebner, *We Were the Ninth*, 139; Bishop, *Story of a Regiment*, 115–16; U.S. War Department, *War of the Rebellion*, Ser. no. 52, p. 152.
389. Keil, *Thirty-fifty Ohio*, 120.
390. Boynton, *Letters*, 12.

nessee.[391]

The honor of being the first unit in the Army of the Cumberland to set foot on the south bank of the Tennessee River was a notable one and was given to a regiment that had had precious few. The Persimmons had waited a long time to be the first at anything, and were more than willing to accept the risks involved. They were lean, weather-beaten, well-trained soldiers who finally had the opportunity as a organization to do something on their own that would make a meaningful contribution to the destruction of the Confederacy. Excited at having been so honored and at being part of a very daring operation, nothing could have prevented them from going.

At midmorning on the thirtieth, the signal was given, and the Persimmons' own little homemade fleet swarmed out from the bushes covering the mouth of Battle Creek and paddled furiously for the south bank. In a matter of minutes, L'Hommedieu and his exhilarated soldiers were across the river having encountered no resistance. The pickets on the riverbank had fled, and after sending out patrols, L'Hommedieu reported back that there were no Confederate soldiers for two miles in any direction. With that information, the crossing commenced in earnest, and as the canoes and rafts returned for additional loads, impatient Persimmons who could swim piled their rifles, clothes, and accouterments on bundles of fence rails and pushed off for the far bank. The next day, Brannan was able to inform General Thomas that the entire Third Brigade was on the south side of the Tennessee River and in control of the planned crossing sites. In the following days, all of the Fourteenth and Twentieth Corps crossed the river on the heels of the Thirty-fifth Ohio without opposition and went into camp near Shellmound.[392]

After crossing the Tennessee River, Brannan's division moved over Sand Mountain and spent the night of September 3 at Graham's Spring at the foot of Raccoon Mountain not far from the monument marking the corners of Tennessee, Georgia, and Alabama. It was a slow march because the slopes were steep and the paths clogged with other units. The column passed Nick-A-Jack Cave, an important source of saltpeter for Confederate munitions, on the fourth but the poor condition of the road and the slow progress of the wagon trains created more delays. The regiment camped on the summit of Raccoon Mountain on the sixth and descended precipitous slopes into Lookout Valley the next day. There were coal pits on top of Raccoon Mountain, and a track ran up the side of the mountain to the mineral seams. John Baxter of Company C, well known as "a wild, reckless fellow," pushed one of the coal cars down the inclined track. Speeding down the slope at a high rate of speed just where the track began to level out, the car "ran into an old mule, which had done duty for many years hauling the cars out of the mine, and mangled it horribly. The car flew to pieces, and one of the wheels was found imbedded in a jack pine tree at a height

391. Keil, *Thirty-fifty Ohio*, 121.
392. Ibid.; Daniel, *Days of Glory*, 293; Boynton, *Letters*, 12.

of twenty-five feet. The balance of the car was strewn around within a radius of fifty yards."[393]

For three days after coming off the mountain, they remained in camp at Boiling Springs five miles below the village of Trenton, Georgia. As the Thirty-fifth Ohio was taking up positions on the western side of Lookout Mountain near Trenton, they learned that Crittenden's Twenty-first Corps had captured Chattanooga. The entire Army of the Cumberland was on the south side of the river ready to strike at the Army of Tennessee's flank. Up to that point, General Rosecrans had been served well by his caution, but now, believing that Bragg was in full retreat, Rosecrans sent his three corps pounding after him. One of the Thirty-fifth's staff officers reported, "The intention I believe, is, to get to the south of Chattanooga and for Bragg to run away as he did at Tullahoma." The regiment left Trenton on September 8 and advanced to Frick's Gap. On September 10, the Confederates nearly cut off and destroyed Negley's division on the west side of Missionary Ridge. The Third Brigade was ordered to cross over Lookout Mountain immediately, but the order was quickly countermanded and they went into camp at the base of Pigeon Mountain. The brigade conducted a reconnaissance toward Dug Gap on the twelfth, going as far as Davis's Crossroads without contacting any enemy. For two days the regiment camped in Chattanooga Valley beside one of the roads crossing the mountains. With no towns nearby, they had nothing to do but watch other units march back and forth behind them "in a way that seemed mysterious and without any definite or intelligible purpose." They were still convinced that no fighting would occur anytime soon. On September 14, Van Derveer's brigade was sent toward Lee and Gordon's Mill where they watched the fords across Chickamauga Creek for three days, bivouacking about six miles south of the mill near the west bank of Chickamauga Creek.[394]

The Persimmons were moving closer and closer to the rebel forces and could see their camps out in front of the Union picket line. The two sides were now looking "defiantly into each others faces." Rations were once again short, but no movement was made on the fifteenth, so foraging parties were able to go out. The corn they brought back was ground down and made into cakes for eating. The boys in Company K came across two hogs and some sweet potatoes that nobody had yet claimed and ate well that night. Weeks of marching had ruined the regiment's footwear, but some shoes arrived in camp so the men who had been going barefoot were reshod. Orders to be prepared to march were

393. Grebner, *We Were the Ninth*, 139; Bishop, *Story of a Regiment*, 117; Bircher, *Drummer Boy's Diary*, 44.

394. Foord Papers, 14–16 September 1863; Grebner, *We Were the Ninth*, 139; Bishop, *Story of a Regiment*, 117–18; U.S. War Department, *War of the Rebellion*, Ser. no. 50, p. 249, Ser. no. 52, pp. 247–48; Judson W. Bishop, "Van Der Veer's Brigade," *National Tribune*, 9 June 1904; Catton, *Hallowed Ground*, 276; Van Derveer to wife, 7 September 1863, Van Derveer Family Collection.

given on September 16, but the order to move did not arrive. Foragers used the delay to good advantage, finding more sweet potatoes and honey, they returned to camp about the time the provision train finally caught up. As the Persimmons were drawing five days rations, skirmishing broke out to the front. The opposing pickets continued firing at each other throughout the night.[395]

Recognizing the danger to his army at last, Rosecrans gave orders for a concentration. Crittenden's Twenty-first Corps was already at Lee and Gordon's Mill, so starting on September 17, General Thomas began to gradually shift his forces in that direction while holding on to Steven's Gap. The pass over the mountain at that place had to be held until the Twentieth Corps had crossed over. There are many accounts that describe the shadow of doom that was slowly spreading through the Army of the Cumberland during the second week of September 1863. The dawning realization of the danger to the army and the moves to avoid it cast a pall on the mood of the men in ranks. The Thirty-fifth Ohio was apparently out of step with the rest of the army in this case. The regimental historian recorded that the Persimmons "were contented, resting quietly under their shelter tents, or foraging roasting ears, sweet potatoes, and honey, with as much unconcern as though they were still north of the mountains and the Tennessee River. There was no dread in their minds that some disaster might happen any hour to the army, as was preying on the spirits of the chief in command. This was one of the instances when ignorance was bliss."[396]

Abraham Landis wasn't quite as sanguine as his fellow soldiers. He had received little news of his family in several weeks and was growing uneasy. Since meeting him in July, Landis had heard only silence about his brother Fred in the Sixty-ninth Ohio, and each successive day brought no letters from home. Knowing that campaigning made it hard for mail to be delivered didn't help much. Still, Abraham Landis was a hard man to keep down, and his letters home describing the beauty of the north Georgia hill country indicated he, too, was unaware of the seriousness of the army's situation.[397]

As the Thirty-fifth Ohio got on the road the men could see heavy clouds of dust on the eastern slope of the Chickamauga Valley. Marching "by the left flank," the Persimmons trod along in parallel to enemy columns marching "by the right flank." The two armies weren't much more than a mile from each other, and after the regiment had gone several miles, a small rebel force made a stab at the column. Dusty rebels skirmished briefly with dust covered Yankees before both resumed the march. The regiment crossed Chickamauga Creek and went into camp, but Confederate soldiers were still prowling around the countryside. Their campfires could be clearly seen to the east, and the men slept with their weapons ready. In the dark of the night, seven pickets, six from Com-

---

395. Foord Papers, 14–16 September 1863; Ohio Roster Commission, *Official Roster.*
396. Keil, *Thirty-fifty Ohio*, 126.
397. Landis, *From Pilgrimage to Promise*, 18.

pany E and one from Company K, were captured by the rebels.[398]

Having slept in the open the night before, the Persimmons decided to erect their tents on the morning of the eighteenth even though they were still under marching orders. Most of the day was spent watching infantry, artillery, and wagon trains pass along the road. Thousands of men passed the camp that day, and sometime during the day, one stopped. Capt. Oliver Parshall of Company F, who had been home on leave for the past few weeks, reported back to the regiment and was temporarily assigned to the brigade staff as one of Van Derveer's aides. It was not until 5:00 p.m. that orders came to move to Kelly's Farm, and tents had to be quickly packed away. It was a long slow march through clouds of dust and smoke. The column would move a few hundred yards, stop long enough to get stiff and cold, and then move on. Every man in the regiment was tired and sleepy, but they kept going. As the sky began to lighten, the Thirty-fifth could see units moving off of the road and into the woods in line of battle, and everyone was sure the fighting was about to begin.[399]

---

398. Foord Papers, 17 September 1863; Bishop, *Story of a Regiment*, 118.
399. Foord Papers, 18 September 1863; Bishop, *Story of a Regiment*, 119.

CHAPTER 9

A Furious Fire

September 19–20, 1863

Fifteen Minutes of Rest

It was a scruffy looking lot of men that moved onto the Lafayette road about 5:00 p.m. on the afternoon of September 18. Nearly all lean men, they wore faded blue blouses, baggy, tattered pants, and badly scuffed shoes. Rolled blankets were draped over one shoulder and tied at the opposite hip, and battered haversacks hung from their straps. The road ran parallel to the creek for several miles until it veered to the northeast toward Rossville three miles further on. The Thirty-fifth was once again participating in a race, this time to prevent the Army of Tennessee from getting around the Army of the Cumberland's left flank and block the road to Chattanooga. Missionary Ridge was to the left of the marching column as it passed through terrain dominated by limestone outcroppings and dense cedar thickets. There were several farms with open fields and log buildings, and from each ran narrow roads and trails to other farms and the bridges, but nowhere was there an open view of the entire area. There was no way to know exactly where the rebels were on the other side of the creek. The country road was choked with soldiers, artillery, and wagons. The Persimmons spent the night "alternately moving and standing, never halting long enough to stack arms and rest, and never moving more than a few rods at a time."[400]

The Thirty-fifth passed General Rosecrans's headquarters at Widow Glenn's house about first light and began to see regiments and batteries moving into the woods on the right side of the road. As they skirted the edge of the Dyer fields, the road was open ahead of them as far as anyone could see. The Persimmons passed by the foot of Snodgrass Hill and took the first road to the right arriving at Kelly's Farm just after sunrise. It had taken fifteen hours to

---

400. Bishop, "Van Der Veer's Brigade," 9 June 1904; Wiley, *Billy Yank*, 65.

cover the seven miles from Crawfish Springs and twenty-one of their number were scattered on the road behind them, having fallen out along the way. A few less than four hundred Persimmons, worn out and covered with dust, stood with the flag at the designated place in line about 7:00 a.m. on September 19. It had been a "most fatiguing march." Baird's division had already arrived at Elijah Kelly's Farm, so Brannan's Third Division marched past the farm to extend the Union line further toward Reed's Bridge Road. Just beyond Kelly's, the brigade was given twenty minutes for breakfast. The men dropped to the ground amid the shadows of early morning and did what veteran campaigners always did in such situations. Some of them were instantly asleep, but most started fires to brew coffee. Few of them noticed the messenger that tipped his hat to Van Derveer before handing over a long envelope.[401]

Bacon was being sliced and the coffee was just starting to get hot when orders rang out up and down the column. General Brannan had ordered Colonel Van Derveer and the Third Brigade to support the advance of McConnell's First Brigade by "move[ing] with haste" along the road that led to Reed's Bridge, seize Daffron Ford, and hold it. The air was rent with sulfurous language as much desired coffee, just starting to get hot, was either poured on the ground or quickly gulped down. Canteens and cartridge boxes were quickly shifted to more comfortable positions and shoulder straps were adjusted. After resting only fifteen minutes, the Thirty-fifth once again went pounding down the road. General Brannan was there to see them off, but the Persimmons probably took little heed of his words of encouragement. Some that had managed to at least warm their coffee sipped the lukewarm brew as they marched. Many more nibbled on hardtack, and every man trod along "relieving his indignant soul at every step of thoughts not to be quoted here, but at the time better uttered than suppressed." Continuing on down the Lafayette road in the direction of Chattanooga, Van Derveer's brigade passed beyond the extreme left of the Union line of battle still forming in the woods to the east.[402]

At McDonald's farm, the brigade turned onto a wagon path that led to Reed's Bridge road and halted. General Thomas had established his headquarters at the farm and watched as the brigade readied itself. Van Derveer's movement down Reed's Bridge Road would have been accomplished much faster had he kept his regiments in a marching formation, but no guide had been provided to him and there had been no time for reconnaissance. The Thirty-fifth Ohio had been caught unawares at Fishing Creek nearly two years before, and since that day, Van Derveer had scrupulously taken every precaution to prevent a repetition of that occurrence. With the knowledge that his brigade was the extreme left of the Army of the Cumberland and would soon face a deadly

---

401. U.S. War Department, *War of the Rebellion*, Ser. no. 50, pp. 427, 434; Boynton, *Military Park,* 28, 170, Bishop, "Van Der Veer's Brigade," 9 June1904; Cozzens, *Terrible Sound*, 127.

402. Bishop, "Van Der Veer's Brigade," 9 June 1904; Cozzens, *Terrible Sound*, 127.

enemy, Van Derveer chose the more cautious approach. He deployed the Third Brigade into a battle formation ensuring a slower advance.[403]

The Thirty-fifth took position to the right of the road with the Second Minnesota on the left. Battery I moved along the road between the two regiments. Skirmishers fanned out in front of the brigade while the Eighty-seventh Indiana formed a line behind the Thirty-fifth. The Ninth Ohio was still in the rear guarding the division wagon train and had not yet arrived. While the formations were squared away, officers walked up and down the ranks checking the men's equipment and speaking encouragingly to them, but with no chaplain on hand, there was no group religious observance. Throughout the ranks, individuals said their own private prayers in lonely silence. The knowledge that they would soon be desperately needed caused every man to give his rifle a serious going-over. Some men with old charges in the barrel called to the file closers to have them drawn out so a fresh round could be loaded. Not wanting to be burdened with excess accouterments on the verge of battle, packs and extraneous equipment were grounded and a small detail was left to guard them. Based on past experience, the men might have been leery of leaving their personal baggage behind, but the prospects for battle were very high. On another account, they had no concerns whatsoever. They had been with the Second Minnesota, Ninth Ohio, and Eighty-seventh Indiana for many long months. The trust in each regiment was implicit. From McDonald's, Van Derveer turned the Third Brigade at right angles, moving southeast down the road toward Reed's Bridge two miles distant.[404]

The Third Brigade left McDonald's and "advanced cautiously, though without losing time" toward Chickamauga Creek. The ground the regiment traversed was the top of a low ridge that sloped gently on either side. While appearing to be flat, it was actually undulating and heavily wooded. Though visibility was as much as two hundred yards in places, the undergrowth of scrub oak and stunted pine trees was enough to mask the rise and fall of the earth. The few clearings were small in size, and speed of movement was a relative thing. The Thirty-fifth moved as quickly as they could in the forest but not as quickly as Brannan would have liked. After progressing about a mile and a half, the men began to hear the rattle of musketry to the south on the right of the line where the First and Second Brigades of Brannan's division were engaging the enemy. Van Derveer had nothing but his own judgment to rely on as he moved toward contact. He had no idea how close he was to Reed's Bridge, but he did know where he needed to go. He moved his brigade toward the sound of battle.[405]

The slow passage through the trees was a time of great tension among the

403. McKinney, *Education in Violence*, 231.
404. U.S. War Department, *War of the Rebellion*, Ser. no. 50, pp. 428, 434; Boynton, *Dedication*, 177, 357; Bishop, "Van Der Veer's Brigade," 9 June 1904; Wiley, *Billy Yank*, 67–68.

men of the Thirty-fifth, but being in motion was much better than standing and waiting. The noise of battle to the front and the movement of the regiment toward that noise made it clear that they were only moments away from fighting. The ranks grew quiet with only calls from officers to "center dress" and "close up those gaps" to break the silence. Veteran campaigners, the Persimmons knew what was coming, but for the moment they could do nothing about it. Fear became a palpable presence, manifesting itself in dry throats, tight chests, and heavy sweat. It is possible that a few members of the regiment took the opportunity to slip away or lag behind. The junior officers of the companies marched behind the rest of the company to act as file-closers, halting any shirkers to get them back into the ranks. It wasn't as easy as it might seem, since they had to keep up with the moving formation and the trees limited vision and mobility. Any man who really wanted to get away could, but the great bulk of the men found a way to continue on. Some found strength in the Lord, while others trusted to chance. Many trusted in fate, believing that if it was their time to go, so be it. There was also a strong feeling that they were doing their bound duty to God and country, and so they kept moving steadily toward their first big battle. Nearly all of them thought of home, friends, and family.[406]

The men's voices may have been silenced, but moving in the woods was a noisy business. The ground was littered with dried leaves and broken tree limbs, so every step produced a distinct cracking sound. Branches scraped across clothing and equipment in the thick undergrowth. Having been bent forward by one man, green vines would come loose and slap into the next man. Over all of the noise being produced by the passage of the brigade, the sound of combat grew louder, and Van Derveer realized that he had passed the rebel line of battle and was in a position to take them on the flank. The brigade wheeled toward the enemy as skirmishers scrambled through the tangled thickets to stay out in front of their regiments. The brigade, coming over the top of a low ridge where the thin soil and rock outcrops formed a natural clearing, began to descend into open end of a U-shaped cove. As the Persimmons' skirmish line, led by Captain Daugherty of Company C that morning, began to advance, the Third Brigade received additional orders from General Brannan. The Second Brigade was hard-pressed and being forced slowly backwards. To support his center, Brannan directed that Van Derveer "should at once make an attack." The Persimmons had gone cold and hungry in Kentucky, marched to Alabama and back with General Buell, guarded fords, roads, and bridges around Nashville, and slogged over the mountains of Tennessee in the summer heat. Now, after two years of strenuous service, the hour of testing had arrived for the Thirty-fifth Ohio Volunteer Infantry.[407]

---

405. U.S. War Department, *War of the Rebellion*, Ser. no. 50, p. 428; Keil, *Thirty-fifth Ohio*, 136; Bishop, "Van Der Veer's Brigade," 9 June 1904.

406. Wiley, *Billy Yank*, 69–71; Nosworthy, *Bloody Crucible*, 247.

407. U.S. War Department, *War of the Rebellion*, Ser. no. 50, p. 428.

Well Directed Fire

About a quarter past nine, after moving a hundred yards or so into the woods, Third Brigade skirmishers began to exchange fire with their rebel counterparts. Word came back that an enemy formation was advancing toward him, and the expressions on men's faces began to tighten. With lips compressed, muscles tightening, and eyes fixed forward, peering anxiously for the enemy, they began to take on a malevolent look. Colonel Van Derveer halted his regiments and prepared to meet the enemy attack. The Thirty-fifth went into battle on the right of the line with the Second Minnesota beside them. Sandwiched in between the two infantry regiments was the first section of Battery I, Fourth U.S. Artillery. The second section was posted on a low rise to the right and sixty yards behind the Thirty-fifth. In line of battle, the soldiers peered through the undergrowth and trees as company officers reminded them to aim low. Behind the guns, the Eighty-seventh Indiana waited in reserve on the high ground in a rather exposed position. To reduce the effect of the enemy fire, they were lying down as Van Derveer had taught them. Skirmishing continued and men began to fall. Among the first was 1st Sgt. George Keever of Company A. The two sides exchanged fire for several minutes before the advancing butternut ranks came into view. As Battery I was moving into its firing positions, Confederate rifle fire began to strike the cannoneers. Lt. Frank Smith, commanding the battery noted that the "firing began before we had fairly taken our position, and 4 of my men were disabled before I could open fire on the enemy." Even so, the second section of Battery I quickly commenced firing, in the words of one observer, "making Rome howl." As the battle opened, clouds of thick gray smoke immediately began to spread murky shadows across the battlefield.[408]

The Confederates, dismounted troopers of George Dibrell's brigade from Forrest's cavalry division, were not looking for Van Derveer. They were attempting their own flanking movement against the Second Brigade, but upon realizing they were the ones being flanked, had turned into the oncoming Third Brigade and "opened a furious fire of artillery and musketry." The Persimmons wasted no time in returning fire and the two sides slugged it out at close range. The commencement of combat was actually a relief, as the fear most men felt was immediately lost in the excitement. Amidst the first few volleys, Sgt. Maj. Lucius Potter had his horse shot out from under him. Another bullet knocked Potter's hat from his head. The second section of Battery I was firing as rapidly as it could, and of necessity, the rounds were passing "uncomfortably near" the Thirty-fifth's line. Principle Musician Clark Castater, formerly of Company B, positioned to the rear of the firing line was so close to the muzzle of the roaring

408. U.S. War Department, *War of the Rebellion*, Ser. no. 50, pp. 428, 436–437; Keil, *Thirty-fifth Ohio*, 136, 140; Bishop, "Van Der Veer's Brigade," 9 June 1904; Cozzens, *This Terrible Sound*, 129; Mitchell, *Civil War Soldiers*, 72; Bogan, *Warren County's Involvement*, 21.

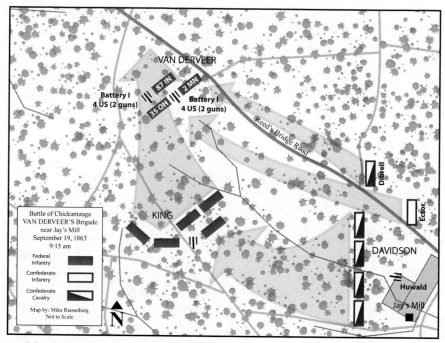

Map 1. *Van Derveer's brigade near Jay's Mill, September 19, 1863, at 9:15 a.m.*

cannons that the concussion caused blood to run from his ear. Dibrell's men were stopped, and their fire began to slacken about a quarter of ten. For several minutes, the firing ceased, but sometime after ten o'clock, a second Confederate brigade commanded by Matthew Ector bored in. In the midst of the heaviest firing, Colonel Boynton rode over to the left side of his line and reined in his horse beside a small tree. As he observed the fighting, a shell from Battery I hit the tree, barely a yard from where Boynton sat his horse, shattering the tree and throwing splinters in all directions.[409]

The Thirty-fifth firmly stood its ground as the violence swirled around them. Confederate artillery sent bursting shells over and into the line of battle. Men in the ranks heard the sound of bullets going by like "large blue flies that sometime flew high and at other times seemed to pass close to one's ears." Closely behind those sounds came the thudding noise of bullets striking flesh and bodies crashing to the ground. The Thirty-fifth Ohio had been in several skirmishes, but nothing in their two years of service compared to this. Military training has always been repetitious and redundant, but it is anything but mind-

409. U.S. War Department, *War of the Rebellion*, Ser. no. 50, pp. 428, 436–437; Keil, *Thirty-fifth Ohio*, 140; *Cyclopaedia of Butler County, Ohio,* 222; Wiley, *Billy Yank*, 71; U.S. Congress, *Congressional Record*, 50th Cong., Report 2629, June 19, 1888, (Washington, D.C.: Government Printing Office, 1880–1901).

less. On the contrary, it is a very well thought out process based on centuries of experience. After a soldier has repeated a task, like loading and firing a rifle, countless times, his subconscious mind remembers the steps when his conscious thought is otherwise engaged or overwhelmed. So it was with the Persimmons that September morning.[410]

The first shock of combat and the quick loss of sixty men staggered the regiment, but the men of the Thirty-fifth adjusted quickly. As the deafening rampage continued, they found that they soon became indifferent to the chaos. A feeling of savage excitement replaced what fear remained, and they began to shout. One of the peculiar characteristics of soldiers in combat was that men who would never utter a single swear word under normal circumstances cursed like sailors in the excitement of battle. Officers and sergeants quickly learned that violent cursing caught the attention of men more surely, and after adding the shouts of those who used it at all times, the firing line was a place of great profanity. Faces became blackened from frantically tearing open cartridges with their teeth, adding an even stranger countenance to features already strained and exaggerated. Among the fallen in the first minutes of battle were Captain Deardorf of Company K and Captain Lewis of Company I, both severely wounded. First Sergeant Richard Foord stepped up and took charge of Company K. Company I had to dig a little deeper into the ranks for a replacement. For the rest of the battle, Sgt. William Vanhorn led that company. Even as officers and men fell, the "accurate fire of the line" began to have a definite effect and enemy fire began to slacken. Nearly destroyed after another thirty minutes of "very fierce" fighting, Ector's rebels were "compelled to fall back." The Persimmons took a deep breath, reloaded, and waited for the next assault.[411]

Van Derveer had proudly watched his regiment perform "with as much coolness and accuracy as if on drill," but it was obvious to him that the Thirty-fifth had "already suffered severely in the engagement" and needed to catch its breath. He ordered the Eighty-seventh Indiana to come forward and replace the Thirty-fifth on the line. The Eighty-seventh laid down to allow the battered Buckeyes to pass through them. The passage of lines was done without incident, but what came next was certainly unexpected. The sound of firing swelled to the southeast. With no warning, retreating Union soldiers began to pass through the regiment's position. The regiments of King's brigade of regulars had been flanked by Confederate attacks and fled the field. Accounts of the mental state of the retreating regulars vary, but according to some first-hand battle reports these fleeing men "ran panic-stricken though and over" the regi-

---

410. Nosworthy, *Bloody Crucible*, 217.

411. U.S. War Department, *War of the Rebellion*, Ser. no. 50, pp. 428, 434, 436–437; Wiley, *Billy Yank*, 71–72; Mitchell, *Civil War Soldiers*, 54, 77; Nosworthy, *Bloody Crucible*, 253; David V. Stroud, *Ector's Texas Brigade and the Army of Tennessee* (Longview: Ranger Publishing, 2004), 135.

ment shouting for them to retreat before they, too, were overrun and disrupting preparations to meet this next rebel attack. Panic is generally contagious in combat, but not a man of the Thirty-fifth left the ranks. The routed soldiers were met with scorn all along the lines. While Van Derveer watched approvingly, Private Savage of Battery I used his rammer staff to pummel and curse a wildly retreating officer who had bumped into his gun after it had just been laid.[412]

The fleeing regulars passed and the Eighty-seventh Indiana arose to its feet just as a new line of butternut soldiers from Brig. Gen. Edward Walthall's Mississippi brigade made a lunge forward. The brigade delivered a "terrible volley" that stopped Walthall's men in their tracks. As the fight intensified, reinforcements began to arrive. Battery D, First Michigan Artillery and the Seventeenth Ohio of the First Brigade were sent to strengthen Van Derveer's right flank. Shortly afterwards, Col. Gustav Kammerling and his Germans had finally arrived from the division trains and rushed forward as quickly as they could into the gap between the Second Minnesota and the Michigan battery. Arriving just as Walthall was withdrawing, a disappointed Gustav Kammerling complained that the Ninth Ohio had missed the fight. Seeing no reason to waste all that enthusiasm, Van Derveer suggested Kammerling and his men could try to recapture the guns lost by the retreating regulars. With bayonets fixed and ready, they charged off to do just that.[413]

The Persimmons had gone into reserve behind the Eighty-seventh Indiana. The change-out of regiments was intended to provide time for the Thirty-fifth to catch its breath and reorganize, but the Confederates weren't cooperating and began to move to the left in order to get behind Van Derveer's line. After being repulsed earlier, Dibrell, a capable and enterprising officer, had taken his cavalrymen across Reed's Bridge Road with the intent of using a ravine north of the road to catch the Third Brigade on the flank. It was while Dibrell was maneuvering between 11:00 and 11:30 that King's retreat had passed through the regiment's position.[414]

The new Confederate attack could have been a very nasty surprise, but true to form, Van Derveer, knowing he was at the extreme end of the Union line, had skirmishers out to guard his flanks. After skirmishers warned of the approach, Dibrell's arrival was detected simultaneously by several officers of the brigade. From his vantage at the end of the line, Colonel Boynton could see that Battery I was now dangerously exposed. Without waiting for orders, Boyn-

412. U.S. War Department, *War of the Rebellion*, Ser. no. 50, pp. 431, 434; Boynton, *National Military Park,* 179.

413. U.S. War Department, *War of the Rebellion*, Ser. no. 50, pp. 428, 1058; Joseph C. McElroy, *Record of the Ohio Chickamauga and Chattanooga National Park Commission* (Cincinnati: Earhart and Richardson, 1896), 29.

414. U.S. War Department, *War of the Rebellion*, Ser. no. 50, pp. 431, 434; Boynton, *National Military Park,* 179.

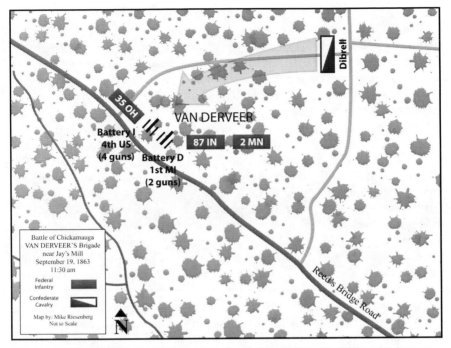

Map 2. Van Derveer's brigade near Jay's Mill, September 19, 1863, at 11:30 a.m.

ton began to shift the Thirty-fifth Ohio to meet the new rebel assault head on, "it being perfectly apparent that this alone could save the battery." Van Derveer had also interpreted the situation the same way and had already given the order for the rest of the brigade to change front. Maneuvering his brigade across the road, Van Derveer had no time to spare, but his well-trained soldiers executed the tricky maneuvers "rapidly and smoothly in the heat of battle." Van Derveer also made skillful use of the terrain and placed his regiments on a slight rise parallel to the road that offered some advantage to the defenders. The Third Brigade now formed an obtuse angle opening toward the enemy. The Second Minnesota was at the far right end of the line with the Eighty-seventh Indiana at the vortex of the angle. Lieutenant Rodney's section of Battery I was again sandwiched in between the two infantry regiments. On the base of the angle, Captain Church's Battery D, Lieutenant Stephenson's section of Battery I, and the Thirty-fifth faced the oncoming butternut lines. The sound of men moving through the woods could be heard clearly, and moments later, gray-clad soldiers in ranks four deep began to materialize under the trees.[415]

415. U.S. War Department, *War of the Rebellion*, Ser. no. 50, pp. 428, 434; Stephen E. Woodworth, *Chickamauga: A Battlefield Guide* (Lincoln: University of Nebraska Press, 1999), 16; Stephen E. Woodworth, "The Other Rock," *Civil War Times* 42 no. 4, 45–46; McElroy, *Record of the Ohio*, 7; Boynton, *Dedication*, 358; Boynton, *Letters*, 29.

The tables had been turned on Dibrell and his men. Expecting to surprise the Federals, they were instead surprised by the quick reaction of the Third Brigade. Van Derveer had the Second Minnesota and Eighty-seventh Indiana lie down and the prone soldiers were apparently unseen by the attacking Confederates. The rebels were entirely focused on the Thirty-fifth Ohio standing before them about a hundred yards away. The Thirty-fifth, with the support of the guns, bore the brunt of the fighting alone for several minutes, falling back slowly as the pressure on them mounted. Finally, as the enemy line drew opposite of Van Derveer's right wing, the Second and Eighty-seventh jumped to their feet and poured "a murderous and enfilading fire" into the rebel line. The rebels were staggered, but they were determined fighters and held their position. A second and third line of Confederates advanced and pushed to within forty yards of the Persimmons. The pressure was intense, and "it seemed as if the limit of human endurance even for iron veterans must soon be reached." For a moment, the Thirty-fifth wavered, and their firing became less regular. The rebels sensed their advantage and pushed even harder, but the men of the Thirty-fifth dug deeper into their hearts and then into their cartridge boxes and continued to fight.[416]

In battle, the world became a very small place for a rifleman in the line. He was able to see the enemy better than he was able to see the rest of his own regiment. With his attention to the front and smoke all around, he could see the few men in line next to him and he could hear officers shouting from behind, but the din of battle prevented normal communication. Once the firing started, the men of the Thirty-fifth didn't worry much about staying in neat ranks. Their primary concern was to load and fire, load and fire, and tight ranks made it difficult to move a rifle around freely. The line began to loosen up and string out and men started to kneel down as soon as the shooting started. At times, it seemed as if the rebels were coming from every direction, and everything was confused.

Communication was also extremely difficult for Colonel Boynton. The field musicians relayed commands as he gave them, but not everyone could hear them over the din of battle. The smoke and terrain made it difficult see. The only way to get a good look at his line companies or the enemy was to move up and down the line. When he moved about, he lost contact with the field musicians but was able to give commands directly to the firing line, at least the portion of it in front of him at that moment. To communicate with the others, he had to continue moving. Staff officers helped by observing, reporting, and carrying orders, but their line of sight and ability to communicate was just as limited as that of their commander. In spite of the difficulties, Boynton and the other regimental commanders on the field that morning did a commendable job of controlling their troops.

---

416. U.S. War Department, *War of the Rebellion*, Ser. no. 50, pp. 429, 436; Boynton, *Military Park*, 36; Boynton, *Letters*, 28–29.

After the battle Colonel Boynton stated that Color Sergeant Mark Price played a major role in holding the line against the rebel attacks. In an age when carrying the unit colors into battle was a virtual guarantee of getting shot, Price, seemingly charmed, stood tall as the battle raged around him. He was wounded as he defiantly waved his banner at the enemy, but the flag neither wavered nor dipped. Soldiers on the firing line loading and firing as fast as they could while clouds of thick gray smoke wafted around them could only see a few feet down the firing line in any direction. They couldn't really tell if the company next to them was still standing or if the other end of the line had been flanked. But, they could see the regimental colors floating above the ranks, and as long as the colors stood, the men in ranks knew the regiment was intact. Both mentally and physically, the colors gave them something to rally around.[417]

Just when it seemed the rebels might break through, the Ninth Ohio returned from its wild charge. Van Derveer had sent several messengers to find Colonel Kammerling and get the Ninth turned around and one of them had evidently made contact. Brave and determined as they were, Dibrell's cavalrymen did not want to give up the fight, but the arrival of the Germans in addition to the heavy rifle fire and double charges of canister from the guns they were already receiving was too much. The effects of the Smith's and Church's batteries were particularly devastating. Having gotten to within fifty yards of the brigade's lines, the rebels "began to 'wabble,' and commenced firing wildly." Sullenly, the rebels began to drift backwards, continuing to fight with "great obstinacy and determination, only retreating when fairly swept by our overwhelming fire." The Eighty-seventh Indiana, returning to the hill from where it had started the battle, continued to fire into the rebels until they retired from view. When the smoke finally drifted away from the battle lines, "it seemed as if the lines of gray had sunk into the earth." With more Federal units arriving, General Brannan used the respite to form his division into a new line, but by twelve thirty the rebels were done for the day on the Union left. Dibrell's Confederate brigade was so badly mauled that it took no further part in the battle of Chickamauga.[418]

After four hours of furious combat, the Thirty-fifth Ohio began to deal with the aftermath of battle. For the first time, the Persimmons realized what hard work combat was. Exhausted both physically and mentally, and soaked with sweat, even the uninjured found that their bodies were sore all over. Every company had suffered losses. In Company K, First Sergeant Foord had only 18 men to command. Nine men, killed during the day's fighting, were gathered together to await burial. Most of them, including George Keever, were buried on the battlefield. Counted among the dead was Capt. Oliver Parshall who had

---

417. U.S. War Department, *War of the Rebellion*, Ser. no. 50, pp. 429, 436; Wiley, *Billy Yank*, 93.

418. U.S. War Department, *War of the Rebellion*, Ser. no. 50, p. 429; *National Tribune*, 9 June 1904; Boynton, *Letters*, 29.

returned from leave barely twenty-four hours before. Acting as an aide to Van Derveer, Parshall had been monitoring the battle near the right end of the regiment's line when he was knocked from his horse by a Confederate bullet. Both a popular and a capable officer, Parshall was eulogized by his superiors. Van Derveer called him a "brave, noble soldier, and upright gentlemen" whose loss would be felt deeply. To Colonel Boynton, Parshall was a man who was able to "secure the confidence and esteem of all."[419]

Ninety-seven men had been wounded. In addition to Deardorf and Lewis, Lieutenant Thompson of Company E had been wounded in the leg. Another four men were missing and unaccounted for, assumed to have been captured by the rebels. The wounded were collected and sent to the rear for what care was available. Nearly empty cartridge and cap boxes were replenished from the division trains, and the few rebel prisoners taken were processed for movement away from the battlefield. Before being taken away, the captured rebels were very talkative and claimed to be part of Longstreet's corps. The significance of the news escaped everyone at the moment. Weary from their first heavy combat, the Thirty-fifth had rested for about an hour before moving a little to the west to form a new line. Around 3:30 p.m., orders arrived for the brigade to report to General Reynolds whose division was being hard-pressed around the Brotherton farm. By the time the Thirty-fifth and the rest of the brigade arrived near sundown, the crisis was over and the regiment went into bivouac on a high ridge perpendicular to the Lafayette road northwest of the Dyer house. The campground had been personally chosen by General Thomas because it commanded the approach along Reed's Bridge Road. The Persimmons had just finished a very strenuous day with nothing to eat, but their new camp offered no comfort. It was a cold night, no fires were permitted, and water was scarce. Their blankets and packs were neatly stacked on the other side of McDonald's farm and would not arrive until it was too late to make any use of them, so each man lay on the hard, gravelly hillside with his rifle at this side and slept as best he could. Nothing had been settled and everyone knew there would be more fighting tomorrow. Throughout the cold, restless night, wounded men could be heard crying out from far away in the frigid darkness.[420]

For the men of the Thirty-fifth who had been wounded, the battle was over, but the ordeal was just beginning. While the fighting continued, there was little help to be found. Surgeons Wright and Landis were at a field hospital set up in "a church, a magazine, and a cooper's shop" over two miles behind the lines at Cloud's Farm. It was no easy task for the wounded to get there. They had to

419. Nosworthy, *Bloody Crucible*, 227; U.S. War Department, *War of the Rebellion*, Ser. no. 50, pp. 432, 435; Foord Papers, 19 September 1863; Bogan, *Warren County's Involvement*, 21.

420. U.S. War Department, *War of the Rebellion*, Ser. no. 50, p. 435; Keil, *Thirty-fifth Ohio*, 134–35; Bircher, *Drummer Boy's Diary*, 47–48; Bishop, "Van Der Veer's Brigade," 9 June 1904; McKinney, *Education in Violence*, 234.

hobble painfully back on their own, hope a roving team of stretcher bearers found them, or wait until the fight was over and members of the regiment came to look for them. In fact, several members of the Thirty-fifth did go out after the first day's fighting to try and find missing comrades. Four of them were captured while searching for their friends and ended up in rebel prisons. That a wounded man might bleed to death before help came was a real possibility, and under any circumstances blood loss would likely be severe. In the wooded terrain of Chickamauga, ground movement was difficult and even being carried on a stretcher was a painful experience. Having once made it to the hospital, the wounded man stood a reasonable chance of survival, but the price was often an amputated limb.[421]

Dr. Landis was busy helping as many men as he could, but he was able to provide a more personal service to a fellow Buckeye. Col. William G. Jones, a graduate of West Point and an officer in the Thirty-sixth Ohio, was brought to the church hospital mortally wounded. Landis cared for Jones on his death bed and then attended to his burial. Just before lowering the colonel's body into the ground, Landis removed his shoulder straps and two one dollar gold coins. Guarding them carefully throughout the rest of his service, Landis returned the mementos to Jones's brother after the war.[422]

Aside from the physical damage of a wound, there was a great deal of mental stress from being in a Civil War hospital. The wounded were taken to a facility where dehumanizing piles of amputated arms and legs were heaped up in plain view, injured men were screaming and crying all around, and where the man beside them might die before ever seeing a doctor. The field hospital was a filthy place filled with flies and the stench of death, and by 11:00 p.m. it was flooded with many more casualties than it could possibly handle. The crush was overwhelming, and the flood of human wreckage prevented doctors from beginning surgical procedures until the next morning. As dedicated as most of the doctors were, their ministrations were "often painful and barbarous." Operating in blood and pus stained coats with instruments that had never been properly disinfected; their treatment was just as likely to cause gangrene as prevent it.[423]

Almost in Their Faces

The Thirty-fifth Ohio awoke "cold, uneasy, and troubled" on ground covered by frost and fog on the morning of September 20. No fires meant no hot food,

---

421. Keil, *Thirty-fifth Ohio*, 160; Grebner, *We Were the Ninth*, 150.

422. Landis, *From Pilgrimage to Promise*, 20.

423. Bircher, *Drummer Boy's Diary*, 49; Grebner, *We Were the Ninth*, 150; Wiley, *Billy Yank*, 147–48; Mitchell, *Civil War Soldiers*, 61; Nosworthy, *Bloody Crucible*, 226.

and more importantly, no hot coffee. For the second morning in a row, the men had been denied the beverage so essential to their morale. Given a cup of hot coffee sweetened by Army-issue yellow sugar, a soldier's mood was generally positive regardless of what might lie ahead. To go without was a great disappointment to the men of the regiment, but they took it in stride. They were prepared to fight again that morning, even without the aid of caffeine.[424]

As darkness fell on the nineteenth, Brannan's Third Division had been designated as the Fourteenth Corps Reserve and was at the right end of Thomas's corps, perpendicular to the line. About 9:00 a.m., Breckenridge's Confederate division attacked the Union left, and Brannan's men were moved into the line next to Reynolds's division. The first two brigades moved forward, while Van Derveer's Third Brigade was held back as the division reserve. During the early morning hours, the Thirty-fifth waited quietly, but about eight o'clock, the men were ordered to once again pile the knapsacks that had just arrived and get ready to move. The canvas bags were obediently placed on the ground, never to be seen again. Van Derveer's brigade formed in two columns *en masse* with the 280 remaining men of the Thirty-fifth Ohio in the right rear of the columns. The brigade began to hack its way slowly through the underbrush to get in position between the Second Brigade and General Reynolds's division. The entire army was shifting gradually to its left, and as they moved, the Persimmons could hear firing in the woods to their front. When the Confederate attack kicked off at nine thirty, the firing increased until "the roar of musketry and artillery was appalling." As Gen. John C. Breckenridge's Confederates assaulted Thomas's extreme left, Van Derveer's brigade was affected two ways.[425]

Gen. Absalom Baird, in command of the corps' left flank, quickly called for reinforcements. Thomas's first response was to send all available artillery to support his left most divisions. Orders arrived and Van Derveer was forced to send Battery I to support Baird. It was with deep misgiving that he watched the red legs go, as the guns of the battery had been invaluable the day before. Van Derveer would have to fight without direct support artillery but there was no help for it. Breckenridge's attack intensified, and another call was made for reinforcements. George Thomas ordered Brannan to bring the Third Division to the Lafayette road. Two of Brannan's brigades had already been committed to the line next to Reynolds' division, but he immediately ordered the Third Brigade to Thomas's aid.[426]

Shortly after Battery I rattled off through the trees, Van Derveer received

---

424. Keil, *Thirty-fifth Ohio*, 142; *Hamilton Republican News*, 1898, Thirty-fifth OVI Collection, Butler County Historical Society; Boynton, *Letters*, 34.

425. U.S. War Department, *War of the Rebellion*, Ser. no. 50, pp. 429, 436; Bishop, "Van Der Veer's Brigade," 9 June 1904; McKinney, *Education in Violence*, 242.

426. U.S. War Department, *War of the Rebellion*, Ser. no. 50, pp. 429, 436; Bishop, "Van Der Veer's Brigade," 9 June 1904; Daniels, *Days of Glory*, 325.

urgent orders from General Brannan to take his brigade and report to General Baird who was being hard pressed around Kelly's Farm. Redeploying into two lines with the Thirty-fifth still on the right rear of the formation, the brigade moved through the shadowy woods toward the Chattanooga road with Lieutenant Miller of Company C leading the skirmishers. The small trees and brush that made up the impenetrable undergrowth contested every human movement. The regiment began to encounter soldiers trying to sneak away from the fighting in front. The stragglers came "singly at first, then in squads, until it seemed that our line in front must be breaking up." As the Persimmons watched these fleeing men, "the enemy's bullets and shells came through the trees and among us in a very disquieting manner." Swinging his units gradually to the left, Van Derveer skillfully maneuvered the brigade so that it struck the road perpendicularly just north of the Kelly house near the barn about two hundred yards behind the battle line of General Reynolds's division in the Kelly fields. It was just after 11:00 a.m.[427]

Looking east into Kelly's field. This is what the Thirty-fifth Ohio would have seen as they arrived on the morning of September 20, 1863.
DEDICATION OF THE CHICAMAUGA AND CHATTANOOGA NATIONAL MILITARY PARK.

For the second time in two days, the situation that Van Derveer strode into was not what he had been led to believe it would be. Expecting to find General Baird and be directed to some position in the line, Van Derveer had unknowingly arrived at Kelly's at a moment of crisis for the left flank of the Army of the Cumberland. The firing lines were fifty yards or more inside the trees, so

427. U.S. War Department, *War of the Rebellion*, Ser. no. 50, pp. 429, 435; Bishop, "Van Der Veer's Brigade," 9 June 1904; Boynton, *Letters*, 38.

Van Derveer had entered the area of utter confusion behind them. Leaving the woods, the Thirty-fifth and the other regiments in the brigade came under fire without warning. The Kelly fields, approximately a quarter mile wide by three quarters of a mile long, didn't look at all like they had the morning before. Supply wagons cluttered fields that were already thick with powder smoke, and burning farm buildings only added to the already thick veil. Everywhere they looked, soldiers were running. Some moved with determination, others with no apparent purpose, and still others who were obviously running away. Wounded and dazed men staggered around amid the tumult. The entire Union line was under attack. Cannon shells and grapeshot crashed through the trees, and "musket balls as thick as hail stones" were coming at them from every direction except the trees they had just left. It was very difficult to for anyone to get a clear picture of what was going on, since there was no overall control of the battle. For the most part, the fighting was being directed by individual brigade, regiment, and battery commanders, all doing the best they could. [428]

It was a problematic situation, but Van Derveer was most steady under trying circumstances. Most of the fire appeared to be coming from the east across the field, so Van Derveer had faced his formation in that direction. The area that the men in ranks now stood in was a thicket, and the soldiers standing on the ground could not see through the underbrush. The rebels could see the regimental colors over the top of the brush and had begun to fire in their direction. On horseback, Van Derveer was able to see this new threat over top the thicket, and he realized the direction of fire was coming from the north, his left. Peering in that direction, Van Derveer saw the rebel brigade of Brig. Gen. Marcellus Stovall advancing in four ranks from the north end of Kelly's fields about three hundred yards distant. The Confederates had gotten beyond the Union left flank and were blocking the only line of retreat into Chattanooga. The attention of Reynolds and Baird was focused entirely to the front. Van Derveer could see that the rebel attack was about to crash into the rear of the Union line possibly sweeping Union forces from the field. There was no time to find Baird as his orders had dictated. On his own initiative and without hesitation, Van Derveer wheeled the Third Brigade into Kelly's cornfield and faced the enemy advance. Under similar circumstances, some Union regiments had already broke and run, but Van Derveer's men responded coolly, under fire the whole time.[429]

Due to the change of front, the Thirty-fifth was now on the left rear of the brigade formation. Two enemy cannons five hundred yards to the front began

428. Woodworth, *Guide*, 45–46; Woodworth, "Rock," 46; Judson Bishop to sister Frank, 29 September 1863, Judson Bishop Papers, Minnesota Historical Society, St. Paul; Cozzens, *This Terrible Sound*, 332; Boynton, *Letters*, 36.

429. U.S. War Department, *War of the Rebellion*, Ser. no. 50, pp. 249, 429, 1068; Grebner, *We Were the Ninth*, 143; McKinney, *Education in Violence*, 242; Woodworth, "Rock," 46–47; Connelly, *Autumn of Glory*, 221; Society of the Army of the Cumberland, *Twenty-fourth Reunion* (Cincinnati: Robert Clarke Co., 1894), 233.

*Looking north into Kelly's field facing north in the direction of the Confederate lines
on the morning of September 20, 1863.*
CHICKAMAUGA NATIONAL MILITARY PARK.

to fire into the blue clad infantry. White puffs of smoke from the exploding shells began to appear above the Third Brigade, and then a heavy volley from the Confederate lines smashed into the Eighty-seventh Indiana standing in front of the Thirty-fifth. Van Derveer immediately ordered the brigade to lie down to avoid most of the fire, but Company F's Lieutenant Harlan was slow in obeying the order and was shot down. As he fell dying, his last words were to cheer his men on. Lt. Phillip Rothenbush was near Harlan when he was struck down. His first thought was to get Harlan's watch and money so it could be sent home to his family, but upon considering the situation a little more, he changed his mind. "I thought, 'Rosy' you're in a pretty damned tight place yourself, and liable to be killed at any minute, and if they find you with any of Harlan's property in your clothes, they'll surely say you robbed the dead." The Persimmons watched as the rebels, moving obliquely to the regiment, exited the trees about one hundred yards away. Grape shot, canister, and bullets whistled overhead as the tension mounted and the butternut ranks drew ever closer. When the Confederates were seventy-five yards away, orders were shouted down the lines.[430]

The Second Minnesota and the Eighty-seventh Indiana stood and brought their weapons to bear. At the other end of the field, the Confederate infantry cringed as the blue ranks rose from the cold ground and aimed at them. On command, the Second and Eighty-seventh fired a volley "almost in their faces," smashing the rebel line as if it had been hit by some great tempest. As soon as the volley crashed across the field, more orders were called out. "Ninth Ohio, Thirty-fifth Ohio; pass lines to the front; fix bayonet; double-quick; march."

430. U.S. War Department, *War of the Rebellion*, Ser. no. 50, pp. 429–430, 435; Keil, *Thirty-fifth Ohio*, 144; *Hamilton Republican News*, 1898, Thirty-fifth OVI Collection.

Passing though the Eighty-seventh Indiana, the men of the Thirty-fifth charged eagerly forward across the corn stubble, spontaneously shouting the Union battle cry at the top of their lungs. The Confederates, already shredded by the first volley, looked at the onrushing line of blue and began to retreat at a run. Prisoners and wounded taken during the battle said it was the first time Stovall's brigade had ever turned its back on an enemy. With the Ninth Ohio keeping pace on the right, the Thirty-fifth drove the rebels back across fields strewn so thick with dead and wounded that the advancing men "could almost step from man to man as they fell." Forty-seven-year-old Pvt. John Brooks of Company I was still carrying a cast iron skillet as the attack began. He held it before his face and shouted, "You may kill me, but you can't spoil my beauty." The Confederates didn't kill him, but sometime during the morning's fighting, Brooks was wounded and captured. As the Thirty-fifth advanced, the company officers tried to keep tight control of their men, but inevitably, gaps began to appear in the ranks. Even so, the men kept up a steady fire that took a toll on the Confederate ranks. On their second day of combat, the Persimmons were performing like veterans of many battles.[431]

Their brigade commander was also demonstrating courage and ability. Mounted and in full view of the enemy, Ferdinand Van Derveer remained in the midst of his advancing brigade. He closely observed the action and continued to give orders as the men raced forward. Bullets whizzed past and whacked into nearby ranks, but there was no sign of agitation or nervousness about him. If Van Derveer felt any fear, it was held quietly in check. The colonel was not a man to act recklessly or to expose himself to no good purpose, but he never avoided necessary risk. If doing his duty required him to be shot at, or even shot down, so be it, and the odds for getting shot were fairly high. Confederate fire from the trees and the nearby battery was heavy, and by the time the brigade entered the forest, all but two of its horses had been disabled.[432]

The closer the Persimmons got to the trees, the wilder the rush became. The last leap for the enemy was partially the result of hot-bloodedness, but mostly it was driven by the desire to get in close under the enemy fire. The rebels had hoped to find cover in the deep woodland shadows, but the Persimmons drove them northeast through the Kelly fields and more than a hundred yards deep into the woods before the attack ground to a halt. Under the trees, it was tough going. Rothenbush remembered that, "There was a very thick undergrowth in our way; pine trees, bushes and all that and as we advanced we had our troubles." The spirited attack by the Third Brigade had given encouragement to other regiments, and the entire Union line surged forward. The Thirty-

---

431. U.S. War Department, *War of the Rebellion*, Ser. no. 50, p. 435; Keil, *Thirty-fifth Ohio*, 144; Bishop to sister Frank, 29 September 1863, Bishop Papers; *Hamilton Republican News*, 1898, Thirty-fifth OVI Collection; Official Roster Commission, *Official Roster*, 628; Wiley, *Billy Yank*, 74; Nosworthy, *Bloody Crucible*, 216.

432. Boynton, *National Military Park*, 47.

fifth entered the woods in a line two deep, but the dense undergrowth broke the momentum of the charge and caused the men to scatter in small groups, so that unit cohesion was momentarily lost. Somewhere in the confused fighting under the leafy canopy, Lieutenant Cottingham of Company E and several of his men were cut off, surrounded, and captured. First Sergeant William Mikesell took command of Company E as the regiment struggled to get reorganized. As the fighting swirled through the woods, Company I's Sgt. John Fenton was captured by the rebels and then released when his company lunged forward one more time.[433]

The Second Minnesota and Eighty-seventh Indiana had quickly reloaded and followed the two Ohio regiments into the forest. Surrounded by tumult as the combat spread under the trees, Lieutenant Rothenbush experienced a surreal moment. He noticed that his shoelace was undone, and in the midst of the charge with bullets flying in all directions, he knelt down to tie his shoe. Attempting to leave the forest and enter the road, the Persimmons came under fire from enemy cannons placed in the road above the woods. With artillery shells "dropping among an around us" like "the throwing of corn to the chickens" the attack was finally halted. The entire brigade, reforming its line, took up positions deep in the forest to repel the expected counterattack. The attack never came, but for over an hour, the regiment engaged in close combat with rebel infantry in the shadows of the northern Georgia forests. In the heavy undergrowth, movement by individuals was difficult and coordinated movement by groups even more so. The natural tendency was to take cover wherever it was available. Van Derveer, sorely missing Battery I at this juncture, had no effective way to deal with the Confederate battery firing into his brigade. The enemy put up an "obstinate and bloody" fight in the woods, but it soon became obvious that the rebels were backing off. Looking around, Van Derveer could see that his brigade had moved too far into the woods to be adequately supported by the friendly units on his flanks. Concerned that the Third Brigade was nearly surrounded, he ordered a retirement to a more defensible position about a quarter after twelve.[434]

The regiment withdrew from its forward position by a passage of lines to the rear while continuing to fire. The front rank would "raise, take aim, fire, lie down and reload while the second line would do the same," both repeating the process over and over until contact was broken. A passage of lines under fire is always a difficult situation. The men were most vulnerable when upright and moving, and the rebel soldiers in the woods simply had to wait for them to rise up. Lieutenant Colonel Boynton's horse was shot out from under him and Lieu-

433. U.S. War Department, *War of the Rebellion*, Ser. no. 50, pp. 430, 436; *Hamilton Republican News*, 1898, Thirty-fifth OVI Collection, Butler County Historical Society; McElroy, *Record of the Ohio*, 15; Boynton, *Dedication*, 358; Wiley, *Billy Yank*, 75.

434. U.S. War Department, *War of the Rebellion*, Ser. no. 50, pp. 430, 435; Grebner, *We Were the Ninth*, 143; *Hamilton Republican News*, 1898, Thirty-fifth OVI Collection.

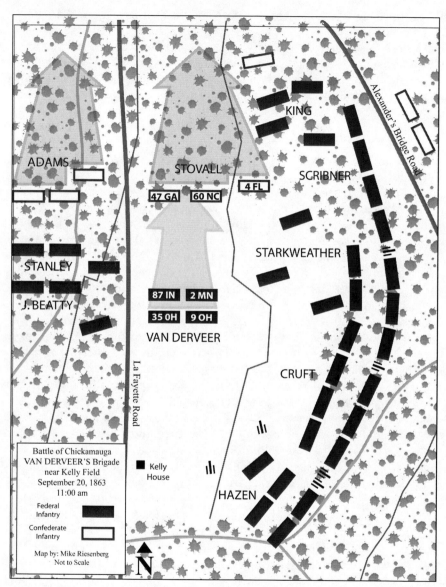

Map 3. Van Derveer's brigade at Kelly's field, September 20, 1863, at 11:00 a.m.

tenant Rothenbush was hit in the left calf. After feeling a sudden "stinging sensation as if my heel was gone," Rothenbush's leg wound was bound with a handkerchief by Sgt. Jim Jackson. The Persimmons took more casualties in this part of the action than in the charge that preceded it, but by placing accurate fire on the enemy, they were able to safely extricate themselves.[435]

As they moved back across the field, the men of the Thirty-fifth saw many pitiful and bone chilling sights. One mortally wounded soldier moaned continually for his mother. Only a few feet away, another man in the last throes of death was literally pulling his brains out through a head wound. Van Derveer moved back near the Kelly house and waited, satisfied that he had supported Baird effectively when the need was greatest. As on the first day, wounded men needed to be attended to, so details went out to carry them to the field hospital at Kelly's house. Others collected the dead. Those not detailed to these tasks took the opportunity to try and get some rest. If cessation of physical activity is rest, then the men of the Thirty-fifth rested. If the definition includes relaxation, none was to be had. Rebel sharpshooters sent bullets whizzing through the air while the rebel battery to the north continued to lob shells at them while they waited.[436]

As the Thirty-fifth fought in the woods north of Kelly's, events were unfolding on other parts of the battlefield. The great Confederate breakthrough engineered by newly arrived Gen. James Longstreet had punched a huge, irreparable hole in the Union lines. As a large part of the Army of the Cumberland was driven from the field, the effects rippled down the left flank of the army. Colonel Van Derveer received some indication of what was beginning to happen all over the field when a detachment of the Fourth Kentucky Infantry, unable to find its parent unit, attached itself to Van Derveer, the first friendly officer they could find.[437]

Back at the division field hospital at the Cloud Church, Doctors Wright and Landis had a more direct knowledge of events. The early morning battles of the twentieth had come within three-quarters of a mile of the hospital, and starting at about nine thirty, indiscriminate Confederate artillery fire began to strike the hospital area. The surgeons were told to get ready to displace to Rossville. Severely wounded were to be loaded on ambulances. The walking wounded were to do just that, walk to the new hospital. Around 11:00 a.m., in the midst of all the confusion, rebel cavalry stormed the hospital, and the word went out for everyone to save themselves. Chaos spread quickly. Ambulances drivers panicked at the sight of the rebels began to drive their teams wildly away. Many of them drove off empty or only partly full. Wounded men, determined not to be captured, ran in every direction. Some doctors mounted horses and abandoned their patients to the enemy, but Wright and Landis chose to stay. Upon realizing that they were attacking a hospital, the bulk of the rebel forces went off, leaving only a small detachment to keep an eye on the doctors. Later in the day, when Granger's Reserve Corps approached the battlefield from Rossville,

435. Keil, *Thirty-fifth Ohio*, 145; U.S. War Department, *War of the Rebellion*, Ser. no. 50, p. 430; Grebner, *We Were the Ninth*, 143; *Hamilton Republican News*, 1898, Thirty-fifth OVI Collection.

436. U.S. War Department, *War of the Rebellion*, Ser. no. 50, p. 430; *Hamilton Republican News*, 1898, Thirty-fifth OVI Collection; Bishop, "Van Der Veer's Brigade," 9 June 1904.

437. U.S. War Department, *War of the Rebellion*, Ser. no. 50, p. 1062.

the rebel squad drew off, and the hospital was left alone for the rest of the day. Landis and Wright continued to treat the wounded in their charge and were still busy when the Confederates entered the hospital again the next morning.[438]

Unexampled Fury

Chickamauga has often been described as a battle in which the generals had minimal influence, and the experience of the Third Brigade bears that out. After receiving initial instructions early in the day, Van Derveer had been without formal guidance. At Kelly's Field, he had never been able to locate General Baird but had sized up the situation and responded in the way he thought best. After the fighting died down, still officially under orders to support Baird's division, he had remained at Kelly's while collecting casualties. Shortly before two o'clock in the afternoon, heavy firing was heard to the west, and word reached Van Derveer that General Brannan was attempting to form a line on the high ground in that direction. As Longstreet's breakthrough expanded, other commanders, alone in similar situations had chosen to retire, but it was not in Ferdinand Van Derveer's makeup to just walk away. He pushed out skirmishers and began moving through woods and cornfields toward the sound of battle, thrusting any rebels who attempted to interfere out of the way. [439]

Arriving in the vicinity of Snodgrass Hill, General Brannan was not where Van Derveer had expected to find him, but he was able to find Gen. George Thomas. The colonel rode up to Thomas and said, "General, I report my brigade. Where shall I place it?" Scrambling to build a line of battle that could stop the Confederate army, Thomas was using every unit he could get, but most of what he was getting was the beat up parts of regiments and brigades. Surrounded by confusion and desperation, the ever-poised Virginian expressed his pleasure at seeing Van Derveer and then asked the question most important to him at that moment, "What condition is your brigade in?" Van Derveer replied, "All in line, save our dead and wounded." At the moment it was most needed, Van Derveer had delivered an intact and fully functional infantry brigade to the critical point in the line.[440]

Van Derveer reported to Brannan somewhere between 2:30 and 3:00 p.m. The division commander was also pleased to see Van Derveer. The brigade was immediately pushed up on the line to replace other exhausted units while the Fourth Kentucky detachment rejoined its own regiment. The hill provided a

---

438. Grebner, *We Were the Ninth*, 151–52; *Cyclopaedia of Butler County, Ohio*, 223.
439. McKinney, *Education in Violence*, 253.
440. Keil, *Thirty-fifth Ohio*, 146; U.S. War Department, *War of the Rebellion*, Ser. no. 50, p. 430; Grebner, *We Were the Ninth*, 143; Boynton, *National Military Park*, 55; McElroy, Record of the Ohio Commission, 18.

good position, one that Van Derveer liked immediately. It ran along the crest of the hill and was "capable of being defended against a heavy force." The men of the Thirty-fifth, now placed on the right end of the brigade line, liked it, as well. They were on high ground with a log barricade to take cover behind. It wasn't very substantial, but it was enough to protect the men if they lay down, and only a few hours of combat had taught them that any cover was a good thing.[441]

After 3:00 p.m. the Confederates tried several times with "almost inconceivable fury and persistence" to take the hill and crush the Army of the Cumberland once and for all. They attacked with "unexampled fury, line after line of fresh troops being hurled against our position with a heroism and persistence that almost dignified their cause," and some of them actually reached the fence line before being shot down. On the crest, Lieutenants Sabin and Adams were wounded Adams, the youngest officer in the regiment, thought he was dying. Looking up at those attending to him, he smiled and said, "I shall die, but that is nothing if we whip the rebels." The Thirty-fifth was as well drilled as any regiment in the Army of the Cumberland and that training now allowed them to stick to the job of fighting for hours on end. Psychologically, there were several factors at work. The men in the ranks had formed intensely personal relationships, and probably the biggest single reason they stayed in the fight was because they didn't want to let their friends down. Some no doubt stayed because they believed this was what they had enlisted to do, still others were caught in the universal dilemma of combat. They were afraid of facing enemy fire, but they were even more afraid of others thinking they were afraid. For whatever reason, the men carried on and any on the verge of running were strengthened by the example of those around them.[442]

For two hours, every rebel attack was beaten back. The bushes on the slope in front of the Thirty-fifth had "been cut down with bullets as if with a mowing machine" as each soldier fired between fifty and sixty rounds apiece. Ammunition began to run critically low. Gen. Gordon Granger commanding the army reserve had brought a small quantity forward, but it wasn't nearly enough. The rebel ranks kept coming up the hill, and cartridge boxes soon emptied again. Boynton and his men were determined to stop the rebels and "clung to [the] hill as if to a rock in the ocean." The Persimmons was ordered to fix bayonets and prepare to repel the next assault with bare steel. While the men hunkered down and waited, several officers took it upon themselves to find more cartridges. Major Budd, Captain L'Hommedieu, Captain Daugherty, and Lieutenant Bone led details to search the dead and wounded for additional cartridges. Even prisoners were searched for whatever might be found on them. Firing continued, but the Persimmons ran out of bullets for a third time.[443]

The camaraderie and professionalism that had developed among the regi-

441. U.S. War Department, *War of the Rebellion*, Ser. no. 50, pp. 430, 436, 1062.
442. Ibid., Ser. no. 50, pp. 430, 436, 1062.

ments of the Third Brigade now worked to the Persimmon's advantage. The men of the brigade had been together for many long months. They knew one another and had learned to trust each other's abilities and intentions. So it was that when the Thirty-fifth ran completely out of ammunition, the Second Minnesota, itself desperately low, found it could spare a few bullets, enough so that with the bullets found on the dead and wounded, each man in the Thirty-fifth received three rounds. After hours of pushing themselves against the Federal lines and suffering terrible losses, the rebels were running out of steam. As the last ammunition was distributed, the battlefield began to quiet down with the increasing darkness.[444]

As the sun fell below the horizon, the Thirty-fifth held a line along the ridge to the ravine that separated Brannan's division from Steedman's. The right end of the Persimmon's line was refused to cover the gap between the two divisions. Unknown to Van Derveer, Steedman had withdrawn his units on the other side of the ravine and the brigade's flank was exposed. There was movement in the ravine, and the men in the firing line informed their commander, that "the enemy had ascended the ravine and gained position near the crest, between Steedman's and Van Derveer's positions." Boynton immediately faced

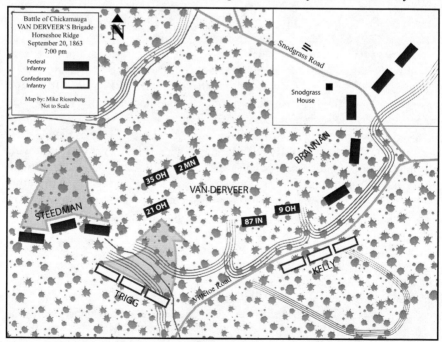

Map 4. Van Derveer's brigade at Horseshoe Ridge, September 20, 1863, at 7:00 p.m.

443. U.S. War Department, *War of the Rebellion*, Ser. no. 50, 430; Grebner, *We Were the Ninth*, 143.

444. U.S. War Department, *War of the Rebellion*, Ser. no. 50, p. 436.

his line to the right to meet the new threat. As the men scrambled to their new positions, more rebels could be seen on the ridge across the ravine. Boynton pushed his line even further to the right so that it's upside down bowl shape allowed him to face both new Confederate threats.[445]

General Brannan had his headquarters set up behind the Second Minnesota, and Boynton reported the situation directly to him. The Ninth Indiana, having just reported to Brannan, was ordered to form a line on the right of the Thirty-fifth Ohio and assume a position to be designated by Boynton. Colonel Suman, the commander of the Ninth Indiana soon learned that Steedman's units were gone and began giving orders to move his regiment to the rear away from the advancing Confederates. Having been given command of the regimental fragments on his right by General Brannan, Boynton stopped the retreat and was forced to shame the colonel into taking his regiment back into the line. No sooner had the Ninth Indiana returned to their position, than a lone rider on horseback came closer and demanded to know whose troops were in front of him. One of the Persimmons obliged him by shouting, "The Thirty-fifth Ohio," and realizing his mistake, the Confederate horseman attempted to turn and flee. The Persimmons, being slightly quicker on the uptake, fired a volley down the slope into the darkened ranks. The rider fell, and the rebels behind him, having had enough for one day, fired a few rounds and quickly withdrew. After this brief skirmish a "painful and awful" stillness descended on the lines. It was about 7:00 p.m. and the battle of Chickamauga was over. Casualties on the second day had also been heavy. Nine more men had died on Sunday, fifty-four had been wounded, and twenty-two others were nowhere to be found.[446]

As the twilight shadows deepened, the battlefield quieted down. Men began to creep down the slope to look for wounded friends. Burning powder had fallen on the dry leaves, and in some places it was smoldering. In others, small flames could be seen. The ground was thick with Confederate dead and wounded, but there was nothing to be done for them. Little more could be done for the few wounded Yankees that were retrieved. They were deposited near the Snodgrass House in the hopes that they could be transported later. By 7:30 p.m. the field had grown quiet. The part of the Army of the Cumberland that remained with General Thomas at Snodgrass Hill had already begun to withdraw under the cover of darkness. The movement was coordinated by one of Van Derveer's staff officers, Captain Cilley of the Second Minnesota, who was the brigade's topographical engineer. The last unit off the hill, the Third Brigade walked down the slope shortly after seven thirty into the darkness and marched without incident to Rossville as the rear guard of Thomas's column. Winding his way in and out among the powder-darkened faces was that dog

445. Boynton to Fullerton, 17 April 1896, Henry V. N. Boynton Correspondence, Chickamauga and Chattanooga National Military Park, Chattanooga, Tennessee.

446. U.S. War Department, *War of the Rebellion*, Ser. no. 50, pp. 431, 436; Boynton to Fullerton, 17 April 1896, Boynton Correspondence; Boynton, *Letters*, 48–49.

Jack. He had stayed with the regiment through all of the fighting, running back and forth along the ranks, yapping and barking. He was now as much a combat veteran as any of them. As the column moved north toward Rossville, most everyone was quiet. Exhaustion filled the ranks, and most of the officers had long since shouted themselves hoarse. As the column moved north on the road, it passed Col. Moses B. Walker of the Thirty-first Ohio who both commended and cautioned his fellow Buckeyes. "Boys," Walker said, "you showed your-selves to be men this day, prepare for still greater action." The Persimmons were willing to fight again if need be, but Walker's comment set them to won-dering. Where were they going to get cartridges to fight with, and when would they get something to eat?[447]

Not everyone escaped the rebels. There was neither time nor conveyances to carry the wounded off the field and certainly no way to transport entire field hospitals in the retreat. Whatever ambulances and wagons might have been available had been swept back to Chattanooga in the headlong retreat of the Army of the Cumberland's right wing. The wounded of the Thirty-fifth remained behind at the field hospital set up at the Snodgrass cabin and were captured by the Confederates. Among the wounded were First Sergeant Foord of Company K, who had performed so admirably during both days fighting, and A Company Pvt. Joseph O'Neall, who was still too young to legally enlist. Foord had been wounded in the hip late in the day as the Thirty-fifth repulsed yet another attack. O'Neall had been wounded at least twice, the last one a blow to the head that left him unconscious. For them and the others left behind with them, the sudden change from "Yankeedom to Dixie" was quite sudden and undesirable. The Confederates didn't have enough medical supplies to care for their own wounded, and in the undeveloped northwest Georgia forests, transportation was impeded by terrible road conditions and no railroad. Under the best conditions, little help would have been available for those wounded and captured, but after Chickamauga, there was next to nothing that could be done. The Confederate surgeons did what they could, but the battle had been over for ten days before some wounded received medical care.[448]

A Strong Light

Even though it was only two of the regiment's one thousand days of existence, the Thirty-fifth Ohio was defined by its experience at Chickamauga. Prior to the battle, the regiment's most noted combat experiences had been the farcical rout at Fishing Creek and the frustrating wait at Perryville. No one had believed

447. Keil, *Thirty-fifth Ohio*, 148–49; Bishop, "Van Der Veer's Brigade," 9 June 1904.
448. Keil, *Thirty-fifth Ohio*, 157; Foord Papers, 20 September 1863; Bogan, *Warren County's Involvement*, 13.

that Fishing Creek was in any way indicative of the regiment's true capability, as the patient endurance under fire at Perryville had indicated, but they had had to wait nearly two years for definitive proof. For two days, in three separate actions, the Thirty-fifth Ohio and the Third Brigade had done "as much as any other brigade—and more than most—to save the Union Army of the Cumberland from destruction at Chickamauga." On the nineteenth, in heavy combat for the first time, the Persimmons stood up under murderous fire, recovered quickly from the initial shock, and responded instantly to changing situations. The next morning in Kelly's field, in the bloodiest fighting of the battle, they mounted a determined counterattack, stopped a dangerous enemy advance, and drove them back into the woods. On the same day at Snodgrass Hill, the Thirty-fifth stayed in line when it was out of ammunition and had enough spirit remaining to defend the hill with bayonets.[449]

The cost of courage had been high. The regiment had taken 391 officers and men into battle on the nineteenth. The next morning, after some of the stragglers had arrived, there were 280 Persimmons still in line. In Rossville, on the morning of the twenty-first, 200 men remained in formation. "Half of the Thirty-fifth are dead or wounded," Boynton sadly stated. As far as he was concerned, this fact "taken in connection with the fact that the regiment never broke and constantly maintained its ground, shows its merits in a strong light and needs no comment." Van Derveer was also greatly pleased with the regiment's performance. His men had "fought like heroes, and have covered themselves with glory," he reported. "More gallantry and indomitable courage was never displayed upon the field of battle."[450]

The junior officers and senior noncommissioned officers had led their companies ably. The incompetent and incapable had been weeded out by two years of campaign experience, and the soldiers had full trust in the men who led them at Chickamauga. Colonel Boynton was entirely satisfied with their performance. "Where all fought so nobly and so well it is impossible to make distinctions," he stated before commending seventeen of them by name in his battle report for being "ever conspicuous in the discharge of every duty." All of the dead and wounded had fallen "at their posts facing the foe." Boynton, himself, had provided solid leadership, particularly in facing Dibrell's unexpected attack on Reed's Bridge Road. Having been vigilant enough to see the enemy approaching, he accepted the fact that he was the man on spot and did what he thought best without waiting for instructions. According to Van Derveer, Boynton had performed with "coolness and great promptness," and "such officers are a credit to the service and our country." General Brannan also lauded Boynton for his actions on the evening of the twentieth when the Thirty-fifth had repulsed the final rebel attack "in the most gallant manner."[451]

---

449. Woodworth, "Rock," 46–47

450. U.S. War Department, *War of the Rebellion*, Ser. no. 50, pp. 431, 436–437; Van Derveer to wife, 23 September 1863, Van Derveer Family Collection.

Chickamauga was the pinnacle of Ferdinand Van Derveer's military career. His actions on those two days exceeded everything he had done before and everything that was to come afterwards. All of the lessons learned in Mexico and during the previous two years had fully prepared him for his supreme moment. On the morning of the nineteenth, he had been ordered into battle without any time to reconnoiter and without any guide. Feeling his way along on vague instructions, he had listened carefully to the sounds of musketry and artillery fire and brought the brigade to the place it needed to be and effectively anchored the left of the Union line. Deliberate by nature, Van Derveer has been questioned for not pushing his attack harder on the morning of the nineteenth and crashing down on the rebel flank, perhaps changing the entire character of the battle. An opportunity might have existed as the Third Brigade first arrived on the battlefield, but in view of his complete lack of information, Van Derveer opted for a cautious approach. A hard, fast attack might have pushed the Confederates back, and it might even forced them to retreat across Chickamauga Creek, but two things make it seem unlikely. The same skirmish line activity that alerted Van Derveer to the Confederate advance, told the rebels that more Federal troops were in the area. The rebels near Reed's Bridge were led by very capable men, among them Nathan Bedford Forrest, who had the skill and forces to punish any new attacker. Had Van Derveer plunged deeper into the enemy lines after Dibrell's first attack, the continuing advance would have exposed his own flank to Dibrell's second assault. That may have changed the character of the battle, but not in the Union's favor. After Dibrell's second assault, Van Derveer had no opportunity to counterattack. In his battle report, General Brannan, commander of the Third Division, described the difficulty he was having maintaining his flanks, one of which was held by the Third Brigade. His interest was in shoring up his line and not in attacking. After clearing the field of dead and wounded, Brannan ordered a withdrawal to a new line nearer the Lafayette road.[452]

On the morning of the twentieth, Van Derveer was again operating on incomplete information. He was ordered to move the Third Brigade to Kelly's field and report to General Baird. The reasonable expectation would have been to move into the area behind Baird's division, find him, and get instructions on what part of the line to support. Instead, Van Derveer walked into a chaotic situation where no one seemed to be in control. Rather than stick to the letter of his orders, he chose to obey the spirit and acted on his own responsibility, preventing an even earlier Union disaster. These two situations may be the origin of one comment in Van Derveer's report, when speaking of his brigade he said, "Without exception they performed all that was required, much more than should have been expected." While caution was definitely part of Van Der-

---

451. U.S. War Department, *War of the Rebellion*, Ser. no. 50, pp. 405, 431, 436–437; Wiley, *Billy Yank*, 94.

452. U.S. War Department, *War of the Rebellion*, Ser. no. 50, pp. 401, 429.

veer's nature, it did not prevent him from acting quickly and decisively when necessary. Three times, with disaster staring the Army of the Cumberland in the face, he brought his brigade to a critical place in the battle. It was brigade commanders like Van Derveer, said Francis F. McKinney, acting on their own responsibility that made the "miracle of Chickamauga."[453]

Through it all, Van Derveer seemed to be charmed. One of his aide's, Captain Parshall had been killed during opening minutes of the battle. His second aide, Captain Moerrson, disappeared some time later and was assumed to be killed or captured. Captain Cilley of the Second Minnesota, the brigade engineer, had two horses shot out from under him. The same went for Captain Beatty, another staff officer. In one of his letters, Van Derveer said, "Nearly everyone in the brigade was shot through the clothes." The fighting had been up close and intense, and as a commander moving about on a horse, he was one of the most conspicuous and exposed men on the field. It was as if Chickamauga was his destiny, his contribution to the nation's unity, and nothing could keep him from it. He had felt it himself. "Through it all, I have passed untouched," he wrote. "It seems providential."[454]

At the time of the battle, Van Derveer's superiors praised his performance. Of his stalwart brigade commander, Gen. John Brannan wrote, "I cannot conclude this report without bringing to the special notice of the commanding general the gallant and meritorious conduct of Colonel Van Derveer, Thirty-fifth Regiment Ohio Volunteer Infantry, commanding Third Brigade, whose fearlessness and calm judgment in the most trying situations added materially to the efficiency of his command, which he handled both days in the most skillful manner, punishing the enemy severely." Including the entire brigade in his praises, Brannan continued, "Colonel Van Derveer's brigade (Third) which having successfully, though with great loss, held its precarious position in the general line, until all its vicinity had retreated, retired in good order, actually cutting its way through the rebels to rejoin my division. The gallant brigade was one of the few who maintained their organization perfect through the hard fought passes of that portion of the field." General George Thomas, already well acquainted with Van Derveer, seconded that opinion. In his own battle report, Thomas wrote, "I am much gratified to find the name of Col. F. Van Derveer, Thirty-fifth Ohio, commanding Third Brigade . . . whom I saw on Saturday, and I can confirm the reports given of [him] by [his] division commander." Thomas, who had long respected Van Derveer's ability, a few weeks after the battle recommended him for promotion to brigadier general for "gallant and meritorious conduct at the battle of Chickamauga." General Rosecrans added his own positive endorsement. Modern historians have also recognized Van Derveer's contributions at Chickamauga. Steven E. Woodworth described

---

453. U.S. War Department, *War of the Rebellion*, Ser. no. 50, p. 431; Cozzens, *This Terrible Sound*, 332; McKinney, *Education in Violence*, 262–63.

454. Van Derveer to wife, 23 September 1863 Van Derveer Family Collection.

Van Derveer as an alert and able commander and wrote that the superior fighting qualities of his brigade allowed it to perform several remarkable services for the Army of the Cumberland. In his words, "No other unit found so many opportunities to change the course of the battle nor used its opportunities so well." Experience, leadership, and "profound mutual trust" had contributed to "one of the greatest combat performances of the war."[455]

As the Third Brigade marched away from the battlefield, all the praise and controversy was still in the future. That night, the men of the Thirty-fifth Ohio had a lot to be proud of but mostly they were just tired. The wearing march on the eighteenth, and two days of combat on the nineteenth and twentieth with its accompanying emotional stress had left them exhausted. They knew they had done well, but they had no idea the army was going all the way back to Chattanooga. After Colonel Walker's exhortation, they assumed the army was moving to a more advantageous place to resume the battle. Despite two very exhausting days of combat and heavy losses, the Thirty-fifth Ohio was ready and willing to continue fighting. Had they known the army was in full retreat, they would probably have been upset. But for the moment, they were too tired to be angry. That would come later.[456]

455. U.S. War Department, *War of the Rebellion*, Ser. no. 50, pp. 80, 255, 404, Ser. no. 56, p. 202, Ser. no. 58, p. 275; Woodworth, *Guide*, 15–16; Woodworth, "Rock," 48.

456. Keil, *Thirty-fifth Ohio*, 149.

CHAPTER 10

This Wretched Place

October and November 1863

Winter All The Time

The Thirty-fifth Ohio went into position near the Rossville Gap early on the morning of September 21, 1863, astride the road from McFarland's Gap. The Confederates were slow to follow, and it was not until eleven o'clock the next morning that they showed up in front of the ridge. There was some small scale skirmishing but no serious stab was made at the Union lines. That night, the Persimmons left Rossville and retired into the newly established lines around the city of Chattanooga. Brannan's division was again the army's rear guard, and it was daylight on the twenty-third before the Thirty-fifth Ohio was in its new camp near the center, and potentially the most likely point of attack, of the Union defenses. The Thirty-fifth was responsible for building and manning fortifications adjacent to and across the Rossville road.[457]

Exhausted from having no appreciable rest since the eighteenth, the men were far from pleased to be handed picks and shovels as soon as they arrived. But they also knew the rebels were out there and resignedly "dug into the red clay, sank trenches, and threw up a line of earthworks." Even the smallest breastwork provided protection and it was entirely possible the rebels would quickly follow up their victory at Chickamauga by trying to capture Chattanooga. If that happened, it was the soldiers who would pay the price, so their digging was as much an instinctive response as it was obedience to orders. The work started with each man digging a simple ditch. As dirt was taken out of the ditch, it was thrown on the side to make an earthen wall in front. Digging continued so that the individual ditches were connected until the regiment had a continuous trench line. The work of fortification never really ended, but this

---

457. Keil, *Thirty-fifth Ohio*, 161; Bishop, *Story of a Regiment*, 131; Boynton, *Military Park*, 89–90; McKinney, *Education in Violence*, 267.

initial line of trenches was done by noon. The speed with which the works went up surprised both the watching Confederates and the Union commanders.[458]

That first day, while they labored, the Persimmons talked among themselves about personal experiences in battle. They talked about how many enemy soldiers they thought they had killed and about the way the rebels had fled before them in Kelly's field. They described the coolness of their favorite officers and how that dog Jack had stayed with them through it all. The eagerness most of them had felt was surprising and even those who had not been enthusiastic about combat had learned that a strong sense of duty was enough to keep them in the firing line. They recounted courageous acts they had seen each other perform and wondered at what it was that possessed anyone to do such things. Now that the danger was passed, the battle had become an exciting experience. In contrast to the tense, anxious faces they had shown in combat, they now laughed and joked about what they had seen and done. They belittled their own fears and were amused by a multitude of "hairbreadth escape" stories. Those who had fled or hidden came in for a more caustic brand of humor.[459]

It was only a matter of a few days before the folks at home heard about the battle and began clamoring for news on casualties. Ferdinand Van Derveer was swamped with requests about how friends and relatives had fared in the fighting, but he couldn't respond to everyone. Van Derveer wrote to his wife knowing she would spread the message for him. "The wounded have been and are being brought in from the neighborhood of the battlefield—There are a great many of them—Many returning with bad wounds, but the great majority of them always are slightly hurt—The battle was a terrific one—the enemy loosing many more in officers and men than we. I have been anxiously inquired of by many with regards to casualties—I have sent a list of the killed and wounded of the brigade for publication in the Cincinnati papers."[460]

Chattanooga sat in the southeast corner of Tennessee where that state, Alabama, and Georgia all come together, and prior to the war, it had burgeoned with railroads and iron foundries. The importance of its railroad connections had caused Chattanooga to become known as the "Gateway to the South." From the city, trains went east to the Atlantic coast, south to Atlanta, north to Knoxville, and west to Memphis. At Bridgeport, Alabama, the western line connected with the tracks coming south out of Nashville. Dozens of trains a day had carried passengers and cargo to and from the rapidly growing and highly optimistic city. The war had changed all that. Most civilians were driven from the city or left of their own accord. Those that remained had little to be happy about. The Army of the Cumberland had taken over all government

458. Keil, *Thirty-fifth Ohio*, 161; Bishop, *Story of a Regiment*, 131; Sword, *Mountains*, 90.

459. Wiley, *Billy Yank*, 81; Mitchell, *Civil War Soldiers*, 72, 80–81.

460. Van Derveer to wife, 30 September 1863, Van Derveer Family Collection.

buildings for military use, churches were turned into hospitals, and private homes became headquarters for high-ranking officers. All the stores were closed, so good food was scarce. The streets were filled with blue uniforms, and every open space had tents in it. The remaining citizens sat behind closed doors and despaired of the future. As one local minister put it, it was winter all the time in Chattanooga.[461]

In addition to being a place of desolation, Chattanooga and Lookout Valley were also physically cut off from the rest of the world. The entire region was dominated by Lookout Mountain, rising more than twenty-one-hundred feet at the southeast edge of the valley. The peak of the mountain, bumped up against Moccasin Bend, stood three miles from Chattanooga. To the east, Missionary Ridge, also about three miles from town, formed one long wall of the valley, and Waldon's Ridge did the same on the north side of the valley. Raccoon Mountain acted as the sentinel to the city at the western end of the vale. The Tennessee River entered at the northwestern end of the valley and exited though a narrow gorge at the end of Missionary Ridge known as the Suck. Elliptical in shape, the low land was several miles wide, and the line of Union earthworks ran across the middle of valley floor. Construction of fortifications occupied most everyone's time for the first few weeks of the siege. The Confederate Army of Tennessee held strong positions on Lookout Mountain and Missionary Ridge and had pushed picket lines down into the valley to conform with the trenches built by the Union commanders.[462]

Scarcely A Murmur or Complaint

The immediate problem faced by the Army of the Cumberland and General Rosecrans in the aftermath of Chickamauga was a continued Confederate advance, but after two days, the Union lines around the city were strong enough to repulse any attack. Colonel Van Derveer was convinced that there "is no present intention on the part of the enemy, I think to attack us—in fact should they do so, they would inevitably be defeated—we have created strong defensive works around the city." There was no way in for the rebel army, but neither was there a way out for the Army of the Cumberland. As the likelihood of an attack became less and less, a new problem became much more visible; logistics. Stocks in the city were low. With commanding positions on the high ground, the rebels dominated the routes in and out of Chattanooga and Federal supplies could not reach the beleaguered troops. Along with the rest of the army, the Thirty-fifth Ohio went on half rations before the end of September for items that were still available. Half the normal ration would not have been

---

461. Sword, *Mountains*, 84–85.
462. Ibid., 86.

unbearable, but as Lieutenant Keil of Company C explained, things weren't normal. "Half rations on the full line of items allowed soldiers, is of a nature that can be submitted to without serious complaint, but when half rations on only half the articles allowed are issued, then affairs grow rather slim: it is only a fourth allowance." When Joseph Wheeler's Confederate cavalry captured a large Union wagon train of supplies destined for Chattanooga, things got worse. The Persimmons went on one-third rations, or more accurately, one-third of half the normal issue, and "starvation was plainly at the door." Meat scraps were stolen from slaughter pens, and hungry mules suffered even more when soldiers stole their corn. Men roamed the town in search of food, but there was none to be had from the residents, who had moved their remaining livestock into their homes with the rest of the family to protect it. Any animal in plain sight was fair game, and one Yankee soldier admitted that, "There is not a pig running loose inside our lines."[463]

The army also lacked just about everything else it needed. The number of campfires burning within the Union lines was astounding. Confederates on Missionary Ridge reported, that some days, the smoke was so thick that they couldn't see the city or the river. Wood for fuel quickly became scarce, and before long, houses were being torn down for fuel and fortification work. When the houses were all stripped, the shade and fruit trees began to disappear. The men had lost most of their tents, blankets, and extra clothing during the battle and subsequent retreat, so it was hard to stay warm after the sun went down. After several weeks, the valley had been stripped of trees all the way out to the picket line. About once a week or so, an operation would be mounted to drive the enemy pickets back fifty to one hundred yards in order to "capture" more trees. The men dug shelters underground and used any materials they could get their hands on to make others above ground. Unfortunately, in spite of all the incredible schemes that were devised for housing, it was impossible to improvise food. Belts were tightened until there were no more notches left, and after that, everyone just did the best they could.[464]

In spite of the difficulties they faced while surrounded by the rebel army, none of the Persimmons were ready to throw in the towel. To a man, they believed the current situation was temporary and would soon be righted. The week after the retreat into the city, the generals in Rosecran's army had worried that the Confederates might try a frontal assault. After a couple of days of digging, the Persimmons hoped the rebels would attack them in their fortifications. In addition to trusting their trenches, they believed in Pap Thomas and in each other and were in agreement with his intention to hold Chattanooga until they all starved. Submitting to short rations "with scarcely a murmur or com-

463. Keil, *Thirty-fifth Ohio*, 162; Sword, *Mountains*, 85, 90–91; Catton, *Hallowed Ground*, 286.

464. Grebner, *We Were the Ninth*, 156; Bishop, *Story of a Regiment*, 132; Sword, *Mountains*, 86.

plaint," they worked hard to make their fortifications as strong as possible and waited for the better days they were convinced were just around the corner. The work required increased as the rations decreased, but the men of the Thirty-fifth never gave in. "'Hard tack and sow belly' were scarce; but, pluck and determination were abundant, and won in the end."[465]

Two years into their enlistment, the men of the regiment had learned that army life was a repeating cycle of feast or famine, and on active campaigns, fasting was more frequent than feasting. The cycle of fasting was normally broken by a successful foraging expedition, but there would be none of those with the rebels surrounding the city. Time that had once been spent in preparing and eating food was now spent talking about it. It was the primary topic of every campfire discussion, and every conversation began and ended with food. Even as their stomachs constantly reminded them of the shortage of rations, the Persimmons remained in an excellent frame of mind. They couldn't do much else, so they complained, but it wasn't the army they complained about. Their anger was directed at "the copperheads of the north." Their discussions about the Northern peace party became "more biting and stinging," and none among them was willing to show "weakness, or signs of yielding" to Copperhead ideas and suggestions. There was no back-up and no lessening of faith that they were doing the right thing. The Thirty-fifth's historian believed that just one day among these hungry but determined men "would have cured any milk and water compromise union man, who lived at the north and out of danger, and the reach of starvation." As part of their resolve, they made sure everyone marked their ballots for state elections on October 13.[466]

Among the bitter-enders was that dog Jack. He had learned well on his campaigns with the Persimmons and was as good a forager as any man in the regiment. A true Union man, Jack "had no respect for confederate hen-roosts or smoke houses. He was fond of nice chickens taken from the southern plantations, and was not averse to a good 'hunk' of sesech ham, when fresh meat was scarce." In spite of his naturally inquisitive ways, Jack had never been one to poke around much in other people's haversacks, at least not until Chattanooga. Fresh meat and everything else was scarce in that barren city, and Jack was just as hungry as his friends. The men did not begrudge Jack his unauthorized investigations, mostly because there was so little for him to steal. Tough times or not, Jack stayed close to home and never considered abandoning his comrades.[467]

Back in Ohio, news of Chickamauga was still filtering slowly back to each community. Newspapers carried accounts of the fighting, but they didn't tell what had happened to individual soldiers. Some news came by telegraph and some by letters from the soldiers, but most of it was rumor. On October 8, Sal-

465. Keil, *Thirty-fifth Ohio*, 162–63; Sword, *Mountains*, 88.
466. Keil, *Thirty-fifth Ohio*, 181–82.
467. Ibid., 223.

That dog Jack
KEIL

lie Rogers got a letter from her brother Jamie, a member of the Eighty-third Ohio, reporting that everyone in the Thirty-fifth Ohio had been "lost, killed, and wounded." Stout-hearted Sallie found it hard to accept that the entire regiment could have been lost and simply refused to believe it.[468]

The randomness of war reared its head again as September ended. Company H's Pvt. Henry Bradford had been detailed to the division ammunition train. As the Union line was collapsing at Chickamauga, Bradford had managed to escape the rout and ended up at the supply depot in Bridgeport, Alabama. On September 30, an artillery shell exploded unexpectedly while being moved, and Bradford was killed. And supply depots were not the only rear echelon areas where a man could get into trouble. John Perrine was a wagoner in Company A. He was part of the wagon trains trying to get enough food and supplies into Chattanooga in early October. On the second of that month, his train was attacked by a band of Wheeler's Confederate cavalry, and Perrine was captured. Uncomfortable with the idea of going to a prison camp, Perrine escaped from his captors at McMinnville and headed for more friendly territory. Taking advantage of the darkness, he traveled by moonlight and walked into the Union lines five days after being captured.[469]

---

468. Rogers Papers, "Country Life," 18.

469. Ohio Roster Commission, *Official Roster*, 625; Bogan, *Warren County's Involvement*, 45.

Not Much Hope for Me

When the Army of the Cumberland retreated into Chattanooga, it left behind hundreds of wounded men. As the rebel wave swept forward, the ambulances and wagon trains that might have moved them were pushed farther and farther away. Many of the Thirty-fifth's wounded were lying in the shadows around the Snodgrass farmhouse and watched as the regiment marched off toward Rossville on the evening of September 20. Among them was 1st Sgt. Richard Foord of Company K, wounded in the hip Sunday afternoon. They expected their friends to return and gather them up, but when rebel soldiers began wandering through the area collecting weapons and other useful equipment, they realized that they were prisoners of war.[470]

The Confederates were barely able to sustain their own minimal medical program and had nothing to offer the Union wounded other than very basic first aid. Few doctors were available to treat them, and those that did come were busy performing amputations on the seriously wounded. Wounded who did not require amputation got almost no care but took consolation in keeping all of their limbs. Richard Foord had spent a miserable night in the open at the Snodgrass farm. His wounded hip was painful and his empty stomach was growling. The Confederates gave the wounded some corn meal, but it did little to stem the hunger. As Foord lay on the ground with this injured comrades, he wanted nothing more than to "make my escape from this wretched place."[471]

The wounded comforted and helped each other as best they could. Foord also received help from Pvt. John Bate of Company A. Bate though a prisoner was unwounded and able to move around. He made some coffee and stewed peaches that provided nourishment to the immobile first sergeant. On September 23, while their comrades were busy digging trenches in Chattanooga, the wounded men of the Thirty-fifth were moved to a camp on the Lafayette road under the limbs of the trees. No other shelter was available. That morning, John Bate and many other unwounded prisoners were taken away and sent to Richmond, Virginia. It was to be the considerate Bate's last journey. He was to die in prison six months later. For two more days, the wounded sat under the trees and watched as rebel regiments marched past on their way to positions around the city. There were a lot of them, and as they told the wounded Yankees, they fully expected to capture the place before much longer. Wounded men were still being brought in from the battlefield, and the rebels had begun to bury the Yankee dead.[472]

Richard Foord's mood went up and down over the next few days. He slept well on the night of the twenty-fourth and his wound seemed greatly improved

470. Keil, *Thirty-fifth Ohio*, 158; Grebner, *We Were the Ninth*, 157.
471. Grebner, *We Were the Ninth*, 157; Foord Papers, 21 September 1863.
472. Grebner, *We Were the Ninth*, 157; Foord Papers, 22–24 September 1863.

the next morning. With Bate gone, all he was getting to eat was cornmeal mush, an inadequate diet for any human, and particularly for a man recovering from serious injury. He was able to visit with other wounded men from Company K, including his company commander. Captain Deardorf was very weak and would eventually die of his wounds three weeks later. More healthy men were pulled out and shipped to rebel prisons, and Foord sent a hastily scribbled letter with one in the hopes that he would be able to mail it from Richmond. The next morning, Foord's wounds were very sore, and his mood plummeted. "My heart's full of trouble and sorrow and pain," he wrote. "I hope I will meet my Dear Friends again." Part of Foord's malaise was his inability to move. He was tired of lying down all day but wasn't yet able to walk around. The sound of heavy artillery fire from the direction of Chattanooga was also disquieting.[473]

September 27 was a beautiful Lord's Day morning, and Foord's disposition brightened considerably. He still desperately wanted to be with friends at home, but he was able to fashion a crutch and move around a little. Mobility and news that they were to be exchanged soon did wonders for his humor. Another good night's sleep made the first sergeant feel even better. Proof of their exchange came when provisions sent from the Union camp arrived and they were formally paroled. After drinking a cup of coffee, that magical beverage, and having his hip wound dressed, Foord remained in good spirits.[474]

On September 29, Foord was loaded into an ambulance for transportation into friendly lines. It was a difficult trip in uncomfortable carts and the men inside were bounced around for six hours or more before they arrived in Chattanooga. The wagons traveled the Rossville road, passing right through the camp of Van Derveer's brigade. Lt. Lewis Lambright and men from Foord's company were guarding the road that day, and Foord was able to speak with them briefly as the ambulances passed. Foord and the other wounded from the Thirty-fifth Ohio ended up at the Reed House, the city's largest hotel now converted into a makeshift hospital. Any man who was expected to die soon was placed outside in the hallways. Some of the wounded men who made it back to the hospital recovered and rejoined the regiment later. Some died within a few days. Others hung on for months before finally succumbing to their wounds. Pvt. Thomas Lyons of Company A lingered until July 1864 before passing away at home in Warren County, Ohio.[475]

Coming back into the Union lines had the feeling of a homecoming for Richard Foord. As soon as he had passed through the camp and spoken to his mates, Foord felt better and was convinced he would soon be well. Visits from friends in Company K increased his feelings of well being immeasurably, but Foord did not stay in Chattanooga for long. After a few days of alternately

---

473. Foord Papers, 25–26 September 1863.
474. Ibid., 27–28 September 1863.
475. Keil, *Thirty-fifth Ohio*, 158; Grebner, *We Were the Ninth*, 158; Foord Papers, 29 September 1863.

lying in a bed made of confiscated cotton bales and hobbling around the hospital, he was loaded into a wagon and sent to Stevenson, Alabama, on October 4. By the thirteenth, Foord was in Nashville reading Cincinnati newspapers and eating good food prepared by the Sisters of Charity. Less than a week later, the steadily healing first sergeant was in Louisville, still sore and starting to feel lonesome. He had left one home far behind in Chattanooga and was still some distance from the place he wanted to be in Middletown. In Louisville, the hospital chaplain came by for a visit. The two men must have disagreed on some topic of theology, because Foord wrote that the chaplain "talked with me sometime on the subject of religion—I am afraid he thought there was not much hope for me." Finally, after several weeks in the Louisville hospital, Foord got what he wanted most and was sent home on leave.[476]

Laurels Will Soon Wither

Henry Boynton had been suffering from an intermittent fever in the days before Chickamauga, but the symptoms "disappeared under the excitement of the fight." Once the regiment took its place in the lines around Chattanooga, the fever returned with a vengeance. In his request for leave, Boynton wrote that his symptoms "in connection with the derangement of the system have completely prostrated me and rendered a respite absolutely necessary to restore me to duty." The positive endorsements of Colonel Van Derveer and General Brannan resulted in approval of the leave. Brannan made it clear that he wanted Boynton back on duty and a restorative leave was necessary to achieve that. The plan worked, and a few weeks later Boynton was back in command of the regiment.[477]

While the wounded Union soldiers were being exchanged, an informal truce had gone into effect all along the lines. For several days, the pickets on both sides had been able to talk things over and exchange goods. They made an agreement among themselves not to shoot at each other unless there was a general advance by one side or the other. Left to their own devices, the truce would have lasted indefinitely, but the Confederate high command had different ideas. On October 5, the Confederate artillery on Lookout Mountain and Missionary Ridge began to bombard the Union position around Chattanooga. As far as the men in the Third Brigade were concerned, the rebel cannonade was useless but slightly amusing. The danger of upsetting a cup of coffee was considered more important than being hit by a piece of flying metal. The Confederate artillery

476. Foord Papers, 29 Sep tember–25 October 1863; Sword, *Mountains*, 85.

477. Compiled service record, Henry V. Boynton, Maj., Staff, 35th Ohio Inf.; Carded Records, Volunteer Organizations, Civil War; Records of the Adjutant General's office, 1780s–1917, Record Group 94; National Archives, Washington, D.C.

did not fire continually, but in sudden spurts. Guards were instructed to watch for muzzle flashes or smoke on the ridge. The muzzle-loading cannon of the Civil War fired its projectiles at a low enough velocity that the shells could actually be observed in flight. When cannon fired on the ridge, sentries called out a warning. At first, everyone would scamper for the nearest hole when the warning came. But as the ineffectiveness of the fire became apparent, each soldier would watch the incoming shell and make his own decision to stand or flee.[478]

Ferdinand Van Derveer regularly toured the positions held by his brigade. It gave him a chance to inspect the works and to think. The Second Minnesota was busy at work on their breastworks one day, while their brigade commander strolled thoughtfully in front of them. Pacing back and forth with his arms folded behind him, momentarily consumed by his thoughts, Van Derveer was oblivious to the world around him when a rebel cannon on Missionary Ridge fired the first round of the day. Men all along the line looked up at the sound of the shot, all except Van Derveer, who continued his contemplative pacing. The shell hurtled its way toward the Union lines, while men hunkering behind earthen mounds tried to gauge its flight. Unmindful of the commotion, Van Derveer never looked up as the enemy shell smashed into the ground a few feet away, showering him with dirt.

It took a lot to ruffle Ferdinand Van Derveer's feathers. As the cannonball rolled to a stop directly in front of him, the stern faced colonel gave no indication of surprise or concern. Gazing at the spent projectile briefly, he reached out, tapped it with his foot, and then spoke loud enough for the Minnesotans to hear. "It looks as though that was intended for me," he stated calmly, "but I serve notice on Longstreet that if that is the best he can do, in spite of his successes on the Potomac, his laurels will soon wither in this climate." With that, he continued his pacing as the men around him smiled and shook their heads. On the same day, Van Derveer wrote to his wife, "We are having no trouble with the rebels except a little artillery firing—which has yet done little harm."[479]

The geography of the Chattanooga area served to add a little something of the spectacular to the siege of Chattanooga. During daylight hours, the Persimmons could look up at Missionary Ridge and Lookout Mountain and see the Confederate lines dug into the hillsides. The positions of the rebel artillery batteries could be made out with the naked eye, and those fortunate enough to have a spyglass could see individual enemy soldiers moving around. All of that was interesting, but at night, it became downright wonderful. "[The] grand semi-circle was lighted up with the enemy's little campfires, whose light was

---

478. Sword, *Mountains*, 92–93; Cozzens, *Shipwreck*, 33.
479. Bishop, *Story of a Regiment*, 133; H. H. Hill, "The Second Minnesota: Reminiscences of Four Years at the Front," *National Tribune*, 13, 20 July 1899; Cozzens, *Shipwreck*, 33–34; Van Derveer to wife, 16 October 1863, Van Derveer Family Collection.

continually intermitted by the squads of shivering, half-clothed rebels standing and moving around them, the spectacle was one we never tired of watching." Added to this marvelous scene were Confederate signal torches that could be seen flashing messages to each other across the valley. Yankees and Confederates alike wrote home about the sight, describing it to the homefolks as impressive and imposing. To some it seemed as if a great celebration was occurring in the valley.[480]

Organizational changes occurred in the Army of the Cumberland in October. General Rosecrans was relieved of command and replaced by General Thomas. The Fourteenth Corps was taken over by Maj. Gen. John M. Palmer. General Brannan also moved on, becoming the chief of artillery for the Army of the Cumberland, and was replaced by Brig. Gen. Absalom Baird. Baird, a career army officer, had served in the Army of the Potomac before coming west. The Third Brigade, Third Division, to which the 35th Ohio had been assigned, was redesignated as the Second Brigade, Third Division. The changes brought new responsibilities for Colonel Van Derveer, further indication of the respect for which he was held at army headquarters. In addition to the Persimmons, the 2nd Minnesota, 9th Ohio, and 87th Indiana remained under his command. Added to those four regiments were three others, the 75th Indiana, 101st Indiana, and the 105th Ohio for a total of 2,116 men. All were veteran units, and the 105th Ohio had distinguished itself at Chickamauga with a daring charge that bought crucial time for the army to form a new line.[481]

In addition to the gnawing hunger, the weather did its part to make life miserable for the Thirty-fifth Ohio. During the months of October and November, it rained about every other day. Trenches filled with water, and the makeshift shelters the men lived in didn't do much to keep it out. Compounding the misery, the temperature fell along with the rain. During the day, everyone foundered around in mud deep enough to cover their shoes. With thousands of soldiers and wagons trampling the ground, it was difficult to walk anywhere in town. Cold nights and frost-covered ground made it hard to sleep comfortably. The need for wood grew even greater.[482]

There has always been a gap between officers and enlisted men when it comes to style of living, and Chattanooga in the fall of 1863 was no exception. Ferdinand Van Derveer didn't get any more to eat than his men did, but he didn't have to live in the mud. He had "coaxed" two ladies living in a nearby house to leave and allow him to stay while they were gone. He told his wife, "I wish you could peep into my domicile this evening and see how comfortably I am provided for." No problems with wood for the colonel. His cozy little house had a grate with plenty of coal. It even had an earthwork in front of it to stop

---

480. Bishop, *Story of a Regiment*, 134; Sword, *Mountains*, 87.

481. U.S. War Department, *War of the Rebellion*, Ser. no. 50, p. 213; McKinney, *Education in Violence*, 258.

482. Sword, *Mountains*, 96–97.

skipping cannon balls. He had also just learned that General Rosecrans had nominated him for elevation to brigadier general. Sitting in "tiresome" Chattanooga and thinking of home left him with mixed feelings about any promotion. "If my own wishes alone were to be consented, I would prefer being only Ferd. V.—and the command I most covet consists of one little woman and four babies."[483]

The work of fortification was never ending, and chief engineer Gen. W. F. "Baldy" Smith pursued it relentlessly. Each regiment was required to provide work details at specified points to work under the direction of designated engineering officers. The commander of Smith's pioneer brigade, General Morton, sent his engineering officers out with tools and orders to supervise the details but not direct them. The line officers in charge of each detail were responsible for accomplishment of the actual work. It was a plan designed to create inaction, because after two years, the officers and men of the Thirty-fifth had learned how to get by in the army. They were also heartily tired of digging. Building forts was very hard work, and some of the logs being used in the walls required thirty men to put them in place. On October 14, Lt. Theodore Mather of Company H reported to the engineering officers with a work party of fifty men. Engineer Lieutenant Gillespie, explained what needed to be done and then left the work to Mather. After one look at the darkening sky, Mather decided the weather was too bad to work, so he and his men went back to camp without turning a single spade full of dirt. The Second Brigade provided four details that morning. Having seen Lieutenant Mather's successful bid for freedom, the other three officers from the 9th Ohio, 87th Indiana, and the 105th Ohio, also packed it in before any work was done. General Smith was not in the least bit amused, but no action was taken against Mather or the others, who had, after all, only taken advantage of the discretion allowed them.[484]

Ever since July, Colonel Van Derveer had been suffering from intestinal inflammation. At the beginning of October his health deteriorated to the point that he felt like he had to ask for leave to recuperate. The brigade's senior surgeon, Dr. Konrad Sollheim of the Ninth Ohio, prepared a medical certificate stating that Van Derveer's best chance of recovery was "rest, together with a change of diet & mode of living" for thirty days. Van Derveer applied for and received a twenty-day leave and rode the train north to his home in Hamilton.[485]

General Rosecrans already had a plan ready for breaking the siege when he was relieved on October 18. Grant reviewed the plans made under Rosecrans's

---

483. Van Derveer to wife, 7 October 1863, Van Derveer Family Collection.

484. U.S. War Department, *War of the Rebellion*, Ser. no. 53, pp. 362–63; Sword, *Mountains*, 88.

485. Compiled service record, Ferdinand Van Derveer, Col., Co. Staff, 35th Ohio Inf.; Carded Records, Volunteer Organizations, Civil War; Records of the Adjutant General's office, 1780s–1917, Record Group 94; National Archives, Washington, D.C.

direction when he arrived on October 22 and ordered them implemented. The Eleventh and Twelfth Corps of the Army of the Potomac, under the command of General Joseph Hooker had been ordered to reinforce Rosecrans and were waiting at Bridgeport. Hooker's forces, in combination with Hazen's brigade of the Army of the Cumberland, pushed the rebels away from the river crossing at Brown's Ferry on November 5 and laid a pontoon bridge. Supplies were shipped by river from Bridgeport, Alabama, and offloaded at Kelly's Ferry. From there, wagons brought them into Chattanooga. It was not the return of abundance, but the threat of starvation was removed forever.

More food wasn't enough to save everyone. When word reached home that Cpl. Benjamin Boatman had been wounded at Chickamauga, his father, Mark, had immediately set off for Chattanooga. If they could get him home, Boatman's family believed he would get better care and be more likely to recover. The elder Boatman found his son in a Chattanooga hospital and got permission to carry him back to Ohio. But when he returned to his home, Mark Boatman was alone. Greatly weakened by his wounds, Ben died en route and was buried in Nashville.[486]

Everybody could agree that wagonmaster Wilkinson Beatty was a unique character. Old Wilk had done well for himself since leaving Hamilton. His obvious competence in choosing and managing animals was reinforced by his quirky, but somehow attractive, personality. Always the oldest man in the regiment, Beatty had been discharged for disability in February 1863 at age sixty-five about the time Colonel Van Derveer took permanent command of the brigade. Somehow, after his discharge, Beatty was given the rank of first lieutenant and made the brigade wagonmaster. There is something a little mysterious about the situation. Everyone acted as if Beatty was an officer, but there is no record of any official service after his discharge. Whatever the case, Beatty accompanied the brigade to Chickamauga and was with the army during the subsequent siege. At Chickamauga, Wilk's health apparently deteriorated to the point that he had to resign and leave the army.[487]

Then again, he may not have resigned at all. It may be that he simply found a better deal, for when he left the army, Beatty opened a hotel in Chattanooga. Beatty had gained the good graces of Pap Thomas in Kentucky and held on to them ever since. Everyone always assumed that "the peculiar make up of the man attracted the general's attention, and the rattling way of talking, so peculiar to Beatty, afforded amusement and recreation to a mind so habitually over-worked." Beatty's connections stood him in good stead when he became a businessman. In spite of the shortages in Chattanooga, Beatty could always get what he needed for his hotel and was able to assist others in getting freight shipped in and out of the city by rail. When he joined the army, Beatty had been "bankrupted by placing his name on too many accommodation papers," but his

---

486. Boatman Family Papers, Butler County Historical Society, Hamilton, Ohio.
487. Keil, *Thirty-fifth Ohio*, 58.

hotel and freight business made him quite comfortable.[488]

Pay was a constant source of irritation to the soldiers of the Thirty-fifth. They were supposed to be paid every other month, but it never seemed to work that way. The paymaster was always late or seemed to arrive at the most inopportune times. To make matters even worse, they were paid in depreciated greenbacks. Since they had to buy things according to specie rates, the thirteen dollars a month they were receiving had the spending power of about five dollars. A year before, they had been in Louisville, a city rich with everything a hungry or bored soldier could want, but the paymaster had not arrived until after the Perryville campaign. Chattanooga was nearly the opposite of Louisville. A city scarred by bombardment and stripped bare by two armies, it offered virtually nothing desirable to a soldier, but here, surrounded by hostile rebels, the paymaster showed up on time. The money he brought was near useless to the Persimmons. There was little to buy in the city, and all indications pointed toward more extended campaigns in the field. Most of the soldier's money was sent home, but a lot of it still ended up in chuck-a-luck games.[489]

Ferdinand Van Derveer was once again on his way to the front. After less than three weeks home, he was back on the train headed south. He was not fully recovered but felt well enough to return to duty. At Nashville, Van Derveer ran into Colonel John Beatty [Note: John Beatty began the war as a captain in the Third Ohio Infantry and eventually rose to the rank of brigadier general. After the war, he served in Congress from 1868 to 1873, and then as president of the Citizen's Savings Bank. He also published his wartime diaries and several historical novels.] a fellow Buckeye, also on his way back to Chattanooga. Both had passes that entitled them to first class accommodations, but the train they were assigned to contained only one passenger car. The rest of the train consisted of freight cars and the caboose "which offered the traveler but little comfort." So, by default, that one passenger car became first class, and the two veteran field commanders climbed aboard. There were plenty of seats available and they took the nearest ones, pleased to have a reasonably comfortable perch for the trip. But all was not well.

Another officer approached, and the two senior officers "were notified rather brusquely by a gentleman in major's uniform that it was a special car, engaged for the accommodation of the paymasters who were in it, and they desired that we should find seats elsewhere." Van Derveer gazed up at the major steely eyed and informed him that since they had tickets for a first class fare and this was the only passenger car on the train, he and Beatty "proposed to continue in it." The paymasters were highly irritated, and fully intended to have the two interlopers off their car. They had no idea who they were dealing with. Both Van Derveer and Beatty were combat veterans with little regard for

488. Keil, *Thirty-fifth Ohio*, 58–59.
489. Grebner, *We Were the Ninth*, 161; Bircher, *Drummer Boy's Diary*, 56; Sword, *Mountains*, 96.

soft living rear echelon officers, even if they were paymasters. John Beatty was also every bit as stubborn as Ferdinand Van Derveer, but the paymasters didn't know that. They began a "consultation" among themselves in which they loudly criticized Van Derveer and Beatty for "obtruding upon a party of gentlemen."

They no doubt hoped that the shame of it all would induce their unwanted guests to disembark, but the two combat veterans would have none of that. A lively exchange ensued with both sides heatedly exchanging personal opinions of the other. After several minutes of debate, the paymasters "finally discovered that they had run against two very obstinate men, who could not be bullied, and who were just as quick and bitter with their tongues" as any paymaster could be. Realizing they had no hope of victory, the paymasters ended the exchange and went back to their part of the car. The quarrel ended amicably. As the train traveled south, the two groups began to converse on a more friendly basis, and by the time they all arrived in Chattanooga, they "were all on tolerably good terms."[490]

Liars and Thieves

Surgeons Landis and Wright were not as fortunate as those captured at Snodgrass Hill. As the Thirty-fifth was retreating into Chattanooga, the two doctors were still working among the wounded at the hospital on the Cloud farm. Confederate general Nathan Bedford Forrest visited the hospital on September 21 and informed the Union doctors that they would be allowed to continue their work unmolested. Forrest also said that wounded northern soldiers were to be collected and brought to the hospital and would receive the same treatment as the Southern wounded. Furthermore, parties had been detailed to bury the dead of both sides. Landis later had a personal conversation with Dr. Fluellan, the medical director of the Confederate Army of Tennessee, and the exact same assurances were given. As Landis soon learned, the "promises may have been in good faith, but from observation I know—and every other medical officer who fell into their hands knows—they were not realized."[491]

Doctor Landis was able to walk over part of the battlefield on September 23, and he found that the Confederate dead had been buried, but the Union dead, many of them stripped of pants and shoes, still lay about the field. After three days of exposure to the sun, their "appearance was most revolting," and "they were so swollen and changed in appearance that recognition was impossible." The remaining Union wounded had also been left scattered about the field

---

490. Ford, Harvey S., ed., "The Diary of John Beatty, January-June 1884," pt. 1, *Ohio History* 58 no. 2 (April 1949): 135–36.

491. *Cyclopaedia of Butler County, Ohio*, 223.

even though the rebel injured had been removed to hospitals. Landis found more than three hundred Northern wounded, some in cabins, some collected in groups, and some scattered about in close proximity to dead comrades. In addition to their injuries, these men were now suffering acutely from hunger. Landis did credit the rebels for providing rations for the wounded the next day.[492]

The most frustrating thing for Landis was his inability to do anything for the wounded men he had found. There were no ambulances or wagons available to transport the wounded to the hospital, and the rebels refused to provide any. Even had they been able to bring these men to the hospital, little could have been done. The hospital was swamped with the injured men already there. Provisions had run out on September 22, and the men there were hungry, too. After two days of begging, the Confederates provided beef, bacon, hardtack, and corn meal. The bacon and crackers were good but arrived in insufficient quantities. The beef, assumed to be "of Pharaoh's lean kine," was stringy and tough, and the corn meal was scarcely fit to eat. But at least it was food, and its arrival was welcomed. The arrangement that allowed the Army of the Cumberland to send food to the wounded held by the rebels changed everything. Beginning on the twenty-eighth, the shadow of hunger lifted and there was plenty of food. Landis reported that "we fared sumptuously" from then on.[493]

The shadows returned on October 2. The wounded men at the hospital were paroled and repatriated through the lines around Chattanooga, but the doctors and able-bodied enlisted men remained prisoners of the Confederates. A party of seven doctors and seventy-three enlisted men were marched seven miles to Chickamauga Station and taken to Atlanta by train. Included in this party was Joseph O'Neall. Conditions at the prison barracks in Atlanta, a two-acre plot surrounded by a twelve-foot high wooden fence, were bad. Upon arrival, the blankets of O'Neall and the other enlisted men were confiscated, forcing them to sleep on the cold ground. The barracks consisted of "two board shanties" in which the new arrivals found some forty wounded men. The wounded men were lying on the floor with but one blanket apiece. One of the surgeons, Dr. Ashman, asked for straw to be used as bedding. As at Chickamauga, promises were made, but no straw appeared. Among the injured prisoners was a Major Morely, who, because he was a resident of Tennessee and considered a traitor by the rebels, received special treatment. Suffering terribly from typhoid fever, Morely was forced to wear a ball and chain until it became obvious he was dying.[494]

On October 5, several hundred other prisoners taken at Chickamauga, including forty surgeons were placed in the Atlanta prison. The next day, nearly all of the surgeons, Landis included, and three hundred enlisted men were put back on railcars. Traveling first through Georgia, South Carolina, and North

---

492. *Cyclopaedia of Butler County, Ohio,* 223.
493. Ibid; Bogan, *Warren County's Involvement,* 13.
494. *Cyclopaedia of Butler County, Ohio,* 223.

Carolina, the train arrived in Richmond, Virginia, on Sunday, October 11. Landis and the other surgeons were taken to Libby Prison. When he entered the prison, Landis was told to hand over any greenbacks, gold, or silver he might have. Confederate captain Turner told Landis that if he needed money while in the prison, his legal money would be exchanged for Confederate money at the rate of seven to one. Upon release, any remaining money would be refunded in kind. Refusal to hand over his money would result in all of it being confiscated. It seemed a fair proposition, and Landis turned his money over to the Confederates.[495]

As described by Landis, Libby Prison was "a substantial brick building, one hundred fifty feet long, and one hundred and ten feet wide, and three stories high besides the basement. The upper two stories are each divided into three rooms, and in these six rooms, before our release, were over one thousand prisoners, all commissioned officers." The stench from the open toilets was "almost unendurable." The glass had been taken out of all the windows, and the fall nights were starting to get good and cold. In response to complaints, the prison commander provided two stoves for each room, but since he provided barely enough fuel to cook with, there was none left for heating. The captured officers got no relief from the cold.[496]

Some of the wounded prisoners from Chickamauga were housed in the room below Landis's. The officers were able to communicate with these enlisted soldiers though a hole in the floor. The desperate soldiers told them they had not been fed for over a day and implored the officers for something to eat. The officers had little themselves, but they divided what they had and gave some to the men below. Captain Turner learned of the exchange and was infuriated. He declared that the men would not be fed for the next two days as punishment for talking with the officers. Landis also learned that the enlisted prisoners at Belle Isle were suffering even more than those incarcerated at Libby. He observed a work party of prisoners on the street in mid-November. "Some men were barefooted, some bareheaded, and I noticed one poor fellow barefooted, bareheaded, and without a shirt. We never were allowed to ask them any questions in reference to their treatment, but the mere appearance of their faces told us starvation and exposure were closing the work of death."[497]

Joseph O'Neall ended up in Castle Pemberton. The youngster found prison life not to his liking and began to dig a tunnel with the help of four other soldiers. They were caught before their underground passage was completed, and O'Neall was forced to stand on his feet for twenty-four hours and was not given any food for two days. Shortly after his punishment, he was transferred to the prisoner-of-war camp at Danville, Virginia, where he immediately began planning for his next escape. Seven soldiers slipped into a drain pipe, followed it as

495. *Cyclopaedia of Butler County, Ohio*, 223–24.
496. Ibid.
497. Ibid., 224.

far as they could, and then tunneled out. Four of the escapees were quickly captured, but O'Neall and two others slipped into the woods. They eluded searching Confederate parties, and after three days of wandering in the forests, the man too young to be in the army heard the baying of the blood hounds. Recaptured only a few hundred yards from friendly positions, O'Neall was stripped to his underwear, or what was left of it, to discourage further escape attempts. He was kept in this "almost nude condition," wearing only the remains of a shirt provided by a generous fellow POW, for about six months. It was during this period that the young Ohioan finally turned eighteen and became eligible to serve in the armed forces of his country. In May 1864, when the Danville stockade became too crowded for the rebels to manage, Joseph O'Neall was shoved into a boxcar with sixty other men, most "suffering with bowel trouble, diarrhea, and dysentery" and shipped further south. It was a long, excruciatingly slow trip. "No matter how often our engine was changed," he recalled, "it was drawn by an old worn out rickety, squeaking, squealing wagon over a worn out, half ballasted railroad." The cars were filthy, the stench nearly unbearable, and several times, the prisoners were forced to detrain and chop wood for the locomotive. After brief stays in the Greensboro, North Carolina, jail, the state penitentiary at Raleigh, another penitentiary at Columbia, South Carolina, and a jail in Macon, Georgia, the imperturbable youth from Warren County was entered on the rolls of the Confederacy's newest hellhole at Andersonville, Georgia.[498]

Landis and the other surgeons were more fortunate than most of the officers who entered Libby Prison. They were exchanged toward the end of November after only a few weeks in confinement. On the way out of the prison, Landis's money was refunded as promised, with one little catch. His legal United States tender was returned to him in worthless Confederate bills. Abraham Landis was a fair-minded, gentle man, but he had nothing good to say about Libby Prison and the men who ran it. "There is no state-prison in North America that can belch forth a more infamous pack of liars and thieves than the officers in charge of Libby Prison." He was convinced that America would never know "how many of her noble sons perished in the dens of Richmond." Time has proven him right.[499]

---

498. Bogan, *Warren County's Involvement*, 13, 62.
499. *Cyclopaedia of Butler County, Ohio*, 224.

CHAPTER 11

Long-Winded Chaps

November 1863 to April 1864

We Wanted that Ridge

Gen. Ulysses S. Grant began his effort to break out of Chattanooga by ordering Gen. William T. Sherman and the Union Army of the Tennessee to join the Army of the Cumberland at Chattanooga. The general plan called for Hooker's easterners to capture Lookout Mountain while Sherman and his army crumpled the Confederate line on Missionary Ridge from the north. The role of the Army of the Cumberland was to demonstrate in front of Missionary Ridge and draw attention away from the main efforts on the flanks. The Cumberlanders were to watch while others did the hard work and not join in until the other Union forces had broken the shoulders of the enemy line. Sherman reached Chattanooga in mid-November, but his army was late in arriving, and even later in getting into position for the attack. The rebels also hindered Union efforts by sending logs down the river to break the pontoon bridge the army was using.

In spite of the delays, Grant clung to his plan of using the Army of the Tennessee as the primary assault force. It was his army. He had commanded it during the Vicksburg campaign and knew all of its idiosyncrasies. Supremely confident of the army's capabilities and that of its commander, General Sherman, Grant did not have the same confidence in the Army of the Cumberland and its new commander, George Thomas. Grant still connected Thomas with his near disgrace after Shiloh and believed him to be overly cautious. Grant also believed that the Army of the Cumberland had been demoralized by the battle of Chickamauga and would not be willing to leave its trenches and make a determined assault.

Grant was wrong on both counts. The men of the Thirty-fifth Ohio had been too tired to be angry after being ordered to leave the field at Chickamauga, but now they got mad. In Grant's mind, it was a question of *if* the Cumberlanders would attack. As far as the Thirty-fifth was concerned, the only question was *when*, and in their minds, Grant's attitude impugned them and the entire army. Nothing could change the fact that they had been beaten in a stand-up fight at Chickamauga, but they were still fully capable of making an attack. Moreover, they were ready to do it just as soon as the orders were given, because they could never be at peace with themselves until they had made up for the whipping the rebels had given them. The Persimmons trusted their own courage and ability and believed that Grant's feelings toward them were "uncalled for and highly unjust." As they saw it, "A more determined and pluckier set of men than those found in the trenches at Chattanooga never shouldered a musket. These were the men who stood on Horseshoe Ridge on the Chickamauga battlefield, hurling Longstreet's veterans back as often as they approached. Braver men with stouter hearts never wore the blue. These men needed no [A]rmy of the Tennessee to show them how to fight." The Army of the Tennessee had admittedly done well at Vicksburg, but they "had never seen fighting like that on Chickamauga's field."[500]

Sherman's attack was originally scheduled for November 21, but the red-haired general was unable to get his army in position. On November 23, a warm pleasant day, orders arrived to be ready to move the next morning. Each man was given two days rations and one hundred rounds of ammunition, and the brigade took up positions in front of one of the earthen forts surrounding Chattanooga. Once again, the Army of the Tennessee was not ready, so ironically, it was the Army of the Cumberland that made the first offensive move. As part of their demonstration to draw attention away from Sherman's effort and determine the strength of the rebel lines in the valley, the Cumberlanders were to drive the rebels from the high ground at Orchard Knob and Indian Hill. As the rebels watched with interest from Missionary Ridge, the regiments in the Army of the Cumberland carefully and deliberately put on a show. Drums and bugles sounded as regiment after regiment moved into position and dressed its ranks. Sunlight flashed on bayonets and in every direction, flags waved in the wind. Every one of Thomas's soldiers was anxious to show that these "demoralized, faint-hearted, enfeebled, and terrified troops, which Grant feared could not be coaxed to leave their entrenchments" would not only leave them, but fight with great élan. With everyone straining at the bit, the entire army moved forward rapidly when the order finally came about one thirty.[501]

As part of the Second Brigade's forward movement, the Thirty-fifth Ohio advanced along the Rossville road to the south of Orchard Knob. The Persimmon's role, and that of Baird's entire division, was to push the rebel picket lines back in support of the attack on Orchard Knob. Baird pushed his troops right up to the rebel lines and then halted. Having been ordered not to bring on a general

---

500. Keil, *Thirty-fifth Ohio*, 166; Catton, *Hallowed Ground*, 293.

501. Keil, *Thirty-fifth Ohio*, 166; Bircher, *Drummer Boy's Diary*, 53; U.S. War Department, *War of the Rebellion*, Ser. no. 55, pp. 533, 537; McKinney, *Education in Violence*, 288.

Missionary Ridges as seen from Orchard Knob
CHICKAMAUGA NATIONAL MILITARY PARK

engagement on his part of the line, he advanced no further.

The Confederates behind the breastworks on the two hills constituted nothing more than a reinforced picket line, and even though all of the Union army's preparations had been conducted in full view of the rebels, their commanders had made no effort to prepare. Some thought a review was being conducted. Others assumed the Yankees just needed more wood. Early in the afternoon, the rebel pickets saw the Union army coming at them in dense compact ranks and immediately fell back on their reserves. The forward movement continued inexorably and the enemy picket's reserve was in turn driven back into the field works. Even the trenches provided no bulwark in which the retreating rebel pickets could regroup. The Federal ranks neither delayed nor hesitated, and immediately followed the Confederate pickets into their trenches. By three o'clock, Orchard Knob and Indian Hill were permanently secured. The Army of the Cumberland completed its attack before Sherman's army, the men who were supposedly going to save it, had fired a shot or could even get across the river. Even so, the soldiers of the Army of the Cumberland were still not happy. The day's fighting had only involved light skirmishing and the real work of driving the Confederates away from Chattanooga still belonged to the outsiders in Hooker's and Sherman's ranks. As night fell, the Thirty-fifth Ohio bivouacked astride the Moore road about three quarters of a mile in front of Fort Phelps.[502]

On November 24, the Union army launched a two-pronged attack at both ends of the Confederate line. Sherman's men attacked the Confederates near the

---

502. Keil, *Thirty-fifth Ohio*, 166-67; Bishop, *Story of a Regiment*, 134; U.S. War Department, *War of the Rebellion*, Ser. no. 55, pp. 527, 537.

railroad tunnel and were stopped in their tracks. Hooker's attack on Lookout Mountain was much more successful and infinitely more spectacular. Standing in formation on the valley floor near the Rossville road, the Persimmons were able to observe the progress of the battle on Lookout Mountain. Fog covered the mountain and had settled thick at the base, but there were enough gaps to allow the men below to monitor Hooker's progress. When the fog was too thick to see through, they could tell how the fighting was going by listening to the sound of musketry from the slopes. When the fog cleared, the Persimmons were treated to an inspiring vista in which they "could observe exactly how the Rebels withdrew northeast along the slopes, with Hooker's troops after them, flags flying." About noon, soldiers in Union blue moved around the point of Lookout Mountain and drove toward the bridge across Chattanooga Creek and the Summertown road. The men in the valley cheered and the cannons in Fort Negley and Fort Wood sounded their own congratulations. The easterners ran out of ammunition in midafternoon, and their trains were unable to get up the steep slopes of the mountain. Hooker had to stop before reaching either the bridge or the road.[503]

The night of the twenty-fourth was quiet, but firing started early the next morning as Sherman made another attempt to roll up the Confederate right. The Persimmons were ordered to perform a reconnaissance along the brigade front and put 221 men in a long, thin, skirmish line. Two years after leaving Ohio, they were down to 25 percent of their original strength. Information that the rebels had abandoned their forward positions was proven correct as the Thirty-fifth advanced for about a mile meeting no real opposition. Nearly all the rebel pickets had withdrawn at daybreak, and "several small parties left for observation" skedaddled as soon as the Yankees appeared, moving back to the base of the ridge. Finding nothing of interest to do, the regiment remained in its advanced position while the "demoralized, frightened, and timid men of the Cumberland army were to look on from the plains below, and see how armies, not demoralized or effeminated behind breast-works fight." Once again, the Thirty-fifth Ohio "stood long, and waited patiently for the object lesson that was to be given them," but no lesson was provided. Hooker's attack never materialized, and Sherman was once again stopped cold. Down in the valley, the indignation intensified. Where's Hooker? Where's Sherman? Why are we just standing here? The sun had reached its highest point in the autumn sky and was well on its path toward the horizon, but still they waited. With nothing in the offing, Pvt. Johnny Doyle of Company C was sent to the rear to get rations for the officer's mess.[504]

Some level of satisfaction was regained later in the day. Sherman had called for reinforcements, and around 11:00 a.m. Baird's division had been

---

503. Grebner, *We Were the Ninth*, 162.
504. Keil, *Thirty-fifth Ohio*, 168; U.S. War Department, *War of the Rebellion*, Ser. no. 55, pp. 527, 537.

ordered to go to Sherman's support. The Thirty-fifth Ohio marched along with the rest of the Third Division, and by noon had reached Citico Creek in the rear of Sherman's lines, when new orders called them back. Just west of the Nashville and Chattanooga Railroad, the brigade formed for battle about half a mile north of Bald Hill and approximately twelve hundred yards from the rebel trenches at the base of the ridge. Everyone was ordered to stack arms and lie down to rest. While the regiment was marching to and fro, Johnny Doyle had stuffed a basket with food and returned to the place he had left, but the Thirty-fifth was nowhere to be found. Undaunted, the luckless private set out to find his comrades and officers waiting to be fed. [505]

The sun was low in the sky when orders came about 4:00 p.m. to make another demonstration against the base of Missionary Ridge with the entire Army of the Cumberland advancing as one unit. Blue-clad Persimmons got to their feet, reclaimed rifles from the stacks, and shuffled into line. Mark Price and his crew began to unfurl the colors, and the regiment's line of battle firmed up. General Baird came to Colonel Van Derveer and told him, "Van Derveer, it is evidently too steep for riding. You had better order your regimental officers to leave their horses." Baird had just completed his orders to Van Derveer when the signal guns announcing the start of the attack were fired. With the 2nd Minnesota acting as skirmishers, the Persimmons were in the center of the brigade lines flanked on either side by the Hoosiers of the 101st and 87th Indiana and the 75th Indiana, the 105th Ohio, and the 9th Ohio following close behind. Seething with nervous energy, the regiment "moved off with a will" toward the enemy trenches at the bottom of the hill, every man shouting the Union battle cry, *Hurrah!* The Persimmons advanced in "fine style" and "pushed briskly forward." Rifle fire came from the lower rebel works where two stands of Confederate colors were clearly visible, while Confederate artillery opened up from the heights with "a terrific fire of spherical case." The sound of cannon fire echoed like thunder across the valley. The ridge seemed to be covered in smoke and flame as grapeshot tore into the ground around them, but there was little or no firing from the blue ranks.[506]

In spite of all the dramatic effects, there were very few casualties. Van Derveer had intentionally held his main battle line three hundred yards behind his skirmishers. Nearly all of the rebel fire overshot the skirmishers and hit the ground between the two groups. The advance was not delayed in the slightest. The excitement and impatience of the men began to show as the regiment reached open ground in front of Orchard Knob where the Confederates had chopped down every last tree. The men-in-ranks "started off on the double quick, and next into a clever run, right at, and into the rebel works."[507]

505. Keil, *Thirty-fifth Ohio*, 173; U.S. War Department, *War of the Rebellion*, Ser. no. 55, pp. 527, 531, 537.

506. Keil, *Thirty-fifth Ohio*, 171; U.S. War Department, *War of the Rebellion*, Ser. no. 55, pp. 528, 538; Cozzens, *Shipwreck*, 257, 260; Boynton, *Annual Address*, 34.

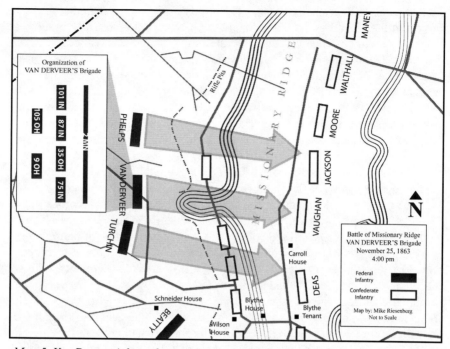

Map 5. Van Derveer's brigade at Missionary Ridge, November 25, 1863, at 4:00 p.m.

The rebels in the trenches at the bottom of the ridge were overwhelmed, physically and psychologically. Watching his skirmishers advance, Colonel Van Derveer related, "As they approached to within 150 yards of the enemy, great uneasiness was apparent among the men in the rifle-pits, and by the time our skirmishers were at a distance of 100 yards they were retreating precipitately up the ridge to their rear." Excited soldiers of the Second Minnesota leaped into the Confederate trenches, as the rebels leaped out and began scurrying up the hill any way they could. By the time the Thirty-fifth Ohio, three hundred yards behind the skirmishers, entered the trenches, the rebels were all scrambling up the hill. The day's objective had been taken so quickly that casualties were few in spite of the heavy "fire of musketry in front, and of case shot from the front and flank." Turchin's brigade had fallen behind in the attack, so Van Derveer had his men lie down to wait for the First Brigade to catch up.[508]

There has always been a debate about who ordered the assault up Missionary Ridge. Generals Grant and Thomas always claimed that their orders

507. U.S. War Department, *War of the Rebellion*, Ser. no. 55, pp. 528, 538; Cozzens, *Shipwreck*, 270.

508. Keil, *Thirty-fifth Ohio*, 171; Grebner, *We Were the Ninth*, 163; Bircher, *Drummer Boy's Diary*, 54; U.S. War Department, *War of the Rebellion*, Ser. no. 55, pp. 527–28, 538; Cozzens, *Shipwreck*, 280.

restricted the attack to the trenches below. General Baird said he was at first told to capture the rifle pits at the base of the slope only, but later, the order was amended to allow him to push on to the top of the ridge. Colonel Van Derveer got his orders directly from Baird, who had mentioned the steepness of the ridge before the attack began. He was to storm the heights and carry the ridge if possible. It would seem, regardless of the offical orders and statments, that from the beginning, the intent was to go to the top. The Persimmons couldn't have stayed in the captured trenches for long at any rate. Only knee-high at the back, the abandoned earthworks offered little protection against plunging fire from the Confederates above. Men ducked as low as they could in the trench or began to scatter for cover behind whatever was available. They were "sheltered somewhat" from the plunging fire, but to every soldier looking up at the ridge looming six hundred feet over them, it was obvious that the best way out was to go up the face of the ridge. When the order came, the Thirty-fifth Ohio began climbing instantly.[509]

The improbable assault up the Carroll house spur of the ridge began about a quarter after four with the men "cheering with hearty good will." What they were doing was truly amazing, even foolhardy, something rational men would never have contemplated, but logic no longer had a part in the story. As Wiley Sword described the Army of the Cumberland, it was "an army rampant, feeding upon its old agony. Somehow, George H. Thomas's troops had found a way to fight the battle they weren't supposed to." The precipitous slope, the enemy's sharpshooters in front, and the terrific enfilading artillery fire upon each flank were forgotten in their eager haste to storm the heights. It was a matter of pride now, made that way by a doubting general, and the Persimmons had no choice but to go up. For the first moment, "the lines moved in pretty good order," but the order didn't last long. Clambering up a steep slope through the undergrowth is not conducive to tight military formations, and after only a few moments, the lines "became less distinct; color bearers were generally in advance, and men drifted toward the colors." Colonel Boynton made the attack on foot with his troops. Rather than make himself an easily visible target in the rush across the open ground in front of the ridge, he had dismounted to gain some anonymity. Leading his horse up the steep slope, shouting and encouraging his rapidly advancing men on, Boynton was hit by a minie ball and was unable to continue. The bullet passed through his scrotum and left a gouge in his thigh. The wounds proved to be minor, but still, they were to take Boynton out of the war for good.[510]

509. Bishop, *Story of a Regiment*, 140; U.S. War Department, *War of the Rebellion*, Ser. no. 55, pp. 534, 538; Cozzens, *Shipwreck*, 260, 273.

510. Bishop, *Story of a Regiment*, 140; U.S. War Department, *War of the Rebellion*, Ser. no. 55, pp. 528, 538; Compiled service record, Henry V. Boynton, Maj., Staff, 35th Ohio Inf.; Civil War; RG 94; NA–Washington; Cozzens, *Shipwreck*, 260, Sword, *Mountains*, 280.

Seen from a distance, as Grant and Thomas saw it, it must have been a heart-stopping view. The slope was lit directly by the setting sun. Ranks of soldiers, forming vees behind their regimental flags, scrambled up the bare slope. When the ground opened a little and enemy fire thickened, they would spread out, only to reform the vee when the slope got steeper again. It all looked very much like geese flying south. The bright colored flags made it possible to follow the progress of units up the ridge, as first one then another sprang forward. Light occasionally flashed off a flag tip, bayonet, or sword, and through it all, the soldiers kept moving up. There was no military science to it. It was the corporate act of thousands of individuals, but it was as powerful as any attack made in the war. It was brilliant.[511]

Casualties were surprisingly light considering the "importance and danger of the undertaking." Sgt. William Stokes of Company K, considered an excellent soldier by the officers over him, "was shot through the head and died at once." Company C Pvt. Simon Kumler was also shot down while climbing the slope. Ferdinand Van Derveer came upon the dying soldier as he lay on the ground. In the midst of the battle still raging around him, the colonel paused for a moment and shook Kumler's hand. The "worthy young" soldier died a short time later.[512]

Drawing of Baird's division attacking Missionary Ridge on November 25, 1863.
KEIL

---

511. McKinney, *Education in Violence*, 296–97.
512. Van Derveer to wife, 30 November 1863, Van Derveer Family Collection.

How a soldier got up the ridge depended a lot on personal agility and stamina. As the regimental historian put it, "the long-winded chaps were in the lead." Most men had to stop at some point to catch their breath, but nothing was going to keep them from reaching the top. The competition with the Army of the Tennessee was momentarily forgotten, and the assault became a race between units in the Army of the Cumberland. Everyone wanted to be the first one on top and "had to find or clear his own way through the entanglement." The "terrible fire of musketry and artillery" directed down the slope by the Tennessee regiments of Vaughn's Brigade had little affect in slowing the momentum of the assault. Even within the Second Brigade, regiments "vied with one another as to which should reach the summit and enter the rebel works." At the forefront of the Thirty-fifth's line were the members of the color guard who bore the national colors with "gallantry and bravery," planting them on the summit half an hour after the charge began. Along the way the banner "got a good many new holes in it." Close behind the colors was that dog Jack. In this uphill race, it was inevitable that unit cohesion would be lost. Even so, the loosely organized mob-like force that crested the ridge was a tide that could not be stemmed. In a matter of minutes, the rebels were out of their fortifications.[513]

"The first blue soldiers came up in 'clumps'" about a quarter to five according to Lieutenant Keil, "but men pushed on as soon as they regained breath." The question of exactly who was first will likely never be settled. In the rush to the top, they had all arrived about the same time. Major Budd, like most every other regimental commander that day, claimed the Thirty-fifth Ohio was first, but that was certainly not the case. Budd also observed that "it was but a very short time before the men from the different regiments became so mixed up (and partly owing to the nature of the ground) it was impossible to maintain anything like an organization." For the most part, the disorganization began to fade rapidly. Company officers collected their men and quickly regained general control. Budd was particularly impressed by the actions of 1st Sgt. Alonzo Fisk, Company B, and Sgt. James Blair of Company K. Both men were commanding companies that had no officers. Colonel Van Derveer was also working to sort out the tangled units whom he admitted were "in some disorder for a short time." As soon as he could restore some semblance of order, he intended to continue the attack north along the top of the ridge.[514]

Using the Confederate trenches on top of the ridge as protection, the Persimmons "opened a vigorous fire on the enemy" and a "short but sharp" fire fight ensued until the Tennesseans were driven out of their fortifications. Con-

---

513. Bishop, *Story of a Regiment,* 140; U.S. War Department, *War of the Rebellion,* Ser. no. 55, pp. 528, 535, 538; Keil, *Thirty-fifth Ohio,* 172; Van Derveer to wife, 7 December 1863, Van Derveer Family Collection.

514. Keil, *Thirty-fifth Ohio,* 171, 173; U.S. War Department, *War of the Rebellion,* Ser. no. 55, p. 538; Cozzens, *Shipwreck,* 329.

federate General Vaughn sent the 19th Alabama, the 11th Tennessee, and the consolidated 13th and 154th Tennessee to retake the spur, where they ran headlong into the 2nd Minnesota, still acting as skirmishers, and units from Turchin's brigade. When Colonel Van Derveer sent the 35th Ohio into the fight to support the Minnesotans, the Persimmons rushed into the swale to the right of the 2nd Minnesota. The regiment's quick response, coupled with a vigorous push by the 9th Ohio and 75th Indiana, drove the butternut soldiers. Suddenly facing several onrushing blue regiments, the confused Confederates were overwhelmed. Not ready to give up yet, Vaughn sent a second counterattack at the 35th and 2nd Minnesota. The Persimmons blazed away at the rebels from a range of a hundred yards for about half an hour. The Tennessee rebels eventually ran out of ammunition and were forced to begin moving down the wooded southern slopes of the ridge to escape the blue onslaught.[515]

As Vaughn's soldiers retreated, Scott's Tennessee battery positioned nearby was left dangerously exposed. They were still firing down the slope at Union regiments hunkered down beneath the battery and were caught unawares when their supporting infantry broke and ran. But since the Yankees directly below them on the ridge were no longer advancing, they decided to stay and keep fighting. Their fortitude cost them dearly, because they did not know that the Thirty-fifth was racing toward them unchecked along the crest of the ridge until the Persimmons began to fire into the battery. As bullets rained among them, the unprotected cannoneers were "caught in the act of loading." Horses hitched to caissons began to crumble to the ground as gunners "were bayoneted or driven off before they could fire their pieces" by the wildly shouting Persimmons. Seven stunned rebels were quickly captured as the rest scattered off the ridge. It was a good haul. With the support of the Second Minnesota, the Persimmons captured three enemy guns, a caisson, half a dozen horses, and the battery guidon. In the rush to continue the advance, the prisoners were hustled off down the hill and the cannon left behind.[516]

The troops following the Thirty-fifth up the ridge were not in as big a hurry as the Persimmons. Men from General Woods's division found the three cannon captured moments before and took possession of them. They hauled the cannon off "thus claiming the honor of capture to which they had no right," but both General Baird and Colonel Van Derveer ensured proper credit was given in their official reports. Somewhere during this time, Pvt. Johnny Doyle reached the summit with his food basket. Not knowing exactly where to look for Company C, Doyle wandered across the summit "into the rebel lines with his dinner for the officers, of which he was promptly relieved, as well as of his hat and silver watch."[517]

515. Keil, *Thirty-fifth Ohio*, 171–72; U.S. War Department, *War of the Rebellion*, Ser. no. 55, pp. 528, 538; Cozzens, *Shipwreck*, 332.

516. U.S. War Department, *War of the Rebellion*, Ser. no. 55, pp. 528, 535, 538; Keil, *Thirty-fifth Ohio*, 171–72; Cozzens, *Shipwreck*, 331.

Darkness and the presence of so many Confederate troops on Bragg's right prevented Van Derveer's brigade from pursuing the rebels down the mountain. Seeing that the only route of advance was quite narrow and worried that his troops were still disorganized, General Baird called off the attack. To the right, some attempt at pursuit was made, but by 6:00 p.m., the Thirty-fifth Ohio had run out of rebels to shoot at. Ferdinand Van Derveer was proud of his men. Sustaining "the reputation it had won at Chickamauga," the Second Brigade had attacked an enemy in an impregnable position, roundly defeated them, and sent them packing in disarray. In the process, "none flinched from their duty," and they had proven that they were warriors as good as any in the U.S. Army. [518]

Organized fighting may have ended, but there were still angry Confederate soldiers out there. Alfred Amlin was a private in Company H and said to be an excellent soldier. Tired from an exhausting fight, he slumped down to the ground and began to eat his supper. A rifle blasted from the other side of the ridge, the bullet struck the resting Amlin, and he died the following day. It had taken two years rather than the two weeks he had naively predicted so long ago, but Alf Amlin was finally going home. The rest of the Thirty-fifth laid down with their rifles in the cool air and slept soundly, convinced that the Confederate Army of Tennessee wasn't going to bother anyone that night.[519]

Once again, Van Derveer was pleased with his soldiers, saying they had fought splendidly. He praised all of his regimental commanders and called Major Budd out for "the energy and skill he exhibited" after assuming command in the middle of the battle. In turn, General Baird declared that Van Derveer's "skill, bravery, and high soldierly qualities" had figured prominently in the division's successful assault of Missionary Ridge. Good as it had been, the day had not been without cost. In addition to Colonel Boynton, Lieutenant Mather had received two minor wounds in the hand and the leg and Lieutenant Lambright of Company K had been very painfully wounded in the shoulder. Six enlisted men had been killed and nineteen others wounded. Among the dead was Company F's John Venard. Venard had enlisted only six weeks before and had been with the regiment barely a month. Johnny Doyle and one other man were missing.[520]

All things being even, the Thirty-fifth Ohio never had a chance of gaining the crest of Missionary Ridge. Confederate soldiers on the heights commanded all the approaches with rifle and cannon fire and could easily have stopped the

517. Keil, *Thirty-fifth Ohio*, 172; U.S. War Department, *War of the Rebellion*, Ser. no. 55, pp. 510, 528, 538.

518. Keil, *Thirty-fifth Ohio*, 172; U.S. War Department, *War of the Rebellion*, Ser. no. 55, pp. 528, 538.

519. Keil, *Thirty-fifth Ohio*, 172; Sword, *Mountains*, 315.

520. Keil, *Thirty-fifth Ohio*, 172; U.S. War Department, *War of the Rebellion*, Ser. no. 55, pp. 511, 529, 538; Van Derveer to wife, 30 November 1863, Van Derveer Family Collection.

assault in its tracks. But, the battle of Missionary Ridge was not decided by rifles and artillery. Rather, it was decided by the most potent weapon in the Army of the Cumberland, the fighting spirit of each soldier. The Persimmons, and every other soldier in the Army of the Cumberland, had taken an emotional and spiritual inventory of themselves during the weeks since Chickamauga. Given the chance, they knew deep in their hearts, that nothing could stop them from getting what they wanted, and what they wanted was to prove they were the best army in the world. Hunkered down in the shallow trenches at the base of the ridge, they got their chance, and as they began moving up the slope toward their enemy, they knew they were going to win. In their own words, "[We] wanted that ridge and believed that we could and would take it, and did." For them, it was no more complicated than that.[521]

The Confederate Army of Tennessee was rife with anger and dissention. Bragg's heavy-handed methods had alienated his soldiers, and his insistence on blaming failures on anyone other than himself, had turned his officers against him. Confederates at all levels were "astonished and disconcerted" when the Yankees started up the slope. The Persimmons admitted that if the rebels had stood and fought, the attack would have quickly failed, and the Thirty-fifth Ohio, and possibly the Army of the Cumberland, would have been wrecked beyond repair. Already sunk in the depths of low morale, the rebels "had just seen us take the first line" and knew they were also being attacked on both flanks. Rebel soldiers in rifle pits and trenches looked into their own hearts and found that they agreed with the Yankees. When they saw the Army of the Cumberland coming up the slope in front of them, they were "convinced we would take the crest also, and they lost their courage and gave it up without half defending it."[522]

On the morning of the twenty-sixth, cleanup from the fighting began. Abandoned weapons and equipment were collected, wounded were sent back down the ridge, and the dead were buried. Four days rations were issued and each man got another hundred rounds. An attempt at pursuit was made in the afternoon, and the Thirty-fifth marched eight miles south into Georgia before stopping for the night at McAfee's Church. The pursuit continued another fifteen miles to Ringgold the next day, before it finally petered out. Confederate skirmishers had harassed the advance all day, and when an Ohio regiment from another brigade tried to force its way into Taylor's Gap, it met a costly repulse. November 28 was cold and saw rain mixed with sleet fall from the sky. Ringgold was abandoned to the Confederates for the time being, but before leaving, the flourmill was destroyed and the railroad tracks torn up. Four days after the battle of Missionary Ridge, the Persimmons marched back to their camp at Chattanooga.[523]

521. Keil, *Thirty-fifth Ohio*, 172.
522. Bishop, *Story of a Regiment*, 140.

Heavy and Irksome

The Thirty-fifth Ohio returned to its camp on Hospital Hill near Chattanooga and settled in for the winter. With the Confederate army back in Georgia, supplies were coming into Chattanooga on a regular basis. The regiment was still not back to full rations. Existing stocks had been completely depleted, and for some time, everything that came in was being immediately consumed. During the siege, the army's logistical effort had focused on rations and ammunition. No clothing had come in and some of the men were reduced to wearing rags. A drummer in the Second Minnesota described the general conditions of all when he said, "[Clothing] was getting to be a serious matter with us. We had not changed clothing for a month or more, and the men were getting filthy and covered with vermin. We thought that we were accomplishing quite a feat to sustain ourselves with the small quantity of rations that were issued to us, without feeding myriads of graybacks." A temporary wagon road had been built around Lookout Mountain, but increased capacity required the railroad from Bridgeport to be repaired. Several long bridges and trestles had to be rebuilt, and it was some time before the storehouses began to fill up. Clothes finally did get issued and rations did increase over time. At any rate, the men were getting enough and were satisfied as much as soldiers can be.[524]

Recently exchanged Surgeon Abraham Landis rejoined the regiment just after Missionary Ridge, arriving in time to help handle the casualties of that battle. One of the melancholy tasks he performed was to make arrangements to have two bodies, Sgt. William Stokes of Company K and Pvt. Simon Kumler of Company C, shipped home for burial. The nineteen-year-old Kumler was Landis's cousin.[525]

Shortly after the battle of Missionary Ridge, another old friend of the Thirty-fifth Ohio was "placed on the invalid list." The flag presented to the regiment by the ladies of Cynthiana had seen two years of rough service in Kentucky, Tennessee, and Georgia. Aside from being stained and frazzled from exposure to all kinds of weather, it had been pierced by bullets at Chickamauga and Missionary Ridge. The shredded cloth was carefully wrapped around its staff, which also bore the marks of several bullets, and was never again unfurled in the breeze. The battered old flag was replaced by new national colors presented by the ladies of Lebanon, Ohio, who also provided an Ohio state flag. From that time on, the regimental color guard carried three sets of colors. The old flag, "a sacred relic, as dear to the men as their own lives," was not discarded. It was lovingly borne by Color Sgt. Mark Price. The newer national

---

523. Bircher, *Drummer Boy's Diary*, 55; U.S. War Department, *War of the Rebellion*, Ser. no. 55, p. 539.

524. Keil, *Thirty-fifth Ohio*, 183; Bircher, *Drummer Boy's Diary*, 55; Bishop, *Story of a Regiment*, 141.

525. Landis, *From Pilgrimage to Promise*, 35.

flag and the state flag were carried by other members of the color guard.[526]

*Thirty-fifth Ohio regimental colors sewn by the ladies of Lebanon, Ohio,
and presented to the regiment at Chattanooga.*
THE OHIO BATTLE FLAG COMMISSION, OHIO HISTORICAL SOCIETY

The winter of 1863/64 was colder than normal around Chattanooga, and the real logistical concern became wood rather than food. The army needed huge amounts of wood everyday for cooking and keeping warm. The valley had already been stripped of most trees, but there were plenty in the hills a few miles away. Chopping wood is hard work, but hauling it two miles is back-breaking labor. A system was devised where fabricated wooden cars were dragged along the railroad line to where the tracks crossed Chattanooga Creek. Wood was cut and dragged down the slopes, loaded onto the cars, and pulled back into the camps. No one in particular managed the system, so carts going in opposite directions sometimes met, requiring one to be unloaded and tipped over for the other to pass. Wood gathering required the men to serve a dual role

526. Keil, *Thirty-fifth Ohio*, 10–11.

as wood cutters and as livestock. The Army of the Cumberland was chronically short on transportation, and the teams it did have were still weak from the previous food shortage. Since any healthy animals were needed exclusively to haul rations, the soldiers hauled the wood cars. As a result, it sometimes took a day and a half to get a load of wood from the mountains down to camp. [527]

An "unusually heavy and irksome" cordon of pickets was retained around the army during the winter at Chattanooga. The low ridges and shallow depressions that made up the floor of Lookout Valley resembled the waves of an ocean, generally running parallel to Missionary Ridge. Pickets usually were placed in lunettes on top of the ridges while the reserve waited in the ravines behind them. Cold weather made things more difficult, as well. On New Years Eve, the temperature dropped throughout the day to ten below zero that night. Pickets had to be relieved every thirty minutes to keep from freezing, and ponds that had to be circumnavigated that morning were frozen solid enough to walk across that night.[528]

To the satisfaction of the enlisted men, picketing was one duty that even the highest ranking officers had to perform, and Ferdinand Van Derveer was no exception. "Yesterday, I was Corps Officer of the Day and spent the greater part of my time among the pickets—the rebel picket lines in many places within one hundred yards of ours—We are on one bank of Chattanooga Creek and they are on the other. There is no firing by either party—and I rode close enough to see the color of their eyes, without molestation."[529]

The Thirty-fifth's company officers viewed picket duty with dread while at Chattanooga, partly because of the weather, but mostly because of Gen. Phil Sheridan. Sheridan apparently liked to slip quietly down the ravines between the picket posts and then "spur his charger over the ridge, and ride down on the post before the men had time to form and receive a general officer, as prescribed in the tactics." Having surprised the unsuspecting pickets, Sheridan would verbally destroy the officer in charge of the picket reserve with "very naughty language" and then move on to the next post "leaving a sulphurous scent that lingered in the air, or rather in the ears of the men." Sheridan made his one-man assaults on the pickets just about every day, and the officers of the Thirty-fifth learned to hate picket duty and Phil Sheridan. The fact that the number of officers on detail or recovering from wounds reduced the number officers available for picket duty only made things worse on those few who could not avoid it.[530]

Lieutenant Keil of Company C had been assigned to court-martial duty in Ohio and had been living the good life for several weeks until the court was dissolved. Immediately upon returning to Chattanooga, he found himself at the

527. Keil, *Thirty-fifth Ohio*, 175–76.
528. Keil, *Thirty-fifth Ohio*, 176; Grebner, *We Were the Ninth*, 159.
529. Van Derveer to wife, 12 November 1863, Van Derveer Family Collection.
530. Keil, *Thirty-fifth Ohio*, 176–77; Cozzens, *Shipwreck*, 50.

top of the picket duty roster. The officers who had been pulling the duty night after night felt no sympathy for him at all. In fact, they were gratified that it was now someone else's turn to face Sheridan and lost no time in congratulating him on his new opportunity. Their explanations of what to expect were terse and consisted mostly of statements that "'Phil' would give him "h——l." There wasn't much Keil could say or do. He knew it was only fair that the duty come to him and the best thing seemed to be as prepared as possible.[531]

Keil's detachment was positioned on a small round hill on a narrow strip of land between the Tennessee River and Citico Creek. The pickets were perched on top of the hill with their reserve in a clump of trees dense with undergrowth at the base of the hill. It was a good place for pickets. A road ran between the creek and the hill, but the distance between the two was very short and cane-brakes filled the open ground. The road was obstructed by felled trees, and riders like Phil Sheridan could not get through. The only way to reach the picket reserve was to circumnavigate the hill. Keil positioned his men to what he believed was his best advantage. Six were stationed on the hill or near the road to watch for signs of Confederate activity. Seven others were ordered to watch for the approach of Phil Sheridan.[532]

Keil had given very explicit instructions to his pickets and watch closely. He made threats that "it would go hard with them" if Sheridan or any other officer approached without warning. So emphatic were Keil's instructions to these guards "watching the approach of an enemy in the rear" that they gave over a dozen warnings during the day. Each time the reserve was called to arms, and each time the alarm proved to be false. It was a very cold day, and anyone who had to be out was dressed in a regulation army overcoat so privates could not be distinguished from generals or any other rank. It may have been that the tense guards remembered Keil's threats and were taking no chances. It is just as likely that they were messing with a nervous officer. Either way, anyone who came anywhere near the pickets was assumed to be General Sheridan and the alarm was given. As it turned out, the only persons who appeared at the post during the day were teamsters who came out to cut the cane to use as fodder for their animals. All of Keil's extra preparations and dread came to naught. Neither Sheridan nor any other officer had appeared at his picket post, and upon returning to camp, the chagrined lieutenant learned that Sheridan, having been promoted, had left the Army of the Cumberland the day before.[533]

Death was not confined to the battlefields around Chattanooga in 1863. In late summer, Capt. David Gans of Company E had been detached on recruiting

---

531. Keil, *Thirty-fifth Ohio*, 177; Compiled service record, Frederick W. Keil, 2nd Lt., Co. C, 35th Ohio Inf.; Carded Records, Volunteer Organizations, Civil War; Records of the Adjutant General's office, 1780s–1917, Record Group 94; National Archives, Washington, D.C.

532. Keil, *Thirty-fifth Ohio*, 177–78.

533. Ibid., 178.

duty. It was a coveted assignment, since recruiting was done at home. Gans had left the regiment in good health and high spirits, but after he arrived in Preble County, he became ill. Things got progressively worse, and on December 10, the regiment was notified by Gans's brother that he had died. "He was a good officer," Van Derveer wrote, "and his death is much regretted" The loss also left Company E in the lurch. Lieutenant Cottingham was in a rebel prison and the company's other officer had been wounded at Missionary Ridge.[534]

With the area free from Confederate forces, Union detachments were once again able to visit the Chickamauga battlefield, and they returned to report that many Federal dead remained unburied on the field or had not been properly interred. On December 16, a detachment from each regiment in the Second (formerly Third) Brigade was sent back to the Chickamauga battlefield to search for and properly bury any of the brigade's dead that had been left behind. They had no trouble finding the fighting positions. Paper from torn cartridges "lay thickly strewn on the ground along the lines that had been held that day." Many bodies were found, and since a lot of them had identifiable marks on the clothing or had names pinned to them, few were buried anonymously. The rocky soil was very thin, and several corpses that had been buried at the time had later been exposed by the weather. The Confederates had shown "reckless indifference in the burial of the union dead," angering the burial parties and creating a strong feeling of disgust for their enemies. Some of the Union dead had been "collected and placed in depressions in the surface of the ground, over which brush, stones, and some soil were thrown." In other places, "a pit was made by placing a number of dead side by side, old logs were placed on the sides and at the head and feet, and then dirt thrown over so as to cover the dead." After two major battles, General Thomas needed a place to bury the army's dead, and a cemetery was begun at Orchard Knob, not far from where he and General Grant had watched the assault on Missionary Ridge.[535]

In December and January, the regiments whose three-year enlistments were approaching an end were asked to reenlist. In exchange, they would be given thirty-day furloughs and a generous bonus. Very few men in the Thirty-fifth Ohio chose to do so. The reasons varied. Some had families they needed to get home to. Others felt that they had fulfilled their obligation and had every right to go home and leave the remaining work to others. The main reason appears to have been that the men of the Thirty-fifth Ohio thought it was time to make the draft work. As one member of the regiment put it, they might have enlisted "if by doing so—the same number would be expected from the draft at home." It may seem a disappointing attitude to latter day observers, but it is hardly unusual. Twentieth century American military history shows that few men will voluntarily reenlist and return to combat when there is an honorable way to avoid it. Having seen the horror and waste of war and having experienced the helpless feeling it often engenders, few men will choose to remain when they

---

534. Van Derveer to wife, 10 December 1863, Van Derveer Family Collection.
535. Keil, *Thirty-fifth Ohio*, 160; Mitchell, *Civil War Soldiers*, 63.

don't have to.[536]

Work had never ceased on the fortifications, roads, and railroads around Chattanooga. The Confederate Army of Tennessee still might decide to try and take the city back, and a solid logistical structure was needed to support future operations in the Deep South. On January 14, all other work stopped as everyone celebrated the arrival of the first train into Chattanooga. From that day on, the army's logistical goal was very simple. Get more. Huge quantities of rations and other supplies began to flood warehouses in the city.[537]

No Longer a Prisoner

It was a very cold winter in Butler County, Ohio, as well, but at least two Persimmons didn't mind. Richard Foord and Henry Moser had both been sent home to recuperate. Moser had been in a Chattanooga hospital since being wounded on Missionary Ridge. His recovery was delayed several weeks by a bout of fever in January, so it was not until the end of February that Henry was given leave to recuperate at home. He sent word of his imminent departure, and Sallie Rogers spent many impatient hours waiting for him to arrive, filling in the time by baking pies and doughnuts.

Moser applied for and received a thirty-day extension to his leave in mid-March. The couple spent as much time together as possible, but the time went all too quickly. Henry hung around the Rogers' home, sharing meals and staying so late on one occasion that he was permitted to spend the night. There were more pleasant buggy rides to church and to Literary Society exhibitions, and on one occasion, the two young lovers visited a neighbor named Mrs. Lance. Sallie felt left out of the conversation as Henry spoke German to their hostess. As the time grew short, Moser bought a portrait of George Washington and presented it to Sallie as a gift. On April 6, Sallie threw a big party at her home that lasted until three o'clock the next morning. On April 11, Henry Moser boarded the train and headed back to Chattanooga.[538]

There is a gap in Richard Foord's diary from October 25, 1863, to January 1, 1864. Sent home to recover from wounds, Foord married his fiancée, Laura Webster, while on leave. For several weeks, he was too caught up in being a newlywed to keep up with his diary. At the start of the new year, perhaps at Laura's urging, Foord once again began making daily entries. He began to describe domestic scenes of the two of them doing laundry and cleaning house together.

---

536. Van Derveer to wife, 27 December 1863, 14 January 1864, Van Derveer Family Collection.

537. Grebner, *We Were the Ninth*, 169.

538. Rogers Papers, "Country Life," 21–22.

Pvt. Henry Moser, Company G.
BUTLER COUNTY HISTORICAL SOCIETY

On New Year's Day, 1864 the thermometer read twenty-two degrees below zero but Foord had "a gay time cutting up in the afternoon." He went to church and to the post office. He watched children skating on the ice of the frozen Hydraulic (a canal built to provide waterpower for local industries), and of course he spent as much time as he could with Laura, helping her to do laundry and save carpet rags. He drove sleds all the way out to places like Blue Ball and Post Town while she leaned against his shoulder and slept. The two of them visited friends around town, took tea together, and even sat together to write letters. After the rough life of the army, the domesticity of it all must have been wonderful to Foord.[539]

Church related activities also occupied a lot of Foord's time at home. It was certainly one way to spend time with his new wife, but he also went several times on his own attending both Sunday worship services and midweek prayer meetings. At the Baptist church he heard "Elder Knapp preached of Hell fire

---

539. Foord Papers, 1–10 January 1864.

and brimstone," and after another meeting, he "retired to bed early and dreamed of snakes." On Sunday, January 17, Foord taught his mother's Sunday school class and then went home with Laura. He tried to take a nap, but Laura would not let him sleep. Perhaps she sensed their time together slipping away.[540]

Foord was still in the army and had to report his location to the state provost marshal and to the regiment. Both of these he did by mail and soon had cause to regret it. On January 18, he was ordered to immediately report to the Provost Marshal in Columbus. It took all day to get there by rail, and Foord reported in the next morning. Foord was a paroled prisoner of war and standard conventions of the day required him to await formal exchange before taking an active part in the war. That exchange had not occurred, yet when he reported to Columbus, he was told he was being sent back to the Thirty-fifth Ohio. Returning to Middletown, he spent his last few days attending church, visiting friends, and sitting with Laura. On one occasion, Foord knitted while Laura mended a dress. It was always difficult to leave family and friends at home and return to the war, but it was made even more difficult when the father of Cpl. Peter Allison asked Foord to send the body of his son home. Allison had been killed at Missionary Ridge.[541]

After bidding friends and Laura goodbye on January 25, Richard Foord boarded the 4:00 p.m. train to Cincinnati. The next night found him in Louisville, where he wrote a letter to Laura, and the train arrived in Nashville in time for supper on the twenty-eighth. Foord had been traveling with Pvt. Frank Kemp of Company H, and the two of them briefly toured the city after supper. Foord felt very tired and decided to retire. His lassitude was probably more loneliness than weariness, because he had enough strength left to write Laura before he went to bed. The Herculean efforts made to improve the railroad system supporting Chattanooga had obviously been very effective. A little over three days after leaving Middletown, Foord's train chugged into Chattanooga.[542]

The maddening aspects of military bureaucracy have changed little over the centuries. The Provost Marshal in Columbus had sent Foord back to the Thirty-fifth Ohio before a formal exchange had taken place, because he had been told to get soldiers back to the field as quickly as possible. When the first sergeant reported in to Captain L'Hommedieu, the acting regimental commander while Colonel Boynton and Major Budd were on furlough, he was told he shouldn't have come back, because he had not been properly exchanged. None other than Gen. George Thomas agreed, and on January 30, Foord received orders to return to Ohio to await exchange. While Foord waited for his travel orders, he looked over the Missionary Ridge battlefield and visited

---

540. Foord Papers, 12–17 January 1864.
541. Ibid., 18–24 January 1864.
542. Ibid., 25–28 January 1864.

friends in the Sixty-ninth Ohio. He also fulfilled the obligation he had made to Mr. Allison. Foord and several other members of Company K exhumed Peter Allison's body and expressed it back to Middletown.[543]

The return trip to Ohio was just as quick. The train left Chattanooga at 12:30 p.m. on January 31, and Foord arrived in Middletown on the night of February 4. That time included most of a day lost when the train derailed several miles south of Nashville. Foord emerged unscathed from the wreck, but five other men had lost their lives. Late as it was, the lovesick soldier rushed home and awoke Laura who had already gone to bed. Though his orders required him to report directly to Camp Chase in Columbus, Foord decided that a few days at home would be appropriate. Those few days somehow stretched into ten.[544]

He did have some serious business to take care of. Foord met the remains of Peter Allison and turned them over to his family. Other than that, he just tried to enjoy himself, and as before, most of his time was spent with Laura. He baked pies with her and made a kite for a boy named Tommy Charles. He loafed around town some on his own, but more often he walked with Laura. The two of them also made more carpet rags, did some housecleaning (anything to be with the woman he loved), and just sat and talked. On February 14, Foord attended Peter Allison's funeral service and apparently decided he had pushed things as far as he could get away with. The next morning, he rode the train to Columbus and reported to Company E, First Parole Battalion at Camp Chase. There he would remain three months waiting to be exchanged.[545]

Foord made daily entries in his diary from the day he arrived at Camp Chase, February 15, until the day he left, May 19, and not one of them mentions work. According to the cartel that existed between the Northern and Southern armies, paroled prisoners were not supposed to perform military duties. So other than a few administrative activities required to feed, house, and clothe the soldiers in his parole company, he had no work to do. Foord did pretty much whatever he wanted to with few restrictions. That was not to say that Foord did nothing. He did a little sales work for his father, read several novels (among them was *The Brother's Secret* by Gus Wood), walked many miles on the roads around Camp Chase, and ate a lot. And of course, he wrote an endless stream of letters to Laura, whom he now called "Lolly." The only official duties Foord performed in February and March were the annual reading of the Articles of War and preparation of payrolls. After the rolls were prepared, it still took more than four weeks to actually get paid for the eight months owed him.[546]

Having learned the ways of a successful first sergeant, Foord strong-armed his way into another furlough at the end of March, and while on leave in Mid-

---

543. Foord Papers, 29–30 January 1864.
544. Ibid., 31 January–4 February 1864.
545. Ibid., 5–15 February 1864.
546. Ibid., 16 February–11 April 1864.

dletown, his military status changed unexpectedly. Foord received a letter from the Ohio Adjutant General on April 12, 1864, informing him that he had been promoted to first lieutenant, an appointment he instantly accepted. He got the first taste of his new status upon his return to Camp Chase where he was placed in command of his parole company. Foord's first official duty was to write out physical descriptions of his men. In the age before photographs were used for identfication, a written description was prepared opf each man's features. As an example, one soldier's descrition was recorded as "born in Belgium. Is 32 years old is five feet 8¼ inches high light complexion. Brown hair and gray eyes by occupation when enlisted a farmer." Hours spent preparing dozens of such descritpions could hardly have been entertaining.[547]

Becoming an officer did not change the fact that he was still a paroled prisoner with little or nothing to do, but it did have one advantage. He got yet another furlough in early May. Foord was in Middletown for about ten days when he learned on May 11 that he had finally been exchanged and returned immediately to Camp Chase. On the night he learned of his exchange, Foord wrote and then underlined in his diary, *"I am no longer a Prisoner."* It is not surprising that he was glad to finally be released from parole. The indolent existence that he had been leading had to have lost its luster, and at that point in his life, he must have been thinking a lot about Laura and his future life with her. It was time to get on with it.[548]

Three Days Rations and Forty Rounds

As 1864 opened, a dull routine had settled over the Thirty-fifth Ohio in Chattanooga. The men weren't exactly growing fat, but the food situation was greatly improved. With all the empty houses in town, there was a more than ample supply of building materials. The lumber from standing houses were stripped and taken where it was needed. One officer reported home that the "men have all built for themselves shanties with fire places or stoves, and are generally better fixed than any previous winter." The folks at home were repeatedly told that there was no news to report and that things were going "on in the same old tread mill style." For most everyone, it was "the same dull muddy round every day" with nothing to "excite and enliven" them. At least there was music to break up the monotony. The Third Brigade had a total of five bands, and it was not uncommon for all five of them to be playing five different tunes at the same time.[549]

The colonel's life wasn't so dull in other ways, as well. One particular let-

547. Foord Papers, 12 April–11 May 1864; Furlough Papers, 1862–1865, Series 2445, Adjutant General Of Ohio State Archives, Ohio Historical Society, Columbus.
548. Ibid., 12 April–11 May 1864.

ter from home gave him something to laugh about. Mrs. Skinner from Hamilton had asked for a lock of Van Derveer's hair. It gave him an opportunity for a little humor at his wife's expense. After stating his uncertainty about the whole idea, Van Derveer wrote, "Might have agreed if it was a pretty, single woman," before divulging the real reason for his refusal. "But as it is, I beg to decline. The fact is, my hair is getting very thin and I don't like the idea of clipping it." Van Derveer was also able to spend an evening with General Thomas. He had intended to call on another officer who was not at his quarters, so he decided to make a courtesy call on the army commander while he was in the vicinity. It turned into a pleasant, evening long chat on a wide variety of subjects.[550]

Emily Van Derveer, ever the dutiful wife, in addition to playfully passing on requests like Mrs. Skinner's, also got involved in local charities and efforts to support the soldiers in the field. One of her efforts was participation in local Sanitary Fairs that provided support to the Sanitary Commission. The Commission was created to improve sanitary and health conditions in the army, and the funds it collected were used to supply hospitals and educate soldiers. After two years in the field, Ferdinand Van Derveer had seen repeatedly that the reality rarely lived up to the ideal, and he informed his wife as to his own cynical opinion of Sanitary Fairs. "I suppose you are all busy with the Fair—if any of the proceeds ever reach the soldiers they will be grateful no doubt —But my experience is that Sanitary stores are usually used up by the Doctors Chaplains and loafers. I know great encomiums are bestowed upon the Sanitary Commission, but I know. If the people of Hamilton want to have their own soldiers benefited—they must not let the Commission get hold of it—the best disposition of the proceeds is to supply and support the families of the soldiers in the service."[551]

In January, Ferdinand Van Derveer once again returned home. The dull routine was wearing him down, and at one point, he had considered resigning, but he decided to stay until the Thirty-fifth's enlistment was up. At midmonth, he was able to come up with a legitimate reason to get out of camp for a while. This time it had nothing to do with his health. When the Persimmons had left Hamilton in September 1861, Van Derveer had left two hundred muskets behind in safe storage. When John Hunt Morgan and his raiders appeared in July 1863, the stored arms had been seized and distributed to local citizens "at the time of an apprehended attack upon the place. Certain citizens had possession of them for some time, but as to their ultimate disposition [Van Derveer had] no knowledge." Apparently having learned of the situation, the Ordnance Department ordered Van Derveer to "forward vouchers" describing the location and condition of the weapons. They only way the colonel could do that was to

549. Van Derveer to wife, 15, 18 November 1863, 7, 30 December 1863, Van Derveer Family Collection.

550. Van Derveer to wife, 13, 18 December 1863, Van Derveer Family Collection.

551. Ibid., 27 December 1863.

go there and inspect the weapons in person. General Palmer approved Van Derveer's request on January 15, and he left for home shortly afterwards. After dispensing of his business with the Ordnance Department and spending some time at home with his wife and children, Van Derveer returned to Chattanooga, rejoining the brigade on February 14.[552]

On January 26, the routine of camp life and picket duty was broken for a few days. The Persimmons were part of a reconnaissance and foraging expedition sent to the town of Harrison, Georgia. Under the command of Lieutenant Col. William O'Brien, commander of the 75th Indiana, the 35th Ohio, 105th Ohio, and O'Brien's Hoosiers spent three uneventful days in the field before returning to camp at Chattanooga.[553]

On February 22, 1864, the Army of the Cumberland left camp for Ringgold, Georgia, to make a reconnaissance in the area of Tunnel Hill. As its part of the operation, Baird's Third Division marched past the Catoosa Platform, down the valley east of Buzzard's Roost Ridge, and on into Ringgold. The residents had already abandoned the town, and only a few of its building still remained standing. Going into camp at the mouth of Taylor's Gap, the Thirtyfifth Ohio could hear cannon fire to the south. On February 24, they made a forward movement toward Tunnel Hill, where entrenched rebels were found in positions on the south side of Crow's Valley. Baird's division pushed across the valley and drove Confederate pickets back into their main line on Buzzard's Roost. The Second Brigade, in the center of the division, saw little action, as most of the enemy resistance occurred on the flanks. Another reconnaissance in the direction of Tunnel Hill on February 27 resulted in a brief but uneventful contact with the rebels, and Ferdinand Van Derveer noted that he had celebrated his forty-second birthday by skirmishing with the enemy.[554]

The Thirty-fifth Ohio actually received new recruits in late winter. They came with very little prior training and had to be instructed individually by their sergeants before they could join in the company and regimental drills. The life of a new recruit was difficult. Aside from the pressure to learn quickly from an impatient or even disinterested sergeant, the newbies took a lot of ribbing from the veterans they were thrown in with. It was all done good naturedly, but it was hard on a proud young man in a new situation. Recruits resented the treatment they got, but they rarely tried to strike back, realizing that the sooner they learned to be soldiers, the sooner the harassment would stop. Once campaigning commenced, a lot of the annoyance went away of its own accord.[555]

---

552. Compiled service record, Ferdinand Van Derveer, Col., Staff, 35th Ohio Inf.; Civil War; RG 94; NA–Washington; Van Derveer to wife, 12 January 1864, Van Derveer Family Collection.

553. U.S. War Department, *War of the Rebellion*, Ser. no. 57, p. 30.

554. Keil, *Thirty-fifth Ohio*, 184; U.S. War Department, *War of the Rebellion*, Ser. no. 57, p. 427; Van Derveer, 29 February 1864.

555. Wiley, *Billy Yank*, 54.

Henry Boynton's wound was healing very slowly. Impatient at being away from his command, the colonel had made more than one attempt to return to duty, but each time, the nagging injury had forced him back into recuperation. In January, he was assigned to a Board of Examination in Cincinnati that was reviewing applicants for commissions in the U.S. Colored Troops. When that board concluded its function, he returned to Chattanooga. By strength of will, Boynton had managed to lead the regiment on the reconnaissance to Ringgold on February 22, but the effort had once again reopened his wound. Returning north, Boynton was detached to serve on the same examination board he had recently left. Even in the much more healthful climate of Cincinnati, Boynton's groin knitted slowly. Boynton did not return to Chattanooga until August, and even then it was not to return to duty. Major Budd assumed command of the regiment, a position he would hold through the regiment's remaining service.[556]

Baggage and other camp equipment came down from Chattanooga, and on March 1st, the Thirty-fifth went into permanent camp at Ringgold. It was a deserted village, where other than the snowball fights afforded by one particularly heavy snowfall, life held few attractions. For the most part it was the regular routine of drilling and inspections. Ferdinand Van Derveer reported that, "We have comfortable quarters here; and close enough to the enemy to keep us awake—I was on the ridge this morning looking at their pickets." He had also learned that his name had been sent to the Senate by President Lincoln for confirmation as a brigadier general. Food was once again plentiful, and the volunteer musicians of the "regimental band" did what they could to make life a little easier. They began a nightly minstrel show and every Persimmon, or anybody else for that matter, was welcome to attend.[557]

On March 14, Van Derveer, five of his officers, and an escort of twenty soldiers went out to "see some of Jeff Davis' folk" under a flag of truce. A civilian named Malone and his family were "excruciatingly anxious" to travel south to assist Mrs. Malone's sister who was expecting, and they had requested permission to cross the lines. Van Derveer explained the long, convoluted process in a letter home. It started when the colonel "sent one man a hundred yards in advance carrying a white flag, that Captain Cilley had made out of our old sheet—We were all dressed in our best clothes wearing our best swords and riding our finest horses—When we came within an hundred yards of the rebel pickets we were ordered to halt and directed to retire to a house close by. We told the officer who I was what rank I hold, and what I wanted. We went to the house of a presbyterian minister named Lockridge—They soon made a fire in the best room and we made ourselves comfortable—Presently a Captain came

---

556. Keil, *Thirty-fifth Ohio*, 237–38; Compiled service record, Henry V. Boyton, Maj., Staff, 35th Ohio Inf.; Civil War; RG 94; NA–Washington.

557. Grebner, *We Were the Ninth*, 171; Bircher, *Drummer Boy's Diary*, 72; Van Derveer to wife, 2, 12, 22 March 1864, Van Derveer Family Collection.

to demand my business, and I gave him a letter for his commanding officer – they had to send nearly or quite to Dalton for a reply and it was almost evening before I received it. Col. King of General Wheeler's staff came with a party of officers to receive me. I was for a while the politest man in Dixie—Col. King however contesting the palm with me. We talked of the unfortunate state of our country, of the weather, and all expressed hopes for the return of peace. They delivered me a note from Gen'l Wheeler, which stated that my communications, had been forwarded to Gen'l Johnston, and we would be notified when a reply was received. So after exchanging newspapers, talking a while longer we all shook hands and parted. The Malones were eventually granted permission to cross the lines, and not long after, Van Derveer was involved in another flag of truce for a similar situation.[558]

The old issue of the draft was still nagging. The great majority of the men had refused to reenlist because they thought the army should be filled up with drafted men. They had seen nothing to convince them anything was being done about their months-old frustration. The commander, Colonel Van Derveer explained his own feelings to his wife. "Every day I talk of resigning, and only lack the courage to do so. It is plain to see that the government does not intend to enforce the draft and put sufficient men into the field to crush the rebellion— So we may look for it to last at least until after the presidential election. Mr. Lincoln appears to be afraid of injuring his popularity with the people—One thing is very sure he will loose many friends in the army by his course. The soldiers will wish the war ended, and have a strong desire to see a larger army in the field—And above all they want to see their copperhead friends carrying muskets."[559]

Van Derveer's situation was aggravated by his wife's oft stated desire for him to resign and come home. She felt the delay in receiving his promotion was cause enough to do it. His response to her made it clear that resignation was not an option. It would make him just like all those other men who had resigned, and Ferdinand Van Derveer was not like other men. He also reminded his wife why he went to war in the first place. "You are anxious that I should resign at once and say that I have been treated unfairly and unjustly. This may be so— and if I was disposed to take advantage of it, might afford a pretext for my leaving the service. But as I did not enter it for the purpose of making money or glory, I feel no great indignation about the matter of promotion—I came to pay a debt I owed my county, and I think no one will say I have not done my duty."[560]

After months of campaigning and siege, even the most basic skills could use a little touch up, so orders came down for each company to conduct individual target practice. These were the same men who had fared so badly at the

---

558. Van Derveer to wife, 15 March 1864, Van Derveer Family Collection.
559. Ibid., 19 March 1864.
560. Ibid., 3 April 1864.

same exercise at Paris, Kentucky, but they were not the same soldiers. They had more than two years of experience now and greatly improved skill learned from using their weapons. The improvements in individual soldiers were matched by the improved Springfield rifles they now carried. Company C marked a tree on the opposite of Chickamauga Creek at the improbable distance of three hundred yards, and each man fired a shot. Lieutenant Keil reported that "each shot was placed so close to the mark, that if a string, six inches long, had been taken as a radius and a circle swept around the centre of the mark it would have enclosed nearly every shot fired at the target."[561]

In April, the pace began to pick up as preparation for the Army of the Cumberland's spring campaign went into full swing. On April 8, General Baird's division was reviewed by General Thomas and General Hooker. The Army Commander was impressed and apparently stated his belief that Baird's was the best division in the army and Van Derveer's brigade was the best brigade in the division. The inference that Van Derveer made sure everyone at home understood was that his brigade was considered the best in the Army of the Cumberland. On another night, he and General Baird spent the evening in his tent looking at stereographic pictures. The owner of the pictures was an unnamed member of the Thirty-fifth Ohio who was apparently making quite a bit of money exhibiting them around camp. Of course, there was no mention of payment for Van Derveer and Baird.[562]

The Second Minnesota returned from veteran furlough on April 10 as the Ninth Ohio was making plans to muster out. All the men were glad to see their old friends from Minnesota return and the Ninth Ohio celebrated by tearing down an abandoned church so the Minnesotans would have building material for their huts. Taking a gentler approach to the situation, the Thirty-fifth's band serenaded the officers of the Second Minnesota and invited them to attend the nightly minstrel show.[563]

Van Derveer had not received his promotion by midmonth, and he was convinced Congressman Robert Shenck of the Third Congressional District, Van Derveer's home district, wasn't trying hard enough to get it through. He was somewhat mollified that General Thomas had told him that he wanted to keep Van Derveer whether he got promoted or not. That seemed to mesh with the news General Baird had. According to Baird, Lincoln was only promoting officers who could help him politically. Van Derveer was a Democrat and Shenck, the man whose support he needed, was a Republican.[564]

As April closed, efforts at discovering the enemy's positions increased. On April 29, the 35th Ohio, in combination with the 2nd Minnesota, 9th Ohio, and 105th Ohio, pushed the rebel pickets about two miles back into their own lines

561. Keil, *Thirty-fifth Ohio*, 21.
562. Van Derveer to wife, 5, 8 April 1864, Van Derveer Family Collection.
563. Bircher, *Drummer Boy's Diary*, 72.
564. Van Derveer to wife, 29 April, 1 May 1864, Van Derveer Family Collection.

to first support and then cover the withdrawal of a cavalry reconnaissance. A similar movement on May 2 toward Tunnel Hill was also inconclusive but earned Colonel Van Derveer a mention for his "fine soldierly qualities." Both affairs were designed to produce information and were uneventful, but the time for another major campaign was obviously approaching. All baggage that was not absolutely essential was to be prepared for storage. Even company records were deemed nonessential and packed up. Doctors went through the camps and identified men whose health would not hold up in a strenuous campaign. They were to be used as garrison troops in towns captured during the advance. The official rosters indicate more than twenty men were transferred to the Veteran Reserve Corps between the time of Missionary Ridge and the start of the Atlanta campaign. The final unmistakable signs of a new campaign showed in early May. Each man in the regiment was ordered to prepare cooked rations for three days and put forty rounds of ammunition in his cartridge box.[565]

---

565. Grebner, *We Were the Ninth*, 174; U.S. War Department, *War of the Rebellion*, Ser. no. 57, pp. 31–32, 690 and Ser. no. 72, p. 732; Wiley, *Billy Yank*, 66.

CHAPTER 12

Little Inconvenience to Ourselves

May to August 1864

Beyond the Control of the Commanding Officer

As it prepared to begin the most exhaustive campaign it had yet participated in, the Thirty-fifth Ohio had lost well over half of its strength. Decreasing manpower was a problem that vexed company officers to no end. It was not uncommon for the list of men assigned but unavailable for duty to be as large as the list of those still with the regiment. The two biggest manpower issues were men unavailable due to illness and men on detached duty. The fact that both of these situations were beyond the control of the company did not prevent the regimental staff from "constantly prodding company officers to look up absent members."[566]

The problem in locating sick men was that the army had no system for accurately tracking and reporting their whereabouts. When surgeons deemed a man too sick for duty, he was sent to a hospital somewhere in the rear. Generally, he went to a hospital reasonably close to the regiment's camp, but once there, that nearby field hospital might decide to send him to another farther in the rear to free up space or because he needed more care than they could provide. The medical department made no effort to let the soldier's unit know where he was, what his condition was, or when he might be expected to return. For all intents and purposes, a soldier sent to the hospital became an invisible man. The only way to get information was to send a tracer back along the "red tape line" until some hospital or headquarters claimed to know where the sick man was.[567]

The army also had no method for recruiting soldiers and officers for staff or headquarters duty, so it pulled men out of regiments in the field. The calls to

---

566. Keil, *Thirty-fifth Ohio*, 220.
567. Ibid.

detach men for special service were unending and multifarious. They might be called out to be clerks on the brigade or division staff. They might become teamsters for division trains or orderlies in a hospital. Whatever job they were given, they were no longer available to be used by the regiment for any duty. Whatever the reason for a man being away from the regiment, official or otherwise, he was of no use to the Thirty-fifth Ohio. The large number of absences only made life harder on the men who were present.[568]

Pvt. Michael Garver of Company I was a man in his midforties with a family back home. His wife either died or became incapacitated, and Garver requested a furlough to go home and arrange for the safekeeping of his children. Army policy at the time required that each request for furlough be accompanied by a tally of enlisted men currently absent from the regiment. If the total number absent from all causes was above 5 percent of the regiment's strength, no new furloughs would be granted. Garver's application included a note that the official strength of the regiment was 557 with 223 men present for duty, so the rate of absence was ten times greater than the 5 percent allowed. The Garver's application was returned from Fourteenth Corps Headquarters with a sharp, written reprimand for Major Budd, the acting commander. For two years, Budd had watched the strength of the regiment dwindle while ever increasing calls for details came in. He had actually been in Ohio on recruiting duty when recalled to the regiment to assume command in Henry Boynton's continuing absence. Sitting in his tent reading General Palmer's reprimand, he had finally had enough.[569]

As a citizen-soldier who was entirely fed up with the soldier part and was increasingly willing to return to being just a citizen, Budd felt compelled to reply to General Palmer and inform him how things really were outside the rarified air of headquarters. He sent Garver's application back to Corps Headquarters with his own tart endorsement. "Respectfully returned to the Major-General commanding the Fourteenth corps," he wrote in the stilted language of military protocol. "As the endorsement of Major-Gen. Palmer contains a reprimand, or charge of negligence on the part of the commanding officer of the Thirty-fifth O.V.I., I have the honor to request that the reason for so doing be stated.

By referring to the list of absentees, as stated on the accompanying paper, it will be seen that a large number of men are absent on detail duty; absent under orders of officers superior to the regimental commander. A still larger number are absent sick in the hospital, wounded, or prisoners. All absent under circumstances entirely beyond the control of the commanding officer of the regiment.

Applications are forwarded almost daily to have men returned to duty, and our

---

568. Keil, *Thirty-fifth Ohio*, 220.

569. Compiled service record, Joseph L. Budd, Capt., Co. A, 35th Ohio Inf.; Carded Records, Volunteer Organizations, Civil War; Records of the Adjutant General's office, 1780s–1917, Record Group 94; National Archives, Washington, D.C.

efforts to keep up an efficient regiment, so far as numerical strength is concerned, are not without success. Immediately after the battle of Chickamauga we were reduced to one hundred and eighty muskets; now we number three hundred and fifty. It is questionable whether any regiment in the army, after two years and eight months of service in the field, and not having their numbers increased by recruits, can make a more favorable showing than the Thirty-fifth Ohio.

By far, the greater number of these men became absentees while the regiment was commanded by Lieut. Col. Boynton, and as the endorsement of Major Gen. Palmer reflects not only upon myself, but upon Col. Boynton, (who is now at home wounded) I respectfully request that we be notified wherein we have been so very negligent.

Perhaps the best indication of the anger created within over-stretched units by the constant requests for men to be detailed comes from Budd's superiors. Not only did Budd's brigade commander, Colonel Van Derveer, and his division commander, Gen. Absalom Baird, forward the indignant letter, they both added positive endorsements. General Palmer's reply to their complaints was less "haughty," but he wasn't willing to back down, either. In a final endorsement that apparently denied Garver's request once again, Palmer expanded on the fact that the Persimmon's reported sixteen men as absent without leave. Most of this number was made up of men that the hospital's had released but not bothered to forward to the regiment, but Budd chose not to prolong the argument.[570]

Nothing could change the fact that the life of a soldier in the field was hard, and that inherent difficulty created a constant churn among the membership of the Thirty-fifth Ohio. Assuming that Company I remained with the bulk of the regiment, even though they were formally mustered in at Cynthiana, Kentucky, a week later, the regiment was about 836 strong when it boarded trains in Hamilton in late September 1861. By the time Company K joined the regiment and was mustered in November 5, 1861, 28 men had already been lost. The muster of Company K put the Thirty-fifth Ohio at its highest strength with about 890 men on hand, but from that day, the numbers dwindled and regimental manpower never again approached maximum strength. Of those 890 men, less than half would stand for the final muster. [Note: Statistical analysis is based on the *Official Roster of Ohio Soldiers* and *A History and Biographical Cylopedia of Butler County, Ohio*.]

Reductions in force began immediately upon entering service. In fact, the regiment had already discharged half a dozen men for various reasons before it left home. Some men decided they had made a mistake, and as many as 40 deserted the regiment in its first two months. For the most part, it would appear the desertions ended after a few months, but as many as 55 men may have deserted over the course of three years. Other administrative, or nonbattle, losses would continue steadily for the next three years. The first deaths and dis-

---

570. Keil, *Thirty-fifth Ohio*, 221–22.

charges for illness came in October, three weeks after leaving Ohio, and continued even after the regiment mustered out three years later. During three years of service, 148 men, or about 1 in 6, died from disease or accident. Another 222 men were discharged prior to completing their enlistment. The vast majority of these men became seriously ill and received a surgeon's certificate of disability, so it is safe to say that 40 percent of the regiment was lost for medical reasons. Officers had an option the enlisted men did not. They had accepted a commission rather than enlisting, and they had the right to resign. Eighteen of them exercised that option. Several of them left for bad health or wounds, at least one accepted assignment to another regiment, but the others left for reasons not recorded.

Disease proved to be a greater enemy to Union soldiers than the Confederates, and thousands more died from sickness than combat. During its three-year history, 1,021 men served in the Thirty-fifth Ohio. They were predominantly young men. Eight out of 10 were under thirty years old, and 65 percent of them were under twenty-five years of age. One in 3 were teenagers. On the other end of the spectrum, there were nearly 70 men over the age of forty. Seven were fifty or older and 2 were over the age of sixty. It would seem logical that younger men would bear up under the rigors of military life better than older men. When it came to early discharges for illness, that did, in fact, prove to be the case. Six of 9 men over the age of fifty, or 67 percent, were discharged for illness. As age decreased, so did the likelihood of being discharged early. Forty-two percent of men in their forties were discharged early, but for men in their thirties, losses fell to 27 percent. For men under the age of twenty-five, the loss rate was 17 percent. Nonbattle deaths did not reflect the same trend. The percentage of men under the age of twenty-five who died from disease was 15 percent. For men over the age of forty, it was 14 percent.[571]

The details that so annoyed Major Budd also had a deleterious affect over the long run. The detachment or detailing of twenty-one officers and men is recorded, but the true number was much higher. At any given point in time, twenty-five to thirty Persimmons were away from the regiment. Some were permanent detachments and were so noted, but most of the men unavailable were on temporary details for some unspecified period of time. The only time a temporary detail would have been permanently recorded was when the soldier detailed was not present when payrolls were prepared. Payrolls were prepared every other month, so a soldier could be away from the regiment and unavailable for up to eight weeks and not have been recorded as such. It is safe to assume that the total number of men away from the regiment for weeks at a time numbered a hundred or more over three years.[572]

Another source of loss was through transfers. Three dozen men transferred from the regiment to other organizations during the Thirty-fifth's term of ser-

---

571. Wiley, *Billy Yank*, 124.
572. Daniel, *Days of Glory*, 127.

vice. A handful of men were discharged to join other branches of service. Several enlisted men joined the Fourth U.S. Artillery. Another joined the Signal Corps and still another joined the Mississippi Marine Brigade. One private with connections got himself a commission in a New Jersey cavalry regiment. But nearly all of the men who left the Thirty-fifth to join other military organizations went into the Veteran Reserve Corps. When the losses of the Thirty-fifth Ohio are totaled, five hundred men, 56 percent of the regiment's maximum field strength, were lost to the regiment for administrative reasons.

Battle losses were much fewer, but the numbers can be deceiving. Up to September 1863, total losses in killed, wounded, and captured numbered fewer than 20 with 17 of those coming from the skirmish at Fishing Creek. At the end of November 1863, battle losses stood at 182. Nearly 150 men were lost in two days at Chickamauga when on-hand strength was below 400. Had the regiment been at full strength, the names on the casualty lists would have numbered about 350. From Fishing Creek to Atlanta, 91 Persimmons were wounded, 41 were killed, and 54 were captured. Killed or not, battle losses were generally permanent. Less than half of the wounded men ever returned and several of those that did were eventually discharged. For prisoners of war, the return rate was only 1 in 5.

On an individual basis, it came down to this. Every man that enlisted in the Thirty-fifth Ohio Volunteer Infantry had a 50–50 chance of completing his enlistment and an 80 percent chance of surviving it. He had a 5 percent chance of getting mad, lonely, or scared enough to run away, a 15 percent chance of dying from disease, and a 25 percent chance of becoming so ill that he was discharged. The same man had a 15 percent chance of getting shot, a 5 percent chance of dying because he got shot, and a 5 percent chance of spending time in a rebel prison.

Major Budd's statement about not receiving any recruits wasn't true if only numbers are considered. Eighty-eight men enlisted in the Thirty-fifth Ohio after Company K was mustered in November 1861. Most came in groups that arrived during the winter of 1862, the fall of 1862, and the winter of 1864. When comparing the number of recruits to the total losses, Major Budd was exactly right. Receiving one recruit for every five men lost can hardly be considered an increase in numbers, but it was typical for Union regiments. The focus of recruitment had always been on raising new regiments, and no useful system of providing replacements for regiments in the field was ever established. Recruitment was left to the regiments, who being generally too short handed or too busy to make a concerted effort, grew weaker and weaker by the month. As the Atlanta campaign began, the Thirty-fifth Ohio was probably near half strength on paper but closer to one-third strength on hand.[573]

---

573. Catton, *America*, 43–44.

A Continued Forest

The Union campaign to capture Atlanta began on the morning of May 7, 1864. The ninety thousand men who headed south under General Sherman were nearly all veterans used to long marches. The Fourteenth Corps, already concentrated around Ringgold, moved directly on Tunnel Hill. During the opening days of the campaign, the role of the Thirty-fifth Ohio seemingly was to conduct "an unusual amount of marching and counter-marching" while other parts of the Fourteenth Corps did some "brilliant skirmishing" at Snake Creek Gap and on Rocky Face Ridge. At night, the Persimmons could follow the action by the muzzle flash of the pickets. This back and forth movement was an indication of things to come. General Sherman intended to maneuver whenever he could and fight only when he had to. May 11 found the regiment on the slope of an unnamed hill from where they could look down into the funnel shaped valley between Rocky Face Ridge and Buzzard Roost. From this vantage, they also saw "the largest and finest assembly of officers of the Union army."[574]

Gen. William T. Sherman had his headquarters in a building at the point between the two ridges where the valley began to widen. As the sun dropped low in the sky, a truly remarkable conclave took place below the Thirty-fifth. Among the relaxed gathering were Generals Sherman, Thomas, Hooker, Oliver Howard, George Stoneman, John Brannan, John Palmer, John Schofield, Judson Kilpatrick, Anson McCook, Jefferson C. Davis, R. W. Johnson, and John Turchin, all surrounded by a covey of staff officers. Discerning observers among the regiment noted that Sherman was the only one among the assemblage that appeared to harbor "a shadow of uncertainty." How much this discernment was affected by the Persimmons' dislike of the man sent to save Chattanooga is hard to tell, and Sherman did have some cause for concern. He was still a long way from Atlanta and the geography definitely favored the Confederates.[575]

Of all those gathered there, the man who most impressed the watching Thirty-fifth Ohio was George H. Thomas. No other general fully commanded the confidence of the Persimmons as he did and their respect, admiration, and affection for him was unbounded. As they looked down the slope at the throng below them, "the eyes of all rested on him, " the "erect form and manly appearance" of the general "who held his corps on the field, when the commander-in-chief with two of his corps commanders had drifted into Chattanooga." Something about the man drew the soldiers of the regiment to him. "No finer figure was found in the western army. There was a curiosity to see the face of the man who could hold his corps to the mark, when half the army had been dispersed."

574. Keil, *Thirty-fifth Ohio*, 187–88; U.S. War Department, *War of the Rebellion*, Ser. no.72, pp. 788–89; Catton, *Hallowed Ground*, 338–39.
575. Keil, *Thirty-fifth Ohio*, 188.

In following years, an effort was made by Grant and his supporters to demean Thomas's abilities. The Thirty-fifth Ohio frowned upon the effort and those who led it. It did not matter what others might say, because they knew better. The Persimmons knew Thomas was "the one commander of a great army of whom it can be said with accuracy from the first day of the war to the close no movement of his miscarried." They knew he had been the first one to crack the Confederate line in the west at Mill Springs, and none of them would ever forget the afternoon of September 20, 1863, when they made history standing with the Rock of Chickamauga. They would not have willingly served under any other commander, and in the years to come, they stood staunchly by his reputation, as he had stood with them on Snodgrass Hill.[576]

The ground the Thirty-fifth Ohio was advancing over was "seemingly, a continued forest of 'scrub oak,' or Georgia pine, we seldom came to a farm which gave evidence of life or enterprise." It was a wild, uncultivated, sparsely populated area. They passed through places like Calhoun, Adairsville, and Kingston marching from two to twenty-five miles a day. A pattern of operations had emerged. When the Confederates settled into a new position, the Army of the Cumberland skirmished with the enemy to hold them in place, while the Army of the Tennessee maneuvered around the flanks. On May 13, the Union forces faced the rebels at Resaca and fought in "a wood with few spots that the enemy could be seen any considerable distance ahead." "A fierce contest" began on the morning of the fourteenth and continued until darkness fell. Baird's division was advancing in support of an attack by the men of Schofield's Army of the Ohio with the Second Brigade on the right end of the line. The Thirty-fifth passed through woods with undergrowth so thick "an individual alone could make his way through it only with difficulty." The organization of the regiment suffered by this transit, but there was no time to stop and reorder when they left the cover of the wood. As Schofield's men pressed on, the Second Brigade had to keep up. The movement forced the Thirty-fifth to descend a hundred feet down a nearly vertical slope and brought them into an open valley directly in front of the Confederate works.[577]

"The tried and true veterans" of the Thirty-fifth Ohio, "who had never failed to accomplish anything that was possible, did not falter" and continued advancing until they ran into a dry creek bed that ran along the edge of a field. On the top of a ridge some distance on the other side of the field, the rebels had dug rifle pits and placed an artillery battery. The cannon were positioned "to our left at a long distance" and were firing as the Persimmons went into line in the bed of the stream. They had no orders to fire, but several men couldn't resist the temptation and fired shots at the battery. To the surprise of the riflemen, they could see puffs of dirt where their shots were striking near the guns. This

---

576. Keil, *Thirty-fifth Ohio*, 187–88; Boynton, *Letters*, 25.

577. Keil, *Thirty-fifth Ohio*, 187–88; U.S. War Department, *War of the Rebellion*, Ser. no. 72, p. 735; Catton, *Hallowed Ground*, 340.

news was shouted along the firing line, and "a fusillade was opened on the gunners." As dozens of bullets began to strike among them, the rebel cannoneers dove for cover. Every time one of them dared show his head, rifle bullets would rain down upon him, and the rebel battery was effectively silenced for the rest of the day.[578]

At midnight, the pickets began to hear the unmistakable noises of the rebel army preparing to move. The men had expected the fighting to continue the next day, so there was some uncertainty as to whether the rebels were preparing to attack or to retreat. The muffled sounds of the commands used to prepare the rebel formations could be heard on the picket line, until at last, one loud voice called out through the nighttime shadows, "Forward: Guide center: March." The pickets had listened quietly to the voices in front of them, but when the last command rang out, one impatient sentry shouted back, "Come on old guide center, we'll give you merry hell!" His shout caused excitement in the camp as men clambered into formation to repel an attack. None came, because the Union Army of the Tennessee had turned the rebel flank and the Confederates were retreating yet again.[579]

At Cassville, the regiment "found the only noticeable country that had marks of value." It was also at Cassville that the Ninth Ohio left the Second Brigade. The Germans from Cincinnati had chosen not to reenlist, and their term of service was about to expire. The Ninth Ohio and the Thirty-fifth Ohio had been together since the brigade had been formed two and a half years before, and the shared experiences of war made those months seem like a lifetime. Of the seven regiments the Thirty-fifth had served with, they had been closest to the Ninth Ohio. Coming from neighboring counties in southwestern Ohio, the two regiments had formed a closeness that would never be broken. As far as the Thirty-fifth was concerned, "We had rather seen any other regiment march away and leave us than the Ninth Ohio." "That regiment had been a constant companion" and "a model regiment in every respect." The relationship between the two regiments had been a bright spot during dark days, and when the Ninth marched out for the last time, a little light went with them.[580]

On May 23, the Thirty-fifth Ohio received rations for twenty days and crossed the Etowah River. The crossing turned out to be a humorous experience. The river bottom was covered with stone and boulders. For men stripped down and trying to hold all of their worldly possessions up out of the flowing water, it was a very slippery surface, and dozens of them tripped and went under. They would go under and then pop back up, sputtering and cursing over getting clothes, rifle, and cartridges wet. No one was hurt in the crossing, so the dunkings were enjoyable, at least for those who didn't get one. South of the

---

578. Keil, *Thirty-fifth Ohio*, 22, 188; U.S. War Department, *War of the Rebellion*, Ser. no. 72, pp. 735, 788–89.

579. Keil, *Thirty-fifth Ohio*, 189, 193.

580. Ibid.

river, the regiment passed though Burnt Hickory and went on to a spot on Pumpkin Vine Creek near Dallas.[581]

When the Confederates got across the Union line of march at Dallas and New Hope Church, Sherman packed his wagons full of supplies, cut loose from the railroad, and marched through the wilderness of north Georgia. Van Derveer's brigade was assigned to guard the long train of wagons that now carried all of the army's supplies. They returned to the small village of Burnt Hickory midway between the railroad and New Hope Church. From this central location, individual regiments were sent out to guard wagon trains on the move. While the Persimmons watched over the army's supply line, the battle of New Hope Church was fought on May 24. A week later, the brigade was relieved of its guard duty and began to move toward the front on June 2 through dense pine forests. There was a little skirmishing everyday. None of the Persimmons were hurt by enemy fire, but friendly fire took its toll. Pvt. George Bowers of Company B accidentally shot himself in the leg on June 1and died six weeks later in Nashville.[582]

The roads were jammed with men, and several halts were necessary to allow the units to sort themselves out. During one halt under the trees, Maj. David Beckett, a resident of Hamilton and familiar to many of the men in the regiment, came by. Seeing familiar faces, Beckett, then serving in the Sixty-first Ohio under Hooker, gladly stopped to visit. As was his way, Beckett was "full of hope, looking only on the sunny side of all subjects," and fully expected the army to be in Atlanta by July 1. He chatted pleasantly with his friends and acquaintances from home until the bugle called the Thirty-fifth back into formation. As the Persimmons fell in to continue marching, Beckett mounted his horse and rode off. Several days later, the men of the Thirty-fifth learned, that David Beckett was dead, killed by a sharpshooter at Kennesaw Mountain.[583]

Nerves Educated to the Work

The Confederates retreated further into Georgia, and the Union army was able to repair and resume its use of the railroad all the way to Big Shanty. Lieutenant Foord, now formally exchanged, caught up with the Thirty-fifth Ohio on June 7 where it was camped about three miles from Acworth. After leaving Columbus, Ohio, on May 18, it had taken three weeks for him to get to the front. During a

581. Bircher, *Drummer Boy's Diary*, 74; U.S. War Department, *War of the Rebellion*, Ser. no. 72, p. 789.

582. Keil, *Thirty-fifth Ohio*, 190; U.S. War Department, *War of the Rebellion*, Ser. no. 72, p. 789; Van Derveer to wife, 3 June 1864, Van Derveer Family Collection.

583. Keil, *Thirty-fifth Ohio*, 190.

layover in Cincinnati, he had been able to visit Colonel Boynton whose wound was still healing very slowly. Rather than traveling the entire way by rail, Foord went by river packet all the way to Nashville, arriving on May 25. Boarding the train in Nashville, Foord's trip to Chattanooga began with a bang, literally. The train suddenly lurched forward throwing the half-awake lieutenant onto the floor. It left him in a bad mood for the rest of the night. He arrived in Chattanooga via Stevenson, Alabama, on the afternoon of the twenty-seventh and immediately ran into Capt. John Van Derveer of Company C and Quartermaster Sgt. Martin Betz. The next day, Foord and Betz made a solemn trip to Orchard Knob to view the graves of several members of the regiment buried there.[584]

It was not until June 3 that Foord and the other exchanged prisoners of the Thirty-fifth were able to get transportation to Kingston, Georgia. He joined the division wagon train there for the trip to the front. It rained steadily, and the trip was an uncomfortable one. During one rest halt, a kind woman put a chair on her porch for him to rest in, but when they stopped for the night, his bed was a rubber sheet thrown over some fence rails. Foord was given little time to acclimate himself to his new surroundings. Formally mustered in as first lieutenant on the morning of the eighth, Foord went back to retrieve the wagon train that afternoon, and was given picket duty that same evening. Fortunately, it was a quiet night.[585]

After receiving his commission, Foord was mustered in as first lieutenant of Company F, but due to the critical shortage of officers, Foord was placed in command of his old company. Captain Deardorf had been killed at Chickamauga. Lt. Lewis Lambright had been wounded at Missionary Ridge and had not yet returned. The only remaining company officer, Lieutenant David Stiles, had been on detached duty for more than a year, so Foord, intimately familiar with Company K, returned to lead it. Since he was the only officer in the company, Foord shared a tent with Lt. David Schaeffer of Company H.[586]

On June 10, the Thirty-fifth Ohio was involved in heavy skirmishing and several men were wounded. Every day seemed like the one before, and Colonel Van Derveer admitted that on one occasion, he had to ask someone what the date was and then what day of the week it was. The dysentery he had struggled with off and on during the war had returned and was troubling him. There was also still no progress on his promotion, and even Governor Brough had failed to have any positive influence. For months he had been hearing that it was the

584. Foord Papers, 17–29 May 1864; U.S. War Department, *War of the Rebellion*, Ser. no. 72, p. 789.

585. Foord Papers, 30 May–8 June 1864.

586. Ibid., 9–10 June 1864; Compiled service record, Richard H. Foord, 1st Sgt., Co. K, 35th Ohio Inf.; Carded Records, Volunteer Organizations, Civil War; Records of the Adjutant General's office, 1780s–1917, Record Group 94; National Archives, Washington, D.C.

politics of the presidential election that was preventing his advancement, but Van Derveer held no grudge against Abraham Lincoln and announced that he intended to vote for him in the fall.[587]

The next several days were spent moving and skirmishing. Sometimes it was just a few shots off to the right or left. Other times, the firing was heavy and lasted for hours. On June 14, the opposing skirmish lines engaged in a running fight that went on for half a mile or more and then continued to trade shots all night long. In his diary, Richard Foord described the night by saying, "Balls flying over our Camp, not very pleasant." He remembered his wife at home and prayed that God would spare him to return to her. Ferdinand Van Derveer was also writing to his wife about an experience with one of the flying balls Foord mentioned. "Saturday night after supper I was lying on my bed inside a tent reading, when a saucy rebel half a mile off seeing the light of the candle fired his rifle at it—the ball passed just over my feet and within a few inches of the candle—Had I been sitting up at the table as anyone but a lazy man would at that time in the evening I would most likely been hit—So you see that laziness sometimes pays."[588]

By June 15, the rebels had withdrawn into strong field works prepared ahead of time along Mud Creek. The Army of the Cumberland pushed right up against the Confederate lines on the eighteenth of June, another rainy day. The skirmish line reached the top of a low ridge about 9:00 a.m. and could see the rebel trenches a few hundred yards to the front. The Thirty-fifth Ohio and Second Minnesota advanced into an open field and prepared fortifications in one of the most exposed points of the Federal line. While the rebels watched and took pot shots at them under a persistent rain, the Persimmons carefully dug their trenches. Once again, the regiment's rifle fire helped silence enemy artillery. In this very dangerous position only a few hundred yards from the rebels, their earthworks were completed without losing a man. Ironically, the only losses came from shots fired over the high ground that fell into the regiment's camp. Sgt. James Blair of Company K was wounded, and 1st Sgt. James Jackson of Company F was killed in the random firing.[589]

As daylight crept over the hills, the Thirty-fifth awoke and peered over their breastworks to see what the rebels were up to. They were up to nothing. During the night, they had once again withdrawn and their trenches were empty. There was no question as to where they had gone. A quick look through the field glass told the Persimmons that their foes were already placing artillery on top of Kennesaw Mountain. The Army of the Cumberland immediately moved to follow the Confederates to the mountain. It rained throughout the

---

587. Van Derveer to wife, 10 June 1864, Van Derveer Family Collection.

588. Foord Papers, 11–17 June 1864; Van Derveer to wife, 7 June 1864, Van Derveer Family Collection.

589. Keil, *Thirty-fifth Ohio*, 192; Bishop, *Story of a Regiment*, 154; Foord Papers, 18 June 1864; U.S. War Department, *War of the Rebellion*, Ser. no. 72, p. 789.

advance, and the men found the summer showers "anything but agreeable." June 19 was spent once again sparring with the Confederate as the Army of the Cumberland advanced to the base of Kennesaw Mountain.[590]

During the skirmishing, Captain L'Hommedieu, on detached duty as Second Brigade inspector since April, found himself in hot water. In his capacity of inspector, L'Hommedieu was in command of the brigade's picket line on June 19. Long known as an expert forager, it may have been that he was a little too successful in finding spirituous liquor that day. Capt. Edward Grosvenor, the inspector for the First Brigade in charge of that brigade's pickets, had been directed by General Baird to conform his line and movement to that of the Second Brigade. Grosvenor, having gone to L'Hommedieu to discuss the joining of the flanks of the two lines, reported that he found L'Hommedieu "in a State of Stupid Intoxication—and apparently oblivious of where or how to position his line." Later in the day, a messenger from L'Hommedieu ordered Grosvenor to move his picket line into a more exposed position. Grosvenor protested the order, and when it resulted in several casualties, he stormed off to accuse L'Hommedieu of not properly supporting his movement. According to Grosvenor, L'Hommedieu's "drunkenness had increased until he was alike incapable of Superintending his Skirmishers—or giving to me a civil answer."

It was a very serious charge, because if true, L'Hommedieu had allowed the brigade "lines to be broken and separated" and caused the pickets to be "criminally exposed." A week later, Grosvenor preferred charges of "gross abuse of trust" against L'Hommedieu in a scathing letter. His brigade commander, Brigadier General Turchin, endorsed the charges, adding charges of "drunkenness and misbehavior before the enemy" and included the names of other officers who would corroborate Grosvenor's charges by describing similar behavior in the days following. If the charges were true, and it would appear they were, Turchin's claim that the brigade's safety was "greatly jeopardized under the supervision of such an officer" was accurate and the court-martial he desired should have been convened.

L'Hommedieu got off on a technicality. Grosvenor and Turchin made the mistake of addressing the charges directly to the Inspector General of the Army of the Cumberland rather than General Baird, the division commander. On July 7, Baird "respectfully returned" Grosvenor's letter to Turchin hotly admonishing him for not addressing the situation directly with Baird before proposing to escalate it to army headquarters. "Gen. Turchin will instruct his Inspector," Baird responded, "that when he sees any irregularities in this command he will report them to me, I being responsible for them—and for their correction—I will not permit any officer in my command to report me to higher authority for permitting irregularities in my command unless after I fail to correct them." Baird did not drop the issue entirely. Turchin could resubmit the charge, provided he limited them to what Grosvenor had written, and a court-martial

590. Keil, *Thirty-fifth Ohio*, 192; Foord Papers, 19 June 1864.

would be convened "as soon as the interests of the service will admit."

The Thirty-fifth, Captain L'Hommedieu included, came off the line a few weeks later as its enlistment expired. Turchin apparently did not resubmit the charges prior to that time, most likely because the army's movements did not allow him time to pursue the matter. There is no obvious reason for L'Hommedieu's behavior in the face of the enemy. He had performed ably up to that time, having been wounded in the skirmishing at Hoover's Gap the year before. A week prior to the incident on the skirmish line, he had commanded the regiment during a demonstration near Dalton. The answer may lie in L'Hommedieu's seeming durability. According to his pay records, he had not been away from the regiment since he enlisted, except for a brief stay in a Tullahoma hospital after being wounded. He had been in a command position all the while, even commanding the regiment for a short period. For all of the Atlanta campaign, one marked by early constant contact with the enemy, L'Hommedieu had been in charge of the brigade skirmish line. Perhaps the stress finally caused him to break down. Then again, heavy drinking was a common problem among Civil War officers.[591]

The Thirty-fifth began digging in "in front of the central knob of Kennesaw" and occupied the forwardmost positions once again. The men of the regiment were now old hands at entrenching and fully capable of building strong fortifications overnight. The undergrowth in front of the trenches was thick and had to be removed. While the men were exposed at this work, Color Sgt. Mark Price decided to air out the regimental flag that had now been damp for several days. The sight of Old Glory waving in front of them was more than the Confederates could stand, and their artillery opened up without warning. The first shot dug into the ground a few feet from the flag, and there was a mad scramble to get into the trenches. The shelling continued regularly for a few days, but the men were old hands at this sort of thing, as well. They came to expect "these complimentary recognitions" and "knew how to receive them with little inconvenience to ourselves." A watch was set up to call out whenever a puff of smoke appeared on the mountain in front of them until the rebels finally tired of wasting ammunition.[592]

The Thirty-fifth Ohio had now been in the field for forty days during which enemy fire was an ever present danger. While casualties were few, no one was ever really safe, not even the doctor. A ricocheting cannonball flew through camp, breaking the leg of Surgeon Abraham Landis on its way and making him one of eighty-three Union surgeons to be wounded in battle. There were non-battle losses as well. Captain Henninger of Company B was seriously hurt in an accident and spent two months in a Chattanooga hospital. Since the rebel lines

---

591. Compiled service record, Samuel L'Hommedieu, Capt., Co. G, 35th Ohio Inf.; Carded Records, Volunteer Organizations, Civil War; Records of the Adjutant General's office, 1780s–1917, Record Group 94; National Archives, Washington, D.C.

592. Keil, *Thirty-fifth Ohio*, 192–93; Bishop, *Story of a Regiment*, 155.

on Kennesaw Mountain were quite formidable, the Union army attempted to extend its lines around the flank of the mountain and the Thirty-fifth changed positions several times as the trenches were extended. All movements were made at night when observers and cannoneers couldn't see them.[593]

On the night of June 22, another movement to the right was made. The men were ordered to sling their rifles over the shoulder with the muzzles down to prevent the rifle barrels from reflecting in the moonlight. The brigade halted shortly before arriving at its new station and as the men formed back into ranks to continue marching, most of them returned their rifles to the normal sling arms position. As feared, the upright barrels reflected the moonlight, and a Confederate battery immediately hurled a volley in the direction of the light. The shells crashed into the Second Minnesota killing and wounding several men. The dead included one man who had been mustered out that day, and had he lived three hours longer, would have been on his way home.[594]

For three days, the Persimmons dug deeper into the Georgia clay and did what they could to strengthen the fortifications in their front. As usual, tents were set up behind the trenches but were rarely occupied. The Confederates continued to fire at odd times, and most men stayed near the earthworks. The rain had stopped but was replaced by oppressive heat that did a lot to bring relative quiet to the lines. The occasional minie ball would fly over, but for the most part there was no firing. Lieutenant Lambright returned to Company K on June 24, but Richard Foord remained with that company. He spent several days and nights in the trenches but managed to sneak off for a bath in a nearby creek.[595]

General Sherman was aware of complaints from the ranks that the army was doing too much marching for their liking. For his part, Sherman thought there was too much digging. Only a few weeks later, Sherman would comment that, "The skill and rapidity with which our men construct these [earthworks] is wonderful and is something new in the art of war," but standing before Kennesaw Mountain, he had other ideas. Having taken note of how men began to dig trenches as soon as they stopped, he worried that the army might become too cautious to fight in the open. Sherman decided that it was time the army came out of its trenches and made a direct assault on Kennesaw Mountain. The Second Brigade was assigned to support the attack, and on the night of June 26, moved into position near the units it would support. It was the fiftieth day of the Atlanta campaign, during which there had been nearly constant skirmishing and little time for resting. Everyone was tired and hoped the rebels would just run away again. The march was a short one, but it still took nearly the entire night to complete the move. At 8:00 a.m. on June 27, the Thirty-fifth moved

593. Foord Papers, 22 June 1864; Wiley, *Billy Yank*, 131; *Cyclopedia of Butler County, Ohio*, 385.

594. Keil, *Thirty-fifth Ohio*, 193–94; Bircher, *Drummer Boy's Diary*, 77.

595. Foord Papers, 23–25 June 1864.

into the works just vacated by the attacking force. No sooner than they had gotten into the trenches, "a most infernal racket of musketry and artillery opened in front." The firing quickly spread up and down the lines, but no one in the trenches could see what was happening. The thick vegetation kept the battle hidden from the waiting Persimmons, but it only required a few moments waiting for the effects to be known. Through the dense foliage, shadowy figures of wounded men slowly limping to the rear began to appear, so that "the open space in our front was filled at once with the wounded that came hobbling back bloody, and they presented a fearful sight."[596]

The anxious Buckeyes found that it was one thing to view the carnage of battle while involved in the fighting, but another thing entirely to view it second hand. While a man was busy fighting, his "attention is occupied with what was going on in front." A soldier firing his rifle as quickly as he can and shouting at the top of his lungs all the while pays little attention to anything else around him, and the condition of the dead and wounded "do not affect a person." At Kennesaw Mountain, the Thirty-fifth Ohio did not take an active part in the fighting, but it had to deal with the sight of fearfully mangled men streaming past. Losses were heavy, and they watched as a moaning stream of wounded men "were carried back in stretchers while the blood ran in streams thought the canvas on which they lay." "It required nerves educated to the work, to stand such sights," and since there was little they could do, they bore it all in a moody silence. All that was accomplished by the attack was to move the Federal lines closer to the base of the mountain. A truce was arranged on June 29 to bury the dead, and a couple of days later on July 2, the Confederates were forced out of their mountain top position by another flanking movement, just as they would have been if the attack at Kennesaw Mountain had never been made.[597]

Watching the scenes at Kennesaw Mountain caused Lieutenant Keil of Company C to ponder the psychology of battle. Having been through numerous skirmishes and fights, he was qualified to make an observation on the subject. Just prior to a battle, Keil wrote that a soldier "would as lief that it were some one else that held his place" and realizes that there were "many positions he would rather be in" than the one he is. Considering his prior experiences and observations of others in the same situation, Keil believed that the "class that are just dying to get into a battle, are not found in the army! Either there is no such class; or they are careful not to be found when the recruiting officer comes along. As a rule, persons prefer to die, not on the battle-field, but somewhere else." Soldiers did not stand up to fire in battle because they liked war or to become heroes. They essentially did it because they felt they had no other choice. The desire not to be considered a coward was vital to their manhood.

596. Keil, *Thirty-fifth Ohio*, 194; Wiley, *Billy Yank*, 85; Van Derveer to wife, 26 June 1864, Van Derveer Family Collection.
597. Keil, *Thirty-fifth Ohio*, 194; Foord Papers, 27–29 June 1864.

Their sense of duty refused to let them run from a battle and training kept them functioning in the midst of it.[598]

When it came to organized fighting, discipline was the single most important factor in success. Discipline, as Keil saw it, was a cohesiveness, or more correctly, an *esprit de corps* created by the combination of duty and training. If discipline "be wanting, the regiment likewise will be wanting in the scale where courage is weighed." If a regiment felt no sense of duty to give it purpose, it would not fight. If it felt it had no effective way to defend itself, even if feeling called to do so, it would not fight. Given a sense of duty and training, men would join together, and then stick together in battle. But experience also proved absolutely that "while a regiment as an organization can be educated to stand under almost any condition, or circumstance, there [sic] are individuals within the organization who are constitutionally wanting in that which constitutes courage; and no discipline, no schooling to danger, can supply such courage." In other words, a man who was unwilling to look beyond the possibility of immediate negative impacts to his own person would always be a coward.[599]

Fear, in and of itself, did not represent a fault in a man's character. The thought of being maimed or killed is frightening to all normal men. Keil felt this idea needed no explanation, as it had been proven over and over again in human experience. "The first rattle of the enemy's musketry; or the screeching of the shell that comes along looking for a person, has an indescribable effect over a person, and produces a weakening about the knees." Physical strength had nothing to do with it. "The legs which carried the soldier thirty miles in one day's march, and came into camp still strong; under the circumstances named, suddenly become weak, and are inclined to let down the body." In fact, a man's body was a contrary vessel to be trapped in just before a battle. "Likewise, there is an unwillingness on the part of the muscles to do duty—unless required to carry the body to the rear, out of danger; in which case, it has been reported by those who have a right to know, that muscles increase in strength, as the distance widens between the person and the danger!"[600]

So how was it that a frightened man was able to stand and fight? The fact of the matter was that for most men, "that indescribable something, which affects a person so peculiarly, is of short duration. One volley from the enemy and a warm response, will do away with squimishness, and make a person feel like taking a hand in the muss." Once a battle starts, the simple reality of having something to do allows most men to function as they have been taught. A man with something to focus his mind on can make his body do what it seemingly does not want to. To sum it all up, "Men wish themselves somewhere else, but they keep right on. Their pride, their sense of duty, their ideas of manhood, the discipline, and the honor of the regiment in which they serve will not allow them to do otherwise than to stand up to the racket."[601]

---

598. Keil, *Thirty-fifth Ohio*, 195.
599. Ibid., 195.
600. Ibid., 195–96.

Reluctant Departure

Ferdinand Van Derveer had been ill for a full year. Two furloughs had allowed him to regain some of his strength, but he had never completely shaken his sickness and was slowly wasting away. The fact that he had lasted as long as he had was a testament to the strength of his will. His desire to remain with his men in the field to the very end was admirable, but the same stubbornness that carried him through every difficult time probably worked against him this time. Refusing to allow himself the time to fully recover from his illness, Van Derveer grew weaker and weaker until there was only one option left. Surgeon Francis Morris did the best he could for his commander, but the stress of command and life in the field continually ate away at Van Derveer's vigor. At last, the colonel made what must have been one of the most difficult decisions of his life.

In the certificate prepared to support a much needed request or furlough, Morris declared that Van Derveer was "unable to perform the duties devolving upon him because of inflammation of the bowels." The doctor fully believed that "unless he can obtain a more nutritious diet and be relieved from the responsibilities of command he will not recover." There it was. With no other reasonable action available to him, Ferdinand Van Derveer once again requested another twenty-day leave to recuperate, knowing fully well what it meant. The Thirty-fifth Ohio only had one month remaining on its enlistment, a month in which he would not be present. Van Derveer's regiment and the soldiers he cared for so deeply would have to finish the war without him.

Van Derveer's reluctance was matched by that of the Third Division commander. Gen. Absalom Baird had developed a very deep respect for Van Derveer, and it pained him personally to see his brigade commander leave. But having been in daily contact and closely observing his subordinate's steadily worsening health, he understood what had to happen. Endorsing Van Derveer's request, Baird wrote, "Col. Van Derveer is a much valued officer and is reluctant to leave but he can be of no use here in his present condition and would probably forfeit his life by attempting to remain." A decent man, Baird could not allow that to happen and earnestly recommended that the request be approved. Whether a sign of the army's increasing efficiency or its respect for a dedicated officer, Van Derveer's requested was routed and approved on the same day it was prepared.[602]

Also a generous man, General Baird made special mention of Colonel Van Derveer's departure in his report on the Atlanta campaign. "On the 27th, Col. F. Van Derveer, commanding my Second Brigade, who had long been suffering

---

601. Keil, *Thirty-fifth Ohio*, 196.

602. Compiled service record, Ferdinand Van Derveer, Col., Staff, 35th Ohio Inf.; Civil War; RG 94; NA–Washington.

from disease, was compelled to go North for relief, and turned over the command of the brigade to Col. N Gleason, of the Eighty-seventh Indiana Volunteers, who has since retained it. In losing Colonel Van Derveer, my command, and the service generally, was deprived of one of its most gallant and best officers and most accomplished gentlemen. Always prompt, judicious, and brave, he had distinguished himself on many fields, and his promotion had been strongly urged on the government, but unaccountably overlooked."[603]

As Colonel Van Derveer departed for home, Maj. Joseph Budd became the only field-grade officer remaining with the Thirty-fifth Ohio. The men were sorry to see Van Derveer go, but they didn't have much time to worry about it. Their war wasn't over yet, and Budd, along with the 273 remaining Persimmons, still had dangerous work to do.

Busily Engaged With Pick and Shovel

Tullahoma and Chickamauga had been campaigns of maneuver after maneuver. The Atlanta campaign was one of fortification after maneuver. The Atlanta campaign also differed from the previous two in the continuous nature of the fighting. From the time the Thirty-fifth Ohio left Ringgold in early May, the skirmishing had never stopped. Heavier fighting occurred nearly every day at one point in the line or another, but rarely did the two armies actually square off. The Persimmons had built defensive works at numerous camps, but never had they dug fortifications to the extent they did in their final campaign. The increased effort required some minor organizational changes. A number of men in each regiment were assigned to carry picks and shovels, and every night, when the regiment halted, field works were thrown up. If it was only an overnight stop, a wall was erected in front of the camp. If the stay was to be longer, the effort was more expansive. Digging had become "almost an instinct," and it was "surprising how rapidly men in the field threw up fortifications, how the work progressed, and what immense results were accomplished by a body of troops in a single night."[604]

The field works were also becoming more elaborate as demonstrated by things like head logs. Head logs were placed along the top of the works with a narrow space between them and the parapet below. They allowed the men to fire their rifles through the gap without exposing their heads. It was possible for artillery to knock a head log from its place back onto the heads of the men it was supposed to protect, so a series of skids were wedged under the head logs and stretched across the trench. If a head log did get knocked loose, it would roll across the trench on the skids rather than fall on the riflemen. One "genius"

603. U.S. War Department, *War of the Rebellion*, Ser. no. 72, p. 739.
604. Keil, *Thirty-fifth Ohio*, 202–3; Bircher, *Drummer Boy's Diary*, 75.

even designed a sighting system of looking glasses that allowed sharpshooters to line up the sights on a rifle and fire it while sitting down inside the trench with his back to the wall.[605]

After abandoning their position on Kennesaw Mountain, the Confederate army fell back behind the Chattahoochee River. The day after the rebel evacuation, the Thirty-fifth traded shots with the rebel rear guard all day, but there were no casualties and the day ended well. A "great many prisoners" were captured, and that evening, they had " a glorious supper of ham." The next day, July 4th, the regimental band awakened everyone with tunes suitable for Independence Day. The regiment began to work on its fortifications, but later in the day they were pulled out of the lines. The Second Brigade had again drawn temporary garrison duty, this time at the new supply depot at Marietta, Georgia. For a week they did "a large amount of work in policing the town and doing guard and picket duty; in receiving and sending North a large number of factory employees from Roswell and other places."[606]

The stay in Marietta turned out to be a "most delightful" eight days. The regiment's camp, on the property of former Georgia governor Charles J. McDonald, was set in "a park of natural forest trees, affording cool shade." The rebel army was on the other side of the river, there was no guerilla activity, and nearly all of the town's citizens had left before the Yankees arrived. The Persimmons had virtually nothing to do, and over the last three years, they had become masters of the art. They lounged in the breeze under the trees, strolled through the local flower gardens, and slept. After eighty days of campaigning, they had been tired for so long that at first, all anyone wanted to do was sleep. With most of the town empty, the men of the Thirty-fifth were "privileged to go where we pleased," and generally made themselves at home in other people's houses. The firing lines were far enough away, that even artillery fire could not be heard. "Nothing now disturbed nature's quiet save the gentle rustle of leaves, as moved by a pleasant breeze."[607]

In exploring the area, McDonald's house was found to contain several packing cases full of books. The occupants had apparently fled as fast as the Confederate army and had not had time to finish packing McDonald's impressive personal library. Gen. George Thomas did his best to care for his men, and one of the things he had done was insist that the army be provided with books and magazines. The Persimmons were used to reading as they rested, and now wandering soldiers "examined his selections at our leisure, and found that he had many of the standard works of English literature, and some of the volumes were placed in most excellent bindings." Making the most of the situation, the books that had once been, and technically still were, the property of an "aristo-

---

605. Keil, *Thirty-fifth Ohio*, 203.

606. Foord Papers, 3–4 July 1864; U.S. War Department, *War of the Rebellion*, Ser. no. 72, p. 790.

607. Keil, *Thirty-fifth Ohio*, 196–97; Bircher, *Drummer Boy's Diary*, 78.

cratic old rebel" became the Thirty-fifth Ohio's own circulating library. For several days, these "agreeable companions" provided stimulating and satisfying company. As to the circulating part, "It cannot positively be stated that all the books 'circulated back' to the owner's house when we left!"[608]

Life was easy in Marietta. Several of the officers, including Captain Daugherty of Company A and Lieutenant Keil of Company C, found a woman who had not left town and who was willing to cook for them. They formed a mess in which they proposed to provide provisions for themselves and for her family. Her part of the bargain was to prepare the meals. The woman's food supplies had been cleaned out as two armies passed through town, so she readily agreed to the arrangement. For the officers, it was a wonderful deal, and they sat down at the woman's dining room table for their first meal with great anticipation. When everyone was seated and ready, the woman spoke from her place at the head of the table. "Now, gentlemen, you are all strangers to me, of course, you are Christian gentlemen, and would not think of eating a meal before saying grace; who shall do it at the table is a matter I leave to you."[609]

The officers were all dumbstruck. Since saying grace was "a ceremony that had been entirely dispensed with" when the regiment took the field three years before, none of the officers had even considered the possibility. While the startled officers looked around the table at each other trying to will one of the others to say the prayer, the woman waited patiently. No one dared eat until the words had been spoken, but no one dared speak them. Finally, after the "affair was becoming somewhat embarrassing, as to who, among such a graceless set, was to say grace," one officer spoke up. One "lieutenant among the number," perhaps Lieutenant Keil, took charge of the situation. This particular lieutenant had been a "Methodist in good standing, before he entered the army—a fact, however, not suspected by any one up to that date," and knew what needed to be done. For the rest of the Thirty-fifth's time in Marietta, the same officer said grace before every meal.[610]

The arrangement with the local woman turned out to be a very positive thing for everyone involved. The officers had not been around children since leaving Hamilton, and the woman's small daughter quickly became a favorite among them. For her part, the little girl quickly warmed up to the visitors in her house and received many favors from them. She was so young that she had no idea what the greenbacks presented to her were. But, in her still simple world, she assumed they must be important, or the nice men would not be giving them to her. Before leaving to rejoin Thomas's troops at the front, the helpful woman was given a "fine supply of provisions," and was ecstatic to find a packet of tea among them.[611]

---

608. McKinney, *Education in Violence*, 302; Keil, *Thirty-fifth Ohio*, 197.
609. Keil, *Thirty-fifth Ohio*, 197.
610. Ibid., 198.
611. Ibid.

The final advance on Atlanta had begun, and on July 17 the Thirty-fifth Ohio crossed the Chattahoochee River near Vining's Station on a pontoon bridge. The entire army had crossed by the end of the next day, and the Confederates had been pushed back to Nancy Creek, between the river and Peachtree Creek. On the evening of July 19, the Persimmons crossed Peachtree Creek at Howell's Mill and prepared to push the rebels back even closer to Atlanta the next day. After things had settled down for the night, Captain Daugherty and his friend Lieutenant Keil sat under a tree on the banks of the creek and talked about what they would do when the war was over. That night, as the "moonbeams came glittering through the fret-work of leaves, casting fantastic shadows upon the ground" around them, they had less than a month left on their enlistment. Daugherty, a conscientious officer who had rarely left his place of duty with the regiment in three years, "spoke feelingly of his family at home," and the two men chatted long into the night. It was a pleasant chat about memories of home and friends there, and neither felt like sleeping.[612]

On July 20, newly appointed Confederate commander, Gen. John Bell Hood, struck the Union army hard along Peachtree Creek. As the battle progressed, the Second Brigade attacked the woody ridge to their front with the intent of capturing and holding the enemy works there. The Thirty-fifth Ohio made the attack with consummate skill learned in dozens of similar actions, but in war, skill is no guarantee of survival. The rebels fought back stoutly, and the Persimmons took casualties. Among them was Captain Daugherty, shot dead in the middle of the fighting. A "faithful and valuable" officer, Lewis Daugherty never made it back to the home he had spoken of with such longing the night before. His body was taken back across Peachtree Creek and buried near Howell's Mill under the shadow of a spreading chestnut tree. Daugherty's grave was later moved to the national cemetery at Marietta. His friend Lieutenant Keil had little time to grieve. The war moved on, and Keil had no choice but to go with it.[613]

A week later, Hood attacked again near Ezra Church. The Thirty-fifth Ohio was busy building fortifications on the other side of Atlanta but could hear the noise of the battle as they worked. As the men were "busily engaged with the pick and shovel," they suddenly became heedful of the presence of General Thomas. The stout man who climbed down from his horse and sat under the shade of some nearby trees was their favorite general, but his presence was of no comfort to them on this occasion. The question "What does Pap want here?" quickly went up and down the lines. Having served under the imperturbable one for two and a half years, they knew his ways. It was Thomas's habit to be present at the place in the line that he felt was most critical, and here he was, watching the Persimmons dig. Thomas had been ordered to send reinforcements to the Army of the Tennessee and they had come from the right end of

---

612. Keil, *Thirty-fifth Ohio*, 199–200.
613. Ibid., 200; U.S. War Department, *War of the Rebellion*, Ser. no. 72, p. 790.

his line, which was farthest from the fighting. That made the Second Brigade the extreme right of the army, and in Thomas's mind, the most likely place for an unexpected Confederate attack. He loitered near the Thirty-fifth's trenches as the men kept a watchful eye on his movements. When the units he had sent to the left returned and had moved back into their positions, Thomas mounted up and returned to his headquarters.[614]

As the siege of Atlanta began, the Persimmons spent the days hunkered down in the trenches waiting while "grim messengers of death and destruction were hurled night and day into the fated city." At night, when the air was still, the men "followed the shells from our siege guns, by their whirr into Atlanta, until the low, dead sound of explosion came back to our ears." The daylight hours found them on the opposite end of the stick. The Confederate artillery was active during the day, and the Thirty-fifth's "attention was more particularly given to the action of the enemy's guns in our vicinity." When the flash or smoke of cannon was observed, they were also given to "making sudden divings" into their holes like startled gophers. The Confederate's were so regular that everyone soon knew their firing schedule, and when that time approached, they all edged closer to their "gopher" holes, ready to dive in at the first sound. "The big shells came thick and fast, and though we occupied a position down the slope, yet the rebels had the range so well, that the projectile force was so far exhausted, when our ridge was reached, that the shells curved rapidly, and dropped uncomfortably close." The heavy enemy shelling in front of Atlanta proved how adept the regiment had become at preparing fortifications. In spite of the hundreds of shells that landed in and around the regiment's position, not a single casualty was reported.[615]

---

614. Keil, *Thirty-fifth Ohio*, 201; U.S. War Department, *War of the Rebellion*, Ser. no. 72, p. 790.

615. Keil, *Thirty-fifth Ohio*, 204.

CHAPTER 13

Men Who Could Do
Somewhat as They Pleased

August to October 1864

Faces Turned Homeward

For several days, the regiment lived in the shadows of the fortifications outside Atlanta, but on the night of August 1 a great commotion swept the camp. At midnight, orders arrived relieving the Thirty-fifth Ohio Volunteer Infantry from further duty at the front. The news spread like wildfire, and within five minutes of its arrival everyone, including the men on the picket line, had heard. No one slept anymore that night. The regimental history states, "There are moments in men's lives when the flow of happy feelings are so strong, that they carry everything before them. Such are the moments when success first crowns continued, persistent, and painstaking efforts. The pains and perplexities are forgotten, because thrust aside by the strong flow of happy emotions." They had honorably fulfilled their enlistment, and having survived dozens of deadly situations, could finally afford to "turn their faces homeward, where loving hearts awaited their coming."[616]

The Thirty-fifth Ohio marched away from the trenches around Atlanta with "gladsome hearts, and smiling faces," but their war wasn't quite finished. With a few days still remaining on their term of enlistment, the regiment was held up at the Chattahoochee River to guard construction crews erecting "the highest bridge known to military art." Released from that duty, the Persimmons marched on to Marietta, where they were held up again. This time, the delay was not caused by Union officials. Marauding rebel cavalry had torn up the railroad between Marietta and the Allatoona Pass. There was nothing they could do about it, but everyone was now anxious to leave the army behind, and the waiting chafed. "To counsel patience is well enough so long as a particle of

---

616. Keil, *Thirty-fifth Ohio*, 203; U.S. War Department, *War of the Rebellion*, Ser. no. 72, p. 790.

that remains; but men returning home, after so long an absence, have never been known to possess an overly amount of the same, as those who have had charge of mustering out men know."[617]

While in Marietta, the group of officers that had been so well fed by a local woman several weeks previous took the opportunity to renew their acquaintance with her. In spite of the difference in their politics, the woman and her daughter had treated them with kindness, gently reminding them of the ways of civilized folk, and they had developed a fondness for her. The unnamed Southern lady, returning the warm feelings of her Northern friends, had heard all of the news about the deadly fighting in and around Atlanta. Genuinely concerned about the welfare of her "Yankee boarders," she was saddened by the death of Captain Daugherty but pleased that the others had come through all right. She was also quite pleased to learn that the war had moved well beyond her home and would not be coming back.[618]

Finally, after a week of waiting, word came down that the tracks had been repaired. At 6:00 a.m. on August 11, the cheerful men jostled their way aboard the cars and set out for Chattanooga. The return trip to the city proved to be a retrospective on the most exciting times of their lives. It had taken the Persimmons three months to fight their way to Atlanta while "scarcely an hour passed during which the boom of cannon, or the sharp rattle of musketry could not be heard." Now they peacefully followed the same path in reverse in a single day. Big Shanty, Allatoona, and Cassville drifted by. The sun was settling behind Lookout Mountain as they crossed Rocky Face Ridge, where they had started on the road to Atlanta amidst heavy skirmishing. From the railcars, they could see Chickamauga Creek flowing through its valley, and just before dark, they were able to make out lights on Missionary Ridge before they went through the tunnel under the mountain. It had been an amazing journey "rich with incidents, long to be remembered."[619]

Good Soldiers

Not everyone was going home. Two officers continued on after the regiment was disbanded. Twenty-seven men had reenlisted and another forty-two men who had enlisted at various times after the regiment had been mustered still had time to serve. Tragically, another dozen enlisted men captured at Chickamauga and Missionary Ridge remained in rebel prisons.

Forty-eight Persimmons had gone into captivity at Chickamauga. Most had been taken in the confusing ebb and flow of the woodland fight at Kelly's. Ten

---

617. Keil, *Thirty-fifth Ohio*, 205.
618. Ibid., 199.
619. Ibid., 205.

others had been wounded and left behind when the army retreated. Seven of the wounded were paroled and returned to the custody of the Union army a few days after the battle. They were the lucky ones. They all survived. For those who entered it, the rebel prison system was a deadly place. By the time their companies mustered out that fall, eighteen of the Thirty-fifth's POWs had already died in rebel custody, most at Andersonville, some at Belle Isle, and a few at Danville. Four souls simply disappeared. They had been taken by the Confederates but were never heard from again. Less than half the men who became prisoners survived the ordeal. They were paroled and released at various times as the war wound down. Even that didn't guarantee survival, and two tired, worn down Persimmons died shortly after gaining their freedom. John Brooks, the private who had held a skillet in front of his face at Chickamauga to protect his beauty didn't get home until January 1865. The dubious honor of being the last man standing went to hapless Pvt. Johnny Doyle of Company C. Captured at Missionary Ridge when he unwittingly carried lunch to the rebels, Doyle ended up at Bell Isle, Virginia. In February 1864, he had been transferred to the hellhole at Andersonville, where he suffered from scurvy but managed to survive. In April of 1865, Doyle was paroled at Jacksonville, Florida. Johnny's wartime journey included a final month of recovery at Camp Chase in Columbus, Ohio, and not until June 2, 1865, did he receive his much belated discharge and head for home.[620]

Pvt. Joseph O'Neall continued to bedevil the Confederate prison system with escape attempts. After arriving at Andersonville, he made five separate attempts to tunnel out of that disease-ridden quagmire. All failed, and his health began failing, as well. Constant exposure to the weather and a starvation diet (he once went nine days without eating) affected him as it did all the other unfortunates trapped in the Andersonville cesspool. In late 1864, he was transferred to a prison pen in Charleston, South Carolina, where he had the dubious privilege of being shelled by Union artillery. While his body was weak and worn, his spirit remained unconquerable, and on December 16, 1864, he made one final and successful escape attempt. Breaking out of the Charleston prison, he made his way to Savannah where he was finally free. His family had long ago given him up for dead, and they were astonished when he came through their Wayne Township door. They almost didn't recognize him. He had left home more than two years before weighing 155 pounds. When he returned from his captivity, he weighed less than 85 pounds. But not even the suffering of prison could keep Joseph O'Neall down. After recovering, he accepted a commission as a second lieutenant in May 1865, but the war ended before he was assigned to a unit.[621]

Lt. Edward Cottingham of Company E had also been captured at Chickamauga. While at Libby Prison, he had made his own escape attempt. After tun-

---

620. Ohio Roster Commission, *Official Roster*, 601–34; Boynton, *Letters*, 26.
621. Bogan, *Warren County's Involvement*, 13.

neling under the street, he had fled north toward the lines held by the Army of Potomac. Less than a mile from freedom, Cottingham had been recaptured and returned to Libby. Finally paroled, he rejoined the regiment and was promoted to captain. Acceptance of a promotion mustered an officer for an additional three years at the rank accepted. As units mustered out, nearly all officers mustered out with their companies by resigning their commissions. Even so, some officers were unwilling to take the chance. For that reason, Lieutenants Saunders, Keil, and Taylor had received promotions but never been mustered in at their new rank. Whether desirous for making up for lost time or wishing another shot at his captors, Cottingham found a staff position and decided to stay in the army a while longer. He was finally discharged in March of 1865.[622]

The only other officer of the Thirty-fifth Ohio to remain in service was Colonel Van Derveer. On August 12, after returning for the mustering out of the Thirty-fifth Ohio, Van Derveer had made one more trip to the front at Atlanta. He was close enough to hear the bullets fly one last time, but the purpose of his visit was to say goodbye to all his friends still with the army. After mustering out, he had initially returned home to Hamilton. Finally, more than a year after being recommended, and after the presidential election was over, he received a promotion to brigadier general and was given command of a brigade of the Fourth Corps in January 1865. The brigade's mission in Alabama was primarily occupation duty with little campaigning and no actual fighting. In the spring of 1865, the rapidly shrinking army reorganized, and the number of brigades assigned to each division was reduced to two. As one of the least senior brigadiers, Van Derveer became supernumerary, and seeing that there was no longer a need for his services, he resigned his commission on June 3, 1865. On June 14, General Thomas prepared Special Order No. 61, announcing Van Derveer's departure. The quiet, bespectacled officer packed his bags and went home for good. It was quiet ending to a solid, if unheralded, military career.[623]

The enlisted men of the Thirty-fifth Ohio who continued their service were transferred to the Eighteenth Ohio. The Eighteenth had a long service record with the western armies, and enough of its members had reenlisted for it to be designated the Eighteenth Ohio Veteran Volunteer Infantry. To bring it back up to a respectable strength, smaller groups of veterans from several regiments that had not reenlisted were transferred into the Eighteenth. Along with other soldiers from the First Ohio, Second Ohio, and Twenty-fourth Ohio, the men of the Thirty-fifth joined the Eighteenth Ohio on garrison duty at Chattanooga. They participated in the battle of Nashville and subsequent pursuit of the retreating Confederate army in December 1864. Following more garrison duty at Nashville, the veteran Eighteenth moved to Augusta, Georgia, where it remained on occupation duty until being mustered out in October 1865.

---

622. Lowry, *History of Preble County*, 214.

623. U.S. War Department, *War of the Rebellion*, Ser. no. 104; Van Derveer to wife, 13 August 1864, Van Derveer Family Collection.

Brig. Gen. Ferdinand Van Derveer (standing left) while serving as a brigade commander in IV Corps in Alabama in 1865.
MASSACHUSETTS COMMANDERY OF MOLLUS AT USAMHI

Sixty-nine Persimmons received orders to the veteran Eighteenth Ohio, but some of them never truly joined it. A handful were either in the hospital or on details elsewhere and never spent a day in camp with the Eighteenth Ohio. Those that actually joined their new regiment were in two distinct groups. There were the original members who had reenlisted and were officially considered veterans. The men who had enlisted after the regiment went into service did not carry that classification, but there was really no other way to consider them. Even the group that had not joined the Thirty-fifth Ohio until February of 1864 had gone through the Atlanta campaign and could in no way be considered recruits.

The Persimmons with time remaining had anywhere from a few weeks to two years left to fulfill. The first of them was discharged four days after the transfer, but the members of the 1864 group of recruits remained with Company C of the Eighteenth Ohio until it was formally mustered out in October 1865. Their service in the Thirty-fifth worked to their advantage. For one thing, they were now much more survivable than they had been. After joining the Eighteenth Ohio, only one Persimmon, William Rogers, died of illness and two others were discharged. Pvt. John Garrison was discharged on a certificate of disability, but Cpl. William Tillson was determined to see it through to the end. When illness weakened him, Tillson transferred to the Veteran Reserve Corps and completed his enlistment. There were no battle losses. The 8 percent loss rate for these veterans compares quite favorably to the 47 percent rate suffered by the Thirty-fifth Ohio during its service. Prior service also made the new members of the Eighteenth Ohio much more skillful and useful. Of the thirty-six who actually joined the Eighteenth, eleven men received promotions after joining their new company. William Burgett was promoted twice, to corporal and then to sergeant. Pvts. William Emrick and David Schellenbarger both received a commission as second lieutenant in December 1864. Emrick received his as a reward for bravery at the battle of Nashville where he rescued the regiment's commander after that officer was wounded.[624]

The record of the Persimmon veterans was even more striking. It has been said that volunteer soldiers were as good as they wanted to be, and the veterans of the Thirty-fifth Ohio wanted to be the best. A remarkable group of men to start with, after three years of war and hard campaigning, they had chosen to stay and do it for three more years. It had to have been a difficult decision, because it was apparent early on that the vast majority of the Persimmons had no intention of reenlisting. The pressure to conform to the group as well as the natural desire to go home must have been powerful. For the same reason, it must also have been a lonely decision. For three years, the regiment had been family, and the shared danger and hardship had made it a very tight knit family. In many cases, the regiment was literally a family affair. All of the Thirty-fifth's company rosters have clumps of men with the same name; fathers, sons, brothers, and cousins all serving together. There are no common names among the veterans, nor did they share names with the time-remaining men, indicating that to reenlist meant to separate themselves from both families, military and blood. When made, even after discussing it with family and friends, it was a decision made alone for private reasons.

Fortunately, if turned out to be a good news story for all of them. All twenty-six Persimmon veterans completed their service in the Eighteenth Ohio and were discharged without loss. None died, none were injured, and there is no record of illness among them. When the Eighteenth Ohio mustered out in October 1865, they were all there. These tough, disease-resistant men also had years of campaign and battlefield experience. The hard-won skills learned in hundreds of camps and skirmish lines were of great value to their new regiment, and the Eighteenth made good use of them. Ten of the twenty-six veterans were promoted in their last year of service. Pvts. Frederick Ewalt, Newton Jones, and Micajah Samuels became corporals. John Bowman and Jacob Foutz were promoted to corporal and then further advanced to sergeant. Pvt. William Shires was promoted directly to sergeant, while Isaac Shaffer rose even more precipitously, going directly from private to first sergeant. Excelling at that rank, Shaffer received a commission and ended the war as a second lieutenant.

---

624. Ohio Roster Commission, *Official Roster*, 589–96; U.S. War Department, *War of the Rebellion*, Ser. no. 93, p. 531.

Joseph Harris, Thomas Sheldon, and William Ware had been sergeants when they reenlisted. Harris was promoted to first sergeant when Isaac Schaffer became an officer. Ware received his commission to first lieutenant and moved to Company D. Thomas Sheldon rose farthest of all. Commissioned as first lieutenant of Company C just before Christmas 1864, he was promoted to captain in the spring and commanded Company I, Eighteenth Ohio Veteran Volunteer Infantry until the regiment was disbanded. Though overshadowed by more famous outfits, the Thirty-fifth Ohio produced some good soldiers.[625]

An Unusually Long Time

Once in Chattanooga, the actual mustering out process began for those who were going home. Not everyone was mustered out at once. Regardless of when they had signed up individually, the official muster date for the men was the date their company was formally accepted into service. Companies A, B, and C had mustered in on August 20, 1861, and were the first to be officially mustered out. As mustering officer, the first three companies were unfortunate enough to draw 1st Lt. George Sanderson, a West Point graduate in the Fifteenth U.S Infantry, and "it became evident that he was not as well versed in his work as he might have been." Four times, the company officers prepared their muster rolls, and four times Sanderson sent them back with an entirely different set of instructions for preparing them. Being young and impressed with his own importance as an officer in the regular army, the young lieutenant was unwilling to admit any deficiency on his part. The company officers of A, B, and C got "quite warm 'under the jacket.'" They had previously prepared dozens of muster rolls, marching in the worst weather imaginable, fighting battles, starving, and then fighting some more while doing it, and they had always been good enough before. After three years, they were in no mood to put up with the inconsistencies of an inexperienced and vainglorious regular officer.[626]

After the fourth rejection of muster rolls, Captains Henninger and Van Derveer, along with Lieutenants Miller, Houser, and Keil, confronted their peer from West Point and let him know how it was going to be. Sanderson was going to give them definite instructions on how he wanted the company muster rolls prepared. The officers of the Thirty-fifth let it be known that before the fifth set of rolls were prepared, they were more than "willing that he should have all of the time he wanted to make up his mind, but declined to take up the pen until he was fully satisfied in his mind how the work was to be done." It was further made known to Lieutenant Sanderson "that when the next set of rolls were

---

625. Ohio Roster Commission, *Official Roster*, 589–96.

626. Keil, *Thirty-fifth Ohio*, 206; Ohio Roster Commission, *Official Roster*, 602, 605, 608.

made not a scratch would be changed." In the presence of those stern, scruffy looking combat veterans, the regular army officer swallowed his pride and decided he could agree to the terms proposed by these lowly volunteers. The rolls were duly prepared and accepted without further incident, and the first three companies were mustered out on August 26, 1864.[627]

Company officers who also had responsibility for unit equipment had an additional hurdle to overcome. Everything had to be counted, listed, and turned over the local quartermaster. It was during this part of the process that they realized most fully how different the sense of urgency was on the front lines. They recalled how a man constantly busy and burdened as was General Thomas was always prepared to do what needed to be done, while a rear echelon quartermaster in comfortable Chattanooga seemed to make it a point to never be available when needed. A frustrated officer from Company C believed that when the quartermasters "saw persons who wanted to get work off their hands, they quietly put them off, to show that they were men who could do somewhat as they pleased. When men have literally nothing to do, it is remarkable how long it takes them to do it!" It was all a tremendous hassle, but eventually everything did get done. Companies D, E, F, and H were mustered out on September 8, and the last to leave service were Companies G, I, and K, all mustered out on September 23. The men of company K got a break. Though they had not formally enlisted until November 1, 1861, it was felt there was no reason to hold one company after the rest of the regiment had mustered out, so they got out five weeks early. On September 27, 1864, all the required paperwork was completed. The regimental staff was formally mustered out, the field officers resigned their commissions, and the Thirty-fifth Ohio Volunteer Infantry went out of existence.[628]

What Are You Going To Do About It?

While the other companies were preparing to be mustered out, Companies A, B, and C were heading home. They found the journey a troublesome one. As they were leaving Chattanooga, Confederate cavalry under Nathan Bedford Forrest was at work cutting the railroad near Wartrace, Tennessee. Rather than taking the direct route to Nashville, the train was rerouted through Decatur, Alabama, and Franklin, Tennessee. At Nashville, the military bureaucracy once again went to work to hinder the homeward journey. The "military authorities" in Nashville that had to review the three companies' documents and issue new transportation orders to Louisville were in no hurry to do that. After waiting an

---

627. Keil, *Thirty-fifth Ohio*, 206.
628. Ibid.; Ohio Roster Commission, *Official Roster*, 612, 615, 618, 621, 624, 627, 630.

LIEUT. COL. CHAS. L.H. LONG.

LIEUT. COL. H.V. BOYNTON.

GEN. (COL.) FERDINAND VAN DERVEER.

MAJOR JOS. L. BUDD.

IN COMMAND OF THE

CAPT. SAM L. L'HOMMEDIEU

REGIMENT AT DIFFERENT TIMES DURING THE SERVICE.

The men who commanded the Thirty-fifth Ohio at various times in its history.
KEIL

"unusually long time," the company officers, having gained some experience in similar matters at Chattanooga with Lieutenant Sanderson, ganged up on the local transportation officer and threatened to telegraph General Thomas if they did not receive orders immediately.[629]

At Louisville, the transportation office was much more cooperative and got orders for A, B, and C ready quickly. The trouble in that city started when the officers in Company C requested transportation for their servant Henry. Henry was an escaped slave who had been with the officers of Company C for many months. Like many other Union officers, they intended to take Henry back to Ohio to use as a household servant. The request was "stoutly declined" by the local provost and "a war of words" ensued. Captain Van Derveer and Lieutenant Keil declared that they had "started with our servant to take him home with us, and that we would do so at all hazard." But, when the provost told them they would be arrested if they tried to take Henry into Indiana, Van Derveer and Keil backed up and left quietly. If the provost thought he had won the battle, he was sadly mistaken.[630]

Both Van Derveer and Keil had been with the Thirty-fifth since the summer of 1861. Between them, they had made every campaign that the regiment had participated in, and along the way, they had learned the value of tactical flexibility. Realizing that they would never get official approval for Henry's transportation to Indiana, they quit asking for it. Upon leaving the district headquarters, the two lieutenants took Henry down to the wharf, and pointed out the railroad depot across the Ohio River at Jeffersonville, Indiana. They left Henry there with directions to "stroll along the river, select a canoe, and when dark wrench it from its moorings, and paddle across" to the Jeffersonville Depot before the train left at 9:00 p.m. When the train pulled out of the Indiana river town, Henry was comfortably stowed on board.[631]

Once Henry was across the Ohio River "in the free north, where pompous Kentucky provost marshals, and Kentucky laws had no authority," the officers of Company C felt compelled to get in one last shot at the provost marshal in Louisville. Sitting safely and anonymously in the Dennison House in Cincinnati, they fired off a very brief note to the provost that said, "DEAR SIR:—We are here with our colored servant. What are you going to do about it?" If the Louisville provost marshal scratched his head trying to figure out who the letter was from, the signature provided no help. To this cryptic message, the mysterious name of Kai Gar was affixed. For his part, Henry lived several years in the north with his wartime benefactors. Eventually, the desire to return to his former home in the south overcame him, and the men of the Thirty-fifth Ohio never heard from him again.[632]

629. Keil, *Thirty-fifth Ohio*, 207.
630. Ibid., 207, Wiley, *Billy Yank*, 110.
631. Keil, *Thirty-fifth Ohio*, 207.
632. Ibid.

The emancipation of slaves was not the end to the issue of race relations. It was one step in a centuries-long process that continues today, but it was a huge stride forward. It represented a social and economic change so radical and so extensive that those who lived through it were unable to comprehend its vast scope. As individuals, they were unable to change their view of the world as rapidly as the implications of what had been done were appearing. Most of what was left to do would have to be done in the future. That is an unsatisfying idea for citizens of the early Twenty-first century, still trying to sort out the complexities of race relations, because it places the burden squarely on them, but it has always been that way. Because of the time and effort involved in changing the attitudes of an entire society, no social issue is ever solved by the generation that identifies it. That generation can only begin the forward progress required for the next generation to carry on. The difficulties of human relations, racial and otherwise, will never be completely solved.

Henry's story is indicative of the attitude the men of the Thirty-fifth Ohio had toward the black men and women they came into contact with. They assisted him in gaining his freedom. As Henry ventured forth into a new existence, he was given personal protection and a means by which he could support himself while he adjusted to being free. He was also taken into the North where, if life was not easy for an African American, it had more possibilities than in the South. The work given to Henry to perform was menial. He was no longer a slave, but he was still a servant with few realistic choices. While gainful, his employment by the officers of the Thirty-fifth Ohio continued his subservient status in life.

The incident in Louisville when John Van Derveer and Frederick Keil fought the authorities to allow Henry to cross the Ohio River is also a mixed story. Van Derveer and Keil fought to make sure Henry got to come north with them, but Keil's account of the incident indicates the fight was not entirely about Henry. It was as much a personal struggle with the provost marshal as it was support of Henry's rights. As he told the story, Keil referred to Henry as "our servant" and "our colored man," but not once did he use Henry's name in describing the event. The note to the provost marshal sent from Cincinnati was done purely out of spite, and there can be little doubt that Henry's presence in Ohio was part of that spite. When the provost threatened to physically prevent Van Derveer and Keil from going home, they immediately backed off. Had their continued journey been forcefully tied to Henry's remaining in Kentucky, Henry might well have been left behind. But, Henry wasn't left behind. He did go to Ohio and work for several years where he no doubt was able to save some money and learn some useful skills. It is likely that the primary motive behind Henry's eventual return to the South was his personal desire to strike out on his own and see what was possible.[633]

The attitude of the men of the Thirty-fifth Ohio toward the African Ameri-

---

633. Keil, *Thirty-fifth Ohio*, 207.

cans they came into contact with can best be described as ambivalent. They believed that slavery was wrong, but they did not believe black men were the equals of white men. Pvt. Benjamin Arnold of Company C wrote, "The soldiers from the northern states were prejudiced, or at least had preconceived ideas of slavery. The thought of anyone laboring for another without recompense, or even reward, was repugnant to us at first. Oh, how we did pity those poor slaves that came into camp for protection. But this, like many other virtues that we had carried with us from our homes, not being found congenial with the surroundings of camp life, became obsolete." So, the Persimmons gave them jobs cooking, carrying wood, bringing water, and washing clothes and enjoyed the fact that someone else was doing their work for them. When they hired these former slaves, they were "fully determined to recompense him for his toil at pay day with the shekels of commerce instead of the shackles of bondage, but somehow as pay day was a long way off, and never did come less than two months apart, our zeal cooled off also, and like the Israelites of old, the 'shekels became enlarged and the measure small.' Wasn't he getting sufficient pay? Wasn't he getting the same food that we ate, who were fighting his battles? Wasn't he getting our old clothes? And, above all, wasn't he getting his freedom—the greatest boon a bondsman could crave?"[634]

Arnold's use of the Israelites as an illustration of Union soldiers' behavior is an appropriate analogy. Israel had vowed to obey the Lord and then turned their back on Him. For many generations, Israel paid the price of rebellion, but eventually, final redemption was made possible. The final redemption of America was a long way off, but it had finally come within sight. Forty-five years after the war, after over four decades of reflection on the Persimmons treatment of their servants, Arnold was able to see things as they truly had been. "[W]e became hardened to the pricking of conscience, the chafing became less and less, and soon we were entirely free from preconceived ideas. In fact, we were seasoning our broth with the identical salt that the slave-holder wavered his with." Just as it had been with Israel, the awareness of sin was growing, but it would take generations for the truth to reach the open air and become generally accepted.[635]

The ambiguity of it all is still frustrating and leaves some lingering doubt. What could they have done about it? Could they have done more? The simple truth of the matter is that they could not. No generation, including those of the twenty-first century, can escape the confines of the society in which they live. In the attitudes they displayed, the men of the Thirty-fifth Ohio were very much a product of their time. To try and judge their actions based on a twenty-first century American society is misleading and unfair. In the end, nothing can change the fact that the men of the Thirty-fifth Ohio Volunteer Infantry willingly, knowingly, and eagerly participated in the complete destruction of slav-

634. Arnold, *Sunshine and Shadows*, 14.
635. Ibid.

ery in the United States. In so doing, they opened the door for even more meaningful changes yet to come.

Perhaps the most important thing that the Persimmons did when they returned home was simply to get on with their lives. They went back to their homes and became productive, useful citizens. Ferdinand Van Derveer returned to his law practice. George T. Earhart of Company G returned to his job with the railroad. Joseph W. Myers went back to carpentry. All of them expected to receive the respect of the community for their service, but they neither expected nor waited for any special treatment. They returned to their families, careers, and farms and "were at once almost imperceptibly absorbed in the ranks of the citizens." Just as quietly, they passed on their stories and their thoughts to their children and grandchildren who cast their own shadows upon the world.[636]

After three years of war, not all of the Persimmons found the transition from soldier to civilian to their liking. William Hopkins of Union Township in Warren County, was only twenty-one when he mustered out. The young man missed the excitement of war, and having an unattached man's freedom of movement, enlisted in the Eighth Ohio Infantry in early 1865. Almost exactly a year later, after having fallen seriously ill, he died in a military hospital outside Washington, D.C. Arthur Barklow, a private in Company K and a year younger than Hopkins, also enlisted again and ended up in the Army of the Potomac. Barklow's tenure in the eastern army was more notable than Hopkins's. He was a member of the security detachment at the execution of Mary Surratt, David Herold, and Lewis Payne. Barklow received his honorable discharge exactly one week before Hopkins died.[637]

---

636. *Williams Hamilton Directory,* 1861 and 1875 (Cincinnati: Williams Directory Co., n.d.) at Butler County Historical Society.

637. Bogan, *Warren County's Involvement,* 24, 45.

CHAPTER 14

In Quiet Possession

After the War

Mustered Out with Company

In Ohio's *Official Roster of the Soldiers of the State of Ohio in the War of the Rebellion, 1861–1866*, volume 3 there are 150 men in the Thirty-fifth Ohio for which the only comment on their service is the statement, "Mustered out with company." They didn't get shot, killed, captured, promoted, demoted, detailed, transferred, sent to the hospital, or discharged early. For three years, they did nothing out of the ordinary. Provided, of course, that a list of ordinary things includes marching fifteen hundred miles over mountains, through swamps, and across rivers, or living in flimsy canvas tents and make shift shanties in the worst possible weather, going without food for days at a time, eating food of questionable quality for many others, wearing the same clothes for weeks on end without changing them, living without money for months, digging miles upon miles of ditches, constructing log roads in swamps, fighting several battles and dozens of skirmishes, and spending long weeks in close proximity to people who were trying to kill them. Along the way, they also helped restore the Union and destroy the institution of slavery.

These men who seemingly did nothing were the kind of men that first sergeants love. Men like Henry Virdoon of Company D who were always present at roll call and available for duty. Men like Pvt. Calvin Schmuts of Company G who never went on sick call and never went AWOL. Men like Musician Frank Ledman of Company K who had plenty of opportunity to run away but didn't. Men like Sgt. Sam Spurgeon of Company A who toughed it out on long marches and stayed awake on picket duty. They grumbled, complained, and dodged hard duty whenever they could, but they believed they were doing the right thing by being in the regiment. Because of that, they were always around when needed, and they always came to scratch when the enemy stood before them. These are the men who most distinctly define the Thirty-fifth Ohio Volunteer Infantry.

In three years of service, the Thirty-fifth Ohio built a reputation for dependability and competence with the people that mattered, it's brigade and division commanders, the other regiments in its brigade, and the people back home, but it was never a darling of the press or of the army. The men themselves were common, work-a-day citizens from a prosperous but very matter-of-fact midwestern state. They did not have a particular ethnic or demographic character that caused them to stand out in a crowd, so they remained in the shadows. There is little doubt that they would have performed as well as the Second Minnesota at Mill Springs. Man for man, they were just as good as their comrades from the Land of 10,000 Lakes. The difference was that the Second Minnesota was on the firing line, while the Persimmons were waiting for the creek to drop. At Chickamauga, they stood up to the pounding and behaved as well as any professional soldiers could, but so did a lot of other regiments. The regimental commanders were capable men, even ambitious men, but none of them made an effort to promote themselves during the war. Ferdinand Van Derveer and Joseph Budd just weren't that kind of men, and Henry Boynton had yet to put his extensive political skills to use.

Nevertheless, they were the kind of regiment a commander loves. Commanders did not necessarily like the flashy units under them, because they tended to be made up of high-strung individuals. Commanders much preferred the quietly reliable regiments that accepted whatever task was assigned to them and did it right; the kind of regiment that could be sent to guard a railroad or a river ford alone without undue concern over their ability to take care of themselves. The kind that could be expected to conduct adequate drills, prepare effective fortifications, and hold their place in the line come what may. The kind that caused no unusual discipline problems, took care of a lot of their own logistical needs, and always arrived at the places they were sent. The Thirty-fifth Ohio was just that kind of regiment. It "never asked for favors, nor sought easy places away from danger; but the regiment stood ready at all times to do whatever duty was assigned." The Thirty-fifth Ohio was a very low-maintenance organization, and that was the one quality its commanders loved more than any other.[638]

The men of the regiment would have no difficulty with that characterization. They believed themselves to be "quiet, sober, substantial citizens; men who entered the service from a sense of duty, and hence could be depended upon, under all circumstances, to do their duty." They would have understood that the biggest reason for their anonymity was their solid dependability. Because they always did what was expected of them, senior commanders spent little time thinking about them and their competence became a matter of routine. It didn't take away from anything they had accomplished, but it obscured the nation's view. Indomitable in war, they became nearly invisible to history.[639]

---

638. Boynton, *Dedication*, 357.
639. Keil, *Thirty-fifth Ohio*, 215.

One of the quietly reliable men who made the Thirty-fifth Ohio what it was. Postwar photograph of Sgt. Jacob Caughell, Company E.
MARCELLA CAUGHELL COLLECTION AT USMHI

Unmistakable Fraternity

Being invisible to historians did not mean that the veterans of the Thirty-fifth Ohio forgot who they were. When it became known that an Indiana regiment also claimed to be the Persimmon Regiment, the men of the Thirty-fifth took umbrage. They did not know the "nature of the facts on which the claim is made," and they didn't really care. The Hoosiers could make all the claims they wanted. The fact remained that "the Thirty-fifth Ohio has a copyright to that name, which antedates all other claimants; and notice is hereby given, that no one will be allowed to infringe on so well earned a title." The price for the right to use the title Persimmon Regiment had been paid on December 8, 1861, with "the death of one comrade, several wounded, and some eighteen prisoners." The boys from Indiana were challenged to produce an earlier claim, and if they could not, the Thirty-fifth Ohio demanded that they be "permitted to wear the honor, and be left in quiet possession of [their] well earned title."[640]

The Persimmons remained close to the veterans of the Ninth Ohio long after the war. Even as a new century dawned, the men of the two regiments remained united by friendship and respect. When the Ninth dedicated a monument to its first commander, Robert L. McCook, they honored Ferdinand Van Derveer, the man who had turned their wrath after the beloved McCook's death by inviting him to the ceremony. On the thirty-third anniversary of Chickamauga, the Ninth Ohio held a special celebration and invited the Persimmons to join them at Turner Hall in Cincinnati. Prominent among the group was Henry Boynton. The Germans had named Boynton an honorary member of the Ninth Ohio, one of only two men to ever be so honored.[641]

The quiet, sober nature that characterized the Thirty-fifth Ohio was also apparent at the annual reunions. While they enjoyed each other's company, the regiment's veterans were always well behaved. Captain Keil later wrote that no member of the regiment ever had any reason to be ashamed of anything that happened when the boys got together. The wholesome nature of the Persimmon's reunions was so obvious that the Cincinnati *Gazette* once recorded, "One feature is worthy of mention, and that is, the strict temperance principle upon which the banquets are conducted. We refer to the absence of liquor. It is certain no one left the banquet unsatisfied, and it is to be said to the credit of the regiment, only one drunken man was present, and it is said, that has been his normal condition for years. There was observed among the boys, an unmistakable fraternity of feeling, a heartiness of greeting, which was infective, and made outsiders feel the better for its influence. No doubt many a looker-on wished he had belonged to the Thirty-fifth, or some other organization with a history to tell and be proud of."[642]

---

640. Keil, *Thirty-fifth Ohio*, 29.
641. Grebner, *We Were the Ninth*, 190, 196.

When the Persimmons gathered, the years faded away, and they became young soldiers again. They were "still boys in spirit, if not in body, but in spirit only, for sadly we realize that the only boys are those who fell out of line during the conflict, and sleep in soldier's graves." Just as time became meaningless, station in life meant little as well. "On these reunion days, we meet as John, George, and Tom," one veteran of the Thirty-fifth said. "We recognize each other notwithstanding the fearful changes that time has made." They compared their memories to the amazing new technology that was emerging around them. Seeing familiar faces was like looking at a photograph of today and seeing through it a picture of yesterday, "for we see through the film of age the same dear, old faces." The bond between them could never be broken, because "when our hands strike palm to palm, a connection is made on the switchboard and the circuit is complete." The recollection of that grand time of their youth was a treasure in a safety deposit box that required two keys to open. When two of them came together and both keys were turned, the "wealth of years was revealed" as the treasure box was opened.[643]

The strength of their relationships did not diminish with time. Long after the war, Benjamin Arnold wrote about his friend John Reel of Dayton. Whenever the two men met, Arnold did not see the retired carpenter he knew now, but "the same John who raised my head so tenderly and gave me a drink of cool water when I was burning with fever. Because I knew at the time that a long, toilsome journey under the sweltering sun had been made to obtain it made it a hundred fold more precious. Like the water brought to David from the well at Bethlehem, it was fit for an oblation. That water, like Elijah's food, not only strengthened me for forty days, but even now, after more than forty years, I feel it's refreshing." The encouragement and strength they had imparted to each other as young soldiers in a noble cause was still just as powerful decades later.[644]

The Persimmons were proud of what they had done and accomplished. As far as they were concerned, the Thirty-fifth Ohio had never done anything that required a defense, and they were convinced that history would so record it. When that history was eventually written, they were certain that not "one of those who served in the regiment . . . will want a single line erased. The regiment has no act registered, that it wants changed, which it enacted while in the face of the enemy; the only regret it has to make is that it could do no greater harm to the foe than it did." Thirty years after the war, they still had no regrets. "[The Thirty-fifth Ohio] has the satisfaction to know that it did its duty, that it stood its ground under all circumstances; not one word of reproach can be uttered against any one. With such a record the organization can be well satisfied."[645]

---

642. Keil, *Thirty-fifth Ohio*, 215.
643. Arnold, *Sunshine and Shadows*, 47.
644. Ibid., 47–48.

So they gathered and celebrated their service on the "third Thursday in September, each year" as a matter of personal and group pride, but there was much more to it than that. Benjamin Arnold had given a lot of thought to what it all really meant. "Have you considered," he wrote, "the fact that Americans are a nation of forgetters? We are neglectful as a whole people in teaching lessons in patriotism. Are we blind to the fact that we are strangling, crushing—yes, even burying inherent love of country when we withhold from our children the rich memories of the past, even in our own individual lives? If this be true, then how much more when we fail to keep before them that which is not solely the heritage of one family, but the common legacy of a whole nation."[646]

In an effort to hold on to that common legacy, the Persimmons remained active in veteran's affairs long after the war. They formed the Thirty-fifth O.V.I. Association in Butler County, but the United States was a nation on the move after the Civil War, and the Persimmons scattered as the years went on. But wherever they went, they joined the local chapter of the Grand Army of the Republic, and their names appear in GAR membership lists for places as far away as Oklahoma, Texas, California, and Illinois. Joseph W. Myers, former first sergeant of Company D, was a very active member of Hamilton's Wetzel-Compton Post no. 96 of the GAR, a group that left a definite mark on its community. Up until the 1920s, its members turned out in force for every Memorial Day parade, every Fourth of July parade, and every patriotic event scheduled. They made a gift of a large plot at Greenwood Cemetery to be used as a resting spot for local war veterans. Known as the "Field of Honor," it is still the site of public observances on Memorial Day, Independence Day, and Veterans Day. They were also the driving force behind the construction of the Hamilton Soldiers and Sailors Monument in the 1890s. Etched in the walls of the monument are the names of every veteran of the Thirty-fifth Ohio Volunteer Infantry. On the outbreak of war with Spain in 1898, the veterans of Post no. 96 put on their old uniforms and escorted Hamilton's Company E, First Ohio Volunteers to the train depot. Not until August 1936 did Post no. 96 finally go inactive when one of its last two surviving members died.[647]

Written Among the Defenders

It was the idea of a national legacy that drove Henry Boynton. After mustering out of the Thirty-fifth Ohio, Boynton became a war correspondent for the Cin-

645. Keil, *Thirty-fifth Ohio*, 216.

646. Arnold, *Sunshine and Shadows*, introduction; 35th OVI Collection, Butler County Historical Society.

647. Grand Army of the Republic Collection, Butler County Historical Society, Hamilton, Ohio.

cinnati *Commercial Gazette*. It was a short-lived assignment, but after the fighting ended, Boynton remained with the newspaper, moving to Washington, D.C. In 1867, Boynton was rewarded for his performance at Chickamauga and Missionary Ridge with a brevet promotion to brigadier general. While serving as the Washington correspondent of the *Gazette* after the war, Boynton earned a reputation as a principled man who wrote cleanly and incisively. His colleagues in the Press Corps admired him for his knowledge and extensive contacts. If it was learned that Boynton had not heard a particular rumor, it was immediately discounted, and his advice to younger reporters was greatly appreciated. [648]

Boynton became famous for "numerous contests" in which he "crossed swords with distinguished men of national reputation" in his articles. His opponents included claims agents, lobbyists, senators, and the Speaker of the House of Representatives. Among his more notable literary opponents were Generals William T. Sherman and Oliver O. Howard, Senator James Harlan, Congressman J. Warren Keifer, and fellow reporter Murat Halstead. It was said that Boynton "seldom came out these contests second best," and in addition to his "biting pen," he was known for having a very good memory. The desire to do things right never left him, so in spite of having a reputation for being one of the most combative reporters Washington had ever seen, Boynton's most lasting role was that of peacemaker. Boynton was instrumental in creating the standing committee of correspondents to regulate the Washington press galleries and in setting up the Gridiron Club in 1890. Boynton was a Republican who made no attempt to cover his partisanship. He was one of the power brokers in James A. Garfield's contested presidential election of 1880, and in 1892, he was the Republican vice presidential candidate, running unsuccessfully with Benjamin Harrison. [649]

Boynton became a member of the Society of the Army of the Cumberland and was very active in its reunions. As early as 1881, the members of the society had discussed the preservation of the Chickamauga battlefield, but nothing had been done. In 1888, Henry Boynton and Ferdinand Van Derveer, then an officer in the society, returned to the scene of their greatest glory. As they rode across the battlefield on a Sunday as it had been in 1863, they could hear a solemn hymn being sung in a nearby church. They contrasted that sound with the noise of battle, and suddenly the events and faces of twenty-five years before flashed back. Boynton located the tree that had been shattered by artillery fire as he stood beside it, but as the pair toured the field, they became concerned by significant changes in its appearance. Time and use of the land was causing the features so meaningful to the veterans of both armies to be lost. The two men decided that it was time to do something. With Van Derveer's support, Boynton

---

648. Donald A. Ritchie, *Press Gallery* (Cambridge: Harvard University Press, 1991), 115.

649. Cone, *Biographical*, 346; *Memorial Record,* 410; Keil, *Thirty-fifth Ohio,* 238–39; Ritchie, *Press Gallery,* 115.

Postwar photograph of Henry V. Boynton
CIVIL WAR LIBRARY AND MUSEUM, MOLLUS, PHILADELPHIA, PENNSYLVANIA AT USAMHI

began writing open letters to veterans that were published in the Cincinnati *Commercial Gazette*. Boynton wrote about the history of the battle, described the deteriorating condition of the field as he and Van Derveer had seen it, and encouraged veterans to support action to preserve the historic character of the battlefield.[650]

Boynton, always a fiery writer, infused his letters with patriotic language directed at the men who had been there. "The survivors of the Army of the Cumberland should awake to the great pride in this notable field of Chickamauga. Why should it not, as well as eastern fields, be marked by monuments, and its lines be accurately preserved by history? There was no more magnificent fighting during the war than both armies did there. Both sides might well unite in preserving the field where both, in a military sense, won such renown." Boynton proposed a plan to protect the battlefield features that still remained, restore others to their 1863 appearance, and place markers and monuments across the area.[651]

The government had begun actions to preserve the Gettysburg battlefield in 1880, but the Chickamauga effort was the first to involve veterans from both the Union and Confederate armies. It began in September 1888 when the Society of the Army of the Cumberland established a committee to investigate the purchase of the land on which the battle had been fought. The following year, on September 20, 1889, thousands of Union and Confederate veterans met at Crawfish Springs to establish the Chickamauga Memorial Association. A committee of fifty veterans and civilians was appointed and went quickly to work. Less than a year later, Congress passed the first ever legislation for the preservation of an American battlefield.

"An Act to establish a National Military Park at the battle-field of Chickamauga" of August 1890 was a landmark piece of legislation that set several important precedents for historic preservation. It defined the national significance of the battlefield, recognized its educational value for historians and soldiers, required the preservation of the land's agricultural use, and appointed a three-member commission to lead the work of restoring and marking the battlefield. The president of the commission was Henry Van Ness Boynton. With Boynton at its head, the commission set about purchasing the land the battlefield sat on. It was tedious, tortuous work to negotiate with over two hundred landowners. Some of them, having made improvements to the land, wanted higher than expected prices for their property, and lengthy condemnation proceedings were required to obtain many plots. Even so, at the end of the first year of operations, the commission had purchased more than four thousand acres of land and identified an additional one thousand acres of land and forty miles of road still needed to meet the requirements established by the legislation.

---

650. Boynton, *Military Park,* 224.
651. Ibid., 219.

The veterans of Chickamauga wanted a place where people could get the feel of what it had been like to be there while they paid respects to the soldiers of both sides who had fought and shed blood. They wanted a place where people could walk the same roads and fields the soldiers had walked, a place where people could feel awe and reverence for what had occurred on the spot where they stood. Veterans of the battle from all over the country were brought in to help reconstruct the battle and accurately locate troop positions. It proved to be a frustrating task. The land itself had changed. Fields once visible were overgrown or hidden by trees and brush and farmers had changed the landscape. The men who had fought at Chickamauga often disagreed on the location of events and landmarks, and men who had been only a few yards apart in battle might locate the same event hundreds of yards distant from each other. Most of them came to a general agreement on things, but some went to their graves convinced it was all wrong.

The work went on in spite of occasional disagreements. Roads, buildings, and fences that had been present on the day of battle were restored. Buildings and fences built after the battle were removed. Overgrown fields were cleared and brush removed from under trees to provide a better view. Markers were placed at troop positions and various states put up tablets that provided visitors with the ability to look around and understand what had happened when the two armies collided. Henry Boynton was right in the thick if it all. As determined as ever to do the right thing and create the park envisioned by his comrades in arms, he met with veterans and walked the fields with them. He worked with the states and hundreds of veteran's organizations to place memorials. Working with the other commissioners, Boynton resolved disputes over locations and particular events. In the process, most parties involved developed a deep respect for the man and his abilities. Others learned to hate him.

Ohio was the first state to create its own park commission, but many others soon followed suit. The first markers were placed in 1890 for headquarters, corps, division, and brigade locations. Condemned cannonballs were used to build pyramid monuments to general officers killed in the battle, and four hundred obsolete cannon were used to mark artillery positions. The park was dedicated in September 1895, on the thirty-second anniversary of the battle. Congress made the event a national dedication. "*Be it enacted by the Senate and House of Representatives of the United States of America in Congress assembled*, That a national dedication of the Chickamauga and Chattanooga National Military Park shall take place on the battle fields" Vice President Adlai Stevenson presided over the ceremonies, joined by more than forty thousand veterans, dignitaries, and visitors. For Henry Boynton, it was a most satisfying day.[652]

The dedication ceremony for the Thirty-fifth Ohio's battlefield monument on Snodgrass Hill opened with a prayer by Reverend J. J. Manker. Henry Boyn-

---

652. Boynton, *Dedication*, 269.

ton made a brief speech about the regiment's record, but his comments were merely to prepare the way for others. Former Ohio governor James E. Campbell described the Persimmons as the "flower of the young men from the garden spot of the earth; and it is no wonder that, with such material, and commanded by that great old warrior, Ferdinand Van Derveer, and that modern Chevalier Bayard, Henry V. Boynton, it should have exhibited on every field the prowess, fortitude, and intelligence which characterize the highest type of Anglo-Saxon soldier." Captain Phillip Rothenbush of Company I explained how the design of the regiment's monument was arrived at, and then Judge J. W. O'Neall, Company A, and comrade Andrew J. Stakebuke, Company E, gave "stirring extemporaneous addresses." It was left to Frederick Keil of Company C, who had just published a history of the regiment, to give a detailed description of the regiment's actions at Chickamauga.

Keil closed his oration with these thoughts. "When the storm broke upon us, it may be said, it was our fortune to be on the stage of action, and we responded to the call of the nation to take part in the contest. We did not court the place, but we responded and served to the best of our abilities. No one who served then regrets now that his name is written among the defenders of the old flag; nor would he exchange his place for that of the man who was able to take the musket and do duty and did not. It will ever stand to the credit of the men that they could and did serve the cause of the nation and of mankind in the most trying capacity known to citizenship.

"While we feel proud of this monument erected to our organization, may we not recall how many comrades died here on this field and baptized the soil with their blood; and likewise those who literally suffered a living death in Confederate prisons, as well as those who pined long months in hospitals on account of heavy wounds. When we have carefully considered all this, then we can estimate somewhat the cost of these memorials."[653]

Recollections of Survivors

One of the unhappy events associated with the establishment of the battlefield park was the controversy surrounding the capture of the Twenty-first Ohio Volunteer Infantry on Horseshoe Ridge at the close of the battle of Chickamauga. When Van Derveer's brigade arrived on Horseshoe Ridge about two thirty on September 20, the Twenty-first Ohio had already been there for as long as two hours. Sent to beef up Brannan's right flank, they had fought off several enemy attacks using their rapid firing Colt revolving rifles and had clung tenaciously to their position on the hill. On September 20, the Twenty-first Ohio fought as hard and as well as any regiment on the field. In fact, a strong argument can be

---

653. Boynton, *Dedication*, 359–60.

The Thirty-fifth Ohio monument at Chickamauga shortly after it was dedicated in 1895.
CHICKAMAUGA RECORD OF THE OHIO COMMISSION

made that they fought better than most. It was unfortunate that the very unique-ness that made their rifles so effective also led directly to the tragedy that befell them. The ammunition required for the revolving rifles was different than that used by the standard infantry rifles of the army. When the Twenty-first fired off all the ammunition it had, it was unable to obtain more.

In a very precarious position as the afternoon wore on, the Twenty-first was holding the hill with nothing more than bayonets as Van Derveer's brigade arrived. Maj. Arnold McMahan, then commanding the Twenty-first, was relieved to see friendly units move onto the ridge behind him and requested that the Second Minnesota relieve the Twenty-first so it could try and replenish its ammunition. The division trains could not be located, so the dead and wounded were searched. Greatly reduced in numbers after heavy fighting, enough ammu-nition was found to give every man one more round. Though they were still essentially out of ammunition, the Twenty-first was ordered to take a position on the right of the Third Brigade's line, covering the flank held by the Thirty-fifth Ohio. The Twenty-first occupied its assigned position, driving out the reb-els who were already there and capturing several of them. The rebels returned, driving the Twenty-first back, but the determined soldiers from northwestern Ohio pushed back. They regained the position they had lost, but in doing so, used all of their remaining ammunition. Once again, they faced the enemy with nothing but cold steel.[654]

About 7:00 p.m., Trigg's Confederate brigade came back up the hill in an attempt to turn the Union flank and roll up the defenders on the hill. In the gath-ering gloom and swirling fog, the men of the Twenty-first were uncertain as to who was approaching their position. Capt. Henry Alban decided to find out. Stepping out in front of his lines, he asked the approaching men who they were. One of them stuck a pistol to his head and told him to be quiet. When Alban did not return, his first sergeant followed him out in front and he too disappeared. Finally, someone in the line called down the hill asking who the advancing troops were. One of them replied that they were "Jeff Davis' troops." Assuming they were from the Union Twentieth Corps, the men of the Twenty-first Ohio relaxed. A few seconds later, Trigg's rebels shoved rifles into their faces, and the color sergeant of the Twenty-first grudgingly handed over the regimental colors.[655]

Captured by deception after such a gallant stand, the Twenty-first Ohio prepared to go into captivity. It was while the Confederates were deciding how to handle their prisoners that Trigg sent his orderly to find out who was still on the hill firing, and the young man was cut down by the Thirty-fifth Ohio's final volley of the battle. Some of the rounds fired landed among Trigg's soldiers and

---

654. U.S. War Department, *War of the Rebellion*, Ser. no. 50, p. 389; Judson W. Bishop, "Van Der Veer's Brigade," *National Tribune*, 16 June 1906.

655. McMahan Prison Memo Book, William J. Sullivan Collection, MS 562, Center for Archival Collections, Bowling Green State University, Bowling Green, Ohio.

the captives from the Twenty-first Ohio. As everyone pushed and shoved to find cover, about half of the men in the Twenty-first were able to break for freedom and made it into the lines of the Thirty-fifth Ohio. Major McMahan was not one of them and went off with the remainder of his men into captivity. While in Libby Prison suffering from poor treatment and an even poorer diet, McMahan had plenty of time to think, and more than enough time to become truly angry over what had happened to his regiment. Convinced that there was no blame to be placed on the Twenty-first Ohio, he came to believe that he and his men had been disgracefully abandoned and set about trying to find out which of his superiors was at fault.[656]

After being paroled, McMahan was determined to find out who had left his regiment on its own with no ammunition. In this effort, he experienced three insurmountable problems. The first problem was simply one of time. Six months had passed. The war and the Army of the Cumberland had moved on while McMahan was in a rebel prison. The senior officers with whom he wanted to confer were all preparing for the coming campaign to capture Atlanta. The officers of Twenty-first Ohio were either still in prison or with the remnant of the regiment in the field. Not only were they all busy with current events, they were all quite distant, as McMahan was preparing his report from Perrysburg, Ohio, while awaiting exchange.

McMahan's second problem was that his version of events did not square with the remembrances of the officers he contacted. By then, they had all prepared and submitted their formal battle reports, and as far as they were concerned, those reports accurately represented what had happened on September 19 and 20. This conflict in memory led to the third and perhaps decisive problem, McMahan's approach in his inquiries. McMahan had already made up his mind as to the events of the battle and wanted information to justify it, and in the process, vindicate himself. Rather than request information to use in preparing his reports, or even requesting copies of reports to use in preparing his own, McMahan wrote accusatory letters that antagonized the men from whom he was requesting information, squandering whatever natural sympathy they may have had for his situation.

From his old division commander, Maj. Gen. James Negley, McMahan requested "a letter from you, showing why I received no orders from you before night, or in time to prevent so severe a loss of my command." Negley was having problems of his own. He had been fiercely criticized by other Union generals after the battle and was at that moment struggling to avoid his own personal disgrace. Negley merely passed McMahan on to Major General John Brannan, saying he had sent the Twenty-first to support Brannan at that officer's request. By shifting the onus to Brannan, Negley took some of the pressure off himself.[657]

---

656. U.S. War Department, *War of the Rebellion*, Ser. no. 50, p. 394; McMahan Prison Memo Book, Sullivan Collection.

From Brannan, McMahan demanded to know "why I was not informed of the withdrawal of the troops on Horseshoe Ridge at dark, and why I received no orders from you in regard to the retreat of my own command." McMahan went on to describe how the units on his flanks had been "stealthily withdrawn" and explained that by being where they were, the Twenty-first Ohio had made the retreat of the Union army "an easy matter after dark." Even worse, McMahan stated that his report was already written but he would be glad to attach any reply Brannan made. The major would magnanimously allow the general to defend himself if he chose to, but the major's mind was already made up.[658]

Brannan gave no ground. He correctly informed McMahan that at the time the Twenty-first had surrendered, the retreat had not yet begun and Federal units still had a solid grip on the ridge. The general then got in his own shot by informing McMahan that rather than covering the army's retreat, McMahan had surrendered his regiment so quietly that no one knew except the regiment to his left. Brannan had had to shift one of his own regiments to fill the gap created by the capture of the Twenty-first Ohio and covered the retreat with his own men. Finally, using the same tactic Negley had, Brannan let McMahan know that the troops on the right that had withdrawn without warning belonged to General Granger's Reserve Corps and not the Third Division. Brannan's claim that the Twenty-first Ohio surrendered meekly cast an unfair aspersion on the men of that regiment who had fought so doggedly at Snodgrass Hill, but it was McMahan who had made it a personal issue. Brannan simply responded in kind.[659]

McMahan returned to his regiment after being formally exchanged and submitted his Chickamauga report in July 1864. It was received and filed away since the official report had long since been written and published. There it remained for more than twenty years. McMahan and the Twenty-first Ohio served out the rest of war under honorable terms and went home. McMahan returned to his law practice but the war had broken his health. By the 1880s, he was an invalid unable to travel, but poor health did not lessen his interest in the former members of his command. He spent considerable time corresponding with them, offering advice, and actively assisting them in receiving government pensions. The events of Chickamauga were never forgotten, but they faded into the background of his life.

All of that changed in 1888 when Henry Boynton began publishing his articles on establishing a national park. Convinced Boynton's interpretation of events was not only inaccurate but demeaning to the Twenty-first Ohio, McMahan started to boil once again and fired off a series of angry letters. He resumed his accusation that Boynton, Van Derveer, and Brannan had negligently abandoned the Twenty-first to its fate. Boynton agreed someone was at fault, but

---

657. U.S. War Department, *War of the Rebellion*, Ser. no. 50, pp. 391–92.

658. Ibid., 392; McMahan to Brannan, 24 April 1864, Sullivan Collection.

659. U.S. War Department, *War of the Rebellion*, Ser. no. 50, p. 393; Brannan to McMahan, 3 May 1864, Sullivan Collection.

believed it was General Granger, "as both he and Steedman talking it over after the battle admitted. The talk was not about you, but involved the omission to notify Van Derveer, who was to the right of Brannan at the time of the withdrawal, and that of course caused the failure to give you notice." Boynton provided a detailed explanation of events as best he could reconstruct them and provided a map to back it up. He believed McMahan had confused Van Derveer with Colonel Le Favour, and that it was Le Favour who ordered the Twenty-first back into the line without ammunition. Boynton made a good faith effort to smooth things over, but his response was unacceptable to McMahan who believed "the numerous errors into which General Boynton has fallen" including times, locations, and the regiments involved, proved his ignorance "beyond question."[660]

McMahan sent a similar letter to Ferdinand Van Derveer. Van Derveer had some forewarning after reading an interview with McMahan in the Toledo *Commercial* and was in no mood to be conciliatory. McMahan referred to a letter he had written in 1864 that Van Derveer had not replied to. The letter had never reached Van Derveer, who responded to McMahan with the fervor of a former editorial writer, "Had I received such a letter, on account of its misstatements at least, I should not have forgotten the fact." Van Derveer was particularly upset by McMahan's claim that the Twenty-first Ohio had sacrificed itself in protecting the retreat of his brigade and replied quite bluntly. "But the most wonderful of your services, was, as you say, you covered my retreat with the bayonet. Of course I cannot tell what you were doing with your bayonets, but as I never retreated, you must have been engaged in taking care of some other brigade. You are laboring under an hallucination about all this matter. In the final place, I never gave you any command whatever. I never promised to make a report of the valuable services of your regiment, for at that time, I knew nothing of what you had done. You were not connected on my right. You did not protect my flank. You did not protect a retreat that was never made."[661]

Gen. John Brannan had also been on McMahan's mailing list. McMahan had asked him to reconsider the statements in his now published official report and Brannan's reply was much more succinct but just as blunt as Van Derveer's had been. "After an elapse of 26 years it is hardly probable that my memory should be as good, in details, as it was when the official report was made. I, therefore, don't see that I can make any alteration or addition to [it]. If I could not give it to you in 1864, it is hardly possible to do so in 1890." Even had he tried a more diplomatic and tactful approach, McMahan never really had any chance of making his version of events the official one. His accusatory approach once again worked against him as did another important factor illus-

---

660. Boynton to McMahan, with comments by McMahan, 26 July 1889, Sullivan Collection.

661. McMahan to Van Derveer, 20 June 1889, Sullivan Collection; Van Derveer to McMahan, 5 July 1889, Sullivan Collection.

trated in Brannan's letter.[662]

The fog of war has often been cited as the basis of confusion and contradiction in describing the events of Chickamauga. In McMahan's case, time also cast a dark shadow on events. Just as Boynton had learned in his efforts to establish the national park, McMahan found that people have difficulty reaching full agreement on events long past. When queried by McMahan, John Mahoney, a former officer in the Twenty-first Ohio, thought he understood what had happened at Chickamauga but admitted, "It is so long ago that many of the points you would like to have me speak of are gone out of my memory." William Didway said that "after diligent search and enquiry fear that I cannot give you the desired information." Wilson Vance, another former officer in the Twenty-first told McMahan, "I was so young at the time of the battle of Chickamauga & so much has happened to me since then to crowd out recollections of details that I fear I cannot be of important services in the matter." Added to the far off shadows were changes in the land wrought by time. Isaac Cusec had gone to Chickamauga to walk the battlefield with other veterans. He was able to find the positions held by the Twenty-first Ohio but informed McMahan that "the ridge does not look natural. The woods that at the time of the Battle were quite open, is covered with undergrowth, much of it very thick. The small field south of the Snodgrass house, where a Battery was located on Sabbath morning and fired over us as we were formed in the lane is completely covered with pine so that you would imagine that there ever was a field there." Cusec also reported disagreements among the veterans of other units related to the events and that Cusec himself disagreed with McMahan on some points.[663]

Yet another factor that worked against McMahan's effort to change the official view was the reputation of the individuals he was attacking. Boynton, Van Derveer, and Brannan were all competent soldiers of proven ability. They were also men known for their personal integrity. The general public held an overwhelmingly positive opinion of all three, so on the position of veracity, they were unassailable. No one who knew the three officers in question would accept that they would intentionally hide or refuse to acknowledge the obvious truth. The final, and perhaps most decisive, force against McMahan was the prevailing attitude of reconciliation that had also come with time. The war had been over for twenty-five years. Reconstruction had ended, and the preeminent thought of the day was national unity. Everyone wanted to put sectional hostility behind them and had little patience for individuals who desired to extend the conflict in any way. McMahan was given his chance, but his unwillingness to consider any view but his own caused those involved to turn away.

The fog of war that obscured events as they happened, and the fog of time that added to the obfuscation, made it extremely difficult to come up with one

---

662. Brannan to McMahan, 4 April 1890, Sullivan Collection.

663. Vance to McMahan, 5 July 1889, Sullivan Collection; Cusac to McMahan, 10 May 1890, Sullivan Collection; Mahoney to McMahan, 12 May 1890, Sullivan Collection.

single, definitive explanation of the events at Chickamauga, but the battlefield commission did the best they could. Sanford Kellogg, a member of the park commission and its chief mapmaker, asked McMahan to visit the battlefield with him. "What now appears obscure to you," he wrote, "has all been satisfactorily worked out from the official reports, recollections of survivors and visits to the ground." Kellogg assured McMahan that Boynton and Van Derveer would be there and the commission's maps would be ready for use. It is unfortunate that McMahan's failing health prevented him from making such a trip. Forced to rely on information from others who could visit the field, and in some cases, had agendas of their own, McMahan could never truly reconstruct the events for himself. If he had been able to revisit the actual ground, some agreement might have been reached that would have prevented the continued feelings of ill will between Van Derveer, Boynton, and McMahan. But then again, perhaps no agreement was possible. Van Derveer and Boynton were as strong willed as McMahan, and both had demonstrated a powerful stubbornness when convinced of their position. After nearly thirty years of settled conviction, a change of view may have been impossible for any of them.[664]

The men of the Twenty-first Ohio and Thirty-fifth Ohio were not affected by the dispute among their former officers. Regardless of the version of events accepted, the performance of both regiments at Chickamauga had been superb. Both had been at their best when the situation of the army had been at its worst, and both had contributed materially to the Army of the Cumberland's successful stand near the Snodgrass house. The Twenty-first Ohio had ferociously continued to fight after it had expended all of its ammunition and been forced to surrender only when no other option was available. The Persimmons had been in the same desperate situation, but chance had dealt them more favorable circumstances. Had they gathered in peacetime, there would have been no animosity. The veterans of each regiment would have shook hands and traded stories with each other as friends and comrades in arms. They had stood unflinchingly in the breech and done the best they possibly could at the time. All of them could understand and respect that in each other.

Legion Across the River

War is a life-altering experience. For some men, it changes everything. They completely change directions on the path of life and no longer resemble the men they used to be. For others, it intensifies what they already were or creates focus on certain aspects of their lives. Something they were never able to fully communicate had happened to them, and they never again felt the same about

---

664. Kellogg to McMahan, 21 June 1889, Sullivan Collection; Dolton to McMahan, 17 May 1890, Sullivan Collection.

life as they had before. Even as they returned to the jobs and lives they had before the war, they were not the same men they had been before they enlisted.

John G. Baxter of Company C was certainly a changed man when he returned home from the war. Although a good soldier and a jolly friend, he was known to his company commander as a wild and reckless man. Among his peers he was remembered for his ravenous appetite and consummate skill in stealing food. But the experience of war had caused him to reconsider his path and turn his heart to spiritual matters. He joined the Methodist church and eventually became the Reverend John G. Baxter, D.D., ministering in the Southern Indiana Conference of the Methodist Episcopal Church. One of Baxter's wartime victims, Col. John Harlan of the Tenth Kentucky, went on to become Chief Justice John Harlan of the United States Supreme Court, and it is hard not to wonder if they ever met and laughed over the incident in Mississippi years before. Others also had spiritual awakenings of a sort after the war. Sometimes, like John Baxter, it was a matter of record. For most others, like Benjamin Arnold, it is identified through the scriptural references and thoughts expressed in their postwar writings.[665]

Americans of the late nineteenth century were very mobile, ever ready to look for something better. The Persimmons were no different. Some, like John Goodier of Company D, sought their fortune in places like Huron, Michigan, but most of those who moved followed the trend of the era and went west. Corporal Robert Blair of Company I ended up in Ralls, Missouri. Lieutenant Ransford Smith went to Ogden, Utah. Company K's Leonidas Butler made it all the way to California, as did Corporal Bill Tillson of the same organization. Tillson was a member of the GAR's McPherson Post no. 51 in Hanford, California, but eventually returned to live at the Soldiers Home in Dayton.

Some even returned to the land they had campaigned in. Captain James Bone became a carpetbagger and moved to Alabama. Entering politics, he became a Commissioner of DeKalb County, where one of his official duties was to investigate pension claims of former Confederate soldiers. He died in 1906 and was buried at Maple Hill Cemetery in Huntsville.[666]

Ferdinand Van Derveer's status as a local hero was greatly enhanced by the Civil War. Aside from his participation in getting the Chickamauga Park effort underway, he was continually called upon to participate and speak at public gatherings and veteran's reunions. Returning to Hamilton in the spring of 1865, he was appointed Internal Revenue Collector for the Third District of Ohio, a post he held for many years, and he was part owner of a local brewery until 1869. Van Derveer was appointed Postmaster in March of 1885, but the position was apparently not to his liking. He resigned after only eight months to run for common pleas judge of Butler County. Easily elected in 1886 and then reelected in 1891, Van Derveer remained a judge until his death in 1892.[667]

---

665. Arnold, *Sunshine and Shadows*, 31.
666. Marik, A. J., and Robert Edwards, eds., *Find a Grave*, www.findagrave.com.

Tenacious in life, Ferdinand Van Derveer remained so at his death. It was his habit to exercise daily by walking around his property on "D" Street. In early November 1892, he suffered a heart attack while on his walk, but the old soldier refused to go down. He was found some time later clinging desperately to the wrought iron fence outside the house but still on his feet. The successful commander won the battle but lost the war a few days later on November 5, 1892. Van Derveer was buried in his uniform after an impressive military funeral and was borne to the grave by survivors of the Thirty-fifth Ohio. "A man of undaunted courage, he was never conquered by an enemy until death came, and it is doubtful if he did not regard his somber guest less as a foe than as a loving messenger from the unseen world, sent to bear him to his home beyond."[668]

Van Derveer's death was formally announced at the annual reunion of the Thirty-fifth Ohio held at Camden, Ohio, in September 1893. The remaining Persimmons who had served him so loyally and capably had much to say about the commander they respected so deeply and formalized their feelings as a resolution:

WHEREAS, In the course of events, our old and respected commander has fought his last battle, and has passed from life's bivouac to that country whence "no traveler ever returned," and now "sleeps the sleep that knows no waking," and,

WHEREAS, We who served him do hereby bear grateful testimony to his manly courage, to his fine military qualifications as a regimental and brigade commander, and to his patriotic devotion to his country and its flag, as the numerous battle fields on which he fought so gallantly, plainly indicate. Therefore,

Resolved, That in the death of Gen. Van Derveer the nation has lost a valuable citizen, one who did his duty in the hour of the nation's greatest peril; that the country has lost a man who could rise above influences of party and could look to the country's welfare, and that we, the survivors of the Thirty-fifth Ohio, have lost a cherished and valued member and comrade.

Resolved, That we point with pride to the man who led us on many a field of battle, and always to success, and that we are proud of our history as made under his command and leadership.

Resolved, That we extend our heartfelt sympathy to the bereaved family, and that these expressions of our sorrow in the death of our respected commander be entered in the minutes of the Thirty-fifth Association and a copy be sent to the family.[669]

Lt. Col. Charles Long returned to Cincinnati after he resigned, remaining there for the next seventeen years. In 1880, in partnership with his brother, Long bought the Lima *Republican*, changed it to a daily newspaper, and served

---

667. Cone, *Biographical*, 345.

668. *Memorial Record*, 410; Van Derveer Family Papers, Butler County Historical Society, Hamilton, Ohio.

669. Keil, *Thirty-fifth Ohio*, 234.

as the paper's editor for ten years. In early 1890, Long sold his interest in the paper and moved back to Cincinnati. Only weeks after his return, he came down with a case of the flu. His condition steadily worsened, the flu turned into pneumonia, and Long passed away in May.[670]

The political and personal feuds that swirled around Henry Boynton after the war had no bearing on his standing with the Persimmons. Regardless of their political persuasion, they genuinely liked him. Boynton was held in "unbroken respect," and to the day he died, none of them "had aught to render against him as a man, or his skill and ability as an officer." He was awarded the Congressional Medal of Honor in 1893 for bravery at Chickamauga and Missionary Ridge. Boynton's courage was unquestioned, but the timing of the award smacks more of politics than anything else. In 1898, Boynton left the Press Corps when War with Spain was declared to reenter the army. After performing administrative duties, he returned to Washington where his wife had just helped establish a patriotic society called the Daughters of Founders and Patriots of America. Boynton became president of the District of Columbia school board, and even though he had retired from the newspaper business, his former colleagues saw fit to elect him president of the Gridiron in 1899. Henry Van Ness Boynton died in 1905 and was buried in Arlington National Cemetery. As exemplary as his press career was, he will always be best known for the Chickamauga–Chattanooga National Military Park. That fact would have caused him no regret.[671]

Joseph Budd returned to Lebanon, Ohio, and operated his business. He lived at 161 Mulberry Street before moving to Hamilton and later to Cincinnati. He lived to be eighty-eight years old and was eulogized as "ripe in years, four score and eight, rich in good deeds and beloved by all who knew him." He was buried in Lebanon Cemetery. Lebanon remembered the sons she sent off to war, one of whom was Oliver Parshall. In honor of her husband, killed at Chickamauga, Mrs. Belle Parshall was appointed postmaster of the Lebanon Post Office. She remained in office until 1878.[672]

Capt. Samuel L'Hommedieu, had operated the G. W. Tapscott and Company flour mill prior to the war, experience that had served him well as an expert forager. Upon his return to Hamilton, he changed careers and became a successful insurance salesman. L'Hommedieu's father, an executive of the Cincinnati, Hamilton, and Dayton Railroad, named one of the line's locomotives in honor of his son. Its arrival in the station always evoked strong memories in

---

670. Keil, *Thirty-fifth Ohio*, 237.

671. Ibid., 239; Ritchie, *Press Gallery,* 130.

672. *Wiggins and McKillop's Directory for Warren County for 1878* (Lebanon, Ohio: Wiggins and McKillop, printers, 1878[?]), 17; *Celebrating 200 Years*, Warren County Historical Society, 124; 35th OVI Collection, Butler County Historical Society; Endres, David J., *Butler County Obituaries*, pt. viii, (http://freepages.genealogy.rootsweb.com/~hamilton/obits8.html)

every Persimmon who saw it.[673]

That dog Jack came home with John West of Company B. Jack had shared the hardships of war with the Persimmons and had amused and encouraged them through many a trying day. He caught small game for food and had done as much damage to the Confederacy as he could by "doing his best to eat the rebels out of house and home." Jack was a regular at the annual reunions, and stories began circulating that the scar on his head had been obtained in battle. No one knew for sure, but it was a good story. At one reunion, the boys voted him a silver collar, but they waited too long to get it. Jack passed on before the award could be made and was buried with appropriate honors.[674]

Lt. George T. Earhart of Company G returned to his job as ticket agent for the Cincinnati Hamilton & Dayton Railroad. An active member of the Wetzel-Compton Post no. 96, he served on the committee that erected the Butler County Solders, Sailors, and Pioneers Monument. Earhart's service had been cut short by illness, and he had resigned in October 1862 with a surgeon's certificate of disability. For the rest of his life, he suffered from poor health, a condition he always attributed to his wartime service in the Thirty-fifth Ohio. Another Persimmon who never recovered from wartime illness was Surgeon Perkins Gordon. For the rest of his life, he suffered from dizziness and partial blindness as a result of his sunstroke during the Tullahoma campaign. He died in Milan, Ohio, in 1892.[675]

Solid Joseph Henninger, captain of Company B, returned home to his wife and twelve children to operate his contracting business. Large families are expensive, and Henninger sold stoves and was a partner in Cole, Gehrman, and Henninger, manufacturers of sashes, doors, and blinds. Somehow, he also found time to participate in the Odd Fellows.[676]

Lt. Julian Fitch of Company C had served for ninety days in the Sixth Ohio prior to joining the Thirty-fifth Ohio. In the spring 1862, he had been detailed to the fledgling Signal Corps, and finding that he liked his new job, never returned to the Thirty-fifth. He accepted a second lieutenant's commission in the regular army in 1863, and did well enough to be brevetted to captain by the end of the war. As the last vestiges of the war were ending in the spring of 1865, Fitch was transferred to the Department of Missouri and sent out to assist the Butterfield Stage Company in surveying the Smokey Hill Trail from Leavenworth to Denver. Fitch's wife, Louisa, accompanied him on the expedition, and Louisa Springs Station in Ellis County, Kansas, was named in her honor.

In February 1866, Fitch transferred to the Seventeenth U.S. Infantry to further his career. Promotions have always come easier in combat arms, and nine

673. Arnold, *Sunshine and Shadows*, 15; *Williams Hamilton Directory for 1860, 1875, and 1876* (Cincinnati: Williams Directory Co., 1876).

674. Keil, *Thirty-fifth Ohio*, 224–25.

675. *Cyclopedia of Butler County, Ohio*, 311, Lowry, *Tarnished Scalpels*, 93.

676. *Cyclopedia of Butler County, Ohio*, 385.

months later, he was promoted to first lieutenant. In August 1869, Lieutenant Fitch transferred to the Fifteenth U.S Infantry. The Fifteenth Infantry was garrisoning several remote locations in Utah, Colorado, and New Mexico, uninviting duty on the best of days, and it was there that something went wrong. For reasons unknown, Fitch's army career ended in January 1873. He was cashiered and dismissed from the service.[677]

After being discharged for wounds received at Chickamauga, Capt. Andrew Lewis of Company I had returned to Butler County, where he and his wife Martha raised their seven children, one of whom died in infancy. It was said that Lewis "generally followed the occupation of a farmer" after the war. *Generally* might be overstating the case, because by the time he retired from farming, Lewis owned the Don Pedro, Silver Lake, Divide, and Premier mines in Colorado and had a controlling interest in the Blanche mine.[678]

Other Persimmons succeeded in business, as well. Henry Moser married Sallie Rogers in 1865 and moved with her to Mount Healthy, Ohio. For forty years, the Mosers operated a very successful store and lived quite comfortably. From 1866 to 1885, they had seven children, and all but one lived well into the twentieth century. Pvt. John M. Bradstreet used the skills he had learned as commissary clerk for the regiment to start his own business, the Bradstreet Produce Company of Dayton, Ohio.[679]

Captain Phillip Rothenbush also saw a future in produce. Rothenbush returned to Hamilton and worked with his father in the grocery business. He married Ollie Ratliff of Oxford, Ohio, in January 1866 and was named assistant U.S. Assessor later that same year. After serving as the U.S. Stock Keeper in 1867 and 1868, Rothenbush returned to the grocery business, entering into a partnership with a local produce dealer. Several years later, he opened his own fruit market on High Street in Hamilton and gained local fame as the first man to bring fresh bananas into the city. The Rothenbush business specialized in handling apples, cabbages, "potatoes by the car load," and the "best and finest line of domestic and tropical fruits." Rothenbush and Ollie had five children, four of whom lived to be adults.[680]

Rothenbush celebrated his fifty-fifth birthday in a big way and invited all of his former comrades from Company I. Written as a mock order, the invitation read:

> You are hereby commanded to appear, with other members of the Regiment, in fatigue uniform, at the home of Mr. and Mrs. Rothenbush, No. 215 Main Street, Wednesday evening, July 7, 1897. No one excused on account of hospital service.

677. Ware, Eugene, "The Indian War of 1864," *The Kansas Collection* <www.kancoll.org>.

678. *Cyclopedia of Butler County, Ohio*, 468.

679. Rogers Papers, "Country Life," 23–24; Arnold, *Sunshine and Shadows*, 31.

680. Bartlow, *Centennial History of Butler County*, 562, Cone, *Biographical*, 348.

Roll call at 8:20 sharp.
Reports of Officers and Privates, 8:30.
Rations furnished at 10:00
Taps at 10:30
Lights out at 11:00, but all night till morning.
By order of: Phillip Rothenbush,
Late Captain Commanding

Rothenbush lived out his life in Hamilton and was known citywide as a man who was "careful and methodical in business, upright and honorable in all his dealings with men, public-spirited and enterprising, and withal a model citizen and valued friend and neighbor." [681]

Pvt. James Cochran of Company A started out in the grocery business in Lebanon after the war, but in 1871 and 1872, he served as the manager of the Lebanon Hotel. His brief career in the hotel management business would have been quickly forgotten except for one unfortunate event. Congressman Clement L. Vallandigham, notorious for his conviction as a traitor during the war, was accidentally killed while staying at Cochran's hotel.[682]

Pvt. Benjamin Arnold had returned to Ohio after being discharged on a surgeon's certificate of disability, but he couldn't stay out of the war. After recovering his health, he reenlisted in the Fourth Ohio Cavalry. When the war ended, Arnold went back to Montgomery County and was active in veterans groups. For the rest of his life he maintained close contact with his friends from Company C and attended the regiment's reunions. As he grew older, he became concerned that the greatness of the men and events of the Civil War wasn't being adequately told to younger generations. Between February and April of 1909, he wrote a series of articles about his experiences in the Thirty-fifth Ohio. Published under the heading "Sunlight and Shadows in the Life of a Private Soldier," the articles described what it was like to be a Thirty-fifth Ohio Persimmon.[683]

First Sergeant Joseph W. Myers returned to carpentry then became involved in manufacturing brooms and the confectionary business. Myers was very active in his community and the local Wetzel-Compton Post no. 96 of the GAR. He served as Hamilton city street commissioner, police captain, and later fire captain. Along the way, he joined the Veteran Guards, a GAR affiliate, and became "Captain" Myers. In 1881, he joined Bentel, Margedant, and Company, where his woodworking skills were used to manufacture woodworking machines. Myers lived long enough to be ticketed for speeding. According to the Hamilton *Evening Journal* of October 13, 1914, "It is charged that Meyers

---

681. 35th OVI Collection, Butler County Historical Society; Bartlow, *Centennial History of Butler County,* 562, Cone, *Biographical,* 348.

682. Bogan, *Warren County's Involvement,* 44.

683. Arnold, *Sunshine and Shadows,* introduction.

Birthday Anniversary

1842

1861

1897

Phillip Rothenbush

Hamilton, Ohio

Fifty-fifth birthday invitation sent out by Capt. Phillip Rothenbush
BUTLER COUNTY HISTORICAL SOCIETY

Photograph of 1923 reunion of the Thirty-fifth OVI Association.
First Sgt. Joseph Myers is third from the right on the top row.
BUTLER COUNTY HISTORICAL SOCIETY

in his effort to spot speed violators during fair week violated the law himself by speeding in his own auto." [684]

When the rebellion began, Pvt. Martin Saum of Company C had been a nineteen-year-old orphan working on the farm of James M. Stokes in Jackson-burg, Ohio. Saum and Stokes's son, William, enlisted together and went south with the Thirty-fifth Ohio. When he fell ill in 1862, Saum went to the Stokes farm to recuperate. One year later, as the pair charged up Missionary Ridge together, twenty-year-old Stokes was cut down by a rebel bullet. After mustering out, Saum returned to farming in Butler County, married a girl from Seven Mile, and raised six sons. Saum named the oldest William after the friend who never returned. [685]

Company B Drummer Clark Castater eventually became the Thirty-fifth Ohio's principle musician. After lying beneath the guns of Battery I at Chickamauga, his hearing had been ruined, and within a few years, he was completely deaf. A skilled mechanic, Castater never applied for the disability pension he was entitled to because he felt he would be able to make a good living for himself and his family without it. In September 1881, walking home from work one evening on the railroad tracks, he didn't hear the train that ran him over and killed him. His wife applied for his pension, and after some wrangling over her eligibility, it was granted. [686]

684. *Cyclopedia of Butler County, Ohio,* 397; *Hamilton Evening Journal,* October 13, 1914.

685. Stokes/Saum Family Papers, Butler County Historical Society, Hamilton, Ohio.

Surgeon Abraham Landis returned to Millville, Ohio, and the business of raising his family. Landis believed that his sons should be fully capable of supporting themselves and their families, so he had given them the best education possible and taught them how to raise corn and hogs. The family moved to Indiana, and when he died, Landis knew that he had done as much as he could to prepare his sons for life. As adults, the five boys went their own way in the world. Charles B. Landis lived in Logansport, Indiana, and was elected to the United States House of Representatives six times. Frederick Landis became an author, newspaper publisher, and served two terms of his own in Congress. Walter Kumler Landis was a journalist like his brother and eventually became the first United States Postmaster for Puerto Rico. John Howard Landis followed in his father's footsteps and became a doctor. He taught medicine at the University of Cincinnati and served as a public health inspector. The public health reforms John initiated soon became standards across the country. Kennesaw Mountain Landis, named after a place his father could never forget, decided to go into the law. After serving as an attorney, he was appointed to a federal judgeship. Ken became the best-known member of the Landis family when he accepted a position as the first commissioner of major league baseball. Their father would have been pleased.[687]

For precocious Joseph O'Neall of Company A, three years of war, one spent as a prisoner of war under the worst possible conditions, was apparently enough. He left the exciting life behind after the war, got married, and settled quietly back into civilian life. Having had only minimal schooling before the war, he bettered his education so that he was able to teach school and study the law. He passed the bar in 1877 and became probate judge of Warren County less than two years later. His prison experiences were a tale he "would to God I could forever blot it from my memory." After trying to do just that for fifty years, he finally told his story in the *Western Star* in 1912. Understandably, he bitterly recalled the "scenes of horror in rebel prison," but some of his rancor was reserved for his own side. Insisting that he and his fellow prisoners had never been properly recognized for their steadfast loyalty amidst indescribable suffering, he angrily declared, "The government should give to each of these men a medal of honor, much more than to the soldiers who accidentally picked up a Rebel flag on some battlefield, as is now done."[688]

Leonidas Butler enlisted in Company K and was immediately made a corporal, but after that, things didn't go as well as Butler had hoped. He was reduced to the ranks in September of 1862 and was discharged in February of 1863. The records give no specific information, but the reduction and discharge were most likely due to sickness. Butler returned home to Middletown and worked in several local paper mills. In his last years, he moved to Van Nuys,

686. U.S. Congress, *Congressional Record*, Report 2629.
687. Landis Family Papers, Butler County Historical Society, Hamilton, Ohio.
688. Bogan, *Warren County's Involvement*, 13, 60, 61.

California, to live with his daughter. On May 3, 1936, Butler died in California at the age of ninety-four. He was said to be the oldest person to be born in Middletown, and it is likely that he was the last surviving member of the Thirty-fifth Ohio.[689]

Richard Foord returned to his wife Laura in Middletown, Ohio, but a few years after the war, the couple joined Laura's sister and her husband, J. B. Nunnelly, in Austin, Texas, in search of new opportunities. When the town of Temple was founded in Bell County, they moved there, and Richard worked as a contractor. Later, he became head bookkeeper for the firm of Nunnelly and Chattin. Foord served in that position until 1889, when President Benjamin Harrison appointed him postmaster. He was active in his community as "a prominent Republican," the president of the local GAR chapter, and an honored member of the Odd Fellows. His Texas neighbors never held Foord's Union service against him. He had been living in Ohio when the war broke out, and it seemed natural that he would join his fellow Buckeyes in defending the Union. After all, the boys from Texas had done the same thing for the Confederacy. When he died in 1916, the writer of his obituary reminded the citizen's of Temple that even though Foord had "fought under a different flag than most of the old soldiers here," it was now "the flag we all love today." The people of Temple did not remember Foord as a Yankee. They remembered him as a neighbor of thirty-five years whose kind words, pleasant smile, and brotherly handshake would be missed. They remembered a "true, honorable man" who fought for what he believed in and did not begrudge him the right to rejoin "his legion across the river."[690]

Soft Shadows

The wind blows softly through the tall hardwood trees. They are very old trees, some having been there for two hundred years. The edge of the shade under the oaks, maples, and walnuts ripples and an occasional spot of sunlight rushes across the ground as the trees dance before the breeze. Beneath them, the upright white stones are set in rows or neatly turning arcs. Robins perch on the arched stones and search for breakfast in the still wet grass. Squirrels wander in and out among them, pausing now and then to stand up and chew on an acorn or just look around. The warm sun, the gentle breeze, the familiar animals, and the soothing touch of the hand of an unseen but ever present God combine to create a place of true serenity. Chattanooga, Hamilton, Arlington, Louisville, Nashville, Marietta, or Riley—It could be any of them. It is all of them.

---

689. Endres, *Butler County Obituaries*, (http://freepages.genealogy.rootsweb.com/˜hamilton/obits8.html).

690. Foord Papers, obituary.

The stone markers are a mix of old and new. Most are stained, pitted, and cracked from decades in the open. Others are new and starkly clean, put there by family and friends who still remember. Those of men who were more fortunate in life are more akin to statuary than grave markers, but there aren't many of that kind. Nearly all of them are the plain white monuments that mark the final resting place of American soldiers. They all have two things in common, a man's name and a man's pride. The names are spelled various ways, indicating the diversity of the men who joined together in a life and death struggle that marked each and every one for life. They left families behind, marching thousands of miles to face incredible hardships. Swallowing their fears, they fought toe to toe with determined enemies. They bled and they died.

The greatest nation on earth exists because they stepped up when called, and so the pride. It's spelled the same way on every stone: "35th OVI." No matter what may have happened to them later in life, every Persimmon carried that identification to the grave. The pride that went with it is still there. Empathetic visitors who are able to make the emotional and spiritual connection with another time can feel it flowing out of the stones. It is not pride in fighting. Rather it is the pride of having fought, a distinction lost on many people. Now they all lay beneath the earth in eternal rest, and their stones cast soft shadows before them.

Roster

Alphabetical Roster of the 35th Ohio Volunteer Infantry

Name	Age	Rank	Date	Co.	Comments
Able, William W.	21	Private	8/9/1861	B	Mustered out with company.
Adams, John	18	Private	9/16/1861	K	Transferred to Co. A on 11/5/1861. Promoted to corporal. Promoted to sgt. maj. on 5/1/1862. Promoted to 2nd Lt. Co. G on 10/4/1862. Wounded 9/20/1863 at Chickamauga, Ga. Mustered out with company.
Ager, Christian	40	Private	9/7/1861	G	Transferred to Co. D on 9/24/1861. Died on 1/5/1862 at Somerset, Ky.
Albert, Charles P.	23	Private	8/9/1861	B	Died on 2/15/1864 in hospital at Nashville, Tenn.
Albright, John	42	Private	9/7/1861	G	Transferred to Co. D on 9/24/1861. Mustered out on 9/23/1864 at Chattanooga, Tenn., on expiration of term of service.
Alexander, John A.		Private	10/16/1861	F	Discharged for disability on 2/8/1862.
Allen, Benjamin	20	Private	8/20/1861	C	On muster roll. No further record found.
Allen, Leonard	39	1st Sgt	8/20/1861	C	Deserted 5/1862. Reduced to ranks 5/1862. Discharged to enlist in Mississippi Marine Brigade.

Alphabetical Roster of the 35th Ohio Volunteer Infantry

Name	Age	Rank	Date	Co.	Comments
Allison, Peter	17	Private	9/12/1861	K	Promoted to corporal on 5/28/1862. Killed on 11/25/1863 at Missionary Ridge, Tenn.
Amlin, Alfred	25	Private	8/26/1861	H	Died on 11/26/1863 of wounds received on 11/25/1863 at Missionary Ridge, Tenn.
Anderson, Benjamin	25	Private	9/7/1861	G	Transferred to Co. D on 9/24/1861. Mustered out on 9/23/1864 at Chattanooga, Tenn, on expiration of term of service.
Anderson, Calvery	18	Private	8/26/1861	D	Wounded 6/14/1864 at Kennesaw Mountain, Ga. Mustered out with company.
Anderson, Isaac	21	Private	9/7/1861	G	Killed on 9/20/1863 at Chickamauga, Ga.
Andrew, William	44	2nd Lt	9/15/1861	I	Resigned on 3/14/1863.
Antrim, George W.	18	Private	2/26/1864	H	Transferred to Co. C, 18th OVI on 11/10/1864.
Applegate, Thomas	21	Private	8/28/1862	B	Transferred to Co. K on 8/26/1864. Transferred to Co. C 18th OVI on 10/24/1864.
Archdeacon, Benjamin F.	19	Private	9/5/1861	F	Discharged for disability on 1/3/1863 at Gallatin, Tenn.
Archdeacon, George	21	Private	9/5/1861	F	Discharged for disability on 1/3/1863 at Gallatin, Tenn.
Armstrong, Francis M.	20	Private	10/8/1861	K	Transferred to Co. C 18th OVI on 10/24/1864, veteran.
Arnold, Benjamin F.	20	Private	8/20/1861	C	Discharged for disability on 7/24/1862 at Tuscumbia, Ala.
Ast, Henry	20	Private	9/24/1861	K	Transferred to Co. C 18th OVI on 10/24/1864, veteran.
Atkinson, Samuel	18	Private	9/5/1861	F	On detached duty at 3rd Division Headquarters, XIV Army Corps. Mustered out on 9/8/1864 by order of War Department.
Austin, Marcus M.	21	Cpl.	9/1/1861	E	Promoted to Sgt. on 11/3/1862. Reduced to ranks on 7/11/1863. Mustered out with company.
Ayers, James M.	19	Private	8/26/1861	H	Discharged for disability on 8/11/1862.

Alphabetical Roster of the 35th Ohio Volunteer Infantry

Name	Age	Rank	Date	Co.	Comments
Ayersman, Daniel	45	Private	8/15/1861	A	Discharged for disability on 12/10/1862 at Louisville, Ky.
Baily, Abraham S.	19	Private	3/25/1862	D	Wounded on 9/19/1863 at Chickamauga, Ga. Transferred to Co. C 18th OVI on 11/10/1864.
Bane, Andrew W.	20	Private	8/9/1861	B	Killed on 10/7/1862 in action near Perryville, Ky.
Barbee, Elias	21	Private	9/7/1861	G	Transferred to Company K on 9/23/1864. Transferred to Co. C 18th OVI on 10/20/1864. Veteran.
Barber, George	19	Private	8/26/1861	D	Transferred to Co. G on 9/21/1861. Died 10/13/1863 in hospital at Nashville, Tenn.
Barchard, Frederick	21	Private	10/18/1861	K	Promoted to corporal on 11/18/1862. Wounded on 9/19/1863 at Chickamauga, Ga, left arm amputated. Discharged for disability on 6/22/1864 at Cincinnati, Ohio.
Barcus, George W.	21	Private	8/20/1861	C	Transferred to Co. F on 9/9/1861. Died 5/30/1862 in hospital at Corinth, Miss.
Bargett, William H.	19	Private	8/28/1862	K	Transferred to Co. C 18th OVI on 10/20/1864.
Barklow, Arthur	17	Private	9/12/1861	K	Mustered out with company.
Barnett, Francis	25	Cpl.	8/25/1861	C	Discharged for disability on 2/18/1863 at Camp Dennison, Ohio.
Barnhiser, William	20	Cpl.	8/26/1861	D	Transferred to Co. C on 9/1861. Temporarily assigned to Co. K on 8/26/1864. Mustered out on 9/8/1864 at Chattanooga, Tenn., on expiration of term of service.
Barore, Charles	18	Private	8/26/1861	D	Discharged for disability 10/1862.
Barr, Hezekiah	20	Private	8/15/1861	A	Wounded on 11/25/1863 at Missionary Ridge. Wounded on 7/20/1864 near Atlanta. In hospital until 12/3/64.
Bate, George	19	Private	9/7/1861	G	Transferred to Co. A in 10/1861. Killed 9/20/1863 at Chickamauga.
Bate, John H.	19	Private	8/15/1861	A	Captured 9/20/1863 at Chickamauga. Died on 3/11/1864 in prison at Richmond, Va.

Alphabetical Roster of the 35th Ohio Volunteer Infantry

Name	Age	Rank	Date	Co.	Comments
Bauer, George	20	Private	8/9/1861	B	Promoted to corporal on 5/12/1863. Mustered out with company.
Baxter, John	19	Private	8/26/1861	D	Transferred to Co. C on 9/9/1861. Temporarily assigned to Co. K on 8/26/1864. Mustered out on 9/23/1864 at Chattanooga, Tenn., on expiration of term of service.
Beachler, William H.	23	Cpl.	8/20/1861	C	Mustered out with company.
Bear, Carlton	22	Private	9/15/1861	I	Transferred to Co. H in 9/1861. Died on 8/26/1862 at his home in Germantown, Ohio.
Bear, John P.	19	Private	8/26/1861	H	Died on 3/12/1863 in hospital at Nashville, Tenn.
Beard, James W.	23	Private	9/12/1861	K	Discharged for disability on 6/11/1862 at Louisville, Ky.
Beard, Jonathan H.	19	Private	9/12/1861	K	Promoted to corporal on 5/28/1862. Mustered out with company.
Beatty, Frederick		Private	9/5/1861	F	Transferred to Co. C 18th OVI on 11/10/1864.
Beatty, Wilkinson	64	Private	9/15/1861	I	Discharged for disability on 2/7/1863 at Concord Church, Tenn.
Beaver, Daniel J.	20	Private	9/7/1861	E	Transferred to Co. I on 9/9/1861. Discharged on 12/1/1862 at Cincinnati, Ohio.
Becker, Emilian	31	Private	8/26/1861	D	Transferred to Co. C on 9/9/1861. Temporarily assigned to Co. K on 8/26/1864. Mustered out on 9/23/1864 at Chattanooga, Tenn., on expiration of term of service.
Beckett, Michael	19	Private	8/9/1861	B	
Beckle. Lewis	34	Private	8/26/1861	H	Died on 10/1/1862 at Camp Chase, Ohio.
Bell, Abraham S.	23	Cpl.	8/9/1861	B	Discharged for disability in 9/16/61 at Hamilton, Ohio.
Bell, Andrew	21	Cpl.	8/26/1861	H	Promoted to Sgt. on 11/1/1862. Mustered out with company.
Bell, James N.	18	Private	8/9/1861	B	Mustered out with company.
Belot, Emile	30	Private	8/15/1861	A	Discharged for disability at Hamilton, Ohio.
Benner, David	19	Private	3/1/1862	K	Transferred to Co. C 18th OVI on 10/24/1864.

Alphabetical Roster of the 35th Ohio Volunteer Infantry

Name	Age	Rank	Date	Co.	Comments
Bennett, John G.	22	Private	9/5/1861	F	Mustered out with company.
Bennett, John L.	22	Private	9/5/1861	F	On detached duty as ambulance driver. Mustered out 9/8/1864 by Order of War Department.
Bents, William L.	39	Private	10/8/1861	K	Transferred to Co. G on 11/5/1861. Mustered out by order of War Department.
Berry, David C.	18	Private	8/26/1861	D	Transferred to Co. C in 9/1861. Wounded on 9/20/1863 at Chickamauga. Promoted to corporal on 4/1/1864. Temporarily assigned to Co. K on 8/26/1864. Mustered out on 9/8/64 at Chattanooga, Tenn., on expiration of term of service.
Berry, John	18	Private	9/7/1861	G	Transferred to Co. C in 9/1861. Temporarily assigned to Co. K on 8/26/1864. Mustered out on 9/23/1864 at Chattanooga, Tenn., on expiration of term of service.
Berry, John A.	17	Private	9/7/1861	G	Transferred to Co. A in 10/1861.
Berry, Wesley	23	Private	8/15/1861	A	Died on 11/2/1863 in hospital in Nashville.
Betz, Martin	22	Private	9/7/1861	G	Promoted to Commissary Sgt. on 9/27/1862. Mustered out on 9/8/1864 at Chattanooga, Tenn.
Bickle, Jacob	42	Private	11/13/1861	E	Captured on 9/20/1863. Paroled on 10/29/1863 Transferred to Veteran Reserve Corps on 3/15/1864.
Bickmore, Charles E.	30	Private	8/28/1862	C	Transferred to Co. K on 8/26/1864. Transferred to Co. C 18th OVI on 10/20/1864.
Billmire, Charles W.	17	Private	8/26/1861	H	Discharged for disability on 10/29/1861 at Camp Bourbon, Ky.
Billmire, David	18	Private	1/21/1864	H	Transferred to Co. C 18th OVI on 11/10/1864.
Bishop, David W.	19	Private	8/15/1861	A	Promoted to corporal. Reduced to Private. Mustered out with company.
Bittner, Charles		Private	10/6/1861	I	Transferred to Co. K on 11/5/1861. Mustered out with company.

Alphabetical Roster of the 35th Ohio Volunteer Infantry

Name	Age	Rank	Date	Co.	Comments
Black, Abraham	52	Private	10/20/1861	K	Transferred to Co. E on 11/5/1861. Temporarily assigned to Co. K on 9/8/1864. Mustered out 9/23/1864 on expiration of term of service.
Black, Benjamin	17	Private	9/15/1861	I	Discharged on 12/9/1862 at Gallatin, Tenn., to enlist in the regular army.
Black, John M.	19	Private	2/26/1862	D	Died 8/18/1864 at Louisville, Ky., of wounds received on 7/20/64 at Atlanta, Ga.
Black, William H.	23	Private	2/28/1862	D	Died on 8/25/1864 at home in Preble Co., Ohio.
Bladner, Phillip	34	Cpl.	9/1/1861	E	Absent from 10/26/1863 in hospital at Louisville, Ky. Mustered out 9/8/1864 by order of War Department.
Blair, James	21	Sgt.	9/12/1861	K	Captured on 12/8/1861 at Somerset, Ky., returned to company on 2/22/1862. Wounded 6/18/1864 near Kennesaw Mountain, Ga. Discharged on 9/23/1864 at Cincinnati, Ohio.
Blair, Robert	31	Cpl.	9/15/1861	I	Discharged for disability on 10/25/64 at Camp Dennison, Ohio.
Blake, Charles A.	20	Private	8/15/1861	A	Mustered out with company.
Bloss, Thomas J.		Private	10/16/1861	F	Killed on 9/20/1863 at Chickamauga, Ga.
Boatman, Benjamin F.	30	Cpl.	9/5/1861	F	Died on 10/30/63 at Nashville, Tenn., of wounds received on 9/20/63 at Chickamauga, Ga.
Boatman, Jeremiah	20	Private	8/20/1861	C	Transferred to Co. F on 9/9/1861. Transferred to Co. I on 11/1/1861. Mustered out on 9/8/1864 at Chattanooga, Tenn.
Bogar, John W.	22	Private	8/15/1861	A	Promoted to corporal on 10/1/1862. Mustered out with company.
Bone, James H.	25	2nd Lt.	8/15/1861	A	Promoted to 1st Lt. on 7/13/1863. Appointed Adjutant on 9/24/1863. Promoted to captain of Co. D on 3/19/1864. Mustered out with company.
Boner, Martin L.	23	Cpl.	9/1/1861	E	Reduced to ranks. Mustered out with company.
Boner, William A.	25	1st Sgt.	9/7/1861	G	Mustered out with company.
Bookwalter, Benjamin F.	19	Private	8/20/1861	C	Mustered out with company.

Alphabetical Roster of the 35th Ohio Volunteer Infantry

Name	Age	Rank	Date	Co.	Comments
Boos, John L.		Private	9/28/1861	K	Transferred from Co. I on 11/5/1861. Transferred to Veteran Reserve Corps on 8/25/1863.
Booth, Albert	20	Private	8/15/1861	A	Promoted to corporal on 8/30/1862. Mustered out with company.
Bower, George	36	Private	9/15/1861	I	
Bowers, George W.	20	Private	8/9/1861	B	Died 7/14/1864 in hospital at Nashville, Tenn., of a leg wound accidentally self-inflicted on 6/1/1864.
Bowles, William H.	20	Cpl.	9/1/1861	E	Died 10/24/1863 at Chattanooga, Tenn., of wounds received on 9/19/1863 at Chickamauga, Ga.
Bowman, Henry	20	Private	8/20/1861	C	Absent without leave. Mustered out with company.
Bowman, John H.	20	Private	9/7/1861	G	Transferred to Company K on 9/23/1864. Transferred to Co. C 18th OVI on 10/20/1864. Veteran.
Bowsman, William	18	Private	10/10/1861	K	Transferred to Co. H on 11/5/1861. Transferred to Co. C 18th OVI on 10/24/1864. Veteran.
Bowyer, Robert	22	Private	8/9/1861	B	Mustered out with company.
Boyle, Elijah J.	28	Private	9/7/1861	G	
Boynton, Henry V. N.	26	Major	7/29/1861	Staff	Promoted to Lt. Col. on 7/16/63. Wounded at Missionary Ridge on 11/25/63. Absent sick from 11/25/63 recovering.
Braddock, Job	43	Private	9/5/1861	F	Died on 6/8/1862 at Pittsburgh Landing, Tenn.
Bradford, Henry A.	20	Sgt.	8/26/1861	H	Reduced to the ranks on 11/4/1861. Killed on 9/30/1863 at Bridgeport, AL by an exploding shell.
Bradstreet, John M.	20	Private	8/20/1861	C	Detailed to Commissary Department. Mustered out with company.
Bradstreet, William H.	24	Music'n	8/17/1861	Band	Discharged on 9/10/1862 by order of War Department at Nashville.
Brady, David H.	21	Sgt.	8/9/1861	B	Reduced to Private. Promoted to corporal on 2/28/63. Absent sick from 9/20/63 in hospital in Nashville, Tenn. Mustered out on 8/26/64 by order of War Department.
Braffet, Volney M.	20	Private	9/1/1861	E	Mustered out with company.

Alphabetical Roster of the 35th Ohio Volunteer Infantry

Name	Age	Rank	Date	Co.	Comments
Branigan, Joseph	18	Private	9/12/1861	K	Promoted to corporal on 11/18/1862. Mustered out with company.
Brant, David	19	Private	10/6/1862	A	Transferred to Co. K on 8/26/1864. Transferred to Co. C 18th OVI on 10/20/1864.
Brate, William H.	19	Private	8/9/1861	B	Discharged on 8/26/1861 at Hamilton, Ohio, on writ of habeas corpus.
Bresenstein, Christian	18	Private	8/26/1861	H	Mustered out with company.
Bridge, Reuben	24	Private	9/1/1861	E	Discharged for disability on 7/8/1862 at Corinth, Miss
Britton, William	19	Cpl.	8/26/1861	H	Transferred to Veteran Reserve Corps in 11/1/1863.
Brock, John		Private	8/20/1861	F	Died on 11/1/1861 at Paris, Ky.
Brooks, John	45	Private	9/15/1861	I	Wounded and captured on 9/20/1863 at Chickamauga, Ga. Mustered out on 1/26/1865 at Columbus, Ohio, on expiration of term of service.
Brooks, John P.	19	Cpl.	9/15/1861	I	Captured on 9/20/63 at Chickamauga, Ga. Mustered out on 1/26/65 at Columbus, Ohio, on expiration of term of service.
Brower, Cassius C.	19	Private	8/26/1861	D	Transferred to Co. C on 9/9/1961. Died 12/5/1863 in hospital in Nashville, Tenn., from wounds received on 9/20/1863 at Chickamauga.
Brown, Alfred	28	Music'n	9/15/1861	I	Discharged for disability on 12/23/1862 at Columbus, Ohio.
Brown, Elmore H.	36	Private	8/26/1861	H	Mustered out on 9/19/1864 at Columbus, Ohio, on expiration of term of service.
Brown, Franklin	18	Private	8/20/1861	C	Mustered out with company.
Brown, Joseph M.	19	Private	9/1/1861	E	Captured 9/17/1863 near Chickamauga, Ga. Paroled. Died 3/26/1864 at Annapolis, Md.
Brown, Lorenzo	26	Private	10/8/1861	G	Transferred to Co. K on 11/5/1861. Promoted to corporal on 5/1/1862. Promoted to Commissary Sgt. on 10/1/1862. Mustered out on 9/23/1864 at Chattanooga, Tenn.
Brown, Richard M.	20	Private	8/26/1861	D	Transferred to Co. A on 9/10/1861. Died 2/25/1862 at Lebanon, Ky.

Alphabetical Roster of the 35th Ohio Volunteer Infantry

Name	Age	Rank	Date	Co.	Comments
Brown, Robert F.	21	Private	9/15/1861	I	Transferred to Co. B in 9/1861. Died 11/9/1863 in hospital at Nashville, Tenn.
Bryan, John A.	23	Private	8/26/1861	D	Transferred to Co. G on 9/24/1861.
Bryant, James P.	26	Private	8/15/1861	A	Discharged for disability 4/1/1862 at Columbia, Tenn.
Bryant, Stephen	21	Private	8/15/1861	A	Transferred to Veteran Reserve Corp on 7/12/1864
Budd, Joseph L.	29	Capt.	8/15/1861	A	Promoted to Maj. on 7/13/1863. Mustered out with regiment on 9/27/1864.
Budge, John	22	Private	9/12/1861	K	Promoted to corporal on 7/25/1862. Reduced to rank on 11/14/1862. Mustered out with company.
Bullard, Charles W.	18	Private	8/9/1861	B	Mustered out with company.
Bunch, John L.	19	Private	8/9/1861	B	Transferred to Co. D on 9/16/1861. No further record found.
Burden, Isaiah	21	Private	9/25/1861	K	Transferred to Co. E on 11/5/1861. Captured 9/17/1863 near Chickamauga, Ga. Paroled and in hospital at Nashville, Tenn. Temporarily assigned to Co. K on 9/8/1864. Mustered out 9/23/1864 on expiration of term of service.
Burgett, William H.	19	Private	8/28/1862	B	Transferred to Co. K on 8/26/1864. Transferred to Co. C 18th OVI in 10/20/1864.
Burr, Alfred H.	24	Cpl.	9/4/1861	C	Discharged for disability on 10/28/1861 at Cynthiana, Ky.
Burrell, George	29	Cpl.	8/26/1861	H	Transferred to Co. I in 9/1861. Promoted to Sgt. on 11/6/62. Mustered out on 9/8/64 at Chattanooga, Tenn., on expiration of term of service.
Burrows, Theodore	18	Private	9/5/1861	F	Transferred to Co. D on 11/1/1861. Mustered out with company.
Bussard, William H.		Private	10/10/1861	K	Transferred to Co. H on 11/5/1861. Promoted to Principle Musician on 1/5/1862. Mustered out 9/23/1864 on expiration of term of service.
Butler, Leonidas H.	20	Cpl.	9/23/1861	K	Reduced to ranks on 9/1/1862. Discharged at Camp Dennison, Ohio.

Alphabetical Roster of the 35th Ohio Volunteer Infantry

Name	Age	Rank	Date	Co.	Comments
Byers, David	20	Private	9/5/1861	F	Wounded 9/19/1863 at Chickamauga, Ga. Transferred to Co. 126 2nd Battalion Veteran Reserve Corps on 1/12/1864. Mustered out on 10/29/1864 at Cincinnati, Ohio.
Byers, Lewis A.	20	Cpl.	9/7/1861	G	Killed on 9/20/1863 at Chickamauga, Ga.
Calaway, William M.	24	Private	9/12/1861	K	Regimental teamster from 10/28/1863. Mustered out with company.
Calvin, Jacob	19	Private	8/15/1861	A	
Calvin, William	18	Private	9/12/1861	K	Died on 5/15/1862 near Corinth, Miss.
Campbell, Hezekiah	21	Cpl.	9/7/1861	G	Transferred to Co. D on 9/24/1861. Discharged for disability on 4/20/1862 at Nashville, Tenn.
Campbell, William B.	22	Sgt.	8/26/1861	H	Killed on 9/20/1863 at Chickamauga, Ga.
Capp, Peter H.	27	Private	9/7/1861	G	Transferred to Co. C in 10/1861. Killed on 11/25/1863 at Missionary Ridge, Tenn.
Carey, Willis	21	Private	9/12/1861	K	
Carle, Hezekiah	20	Private	8/26/1861	C	Discharged for disability on 10/6/1862 at Louisville, Ky.
Carney, William	34	Private	8/20/1861	C	Transferred to Co. F on 9/9/1861. Absent sick from 9/16/1862 in hospital in Nashville, Tenn. Discharged for disability on 1/15/1863 at Gallatin, Tenn.
Carpenter, Thomas	18	Private	8/26/1861	D	Transferred to Co. C on 9/9/1861. Transferred to Co. G on 11/6/1861. Mustered out on 9/8/1864 on expiration of term of service.
Case, Daniel	27	Private	8/9/1861	B	Absent sick from 7/6/1864. Discharged on 8/26/1864 by order of the War Department.
Case, Thomas	20	Private	8/20/1861	C	Promoted to corporal on 10/5/1862. Wounded on 9/20/1863 at Chickamauga. Mustered out with company.
Castater, Clark J.	18	Music'n	8/9/1861	B	Promoted to Principle Musician on 5/1/1863. Mustered out with company.

Alphabetical Roster of the 35th Ohio Volunteer Infantry

Name	Age	Rank	Date	Co.	Comments
Castater, David	20	Private	8/26/1861	I	Transferred to Co. H in 9/1861. Promoted to corporal. Wounded 9/19/1863 at Chickamauga, Ga. Mustered out on 9/8/1864 at Chattanooga, Tenn., as Daniel Castator.
Castater, John	18	Private	8/26/1861	H	Transferred to Co. I in 9/1861. Discharged for disability on 3/30/1863 at Nashville, Tenn.
Castater, William	18	Private	8/26/1861	H	Transferred to Co. I in 9/1861. Discharged for disability on 3/30/1863 at Nashville, Tenn.
Castle, George W.	20	Private	8/20/1861	C	Transferred to Co. K on 8/26/1864. Transferred to Co. C 18th OVI on 10/20/1864. Veteran.
Cattlehoch, Frederick J.	22	Private	8/15/1861	A	Captured on 9/20/1863 at Chickamauga. Died on 9/11/1864 in rebel prison at Andersonville, Ga.
Caughey, John	28	Private	9/1/1861	E	Transferred to Co. K on 9/8/1863. Transferred to Co. 18th OVI on 10/20/1864. Veteran.
Caughell, Jacob	21	Private	9/7/1861	G	Transferred to Co. D on 9/24/1861. Promoted to corporal. Promoted to Sgt. on 4/1/1863. Mustered out on 9/23/1863 at Chattanooga, Tenn., on expiration of term of service.
Christine, Benjamin	44	Private	9/15/1861	I	Transferred to Co. H in 9/1861. Mustered out on 9/23/1864 at Chattanooga, Tenn., on expiration of term of service.
Christine, Solomon	18	Private	1/21/1864	H	Transferred to Co. C 18th OVI on 11/10/1864.
Clancey. James	21	Private	9/7/1861	G	Promoted to corporal on 1/20/1862. Promoted to Sgt. on 11/30/1863. Mustered out with company.
Clark, Benejah	22	Private	8/15/1861	A	Died 3/7/1862 in hospital at Bardstown, Ky.
Clark, Benjamin F.	21	Sgt Maj	9/8/1861	Staff	Reduced to ranks in Co. B on 5/1/62. Discharged on 8/5/62 at Hamilton, Ohio.
Clark, David	27	Private	8/9/1861	B	Discharged for disability on 8/5/1862 at Hamilton, Ohio.

Alphabetical Roster of the 35th Ohio Volunteer Infantry

Name	Age	Rank	Date	Co.	Comments
Clark, David M.	18	Private	12/30/1862	G	Captured on 9/19/1863 at Chickamauga, Ga. Transferred to Co. K on 9/23/1864. Transferred to Co. C 18th OVI on 10/20/1864.
Clark, Jonathan	44	Private	9/15/1861	I	Discharged for disability on 12/15/1862 at Bowling Green, Ky.
Clark, Peyton F.	31	Private	8/15/1861	A	Mustered out with company.
Clark, Sylvester	28	Private	10/18/1861	K	Wounded on 9/19/1863 at Chickamauga, Ga. Transferred to 152nd Co., 2nd Battalion Veteran Reserve Corps on 1/26/1864. Mustered out on 11/7/1864 at Nashville, Tenn.
Clary, Tipton W.	20	Sgt.	8/20/1861	C	Transferred to Co. D on 9/9/1861. Promoted to 1st Sgt. Discharged for disability on 1/15/1863 at Gallatin, Tenn.
Clatterbuck, George	20	Private	9/1/1861	E	Wounded on 9/19/1863 at Chickamauga, Ga. Returned to company on 11/25/1863. Transferred to Co. K on 9/8/1863. Transferred to Co. C 18th OVI on 10/20/1864. Veteran.
Claypool, Joseph S.	23	Sgt.	8/20/1861	C	Promoted to Commissary Sgt. on 6/30/1862. Promoted to 2nd Lt. Co. B on 6/6/1862. Resigned 1/20/1863.
Cleaver, Mordecai T.	29	Private	9/5/1861	F	Promoted to Hospital Steward on 1/1/1862. Mustered out on 9/8/1864 at Chattanooga, Tenn.
Clenzy, John W.	18	Private	2/26/1864	H	Transferred to Co. C 18th OVI on 11/10/1864.
Clenzy, Joseph	23	Private	8/26/1861	H	Discharged for disability on 4/20/1862 at camp near Nashville, Tenn. Died a few weeks after returning home at Germantown, Ohio.
Clingers, Anthony	43	Private	8/26/1861	D	Discharged for disability on 9/10/1862.
Clouseman, Joseph	34	Private	8/15/1861	A	Mustered out 9/21/1864 at Columbus, Ohio, on expiration of term of service.
Cobb, Charles	25	Cpl.	8/15/1861	A	Reduced to private. Absent sick 6/28/1864 in hospital at Nashville. Mustered out 8/26/1864 by order of War Department.

Alphabetical Roster of the 35th Ohio Volunteer Infantry

Name	Age	Rank	Date	Co.	Comments
Cochran, George W.	23	Private	8/26/1861	D	Transferred to Co. A in 10/1861. Temporarily assigned to Co. K on 8/26/1864. Mustered out 8/8/1864 on expiration of term of service.
Cochran, James T.	27	Private	8/15/1861	A	Mustered out with company.
Cochran, John C.	19	Private	8/28/1862	B	Transferred to Co. K on 8/26/1864. Transferred to Co. C 18th OVI in 10/20/1864.
Cohen, Isaac D.	28	Cpl.	8/9/1861	B	Reduced to ranks. Discharged for disability on 7/26/1862 at Hamilton, Ohio.
Coleman, George F.	23	Private	8/26/1861	H	Mustered out with company.
Collins, Milo	18	Private	8/15/1861	A	Discharged 9/20/1861 on writ of habeas corpus
Colter, John	21	Private	8/20/1861	C	Transferred to Co. F on 9/9/1861. Wounded 9/20/1863 at Chickamauga. Mustered out with company.
Comens, Wilson	18	Private	9/15/1861	I	Deserted 9/20/1862. Sentenced by court-martial and confined to penitentiary at Jefferson, IN for the duration of the war.
Comfort, Henry	26	Private	2/14/1862	K	Transferred to Co. C 18th OVI on 10/20/1864.
Cone, William H.	18	Private	8/9/1861	B	Mustered out with company.
Conklin, Thomas	18	Private	9/7/1861	G	Promoted to corporal on 6/19/1864. Mustered out with company.
Conelly, James	26	Private	9/5/1861	F	Absent sick from 10/20/1863 in hospital in Chattanooga, Tenn. Discharged for disability on 9/25/1864 at Cincinnati, Ohio.
Conner, Moses	18	Private	9/15/1861	I	Transferred to 152nd Co., 2nd Battalion Veteran Reserve Corps on 1/30/1864. Mustered out on 9/24/1864 at Nashville, Tenn.
Conner, Robert	19	Private	8/15/1861	A	Captured 9/20/63 at Chickamauga. Absent sick in hospital at Annapolis, Md. Discharge 8/26/1864 by order of War Department.
Cook, John	18	Private	9/15/1861	I	Mustered out with company.
Cooper, Daniel	21	Cpl.	9/7/1861	G	Transferred to Co. C in 10/1861. Discharged 7/16/1864 for wounds received 9/20/1863 at Chickamauga.

Alphabetical Roster of the 35th Ohio Volunteer Infantry

Name	Age	Rank	Date	Co.	Comments
Coppage, James M.	21	Private	8/9/1861	B	Promoted to corporal. Discharged for disability 4/5/1863 at Nashville, Tenn.
Coppage, Robert	18	Private	8/9/1861	B	Mustered out with company.
Coppage, William R.	19	Private	9/2/1861	D	Transferred to Co. B on 9/9/1861. Temporarily assigned to Co. K on 8/26/1864. Mustered out on 9/8/1864 on expiration of term of service.
Cornelius, John D.	25	Cpl.	8/20/1861	C	Transferred to Co. F on 9/9/63. No further record found.
Corwin, Asa	28	Cpl.	8/9/1861	B	Transferred to Veteran Reserve Corps on 9/14/1863.
Cotter, John	34	Private	8/26/1861	H	Mustered out with company.
Cottingham, Edward	28	1st Lt.	9/1/1861	E	Captured on 9/20/1863 at Chickamauga, Ga. Promoted to captain Co. F on 3/19/1864. Mustered out 3/11/1865 on expiration of term of service.
Cottingham, John W.	22	Cpl.	9/1/1861	E	Captured 8/7/1862. Paroled 8/8/1862. Exchanged 4/1863. Killed 9/20/1863 at Chickamauga, Ga.
Courtney, Henry	44	Private	9/15/1861	I	Transferred to Co. E on 9/24/1861. Discharged for disability on 3/28/1863 at Cincinnati, Ohio.
Covens, Barney	25	Cpl.	8/26/1861	H	Reduced to ranks on 12/1/1862. Mustered out with company.
Cox, Crittendon A.	18	Private	9/1/1861	E	Discharged for disability on 9/16/1862 at Nashville, Tenn.
Coy, Joseph	18	Private	9/15/1861	I	Mustered out with company.
Coy, Thomas	19	Private	11/24/1863	I	Transferred to Co. C 18th OVI on 11/10/1864.
Crane, Charles W.	27	Private	10/8/1861	K	Transferred to Co. B on 11/5/1861. Temporarily assigned to Co. K on 8/26/1864. Mustered out on 9/8/1964 at Chattanooga, Tenn., upon expiration of term of service.
Crane, Joseph H.	19	Private	8/26/1861	D	Transferred to Co. G on 9/24/1861. Transferred to Veteran Reserve Corps.
Craner, William L. M.	28	Music'n	9/9/1861	Band	Discharged on 9/10/1862 by order of War Department at Nashville.

Alphabetical Roster of the 35th Ohio Volunteer Infantry

Name	Age	Rank	Date	Co.	Comments
Crawford, Alonzo	35	Private	10/8/1861	K	Transferred to Co. K, 11th Battalion Veteran Reserve Corps on 4/10/1864. Mustered out on 11/5/1864 at Point Lookout, Md.
Crawford, Charles C.	40	Private	9/15/1861	I	Transferred to Veteran Reserve Corps on 9/17/1863.
Crawford, Solomon	18	Private	10/8/1861	K	Mustered out with company.
Creager, William O.	18	Private	9/7/1861	G	Discharged in 2/1862 for wounds received on 12/14/1861 at Somerset, Ky.
Cregan, Henry N.	18	Private	8/20/1861	C	Transferred to Co. F on 9/9/1861. Discharged on 6/26/1865 for wounds received 7/20/1864 at Peachtree Creek, Ga. Leg amputated.
Crist, James	32	Private	9/7/1861	G	Transferred to Co. A in 10/1861. Temporarily assigned to Co. K on 8/26/64. Mustered out 8/8/1864 on expiration of term of service.
Crow, Joshua	36	Private	9/5/1861	F	Discharged on 5/15/1862 at Pittsburgh Landing, Tenn.
Crume, Levi	18	Private	9/1/1861	E	Discharged for disability on 4/3/1863 at Louisville, Ky.
Cummings, Benjamin	18	Private	8/15/1861	A	Mustered out with company.
Darrah, William	18	Music'n	9/7/1861	G	Transferred to Co. C in 9/1861. Temporarily assigned to Co. K on 8/26/1864. Mustered out on 9/23/1864 at Chattanooga, Tenn., on expiration of term of service.
Daugherty, Charles	19	Private	9/23/1862	I	Wounded on 9/19/1863 at Chickamauga, Ga. Transferred to Co. C 18th OVI on 11/10/1864.
Daugherty, Lewis F.	35	1st Lt.	8/15/1861	A	Promoted to captain on 7/13/1863. Killed at Battle of Peachtree Creek on 7/20/1864.
David, Elihu	33	Music'n	8/17/1861	Band	Discharged on 9/10/1862 by order of War Department at Nashville.
Davidson, Robert B.	18	Cpl.	8/9/1861	B	Promoted to Sgt. on 10/2/1861. Promoted to 1st Sgt. on 2/24/1863. Promoted to 2nd Lt. on 2/12/1863. Promoted to 1st Lt. Co. I on 3/19/1864. Mustered out with company.

Alphabetical Roster of the 35th Ohio Volunteer Infantry

Name	Age	Rank	Date	Co.	Comments
Davis, Albert	18	Private	2/4/1862	F	Transferred to Co. C 18th OVI on 11/10/1864.
Davis, Ellis	18	Private	8/15/1861	A	Discharged for disability 4/20/1862 at Nashville, Tenn
Davis, Isaac H.	20	Private	10/20/1861	C	Discharged for disability on 5/2/1862 at Nashville, Tenn.
Davis, John M.	22	Private	9/7/1861	G	Transferred to Co. C in 10/1861. Promoted to corporal. Promoted to Sgt. on 12/31/1863. Temporarily assigned to Co. K on 8/26/1864. Mustered out on 9/8/1864 at Chattanooga, Tenn., on expiration of term of service.
Davis, John S.	41	Private	10/20/1861	C	Discharged for disability on 7/24/1862 at Tuscumbia, AL.
Davis, Joshua	18	Private	9/7/1861	G	Detailed as hospital steward in spring of 1863. Mustered out with company.
Davis, Martin	26	Private	9/15/1861	I	On muster-in roll. No further record found.
Day, Ephraim A.	26	Sgt.	9/7/1861	G	Died on 11/27/1863 in hospital at Chattanooga, Tenn.
Dayhoff, Martin	18	Private	9/7/1861	G	Mustered out with company.
Deardorf, Joel K.	25	Capt.	9/12/1861	K	Died on 10/8/63 of wounds received on 9/19/63 at Chickamauga, Ga.
Deardorff, Wilson P.	20	Private	9/15/1861	I	Transferred to Co. H in 9/1861. Mustered out on 9/23/1864 at Chattanooga, Tenn., on expiration of term of service.
Debolt, Thomas J.	23	Private	9/12/1861	K	Transferred to Co. C on 11/5/1861. Temporarily assigned to Co. K on 8/26/1864. Discharged on 9/23/1864 at Chattanooga, Tenn., on expiration of term of service. Regimental butcher.
Dedonell, James	16	Private	8/20/1861	C	Transferred to Co. F on 9/9/1861. Died on 4/10/1862 at Lebanon, Ky.
Deiter, Charles	18	Private	9/7/1861	G	Discharged on 3/29/1864 at Columbus, Ohio, for wounds received on 9/19/1863 at Chickamauga, Ga.
Delawter, Davis	30	Music'n	9/9/1861	Band	Discharged on 9/10/1862 by order of War Department at Nashville.
Dennis, Leander	25	Music'n	8/17/1861	Band	Discharged on 9/10/1862 by order of War Department at Nashville.

Alphabetical Roster of the 35th Ohio Volunteer Infantry

Name	Age	Rank	Date	Co.	Comments
Dennis, Samuel	26	Private	9/7/1861	I	Transferred to Co. G in 10/1861. Detailed as hospital steward in spring of 1863. Mustered out with company.
Denny, James M.	22	Sgt.	9/12/1861	K	Absent sick from 4/25/1863 in hospital in Nashville, Tenn. Mustered out with company.
Denny, Samuel M.	29	Cpl.	9/5/1861	F	Promoted to Sgt. on 2/3/62. Discharged for disability on 11/9/62 at Nashville, Tenn.
Desch, Charles	31	Private	9/15/1861	I	
Dickey, James A.	22	Private	9/25/1861	K	Transferred to Co. C on 11/5/1861. Died 3/3/1862 at Somerset, Ky.
Dickey, Jonah	20	Private	9/30.1861	K	Transferred to Co. C on 11/5/1861. Died 11/19/1861 at Paris, Ky.
Diefenbaugh, Daniel	18	Private	11/27/1863	D	Transferred to Co. C 18th OVI on 11/10/1864.
Dilge, George D.	18	Private	8/20/1861	C	Transferred to Co. D on 9/9/1861. No further record found.
Dillon, Samuel P.	18	Private	8/9/1861	B	Mustered out with company.
Dills, Philip	23	Private	9/15/1861	I	Transferred to Co. E on 9/24/1861. Discharged for disability on 12/16/1862 at Nashville, Tenn.
Dine, Robert	19	Private	9/15/1861	I	Transferred to Co. G, 16th Battalion Veteran Reserve Corps on 2/15/1864. Mustered out on 10/7/1864 at Harrisburg, PA.
Dine, William C.	34	1st. Lt.	8/26/1861	D	Resigned on 2/12/1863.
Dinkins, John W.	24	Sgt.	9/15/1861	I	Transferred to Co. E on 9/24/1861. Died on 10/10/1863 at Chattanooga, Tenn., of wounds received on 9/19/1863 at Chickamauga, Tenn.
Dinkins, Anderson A.	18	Private	9/1/1861	E	Discharged on 12/23/1862 at Gallatin, Tenn., to enlist in 4th US Artillery.
Disbro, John	18	Private	9/5/1861	F	Died on 2/23/1862 in hospital at Lebanon, Ky.
Dodd, William R.	27	Private	12/10/1861	C	Temporarily assigned to Co. K on 8/26/1864. Discharged on 12/23/1864 at Columbus, Ohio, on expiration of term of service.

Alphabetical Roster of the 35th Ohio Volunteer Infantry

Name	Age	Rank	Date	Co.	Comments
Doil, Patrick	17	Private	9/15/1861	I	Deserted 9/29/1861 at Cynthiana.
Dominick, Leopold	35	Private	8/15/1861	A	Discharged for disability 11/9/1863 at Chattanooga, Tenn
Dorse, John	22	Private	9/7/1861	G	Died on 11/12/1863 in hospital at Nashville, Tenn.
Doskey, Silas F.	27	Private	8/26/1861	C	Mustered out with company.
Dowler, Uriah	19	Private	9/1/1861	E	Discharged for disability on 4/3/1862 at Nashville, Tenn.
Downs, Benjamin F.	23	Private	8/15/1861	A	Mustered out with company.
Doyle, John	18	Private	8/26/1861	D	Transferred to Co. C on 9/9/1861. Captured on 11/25/1863 at Missionary Ridge, Tenn. Mustered out on 6/2/1865 in Columbus, Ohio, on expiration of term of service.
Drake, Franklin	22	Private	9/5/1861	F	Promoted to corporal on 3/1/1863. Mustered out with company.
Duke, Franklin	24	Music'n	9/5/1861	F	Died 3/30/62 in hospital at Nashville, Tenn.
Duke, Joseph	18	Private	9/5/1861	F	Transferred to Co. D on 11/1/1861. Wounded on 9/20/1863 at Chickamauga, Ga. Discharged for disability on 5/30/1864 at Camp Dennison, Ohio.
Durkill, Joseph	25	Private	9/7/1861	G	Mustered out with company.
Dye, William S.	18	Private	3/1/1862	D	Transferred to Co. C 18th OVI on 11/10/1864.
Eacott, William H.	23	2nd Lt.	8/9/1861	B	Promoted to 1st Lt. on 6/6/62. Resigned on 1/30/63.
Earhart, George T.	28	2nd Lt.	9/7/1861	G	Resigned 10/17/1862 on Surgeon's certificate of disability.
Earhart, George W.	18	Private	8/26/1861	H	Died on 2/3/1862 at Somerset, Ky.
Earhart, John	18	Private	8/26/1861	H	Discharged on 4/3/1863 to enlist in Mississippi Marine Brigade.
Earhart, John S.	37	Capt.	8/20/1861	C	Assigned as Brigade Topographical Engineer in 2/1863. Promoted to Diviison Engineer in Spring 1863. Died on 8/10/1863 at Winchester, Tenn.
Earhart, William	26	Private	8/26/1861	H	Promoted to corporal. Reduced on 6/1/1862. Deserted 6/10/1862.

Alphabetical Roster of the 35th Ohio Volunteer Infantry

Name	Age	Rank	Date	Co.	Comments
East, William M.	22	Private	9/15/1861	I	Transferred to Co. H in 9/1861. Discharged for disability on 7/20/1862 at Camp Dennison, Ohio.
Eberts, David	19	Private	9/1/1861	E	Transferred to Co. K on 9/8/1862. Transferred to Co. C 18th OVI on 10/20/1864. Veteran.
Eby, Martin I.	24	Private	8/26/1861	D	Transferred to Co. A on 9/1/1861. Captured 9/20/1863 at Chickamauga. No further record found.
Eby, William S.	23	Private	8/26/1861	H	Discharged for disability on 3/26/1863 at Camp Dennison, Ohio.
Edens, Henry	18	Private	8/26/1861	D	Mustered in as Henry Eaton. Mustered out with company.
Eliason, William	18	Private	9/15/1861	I	Transferred to Veteran Reserve Corps on 11/1/1863.
Elkins, Erastus L.	17	Private	8/26/1861	H	Died on 5/30/1862 in hospital near Corinth, Miss.
Elkins, Stephen H.	18	Private	9/15/1861	I	Wounded and captured on 9/20/1863 at Chickamauga, Ga. Paroled 10/29/1864. Discharged on 8/31/1865 at Camp Chase, Ohio.
Ell, Mathias	29	Private	9/5/1861	F	Mustered out with company.
Ellingham, James	22	Private	8/26/1861	C	Temporarily assigned to Co. K on 8/26/1864. Transferred to Co. C 18th OVI on 10/20/1864. Veteran.
Elliott, Harvey	24	Cpl.	10/12/1861	K	Promoted to Sgt. on 5/24/1862. Killed on 9/19/1863 at Chickamauga, Ga.
Ellmore, Samuel O.	24	Private	9/5/1861	F	Discharged for disability on 2/3/1863.
Embody, John	36	Private	8/26/1861	C	Discharged for disability on 10/6/1862 at Camp Dennison, Ohio.
Emmenger, Edward	21	Private	8/9/1861	B	Wounded and captured on 9/20/1863 at Chickamauga. Paroled and last heard from at Camp Chase, Ohio.
Emmons, John R.	20	Cpl.	8/26/1861	D	Transferred to Co. C on 9/9/1861. Discharged for disability on 2/26/1863 at Nashville, Tenn.
Emrick, Daniel P.		Private	10/10/1861	K	Transferred to Co. H on 11/5/1861. Mustered out on 9/23/1864 on expiration of term of service.

Alphabetical Roster of the 35th Ohio Volunteer Infantry

Name	Age	Rank	Date	Co.	Comments
Emrick, Henry S.	18	Private	8/26/1861	H	Mustered out on 1/28/1865 at Columbus, Ohio, on expiration of term of service.
Emrick, John	23	Private	8/26/1861	D	Transferred to Co. C on 9/9/1861. Wounded on 11/25/1863 at Missionary Ridge, Tenn. Temporarily assigned to Co. K on 8/26/1864. Transferred to Co. H, 19th Battalion Veteran Reserve Corps on 3/22/1864. Veteran.
Emrick, John	36	Private	10/15/1861	K	Mustered out with company.
Emrick, William H.	21	Private	8/22/1862	C	Temporarily assigned to Co. K on 8/26/1864. Transferred to Co. C 18th OVI on 10/20/1864.
Erisman, Abraham	27	Private	8/26/1861	H	Died on 4/14/1862 in hospital at Lebanon, Ky.
Evans, George	23	Private	8/9/1861	B	Transferred to Co. D on 9/2/1861. Promoted to corporal on 4/7/1863. Mustered out with company.
Evans, John H.	24	Private	8/26/1861	H	Discharged for disability on 8/11/1863 at Nashville, Tenn. Died a few weeks after reaching his home in Montgomery Co., Ohio.
Evans, John M.	18	Private	9/1/1861	E	Captured 9/20/63 at Chickamauga, Ga. Died 12/14/63 in rebel prison at Danville, Va.
Everhart, John	27	Private	9/5/1861	F	Mustered out with company.
Ewalt, Frederick	23	Private	9/1/1861	E	Transferred to Co. K on 9/8/1862. Transferred to Co. C 18th OVI on 10/20/1864. Veteran.
Falk, Charles		Private	9/5/1861	F	Discharged for disability on 10/18/1862 at Louisville, Ky.
Falkner, Daniel C.	21	Private	9/1/1861	E	Mustered out with company.
Fenton, John M.		Private	10/6/1861	K	Transferred to Co. I on 11/5/1861. Promoted to Sgt. on 11/4/1862. Captured on 9/20/1863 at Chickamauga, Ga. Died on 6/25/1864 in rebel prison at Andersonville, Ga.

Alphabetical Roster of the 35th Ohio Volunteer Infantry

Name	Age	Rank	Date	Co.	Comments
Ferguson, Daniel W.	27	Private	9/15/1861	I	Transferred to Co. B in 9/1861. Died 6/19/1864 in field hospital near Big Shanty, Ga., of wounds received on 6/19/1864 in battle of Pine Knob, Ga.
Fielding, Charles	17	Private	10/15/1861	K	Discharged at Camp Dennison, Ohio.
Finley, Webster	30	Private	9/5/1861	F	Died on 3/30/1862 in hospital at Nashville, Tenn.
Fisher, Charles O.	19	Private	9/15/1861	I	Transferred to Co. H in September 1861. Detailed as hospital steward in spring of 1863. Mustered out on 9/23/1864 at Chattanooga, Tenn., on expiration of term of service.
Fisher, Isaac L.	42	Sgt.	9/7/1861	E	Transferred to Co. I on 9/9/1861. Promoted to 1st Sgt. on 11/6/1862. Transferred to Veteran Reserve Corps on 8/25/1863.
Fisher, John T.	30	Private	9/5/1861	F	Discharged for disability on 12/2/1862 at Gallatin, Tenn.
Fisher, Robert	18	Private	9/12/1861	K	Died on 6/26/1862 at Camp Dennison, Ohio.
Fisk, Alonzo	24	Sgt.	8/9/1861	B	Promoted to 1st Sgt. on 5/12/1863. Mustered out with company.
Fitch, Julian R.	23	2nd Lt.	8/26/1861	D	Detailed to Signal Service on 1/29/1862. Promoted to 1st Lt. on 2/18/1863. Discharged on 9/8/1864. Accepted commission as 2nd Lt. in Regular Army Signal Corps.
Fitton, James	18	Private	8/26/1861	C	Promoted to corporal on 4/1/1864. Absent on detached duty. Mustered out on 8/26/1864 by order of War Department.
Flack, William R.	24	Private	9/7/1861	G	Wounded on 9/19/1863 at Chickamauga, Ga. Sent to hospital in Nashville, Tenn. Mustered out on 9/23/1864 by order of War Department.
Flanigan, John	43	Private	9/7/1861	G	Transferred to Co. D on 9/24/1861. Discharged for disability on 7/24/1862 at Cincinnati, Ohio.
Flemming, Walter C.	19	Private	9/1/1861	E	Killed 9/20/1863 at Chickamauga, Ga.

Alphabetical Roster of the 35th Ohio Volunteer Infantry

Name	Age	Rank	Date	Co.	Comments
Flemming, William T.	17	Private	9/15/181	I	Transferred to Co. E on 9/24/1861. Captured 9/17/1863 near Chickamauga, Ga. Paroled Absent sick in hospital at Annapolis, Md. Temporarily assigned to Co. K on 9/8/1864. Mustered out on 9/23/1864 at Chattanooga, Tenn
Focht, John B.	20	Private	9/7/1861	G	Discharged for disability on 11/14/1862 at South Tunnel, Tenn.
Foltz, William H.	18	Private	8/26/1861	H	Mustered out with company.
Foord, Richard S.	21	1st Sgt.	9/12/1861	K	Wounded and captured on 9/20/63 at Chickamauga, Ga. Paroled on 10/29/63. Promoted to 1st Lt. in Co. F on 3/19/64. Mustered out on 9/20/64 at Chattanooga, Tenn.
Ford, David		Private	10/1/1861	F	Transferred to Veteran Reserve Corps in 1864.
Ford, Henry	21	Private	9/5/1861	F	Discharged for disability on 11/30/1863 at Nashville, Tenn.
Ford, John	44	Private	9/5/1861	F	Discharged 12/1/1861 at Paris, Ky.
Fornshell, Lurten D.	16	Private	8/26/1861	D	On muster in roll. No further record found.
Fort, Gooldy	26	Private	9/7/1861	G	Transferred to Co. C in 10/1861. Temporarily assigned to Co. K on 8/26/1864. Mustered out 9/23/1864 at Chattanooga, Tenn., on expiration of term of service
Fort, Jacob S.	19	Private	10/30/1861	K	Transferred to Co. C on 11/5/1861. Temporarily assigned to Co. K on 8/26/1864. Mustered out 9/23/1864 at Chattanooga, Tenn., on expiration of term of service.
Foster, John	17	Private	9/7/1861	G	Promoted to corporal in 10/1861. Killed on 7/20/1864 near Atlanta, Ga.
Foutz, Jacob B.	24	Private	8/26/1861	C	Temporarily assigned to Co. K on 8/26/1864. Transferred to Co. C 18th OVI on 10/20/1864. Veteran.
Fox, Benjamin F.	19	Private	8/26/1861	C	Discharged for disability on 10/11/1862 at Camp Dennison, Ohio.
Frank, George W.	19	Private	8/9/1861	B	Died on 8/16/1862 at Germantown, Ohio.

Alphabetical Roster of the 35th Ohio Volunteer Infantry

Name	Age	Rank	Date	Co.	Comments
French, Marvin	48	Private	9/15/1861	I	Transferred to Co. H in 9/1861. Discharged for disability on 4/20/1862 at Nashville, Tenn.
Fridger, Daniel	21	Private	8/15/1861	A	
Fritch, Charles	21	Private	9/7/1861	G	Transferred to Co. D on 9/24/1861. Wounded and captured on 9/20/1863 ay Chickamauga, Ga. Paroled on 10/29/1863. Mustered out on 9/23/1864 at Chattanooga, Tenn., on expiration of term of service.
Fritch, Joseph	26	Private	9/7/1861	G	Transferred to Co. D on 9/24/1861. Mustered out on 9/23/1864 at Chattanooga, Tenn., on expiration of term of service.
Fritch, Matthew	23	Private	9/7/1861	G	Transferred to Co. D on 9/24/1861. Mustered out on 9/23/1864 at Chattanooga, Tenn., on expiration of term of service.
Fritz, Joseph	21	Private	8/20/1861	C	Transferred to Co. D on 9/9/1861. Discharged for disability on 9/10/1862 at Nashville, Tenn.
Frost, James R.	29	Sgt.	9/5/1861	F	Mustered out with company.
Gable, Adam	22	Private	8/20/1861	C	Transferred to Co. F on 9/9/1861. Wounded on 9/19/1863 at Chickamauga, Ga. Returned to company on 11/26/1863. Transferred to Co. K on 9/8/1864. Transferred to Co. C 18th OVI on 10/20/1864. Veteran.
Gans, David M.	24	Capt.	9/1/1861	E	Died on 11/25/1863 at Eaton, Ohio, while home on recruiting duty.
Gardner, Thomas N.	43	Private	8/26/1861	H	Died on 3/17/1862 in hospital at Nashville, Tenn.
Gardner, William H.	27	Private	9/1/1861	E	Transferred to Co. K on 9/8/1862. Transferred to Co. C 18th OVI on 10/20/1864. Veteran.
Garreth, James W.	18	Private	8/26/1861	D	Transferred to Co. C in 9/1861. Promoted to corporal on 4/1/1864. Temporarily assigned to Co. K on 8/26/1864. Mustered out on 9/8/64 at Chattanooga, Tenn., on expiration of term of service.

Alphabetical Roster of the 35th Ohio Volunteer Infantry

Name	Age	Rank	Date	Co.	Comments
Garrison, John M.	19	Private	8/9/1861	B	Transferred to Co. K on 8/26/1864. Transferred to Co. C 18th OVI on 10/20/1864. Veteran.
Garver, Jacob	21	Private	8/9/1861	B	Absent sick from 8/6/1864 in Hospital at Nashville, Tenn. Mustered out 8/26/1864 by order of War Department.
Garver, James K. P.	18	Private	9/7/1861	E	Transferred to Co. I on 9/9/1861. Died on 7/15/1862 at Hamilton, Ohio.
Garver, John	19	Private	9/15/1861	I	Mustered out with company.
Garver, Michael D.	44	Private	8/26/1861	H	Transferred to Co. I in 9/1861. Mustered out on 9/8/1864 at Chattanooga, Tenn., on expiration of term of service.
Gavin, Charles C.	21	Private	9/1/1861	E	Mustered out with company.
Gearhart, Frederick	31	Priavte	8/9/1861	B	Discharged for disability on 11/10/1862 at Nashville, Tenn.
Gebheart, Sidney	20	Private	9/5/1861	F	Discharged for disability on 7/16/1862.
Gibson, William, Jr.	20	Private	8/9/1861	B	
Gibson, William, Sr.	40	Private	8/9/1861	B	Transferred to Co. D in 9/1861. Discharged in 1/1863 at Camp Dennison, Ohio.
Giffin, John S.	22	Cpl.	8/26/1861	H	Transferred to Co. I in in 9/1861. Promoted to Sgt. on 8/9/1862. Died on 11/6/1862 at Hamilton, Ohio.
Gilbert, Isaac J.	21	Private	8/26/1861	D	Transferred to Co. B on in 9/1861. Killed 12/8/1861 in skirmish near Somerset, Ky.
Giller, John	26	Sgt.	8/26/1861	H	Promoted to 1st Sgt. on 10/24/1862. Mustered out with company.
Gillespie, Arthur	33	Private	2/4/1862	F	Transferred to Co. C 18th OVI on 11/10/1864.
Gillespie, Joseph C.	19	Sgt.	8/26/1861	D	Transferred to Co. G on 9/24/61. Promoted to Sgt. Reduced to ranks on 4/30/1862. Died on 10/3/1863 in hospital at Chattanooga, Tenn., of wounds received on 9/19/6183 at Chattanooga, Tenn.

Alphabetical Roster of the 35th Ohio Volunteer Infantry

Name	Age	Rank	Date	Co.	Comments
Gillespie, Josiah	25	Private	8/15/1861	A	Absent sick from 6/30/1864 in hospital at Nashville, Tenn. Mustered out at Columbus, Ohio, on 10/1/1864 on expiration of term of service.
Gillespie, Thomas	23	Private	8/15/1861	A	Promoted to corporal on 7/1/1862. Mustered out with company.
Gilmore, George W.	23	Cpl.	9/12/1861	K	Reduced from corporal on 11/20/1862 at his own request. Killed on 9/19/1863 at Chickamauga, Ga.
Glady, Henry	23	Cpl.	8/15/1861	A	Reduced to Private. Mustered out with company.
Goodyear, John R (Goodier)	23	Private	8/20/1861	C	Transferred to Co. D on 9/9/1861. Mustered out with company.
Gordon, Perkins A.	39	Surg'n	9/7/1861	Staff	Resigned 11/3/1863 due to affects of sunstroke suffered during the Tullahoma campaign.
Gore, William	34	Private	8/15/1861	A	Discharged for disability 9/16/1862 at Columbus, Ohio
Gorman, James H.	18	Private	10/15/1861	K	Killed on 9/19/1863 at Chickamauga, Ga.
Gorman, John C.	21	Private	10/15/1861	K	Discharged for disability on 6/11/1862 at Louisville, Ky.
Gorman, William	43	Private	8/20/1861	C	Transferred to Co. D on 9/9/1861. Discharged for disability on 8/8/1863.
Gover, George W.	29	Private	9/7/1861	G	Transferred to Veteran Reserve Corps. Mustered out on 11/15/1864 at Columbus, Ohio, on expiration of term of service.
Graham, William H.	44	Private	8/26/1861	C	Detailed to the Ambulance Corps. Mustered out with company.
Gratz, Emanuel	20	Private	8/25/1862	I	Died on 10/19/1863 at Stevenson, Ala., of wounds received on 9/19/1863 at Chickamauga, Ga.
Gratz, Morris	20	Sgt.	9/5/1861	F	Reduced to ranks on 11/15/1862. Wounded 9/19/1863 at Chickamauga, Ga. Mustered out with company.
Greenwood, William	18	Private	8/26/1861	D	Absent sick from 6/20/1864 at Marietta, Ga. Mustered out 8/8/1864 by order of the War Department

Alphabetical Roster of the 35th Ohio Volunteer Infantry

Name	Age	Rank	Date	Co.	Comments
Gregg, Perry	21	Sgt.	8/15/1861	A	Promoted to 1st Lt. in Mississippi Marine Brigade.
Grenham, Nicholas	26	Private	9/12/1861	K	Died on 1/26/1864 in hospital at Nashville, Tenn.
Grey, Lewis	44	Private	8/26/1861	D	
Griffin, Andrew J.	18	Private	9/5/1861	F	Promoted to corporal on 7/19/1863. Mustered out with company.
Grimes, Daniel A.		Private	2/26/1864	H	Transferred to Co. C 18th OVI on 11/10/1864.
Grosch, Samuel	18	Private	9/7/1861	G	Mustered out with company.
Grunden, Thomas A.	25	Private	9/12/1861	K	Discharged for disability on 2/28/1864.
Gugel, Christian	20	Private	9/7/1861	G	Mustered out with company.
Guillaum, Joseph P.	29	Private	10/18/1861	K	Captured on 9/20/1863 at Chickamauga, Ga. Died on 6/27/1864 in rebel prison at Andersonville, Ga.
Gunckel, James	18	Private	8/26/1861	H	Promoted to corporal on 12/5/1863. Mustered out with company.
Gunckel, Michael	42	Capt.	8/26/1861	H	Resigned on 10/24/1862 on surgeons certificate of disability. Afterward appointed Paymaster, U.S.A
Gunckel, Phillip	36	Private	1/24/1864	H	Transferred to Co. C 18th OVI on 11/10/1864. Discharged on 5/29/1865 at Camp Dennison, Ohio.
Hafer, John	23	Private	8/15/1861	A	Discharged for disability at Hamilton, Ohio
Hagerman, Henry	30	Wagnr	9/5/1861	F	Discharged on 4/20/1862 at Pittsburgh Landing, Tenn
Hailmick, Jackson		Private	10/6/1861	I	Died on 2/8/1862 at Somerset, Ky.
Haines, Samuel	20	Private	9/5/1861	F	Wounded 9/19/1863 at Chickamauga, Ga. In hospital at Chattanooga, Tenn. Transferred to Co. G 7th Veteran Reserve Corps. Mustered out on 9/9/1864 at Washington, DC.
Halderman, Joseph	18	Private	3/17/1862	D	Transferred to Co. C 18th OVI on 11/10/1864 while absent sick. Mustered out 3/17/1865 at Cincinnati, Ohio, as of Co. D 35 OVI.
Hale, Miles M.	27	Cpl.	10/12/1861	K	Promoted to Sgt. on 1/10/1862. Deserted 8/31/1863.

Alphabetical Roster of the 35th Ohio Volunteer Infantry

Name	Age	Rank	Date	Co.	Comments
Hall, Andrew J.	32	Private	9/7/1861	G	Transferred to Co. C in 10/1861. Temporarily assigned to Co. K on 8/26/1864. Mustered out 9/23/1864 at Chattanooga, Tenn., on expiration of term of service.
Hall, Charles	40	Private	8/26/1861	G	Absent sick Discharged for disability on 12/9/1864.
Hall, Cyrus	22	Private	2/28/1861	D	Transferred Co. C 18th OVI on 11/10/1864.
Hall, David	43	Private	1/21/1864	H	Discharged on 5/27/1865 at Cincinnati, Ohio.
Haller, John	25	Private	8/20/1861	C	Promoted to corporal. Promoted to Sgt. Died 11/23/1863 in hospital at Nashville, Tenn.
Halliman, William	39	Private	8/26/1861	C	Transferred to Co. B in 9/1861. Killed 9/19/1863 at Chickamauga.
Halloway, Thomas	20	Private	9/5/1861	F	Captured 12/8/1861 at Somerset, Ky. In rebel prison at Salisbury, N.C., for eight months. Paroled on 5/15/1863. Mustered out with company.
Hamilton, Charles	19	Sgt.	8/26/1861	H	Reduced to ranks on 10/12/1862. Mustered out with company.
Hamilton, Francis	21	Private	10/6/1862	F	Transferred to Co. C 18th OVI on 11/10/1864.
Hamilton, Joseph	20	Private	9/5/1861	F	Discharged on 5/16/1862 at Pittsburgh Landing, Tenn.
Hanilton, William	29	Cpl.	9/5/1861	F	Promoted to Sgt. on 11/1/1862. Mustered out with company.
Harlan, Sock	20	Cpl.	9/5/1861	F	Absent sick from 9/18/1863 in hospital at Chattanooga, Tenn. Transferred to Co. K, 15th Battalion Veteran Reserve Corps. Mustered out 9/8/1864 at Chicago, Ill.
Harlan, Thomas M.	27	2nd Lt.	9/5/1861	F	Promoted to 1st Lt. on 1/1/1863. Killed on 9/20/1863 at Chickamauga, Ga.
Harper, William	55	Private	11/13/1861	E	Discharged for disability on 6/16/1863 at Nashville, Tenn.
Harriman, Thomas F.	18	Private	9/1/1861	E	Mustered out with company.
Harris, David	23	Private	9/7/1861	G	Transferred to Co. D on 9/24/1861. Discharged for disability on 10/29/1862 at Nashville, Tenn.

Alphabetical Roster of the 35th Ohio Volunteer Infantry

Name	Age	Rank	Date	Co.	Comments
Harris, James E.	20	Sgt.	8/20/1861	C	Promoted to 1st Sgt. Promoted to 1st Lt. and Adjutant on 3/19/1864. Mustered out with regiment 9/27/1864.
Harris, John	30	Private	9/5/1861	F	Wounded and captured on 9/20/1863 at Chickamauga, Ga. Paroled 10/29/1863. Mustered out with company.
Harris, John W.	18	Private	8/9/1861	B	Mustered out with company.
Harris, Joseph	36	Sgt.	9/5/1861	F	Wounded at 9/19/1863 at Chickamauga, Ga. Transferred to Co. K on 9/8/1864. Transferred to Co. C 18th OVI on 10/20/1864. Veteran.
Hart, Samuel	43	Hs Std	9/5/1861	Staff	Discharged for disability on 9/10/1861
Hart, Samuel S.		Private	9/5/1861	F	Discharged on 6/26/1862 at Corinth, Miss.
Hartman, James	39	Private	9/5/1861	F	Mustered out with company.
Hathaway, Andrew	29	Private	8/15/1861	A	Mustered out with company.
Hathaway, Patrick C.	20	Private	8/5/1862	A	Transferred to Co. K on 8/26/1864. Transferred to Co. C 18th OVI on 10/20/1864.
Haven, Frank	25	Private	8/26/1861	H	Mustered out with company.
Havens, John B.	19	Private	8/26/1861	D	Transferred to Co. G on 9/24/1861.
Hawkins, John O.	20	Private	8/20/1861	C	Transferred to Co. F on 9/9/1861. Died on 12/23/1863 in hospital at Nashville, Tenn.
Hellrigle, Thomas I.	39	Bd Ldr	9/5/1861	Band	Discharged on 9/10/1862 by order of War Department at Nashville.
Helmer, William H.	22	Private	8/26/1861	D	Transferred to Co. G on 9/24/1861. Promoted to corporal in 10/1861. Mustered out with company.
Henderson, William C.	26	Private	8/26/1861	H	Mustered out with company.
Henning, Frederick	45	Private	8/26/1861	H	On muster-in roll, but no further record found.
Henning, Wesley	19	Private	8/26/1861	H	Promoted to corporal on 10/12/1862. Killed on 9/20/1863 at Chickamauga, Ga.
Henninger, Joseph	32	1st Sgt	8/9/1861	B	Promoted to 1st Lt. on 1/30/1863. Promoted to captain on 2/18/1863. Mustered out with company.

Alphabetical Roster of the 35th Ohio Volunteer Infantry

Name	Age	Rank	Date	Co.	Comments
Henry, Isaac R.	55	Private	10/20/1861	K	Transferred to Co. C on 11/5/1861. Died 3/16/1862 at Nashville, Tenn.
Henry, Mathias	24	Private	8/20/1861	C	Transferred to Co. F on 9/9/1861. Captured 12/16/1861 at Somerset, Ky. In rebel prison at Salisbury, N.C., for eight months. Returned to regiment on 5/15/1863. Wounded 9/19/1863 at Chickamauga, Ga.
Herman, Lewis D.	23	Cpl.	9/15/1861	I	Promoted to Sgt. Mustered out with company.
Herman, Richard	26	Private	9/15/1861	I	Wounded on 9/19/1863 at Chickamauga, Ga. Discharged on 12/31/1863 at Camp Dennison, Ohio.
Hersch, Henry	30	Private	8/26/1861	D	Transferred to Co. I in 9/1861. Mustered out on 9/8/1864 on expiration of term of service.
Hetzler, Andrew J.	21	Private	8/26/1861	H	Promoted to corporal on 1/30/1864. Mustered out with company.
Higgins, James	25	Private	8/9/1861	B	Transferred to Co. D on 9/16/1861. Captured 9/20/1863 at Chickamauga. Died 8/19/1864 in rebel prison at Andersonville, Ga.
Hill, Thaddeus	23	Music'n	12/17/1861	E	Temporarily assigned to Co. K on 9/8/1864. Mustered out 10/26/1864 at Chattanooga Tenn., on expiration of term of service.
Hillman, Frank W.	21	Private	9/15/1861	I	Died on 10/11/1863 at Chattanooga, Tenn., of wounds received on 9/20/1863 at Chickamauga, Ga.
Hime, Emmanuel E.	17	Private	10/8/1861	K	Transferred to Co. G on 11/5/1961. Discharged by order of War Department.
Hime, George	19	Private	9/7/1861	G	Transferred to Co. C in 10/1861. Died 4/23/1862 near Pittsburgh Landing, Tenn.
Hippard, Samuel M.	27	Sgt.	8/20/1861	C	Promoted to 1st Sgt. on 3/31/1864. Mustered out with company.
Hoblet, Joshua C.	unk	Chapl'n	1/13/1862	Staff	Resigned 2/19/1863 to accept civilian hospital position in Nashville.

Alphabetical Roster of the 35th Ohio Volunteer Infantry

Name	Age	Rank	Date	Co.	Comments
Hoffman, Abiah Z.	19	Private	9/15/1861	I	Transferred to Co. H in 9/1861. Promoted to corporal on 4/1/1863. Mustered out on 9/23/1864 on expiration of term of service.
Hoffman, James P.	22	Private	8/15/1861	A	Mustered out with company.
Hoffman, James S.	25	Private	10/12/1861	K	
Hoglan, George	22	Private	8/26/1861	D	Wounded on 9/20/1863 at Chickamauga, Ga. Absent on furlough. Mustered out 9/8/1864 by order of War Department.
Holbrook, Heber R.	16	Private	8/26/1861	D	Transferred to Co. A in 9/1861. Transferred to Signal Corps.
Holmes, John		Private	9/25/1861	I	Discharged for disability on 1/16/1863 at Nashville, Tenn
Holsaple, Moses	27	Private	8/26/1861	C	Promoted to corporal on 8/9/1863. Wounded on 9/20/1863 at Chickamauga. Mustered out with company.
Holt, Robert	18	Private	9/5/1861	F	Mustered out with company.
Hopkins, William F.	18	Private	8/15/1861	A	Absent sick from 7/26/1864 in hospital at Nashville, Tenn. Mustered out 12/1/1864 at Columbus, Ohio, on expiration of term of service.
Houser, Jacob	57	Private	9/15/1861	I	Absent without leave on 4/20/1862. No record of muster-out found.
Houser, Jacob W.	19	Private	8/9/1861	B	Promoted to corporal on 7/16/1863. Mustered out with company.
Houser, John B.	25	Private	8/9/1861	B	Discharged 10/14/1861 at Cynthiana, Ky.
Houser, Samuel L.	26	Private	8/9/1861	B	Promoted to corporal on 10/16/1861. Promoted to Sgt. on 10/16/1862. Promoted to 2nd Lt. on 1/20/1863. Promoted to 1st Lt. on 2/13/1863. Mustered out with company.
Howard, Charles R.	17	Cpl.	9/12/1861	K	Discharged for disability on 5/18/1862.
Howell, Harry	23	Private	9/7/1861	G	Absent sick from 7/1/1864 in hospital at Nashville, Tenn. Mustered out on 9/28/1864 at Columbus, Ohio, on expiration of term of service.
Howland, Albert	18	Private	9/5/1861	F	Died on 11/5/1863 in hospital at Chattanooga, Tenn.

Alphabetical Roster of the 35th Ohio Volunteer Infantry

Name	Age	Rank	Date	Co.	Comments
Howland, James	21	Private	9/5/1861	F	Mustered out with company.
Hoyt, Daniel C.	35	Private	2/17/1862	F	Transferred to Co. C 18th OVI on 11/10/1864. Mustered out on 5/22/1865 at Columbus, Ohio, as of Co. F 35th OVI.
Huber, David	20	Private	8/26/1861	H	Promoted to corporal on 7/1/1862. Absent sick from 10/28/1863 in hospital at Chattanooga, Tenn. Mustered out 9/8/1864 by order of War Department.
Huber, John H.	21	Private	9/7/1861	G	Promoted to corporal in 10/1861. Promoted to Sgt. on 11/25/1863. Mustered out with company.
Hudgel, Henry	21	Private	8/26/1861	D	Transferred to Co. G on 9/24/1861. Mustered out on 9/8/1864 at Chattanooga, Tenn., on expiration of term of service.
Hughes, William	19	Private	9/5/1861	F	Transferred to Co. D on 11/1/1861.
Hugunin, James A.	27	Sgt.	8/20/1861	C	Reduced to ranks. Died 2/13/1863 at Winchester, Ohio.
Hull, John	23	Cpl.	8/26/1861	H	Transferred to Co. I in September 1861. Died 3/20/1862 at Nashville, Tenn.
Hulse, Samuel	43	Private	8/15/1861	A	Discharged 10/10/1861 at Cynthiana, Ky.
Hunsaker, Charles	19	Private	8/26/1861	D	Transferred to Co. G on 9/24/1861. Promoted to Sgt. on 9/26/1861. Mustered out on 9/8/1864 on expiration of term of service.
Hunter, George W.		Private	10/21/1862	G	Transferred to Co. K on 9/23/1864. Transferred to Co. C 18th OVI on 10/20/1864.
Hutchings, Allen	18	Private	8/26/1861	H	Died on 2/4/1862 at Somerset, Ky.
Hutchings, Dayton P.	24	Private	9/1/1861	I	Transferred to Co. H in September 1861. Promoted to corporal on 11/9/1861. Reduced to ranks on 7/1/1862. Died on 1/27/1863 in hospital at Nashville, Tenn.
Hutchings, Horatio S.	23	Private	8/26/1861	H	Discharged for disability on 2/3/1864 at Chattanooga, Tenn.
Hutchinson, Tomas H.	25	Private	8/20/1861	C	Mustered out with company.
Hyde, Francis H.	19	Private	9/1/1861	E	Died on 8/18/1863 at Cowan, Tenn.

Alphabetical Roster of the 35th Ohio Volunteer Infantry

Name	Age	Rank	Date	Co.	Comments
Hyde, Hiram B.	18	Private	9/1/1861	E	Captured 9/17/1863 near Chickamauga. Died at Belle Isle, Va.
Hydee, George	19	Private	9/15/1861	A	Mustered out with company.
Inman, Job	19	Private	8/20/1861	C	On muster roll as John Inman. Discharged on writ of habeas corpus in September 1861.
Ince, Albert	21	Wagnr	9/1/1861	E	
Ingram, John	20	Private	8/26/1861	H	Mustered out with company.
Jackson, David A.	18	Private	9/1/1861	E	Captured on 9/20/1863 at Chickamauga. Mustered out 3/17/1865 at Columbus, Ohio, on expiration of term of service.
Jackson, George B.	23	Private	9/15/1861	I	Transferred to Co. B on 9/24/1861. Temporarily assigned to Co. K on 8/26/1864. Mustered out on 9/23/1864 at Chattanooga upon expiration of tern of service.
Jackson, Jacob (Chip)	19	Music'n	8/9/1861	B	Wounded 6/18/1864 in skirmishing along Mud Creek near Marietta, Ga. Mustered out with company.
Jackson, James	22	Sgt.	9/5/1861	F	Promoted to 1st Sgt. on 6/19/1863. Wounded on 9/20/1863 at Chickamauga, Ga. Killed on 6/18/1864 at Pine Ridge near Kennesaw Mountain, Ga.
Jackson, James A.	21	Private	8/9/1861	B	Wounded 6/18/1864 at Pine Knob, Ga. In hospital on 7/24/1864 at Louisville, Ky. Mustered out 8/26/1864 by order of War Department.
Jackson, Stiles H.	20	Private	8/26/1861	H	Mustered out with company.
Jacoby, Benjamin F.	19	Private	9/5/1861	F	Died 1/2/1863 in hospital at Gallatin, Tenn.
Jacquemin, John F.	32	Private	10/8/1861	K	Discharged for disability on 8/15/1862 at Columbus, Ohio.
Jamison, Levi F.	22	Private	9/5/1861	F	Discharged for disability on 10/4/1862 at Nashville, Tenn.
Jeffries, Thomas A.	20	Private	8/15/1861	A	Mustered out with company.
Jenkins, George T.		Sgt.	9/28/1861	K	Transferred to Co. I on 11/5/1861. Reduced to the ranks on 11/6/1862 after deserting from Bowling Green, Ky.
Jessup, Jerome B.	22	Private	9/7/1861	G	Died on 3/15/1862 at Bardstown, Ky.

Alphabetical Roster of the 35th Ohio Volunteer Infantry

Name	Age	Rank	Date	Co.	Comments
Johnson, Clayton C.	23	Music'n	8/26/1861	E	Temporarily assigned to Co. K on 9/8/1864. Transferred to Co. C 18th OVI on 10/20/1864. Veteran.
Johnson, William	20	Private	9/5/1861	F	Transferred to Veteran Reserve Corps in 1863 at Camp Dennison, Ohio.
Johnston, Francis E.	21	Private	3/10/1862	E	Discharged for disability on 11/5/1863 at Columbus, Ohio.
Jones, Newton	37	Private	8/20/1861	C	Transferred to Co. K on 8/26/1864. To Co. C 18th OVI on 10/11/1864. Veteran.
Jones, William D.	21	Private	9/1/1861	E	Mustered out with company.
Jordan. Douglas	43	Private	8/26/1861	H	Discharged for disability on 6/5/1862 at Louisville, Ky.
Jospeh, James B.	38	Private	8/9/8161	B	On muster roll. No further record found.
Kapp, John A.	18	Private	9/15/1861	I	Wounded on 9/19/1863 at Chickamauga, Ga. Mustered out with company.
Karshner, Loammi	21	Private	9/15/1861	I	Discharged for disability on 10/16/1862 at Cincinnati, Ohio.
Kay, Joseph	39	Private	9/7/1861	G	Died on 8/9/1863 at Winchester, Tenn.
Keck, Albert C.	18	Private	8/9/8161	B	Discharged for disability on 8/6/1862 at Columbus, Ohio.
Keen, Ayres	21	Private	8/26/1861	H	Transferred to Co. I in September 1861. Discharged for disability on 11/19/62 at Bowling Green, Ky.
Keen, James	20	Private	9/15/1861	I	Transferred to Veteran Reserve Corps on 1/15/1864.
Keever, George W.	21	Cpl.	8/15/1861	A	Promoted to 1st Sgt. Killed 9/20/1863 at Chickamauga
Keil, Benjamin F.	21	Cpl.	8/20/1861	C	Promoted to Sgt. on 3/21/1863, Captured 9/19/1863 at Chickamauga. No further record found.
Keil, Frederick W.	28	2nd Lt.	8/20/1861	C	Promoted to captain on 6/14/1864 but not mustered. Mustered out with company.
Keiser, Levi	20	Private	8/20/1861	C	Detailed as hospital orderly. Mustered out with company.
Keller, Adam	21	Private	8/9/8161	B	Mustered out with company.

Alphabetical Roster of the 35th Ohio Volunteer Infantry

Name	Age	Rank	Date	Co.	Comments
Kelly, Jeremiah	21	Private	10/15/1861	K	Promoted to corporal on 11/15/1862. Reduced to ranks on 4/28/1863. Mustered out with company.
Kelly, John H.	19	Private	8/26/1861	H	Mustered out with company.
Kelly, Martin J.	20	Private	8/20/1861	C	Transferred to Co. D on 9/9/1861. Drowned 5/1862 at Pittsburgh Landing, Tenn.
Kemp, Benjamin F.	19	Sgt.	9/1/1861	E	Mustered out with company.
Kemp, Frank M.	20	Private	9/15/1861	H	Transferred from Co. I in September 1861. Mustered out on 9/23/1864 at Chattanooga, Tenn., on expiration of term of service.
Kemp, John W.	25	Private	9/5/1861	F	Promoted to corporal on 2/3/1862. Absent sick from 6/4/1863 in hospital in Nashville, Tenn. Transferred to Company 154, 2nd Battalion Veteran Reserve Corps. Mustered out 9/4/1864 at Nashville, Tenn.
Kenler, Matthias	44	Private	8/26/1861	D	Discharged 9/23/1864 at Chattanooga, Tenn., on expiration of term of service.
Kettle, Tunis W.	32	Private	9/1/1861	E	Discharged for disability on 10/1/1861 at Cynthiana, Ky.
Keys, William S.	41	Private	9/5/1861	F	Captured at Somerset, Ky., 12/8/1861. In prison at Salisbury, N.C. Paroled May 1863. Rejoined regiment in August 1863. Died 1/4/1864 in hospital at Chattanooga, Tenn.
Killian, Frederick	19	Private	9/15/1861	I	Mustered out with company.
Kimball, William	31	Private	9/15/1861	I	Discharged for disability on 10/15/1862 at Cincinnati, Ohio.
Kimble, George W.	20	Cpl.	8/9/1861	B	Promoted to Sgt. on 2/24/1863. Mustered out with company.
Kimble, William H.H.	44	Sgt.	9/15/1861	I	Reduced to the ranks on 11/4/1862. Died on 2/20/1864 at Hamilton, Ohio.
King, James P.	20	Private	9/1/1861	E	Wounded on 9/20/1863 at Chickamauga, Ga., and on 5/14/1864 at Resaca, Ga. Absent in hospital at Nashville, Tenn. Mustered out on 9/8/1864 by order of War Department.

Alphabetical Roster of the 35th Ohio Volunteer Infantry

Name	Age	Rank	Date	Co.	Comments
Kinsey, Joseph	18	Private	8/9/1861	B	Died on 3/12/1864 in hospital at Louisville, Ky.
Kinsey, Levi	34	Private	8/28/1861	K	Transferred to Co. B on 11/5/1861. Transferred to Veteran Reserve Corps on 2/15/1864.
Kissinger, Charles M.	23	Private	9/7/1861	G	Absent sick from 10/30/1863 in hospital at Nashville, Tenn. Mustered out on 8/23/1864 by order of War Department.
Kitchen, George G.	20	Private	8/15/1861	A	Mustered out with company.
Kite, James F.	28	Private	8/9/1861	B	Died on 4/13/1864 in hospital at Camp Dennison, Ohio.
Kline, William H.	21	Private	8/26/1861	H	Mustered out with company.
Knox, Enoch	44	Wagnr	9/15/1861	I	Regimental wagon master. Discharged for disability on 3/7/1864 at Ringgold, Ga.
Knox, Enoch, Jr.	23	Private	8/9/1861	B	Mustered out with company.
Koble, David P.	21	Private	8/15/1861	A	Mustered out with company.
Kobler, Christian	32	Private	8/26/1861	H	
Koortz, John	24	Private	9/15/1861	I	Died at Nashville, Tenn.
Korner, John G.	19	Private	9/5/1861	F	Mustered out with company.
Korpal, Anthony	24	Private	9/26/1861	K	Mustered out with company.
Krebs, Charles	24	Private	9/7/1861	G	Discharged for disability on 10/17/1862 at Louisville, Ky.
Kretzler, Emmanuel	18	Private	8/26/1861	H	Died on 2/14/1862 at Somerset, Ky.
Kumler, Abraham N.	18	Private	8/26/1861	D	Transferred to Co. C in October 1861. Temporarily assigned to Co. K on 8/26/1864. Mustered out 9/8/1864 at Chattanooga, Tenn., on expiration of term of service.
Kumler, Franklin W.	22	Private	8/26/1861	G	Transferred to Co. C in October 1861. Temporarily assigned to Co. K on 8/26/1864. Mustered out 9/23/1864 at Chattanooga, Tenn., on expiration of term of service.
Kumler, Simon	19	Private	8/20/1861	C	Killed on 11/25/1863 at Missionary Ridge, Tenn.

Alphabetical Roster of the 35th Ohio Volunteer Infantry

Name	Age	Rank	Date	Co.	Comments
Kurtz, Daniel F.	24	Private	9/15/1861	I	Transferred to Co. E on 9/24/1861. Wounded on 9/19/1863 at Chickamauga, Ga. Temporarily assigned to Co. K on 9/8/1864. Mustered out on 9/23/1864 on expiration of term of service.
Kurtz, Henry C.	19	Private	8/26/1861	H	Mustered out with company.
Lackey, Ira	27	Private	8/15/1861	A	Promoted to corporal on 5/1/1863. Mustered out with company.
Ladd, John A.	28	Cpl.	8/26/1861	H	Promoted to Sgt. on 2/9/1863. Mustered out with company.
Lake, Lorenze	26	Private	8/26/1861	H	Transferred to Co. B on 9/24/1861. Temporarily assigned to Co. K on 8/26/1864. Mustered out on 9/23/1864 at Chattanooga, Tenn., on expiration of term of service.
Lambright, Lewis	38	1st Lt.	9/12/1861	K	Wounded on 11/25/1863 at Missionary Ridge, Ga. Mustered out with company.
Lander, Orange	22	Private	8/26/1861	D	Transferred to Co. G on 9/24/1861. Mustered out on 9/8/1864 on expiration of term of service.
Lander, Phillip	20	Cpl.	8/9/1861	B	Promoted to Sgt. on 5/1/1862. Reduced to ranks on 10/16/1862 at his own request. Mustered out with company.
Landis, Abraham H.	unk	Ast Srg	11/16/1862	Staff	Captured 9/20/1863 at Chickmauga, Ga. Sent to Libby Prison in Richmond, Va. Paroled in November 1863. Wounded near Kennesaw Mountain, Ga. in June 1864. Leg broken by cannonball. Mustered out with regiment on 9/27/1864.
Lane, Albert	18	Private	9/7/1861	G	Mustered out with company.
Larrison, Joseph	30	Private	9/1/1863	E	Promoted to corporal on 1/1/1862. Reduced to ranks. Transferred to Co. K on 9/8/1864. Transferred to Co. C 18th OVI on 10/20/1864. Veteran.
Law, William C.	18	Private	8/26/1861	D	Transferred to Co. C in September 1861. Temporarily assigned to Co. K on 8/26/1864. Mustered out 9/8/1864 at Chattanooga, Tenn., on expiration of term of service.

Alphabetical Roster of the 35th Ohio Volunteer Infantry

Name	Age	Rank	Date	Co.	Comments
Lawder, James M.	17	Private	9/7/1861	G	Transferred to Signal Service at Georgetown, D.C.
Lawson, Alexander	37	Private	8/9/1861	B	Mustered out with company.
Leach, Bazil R.	24	Private	9/5/1861	F	Died 2/18/1864 in hospital at Louisville, Ky.
Leach, John	36	Private	8/15/1861	A	Detailed as hospital steward in spring of 1863. Captured 9/20/1863 at Chickamauga. No further record found.
Leary, Dennis	25	Private	2/28/1862	D	Promoted to corporal. Transferred to Co. C 18th OVI while on detached duty. Mustered out as of 35th OVI on 3/18/1865 at Fayetteville, N.C.
Ledman, Francis M.	17	Music'n	9/16/1861	K	Mustered out with company.
Ledwell, James	18	Private	8/20/1861	C	Transferred to Co. F on 9/9/1861. Died on 3/29/1862 in hospital at Lebanon, Ky.
Lefever, Elias	22	Private	8/15/1861	A	Mustered out with company.
Leggett, Thompson	31	Private	9/7/1861	E	Transferred to Co. I on 9/9/1861. Killed on 9/20/1863 at Chickamauga, Ga.
Leiber, Jacob	21	Sgt.	9/12/1861	K	Reduced from Sgt. on 5/28/1862 at his own request. Discharged for disability on 6/18/1862 at Corinth, Miss.
Leisner, Bernard	20	Private	8/9/1861	B	Wounded and captured on 9/19/1863 at Chickamauga. Paroled on 1/29/1863 and sent to hospital at Jeffersonville, IN. Mustered out on 9/20/1864 at Columbus, Ohio, on expiration of term of service.
Leitch, George W.	20	Cm Sgt	8/9/1861	Staff	Discharged for disability on 6/30/1862
Lewis, Andrew J.	28	1st Lt.	9/15/1861	I	Promoted to captain on 2/17/1862. Wounded on 9/19/1863 at Chickamauga, Ga. Resigned on 1/2/1864.
Lewis, George	19	Private	8/9/1861	B	Promoted to corporal. Transferred to Veteran Reserve Corps on 3/15/1864.
L'Hommedieu, Samuel	26	Capt.	9/7/1861	G	Wounded on 6/29/1863 at Hoover's Gap, Tenn. On detached duty from 4/1/1864 as Brigade Inspector. Mustered out with company.

Alphabetical Roster of the 35th Ohio Volunteer Infantry

Name	Age	Rank	Date	Co.	Comments
Lidy, John G.	33	Private	8/26/1861	C	Transferred to Co. K on 8/26/1864. Transferred to Co. C 18th OVI on 10/24/1864. Veteran
Lighter, Franklin A.	16	Private	8/26/1861	C	Regimental postmaster. Mustered out with company.
Lightfoot, William	45	Private	9/12/1861	K	Discharged for disability on 11/30/1862 at Louisville, Ky.
Limber, John	22	Sgt.	8/15/1861	A	Died 9/15/1862 in hospital in Nashville, Tenn., after being discharged for disability on 8/9/1862.
Lindner, Joseph	39	Private	8/15/1861	A	Discharged on 12/15/1862 at Cincinnati, Ohio, by order of War Department
Littlejohn, Thomas F.	19	Private	8/9/1861	B	Captured 9/20/1863 at Chickamauga. Mustered out on 11/1/1864 at Columbus, Ohio, on expiration of term of service.
Livingood, Calvin	25	Private	9/7/1861	G	Promoted to corporal in 10/1861. Captured 9/19/1863 at Chickamauga, Ga. Died on 12/16/1864 in rebel prison at Andersonville, Ga.
Livingood, Peter	17	Music'n	9/7/1861	G	Mustered out with company.
Livingston, Robert J.	21	Private	9/2/1861	D	Transferred to Co. B on 9/9/1861. Promoted to corporal on 10/2/1861. Promoted to Sgt. on 2/24/1863. Temporarily assigned to Co. K on 8/26/1864. Mustered out 9/8/1864 at Chattanooga, Tenn., on expiration of term of service.
Llewellyn, William M.	27	Cpl.	9/15/1861	I	Deserted 11/4/1862 at Bowling Green, Ky.
Logue, Sharon B.	24	Private	9/5/1861	F	Wounded and captured on 9/19/1863 at Chickamauga, Ga. Died in rebel prison at Andersonville, Ga.
Lohmaear, August	21	Wagnr	9/24/1861	K	Captured on 9/20/1863 at Chickamauga, Ga. Died on 12/2/1864 in rebel prison at Andersonville, Ga.
Long, Charles L. H.	33	Lt. Col.	7/27/1861	Staff	Resigned on 7/13/1863 for disability.
Long, George W.	18	Private	8/20/1861	C	Transferred to Co. D in September 1861. Mustered out with company.
Long, William B.	23	Cpl.	8/20/1861	C	Transferred to Co. D on 9/9/1861. Mustered out with company.

Alphabetical Roster of the 35th Ohio Volunteer Infantry

Name	Age	Rank	Date	Co.	Comments
Loop, William M. C.	22	Private	8/9/1861	B	Discharged for disability on 4/5/1863 at Nashville, Tenn.
Lorentz, Michael		Private	8/26/1861	H	Discharged for disability on 10/23/1861 at Camp Frazier near Cynthiana, Ky.
Lucas, Andrew J.	29	Private	8/15/1861	A	Mustered out with company.
Lucas, Caleb	20	Private	8/15/1861	A	Mustered out with company.
Luce, Joseph	20	Private	8/15/1861	A	Mustered out 8/26/1864 at Columbus, Ohio, on expiration of term of service.
Lyday, John	20	Private	8/26/1861	D	Transferred to Co. G on 9/24/1861. Mustered out on 9/8/1864 on expiration of term of service.
Lyons, Thomas	19	Private	8/15/1861	A	Died on 7/1/1864 at his home in Warren Co., Ohio, of wounds received on 9/20/1863 at Chickamauga.
Mackey, Samuel D.	28	Private	9/1/1861	E	Discharged for disability on 3/30/1863 at Gallatin, Tenn.
Mallory, Henry	39	Capt.	9/15/1861	I	Resigned on 2/17/1862 to accept appointment as Surgeon of the 4th Kentucky Cavalry
Mann, Isaac	19	Private	8/9/1861	B	Died on 10/10/1861 at Cynthiana, Ky.
Mantelbaum, Solomon	18	Private	9/15/1861	I	Deserted 11/6/1862 at Bowling Green, Ky.
Mars, Samuel A.	40	Private	8/9/1861	B	Discharged for disability on 2/20/1864 at Chattanooga, Tenn.
Mars, William G.	19	Private	8/9/1861	B	Promoted to corporal on 2/28/1864. Mustered out with company.
Marsh, Jacob	39	Private	9/15/1861	I	Discharged for disability on 12/14/1862 at Bowling Green.
Marsh, John L.	44	Private	8/26/1861	H	Transferred to Co. I in 9/1861. Discharged for disability on 12/19/1862 at Cincinnati, Ohio.
Marshall, Edmund	24	Private	9/15/1861	I	Transferred to Co. E on 9/24/1861. Died on 6/11/1863 at Triune, Tenn.
Marshall, William H.	24	Cpl.	9/1/1861	E	Discharged for disability on 10/27/1862 at Nashville, Tenn.
Martin, David	23	Private	9/15/1861	I	Transferred to Co. E on 9/24/1861. Died on 8/6/1862 at Salem, Tenn.

Alphabetical Roster of the 35th Ohio Volunteer Infantry

Name	Age	Rank	Date	Co.	Comments
Martin, Lewis		Private	9/26/1861	K	Transferred to Co. D on 11/5/1861. Mustered out on 9/23/1864 at Chattanooga, Tenn., on expiration of term of service.
Martindale, Abraham	19	Private	8/25/1861	I	Captured on 9/20/1863 at Chickamauga, Ga. Died on 2/2/1864 in rebel prison at Richmond, Va.
Martindale, Samuel	31	1st Lt.	8/26/1861	H	Promoted to captain on 10/24/1862.
Martindale, Wakefield		Private	10/6/1861	K	Transferred to Co. F on 11/5/1861. Also listed in Co. I. Deserted 11/6/1862 at Bowling Green, Ky.
Marts, Abraham	30	Private	8/26/1861	D	Discharged for disability on 8/20/1862.
Mather, Theodore D.	21	2nd Lt.	8/26/1861	H	Promoted to 1st Lt. on 10/24/1862. Promoted to captain on 3/19/1864. Mustered out with company.
Mathers, Isaac	45	Private	9/15/1861	I	Discharged for disability on 2/24/1863 at Columbus, Ohio.
Matthews, Jesse G.	27	Private	8/26/1861	D	Transferred to Co. C in 9/1861. Detailed to Ambulance Corps. Died 1/12/1864 at Louisville, Ky.
May, William S.	21	Private	11/27/1863	D	Transferred to Co. C 18th OVI on 11/10/1864
Mayers, John	21	Private	8/15/1861	A	Mustered out with company.
Mayhew, Albert	19	Private	8/26/1861	D	Died 10/1861 at Paris, Ky.
McBride, James	39	Private	9/15/1861	I	Mustered out with company.
McCain, James L.	31	Private	8/15/1861	A	Promoted to corporal on 1/1/1862. Mustered out with company.
McCarthy, James	44	Private	8/26/1861	H	
McCarthy, John	20	Private	8/9/1861	B	Mustered out with company.
McCleod, Archibald	18	Private	9/15/1861	I	
McCrarie, Charles		Private	10/8/1861	K	On muster-in roll, no further record found.
McDevitt, Isaac R.	18	Private	9/1/1861	E	Discharged for disability on 12/1/1862 at Bowling Green, Ky.
McDonald, Henry	21	Private	8/20/1861	C	Transferred to Co. D on 9/9/1861. Wounded 6/9/1864 near Marietta, Ga. Leg amputated. Died 8/2/1864 at Chattanooga, Tenn.

Alphabetical Roster of the 35th Ohio Volunteer Infantry

Name	Age	Rank	Date	Co.	Comments
McFadden, David	37	Private	9/1/1861	E	Discharged for disability on 1/5/1864 at Chattanooga, Tenn.
McGinley, Horace	22	Private	9/5/1861	F	Discharged on 7/9/1862 at Corinth, Miss.
McGriff, Emberson	19	Private	9/7/1861	G	Died on 12/7/1863 in hospital at Nashville, Tenn.
McGriff, John W.	19	Private	11/25/1863	D	Transferred to Co. C 18th OVI on 11/10/1864
McKasson, Frederick D.	19	Private	8/20/1861	C	Discharged for disability on 10/1/1862 at Camp Dennison, Ohio.
McKean, William	18	Private	9/12/1861	K	Transferred to Co. G on 9/24/1861. Mustered out by order of the War Department.
McKee, James H.	23	Private	8/15/1861	A	Captured 9/20/1863 at Chickamauga. Exchanged on 5/7/1864. Mustered out on 12/8/1864 at Columbus, Ohio, on expiration of term of service.
McKelly, James		Private	9/9/1861	D	No record of muster out found.
McKinney, Eli	21	Private	2/15/1862	D	Discharged for disability on 7/8/1862 at Corinth, Miss.
McLaughlin, William	26	Private	9/7/1861	I	Transferred to Co. I on 9/9/1861. Discharged on 1/3/1864 for wounds received on 9/20/1863 at Chickamauga, Ga.
McMahon, Matthew	24	Private	2/14/1862	K	Transferred to Co. C 18th OVI on 10/20/1864.
McNamee, Harvey	25	Private	8/30/1862	I	Transferred to Co. C 18th OVI on 11/10/1864.
McNelly, James	19	Private	9/5/1861	F	Transferred to Co. D on 11/1/1861. Mustered out with company.
McShane, Francis M.	18	Private	8/26/1861	C	Mustered out with company.
Mears, George	18	Private	8/26/1861	H	Discharged on 5/31/1863 at Cincinnati, Ohio
Mehan, Alfred	20	Private	8/26/1861	C	Mustered out with company.
Mench, William	20	Private	8/9/1861	B	Mustered out with company.
Mercer, Albert S.	19	Private	8/15/1861	A	Promoted to sergeant on 7/1/1862. Mustered out with company.
Michael, Henry	23	Music'n	8/17/1861	Band	Discharged on 9/10/1862 by order of War Department at Nashville.
Michaels, Adolph	18	Private	8/26/1861	H	

Alphabetical Roster of the 35th Ohio Volunteer Infantry

Name	Age	Rank	Date	Co.	Comments
Michaels, Philip	19	Private	8/26/1861	H	Mustered out with company.
Mikesell, David A.	19	Private	9/1/1861	E	Captured 9/20/1863 at Chickamauga, Ga. Paroled on 10/4/1863. Discharged for disability on 7/15/1864 at Columbus, Ohio.
Mikesell, John I.	29	Private	9/7/1861	G	Discharged for disability on 10/11/1862.
Mikesell, William B.	25	1st Sgt.	9/1/1861	E	Mustered out with company.
Milford, Augustus E.	23	Private	8/15/1861	A	Mustered out with company.
Miller, Benjamin F.	25	2nd Lt.	8/20/1861	C	Promoted to 1st Lt. on 3/19/1864 but not mustered. Transferred to Co. A on 7/21/1864. Mustered out with company.
Miller, George	18	Private	1/21/1864	H	Transferred to Co. C 18th OVI on 11/10/1864.
Miller, James B.	23	Private	8/9/1861	B	Died on 3/11/1862 at Louisville, Ky.
Miller, James P.	18	Private	8/20/1861	C	Transferred to Co. D on 9/9/1861. Discharged in 3/1862 at Nashville, Tenn.
Miller, John	18	Private	9/7/1861	I	Transferred to Co. I on 9/9/1861. Captured on 9/19/1863 at Chickamauga, Ga. Mustered out on 9/8/1864 at Chattanooga, Tenn., on expiration of term of service.
Miller, John A.	21	Private	9/1/1861	E	Mustered out with company.
Miller, Martin	40	Private	8/26/1861	H	Promoted to corporal on 2/1/1863. Mustered out with company.
Miller, Moses H.	33	Private	8/26/1861	H	Mustered out with company.
Miller, Nimrod	45	Private	9/16/1861	K	Promoted to corporal on 11/18/1862. Discharged for disability on 1/4/1864.
Miller, Richard	15	Cpl.	9/15/1861	I	Transferred to Co. H in 9/1861. Promoted to sergeant on 10/12/1862. Mustered out on 9/23/1864 at Chattanooga on expiration of term of service.
Milllikin, William B.	19	Private	8/26/1861	C	Discharged for disability on 3/9/1863 at Triune, Tenn.

Alphabetical Roster of the 35th Ohio Volunteer Infantry

Name	Age	Rank	Date	Co.	Comments
Mills, Francis M.	18	Private	8/26/1861	G	Transferred to Co. G on 9/24/1861. Mustered out on 9/8/1864 at Chattanooga, Tenn., on expiration of term of service.
Mills, Robert	18	Private	8/26/1861	D	Transferred to Co. G on 9/24/1861. Discharged for disability on 1/6/1862.
Mooney, Commodore P.	44	Private	8/26/1861	H	Mustered out on 12/30/1864 at Columbus, Ohio, on expiration of term of service.
Moore, Aaron	18	Private	9/15/1861	I	Promoted to sergeant on 10/1/1863. Mustered out with company.
Moore, Charles	26	Private	8/9/1861	B	Discharged for disability on 10/13/1862 at Hamilton, Ohio.
Moore, John P.	25	Music'n	8/17/1861	Band	Discharged on 9/10/1862 by order of War Department at Nashville.
Moore, Jonathan	34	Private	8/20/1861	F	
Morgan, Alfred S.	35	1st Sgt.	8/20/1861	C	Transferred to Co. D on 8/26/1861 as Albert S. Morgan. Promoted to first sergeant. Reduced to sergeant on 12/9/1861. Discharged for disability on 5/17/1862 at Pittsburgh Landing, Tenn.
Morgan, Joel T.	18	Private	8/26/1861	C	Wounded on 9/20/1863 at Chickamauga. Temporarily assigned to Co. K on 8/26/1864. Discharged on 9/8/1864 at Chattanooga, Tenn., on expiration of term of service.
Morris, Charles M.	19	Private	8/20/1861	C	Transferred to Co. I on 9/24/1861. Discharged on 11/18/1862 at Bowling Green, Ky.
Morris, David	19	Private	2/19/1862	K	Died on 1/13/1863 in hospital at Nashville, Tenn.
Morris, Francis D.	30	Asst. Sgt.	8/21/1861	Staff	Resigned for disability on 8/6/1862. Commissioned as surgeon on 11/1/1863. Mustered out with regiment on 9/27/1864.
Morris, Levi W.	52	Private	9/15/1861	I	Discharged for disability on 7/22/1862 at Columbus, Ohio.
Morris, Samuel	19	Private	1/21/1864	H	Transferred to Co. C 18th OVI on 11/10/1864.

Alphabetical Roster of the 35th Ohio Volunteer Infantry

Name	Age	Rank	Date	Co.	Comments
Morrison, William A.	20	Cpl.	9/1/1861	E	Reduced to ranks. Mustered out with company.
Morrow, Samuel S.	19	Private	9/5/1861	F	Mustered out with company.
Morrow, William M.	26	Private	9/1/1861	E	Mustered out with company.
Morten, Thomas B.	20	Private	8/26/1861	D	Transferred to Co. B on 9/9/1861. Temporarily assigned to Co. K on 8/26/1864. Mustered out on 9/8/1864 at Chattanooga, Tenn., on expiration of term of service.
Moser, Henry	24	Private	8/26/1861	D	Transferred to Co. G on 9/24/1861. Wounded on 11/25/1863 at Missionary Ridge, Tenn. Mustered out on 9/8/1864 at Chattanooga, Tenn., on expiration of term of service.
Mosler, Christopher R.	34	Private	9/12/1861	K	Transferred to Co. G on 11/5/1861. Absent sick from 10/1/1863 in hospital at Nashville, Tenn. Mustered out 9/23/1864 by order of War Department.
Motter, John E.	24	Private	8/26/1861	D	Transferred to Co. C in September 1861. Temporarily assigned to Co. K on 8/26/1864. Discharged on 9/8/1864 at Chattanooga, Tenn., on expiration of term of service.
Mount, Symmes H.	22	Private	8/26/1861	D	Mustered out with company.
Mountjoy, George	28	Private	9/5/1861	F	Died on 12/15/1862 at Clarkesville, Ohio.
Mowry, Joseph W.	22	Private	9/5/1861	F	Discharged on 2/4/1862 at Columbus, Ohio.
Mudford, William	33	Private	9/7/1861	G	Mustered out with company.
Mullinix, William C.	40	Cpl.	9/16/1861	K	Died on 6/22/1862 in hospital at Corinth, Miss.
Myers, Frederick	41	Private	3/16/1862	K	Died on 1/31/1863 in hospital at Nashville, Tenn.
Myers, Jacob F.	18	Wagnr	8/9/1861	B	Mustered out with company.
Myers, John	31	Private	8/20/1861	C	Transferred to Co. D on 9/9/1861. Discharged for disability on 9/3/1862 at Camp Chase, Ohio.
Myers, Joseph W.	18	1st Sgt.	8/26/1861	D	Mustered out with company.
Myers, Parker		Private		D	

Alphabetical Roster of the 35th Ohio Volunteer Infantry

Name	Age	Rank	Date	Co.	Comments
Nall, Levi	22	Private	9/7/1861	G	Absent sick from 2/20/1864 at Johnsville, Ohio. Mustered out on 9/23/1864 by order of War Department.
Neff, Cornelius	36	Music'n	8/17/1861	Band	Discharged on 9/10/1862 by order of War Department at Nashville.
Neff, Orrion L.	13	Music'n	8/17/1861	Band	Discharged on 9/10/1862 by order of War Department at Nashville.
Nelson, James K.	27	Private	2/25/1862	K	Promoted to corporal on 8/9/1862. Reduced to ranks on 11/18/1862. Discharged for disability on 2/3/1863 at Gallatin, Tenn.
Newhall, Charles O.	22	Private	9/15/1861	I	Transferred to Co. B in September 1861. Discharged for disability on 11/14/1862 at Louisville, Ky.
Newman, John L.	27	Private	8/15/1861	A	Died on 2/11/1863 in hospital at Nashville, Tenn.
Newsock, William	19	Private	8/26/1861	D	Transferred to Co. G on 9/24/1861. Promoted to corporal in 10/1861. Killed on 11/25/1863 at Missionary Ridge, Tenn.
Nicholas, James F.	18	Private	9/15/1861	I	Transferred to Co. B on 9/24/1861. Temporarily assigned to Co. K on 8/26/1864. Mustered out on 9/23/1864 at Chattanooga, Tenn., on expiration of term of service.
Nicholas, Robert C.	21	Cpl.	9/15/1861	I	Transferred to Co. B in September 1861. Promoted to sergeant. Temporarily assigned to Co. K on 8/26/1864. Mustered out 9/23/1864 at Chattanooga, Tenn., on expiration of term of service.
Norris, Andrew M.	20	Private	9/5/1861	F	Absent sick from 3/27/1863 in hospital at Nashville, Tenn.
Norris, Robert L.	22	Private	9/5/1861	F	Discharged for disability at 11/10/1862 at Nashville, Tenn.
Norris, Thomas	18	Private	9/5/1861	F	Transferred to Co. D on 11/1/1861. Transferred to Co. C 18th OVI on 11/10/1864. Veteran.
O'Conner, James	30	Private	9/25/1861	K	Mustered out with company.
O'Conner, John	32	Private	9/16/1861	K	Mustered out with company.

Alphabetical Roster of the 35th Ohio Volunteer Infantry

Name	Age	Rank	Date	Co.	Comments
Odell, Henry C.	20	Private	2/28/1862	E	Transferred to Co. K on 9/8/1864. Transferred to Co. C 18th OVI on 10/24/1864.
Ogden, David D.	24	Private	9/1/1861	E	Mustered out with company.
O'Kane, Joseph	19	Private	8/26/1861	D	On muster roll. No further record found.
Oliver, John	18	Private	9/15/1861	I	Wounded and missing on 9/20/1863 at Chickamauga, Ga. No further record found.
O'Neall, Joseph W.	18	Private	8/5/1862	A	Wounded and captured 9/20/1863 at Chickamauga. Six months in prison at Castle Pemberton and Danville and four months at Andersonville. Transferred to Charleston, S.C., jail where he escaped in December 1864.
Overholtz, William H.	19	Private	8/9/1861	B	Absent sick on 6/26/1863 in hospital at Louisville, Ky. Mustered out 8/26/1864 by order of War Department.
Oxley, Fielding	19	Private	8/15/1861	A	Captured 9/20/1863 at Chickamauga. Mustered out on 8/26/1864 at Columbus, Ohio, on expiration of term of service.
Oxley, John M.	20	Private	8/15/1861	A	Mustered out with company.
Packer, Alexander	23	Private	9/7/1861	G	
Page, Milo P.	32	Music'n	8/17/1861	Band	Discharged on 9/10/1862 by order of War Department at Nashville.
Paine, William O.	20	Private	8/26/1861	D	Transferred to Co. G on 9/24/1861. Promoted to corporal on 9/10/1862. Died on 1/5/1864 in hospital at Louisville, Ky.
Painter, William	23	Private	8/26/1861	D	Transferred to Co. G on 9/24/1861. Died on 3/12/1862 at Nashville, Tenn.
Parker, John B.	20	Private	8/15/1861	A	
Parker, Samuel	27	Private	8/26/1861	D	Transferred to Co. C in September 1861. Died 5/17/1862 at Seven Mile, Ohio.
Parshall, Oliver O.	37	Capt.	8/15/1861	F	Originally sergeant. Promoted to captain on 9/5/1861. Transferred from Co. A on 9/5/1861. Killed 9/19/1863 at Chickamauga, Ga.

Alphabetical Roster of the 35th Ohio Volunteer Infantry

Name	Age	Rank	Date	Co.	Comments
Patterson, James P.	50	Music'n	8/17/1861	Band	Discharged on 9/10/1862 by order of War Department at Nashville.
Pauluss, Adam	36	Private	2/28/1862	D	Promoted to sergeant. Transferred to Co. C 18th OVI on 11/10/1864.
Payne, Leonidas	20	Private	8/15/1861	A	Died on 6/16/1862 in hospital at Cincinnati, Ohio.
Pearson, Henry C.	19	Private	12/1/1861	K	Died on 3/17/1864 in hospital at Nashville, Tenn.
Pearson, Thomas C.	21	Sgt.	9/12/1861	K	Wounded on 9/20/1863 at Chickamauga, Ga. Died of smallpox on 12/11/1863 in hospital at Nashville, Tenn.
Peckinpaugh, Robert	18	Private	8/15/1861	A	Discharged for disability on 9/12/1862 at Columbus, Ohio.
Pegan, David S.	24	Cpl.	8/26/1861	D	Reduced from corporal. Wounded 9/19/1863 at Chickamauga, Ga. Absent sick from 5/2/1864 at Ringgold, Ga. Mustered out on 9/8/1864 by order of War Department.
Peppin, Benjamin F.	18	Private	9/1/1861	E	Discharged for disability on 4/3/1862 at Nashville, Tenn.
Perrine, John	34	Wagnr	8/15/1861	A	Mustered out with company.
Perrine, Joseph C.	30	Private	8/15/1861	A	Died on 7/9/1864 in hospital at Chattanooga, Tenn.
Perrine, Thomas V.	18	Private	8/26/1861	C	Transferred to Co. D on 9/9/1861. Mustered out with company.
Perry, John W.	28	Private	9/5/1861	F	On detached duty as ambulance driver at 3rd Division HQ, 14th Army Corps . Mustered out 9/8/1864 by Order of War Department.
Phasic, William C.	18	Private	8/26/1861	H	Mustered out with company.
Phillips, Thomas	23	Private	8/15/1861	A	Mustered out with company.
Phillips, William J.	21	Private	8/9/1861	B	Transferred to Veteran Reserve Corps on 1/15/1864.
Pierson, Benjamin	18	Private	8/9/1861	B	Discharged for disability on 8/27/1863 at Louisville, Ky.
Pierson, William H. H.	19	Private	8/9/1861	B	Wounded on 9/19/1863 at Chickamauga. In hospital at Covington, Ky. Mustered out 8/26/1864 at Columbus, Ohio, on expiration of term of service.

Alphabetical Roster of the 35th Ohio Volunteer Infantry

Name	Age	Rank	Date	Co.	Comments
Pope, William	20	Private	9/5/1861	F	Discharged for disability on 3/25/1862 at Nashville, Tenn.
Porterfield, John W.	18	Private	9/1/1861	E	Discharged for disability on 4/3/1862 at Nashville, Tenn.
Potter, Lucius B.	18	Private	8/20/1861	C	Promoted to sergeant major on 10/14/1862. Mustered out 8/26/1864 at Chattanooga, Tenn.
Price, James	41	Private	9/7/1861	G	
Price, Mark B.	21	Private	8/20/1861	C	Promoted to sergeant on 5/1/1862. Served as regimental color sergeant. Mustered out with company.
Price, Thomas P.	26	Cpl.	9/15/1861	I	Deserted 11/4/1862, sentenced to he shot but mitigated to imprisonment by President Lincoln.
Printz, Edward O.	32	Private	9/5/1861	F	Discharged on 5/15/1862 at Corinth, Miss.
Proctor, John D.	28	Private	8/15/1861	A	Mustered out with company.
Puttifer, Joseph	21	Private	8/9/1861	B	Mustered out with company.
Quinn, Francis	25	Private	9/7/1861	G	Discharged on 12/2/1863 to accept appointment as 2nd Lt. in the 7th NJ Cav.
Raaf, Jacob	24	Private	8/26/1861	H	Died on 10/10/1863 in hospital at Chattanooga, Tenn., of wounds received on 9/20/1863 at Chickamauga, Ga.
Randall, Jesse K.	41	Cpl.	9/5/1861	F	Died on 12/3/1861 in hospital at Paris, Ky.
Randall, Wesley	19	Private	9/5/1861	F	Promoted to corporal on 11/2/1863. Mustered out with company.
Ratliff, James D.	21	Private	10/8/1861	K	Transferred to Co. B on 11/5/1861. Promoted to corporal on 11/12/1861. Promoted to sergeant on 5/12/1863. Temporarily assigned to Co. K on 8/26/1864. Mustered out 9/23/1864 at Chattanooga, Tenn., on expiration of term of service.
Ray, Henry C.	18	Private	8/26/1861	D	Transferred to Co. C in October 1861. Killed on 9/20/1863 at Chickamauga.

Alphabetical Roster of the 35th Ohio Volunteer Infantry

Name	Age	Rank	Date	Co.	Comments
Reeder, Nathaniel	45	Capt.	8/26/1861	D	Sick in hospital at Somerset, Ky from February 1862. On unofficial detached duty from August 1862, carried AWOL by the regiment. Court-martialed and dismissed from service in August 1863. Later reinstated but did not return to regiment.
Reel, Benjamin A.	18	Private	8/26/1861	D	Transferred to Co. C in October 1861. Killed on 9/20/1863 at Chickamauga.
Reel, John M.	25	Private	8/26/1861	K	Transferred to Co. C on 11/5/1861. Temporarily assigned to Co. K on 8/26/1864. Mustered out on 9/23/1864 at Chattanooga, Tenn., on expiration of term of service.
Reese, Thomas H.	29	Private	9/20/1861	K	Discharged for disability on 3/9/1864 at Camp Dennison, Ohio.
Relter, George	39	Private	8/26/1861	D	On muster roll. No further record found.
Relter, John	45	Private	9/7/1861	G	Transferred to Co. D on 9/24/1861. Mustered out with company.
Rentz. Jacob	27	Private	8/26/1861	C	Wounded on 9/20/1864 at Chickamauga. Mustered out with company.
Rhodes, William	21	Private	8/26/1861	H	Wounded on 9/19/1863 at Chickamauga, Ga. Died the same night.
Rhrorer, Albert G.	23	Private	8/9/1861	B	Captured 9/20/1863 at Chickamauga. Mustered out on 1/23/1865 at Columbus, Ohio, on expiration of term of service.
Rice, Adam A.	19	Private	8/20/1863	C	Company bugler. Mustered out with company.
Richard, John P.	37	Music'n	8/17/1861	Band	Discharged on 9/10/1862 by order of War Department at Nashville.
Richardson, Alex P.	39	Private	8/26/1863	C	Discharged for disability on 5/18/1862.
Richardson, David S.	28	Private	9/15/1861	I	Captured on 9/19/1863 at Chickamauga, Ga. Died on 3/21/1864 in rebel prison in Richmond, Va.
Richster, Henry	22	Cpl.	9/5/1861	F	
Rickets, Miner	18	Private	8/15/1861	A	Mustered out with company.
Ridgeley, Frederick W. G.	18	Sgt.	9/1/1861	E	Died on 7/19/1863 at Nashville, Tenn.

Alphabetical Roster of the 35th Ohio Volunteer Infantry

Name	Age	Rank	Date	Co.	Comments
Ridgeley, Levi	27	Private	2/26/1862	K	
Riggle, David	22	Private	9/7/1861	G	Killed on 9/19/1863 at Chickamauga, Ga.
Ritter, Jacob	45	Private	9/16/1861	K	Died on 1/1/1864 in hospital in Louisville, Ky.
Roberts, David	23	Private	8/28/1862	B	Transferred to Co. K on 8/26/1864. Transferred to Co. C 18th OVI on 10/24/1864.
Robinson, Joseph	20	Private	9/7/1861	G	Transferred to Co. C in October 1861. Died on 4/14/1862 at Indian Creek Hospital, Tenn.
Robinson, Walter S.	19	Private	3/3/1862	K	Promoted to corporal on 11/18/1862. Died on 12/9/1862 in hospital at Gallatin, Tenn.
Rogers, Francis	42	Private	8/26/1861	C	Transferred to Co. D on 9/9/1861. Transferred to Veteran Reserve Corps in 1/1864.
Rogers, James	22	Private	2/16/1862	A	Discharged for disability on 1/9/1863 at Gallatin, Tenn.
Rogers, William H.	33	Cpl.	8/9/1861	B	Reduced to ranks. Mustered out with company.
Rohrer, John H.	25	Private	8/20/1861	C	Mustered out with company.
Rollf, George B.	20	Private	8/26/1861	D	Transferred to Co. C in 9/1861. Temporarily assigned to Co. K on 8/26/1864. Discharged on 9/8/1864 at Chattanooga, Tenn., on expiration of term of service.
Romine, John	24	Private	9/5/1861	F	Died on 9/29/1863 in hospital at Chattanooga, Tenn.
Rose, David G.	44	Private	4/16/1862	K	On detached duty in brigade hospital. Transferred to Co. C 18th OVI on 10/20/1864.
Rose, Thomas W.	28	Cpl.	9/5/1861	F	Discharged on 5/15/1864 at Columbus, Ohio, for wounds received on 9/20/1863 at Chickamauga, Ga.
Ross, Albert A.	21	Private	8/20/1861	C	Transferred to Co. D on 9/9/1861.
Rothenbush, Frederick	18	Private	9/7/1861	E	Transferred to Co. I on 9/9/1861. Mustered out with company.

Alphabetical Roster of the 35th Ohio Volunteer Infantry

Name	Age	Rank	Date	Co.	Comments
Rothenbush, Phillip	19	1st Sgt.	9/15/1861	I	Promoted to 1st Lt. on 2/17/1862. Wounded on 9/19/1863 at Chickamauga, Ga. Promoted to captain on 3/19/1964. Mustered out with company.
Ruch, David S.	19	Private	8/15/1861	A	Died on 5/20/1862 at his home in Monroe, Ohio.
Runyon, Alonzo	18	Private	8/26/1861	D	Transferred to Co. B in 9/1861. Promoted to corporal. Transferred to Veteran Reserve Corps on 4/30/1864.
Russell, Samuel	18	Cpl.	8/26/1861	D	Reduced to ranks. Mustered out with company.
Rutledge, William	17	Private	9/15/1861	I	Mustered out with company.
Ryan, James	32	Private	8/25/1861	B	Died on 12/16/1863 at Riley, Ohio.
Sabin, James	24	Sgt.	8/15/1861	A	Promoted to first sergeant on 7/1/1862. Promoted to 2nd Lt. on 7/13/1863. Promoted to 1st Lt. on 3/18/1864. Died 6/16/1864 of wound to the groin received on 6/9/1864 near Marietta, Ga.
Samsell, David D.	32	Private	9/7/1861	G	Died on 1/2/1864 in hospital at Nashville, Tenn.
Samuels, Micajah L.	24	Private	8/26/1861	C	Temporarily assigned to Co. K on 8/26/1864. Transferred to Co. C 18th OVI on 10/24/1864. Veteran.
Samuels, Nathan R.	18	Private	8/26/1861	C	Wounded 9/20/1863 at Chickamauga. Mustered out with company.
Samuels, Thomas F.	22	Private	8/26/1861	C	Mustered out with company.
Sands, Samuel	18	Private	9/1/1861	E	Mustered out with company.
Saum, Martin	19	Private	9/7/1861	G	Transferred to Co. C in 10/1861. Absent sick for five months in 181862. Temporarily assigned to Co. K on 8/26/1864. Discharged on 9/23/1864 at Chattanooga, Tenn., on expiration of term of service.
Saunders, Joseph F.	19	Qm Sgt	8/9/1861	Staff	Promoted to 2nd Lt. Co. D on 11/19/1862. Promoted to 1st Lt. on 3/19/1864 but not mustered. On detached duty. Mustered out with company.

Alphabetical Roster of the 35th Ohio Volunteer Infantry

Name	Age	Rank	Date	Co.	Comments
Saylor, Samuel	18	Private	8/26/1861	C	Temporarily assigned to Co. K on 8/26/1864. Discharged on 9/23/1864 at Chattanooga, Tenn., on expiration of term of service.
Schadwick, George	23	Private	9/7/1861	G	Mustered out with company.
Schaeffer, Nathan	22	Private	9/5/1861	F	Wounded on 9/20/1863 at Chickamauga, Ga. Mustered out with company.
Scheisler, John	23	Private	8/9/1861	B	Died on 4/6/1864 at Camp Washington near Cincinnati, Ohio.
Schmeltzer, John G.	19	Private	8/26/1861	H	Promoted to corporal on 11/12/1863. Mustered out with company.
Schmuts, Calvin I.	21	Private	9/7/1861	G	Mustered out with company.
Schramm, Charles C.	25	Music'n	9/7/1861	G	Mustered out with company.
Schumaker, Michael	23	Private	8/9/1861	B	Mustered out with company.
Scrackengast, Lewis	23	Private	8/9/1861	B	Died on 2/20/1863 at Gallatin, Tenn.
Seits, John	22	Private	9/15/1861	I	Wounded on 9/19/1863 at Chickamauga, Ga. Mustered out with company.
Shaeffer, David W.	35	1st Sgt	9/15/1861	H	Transferred from Co. I in 9/1861. Promoted to 2nd Lt. on 10/24/1862. Promoted to 1st Lt. on 3/19/1864. Mustered out with company.
Shaeffer, Michael N.	21	Private	8/26/1861	H	Discharged for disability on 4/20/1862 at camp near Nashville, Tenn.
Shaffer, Isaac A.	18	Private	9/7/1861	G	Transferred to Co. C on 10/1861. Temporarily assigned to Co. K on 8/26/1864. 18th OVI on 11/10/1864. Veteran.
Shalenberger, David S.	25	Private	8/18/1862	C	Wounded on 9/20/1863 at Chickamauga. Temporarily assigned to Co. K on 8/26/1864. Transferred to Co. C 18th OVI on 10/20/1864.
Shally, Damiel	24	Private	8/26/1861	H	Mustered out with company.
Shank, William	22	Private	9/12/1861	K	Died on 1/20/1862 at Somerset, Ky.
Shannon, Edward	22	Private	2/16/1862	A	Captured on 9/20/1863 at Chickamauga. No further record found.
Sharer, William H.	22	Private	8/9/1861	B	Mustered out with company.

Alphabetical Roster of the 35th Ohio Volunteer Infantry

Name	Age	Rank	Date	Co.	Comments
Shaw, Joshua	19	Private	8/20/1861	C	Transferred to Co. F on 9/9/1861. Discharged 2/15/1865 at Columbus, Ohio, on expiration of term of service.
Shaw, Lester	29	Private	9/7/1861	G	Promoted to corporal on 9/25/1861. Wounded on 9/19/1863 at Chickamauga, Ga. Sent to hospital at Nashville, Tenn., on 9/25/1863. Mustered out in 9/1864 at Columbus, Ohio, on expiration of term of service.
Shay, John B.	20	Private	8/15/1861	A	Promoted to corporal on 1/1/1863. Mustered out with company.
Shearer, Henry	37	Private	10/6/1861	K	Transferred to Co. I in September 1861. Transferred to Co. D. on 1/1/1862. Discharged for disability on 9/11/1864 at Chattanooga, Tenn.
Shedd, Hiram	18	Cpl.	8/20/1861	C	Transferred to Co. D on 9/9/1861. Promoted to corporal on 4/1/1863. Absent sick at Hamilton, Ohio. Mustered out 9/8/1864 by order of War Department.
Shedd, John S.	20	Sgt.	8/20/1861	C	Transferred to Co. D on 9/9/1861. Reduced to ranks. Died 3/14/1864 at Hamilton, Ohio.
Sheehy, Jeremiah	17	Private	9/12/1861	K	Transferred from Co. B.
Sheets, William	42	Private	8/26/1861	D	Transferred to Co. G on 9/24/1861. Mustered out on 9/8/1864 on expiration of term of service.
Sheldon, Thomas C.	18	Private	9/7/1861	G	Promoted to Sgt. 6/19/1864. Transferred to Co. K on 9/23/1864. Veteran.
Shellhouse, Isaac	20	Private	8/26/1861	H	Transferred to Co. I in 9/1861. Died on 1/30/1863 at Gallatin, Tenn.
Sherde, Charles (Sheid)	33	Private	8/19/1862	I	Deserted 11/6/1862 at Bowling Green, Ky.
Sherer, Christopher	18	Private	9/7/1861	G	Mustered out with company.
Sherer, George H.	19	Private	9/7/1861	C	Transferred to Co. C on 10/1861. Temporarily assigned to Co. K on 8/26/1864. Discharged on 9/23/64 at Chattanooga, Tenn., on expiration of term of service.

Alphabetical Roster of the 35th Ohio Volunteer Infantry

Name	Age	Rank	Date	Co.	Comments
Shields, Henry	18	Private	9/1/181	E	Captured on 9/17/1863 near Chickamauga, Ga. Paroled. Died on 4/15/1864 at Annapolis, Md.
Shipman, Charles T.	20	Cpl.	8/26/1861	H	Reduced to ranks on 11/4/1861 after deserting.
Shires, William H.	26	Private	9/1/181	E	Transferred to Co. K on 9/8/1864. Transferred to Co. C 18th OVI on 10/20/1864. Veteran.
Short, Henry L.	32	Private	8/26/1861	H	Discharged for disability on 12/15/1863 at Gallatin, Tenn.
Showalter, George M.	25	Private	9/1/181	E	Absent sick in hospital at Nashville, Tenn., from 5/8/1864. Mustered out on 9/8/1864 by order of War Department
Shumaker, Isaac	21	Private	9/1/181	E	Mustered out with company.
Shumaker, James	30	Private	9/1/181	E	Mustered out with company.
Shumaker, William	18	Private	9/1/181	E	Killed on 9/20/1863 at Chickamauga, Ga.
Shurts, Andrew W.	34	Cpl.	8/15/1861	A	Reduced to private. Mustered out with company.
Sieker, Henry	22	Private	9/24/1861	K	Died on 10/17/1863 in hospital at Chattanooga, Tenn., of wounds received on 9/19/1863 at Chickamauga, Ga.
Sigman, John	18	Private	9/12/1861	K	Mustered out with company.
Sindall, John	29	Private	9/1/181	E	Discharged for disability on 4/3/1862 at Nashville, Tenn.
Singer, William H.	19	Private	11/27/1863	D	Transferred to Co. C 18th OVI on 11/10/1864
Skiles, John	20	Private	9/1/181	E	Absent sick in hospital at Nashville, Tenn., from 2/28/1864. Mustered out on 9/8/1864 by order of War Department
Slagenhauf, Jacob	19	Private	8/26/1861	H	Mustered out with company.
Sliver, Levi J.	33	Private	9/1/181	E	Mustered out with company.
Small, Joseph H.	20	Private	8/9/1861	B	Died on 10/27/1861 at Somerville, Ohio.
Smith, David	19	Private	9/5/1861	F	Killed on 9/19/1863 at Chickamauga, Ga.

Alphabetical Roster of the 35th Ohio Volunteer Infantry

Name	Age	Rank	Date	Co.	Comments
Smith, Edward	22	Private	9/5/1861	F	Discharged for disability on 4/20/1862.
Smith, John	22	Private	9/15/1861	I	Died on 10/5/1863 at Chattanooga, Tenn., of wounds received on 9/20/1863 at Chickamauga, Ga.
Smith, John D.	23	Cpl.	8/15/1861	A	Discharged for disability on 4/1/1862 at Somerset, Ky.
Smith, John R.	19	Private	8/15/1861	A	Mustered out with company
Smith. Milton	30	Private	9/5/1861	F	Mustered out with company
Smith, Peter A.	18	Private	8/26/1861	D	Transferred to Co. A in September 1861. Temporarily assigned to Co. K on 8/26/1864. Mustered out on 9/8/1864 at Chattanooga, Tenn.
Smith, Ransford	27	1st Lt.	8/9/1861	B	Appointed brigade commissary in January 1862. Promoted to captain on 6/6/1862. Resigned on 2/18/1863.
Smith, Solomon	20	Private	9/15/1861	I	Transferred to Co.B in 9/1861. Promoted to corporal. Died on 11/19/1863 in hospital at Nashville, Tenn.
Smith, Thomas I.	18	Private	8/9/1861	B	Killed on 9/19/1863 at Chickamauga.
Smith, William C.	18	Private	9/7/1861	G	Transferred to Co. C in October 1861. Temporarily assigned to Co. K on 8/26/1864. Discharged on 9/23/1864 at Chattanooga, Tenn., on expiration of term of service.
Smith, William H.	18	Private	8/15/1861	A	Mustered out with company
Snavely, David L.	20	Private	8/26/1861	D	Transferred to Co. C on 9/24/1861. Mustered out on 9/8/1864 on expiration of term of service.
Snediker, James	28	Private	9/15/1861	I	Transferred to Co. E on 9/24/1861. Discharged for disability on 1/30/1864 at Nashville, Tenn.
Snider, Louis P.	22	Private	9/7/1861	G	Mustered out with company.
Snively, Henry L.	29	Private	9/7/1861	G	Transferred to Co. C in October 1861. Temporarily assigned to Co. K on 8/26/1864. Discharged on 9/23/1864 at Chattanooga, Tenn., on expiration of term of service.
Snook, James M.	18	Private	8/15/1861	A	Died on 10/16/1862 in hospital at Nashville, Tenn.

Alphabetical Roster of the 35th Ohio Volunteer Infantry

Name	Age	Rank	Date	Co.	Comments
Snyder, George	23	Private	8/26/1861	H	Discharged for disability on 4/1/1863 at Triune, Tenn.
Snyder, Winfield S.	18	Private	11/27/1862	D	Transferred to Co. C 18th OVI on 11/10/1864
Sortman, Benjamin F.	22	Music'n	9/15/1861	I	Discharged for disability on 5/20/1862 at Corinth, Miss.
Speitel, Joseph	24	Private	8/26/1861	H	Promoted to corporal on 2/1/1863. Died on 11/14/1863 at Stevenson, AL of wounds received on 9/19/1863 at Chickamauga, Ga.
Spellman, Solomon H.	23	Private	9/1/1861	E	Discharged for disability on 4/11/1863 at Triune, Tenn.
Spencer, John	22	Cpl.	8/9/1861	B	Transferred to Co. D on 9/2/1861. Wounded on 9/20/1863 at Chickamauga, Ga. Mustered out with company.
Spohn, Levi W.	30	Private	1/21/1864	H	Transferred to Co. C 18th OVI on 11/10/1864.
Spurgeon, Samuel A.	24	Sgt.	8/15/1861	A	Mustered out with company.
St. John, Thomas J.	27	Private	9/7/1861	G	Transferred to Co. C in October 1861. Detailed to the Commissary Department. Temporarily assigned to Co. K on 8/26/1864. Discharged on 9/23/1864 at Chattanooga, Tenn., on expiration of term of service.
Stakebake, Henry H.	20	Private	9/7/1861	E	Transferred to Veteran Reserve Corps on 3/15/1864.
Stakebuke, Andrew J.	18	Private	9/1/1861	E	Promoted to corporal on 10/1/1862. Wounded on 11/25/1863 at Missionary Ridge, Tenn. Absent in hospital at New Albany, IN. Mustered out 9/8/1864 by order of War Department.
Starr, Richard W.	21	Private	8/26/1861	D	Transferred to Co. G on 9/24/1861. Wounded on 9/19/1863 at Chickamauga, Ga. Transferred to Veteran Reserve Corps.
Starrett, Alexander	43	Private	9/15/1861	K	Transferred to Co. I on 11/5/1861. Wounded on 9/20/1863 at Chickamauga, Ga. Mustered out with company.
Starry, Thomas	26	Cpl.	8/15/1861	A	Promoted to Sgt. on 9/3/1863. Mustered out with company.

Alphabetical Roster of the 35th Ohio Volunteer Infantry

Name	Age	Rank	Date	Co.	Comments
Stubb, William O.	18	Private	8/26/1861	D	Transferred to Co. G on 9/24/1861. Killed on 9/19/1863 at Chickamauga, Ga.
Stead, Smith W.	22	Private	9/15/1861	I	Discharged for disability on 9/25/1862 at Nashville, Tenn.
Steele, William H. C.	36	1st Lt.	9/7/1861	G	Promoted captain Co. E from 1st Lt. Co. G on 3/19/1864. Mustered out with company.
Stephens, Eliphalet H.	24	Private	8/26/1861	D	Transferred to Co. A on 9/1861. Discharged for disability at Hamilton, Ohio.
Sterritt, George D. A.	19	Private	8/26/1861	D	Transferred to Co. B on 9/9/1861. Temporarily assigned to Co. K on 8/26/1864. Mustered out on 9/8/1864 at Chattanooga, Tenn., on expiration of term of service.
Stetler, Henry B.	21	Private	9/12/1861	K	Promoted to corporal on 5/28/1862. Mustered out with company.
Stevens, Andrew	22	Private	8/9/1861	B	Discharged for disability on 1/31/1863 at Nashville, Tenn.
Stewart, Eli	18	Private	8/15/1861	A	Discharged for disability at Corinth, Miss
Stiles, Benjamin F.	22	Cpl.	10/8/1861	K	Reduced from corporal on 9/1/1862. Transferred to 87th Co., 2nd Battalion Veteran Reserve Corps on 3/24/1864. Mustered out on 11/4/1864 at Cincinnati, Ohio, on expiration of term of service.
Stiles, David	34	2nd Lt.	10/8/1861	K	On detached duty from 7/3/1863 as Brigade Acting Commissary of Musters. Mustered out with company.
Stineman, Edward		Private	8/26/1861	H	Sent to Columbus, Ohio, in 10/1861, and dropped from the company rolls.
Stitzel, Sanford P.		Private	10/6/1861	K	Transferred from Co. I on 11/5/1861. Discharged for disability on 11/22/1861 at Paris, Ky.
Stoddard, Alfred	19	Private	9/12/1861	K	Wounded on 11/25/1863 at Missionary Ridge, Tenn. Absent in hospital at Nashville, Tenn. Discharged on 10/24/1864 to date 9/23/1864 at Cincinnati, Ohio.

Alphabetical Roster of the 35th Ohio Volunteer Infantry

Name	Age	Rank	Date	Co.	Comments
Stoker, William R.	18	Private	8/26/1861	H	Died on 1/1/1863 in hospital at Gallatin, Tenn.
Stokes, William C.	18	Private	8/26/1861	K	Transferred to Co. C on 11/5/1861. Promoted to corporal. Promoted to Sgt. Killed on 11/25/1863 at Missionary Ridge, Tenn.
Stone, Thomas	38	Capt.	8/9/1861	B	Resigned on 6/6/1862
Stow, Lyman W.	28	Private	8/9/1861	B	Transferred to Co. K on 9/16/1861. Mustered out on 9/8/1864 at Chattanooga, Tenn., on expiration of term of service.
Stricker, John M.	21	Private	8/15/1861	A	Mustered out with company.
Strickler, Archulus D.	20	Cpl.	8/15/1861	A	Promoted to Sgt. on 8/20/1862. Mustered out with company.
Strickler, Thomas G.	19	Private	8/15/1861	A	Promoted to corporal. Killed 9/20/1863 at Chickamauga.
Strode, James H.	19	Private	9/15/1861	I	Died on 1/2/1863 at Hamilton, Ohio.
Strong, Nathaniel	23	Private	8/26/1861	D	Transferred to Co. G on 9/24/1861. Absent sick from 9/3/1864 in hospital at Chattanooga, Tenn. Mustered out 9/23/1864 by order of War Department.
Stump, Lemuel B.	20	Private	8/26/1861	D	Transferred to Co. A in 10/1861. Promoted to corporal. Transferred to Co. K on 8/26/1864. Discharged for disability on 9/25/1864 in Cincinnati, Ohio.
Sturr, Richard W.	18	Private	8/26/1861	G	Transferred to Co. D on 9/24/1861. Wounded 9/19/1863 at Chickamauga, Ga. Transferred to Veteran Reserve Corps.
Sully, John	25	Private	8/9/1861	B	Discharged for disability on 11/13/1862 at Nashville, Tenn.
Surface, Eli	21	Private	2/28/1862	E	Transferred to Co. K on 9/8/1864. Transferred to Co. C 18th OVI on 10/24/1864.
Surface, Isaiah	18	Private	9/1/1861	E	Captured on 9/20/1863 at Chickamauga, Ga. Died on 3/23/64 in rebel prison at Danville, Va.
Swainy, Charles	28	Private	8/9/1861	B	Discharged for disability on 12/15/1862 at Hamilton, Ohio.
Swainy, Constantine	37	Private	8/9/1861	B	Mustered out with company.

Alphabetical Roster of the 35th Ohio Volunteer Infantry

Name	Age	Rank	Date	Co.	Comments
Swallow, Simpson	32	Private	8/26/1861	H	On muster-in roll, but no further record found.
Sweeny, Fletcher	26	Private	9/5/1861	F	Absent sick on 12/6/1862 in hospital at Gallatin, Tenn. Mustered out with company.
Tapscott, James C.	24	Cpl.	8/9/1861	B	Reduced to ranks. Mustered out with company.
Tate, Robert V.	25	Private	8/26/1861	B	Transferred to Veteran Reserve Corps on 2/15/1864.
Taylor, Charles C.	20	Private	9/15/1861	I	Transferred to Co. H on 9/1861. Discharged for disability on 6/20/1864 at Columbus, Ohio.
Taylor, Joseph	H.	1st Sgt.	9/5/1861	F	Promoted to 2nd Lt. on 1/1/1863. Promoted to 1st Lt. on 3/19/1864 but never mustered. Mustered out with company.
Temple, John	18	Private	9/12/1861	K	Died on 9/19/1862 in hospital at Nashville, Tenn.
Thomas, Alfred	43	Private	9/5/1861	F	Injured on 12/4/1861 in an accident at Nicholasville, Ky. Detached as nurse in regimental hospital. Mustered out on 9/8/1864 by order of the War Department.
Thomas, James B.	38	Private	8/26/1861	B	Mustered out with company.
Thomas, James L.	27	Music'n	8/17/1861	Band	Discharged on 9/10/1862 by order of War Department at Nashville.
Thomas, John G.	28	Bd Ldr	8/17/1861	Band	Discharged on 9/10/1862 by order of War Department at Nashville.
Thompson, Charles H.	20	Private	9/1/1861	E	Promoted to corporal. Killed on 9/27/1863 at Chattanooga, Tenn., by accidental musket shot.
Thompson, Clark S.	23	Sgt.	8/26/1861	K	Transferred to Co. D on 11/5/1861. Reduced to ranks. Mustered out on 9/23/1864 on expiration of term of service.
Thompson, Jesse	21	Private	9/1/1861	E	Discharged for disability on 10/7/1862 at Nashville, Tenn.
Thompson, Levi P.	23	2nd Lt.	9/1/1861	E	Promoted to 1st Lt. Co. G on 3/19/1864. Transferred back to Co. E on 6/10/1864. Transferred back to Co. G on 9/8/1864. Mustered out with company.

Alphabetical Roster of the 35th Ohio Volunteer Infantry

Name	Age	Rank	Date	Co.	Comments
Thompson, Lewis	25	Private	2/15/1862	K	Promoted to corporal on 5/4/1862. Reduced to ranks on 7/25/1862. Discharged for disability on 2/24/1863 at Cincinnati, Ohio
Thompson, Moses	26	Private	9/1/1861	E	Promoted to Sgt. on 1/1/1862. Mustered out with company.
Thompson, Nelson S.	22	Private	9/7/1861	G	Promoted to corporal in 10/1861. Discharged for disability on 3/19/1862.
Thompson, Newton	42	Private	9/7/1861	G	Discharged for disability on 3/19/1862.
Thompson, Oscar F.		Private	9/5/1861	F	Discharged on 5/15/1862 at Pittsburgh Landing, Tenn.
Thoms, Joseph C.	22	2nd Lt.	9/5/1861	F	Resigned on 11/3/1862.
Tillson, William I.	18	Private	2/28/1862	K	Promoted to corporal on 11/18/1862. Wounded and captured on 9/19/1863 at Chickamauga, Ga, paroled. Transferred to Co. C 18th OVI on 10/20/1864.
Tobias, Henry	18	Private	1/26/1861	H	Mustered out with company.
Towhey, Patrick	17	Private	10/15/1861	K	Wounded and captured on 9/19/1963 at Chickamauga, Ga. Paroled on 10/29/1864. Discharged on 11/12/1864 at Columbus, Ohio, on expiration of term of service.
Tracy, Edward	18	Private	2/28/1862	K	Died on 6/17/1862 at Corinth, Miss.
Tracy, Isaiah	30	Private	9/1/1861	E	Captured on 9/17/1863 at Pigeon Ridge, Ga. Died at Belle, Island, Va.
Vam Camp, John	51	Private	9/15/1861	I	Discharged for disability in 6/1862 at Iuka, Miss.
Van Camp, Samuel	21	Private	9/28/1861	K	Transferred to Co. I on 11/5/1861. Mustered out with company.
Van Derveer, Ferdinand	38	Colonel	7/26/1861	Staff	Brigade command from 2/28/1863. Mustered out on 8/26/1864 at Chattanooga, Tenn.
Van Derveer, Henry E.	20	Sgt.	8/9/1861	B	Discharged for disability on 7/26/1862 at Hamilton, Ohio.
Van Derveer, John	24	Qtrmstr	8/2/1861	Staff	Promoted to captain of Co. C on 3/19/1864. On detached duty in Chattanooga in summer 1864. Mustered out with company.

Alphabetical Roster of the 35th Ohio Volunteer Infantry

Name	Age	Rank	Date	Co.	Comments
Vandine, John	38	Cpl.	8/26/1861	C	Discharged for disability on 12/24/1862.
Vanhorn, William R.	32	Cpl.	9/15/1861	I	Promoted to 1st Sgt. on 8/25/1863. Wounded on 11/25/1863 at Missionary Ridge, Tenn. Mustered out with company.
Vannatta, Daniel	44	Private	9/7/1861	E	Transferred to Co. I on 9/9/1861. Discharged for disability on 10/16/1862 at Cincinnati, Ohio.
Vannatta, Joseph H.	18	Private	8/15/1861	C	Killed on 9/20/1863 at Chickamauga, Ga.
Vannatta, Squire H.	19	Private	9/7/1861	G	Transferred to Co. C in 10/1861. Captured on 9/20/1963 at Chickamauga. No further record found.
Vansar, Marinas	38	Private	10/15/1861	K	Mustered out with company.
Venard, John		Private	10/6/1862	F	Died on 12/26/1863 at Chattanooga, Tenn., of wounds received on 11/25/1863 at Missionary Ridge, Tenn.
Vickers, Joseph W.	18	Private	9/5/1861	F	Mustered out with company.
Vickers, William H.		Private	8/26/1861	K	Transferred to Co. H on 11/5/1861. Mustered out on 9/23/1864 at Chattanooga, Tenn., on expiration of term of service.
Victor, Anney		Private	8/26/1861	D	
Vinson, John T.	29	Private	9/5/1861	F	Promoted to corporal on 1/3/1862. Promoted to Sgt. on 7/2/1863. Mustered out with company.
Virdoon, Henry J.	22	Private	8/26/1861	D	Mustered out with company.
Vorhees, Jerome	19	Private	8/26/1861	B	Discharged for disability on 4/5/1863 at Nashville, Tenn.
Vorhes, Edward	17	Private	9/12/1861	K	Died on 1/4/1864 in hospital at Murfreesboro, Tenn.
Vorhes, Ralph	21	Private	9/12/1861	K	Discharged for disability on 5/26/1862 near Corinth, Miss.
Vortman, David W.	26	Music'n	9/9/1861	Band	Discharged on 9/10/1862 by order of War Department at Nashville.
Wagner, John	18	Private	8/26/1861	D	Discharged for disability on 2/20/1862 at Somerset, Ky.
Wahl, Lewis	32	Private	8/26/1861	H	Transferred to Co. F on 11/1/1861. Mustered out with company.

Alphabetical Roster of the 35th Ohio Volunteer Infantry

Name	Age	Rank	Date	Co.	Comments
Walburn, William	21	Private	8/26/1861	D	Transferred to Co. A in 9/1861. Mustered out with company.
Walker, John S.	22	Private	8/28/1862	B	Died on 12/11/1863 at Gallatin, Tenn.
Walker, John W.	60	Private	9/15/1861	I	Discharged for disability on 6/13/1862 at Corinth, Miss.
Wallace, John	25	Private	8/20/1861	C	Transferred to Co. D on 9/9/1861. Discharged for disability 3/20/1862 at Nashville, Tenn.
Walsh, Patrick	23	Private	8/20/1861	C	Transferred to Co. F on 9/9/1861. Killed on 9/19/1863 at Chickamauga, Ga.
Walter, William	32	Private	8/20/1861	C	Transferred to Co. D on 9/9/1861. Promoted to corporal. Reduced to ranks.
Ward, Thomas	32	Private	8/20/1861	D	Mustered out on 5/12/1864 at Cairo, Ill., to enlist in U.S. Navy.
Ware, William S.	28	Cpl.	9/1/1861	E	Promoted to sergeant on 7/11/1863. Temporarily assigned to Co. K on 9/8/1864. Transferred to Co. C 18th OVI on 10/20/1864. Veteran.
Warner, Benjamin F.	18	Private	9/1/1861	E	Captured on 9/20/1863 at Chickamauga, Ga. Died on 1/25/1864 at Andersonville, Ga.
Warner. Frederick S.	39	Private	8/26/1861	D	Transferred to Co. G on 9/24/1861. Died 5/1/1863 at home in Butler County, Ohio.
Warner, Joseph	30	Private	8/26/1861	H	Died on 12/20/1863 in hospital in Chattanooga, Tenn., of wounds received on 11/25/1863 at Missionary Ridge, Tenn.
Warwick, William	21	Private	8/26/1861	D	Transferred to Co. A in September 1861. Died on 3/21/1862 in Warren Co., Ohio
Watts, Isaac	25	Private	9/12/1861	K	Discharged for disability on 5/26/1862 near Corinth, Miss.
Watts, William H.	19	Private	9/7/1861	G	Killed on 9/20/1863 at Chickamauga, Ga.
Waugh, Sereno	18	Private	8/26/8161	C	Wounded on 9/19/1863 at Chickamauga. Mustered out with company.
Weakly, Edward S.	19	Cpl.	8/26/1861	H	Promoted to Sgt. on 7/1/1862. Mustered out with company.

Alphabetical Roster of the 35th Ohio Volunteer Infantry

Name	Age	Rank	Date	Co.	Comments
Weaver, John (Warner)	29	Private	8/15/1861	A	Mustered out on 8/26/1864 at Columbus, Ohio, on expiration of term of service.
Webb, Foster	19	Private	8/9/1861	B	Mustered out with company.
Webb, William	41	Private	8/20/1861	C	Transferred from Co. D on 9/9/1861. Discharged for disability 7/1862 at Camp Dennison, Ohio.
Weinmeister, Augustus	29	Private	8/26/1861	H	Killed on 9/19/1863 at Chickamauga, Ga.
Weiser, Frederick J.	27	Private	8/15/1861	A	Captured on 9/20/1863 at Chickamauga. Died on 8/20/1864 in rebel prison at Andersonville, Ga.
Wellborn, William H.	22	Private	8/9/1861	B	Wounded 9/19/1863 at Chickamauga. In hospital at Nashville, Tenn. Mustered out 8/26/1864 by order of War Department.
Wescott, Peter M.	22	Private	8/9/1861	B	Mustered out with company.
West, John	28	Private	8/9/1861	B	Promoted to corporal on 1/20/1862. Mustered out with company.
West, William	38	Private	9/5/1861	F	Promoted to corporal on 10/4/1862. Died on 1/3/1863 in hospital at Gallatin, Tenn.
Weston, Charles S.	19	Private	9/7/1861	G	Died on 3/19/1862 at Louisville, Ky.
Wetzel, Moses J.	25	Private	9/7/1861	E	Transferred to Co. I on 9/9/1861. Promoted to corporal. Promoted to Sgt. Absent sick in hospital at Chattanooga, Tenn., from 2/22/1864. Mustered out 9/23/1864 by order of War Department.
Wheely, William B.	28	Private	8/15/1861	A	Mustered out with company.
White, Andrew J.	44	Private	8/26/1861	D	Transferred to Co. G on 9/24/1861. Died 12/16/1863 at Nashville, Tenn.
White, John W.	35	Private	9/5/1861	F	Discharged for disability on 11/7/1863 at Chattanooga, Tenn.
Whitkenstien, Henry	45	Private	9/15/1861	I	Transferred to Co. H in September 1861. Discharged for disability on 3/30/1863 at Nashville, Tenn.
Whitaker, John A.	28	Sgt.	9/7/1861	E	Transferred to Co. I on 9/9/1861. Reduced to ranks on 8/9/1862. Transferred to Veteran Reserve Corps on 12/1/1863.

Alphabetical Roster of the 35th Ohio Volunteer Infantry

Name	Age	Rank	Date	Co.	Comments
Whitzel, James	20	Private	9/5/1861	F	On detached duty at 3rd Division Headquarters, 14th Army Corps. Mustered out on 9/8/1864 by order of War Department.
Wilborn, George W.	24	Private	9/5/1861	F	Died on 9/5/1863 at Hospital No. 13 at Nashville, Tenn.
Wiley, Selby	19	Private	8/15/1861	A	Promoted to 1st Sgt. on 9/21/1863. Mustered out with company.
Williams, Charles O.	29	Private	8/26/1861	D	Transferred to Co. A in 9/1861. Discharged Camp Dennison, Ohio
Williams, James W.	33	Private	9/12/1861	K	Transferred to Veteran Reserve Corps on 3/12/1864.
Williams, Richard	19	Private	8/15/1861	A	Discharged for disability on 2/2/1864 at Louisville, Ky.
Williams, Simeon	40	Music'n	8/15/1861	A	Mustered out with company.
Williams, Thomas P.		Private	2/4/1862	F	Captured 11/19/1862 near Gallatin, Tenn. No further record found.
Williamson, Abel	23	Private	9/7/1861	G	Discharged
Williamson, Amos	20	Private	8/20/1861	C	On muster roll. No further record found. Probably Amos A. Williamson.
Williamson, Amos A.	20	Music'n	8/20/1861	C	Mustered out with company.
Willis, Clem	18	Private	8/9/1861	B	Mustered out with company.
Willis, Henry	39	Private	9/15/1861	I	Wounded on 9/19/1863 at Chickamauga, Ga. Discharged for disability on 5/22/1864 at Kingston, Ga.
Wilson, Andrew	30	Private	8/15/1861	A	Died on 5/22/1862 in camp near Corinth, Miss.
Wilson, Charles Lee	22	Private	9/26/1861	K	Transferred to Co. D on 11/5/1861. Mustered out on 9/23/1864 at Chattanooga, Tenn., on expiration of term of service.
Wilson, Enos	19	Cpl.	8/9/1861	B	Promoted to corporal on 9/24/1862. Mustered out with company.
Wison, John	18	Private	8/15/1861	A	Mustered out with company.
Wison, John	29	Private	8/9/1861	B	Absent sick from 7/20/1864 in hospital at Louisville, Ky. Mustered out 8/26/1864 by order of War Department.

Alphabetical Roster of the 35th Ohio Volunteer Infantry

Name	Age	Rank	Date	Co.	Comments
Wilson, Theodore	39	Private	8/9/1861	B	Transferred to Co. D on 9/16/1861. Mustered out with company.
Wilson, William	18	Private	9/1/1861	E	Promoted to corporal on 7/1/1863. Captured 9/17/1863 near Chickamauga, Ga. Paroled and in Parole Camp at Annapolis, Md. No further record found.
Wilt, John	21	Private	9/1/1861	E	Discharged on 12/23/1862 at Pilot Knob, Tenn., to enlist in the 4th US Artillery.
Winterstein, James	18	Private	8/9/1861	B	Mustered out with company.
Whiterow, Dennis P.	21	Private	9/7/1861	G	Transferred to Co. C in 10/1861. Temporarily assigned to Co. K on 8/26/1864. Discharged on 9/23/1864 at Chattanooga, Tenn., on expiration of term of service.
Withers, Charles H.	18	Private	3/3/1862	K	Transferred to Co. C 18th OVI on 10/20/1864.
Wolverton, John	37	Private	10/9/1861	K	Transferred to Co C. on 11/5/1861. Died on 1/1/1864 at Jacksboro, Ohio.
Woodhurst, Daniel F.	19	Private	9/7/1861	G	Transferred to Co. C in 10/1861. Promoted to corporal. Promoted to Sgt. on 12/31/1863. Temporarily assigned to Co. K on 8/26/1864. Mustered out on 9/8/1864 at Chattanooga, Tenn., on expiration of term of service.
Woodhurst, Hazarel	26	Private	10/30/1861	C	Discharged for disability on 10/16/1862 at Nashville, Tenn.
Woodring, Levi	24	Wagnr	8/20/1861	C	Mustered out with company.
Woods, John	24	Chapl'n	9/23/1861	Staff	Resigned 11/19/1862
Woods, Samuel A.	18	Private	8/26/1861	D	Mustered out with company.
Wright, Charles O.		Asst. Sgt.	8/15/1861	Staff	Resigned 6/18/1864
Wright, George B.	24	Adj.	8/2/1861	Staff	Resigned 9/18/1863
Wright, William	21	Private	8/26/1861	D	
Wroten, James W.	18	Private	9/7/1861	G	Transferred to Co. A in 9/1861.
Wroten, William H.	21	Private	8/15/1861	A	Mustered out with company.
Wunderlick, John	32	Private	8/9/1861	B	Mustered out with company.

Alphabetical Roster of the 35th Ohio Volunteer Infantry

Name	Age	Rank	Date	Co.	Comments
Wyrick, James M.	31	Private	9/7/1861	G	Promoted to corporal in 10/1861. Promoted to Sgt. on 5/1/1862. Died on 11/30/1863 in hospital at Nashville, Tenn.
Yowler, Ephraim J.	17	Private	8/26/1861	H	Mustered out with company.
Zehring, Henry	22	Private	8/26/1861	D	Transferred to Co. G on 9/24/1861. Promoted to corporal. Reduced to ranks on 9/10/1862. Mustered out on 9/8/1864 on expiration of term of service.
Zehrling, Samuel P.	18	Private	8/26/1861	H	Mustered out with company.
Zeller, Abia	21	Private	8/26/1861	H	Discharged for disability caused by dysentery in 1863.
Zeller, Joseph S.	20	Cpl.	8/20/1861	C	Mustered out with company.
Zellers, John A.	20	Music'n	8/17/1861	Band	Discharged on 9/10/1862 by order of War Department at Nashville.
Zilliox, Philip	22	Private	8/26/1861	D	Transferred to Co. G on 9/24/1861. Discharged for disability for 1/22/1863 at Gallatin, Tenn.
Zincroft, Frederick	27	Private	9/15/1861	I	Transferred to Co. H in 9/1861. Discharged for disability on 10/17/1862 at Louisville, Ky.

Bibliography

PRIMARY SOURCES

Arnold, Benjamin. *Sunshine and Shadows in the Life of a Private Soldier.* 1909. Reprint, Dayton: Curt Dalton, 1995.

Bishop, Judson W. *The Story of a Regiment.* 1890. Reprint, St. Cloud: North Star Press, 2000.

———. "Van Der Veer's Brigade." *National Tribune* (Washington, D.C.), June 9, 1904; June 16, 1904.

Bircher, William. *A Drummer Boy's Diary.* 1889. Reprint, St. Cloud: North Star Press, 1995.

Boynton, H. V. *Annual Address Delivered at the Twenty-Third Reunion of the Society of the Army of the Cumberland.* Cincinnati: Robert Clarke Company, 1892.

———. *Chattanooga and Chickamauga, Reprint of Gen. H. V. Boynton's Letter to the Cincinnati Commercial Gazette, August 1888.* Washington, D. C., George R Gray, 1891.

———. *Dedication of the Chickamauga and Chattanooga National Military Park.* Washington, DC: Government Printing Office, 1896.

———. *The National Military Park, Chickamauga-Chattanooga.* Cincinnati: Robert Clarke Company, 1895.

Cist, Henry M., *The Army of the Cumberland.* 1882. Reprint, Wilmington, Broadfoot Publishing, 1989.

Daily Republican News (Hamilton, Ohio), 1898.

Grebner, Constantine. *We Were the Ninth.* 1897. Reprint, Kent, Ohio: Kent State University Press, 1997.

Hamilton [Ohio] Evening News, October 13, 1914. Butler County Historical Society, Hamilton, Ohio.

Hamilton [Ohio] Telegraph. October 17, 1861; November 21, 1861; December 5, 1861.

Hill, H. H. "The Second Minnesota: Reminiscences of Four Years at the Front." *National Tribune*, July 13, 1899; July 20, 1899.

Hunt, Roger D. Collection. U.S. Army Military History Institute, Carlisle, Pennsylvania.

Keil, Frederick W. *Thirty-Fifth Ohio, A Narrative of Service from August, 1861 to 1864.* South Bend: Archer Housh and Company, 1894.

Massachusetts Commandery of the Military Order of the Loyal Legion of the United States Collection. U.S. Army Military History Institute, Carlisle, Pennsylvania.

McElroy, Joseph C. *Record of the Ohio Chickamauga and Chattanooga National Park Commission.* Cincinnati: Earhart and Richardson, 1896.

Ohio Battle Flag Collection. Ohio Historical Society, Columbus.

Ohio Roster Commission. *Official Roster of the Soldiers of the State of Ohio in the War of the Rebellion, 1861–1866, Volume III.* Ohio General Assembly, 1886.

Reid, Whitelaw, *Ohio in the War, Her Statesmen, Her Generals and Soldiers.* vol 1. Cincinnati: Robert Clarke Company, 1895.

United States Congress. *Congressional Record, Fiftieth Congress, Report 2629, June 19, 1888.* Washington, D.C.: Government Printing Office, n.d.

United States War Department. *The War of the Rebellion: A Compilation of the Official Records of the Union and Confederate Armies.* 70 vols. in 128 parts. Washington, D.C.: Government Printing Office, 1880–1901.

SECONDARY SOURCES

Baird, John A. Jr. *Profile of a Hero, The Story of Absalom Baird.* Philadelphia: Burrance and Co., 1977.

Bartlow, B. S. *Centennial History of Butler County, Ohio.* Indianapolis: B. F. Bowen, 1905.

Beers, W. H. *The History of Montgomery County, Ohio.* Chicago: W. H. Beers, 1881.

Berg, Gordon. "The Battle of Chickamauga and Gordon Granger's Reserve Corps." *America's Civil War*, November 28, 2006.

Blount, Jim. *The Civil War and Butler County.* Hamilton: Past/Present/Press, 1998.

———. *Rossville, Hamilton's West Bank.* Hamilton: Past/Present/Press, 1994.

———. "Hamilton on alert as Confederate raiders bypass city." *Journal-News*, July 9, 2003.

Bogan, Dallas R. *Warren County's Involvement in the Civil War.* Lebanon: Warren County Quickprint, 1991.

Bradley, Michael R. *Tullahoma, the 1863 Campaign for the control of Middle Tennessee.* Shippensburg: Burd Street Press, 2000.

Catton, Bruce. *America Goes to War.* New York: MJF Books, 1958.

———. *This Hallowed Ground.* New York: Doubleday & Company, 1956.

Cone, Stephen D., *Biographical and Historical Sketches, A Narrative of Hamilton and its Residents from 1792 to 1896.* Hamilton: Republican Publishing Company, 1896 (Butler County Historical Society).

———, *A Concise History of Hamilton, Ohio. Middletown:* G. Mitchell, 1901 (Butler County Historical Society).

Connelly, Thomas Lawrence. *Autumn of Glory, The Army of Tennessee, 1862–1865.* Baton Rouge: Louisiana State University Press, 1971.

Cozzens, Peter. *The Shipwreck of Their Hopes.* Urbana: University of Illinois Press, 1994.

———. *This Terrible Sound.* Urbana: University of Illinois Press, 1992.

Crout, George C. *Middletown Diary.* Middletown: George C. Crout, 1965.

Daniel, Larry J. *Days of Glory, The Army of the Cumberland. 1861–1865*, Baton Rouge: Louisiana University Press, 2004.

Dee, Christine. *Ohio's War, The Civil War in Documents*. Athens: Ohio University Press, 2006.

Dunkelman, Mark H. *Brothers One and All*. Baton Rouge: Louisiana State University Press, 2004.

Endres, David J., ed. *Butler County Obituaries*, pt. 8, www.freepages.geneaogy.rootsweb.com/~hamilton/obits8.htm.

Ford, Harvey S., ed. "The Diary of John Beatty, January–June 1884, Part I." *Ohio History* 58 no. 2 (April 1949): 119–151.

Griffith, Paddy. *Battle in the Civil War: Generalship and Tactics in America, 1861–1865*. Fieldbooks, 1986.

Hafendorfer, Kenneth A. *Mill Springs, Campaign and Battle of Mill Springs*. Louisville: KH Press, 2001.

History and Biographical Cyclopedia of Butler County, Ohio. Cincinnati: Western Biographical Publishing, 1882.

Kaser, James A. *At the Bivouac of Memory*. New York: Peter Lang, 1996.

Landis, Lincoln. *From Pilgrimage to Promise*. Westminster: Heritage Books, 2007.

Lebanon, Ohio: Celebrating 200 Years. Lebanon: Warren County Historical Society, 2002.

Lowry, R. E. *History of Preble County, Ohio, Her People, Industries, and Institutions*. Indianapolis: B. F. Bowen, 1915.

Lowry, Thomas P. and Jack D. Welsh. *Tarnished Scalpels*. Mechanicsburg: Stackpole Books, 2000.

Marik, A. J., and Robert Edwards, eds. *Find A Grave*. www.findagrave.com.

McGinnis, Ralph J. *The History of Oxford, Ohio*. Oxford: Stewart Press, 1930.

McKinney, Francis F. *Education in Violence*. Chicago: Americana House, Inc., 1991.

McPherson, James M. *Battle Cry of Freedom, The Civil War Era*. New York: Oxford University Press, 1988.

Memorial Record of Butler County, Ohio. Chicago: Record Publishing, 1894.

Mitchell, Reid. *Civil War Soldiers*. New York:, Viking Press, 1988.

Nosworthy, Brent. *The Bloody Crucible of Courage*. New York: Carroll and Graf Publishers, 2002.

Prokopowicz, Gerald J. *All for the Regiment*. Chapel Hill: University of North Carolina Press, 2001.

Ritchie, Donald A. *Press Gallery*. Cambridge: Harvard University Press, 1991.

Schwartz, James. *Hamilton, Ohio: Its Architecture and History*. Hamilton: American Printing, 1986.

Stroud, David V. *Ector's Texas Brigade and the Army of Tennessee*. Longview: Ranger Publishing, 2004.

Sword, Wiley. *Mountains Touched With Fire*. New York: St. Martin's Press, 1995.

Trelvik, Arne H., ed. *Obituaries with Warren County Connections*. www.rootsweb.com/~ohwarren/Obits/budd.htm.

Tucker, Glenn. *Chickamauga, Bloody Battle of the West*. New York: Konecky and Konecky, 1961.

Ware, Eugene. "The Indian War of 1864." *The Kansas Collection*. http://www.kancoll.org/books/ware/ew_appb.htm.

Warner, Ezra J. *Generals in Blue*. Baton Rouge: Louisiana State University Press, 1997.

Wiggins and Killop's Directory for Warren County for 1878. Lebanon: Wiggins and Killop Printers.

Wiley, Bell I. *The Life of Billy Yank*. Baton Rouge: Louisiana State University Press, 1994.

Williams Hamilton Directory for 1860, 1875, and 1876. Cincinnati: Williams Directory.

Woodworth, Stephen E. *Chickamauga, A Battlefield Guide.* Lincoln: University of Nebraska Press, 1999.

———. "The Other Rock." *Civil War Times* 42, no. 4.

UNPUBLISHED PRIMARY SOURCES

Adjutant General of Ohio State Archives. Series 147. Correspondence to the Governor and the Adjutant General of Ohio, 1861–1866. Ohio Historical Society, Columbus.

———. Series 2445 Furlough Papers, 1862-1865. Ohio Historical Society, Columbus.

———. Quartermaster General Report for 1862. Ohio Historical Society, Columbus.

Amlin, Alfred, Correspondence. Smith Library of Regional History, Oxford, Ohio.

Bishop, Judson, Papers. Minnesota Historical Society, St. Paul.

Boatman Family Papers. Butler County Historical Society, Hamilton, Ohio.

Boynton, Henry V. N. Correspondence. Chickamauga and Chattanooga National Military Park, Chattanooga, Tennessee.

Caughell, Marcella, Collection. U.S. Army Military History Institute, Carlisle, Pennsylvania.

Civil War Library and Museum, Military Order of the Loyal Legion of the United States, Philadelphia, Pennsylvania. U.S. Army Military History Institute, Carlisle, Pennsylvania.

Foord, Richard H., Papers. Center for Archival Collections, Bowling Green State University.

Grand Army of the Republic Collection. Butler County Historical Society, Hamilton, Ohio.

Hunt, Roger D., Collection. U.S. Army Military History Institute, Carlisle, Pennsylvania.

Landis Family Papers. Butler County Historical Society, Hamilton, Ohio.

Mathews, Alfred E., Lithograph Collection. Ohio Historical Society, Columbus.

National Archives and Records Administration, Washington, D.C.

Rogers, Sarah Elizabeth, Papers. Country Life During the Civil War. Butler County Historical Society, Hamilton, Ohio.

Smith, J. W. C. and William C. Dine Broadside. Ohio Historical Society, Columbus.

Stokes/Saum Family Papers. Butler County Historical Society, Hamilton, Ohio.

Sullivan, William J., Collection. Center for Archival Collections, Bowling Green State University.

Thirty-fifth OVI Collection, Butler County Historical Society, Hamilton, Ohio.

Van Derveer Family Collection. Smith Library of Regional History, Oxford, Ohio.

Van Derveer Family Papers. Butler County Historical Society, Hamilton, Ohio.

Zeller, Abia M., Papers. Ohio Historical Society, Columbus.

Index